MATLAB FOR ENGINEERS – APPLICATIONS IN CONTROL, ELECTRICAL ENGINEERING, IT AND ROBOTICS

Edited by **Karel Perutka**

MATLAB for Engineers – Applications in Control, Electrical Engineering, IT and Robotics
Edited by Karel Perutka

Published by InTech

Janeza Trdine 9, 51000 Rijeka, Croatia

Publishing Process Manager Davor Vidic

Technical Editor Teodora Smiljanic

Cover Designer InTech Design Team

Additional hard copies can be obtained from orders@intechopen.com

MATLAB for Engineers – Applications in Control, Electrical Engineering, IT and Robotics,
Edited by Karel Perutka
p. cm.
ISBN 978-953-307-914-1

For EU product safety concerns:
IN TECH d.o.o., Prolaz Marije Krucifikse Kozulić 3, 51000 Rijeka, Croatia,
info@intechopen.com or visit our website at intechopen.com.

Meet the editor

Dr. Karel Perutka received his Ph.D. degree in 2007 at Tomas Bata University in Zlin, Faculty of Applied Informatics, Czech Republic, where he is a senior lecturer. Technical Cybernetics was the principal branch of his thesis. Dr. Perutka is the author of one monograph about MATLAB, several book chapters about MATLAB and control theory, and author or co-author of more than fifty papers in the conference proceedings. He is a member of the organizing and reviewing committees of several conferences. Dr. Perutka is teaching MATLAB programming, electronics, microelectronics, diagnosis of digital systems and modulations and demodulations of signals. His main research interests are: adaptive control, real-time control, control of multivariable systems, applications of theory at FEC codes (turbo codes).

Contents

Preface

MATLAB is a powerful software package developed by the MathWorks, Inc., the multi-national corporation with the company's headquarters in Natick, Massachusetts, United States of America. The software is a member of the family of the mathematical computing software together with Maple, Mathematica, Mathcad etc. and it became the standard for simulations in academia and practice. It offers easy-to-understand programming language, sharing source code and toolboxes which solve the selected area from practice. The software is ideal for light scientific computing, data processing and math work. Its strength lies in toolboxes for Control and Electrical Engineering.

This book presents interesting topics from the area of control theory, robotics, power systems, motors and vehicles, for which the MATLAB software was used. The book consists of six parts.

First part of the book deals with control theory. It provides information about numerical inverse Laplace transform, control of time-delay systems and distributed parameters systems.

There are two chapters only in the second part of the book. One is about the application of MATLAB for modern chips improvement, and the other one describes results of MATLAB usage for photonics applications.

Next part of the book consists of chapters which have something in common with the power systems applications, for example two chapters are about power supply systems and one is about application of optimal control in power systems.

This part is followed by the part about MATLAB applications used in fault diagnosis of induction motor, implementation of induction motor drive control and linearization of permanent magnet synchronous motors.

The last but one part of the book provides the application for vehicles, namely the guided vehicle simulation, new configuration of machine, behavior of module for electric vehicle and control of vehicle suspension system.

The last part deals with MATLAB usage in robotics, with the modeling, simulation and control of power assist robot and legged walking robot.

This book provides practical examples of MATLAB usage from different areas of engineering and will be useful for students of Control Engineering or Electrical Engineering to find the necessary enlargement of their theoretical knowledge and several models on which theory can be verified. It helps with the future orientation to solve the practical problems.

Finally, I would like to thank everybody who has contributed to this book. The results of your work are very interesting and inspiring, I am sure the book will find a lot of readers who will find the results very useful.

Karel Perutka
Tomas Bata University in Zlín
Czech Republic

Part 1

Theory

1

Implementation of a New Quasi-Optimal Controller Tuning Algorithm for Time-Delay Systems

Libor Pekař and Roman Prokop
Tomas Bata University in Zlín
Czech Republic

1. Introduction

Systems and models with dead time or aftereffect, also called hereditary, anisochronic or time-delay systems (TDS), belonging to the class of infinite dimensional systems have been largely studied during last decades due to their interesting and important theoretical and practical features. A wide spectrum of systems in natural sciences, economics, pure informatics etc., both real-life and theoretical, is affected by delays which can have various forms; to name just a few the reader is referred e.g. to (Górecki et al., 1989; Marshall et al., 1992; Kolmanovskii & Myshkis, 1999; Richard, 2003; Michiels & Niculescu, 2008; Pekař et al., 2009) and references herein. Linear time-invariant dynamic systems with distributed or lumped delays (LTI-TDS) in a single-input single-output (SISO) case can be represented by a set of functional differential equations (Hale & Verduyn Lunel, 1993) or by the Laplace transfer function as a ratio of so-called quasipolynomials (El'sgol'ts & Norkin, 1973) in one complex variable s, rather than polynomials which are usual in system and control theory. Quasipolynomials are formed as linear combinations of products of s-powers and exponential terms. Hence, the Laplace transform of LTI-TDS is no longer rational and so-called meromorphic functions have to be introduced. A significant feature of LTI-TDS is (in contrast to undelayed systems) its infinite spectrum and transfer function poles decide - except some cases of distributed delays, see e.g. (Loiseau, 2000) - about the asymptotic stability as in the case of polynomials.

It is a well-known fact that delay can significantly deteriorate the quality of feedback control performance, namely stability and periodicity. Therefore, design a suitable control law for such systems is a challenging task solved by various techniques and approaches; a plentiful enumeration of them can be found e.g. in (Richard, 2003). Every controller design naturally requires and presumes a controlled plant model in an appropriate form. A huge set of approaches uses the Laplace transfer function; however, it is inconvenient to utilize a ratio of quasipolynomials especially while natural requirements of internal (impulse-free modes) and asymptotic stability of the feedback loop and the feasibility and causality of the controller are to be fulfilled.

The meromorphic description can be extended to the fractional description, to satisfy requirements above, so that quasipolynomials are factorized into proper and stable meromorphic functions. The ring of stable and proper quasipolynomial (RQ) meromorphic functions ($\mathbf{R}_{MS}$) is hence introduced (Zítek & Kučera, 2003; Pekař & Prokop, 2010). Although the ring can be used for a description of even neutral systems (Hale & Verduyn Lunel, 1993), only systems with so-called retarded structure are considered as the admissible class of systems in this contribution. In contrast to many other algebraic approaches, the ring enables to handle systems with non-commensurate delays, i.e. it is not necessary that all system delays can be expressed as integer multiples of the smallest one. Algebraic control philosophy in this ring then exploits the Bézout identity, to obtain stable and proper controllers, along with the Youla-Kučera parameterization for reference tracking and disturbance rejection.

The closed-loop stability is given, as for delayless systems, by the solutions of the characteristic equation which contains a quasipolynomial instead of a polynomial. These infinite many solutions represent closed-loop system poles deciding about the control system stability. Since a controller can have a finite number of coefficients representing selectable parameters, these have to be set to distribute the infinite spectrum so that the closed-loop system is stable and that other control requirements are satisfied.

The aim of this chapter is to describe, demonstrate and implement a new quasi-optimal pole placement algorithm for SISO LTI-TDS based on the quasi-continuous pole shifting - the main idea of which was presented in (Michiels et al., 2002) - to the prescribed positions. The desired positions are obtained by overshoot analysis of the step response for a dominant pair of complex conjugate poles. A controller structure is initially calculated by algebraic controller design in $\mathbf{R}_{MS}$. Note that the maximum number of prescribed poles (including their multiplicities) equals the number of unknown parameters. If the prescribed roots locations can not be reached, the optimizing of an objective function involving the distance of shifting poles to the prescribed ones and the roots dominancy is utilized. The optimization is made via Self-Organizing Migration Algorithm (SOMA), see e.g. (Zelinka, 2004). Matlab m-file environment is utilized for the algorithm implementation and, consequently, results are tested in Simulink on an attractive example of unstable SISO LTI-TDS.

The chapter is organized as follows. In Section 2 a brief general description of LTI-TDS is introduced together with the coprime factorization for the $\mathbf{R}_{MS}$ ring representation. Basic ideas of algebraic controller design in $\mathbf{R}_{MS}$ with a simple control feedback are presented in Section 3. The main and original part of the chapter - pole-placement shifting based tuning algorithm - is described in Section 4. Section 5 focuses SOMA and its utilization when solving the tuning problem. An illustrative benchmark example is presented in Section 6.

2. Description of LTI-TDS

The aim of this section is to present possible models of LTI-TDS; first, that in time domain using functional differential equations, second, the transfer function (matrix) via the Laplace transform. Then, the latter concept is extended so that an algebraic description in a special ring is introduced. Note that for the further purpose of this chapter the state-space functional description is useless.

2.1 State-space model

A LTI-TDS system with both input-output and internal (state) delays, which can have point (lumped) or distributed form, can be expressed by a set of functional differential equations

$$\begin{aligned}
\frac{\mathrm{d}\mathbf{x}(t)}{\mathrm{d}t} &= \sum_{i=1}^{N_H}\mathbf{H}_i\frac{\mathrm{d}\mathbf{x}(t-\eta_i)}{\mathrm{d}t} + \mathbf{A}_0\mathbf{x}(t) + \sum_{i=1}^{N_A}\mathbf{A}_i\mathbf{x}(t-\eta_i) + \mathbf{B}_0\mathbf{u}(t) \\
&\quad + \sum_{i=1}^{N_B}\mathbf{B}_i\mathbf{u}(t-\eta_i) + \int_0^L \mathbf{A}(\tau)\mathbf{x}(t-\tau)d\tau + \int_0^L \mathbf{B}(\tau)\mathbf{u}(t-\tau)d\tau \\
\mathbf{y}(t) &= \mathbf{C}\mathbf{x}(t)
\end{aligned} \tag{1}$$

where $\mathbf{x} \in \mathbb{R}^n$ is a vector of state variables, $\mathbf{u} \in \mathbb{R}^m$ stands for a vector of inputs, $\mathbf{y} \in \mathbb{R}^l$ represents a vector of outputs, $\mathbf{A}_i$, $\mathbf{A}(\tau)$, $\mathbf{B}_i$, $\mathbf{B}(\tau)$, $\mathbf{C}$, $\mathbf{H}_i$ are matrices of appropriate dimensions, $0 \le \eta_i \le L$ are lumped (point) delays and convolution integrals express distributed delays (Hale & Verduyn Lunel, 1993; Richard, 2003; Vyhlídal, 2003). If $\mathbf{H}_i \neq \mathbf{0}$ for any $i = 1,2,...N_H$, model (1) is called neutral; on the other hand, if $\mathbf{H}_i = \mathbf{0}$ for every $i = 1,2,...N_H$, so-called retarded model is obtained. It should be noted that the state of model (1) is given not only by a vector of state variables in the current time instant, but also by a segment of the last model history (in functional Banach space) of state and input variables

$$\mathbf{x}(t+\tau),\ \mathbf{u}(t+\tau),\ \tau \in \langle -L, 0 \rangle \tag{2}$$

Convolution integrals in (1) can be numerically approximate by summations for digital implementation; however, this can destabilize even a stable system. Alternatively, one can integrate (1) and add a new state variable to obtain derivations on the right-hand side only. In the contrary, the model can also be expressed in more consistent functional form using Riemann-Stieltjes integrals so that both lumped and distributed delays are under one convolution. For further details and other state-space TDS models the reader is referred to (Richard, 2003).

2.2 Input-output model

This contribution is concerned with retarded delayed systems in the input-output formulation governed by the Laplace transfer function matrix (considering zero initial conditions) as in (3). Hence, in the SISO case (we are concerning about here), the transfer function is no longer rational, as for conventional delayless systems, and a meromorphic function as a ratio of retarded quasipolynomials (RQ) is obtained instead.

$$\begin{aligned}
\mathbf{Y}(s) &= \mathbf{G}(s)\mathbf{U}(s) = \frac{\mathbf{\Gamma}_1\mathbf{\Gamma}_2}{\Delta}\mathbf{U}(s) \\
\Delta &= \det\left[s\mathbf{I} - \mathbf{A}_0 - \sum_{i=1}^{N_A+1}\mathbf{A}_i\exp(-s\eta_i) - \int_0^L \mathbf{A}(\tau)\exp(-s\tau)\mathrm{d}\tau \right] \\
\mathbf{\Gamma}_1 &= \mathbf{C}\mathrm{adj}\left[s\mathbf{I} - \mathbf{A}_0 - \sum_{i=1}^{N_A+1}\mathbf{A}_i\exp(-s\eta_i) - \int_0^L \mathbf{A}(\tau)\exp(-s\tau)\mathrm{d}\tau \right] \\
\mathbf{\Gamma}_2 &= \mathbf{B}_0 + \sum_{i=1}^{N_B+1}\mathbf{B}_i\exp(-s\eta_i) + \int_0^L \mathbf{B}(\tau)\exp(-s\tau)\mathrm{d}\tau
\end{aligned} \tag{3}$$

A (retarded or neutral) quasipolynomial of degree n has the generic form

$$q(s) = s^n + \sum_{i=0}^{n}\sum_{j=1}^{h} x_{ij} s^i \exp(-\vartheta_{ij} s), \vartheta_{ij} \geq 0 \tag{4}$$

where $x_{nj} \neq 0$ in the neutral case for some *j*, whereas a RQ owns $x_{nj} = 0$ for all *j*.

However, the transfer function representation in the form of a ratio of two quasipolynomials is not suitable in order to satisfy controller feasibility, causality and closed-loop (Hurwitz) stability (Loiseau 2000; Zítek & Kučera, 2003). Rather more general approaches utilize a field of fractions where a transfer function is expressed as a ratio of two coprime elements of a suitable ring. A ring is a set closed for addition and multiplication, with a unit element for addition and multiplication and an inverse element for addition. This implies that division is not generally allowed.

2.3 Plant description in $\mathbf{R}_{MS}$ ring

A powerful algebraic tool ensuring requirements above is a ring of stable and proper RQ-meromorphic functions ($\mathbf{R}_{MS}$). Since the original definition of $\mathbf{R}_{MS}$ in (Zítek & Kučera, 2003) does not constitute a ring, some minor changes in the definition was made in (Pekař & Prokop, 2009). Namely, although the retarded structure of TDS is considered only, the minimal ring conditions require the use of neutral quasipolynomials at least in the numerator as well.

An element $T(s) \in \mathbf{R}_{MS}$ is represented by a proper ratio of two quasipolynomials

$$T(s) = \frac{y(s)}{x(s)} \tag{5}$$

where a denominator $x(s)$ is a quasipolynomial of degree n and a numerator can be factorized as

$$y(s) = \tilde{y}(s)\exp(-\tau s) \tag{6}$$

where $\tilde{y}(s)$ is a quasipolynomial of degree l and $\tau \geq 0$. $T(s)$ is stable, which means that there is no pole s_0 such that $\text{Re}\{s_0\} \geq 0$; in other words, all roots of $x(s)$ with $\text{Re}\{s_0\} \geq 0$ are those of $y(s)$. Moreover, the ratio is proper, i.e. $l \leq n$.

Thus, $T(s)$ is analytic and bounded in the open right half-plane, i.e.

$$\sup_{\text{Re}\{s\} \geq 0} |T(s)| < \infty \tag{7}$$

As mentioned above, in this contribution only retarded systems are considered, i.e. $x(s)$, $y(s)$ are RQs. Let the plant be initially described as

$$G(s) = \frac{b(s)}{a(s)} \tag{8}$$

where $a(s)$, $b(s)$ are RQs. Hence, using a coprime factorization, a plant model has the form

$$G(s) = \frac{B(s)}{A(s)} \tag{10}$$

where $A(s), B(s) \in \mathbf{R}_{MS}$ are coprime, i.e. there does not exist a non-trivial (non-unit) common factor of both elements. Note that a system of neutral type can induce problem since there can exist a coprime pair $A(s), B(s)$ which is not, however, Bézout coprime - which implies that the system can not be stabilized by any feedback controller admitting the Laplace transform, see details in (Loiseau et al., 2002).

3. Controller design in RMS

This section outlines controller design based on the algebraic approach in the $\mathbf{R}_{MS}$ ring satisfying the inner Hurwitz (Bounded Input Bounded Output - BIBO) stability of the closed loop, controller feasibility, reference tracking and disturbance rejection.
For algebraic controller design in $\mathbf{R}_{MS}$ it is initially supposed that not only the plant is expressed by the transfer function over $\mathbf{R}_{MS}$ but a controller and all system signals are over the ring. As a control system, the common negative feedback loop as in Fig. 1 is chosen for the simplicity, where $W(s)$ is the Laplace transform of the reference signal, $D(s)$ stands for that of the load disturbance, $E(s)$ is transformed control error, $U_0(s)$ expresses the controller output (control action), $U(s)$ represents the plant input, and $Y(s)$ is the plant output controlled signal in the Laplace transform. The plant transfer function is depicted as $G(s)$, and $G_R(s)$ stands for a controller in the scheme.

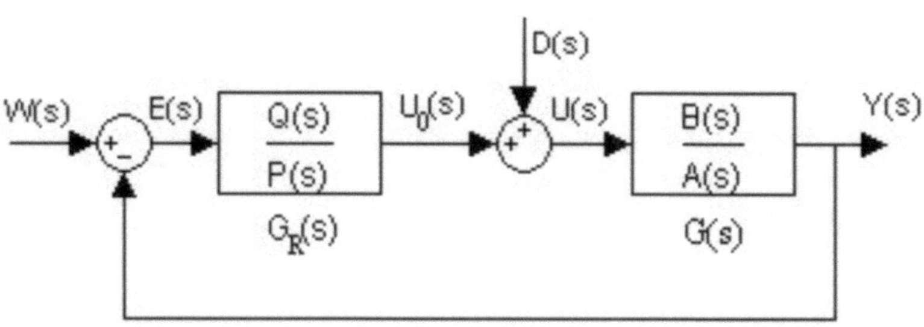

Fig. 1. Simple control feedback loop

Control system external inputs have forms

$$W(s) = \frac{H_W(s)}{F_W(s)},\ D(s) = \frac{H_D(s)}{F_D(s)} \tag{11}$$

where $H_W(s)$, $H_D(s)$, $F_W(s)$, $F_D(s) \in \mathbf{R}_{MS}$.
The following basic transfer functions can be derived in the control system in general

$$\begin{aligned} G_{WY}(s) &= \frac{Y(s)}{W(s)} = \frac{B(s)Q(s)}{M(s)},\ G_{DY}(s) = \frac{Y(s)}{D(s)} = \frac{B(s)P(s)}{M(s)} \\ G_{WE}(s) &= \frac{E(s)}{W(s)} = \frac{A(s)P(s)}{M(s)},\ G_{DE}(s) = \frac{E(s)}{D(s)} = -\frac{B(s)P(s)}{M(s)} \end{aligned} \tag{12}$$

where

$$G_R(s) = \frac{Q(s)}{P(s)} \tag{13}$$

$$M(s) = A(s)P(s) + B(s)Q(s) \tag{14}$$

and $Q(s)$, $P(s)$ are from $\mathbf{R}_{MS}$ and the fraction (13) is (Bézout) coprime (or relatively prime). The numerator of $M(s) \in \mathbf{R}_{MS}$ agrees to the characteristic quasipolynomial of the closed loop.

Following subsections describes briefly how to provide the basic control requirements.

3.1 Stabilization

According to e.g. (Kučera, 1993; Zítek & Kučera, 2003), the closed-loop system is stable if and only if there exists a pair $P(s), Q(s) \in \mathbf{R}_{MS}$ satisfying the Bézout identity

$$A(s)P(s) + B(s)Q(s) = 1 \tag{15}$$

a particular stabilizing solution of which, $P_0(s), Q_0(s)$, can be then parameterized as

$$\begin{aligned} P(s) &= P_0(s) \pm B(s)T(s) \\ Q(s) &= Q_0(s) \mp A(s)T(s),\ T(s) \in \mathbf{R}_{MS} \end{aligned} \tag{16}$$

Parameterization (16) is used to satisfy remaining control and performance requirements.

3.2 Reference tracking and disturbance rejection

The question is how to select $T(s) \in \mathbf{R}_{MS}$ in (16) so that tasks of reference tracking and disturbance rejection are accomplished. The key lies in the form of $G_{WE}(s)$ and $G_{DY}(s)$ in (12). Consider the limits

$$\begin{aligned} \lim_{t\to\infty} y_D(t) &= \lim_{s\to 0} sY_D(s) = \lim_{s\to 0} sG_{DY}(s)D(s) \\ &= \lim_{s\to 0} sB(s)P(s)\frac{H_D(s)}{F_D(s)} \end{aligned} \tag{17}$$

$$\begin{aligned} \lim_{t\to\infty} e_W(t) &= \lim_{s\to 0} sE_W(s) = \lim_{s\to 0} sG_{WE}(s)W(s) \\ &= \lim_{s\to 0} sA(s)P(s)\frac{H_W(s)}{F_W(s)} \end{aligned} \tag{18}$$

where $\cdot_D$ means that the output is influenced only by the disturbance, and symbol $\cdot_W$ expresses that the signal is a response to the reference. Limit (17) is zero if $\lim_{s\to 0} Y_D(s) < \infty$ and $Y_D(s)$ is analytic in the open right half-plane. Moreover, for the feasibility of $y_D(t)$, $Y_D(s)$ must be proper. This implies that the disturbance is asymptotically rejected if $Y_D(s) \in \mathbf{R}_{MS}$. Similarly, the reference is tracked if $E_W(s) \in \mathbf{R}_{MS}$.

In other words, $F_D(s)$ must divide the product $B(s)P(s)$ in $\mathbf{R}_{MS}$, and $A(s)P(s)$ must be divisible by $F_W(s)$ in $\mathbf{R}_{MS}$. Details about divisibility in $\mathbf{R}_{MS}$ can be found e.g. in (Pekař & Prokop, 2009). Thus, if neither $B(s)$ has any common unstable zero with $F_D(s)$ nor $A(s)$

has any common unstable zero with $F_W(s)$, one has to set all unstable zeros of $F_D(s)$ and $F_W(s)$ (with corresponding multiplicities) as zeros of $P(s)$. Note that zeros mean zero points of a whole term in $\mathbf{R}_{MS}$, not only of a quasipolynomial numerator. Unstable zeros agrees with those with $\mathrm{Re}\{s\} \geq 0$.

4. Pole-placement shifting based controller tuning algorithm

In this crucial section, the idea of a new pole-placement shifting based controller tuning algorithm (PPSA) is presented. Although some steps of PPSA are taken over some existing pole-shifting algorithms, the idea of connection with pole placement and the SOMA optimization is original.

4.1 Overview of PSSA

We first give an overview of all steps of PPSA and, consequently, describe each in more details. The procedure starts with controller design in $\mathbf{R}_{MS}$ introduced in the previous section. The next steps are as follows:

1. Calculate the closed-loop reference-to-output transfer function $G_{WY}(s)$. Let l_{num} and l_{den}, respectively, be numbers of unknown (free, selectable) real parameters of the numerator and denominator, respectively. Sign $l = l_{num} + l_{den}$.
2. Choose a simple model of a stable LTI system in the form of the transfer function $G_{WY,m}(s)$ with a numerator of degree n_{num} and the denominator of degree n_{den}. Calculate step response maximum overshoots of the model for a suitable range of its n_{num} zeros and n_{den} poles (including their multiplicities). If $\overline{n}_{num} \leq n_{num}$ and $\overline{n}_{den} \leq n_{den}$, respectively, are numbers of all real zeros (poles) and pairs of complex conjugate zeros (poles) of the model, it must hold that $\overline{n}_{num} \leq l_{num}$ and $\overline{n}_{den} \leq l_{den}$, respectively.
3. Prescribe all poles and zeros of the model with respect to calculated maximum overshoots (and maximal overshoot times). If the poles and zeros are dominant (i.e. the rightmost), the procedure is finished. Otherwise do following steps.
4. Shift the rightmost (or the nearest) zeros and poles to the prescribed locations successively. If the number of currently shifted poles and conjugate pairs $\overline{n}_{den} \leq n_{sp} \leq l_{den}$ is higher then $\overline{n}_{den}$, try to move the rest of dominant (rightmost) poles to the left. The same rule holds for shifted zeros, analogously.
5. If all prescribed poles and zeros are dominant, the procedure is finished. Otherwise, select a suitable cost function reflecting the distance of dominant poles (zeros) from prescribed positions and distances of spectral abscissas of both, prescribed and dominant poles (zeros).
6. Minimize the cost function, e.g. via SOMA.

Now look at these steps of the algorithm at great length.

4.2 Characteristic quasipolynomial and characteristic entire function

Algebraic controller design in the $\mathbf{R}_{MS}$ ring introduced in Section 3 results in a controller owning the transfer function $G_R(s)$ containing a finite number of unknown (free, selectable) parameters. The task of PPSA is to set these parameters so that the possibly infinite spectrum of the closed loop has dominant (rightmost) poles located in (or near by) the prescribed positions. If possibly, one can prescribe and place dominant zeros as well. Note that controller design in $\mathbf{R}_{MS}$ using the feedback system as in Fig. 1 results in infinite spectrum of the feedback if the controlled plant is unstable.

If the (quasi)polynomial numerator and denominator of $G(s)$ have no common roots in the open right-half plane, the closed-loop spectrum is given entirely by roots of the numerator $m(s)$ of $M(s)$, the so called characteristic quasipolynomial. In the case of distributed delays, $G(s)$ has some common roots with $\operatorname{Re}\{s\} \geq 0$ in both, the numerator and denominator, and these roots do not affect the system dynamics since they cancel each other. In this case, the spectrum is given by zeros of the entire function $m(s)/m_U(s)$, i.e. the characteristic entire function, where $m_U(s)$ is a (quasi)polynomial the only roots of which are the common unstable roots.

The (quasi)polynomial denominator of $G_{WY}(s)$ agrees with $m(s)$. Its role is much more important than the role of the numerator of $G_{WY}(s)$ since the closed-loop zeros does not influence the stability. In the light of this fact, the setting of closed-loop poles has the priority. Therefore, one has to set l_{den} free denominator parameters first. Free (selectable) parameters in the numerator of $G_{WY}(s)$ are to be set only if there exist those which are not contained in the denominator. The number of such "additional" parameters is l_{num}.

4.3 Closed-loop model and step response overshoots

The task now is how to prescribe the closed-loop poles appropriately. We choose a simple finite-dimensional model of the reference-to-output transfer function and find its maximum overshoots and overshoot times for a suitable range of the model poles.

Let the prescribed (desired) closed-loop model be of the transfer function

$$G_{WY,m}(s) = k_1 \frac{b_1 s + b_0}{s^2 + a_1 s + a_0} = k_2 \frac{s - z_1}{(s - s_1)(s - \overline{s}_1)} \tag{19}$$

where $k_1, k_2, b_1, b_0, a_1, a_0 \in \mathbb{R}$ are model parameters $z_1 \in \mathbb{R}^-$ stands for a model zero and $s_1 \in \mathbb{C}^-$ is a model stable pole where $\overline{s}_1$ expresses its complex conjugate. To obtain the unit static gain of $G_{WY,m}(s)$ it must hold true

$$k_1 = \frac{a_0}{b_0}, k_2 = -\frac{|s_1|^2}{z_1} \tag{20}$$

Sign $s_1 = \alpha + \omega\mathrm{j}, \alpha < 0, \omega \geq 0$ and calculate the impulse function $g_{WY,m}(t)$ of $G_{WY,m}(s)$ using the Matlab function *ilaplace* as

$$g_{WY,m}(t) = k_2 \exp(\alpha t) \left[\cos(\omega t) - \frac{z_1 - \alpha}{\omega} \sin(\omega t) \right] \tag{21}$$

Since $i_{WY,m}(t) = h'_{WY,m}(t)$, where $h_{WY,m}(t)$ is the step response function, the necessary condition for the existence of a step response overshoot at time t_O is

$$i_{WY,m}(t_O) = 0, t_O > 0 \tag{22}$$

The condition (22) yields these two solutions: either $t_O \to -\infty$ (which is trivial) or

$$t_O = \frac{1}{\omega}\arccos\left(\pm\frac{|\alpha - z_1|}{\sqrt{(\alpha - z_1)^2 + \omega^2}}\right) \tag{23}$$

when considering $\arccos(x) \in [0,\pi]$. Obviously, (23) has infinitely many solutions. If $\alpha < 0, z_1 < 0$, the maximum overshoot occurs at time

$$t_{\max} = \min(t_O) \tag{24}$$

One can further calculate the step response function $h_{WY,m}(t)$ as

$$h_{WY,m}(t) = \frac{k_2}{|s_1|^2}\left[\exp(\alpha t)\left(z_1\cos(\omega t) - \frac{z_1\alpha - |s_1|^2}{\omega}\sin(\omega t)\right) - z_1\right] \tag{25}$$

Define now the maximum relative overshoot as

$$\Delta h_{WY,m,\max} := \frac{h_{WY,m}(t_{\max}) - h_{WY,m}(\infty)}{h_{WY,m}(\infty)} \tag{26}$$

see Fig. 2.

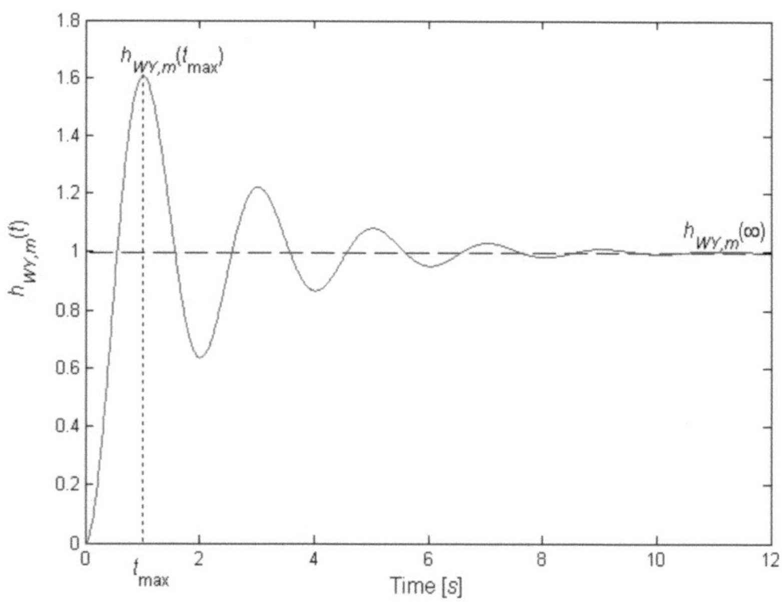

Fig. 2. Reference-to-output step response characteristics and the maximum overshoot
Using definition (26) one can obtain

$$\Delta h_{WY,m,\max} = \exp(\alpha t)\left(\frac{-z_1\omega\cos(\omega t) + \left(z_1\alpha - |s_1|^2\right)\sin(\omega t)}{z_1\omega}\right)\Bigg|_{t=t_{\max}} \tag{27}$$

Obviously, $\Delta h_{WY,m,\max}$ is a function of three parameters, i.e. n_1,α,ω, which is not suitable for a general formulation of the maximal overshoot. Hence, let us introduce new parameters ξ_α,ξ_z as

$$\xi_\alpha = -\frac{\alpha}{\omega},\ \xi_z = -\frac{z_1}{\omega} \tag{28}$$

which give rise from (23), (24) and (27) to

$$\begin{aligned} \Delta h_{WY,m,\max} &= \frac{1}{\xi_z}\exp\left(-\xi_\alpha t_{\max,norm}\right)\left(-\xi_z\cos\left(t_{\max,norm}\right)+\left(\xi_\alpha^2+1-\xi_\alpha\xi_z\right)\sin\left(t_{\max,norm}\right)\right) \\ t_{\max,norm} &= \omega t_{\max} = \min\left(\arccos\left(\pm\frac{\left|\xi_\alpha-\xi_\omega\right|}{\sqrt{\left(\xi_\alpha-\xi_\omega\right)^2+1}}\right)\right) \end{aligned} \tag{29}$$

where $t_{\max,norm}$ represents the normalized maximal overshoot time.
We can successfully use Matlab to display function $\Delta h_{WY,m,\max}(\xi_\alpha,\xi_z)$ and $t_{\max,norm}(\xi_\alpha,\xi_z)$ graphically, for suitable ranges of ξ_α,ξ_z as can be seen from Fig. 3 – Fig. 7.
Recall that model (19) gives rise to $n_{num}=1, n_{den}=2, \overline{n}_{num}=1, \overline{n}_{den}=1$.

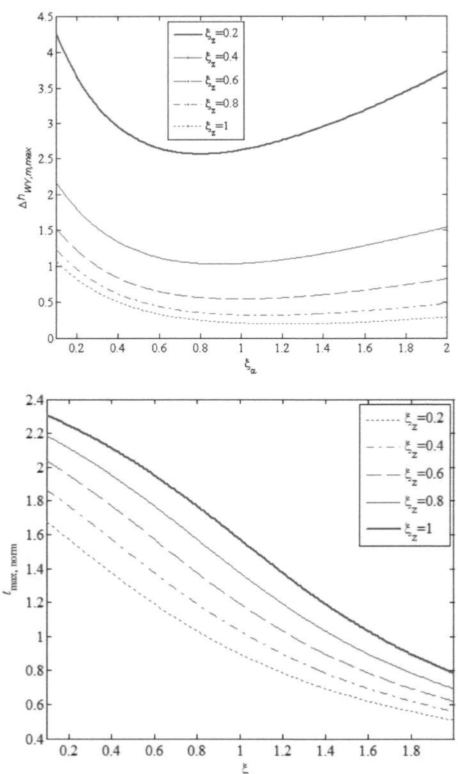

Fig. 3. Maximum overshoots $\Delta h_{WY,m,\max}(\xi_\alpha,\xi_z)$ (a) and normalized maximal overshoot times $t_{\max,norm}(\xi_\alpha,\xi_z)$ (b) for $\xi_\alpha=[0.1,2]$, $\xi_z=\{0.2,0.4,0.6,0.8,1\}$.

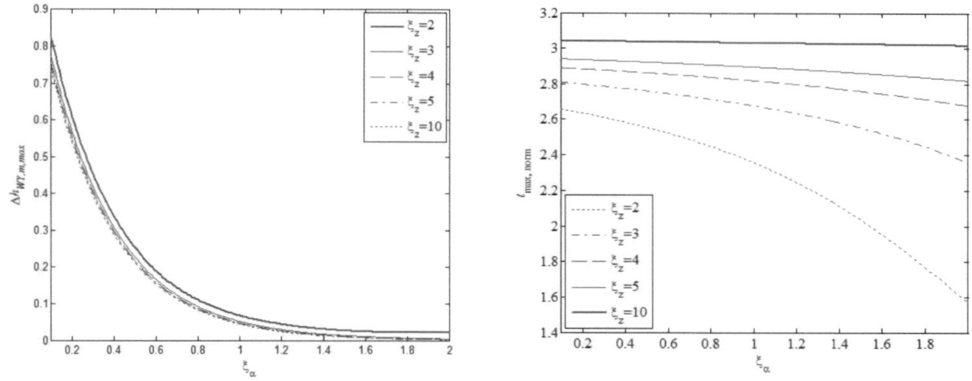

Fig. 4. Maximum overshoots $\Delta h_{WY,m,\max}(\xi_\alpha,\xi_z)$ (a) and normalized maximal overshoot times $t_{\max,norm}(\xi_\alpha,\xi_z)$ (b) for $\xi_\alpha = [0.1,2]$, $\xi_z = \{2,3,4,5,10\}$.

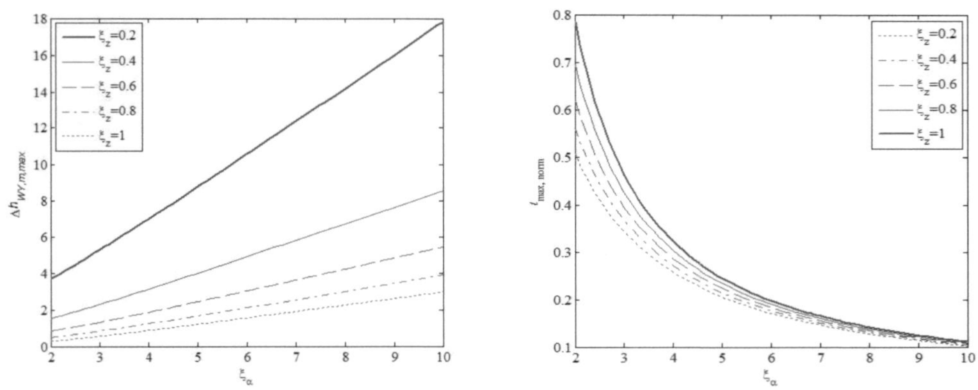

Fig. 5. Maximum overshoots $\Delta h_{WY,m,\max}(\xi_\alpha,\xi_z)$ (a) and normalized maximal overshoot times $t_{\max,norm}(\xi_\alpha,\xi_z)$ (b) for $\xi_\alpha = [2,10]$, $\xi_z = \{0.2,0.4,0.6,0.8,1\}$.

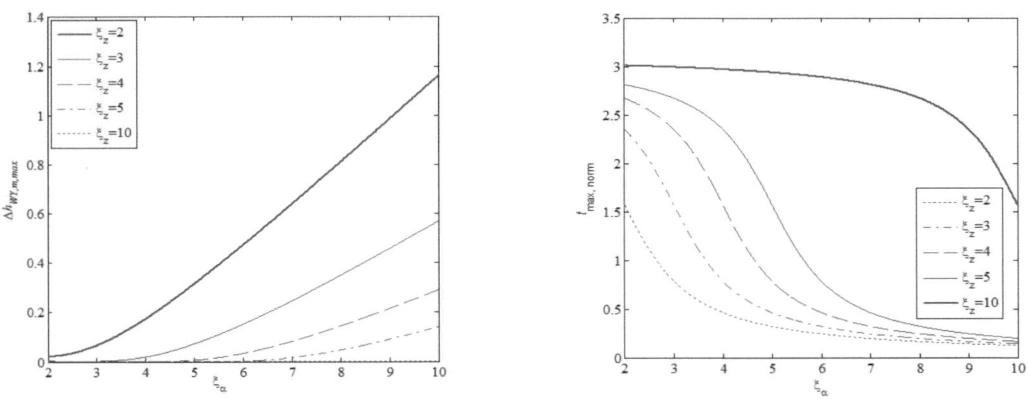

Fig. 6. Maximum overshoots $\Delta h_{WY,m,\max}(\xi_\alpha,\xi_z)$ (a) and normalized maximal overshoot times $t_{\max,norm}(\xi_\alpha,\xi_z)$ (b) for $\xi_\alpha = [2,10]$, $\xi_z = \{2,3,4,5,10\}$.

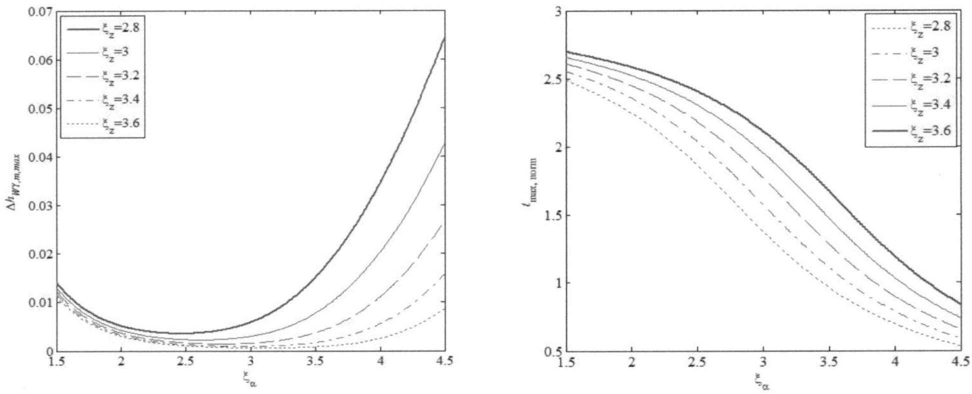

Fig. 7. Maximum overshoots $\Delta h_{WY,m,\max}(\xi_\alpha,\xi_z)$ (a) and normalized maximal overshoot times $t_{\max,norm}(\xi_\alpha,\xi_z)$ (b) for $\xi_\alpha=[1,5,4.5]$, $\xi_z=\{2.8,3,3.2,3.4,3.6\}$ - A detailed view on "small" overshoots.

The procedure of searching suitable prescribed poles can be done e.g. as in the following way. A user requires $\Delta h_{WY,m,\max}=0.03$ (i.e. the maximal overshoot equals 3 %), $\xi_\alpha=4$ (i.e. "the quarter dumping") and $t_{\max}=5\,\mathrm{s}$. Fig. 7 gives approximately $\xi_z=2.9$ which yields $t_{\max,norm}\approx 1.2$. These two values together with (28) and (29) result in $s_1=-0.96+0.24\mathrm{j},\ z_1=-0.7$.

4.4 Direct pole placement

This subsection extends step 3 of PPSA from Subsection 4.1. The goal is to prescribe poles and zeros of the closed-loop "at once". The drawback here is that the prescribed poles (zeros) might not be dominant (i.e. the rightmost). The procedure was utilized to LTI-TDS e.g. in (Zítek & Hlava, 2001).

Given quasipolynomial $m(s)$ with a vector $\mathbf{v}=[v_1,v_2,...,v_l]^T\in\mathbb{R}^l$ of l free parameters, the assignment of n prescribed single roots σ_i, $i=1...n$, can be done via the solution of the set of algebraic equations in the form

$$[m(\sigma_i,\mathbf{v})]_{s=\sigma_i}=0,\ i=1...n \tag{30}$$

In the case of complex conjugate poles, one has to take the real and imaginary part separately as

$$\mathrm{Re}\left\{[m(\sigma_i,\mathbf{v})]_{s=\sigma_i}\right\}=0,\mathrm{Im}\left\{[m(\sigma_i,\mathbf{v})]_{s=\sigma_i}\right\}=0 \tag{31}$$

for every pair of roots.

If a root σ_i has the multiplicity p, it must be calculated

$$\left[\frac{\mathrm{d}^j}{\mathrm{d}s^j}m(\sigma_i,\mathbf{v})\right]_{s=\sigma_i}=0,\ j=0...p-1 \tag{32}$$

or

$$\operatorname{Re}\left[\frac{\mathrm{d}^j}{\mathrm{d}s^j}m(\sigma_i,\mathbf{v})\right]_{s=\sigma_i}=0,\ \operatorname{Im}\left[\frac{\mathrm{d}^j}{\mathrm{d}s^j}m(\sigma_i,\mathbf{v})\right]_{s=\sigma_i}=0, j=0...p-1 \tag{33}$$

Note that if $m(s)$ is nonlinear with respect to $\mathbf{v}$, one can solve a set on non-linear algebraic equations directly, or to use an expansion

$$m(\sigma_i,\mathbf{v})\approx m(\sigma_i,\mathbf{v}_0)+\sum_{j=1}^{k}\Delta v_j\left[\frac{\partial m(s,\mathbf{v}_0)}{\partial v_j}\right]_{\substack{s=\sigma_i\\ \mathbf{v}=\mathbf{v}_0}} \tag{34}$$

where $\mathbf{v}_0$ means a point in which the expansion is made or an initial estimation of the solution and $\Delta\mathbf{v}=\left[\Delta v_1,\Delta v_2,...,\Delta v_l\right]^T$ is a vector of parameters increments. Equations (34) should be solved iteratively, e.g. via the well-known Newton method. Note, furthermore, that the algebraic controller design in $\mathbf{R}_{MS}$ for LTI-TDS results in the linear set (30)-(34) with respect to selectable parameters - both, in the numerator and denominator of $G_{WY}(s)$.
It is clear that a unique solution is obtained only if the set of $n=l$ independent equations is given. If $n<l$, equations (30)-(34) can be solved using the Moore-Penrose (pseudo)inverse minimizing the norm $\|\mathbf{v}\|_2=\sum_{i=1}^{k}v_i^2$, see (Ben Israel & Greville, 1966). Contrariwise, whenever $n>l$, it is not possible to place roots exactly and the pseudoinverse provides the minimization of squares of the left-hand sides of (30)-(34).
The methodology described in this subsection is utilized on both, the numerator and denominator.

4.5 Continuous poles (zeros) shifting

Once the poles (zeros) are prescribed, it ought to be checked whether these roots are the rightmost. If yes, the PPSA algorithm stops; if not, one may try to shift poles so that the prescribed ones become dominant. There are two possibilities. First, the dominant roots move to the prescribed ones; second, roots nearest to the prescribed ones are shifted - while the rest of the spectrum (or zeros) is simultaneously pushed to the left. The following describes it in more details.
We describe the procedure for the closed-loop denominator and its roots (poles); the numerator is served analogously for all its free parameters which are not included in the denominator. Recall that l_{den} is the number of unknown (selectable) parameters, n_{den} stands for the number of model (prescribed) poles (including their multiplicities), $\overline{n}_{den}$ represents the number of real poles and conjugate pairs of prescribed poles and n_{sp} is the number of currently shifted real poles and conjugate pairs. Generally, it holds that

$$\overline{n}_{den}\le n_{sp}\le l_{den} \tag{35}$$

The idea of continuous poles shifting described below was introduced in (Michiels et al., 2002). Similar procedure which, however, enables to shift less number of poles since $n_{sp}\le l_{den}$ includes every single complex pole instead of a conjugate pair, was investigated in (Vyhlídal, 2003). Roughly speaking, the latter is based on solution of (30) - (34) where $\mathbf{v}_0$ represents the vector of actual controller parameters, $\mathbf{v}=\mathbf{v}_0+\Delta\mathbf{v}$ are new controller

parameters and σ_i means prescribed poles (in the vicinity of the actual ones) here. Now look at the former methodology in more details.
The approach (Michiels et al., 2002) is based on the extrapolation

$$m(\sigma_i,\mathbf{v}) \approx \underbrace{m(\sigma_i,\mathbf{v}_0)}_{=0} + \Delta\sigma_i \left[\frac{\partial m(s,\mathbf{v})}{\partial s}\right]_{\substack{s=\sigma_i \\ \mathbf{v}=\mathbf{v}_0}} + \Delta v_j \left[\frac{\partial m(s,\mathbf{v})}{\partial v_j}\right]_{\substack{s=\sigma_i \\ \mathbf{v}=\mathbf{v}_0}} = 0,\ i=1...n_{sp},\ j=1...l_{den} \quad (36)$$

yielding

$$\frac{\Delta\sigma_i}{\Delta v_j} \approx -\left[\frac{\partial m(s,\mathbf{v})}{\partial s}\right]^{-1}_{\substack{s=\sigma_i \\ \mathbf{v}=\mathbf{v}_0}} \left[\frac{\partial m(s,\mathbf{v})}{\partial v_j}\right]_{\substack{s=\sigma_i \\ \mathbf{v}=\mathbf{v}_0}} \quad (37)$$

where $\mathbf{v}_0$ represents the vector of actual controller parameters, σ_i means actual poles and $\Delta\sigma_i$ and Δv_j are increments of poles and controller parameters, respectively. In case of a p-multiple pole, the following term is inserted in (36) and (37) instead of $m(s)$

$$\frac{\mathrm{d}^p}{\mathrm{d}s^p} m(s) \quad (38)$$

However, (38) can be used only if the pole including all multiplicities is moved. If, on the other hand, the intention is to shift a part of poles within the multiplicity to the one location and the rest of the multiplicity to another (or other) location(s), it is better to consider a multiple pole as a "nest" of close single poles.
Then a matrix

$$\mathbf{S} = \left[\frac{\Delta\sigma_i}{\Delta v_j}\right] \in \mathbb{R}\ n_{sp} x l_{den} \quad (39)$$

is called the sensitivity matrix satisfying

$$\Delta\mathbf{v} = \mathbf{S}^{+}\Delta\boldsymbol{\sigma} \quad (40)$$

where $\Delta\boldsymbol{\sigma} = \left[\Delta\sigma_1, \Delta\sigma_2, ..., \Delta\sigma_{n_{sp}}\right]^T$ and $\mathbf{S}^{+}$ means the pseudoinverse.
It holds that

$$\frac{\Delta \mathrm{Re}\{\sigma_i\}}{\Delta v_j} = \mathrm{Re}\left\{\frac{\Delta\sigma_i}{\Delta v_j}\right\} \quad (41)$$

thus, if poles are shifted in a real axis only, it can be calculated

$$\Delta\mathbf{v} = \mathrm{Re}\{\mathbf{S}\}^{+}\,\mathrm{Re}\{\Delta\boldsymbol{\sigma}\} \quad (42)$$

Otherwise, the following approximation ought to be used

$$\Delta\mathbf{v} \approx \mathrm{Re}\left\{\mathbf{S}^{+}\Delta\boldsymbol{\sigma}\right\} \quad (43)$$

The continuous shifting starts with $n_{sp} = \overline{n}_{den}$. Then, one can take the number of $\overline{n}_{den}$ rightmost poles and move them to the prescribed ones. The rightmost closed-loop pole moves to the rightmost prescribed pole etc. Alternatively, the same number of dominant poles (or conjugated pairs) can be considered; however, the nearest poles can be shifted to the prescribed ones. If two or more prescribed poles own the same dominant pole, it is assigned to the rightmost prescribed pole and removed from the list of moved poles. The number $n_{sp} \in \{\overline{n}_{den}, l_{den}\}$ is incremented whenever the approaching starts to fail for any pole. If $n_{sp} > \overline{n}_{den}$, the rest of dominant poles is pushed to the left. More precisely, shifting to the prescribed poles is described by the following formula

$$\Delta\sigma = \frac{\sigma_p - \sigma_s}{|\sigma_p - \sigma_s|}\delta \tag{44}$$

and pushing to the left agrees with

$$\Delta\sigma = -\delta \tag{45}$$

where δ is a discretization step in the space of poles, e.g. $\delta = 0.001$, σ_p is a prescribed pole and σ_s means a pole moved to the prescribed one.
If $n_{sp} = l_{den}$ and all prescribed poles become the rightmost (dominant) ones, PPSA is finished. Otherwise, do the last step of PPSA introduced in the following subsection.

5. Minimization of a cost function via SOMA

This step is implemented whenever the exact pole assignment even via shifting fails. In the first part of this subsection we arrange the cost function to be minimized. Then, SOMA algorithm (Zelinka, 2004) belonging to the wide family of evolution algorithms is introduced and briefly described. Again, the procedure is given for the pole-optimization; the zero-optimization dealing with the closed-loop numerator is done analogously.

5.1 Cost function

The goal now is to rearrange feedback poles (zeros) so that they are "sufficiently close" to the prescribed ones and, concurrently, they are "as the most dominant as possible". This requirement can be satisfied by the minimizing of the following cost function

$$F(\mathbf{v}) = d_\sigma(\mathbf{v}) + \lambda d_R(\mathbf{v}) = \sum_{i=1}^{\overline{n}_{den}} |\sigma_{s,i} - \sigma_{p,i}| + \lambda \operatorname{Re}\{\sigma_{d,i} - \sigma_{p,i}\} \tag{46}$$

where $d_\sigma(\mathbf{v})$ is the distance of prescribed poles $\sigma_{p,i}$ from the nearest ones $\sigma_{s,i}$, $d_R(\mathbf{v})$ expresses the sum of distances of dominant poles from the prescribed ones and $\lambda > 0$ represents a real weighting parameter. The higher λ is, the pole dominancy of is more important in $F(\mathbf{v})$. Recall that (when the dominant poles were moved)

$$\sigma_{s,1} \geq \sigma_{s,2} \geq \ldots \geq \sigma_{s,\overline{n}_{den}}, \sigma_{p,1} \geq \sigma_{p,2} \geq \ldots \geq \sigma_{p,\overline{n}_{den}}, \sigma_{d,1} \geq \sigma_{d,2} \geq \ldots \geq \sigma_{d,\overline{n}_{den}} \tag{47}$$

Alternatively, one can include both, the zeros and poles, in (46), not separately.

Poles can be found e.g. by the quasipolynomial mapping root finder (QPMR) implemented in Matlab, see (Vyhlídal & Zítek, 2003).
Hence, the aim is to solve the problem

$$\mathbf{v}_{opt} = \arg\min F(\mathbf{v}) \tag{48}$$

We use SOMA algorithm based on genetic operations with a population of found solutions and moving of population specimens to each other. A brief description of the algorithm follows.

5.2 SOMA

SOMA is ranked among evolution algorithms, more precisely genetic algorithms, dealing with populations similarly as differential evolution does. The algorithm is based on vector operations over the space of feasible solutions (parameters) in which the population is defined. Population specimens cooperate when searching the best solution (the minimum of the cost function) and, simultaneously, each of them tries to be a leader. They move to each other and the searching is finished when all specimens are localized on a small area.
In SOMA, every single generation, in which a new population is generated, is called a migration round. The notion of specific control and termination parameters, which have to be set before the algorithm starts, will be explained in every step of a migration round below.
First, population $P = \{\mathbf{v}_1, \mathbf{v}_2, ..., \mathbf{v}_{PopSize}\}$ must be generated based on a prototypal specimen. For PPSA, this specimen is a vector of controller free parameters, $\mathbf{v}$, of dimension $D = l_{den}$. The prototypal specimen equals the best solution from Subsection 4.5. One can choose an initial radius (*Rad*) of the population in which other specimens are generated. The size of population (*PopSize*), i.e. the number of specimens in the population, is chosen by the user. Each specimen is then evaluated by the cost function (46).
The simplest strategy called "All to One" implemented here then selects the best specimen - leader, i.e. that with the minimal value of the cost function

$$\mathbf{v}_L^{mr} = \arg\min_i F\left(\mathbf{v}_i^{mr}\right) \tag{49}$$

where L denotes the leader, i is i-th of specimen in the population and mr means the current migration round. Then all other specimen are moved towards the leader during the migration round. The moving is given by three control parameters: *PathLength, Step, PRT*. *PathLength* should be within the interval $[1.1, 5]$ and it expresses the length of the path when approaching the leader. *PathLength* = 1 means that the specimen stops its moving exactly at the position of the leader. *Step* represents the sampling of the path and ought to be valued $[0.11, PathLength]$. E.g. a pair *PathLength* = 1 and *Step* = 0.2 agrees with that the specimen makes 5 steps until it reaches the leader. $PRT \in [0,1]$ enables to calculate the perturbation vector *PRTVector* which indicates whether the active specimen moves to the leader directly or not. *PRTVector* is defined as

$$\begin{aligned} &PRTVector = \left[p_1, p_2, ..., p_{l_{den}}\right]^T \in \{0,1\}^{l_{den}} \\ &p_i = 1 \qquad \text{if } rnd_i < PRT \\ &p_i = 0 \qquad \text{else} \end{aligned} \tag{50}$$

where $rnd_i \in [0,1]$ is a randomly generated number for each dimension of a specimen. Although authors of SOMA suggest to calculate *PRTVector* only once in migration round for every specimen, we try to do this in every step of the moving to the leader. Hence, the path is given by

$$\begin{gathered}\mathbf{v}_{i,k+1}^{mr} = \mathbf{v}_{i,0}^{mr} + (i-1)Step\left(\mathbf{v}_{L}^{mr} - \mathbf{v}_{i,0}^{mr}\right) + \mathrm{diag}(PRTVector)Step\left(\mathbf{v}_{L}^{mr} - \mathbf{v}_{i,0}^{mr}\right) \\ i = 1,2,...PopSize; k = 0,1,...round(PathLength / Step) - 1\end{gathered} \tag{51}$$

where $\mathrm{diag}(PRTVector)$ means the diagonal square matrix with elements of $PRTVector$ on the main diagonal and k is k-th step in the path.
If $PRTVector = [1,1,...1]^T$, the active specimen goes to the leader directly without "zig-zag" moves.
For every specimen of the population in a migration round, the cost function (i.e. value of the specimen) is calculated in every single step during the moving towards the leader. If the current position is better then the actual best, it becomes the best now. Hence, the new position of an active specimen for the next migration round is given by the best position of the specimen from all steps of moving towards the leader within the current migration round, i.e.

$$\mathbf{v}_{i}^{mr+1} = \arg\min_{k} F\left(\mathbf{v}_{i,k}^{mr}\right) \tag{52}$$

These specimens then generate the new population.
The number of migration round are given by user at the beginning of SOMA by parameter *Migration*, or the algorithm is terminated if

$$\max_{i} F(\mathbf{v}_i) - \min_{i} F(\mathbf{v}_i) < MinDiv \tag{53}$$

where $MinDiv$ is the selected minimal diversity.
The final value $\mathbf{v}_{opt}$ is equal to $\mathbf{v}_L$ from the last migration round. We implemented the whole PPSA with SOMA in two Matlab m-files.

6. Illustrative example

In this closing session, we demonstrate the utilization of the PPSA and the methodology described above in Matlab on an attractive example.
Consider an unstable system describing roller skater on a swaying bow (Zítek et al., 2008) given by the transfer function

$$G(s) = \frac{Y(s)}{U(s)} = \frac{b\exp(-(\tau+\vartheta)s)}{s^2\left(s^2 - a\exp(-\vartheta s)\right)} \tag{54}$$

see Fig. 8, where $y(t)$ is the skater's deviation from the desired position, $u(t)$ expresses the slope angle of a bow caused by force P, delays τ, ϑ mean the skater's and servo latencies and b, a are real parameters. Skater controls the servo driving by remote signals into servo electronics.
Let b = 0.2, a = 1, $\tau = 0.3$ s, $\vartheta = 0.1$ s, as in the literature, and design the controller structure according to the approach described in Section 3. Consider the reference and load disturbance in the form of a step-wise function.

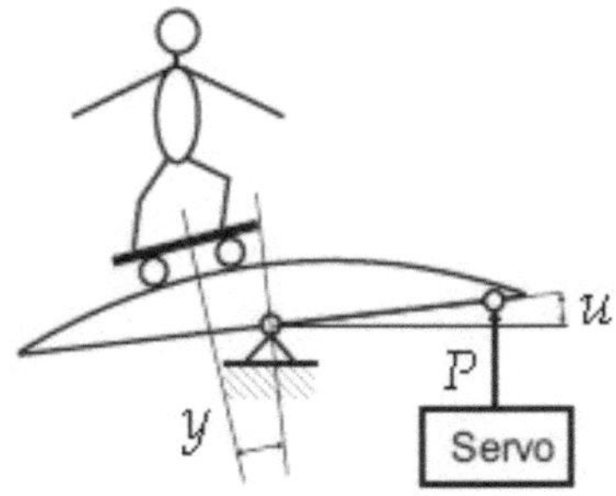

Fig. 8. The roller skater on a swaying bow

Hence, coprime factorization over $\mathbf{R}_{MS}$ can be done e.g. as

$$G(s)=\frac{B(s)}{A(s)}=\frac{\dfrac{b\exp(-(\tau+\vartheta)s)}{(s+m_0)^4}}{\dfrac{s^2(s^2-a\exp(-\vartheta s))}{(s+m_0)^4}}, W(s)=\frac{H_W(s)}{F_W(s)}=\frac{\dfrac{k_W}{s+m}}{\dfrac{s}{s+m}},\ D(s)=\frac{H_D(s)}{F_D(s)}=\frac{\dfrac{k_D}{s+m}}{\dfrac{s}{s+m}} \tag{55}$$

where $m_0>0$, k_W, $k_D\in\mathbb{R}$. Stabilization via the Bézout identity (15) results e.g. in the following particular solution

$$\begin{aligned}Q_0(s)&=\frac{(q_3s^3+q_2s^2+q_1s+q_0)(s+m_0)^4}{s^2(s^2-a\exp(-\vartheta s))(s^3+p_2s^2+p_1s+p_0)+b\exp(-(\tau+\vartheta)s)(q_3s^3+q_2s^2+q_1s+q_0)}\\P_0(s)&=\frac{(s^3+p_2s^2+p_1s+p_0)(s+m_0)^4}{s^2(s^2-a\exp(-\vartheta s))(s^3+p_2s^2+p_1s+p_0)+b\exp(-(\tau+\vartheta)s)(q_3s^3+q_2s^2+q_1s+q_0)}\end{aligned} \tag{56}$$

using the generalized Euclidean algorithm, see (Pekař & Prokop, 2009), where p_2, p_1, p_0, q_3, q_2, q_1, $q_0\in$ ○ are free parameters. In order to provide reference tracking and load disturbance rejection, use parameterization (16) while both, $F_W(s)$ and $F_D(s)$, divide $P(s)$; in other words, the numerator of $P(s)$ must satisfy $P(0)=0$. If we take

$$T=\frac{t_0(s+m_0)^4}{s^2(s^2-a\exp(-\vartheta s))(s^3+p_2s^2+p_1s+p_0)+b\exp(-(\tau+\vartheta)s)(q_3s^3+q_2s^2+q_1s+q_0)} \tag{57}$$

$P(s)$ is obtained in a quite simple form with a real parameter t_0 which must be set as

$$t_0=\frac{-p_0m_0^4}{b} \tag{58}$$

Finally, the controller numerator and denominator in $\mathbf{R}_{MS}$, respectively, have forms

$$Q(s)=\frac{b\left(q_3s^3+q_2s^2+q_1s+q_0\right)\left(s+m_0\right)^4+p_0m_0^4s^2\left(s^2-a\exp(-\vartheta s)\right)}{b\left[s^2\left(s^2-a\exp(-\vartheta s)\right)\left(s^3+p_2s^2+p_1s+p_0\right)+b\exp(-(\tau+\vartheta)s)\left(q_3s^3+q_2s^2+q_1s+q_0\right)\right]}$$
$$P(s)=\frac{\left(s^3+p_2s^2+p_1s+p_0\right)\left(s+m_0\right)^4-p_0m_0^4\exp(-(\tau+\vartheta)s)}{s^2\left(s^2-a\exp(-\vartheta s)\right)\left(s^3+p_2s^2+p_1s+p_0\right)+b\exp(-(\tau+\vartheta)s)\left(q_3s^3+q_2s^2+q_1s+q_0\right)} \quad (59)$$

Hence, the controller has the transfer function

$$G_R(s)=\frac{b\left(q_3s^3+q_2s^2+q_1s+q_0\right)\left(s+m_0\right)^4+p_0m_0^4s^2\left(s^2-a\exp(-\vartheta s)\right)}{b\left[\left(s^3+p_2s^2+p_1s+p_0\right)\left(s+m_0\right)^4-p_0m_0^4\exp(-(\tau+\vartheta)s)\right]} \quad (60)$$

and the reference-to-output function reads

$$G_{WY}(s)=\frac{b\left[b\left(q_3s^3+q_2s^2+q_1s+q_0\right)\left(s+m_0\right)^4+p_0m_0^4s^2\left(s^2-a\exp(-\vartheta s)\right)\right]\exp(-(\tau+\vartheta)s)}{\left(s+m_0\right)^4\left[s^2\left(s^2-a\exp(-\vartheta s)\right)\left(s^3+p_2s^2+p_1s+p_0\right)+b\exp(-(\tau+\vartheta)s)\left(q_3s^3+q_2s^2+q_1s+q_0\right)\right]} \quad (61)$$

which gives rise to the characteristic quasipolynomial

$$m(s)=\left(s+m_0\right)^4\left[s^2\left(s^2-a\exp(-\vartheta s)\right)\left(s^3+p_2s^2+p_1s+p_0\right)+b\exp(-(\tau+\vartheta)s)\left(q_3s^3+q_2s^2+q_1s+q_0\right)\right] \quad (62)$$

Obviously, the numerator of $G_{WY}(s)$ does not have any free parameter not included in the denominator, i.e. $l_{num}=0$. Moreover, the factor $\left(s+m_0\right)^4$ has a quadruple real pole; to cancel it, it must hold that $m_0>>-\mathrm{Re}\{s_1\}=-\alpha$. Hence $l_{den}=7$. Now, there are two possibilities - either set zero exactly to obtain constrained controller parameter (then $l_{den}=6$) or to deal with the numerator and denominator of (61) together in (46) - we decided to utilize the former one. Generally, one can obtain e.g.

$$p_0=-\frac{b\left(z_1+m_0\right)^4\left(q_3z_1^3+q_2z_1^2+q_1z_1+q_0\right)}{m_0^4z_1^2\left(z_1^2-a\exp(-\vartheta z_1)\right)} \quad (63)$$

from (61).
Choose $\Delta h_{WY,m,\max}=0.5$, $\xi_\alpha=0.5$ and $t_{\max}=10$ s. From Fig. 3 we have $\xi_z=0.9$, $t_{\max,norm}\approx 2$ which gives $\omega=0.2, z_1=-0.18, \alpha=-0.1$. Then take e.g. $m_0=5$. Inserting plant parameters in (63) yields

$$p_0=5.4078\left(q_0-0.18q_1+0.0324q_2-0.005832q_3\right) \quad (64)$$

The concrete quasipolynomial which roots are being set, thus, reads

$$m_1(s)=s^2\left(s^2-\exp(-0.1s)\right)\left(s^3+p_2s^2+p_1s+5.4078\left(q_0-0.18q_1+0.0324q_2-0.005832q_3\right)\right)$$
$$+0.2\exp(-0.4s)\left(q_3s^3+q_2s^2+q_1s+q_0\right) \quad (65)$$

Initial direct pole placement results in controller parameters as

$$q_3 = 1.0051, q_2 = 0.9506, q_1 = 1.2582, q_0 = 0.2127, p_2 = 1.1179, p_1 = 0.4418, p_0 = 0.0603 \quad (66)$$

and poles locations in the vicinity of the origin are displayed in Fig. 9.

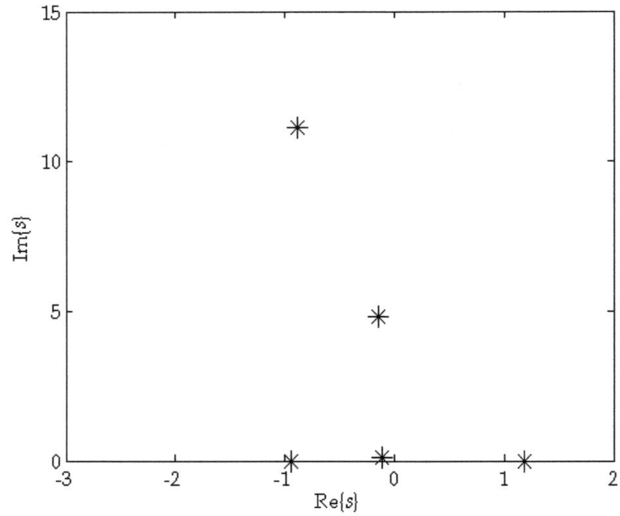

Fig. 9. Initial poles locations

The process of continuous roots shifting is described by the evolution of controller parameters, the spectral abscissa (i.e. the real part of the rightmost pole $\sigma_{d,1}$) and the distance of the dominant pole from the prescribed one $|\sigma_{d,1} - \sigma_{p,1}|$, as can be seen in Fig. 10 - Fig. 12, respectively. Note that p_0 is related to shifted parameters according to (64).

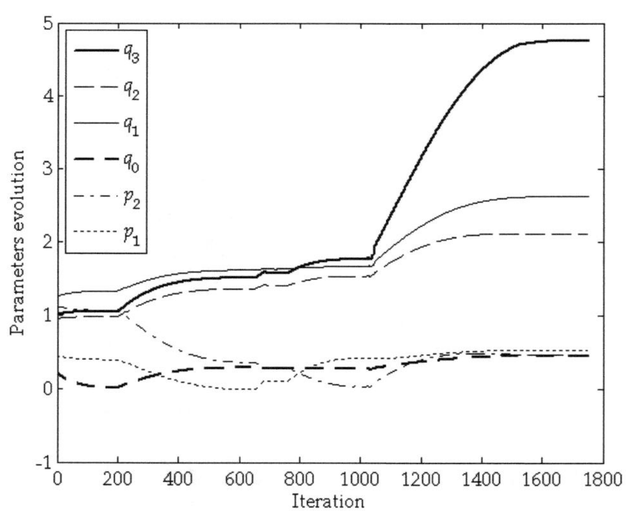

Fig. 10. Shifted parameters evolution

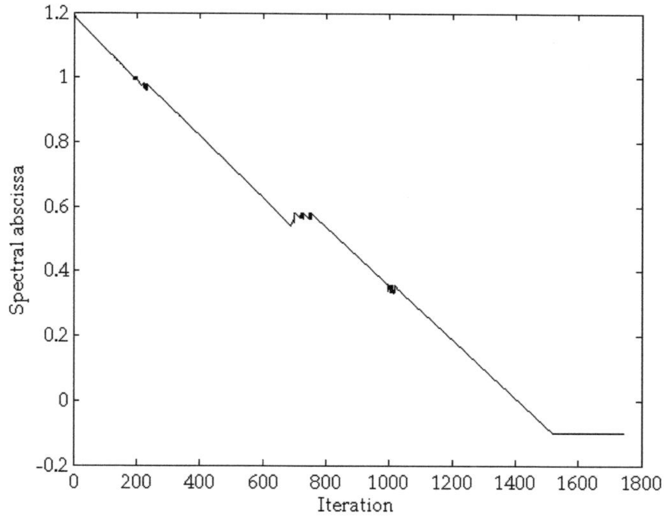

Fig. 11. Spectral abscissa evolution

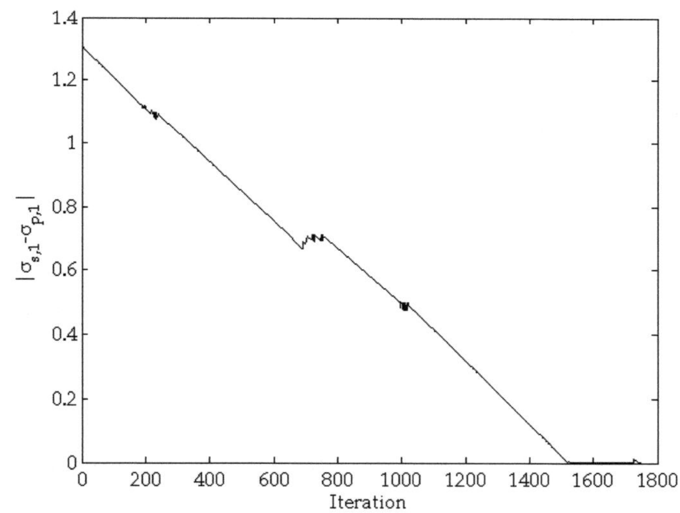

Fig. 12. Distance of the rightmost pole from the prescribed one

When shifting, it is suggested to continue in doing this even if the desired poles locations are reached since one can obtain a better poles distribution - i.e. non-dominant poles are placed more left in the complex space. Moreover, one can decrease the number of shifted poles during the algorithm whenever the real part of a shifted pole becomes "too different" from a group of currently moved poles.
The final controller parameters from the continuous shifting are

$$q_3 = 4.7587, q_2 = 2.1164, q_1 = 2.6252, q_0 = 0.4482, p_2 = 0.4636, p_1 = 0.529, p_0 = 4.6164 \quad (67)$$

and the poles location is pictured in Fig. 13.

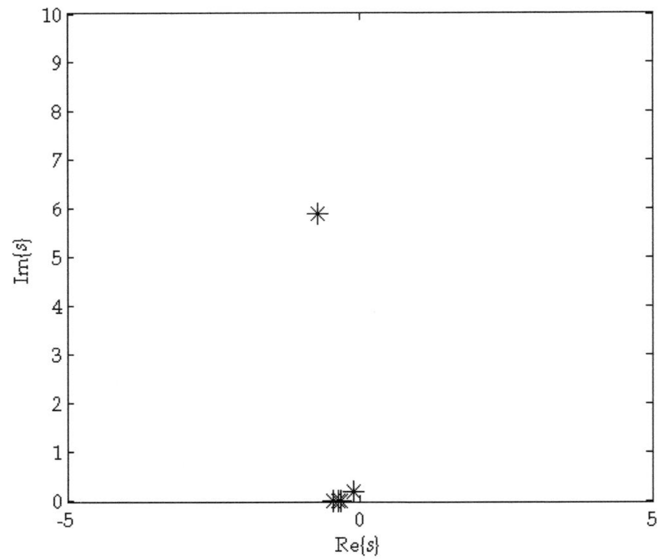

Fig. 13. Final poles locations

As can be seen, the desired prescribed pole is reached and it is also the dominant one. Thus, optimization can be omitted. However, try to perform SOMA to find the minimal cost function (16) with this setting: *Rad* = 2, *PopSize* = 10, *D* = 6, *PathLength* = 3, *Step* = 0.21, *PRT* = 0.6, *Migration* = 10, *MinDiv* = 10^{-6}, . Yet, the minimum of the cost function remains in the best solution from continuous shifting, i.e. according to (67), with the value of the cost function as $F(\mathbf{v}) = 2.93 \cdot 10^{-4}$.

7. Conclusion

This chapter has introduced a novel controller design approach for SISO LTI-TDS based on algebraic approach followed by pole-placement-like controller tuning and an optimization procedure. The methodology has been implemented in Matlab-Simulink environment to verify the results.

The initial controller structure design has been made over the ring of stable and proper meromorphic functions, $\mathbf{R}_{MS}$, which offers to satisfy properness of the controller, reference tracking and rejection of the load disturbance (of a nominal model). The obtained controller has owned some free (unset) parameters which must have been set properly.

In the crucial part of the work, we have chosen a simple finite-dimension model, calculated its step-response maximum overshoots and times to the overshoots. Then, using a static pole placement followed by continuous pole shifting dominant poles have been attempted to be placed to the desired prescribed positions.

Finally, optimization of distances of dominant (the rightmost) poles from the prescribed ones has been utilized via SOMA algorithm. The whole methodology has been tested on an attractive example of a skater on a swaying bow described by an unstable LTI TDS model.

The procedure is similar to the algorithm introduced in (Michiels et al., 2010); however, there are some substantial differences between them. Firstly, the presented approach is made in input-output space of meromorphic Laplace transfer functions, whereas the one in (Michiels et al., 2010) deals purely with state space. Second, in the cited literature, a number

poles less then a number of free controller parameters is set exactly and the rest of the spectrum is pushed to the left as much as possible. If it is possible it is necessary to choose other prescribed poles. We initially place the poles exactly; however, they can leave their positions during the shifting. Anyway, our algorithm does not require reset of selection assigned poles. Moreover, we suggest unambiguously how the prescribed poles (and zeros) positions are to be chosen - based on model overshoots. Last but not least, in (Michiels et al., 2010), the gradient sampling algorithm (Burke et al., 2005) on the spectral abscissa was used while SOMA together with more complex cost function is considered in this chapter.
The presented approach is limited to retarded SISO LTI-TDS without distributed delays only. Its extension to neutral systems requires some additional conditions on stability and existence of a stabilizing controller. Systems with distributed delays can be served in similar way as it is done here, yet with the characteristic meromorphic function instead of quasipolynomial. Multivariable systems would require deeper theoretic analysis of the controller structure design. The methodology is also time-comsupting and thus useless for online controller design (e.g. for selftuners).
In the future research, one can solve the problems specified above, choose other reference-to-output models and control system structures. There is a space to improve and modify the optimization algorithm.

8. Acknowledgment

The authors kindly appreciate the financial support which was provided by the Ministry of Education, Youth and Sports of the Czech Republic, in the grant No. MSM 708 835 2102 and by the European Regional Development Fund under the project CEBIA-Tech No. CZ.1.05/2.1.00/03.0089.

9. References

Ben-Israel, A. & Greville, T.N.E (1966). *Generalized Inverses: Theory and Applications*. Wiley, New York

Burke, J.; Lewis, M & Overton, M. (2005). A Robust Gradient Sampling Algorithm for Nonsmooth Nonconvex Optimization. *SIAM Journal of Optimization*, Vol. 15, Issue 3, pp. 751-779, ISSN 1052-6234

El'sgol'ts, L.E. & Norkin, S.B. (1973). *Introduction to the Theory and Application of Differential Equations with Deviated Arguments*. Academic Press, New York

Górecki, H.; Fuksa, S.; Grabowski, P. & Korytowski, A. (1989). *Analysis and Synthesis of Time Delay Systems*, John Wiley & Sons, ISBN 978-047-1276-22-7, New York

Hale, J.K., & Verduyn Lunel, S.M. (1993). Introduction to Functional Differential Equations. *Applied Mathematical Sciences*, Vol. 99, Springer-Verlag, ISBN 978-038-7940-76-2, New York

Kolmanovskii, V.B. & Myshkis, A. (1999). *Introduction to the Theory and Applications of Functional Differential Equations*, Cluwer Academy, ISBN 978-0792355045, Dordrecht, Netherlands

Kučera, V. (1993). Diophantine equations in control - a survey. Automatica, Vol. 29, No. 6, pp. 1361-1375, ISSN 0005-1098

Marshall, J.E.; Górecki, H.; Korytowski, A. & Walton, K. (1992). *Time Delay Systems, Stability and Performance Criteria with Applications*. Ellis Horwood, ISBN 0-13-465923-6, New York

Michiels, W.; Engelborghs, K; Vansevenant, P. & Roose, D. (2002). Continuous Pole Placement for Delay Equations. *Automatica*, Vol. 38, No. 6, pp. 747-761, ISSN 0005-1098

Michiels, W.; Vyhlídal, T. & Zítek, P. (2010). Control Design for Time-Delay Systems Based on Quasi-Direct Pole Placement. *Journal of Process Control*, Vol. 20, No. 3, pp. 337-343, 2010.

Loiseau, J.-J. (2000). Algebraic Tools for the Control and Stabilization of Time-Delay Systems. *Annual Reviews in Control*, Vol. 24, pp. 135-149, ISSN 1367-5788

Loiseau, J.-J. (2002). Neutral-Type Time-Delay Systems that are not Formally Stable are not BIBO Stabilizable. *IMA Journal of Mathematical Control and Information*, Vol. 19, No. 1-2, pp. 217-227, ISSN 0265-0754

Michiels, W. & Niculescu, S. (2008). Stability and Stabilization of Time Delay Systems: An eigenvalue based approach. *Advances in Design and Control*, SIAM, ISBN 978-089-8716-32-0, Philadelphia

Pekař, L. & Prokop, R. (2009). Some observations about the RMS ring for delayed systems, Proceedings of the 17th International Conference on Process Control '09, pp. 28-36, ISBN 978-80-227-3081-5, Štrbské Pleso, Slovakia, June 9-12, 2009.

Pekař, L.; Prokop, R. & Dostálek, P. (2009). Circuit Heating Plant Model with Internal Delays. *WSEAS Transaction on Systems*, Vol. 8, Issue 9, pp. 1093-1104, ISSN 1109-2777

Pekař, L. & Prokop, R. (2010). Control design for stable systems with both input-output and internal delays by algebraic means, *Proceedings of the 29th IASTED International Conference Modelling, Identification and Control (MIC 2010)*, pp. 400-407, ISSN 1025-8973, Innsbruck, Austria, February 15-17, 2010

Richard, J.P. (2003). Time-delay Systems: an Overview of Some Recent Advances and Open Problems. *Automatica*, Vol. 39, Issue 10, pp. 1667-1694, ISSN 0005-1098

Vyhlídal, T. (2003). *Analysis and Synthesis of Time Delay System Spectrum*, Ph.D. Thesis, Faculty of Mechanical Engineering, Czech Technical University in Prague, Prague

Vyhlídal, T. & Zítek, P. (2003). Quasipolynomial mapping based rootfinder for analysis of time delay systems, *Proceedings IFAC Workshop on Time-Delay systems, TDS'03*, pp. 227-232, Rocquencourt, France 2003.

Zelinka, I. (2004). SOMA-Self Organizing Migrating Algorithm. In: *New Optimization Techniques in Engineering*, G. Onwubolu, B.V.Babu (Eds.), 51 p., Springer-Verlag, ISBN 3-540-20167X, Berlin

Zítek, P. & Kučera, V. (2003). Algebraic Design of Anisochronic Controllers for Time Delay Systems. *International Journal of Control*, Vol. 76, Issue 16, pp. 905-921, ISSN 0020-7179

Zítek, P. & Hlava, J. (2001). Anisochronic Internal Model Control of Time-Delay Systems. *Control Engineering Practice*, Vol. 9, No. 5, pp. 501-516, ISSN 0967-0661

Zítek, P.; Kučera, V. & Vyhlídal, T. (2008). Meromorphic Observer-based Pole Assignment in Time Delay Systems. *Kybernetika*, Vol. 44, No. 5, pp. 633-648, ISSN 0023-5954

2

Control of Distributed Parameter Systems - Engineering Methods and Software Support in the MATLAB & Simulink Programming Environment

Gabriel Hulkó, Cyril Belavý, Gergely Takács, Pavol Buček and Peter Zajíček
Institute of Automation, Measurement and Applied Informatics Faculty of Mechanical Engineering
Center for Control of Distributed Parameter Systems
Slovak University of Technology Bratislava
Slovak Republic

1. Introduction

Distributed parameter systems (DPS) are systems with state/output quantities X(**x**,t) /Y(**x**,t) – parameters which are defined as quantity fields or infinite dimensional quantities distributed through geometric space, where **x** – in general is a vector of the three dimensional Euclidean space. Thanks to the development of information technology and numerical methods, engineering practice is lately modelling a wide range of phenomena and processes in virtual software environments for numerical dynamical analysis purposes such as ANSYS - www.ansys.com, FLUENT (ANSYS Polyflow) - www.fluent.com , ProCAST www.esi-group.com/products/casting/, COMPUPLAST – www.compuplast.com, SYSWELD – www.esi-group.com/products/welding, COMSOL Multiphysics - www.comsol.com, MODFLOW, MODPATH,... www.modflow.com , STAR-CD - www.cd-adapco.com, MOLDFLOW - www.moldflow.com, ... Based on the numerical solution of the underlying partial differential equations (PDE) these virtual software environments offer colorful, animated results in 3D. Numerical dynamic analysis problems are solved both for technical and non-technical disciplines given by numerical models defined in complex 3D shapes. From the viewpoint of systems and control theory these dynamical models represent DPS. A new challenge emerges for the control engineering practice, which is the objective to formulate control problems for dynamical systems defined as DPS through numerical structures over complex spatial structures in 3D.

The main emphasis of this chapter is to present a philosophy of the engineering approach for the control of DPS - given by numerical structures, which opens a wide space for novel applications of the toolboxes and blocksets of the MATLAB & Simulink software environment presented here.

The first monographs in the field of DPS control have been published in the second half of the last century, where mathematical foundations of DPS control have been established. This mathematical theory is based on analytical solutions of the underlying PDE (Butkovskij, 1965; Lions, 1971; Wang, 1964). That is the decomposition of dynamics into time and space components based on the eigenfunctions of the PDE. Recently in the field of mathematical control theory of DPS, publications on control of PDE have appeared (Lasiecka & Triggiani, 2000;...).

An engineering approach for the control of DPS is being developed since the eighties of the last century (Hulkó et al., 1981-2010). In the field of lumped parameters system (LPS) control, where the state/output quantities $\mathbf{x}(t)/\mathbf{y}(t)$ - parameters are given as finite dimensional vectors, the actuator together with the controlled plant make up a controlled LPS. In this sense the actuators and the controlled plant as a DPS create a controlled lumped-input and distributed-parameter-output system (LDS). In this chapter the general decomposition of dynamics of controlled LDS into time and space components is introduced, which is based on numerically computed distributed parameter transient and impulse characteristics given on complex shape definition domains in 3D. Based on this decomposition a methodical framework of control synthesis decomposition into space and time tasks will be presented where in space domain approximation problems are solved and in time domain synthesis of control is realized by lumped parameter control loops. For the software support of modelling, control and design of DPS, the **Distributed Parameter Systems Blockset for MATLAB & Simulink (DPS Blockset)** - www.mathworks.com/products/connections/ has been developed within the CONNECTIONS program framework of The MathWorks, as a Third-Party Product of The MathWorks Company (Hulkó et al., 2003-2010). When solving problems in the time domain, toolboxes and blocksets of the MATLAB & Simulink software environment such as for example the Control Systems Toolbox, Simulink Control Design, System Identification Toolbox, etc. are utilized. In the space relation the approximation task is formulated as an optimization problem, where the Optimization Toolbox is made use of. A web portal named **Distributed Parameter Systems Control** - www.dpscontrol.sk has been created for those interested in solving problems of DPS control (Hulkó et al., 2003-2010). This web portal features application examples from different areas of engineering practice such as the control of technological and manufacturing processes, mechatronic structures, groundwater remediation etc. Moreover this web portal offers the demo version of the **DPS Blockset** with the **Tutorial, Show, Demos** and **DPS Wizard** for download, along with the **Interactive Control** service for the interactive solution of model control problems via the Internet.

2. DPS – DDS – LDS

Generally in the control of lumped parameter systems the actuator and the controlled plant create a lumped parameter controlled system. In the field of DPS control the actuators together with the controlled plant - generally being a distributed-input and distributed-parameter-output system (DDS) create a controlled lumped-input and distributed-parameter-output system (LDS). Fig. 1.-3. and Fig. 6., 11., 14.

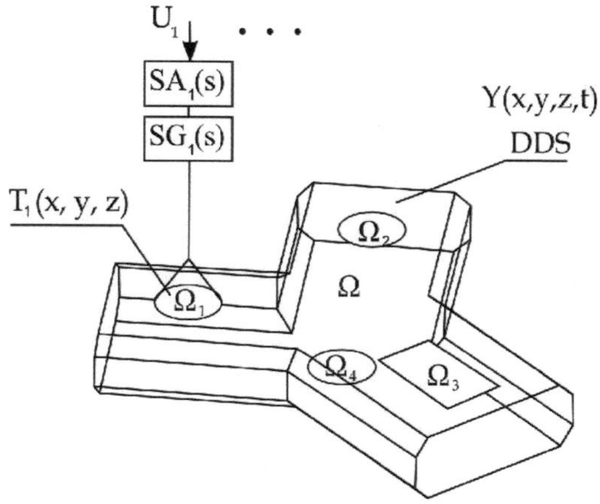

Fig. 1. Controlled DPS as LDS - heating of metal body of complex-shape

$\{SA_i(s)\}_i$, $\{SG_i(s)\}_i$, $\{T_i(x,y,z)\}_i$ - models of actuators

DDS - distributed-input and distributed-parameter-output system

$\{U_i\}_i$ - lumped actuating quantities

Ω / $\{\Omega_i\}_i$ - complex-shape definition domain in 3D / actuation subdomains

Y(x,y,z,t) – temperature field – distributed output quantity

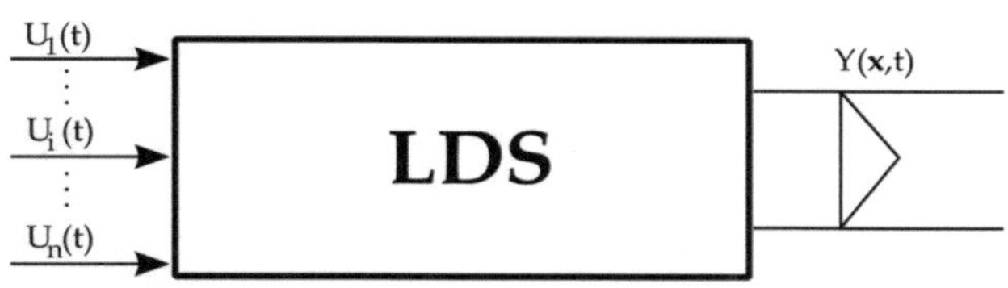

Fig. 2. Lumped-input and distributed-parameter-output system – LDS

$\{U_i(t)\}_i$ – lumped input quantities

$Y(\mathbf{x},t) = Y(x,y,z,t)$ – distributed output quantity

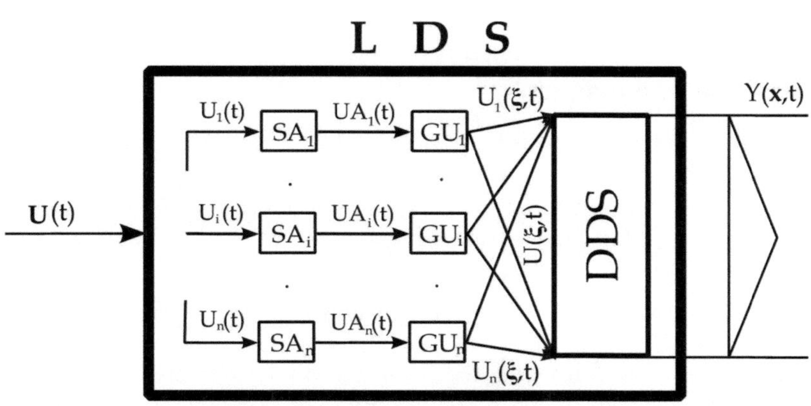

Fig. 3. General structure of lumped-input and distributed-parameter-output systems

LDS - lumped-input and distributed-parameter-output system

$\{SA_i\}_i$ - actuating members of lumped input quantities

$\{GU_i\}_i$ - generators of distributed input quantities

DDS - distributed-input and distributed-parameter-output system

$\mathbf{U}(t) = \{U_i(t)\}_i$ - vector of lumped input quantities of LDS

$\{UA_i(t)\}_i$ - output quantities of lumped parameter actuators

$\{U_i(\xi,t)\}_i$ - distributed output quantities of generators $\{GU_i\}_i$

$U(\xi,t)$ - overall distributed input quantity for DDS

$Y(\mathbf{x},t) = Y(x,y,z,t)$ - distributed output quantity

Input-output dynamics of these DPS can be described, from zero initial conditions, by

$$Y(\mathbf{x},t) = \sum_{i=1}^{n} Y_i(\mathbf{x},t) = \sum_{i=1}^{n} \mathcal{G}_i(\mathbf{x},t) \otimes U_i(t) = \sum_{i=1}^{n} \int_0^t \mathcal{G}_i(\mathbf{x},\tau) U_i(t-\tau) d\tau \tag{1}$$

or in discrete form

$$Y(\mathbf{x},k) = \sum_{i=1}^{n} Y_i(\mathbf{x},k) = \sum_{i=1}^{n} \mathcal{G}H_i(\mathbf{x},k) \oplus U_i(k) = \sum_{i=1}^{n} \sum_{q=0}^{k} \mathcal{G}H_i(\mathbf{x},q) U_i(k-q) \tag{2}$$

where $\otimes$ marks convolution product and $\oplus$ marks convolution sum, $\mathcal{G}_i(\mathbf{x},t)$ – distributed parameter impulse response of LDS to the i-th input, $\mathcal{G}H_i(\mathbf{x},k)$ – discrete time (DT) distributed parameter impulse response of LDS with zero-order hold units H - HLDS to the i-th input, $Y_i(\mathbf{x},t)$ - distributed output quantity of LDS to the i-th input, $Y_i(\mathbf{x},k)$ – DT distributed output quantity of HLDS to the i-th input. For simplicity in this chapter distributed quantities are considered mostly as continuous scalar quantity fields with unit sampling interval in time domain. Whereas DT distributed parameter step responses $\{\mathcal{H}H_i(\mathbf{x},k)\}_{i,k}$ of HLDS can be computed by common analytical or numerical methods then DT distributed parameter impulse responses can be obtained as

$$\{\mathcal{G}H_i(\mathbf{x},k) = \mathcal{H}H_i(\mathbf{x},k) - \mathcal{H}H_i(\mathbf{x},k\text{-}1)\}_{i,k} \tag{3}$$

3. Decomposition of dynamics

The process of dynamics decomposition shall be started from DT distributed parameter step and impulse responses of the analysed LDS. For an illustration, procedure of decomposition of dynamics and control synthesis will be shown on the LDS with zero-order hold units H – HLDS – distributed only on the interval $[0,L]$, with output quantity $Y(x,k) = \sum_{i=1}^{n} Y_i(x,k)$ discretised in time relation and continuous in space relation on this interval. Nevertheless the following results are valid in general both for continous or discrete distributed quantities in space relation given on compex-shape definition domains over 3D as well.

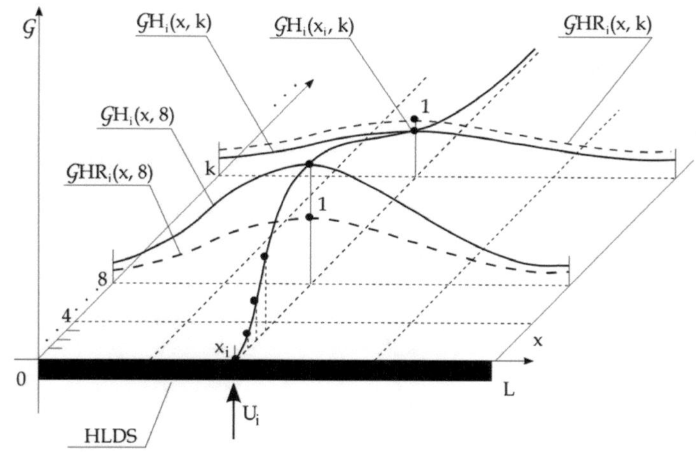

Fig. 4. i-th discrete distributed parameter impulse response of HLDS

$\mathcal{G}H_i(x_i,k)$ - partial DT impulse response in time, t - relation to the i-th input considered as response with maximal amplitude in point $x_i \in [0,L]$

$\{\mathcal{G}H_i(x,k)\}_{i,k}$ - partial DT impulse responses to the i-th input in space - x - relation

$\{\mathcal{G}HR_i(x,k)\}_{i,k}$ – reduced partial DT impulse responses to the i-th input in space, x – relation for timesteps $\{k\}_k$

If the reduced DT partial distributed parameter impulse responses are defined as

$$\left\{\mathcal{G}HR_i(x,k) = \frac{\mathcal{G}H_i(x,k)}{\mathcal{G}H_i(x_i,k)}\right\}_{i,k} \tag{4}$$

for $\{\mathcal{G}H_i(x_i,k) \neq 0\}_{i,k}$, then the i-th DT distributed output quantiy in (2) can be rewritten by the means of the reduced characteristics as follows

$$Y_i(x,k) = \mathcal{G}H_i(x_i,k)\mathcal{G}HR_i(x,k) \oplus U_i(k) \tag{5}$$

At fixed x_i the partial DT distributed output quantity in time direction $Y_i(x_i,k)$ is given as the convolution sum $\mathcal{G}H_i(x_i,k) \oplus U_i(k) = \sum_{q=0}^{k} \mathcal{G}H_i(x_i,q)U_i(k-q)$, in case the relation $\{\mathcal{G}HR_i(x_i,q) = 1\}_{q=0,k}$ holds at the fixed point x_i. At fixed k, the partial discrete distributed output quantity in space direction $Y_i(x,k)$ is given as a linear combination of elements $\{\mathcal{G}HR_i(x,q)\}_{q=0,k}$, where the reduced discrete partial distributed characteristics $\{\mathcal{G}HR_i(x,q)\}_{q=0,k}$ are multiplied by corresponding elements of the set $\{\mathcal{G}H_i(x_i,q)U_i(k-q)\}_{q=0,k}$., see Fig. 5.

This decomposition is valid for all given lumped input $\{U_i\}_i$ and corresponding output quantities $\{Y_i(x,k)\}_{i,k}$ - thus we obtain time and space components of HLDS dynamics in the following form:

Time Components of Dynamics $\{\mathcal{G}H_i(x_i,k)\}_{i,k}$ – for given i and chosen x_i - variable k

Space Components of Dynamics $\{\mathcal{G}HR_i(x,k)\}_{i,k}$ – for given i and chosen k – variable x

Also reduced components of single distributed output quantities are

$$\{YR_i(x,k)\}_i = \left\{ \frac{Y_i(x,k)}{Y_i(x_i,k)} \right\}_{i,k} \tag{6}$$

then $\{Y_i(x_i,k) \neq 0\}_{i,k}$ can be considered as time components and $\{YR_i(x,k)\}_{i,k}$ as space components of the output quantities.

When reduced steady-state distributed parameter transient responses are introduced $\{\mathcal{H}HR_i(x,\infty)\}_i = \{\mathcal{H}H_i(x,\infty) / \mathcal{H}H_i(x_i,\infty)\}_i$ - for $\{\mathcal{H}H_i(x_i,\infty) \neq 0\}_i$ - and discrete transfer functions $\{SH_i(x_i,z)\}_i$ are assigned to partial distributed parameter transient responses with maximal amplitudes at points $\{x_i\}_i$ on the interval $[0,L]$, we obtain time and space components of HLDS dynamics for steady-state as:

Time Components of Dynamics $\{SH_i(x_i,z)\}_i$ - for given i and chosen x_i - variable z

Space Components of Dynamics $\{\mathcal{H}HR_i(x,\infty)\}_i$ - for given i in ∞ – variable x

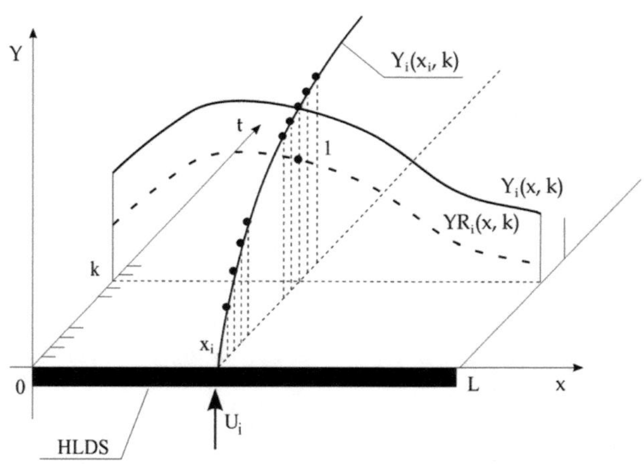

Fig. 5. Partial distributed output quantities in time and space direction

U_i - i-th DT lumped input quantity

$Y_i(x_i,k)$ - i-th partial DT distributed output quantity in time domain at chosen point x_i

$Y_i(x,k) / YR_i(x,k)$ - i-th partial distributed output/reduced output quantity in space direction

For the steady-state, when $k \to \infty$

$$\left\{ YR_i(x,\infty) \to \mathcal{H}HR_i(x,\infty) \right\}_{i,k} \tag{7}$$

then in the steady-state

$$Y(x,\infty) = \sum_{i=1}^{n} Y_i(x_i,\infty) YR_i(x,\infty) = \sum_{i=1}^{n} Y_i(x_i,\infty) \mathcal{H}HR_i(x,\infty) \tag{8}$$

When distributed quantities are used in discrete form as finite sequences of quantities, the discretization in space domain is usually considered by the computational nodes of the numerical model of the controlled DPS over the compex-shape definition domain in 3D.

4. Distributed parameter systems of control

Based on decomposition of HLDS dynamics into time and space components, possibilities for control synthesis are also suggested by an analogous approach. In this section a methodical framework for the decomposition of control synthesis into space and time problems will be presented by select demonstration control problems. In the space domain control synthesis will be solved as a sequence of approximation tasks on the set of space components of controlled system dynamics, where distributed parameter quantities in particular sampling times are considered as continuous functions on the interval $[0,L]$ as elements of strictly convex normed linear space **X** with quadratic norm. It is necessary to note as above that the following results are valid in general for DPS given on compex-shape definition domains in 3D both for continous or discrete distributed quantities, in the space relation as well.
In the time domain, the control synthesis solutions are based on synthesis methods of DT lumped parameter systems of control.

4.1 Open-loop control

Assume the open-loop control of a distributed parameter system, where dynamic characteristics give an ideal representation of controlled system dynamics and $V(x,t)=0$, that is with zero initial steady-state, in which all variables involved are equal to zero - see see Fig. 6 for reference. Let us consider a step change of distributed reference quantity - $W(x,k)=W(x,\infty)$, see Fig. 7. For simplicity let the goal of the control synthesis is to generate a sequence of control inputs $\bar{U}(k)$ in such fashion that in the steady-state, for $k \to \infty$, the control error $E(x,k)=W(x,\infty)-Y(x,k)$ will approach its minimal value $\breve{E}(x,\infty)$ in the quadratic norm:

$$\min \left\| E(x,\infty) \right\| = \min \left\| W(x,\infty) - Y(x,\infty) \right\| = \left\| \breve{E}(x,\infty) \right\| \tag{9}$$

First, an approximation problem will be solved in the space synthesis (SS) block:

$$\min \left\| W(x,\infty) - \sum_{i=1}^{n} W_i(x_i,\infty) \mathcal{H}HR_i(x,\infty) \right\| \tag{10}$$

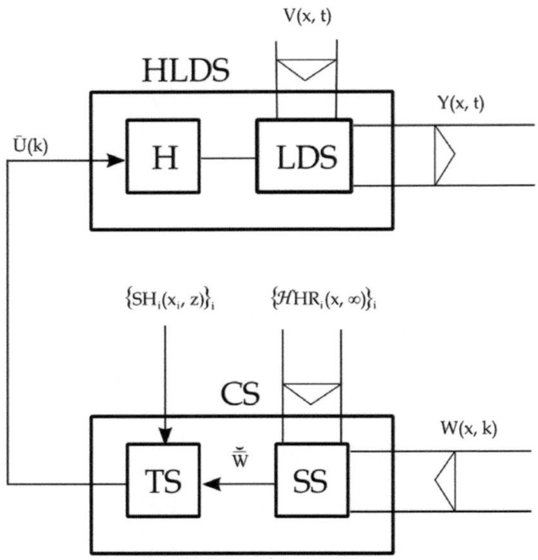

Fig. 6. Distributed parameter open-loop system of control

LDS - lumped-input and distributed-parameter-output system
H - zero-order hold units
HLDS - controlled system with zero-order hold units
CS - control synthesis
TS - time part of control synthesis
SS - space part of control synthesis
$Y(x,t)\,/\,W(x,k)=W(x,\infty)$ - distributed controlled/reference quantity

$V(x,t)$ - distributed disturbance quantity

$\bar{\breve{W}}=\left\{\breve{W}_i(x_i,\infty)\right\}_i$ - vector of lumped reference quantities

$\bar{U}(k)$ - vector of lumped control quantities

$\left\{SH_i(x_i,z)\,/\,\mathcal{H}HR_i(x,\infty)\right\}_i$ - time/space components of controlled system dynamics

where $\left\{\mathcal{H}HR_i(x,\infty)\right\}_i$ are steady-state reduced distributed parameter transient responses of the controlled system – HLDS and $\left\{W_i(x_i,\infty)\right\}_i$ are parameters of approximation. Functions $\left\{\mathcal{H}HR_i(x,\infty)\right\}_i$ form a finite-dimensional subspace of approximation functions *Fn* in the strictly convex normed linear space of distributed parameter quantities **X** on $[0,L]$ with quadratic norm, where the approximation problem is to be solved, see Fig. 8. for reference. From approximation theory in this relation is known the theorem:

Let Fn be a finite-dimensional subspace of a strictly convex normed linear space **X**. *Then, for each f∈* **X**, *there exists a unique element of best approximation.*

(Shadrin, 2005). So the solution of the approximation problem (10) is guaranteed as a unique best approximation $\breve{W}O(x,\infty)=\sum_{i=1}^{n}\breve{W}_i(x_i,\infty)\mathcal{H}HR_i(x,\infty)$, where $\bar{\breve{W}}=\left\{\breve{W}_i(x_i,\infty)\right\}_i$ is the vector of optimal approximation parameters. Hence:

$$\min\left\| W(x,\infty) - \sum_{i=1}^{n} W_i(x_i,\infty)\mathcal{H}HR_i(x,\infty) \right\| = \\ = \left\| W(x,\infty) - \sum_{i=1}^{n} \breve{W}_i(x_i,\infty)\mathcal{H}HR_i(x,\infty) \right\| = \left\| W(x,\infty) - \breve{W}O(x,\infty) \right\| \tag{11}$$

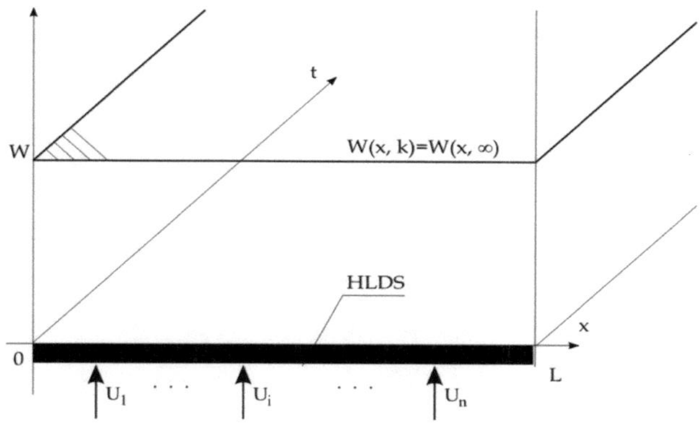

Fig. 7. Step change of distributed reference quantity

HLDS - controlled system with zero-order hold units

$\{U_i\}_i$ - lumped control quantities

$W(x,k) = W(x,\infty)$ - step change of distributed reference quantity

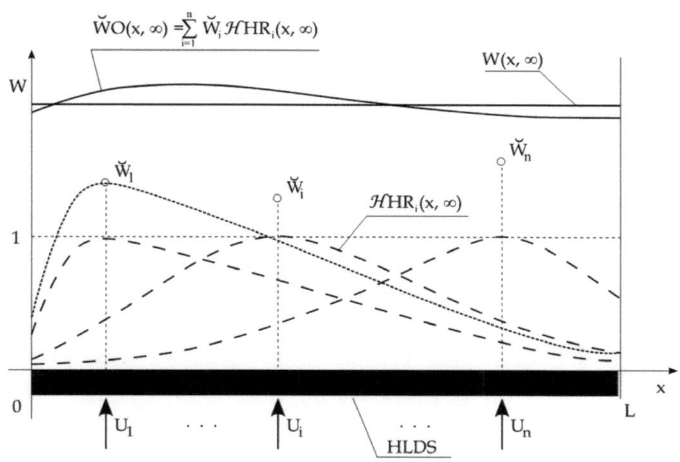

Fig. 8. Solution of the approximation problem

HLDS - controlled system with zero-order hold units

$\{U_i\}_i$ - lumped control quantities

$\{\breve{W}_i\}_i = \{\breve{W}_i(x_i,\infty)\}_i$ - optimal approximation parameters, lumped references

$\{\mathcal{H}HR_i(x,\infty)\}_i$ - reduced steady-state distributed parameter transient responses

$W(x,\infty)$ - distributed reference quantity

$\breve{W}O(x,\infty)$ - unique best approximation of reference quantity

Let us assume vector $\bar{\breve{W}}$ enters the block of time synthesis (TS). In this block, there are „n" single-input / single-output (SISO) lumped parameter control loops: $\{SH_i(x_i,z),R_i(z)\}_i$, see Fig. 9. for reference. The controlled systems of these loops are lumped parameter systems assigned to HLDS as time components of dynamics: $\{SH_i(x_i,z)\}_i$. Controllers, $\{R_i(z)\}_i$, are to be chosen such that for $k \to \infty$ the following relation holds:

$$\left\{\lim_{k\to\infty} \breve{E}_i(x_i,k) = \lim_{k\to\infty}\left[\breve{W}_i(x_i,\infty) - Y_i(x_i,k)\right] = 0\right\}_{i,k} \tag{12}$$

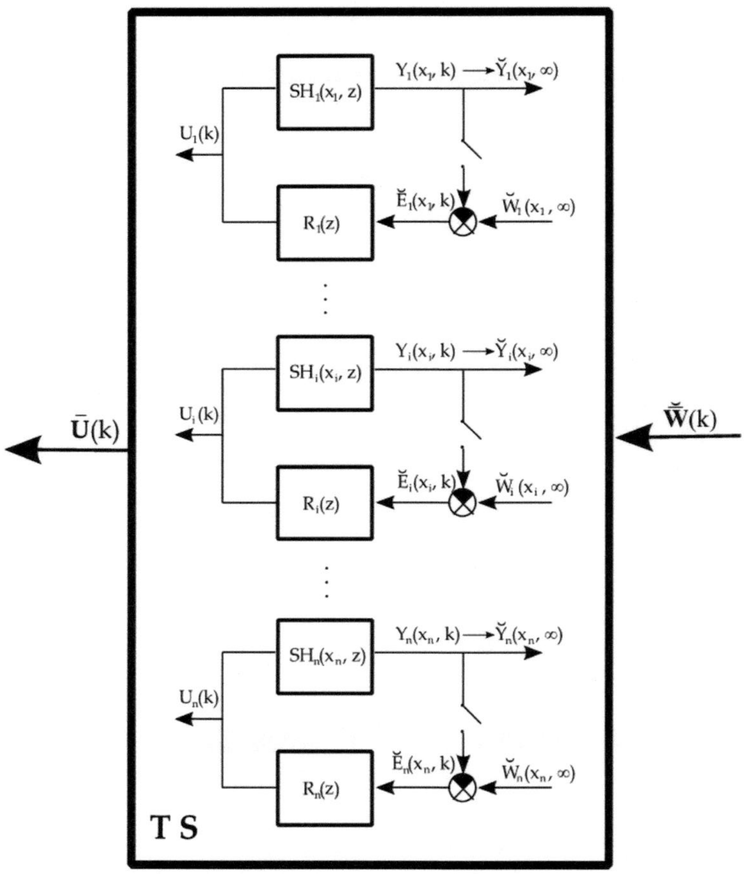

Fig. 9. SISO lumped parameter control loops in the block TS

TS - time part of control synthesis

$\{SH_i(x_i,z)\}_i$ - time components of HLDS dynamics

$\{R_i(z)\}_i$ - lumped parameter controllers

$\{Y_i(x_i,k)\}_{i,k} / \{\breve{W}_i\}_i = \{\breve{W}_i(x_i,\infty)\}_i$ - controlled/reference quantities

$\{\breve{E}_i(x_i,k)\}_{i,k}$ - lumped control errors

$\{U_i(k)\}_{i,k}$ - lumped control quantities

$\bar{\breve{W}}(k) / \bar{U}(k)$ - vector of lumped reference/control quantities

When the individual components of the vector $\bar{\breve{W}} = \{\breve{W}_i(x_i,\infty)\}_i$ are input in the particular control loops: $\{SH_i(x_i,z), R_i(z)\}_i$, the control processes take place. The applied control laws result in the sequences of control inputs: $\{U_i(k)\}_{i,k}$, and respectively the output quantities, for $k \to \infty$ converging to reference quantities

$$\{Y_i(x_i,k) \to Y_i(x_i,\infty) = \breve{W}_i(x_i,\infty)\}_{i,k} \tag{13}$$

Values of these lumped controlled quantities in new steady-state will be further denoted as

$$\{\breve{Y}_i(x_i,\infty) = \breve{W}_i(x_i,\infty)\}_i \tag{14}$$

see Fig. 9. - 10. for reference.

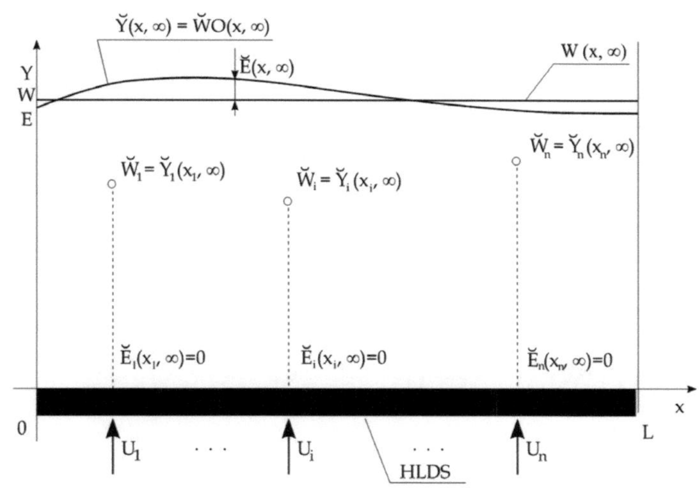

Fig. 10. Quantities of distributed parameter open-loop control in new steady-state

HLDS - controlled system with zero-order hold units

$\{U_i\}_i$ - lumped control quantities

$\{\breve{Y}_i(x_i,\infty) / \breve{W}_i = \breve{W}_i(x_i,\infty)\}_i$ - controlled/reference quantities in new steady-state

$\{\breve{E}_i(x_i,\infty)\}_i$ - lumped control errors

$\breve{Y}(x,\infty)$ - controlled distributed quantity in new steady-state

$W(x,\infty)$ - distributed reference quantity

$\breve{W}O(x,\infty)$ - unique best approximation of reference quantity

$\breve{E}(x,\infty)$ - distributed control error with minimal norm

Then according to equations (12-14) for the new steady-state it holds: $\left\{\breve{Y}_i(x_i,\infty)\mathcal{H}HR_i(x,\infty)=\breve{W}_i(x_i,\infty)\mathcal{H}HR_i(x,\infty)\right\}_i$, which implies that the overall distributed output quantity at the time $k\rightarrow\infty$: $\breve{Y}(x,\infty)$ gives the unique best approximation of the distributed reference variable: $W(x,\infty)$

$$\breve{Y}(x,\infty)=\sum_{i=1}^{n}\breve{Y}_i(x_i,\infty)\mathcal{H}HR_i(x,\infty)=\sum_{i=1}^{n}\breve{W}_i(x_i,\infty)\mathcal{H}HR_i(x,\infty)=\breve{W}O(x,\infty) \tag{15}$$

Therefore the control error has a unique form as well, with minimal quadratic norm

$$\begin{gathered}\left\|\breve{E}(x,\infty)\right\|=\left\|W(x,\infty)-\breve{Y}(x,\infty)\right\|=\left\|W(x,\infty)-\sum_{i=1}^{n}\breve{Y}_i(x_i,\infty)\mathcal{H}HR_i(x,\infty)\right\|= \\ \left\|W(x,\infty)-\sum_{i=1}^{n}\breve{W}_i(x_i,\infty)\mathcal{H}HR_i(x,\infty)\right\|=\left\|W(x,\infty)-\breve{W}O(x,\infty)\right\|\end{gathered} \tag{16}$$

Thus the control task, defined at equation (9), is accomplished with $\left\{\breve{E}_i(x_i,\infty)=0\right\}_i$ - see Fig. 10. for reference. As the conclusion of this section we may state that the control synthesis in open-loop control system is realized as:

Time Tasks of Control Synthesis – in lumped parameter control loops

Space Tasks of Control Synthesis – as approximation task.

When mathematical models cannot provide an ideal representation of controlled DPS dynamics and disturbances are present with an overall effect on the output in steady-state expressed by $EY(x,\infty)$ then

$$\begin{gathered}\left\|W(x,\infty)-\breve{Y}(x,\infty)\pm EY(x,\infty)\right\|\leq\left\|W(x,\infty)-\breve{Y}(x,\infty)\right\|+\left\|EY(x,\infty)\right\|= \\ \left\|W(x,\infty)-\breve{W}O(x,\infty)\right\|+\left\|EY(x,\infty)\right\|=\left\|\breve{E}(x,\infty)\right\|+\left\|EY(x,\infty)\right\|\end{gathered} \tag{17}$$

Finally at the design stage of a control system, for a given desired quality of control δ in space domain, it is necessary to choose appropriate number and layout of actuators for the fulfillment of this requirement

$$\left\|\breve{E}(x,\infty)\right\|+\left\|EY(x,\infty)\right\|\leq\delta \tag{18}$$

4.2 Closed-loop control with block RHLDS

Let us consider now a distributed parameter feedback control loop with initial conditions identical as the case above, see Fig. 11. In blocks SS1 a SS2 approximation problems are solved while in block RHLDS reduced distributed output quantities $\left\{YR_i(x,k)\right\}_{i,k}$ are generated. Block TS in Fig. 12., contains the controllers $\{R_i(z)\}_i$ designed as the controllers for SISO lumped parameter control loops $\{SH_i(x_i,z),R_i(z)\}_i$ with respect to the request formulated by equation (12). In the k-th step in block SS2 at approximation of $Y(x,k)$ on the subspace of $\{YR_i(x,k)\}_{i,k}$

$$\min\left\|Y(x,k)-\sum_{i=1}^{n}Y_i(x_i,k)YR_i(x,k)\right\| \tag{19}$$

time components of partial output quantities $\{\breve{Y}_i(x_i,k)\}_i$ are obtained, in block SS1 reference quantities $\{\breve{W}_i(x_i,\infty)\}_i$ are computed. Then on the output of the algebraic block is $\{\breve{E}_i(x_i,k)=\breve{W}_i(x_i,\infty)-\breve{Y}_i(x_i,k)\}_i$. These sequences $\{\breve{E}_i(x_i,k)\}_i$ enter into the TS on $\{R_i(z)\}_i$ and give $\{U_i(k)\}_i$, which enter into HLDS with $\{\breve{Y}_i(x_i,k)\}_i$ on the SS2 output - among $\{U_i(k)\}_i$ and $\{\breve{Y}_i(x_i,k)\}_i$ there are relations $\{SH_i(x_i,z)\}_i$. - This analysis of control synthesis process shows that synthesis in time domain is realized on the level of one parameter control loops $\{SH_i(x_i,z),R_i(z)\}_i$, Fig. 9.

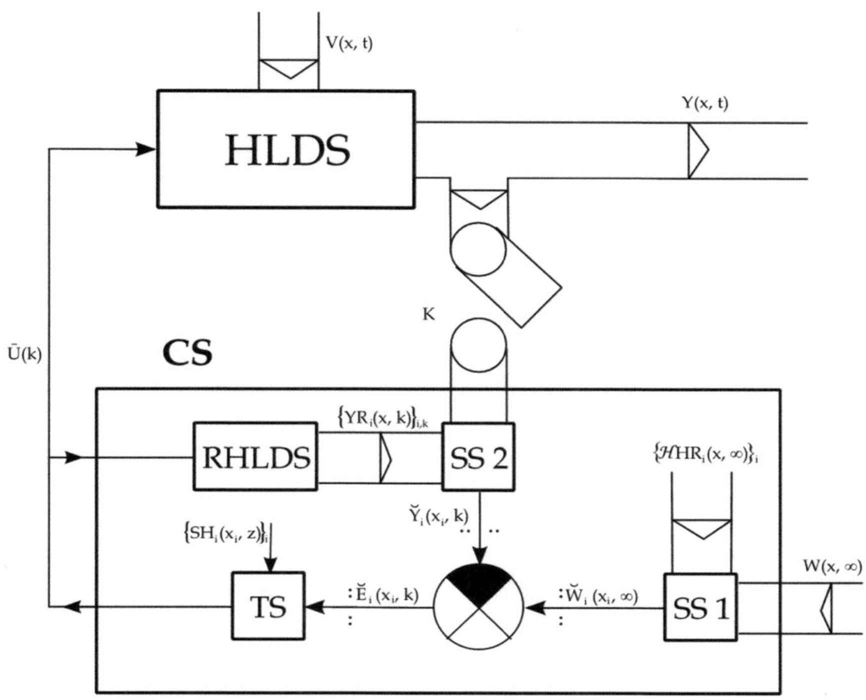

Fig. 11. Distributed parameter closed-loop system of control with reduced space components of output quantity

HLDS - controlled system with zero-order hold units
RHLDS - model for reduced space components: $\{YR_i(x,k)\}_{i,k}$
CS - control synthesis
TS/SS1,SS2 - time/space parts of control synthesis
K - time/space sampling
$Y(x,t)$ - distributed output quantity
$W(x,\infty),V(x,t)$ - reference and disturbance quantities
$\{Y_i(x_i,k)\}_{i,k} = \{\breve{Y}_i(x_i,k)\}_{i,k}$ – time components of output quantity
$\{\breve{W}_i = \breve{W}_i(x_i,\infty)\}_i / \{\breve{E}_i(x_i,k)\}_{i,k}$ - reference quantities/control errors
$\bar{U}(k)$ - vector of lumped control quantities

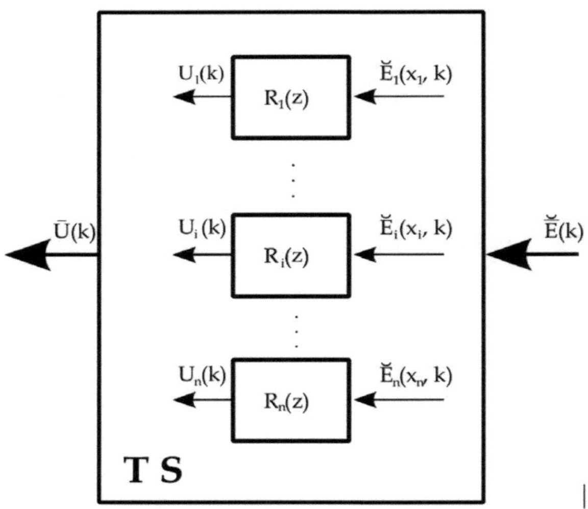

Fig. 12. The block of time synthesis

TS - time part of control synthesis
$\{R_i(z)\}_i$ - lumped parameter controllers
$\breve{E}(k) = \{\breve{E}_i(x_i,k)\}_{i,k}$ - vector of lumped control errors
$\bar{U}(k) = \{U_i(k)\}_{i,k}$ - vector of lumped control quantities

For $k \to \infty$ $\{YR_i(x,k) \to \mathcal{H}HR_i(x,\infty)\}_{i,k}$, $\{\breve{Y}_i(x_i,k)\}_{i,k} \to \{\breve{Y}_i(x_i,\infty) = \breve{W}_i(x_i,\infty)\}_i$ along with $\{\breve{E}_i(x_i,k) \to \breve{E}_i(x_i,\infty) = 0\}_{i,k}$. Thus the control task, defined by equation (9) is accomplished as given by relation (16). In case of the uncertainty of the control process relations similar to (17-18) are also valid.

Let´s consider now the approximation of $W(x,\infty)$ in the block SS1 in timestep k, on the set of $\{YR_i(x,k)\}_{i,k}$. Then in the control process sequences of quantities $\{\breve{W}_i(x_i,k)\}_{i,k}$ are obtained, as desired quantities of SISO control loops $\{SH_i(x_i,z),R_i(z)\}_i$ which are closed throughout the blocks TS, HLDS and SS2, see Fig. 13.

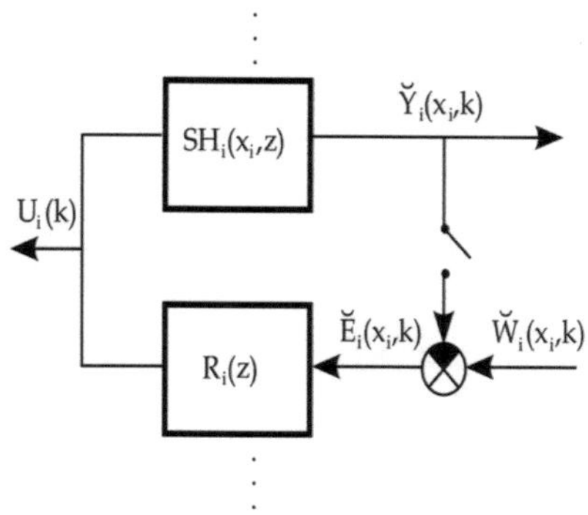

Fig. 13. Lumped parameter SISO control loops – i-th control loop

$SH_i(x_i,z)$ - i-th time component of HLDS dynamics

$R_i(z)$ - i-th lumped parameter controller

$\breve{Y}_i(x_i,k)/U_i(k)$ - i-th controlled/control quantity

$\breve{W}_i(x_i,k)/\breve{E}_i(x_i,k)$ - i-th desired quantity/control error

If for $k \to \infty$ $\{YR_i(x,k) \to \mathcal{H}HR_i(x,\infty)\}_{i,k}, \{Y_i(x_i,k) = \breve{Y}_i(x_i,k)\}_{i,k} \to \{\breve{Y}_i(x_i,\infty) = \breve{W}_i(x_i,\infty)\}_i$ along with $\{\breve{E}_i(x_i,k) \to \breve{E}_i(x_i,\infty) = 0\}_{i,k}$ - this actually means that the control task defined in equation (9), is accomplished as given by relation (16).

Finally we may state as a summary, that in closed-loop control with RHLDS the control synthesis is realized as:

Time Tasks of Control Synthesis – on the level of lumped parameter control loops

Space Tasks of Control Synthesis – as approximation tasks.

At the same time the solution of the approximation problem in block SS1 on the approximation set $\{YR_i(x,k)\}_{i,k}$

$$\min\left\|W(x,\infty) - \sum_{i=1}^{n} W_i(x_i,k)YR_i(x,k)\right\| \tag{20}$$

in timestep k is obtained

$$W(x,\infty) = \sum_{i=1}^{n} \breve{W}_i(x_i,k)YR_i(x,k) + \breve{E}(x,k) \tag{21}$$

where $\breve{E}(x,k)$ is the unique element at the best approximation of $W(x,\infty)$ on the set of approximate functions $\{YR_i(x,k)\}_i$. Similary by the solution of approximation problem in the block SS2 - $\{\breve{Y}_i(x_i,k)\}_i$ in the timestep k distributed output quantity $Y(x,k)$ is given as

$$Y(x,k) = \sum_{i=1}^{n} \breve{Y}_i(x_i,k)YR_i(x,k) \tag{22}$$

4.3 Closed-loop control

Let us now consider a distributed parameter feedback loop as featured in Fig. 14. with initial conditions as above, where in timestep k an approximation problem is solved

$$\min\left\| E(x,k) - \sum_{i=1}^{n} E_i(x_i,k) YR_i(x,k) \right\| \tag{23}$$

and as a result in timestep k a vector $\breve{\bar{E}}(k) = \left\{ \breve{E}_i(x_i,k) \right\}_i$ is obtained. By relations (20-22) the further equations are valid

$$\begin{aligned} &\min\left\| E(x,k) - \sum_{i=1}^{n} E_i(x_i,k) YR_i(x,k) \right\| = \\ &= \min\left\| W(x,\infty) - Y(x,k) - \sum_{i=1}^{n} E_i(x_i,k) YR_i(x,k) \right\| = \\ &= \min\left\| W(x,\infty) - \sum_{i=1}^{n} \left[\breve{Y}_i(x_i,k) + E_i(x_i,k) \right] YR_i(x,k) \right\| = \\ &= \left\| W(x,\infty) - \sum_{i=1}^{n} \left[\breve{Y}_i(x_i,k) + \breve{E}_i(x_i,k) \right] YR_i(x,k) \right\| \end{aligned} \tag{24}$$

The problem solution $W(x,\infty) = \sum_{i=1}^{n} \left[\breve{Y}_i(x_i,k) + \breve{E}_i(x_i,k) \right] YR_i(x,k) + \breve{E}(x,k)$ is obtained by approximation.

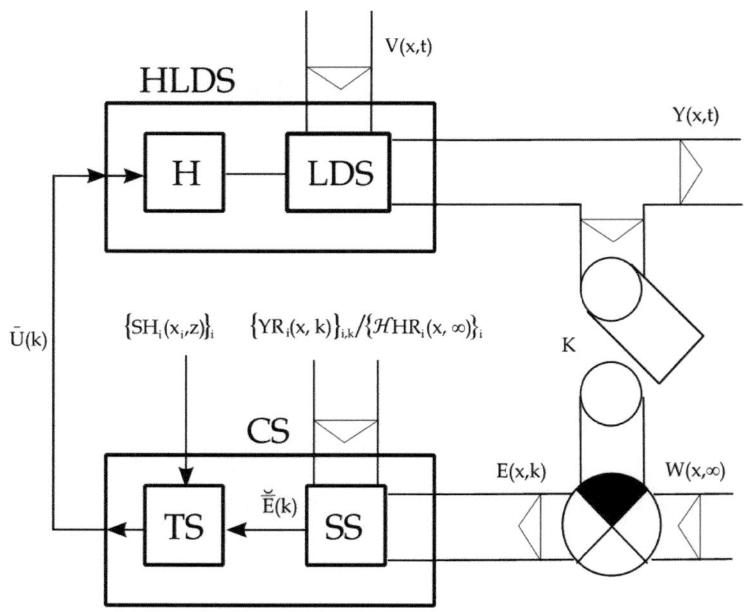

Fig. 14. Distributed parameter closed-loop system of control

HLDS - LDS with zero-order hold units

CS - control synthesis
TS /SS - time/space control synthesis
K - time/space sampling
$Y(x,t) / W(x,\infty)$ - distributed controlled/reference quantity
$\{SH_i(x_i,z)\}_i$ - transfer functions - dynamic characteristics of HLDS in time domain
$\{YR_i(x,k)\}_i / \{\mathcal{H}HR_i(x,\infty)\}_i$ - reduced characteristics in space domain
$E(x,k)$ - distributed control error
$V(x,t)$ - distributed disturbance quantity
$\breve{\bar{E}}(k)$ - vector of control errors
$\bar{U}(k)$ - vector of control quantities

Comparison of relation (21) and result of the approximation problem (24) gives $\sum_{i=1}^{n} \breve{W}_i(x_i,k) YR_i(x,k) + \breve{E}(x,k) = \sum_{i=1}^{n} \left[\breve{Y}_i(x_i,k) + \breve{E}_i(x_i,k)\right] YR_i(x,k) + \breve{E}(x,k)$ and then $\sum_{i=1}^{n} \breve{W}_i(x_i,k) YR_i(x,k) = \sum_{i=1}^{n} \left[\breve{Y}_i(x_i,k) + \breve{E}_i(x_i,k)\right] YR_i(x,k)$, finally $\left\{\breve{W}_i(x_i,k) = \breve{Y}_i(x_i,k) + \breve{E}_i(x_i,k)\right\}_{i,k}$ is obtained. Now in vector form this means

$$\breve{\bar{W}}(k) = \breve{\bar{Y}}(k) + \breve{\bar{E}}(k) \Rightarrow \breve{\bar{E}}(k) = \breve{\bar{W}}(k) - \breve{\bar{Y}}(k) = \left\{\breve{E}_i(x_i,k) = \breve{W}_i(x_i,k) - \breve{Y}_i(x_i,k)\right\}_{i,k} \tag{25}$$

Then sequences $\left\{\breve{E}_i(x_i,k)\right\}_{i,k}$ enter into the block TS on $\{R_i(z)\}_i$ and give $\{U_i(k)\}_i$, among $\{U_i(k)\}_i$ and $\left\{\breve{Y}_i(x_i,k)\right\}_i$ there are relations $\{SH_i(x_i,z)\}_i$. Finally this analysis of control synthesis process shows that synthesis in time domain is realized on the level of one parameter control loops $\{SH_i(x_i,z), R_i(z)\}_i$, Fig. 13. - closed throughout the structure of distributed parameter control loop, Fig. 14. If for $k \to \infty$ $\{YR_i(x,k) \to \mathcal{H}HR_i(x,\infty)\}_i$ and $\left\{\breve{Y}_i(x_i,k)\right\}_{i,k} \to \left\{\breve{Y}_i(x_i,\infty) = \breve{W}_i(x_i,\infty)\right\}_i$ along with $\left\{\breve{E}_i(x_i,k) \to \breve{E}_i(x_i,\infty) = 0\right\}_{i,k}$ then

$$\begin{aligned}
\min\left\| E(x,\infty) - \sum_{i=1}^{n} E_i(x_i,\infty)\mathcal{H}HR_i(x,\infty)\right\| &= \left\| W(x,\infty) - \breve{Y}(x,\infty) - \sum_{i=1}^{n} \breve{E}_i(x_i,\infty)\mathcal{H}HR_i(x,\infty)\right\| = \\
= \left\| \sum_{i=1}^{n} \breve{W}_i(x_i,\infty)\mathcal{H}HR_i(x,\infty) + \breve{E}(x,\infty) - \sum_{i=1}^{n} \breve{Y}_i(x_i,\infty)\mathcal{H}HR_i(x,\infty) - \sum_{i=1}^{n} \breve{E}_i(x_i,\infty)\mathcal{H}HR_i(x,\infty)\right\| &= \\
= \left\| \sum_{i=1}^{n} \left[\breve{W}_i(x_i,\infty) - \breve{Y}_i(x_i,\infty)\right]\mathcal{H}HR_i(x,\infty) + \breve{E}(x,\infty) - \sum_{i=1}^{n} \breve{E}_i(x_i,\infty)\mathcal{H}HR_i(x,\infty)\right\| &= \left\|\breve{E}(x,\infty)\right\|
\end{aligned} \tag{26}$$

is valid, so the above given control task (9) is accomplished - whereas in the steady-state $\left\{\breve{W}_i(x_i,\infty) - \breve{Y}_i(x_i,\infty) = \breve{E}_i(x_i,\infty) = 0\right\}_i$. By concluding the above presented discussion, the control synthesis in closed-loop control is realized as:

Time Tasks of Control Synthesis – on the level of lumped parameter control loops
Space Tasks of Control Synthesis – as approximation tasks.
When mathematical models cannot provide an ideal description of controlled DPS dynamics and disturbances are present with an overall effect on the output in steady-state, expressed by $EY(x,\infty)$ then the realtions similar to (17-18) are also valid here.
In practice mostly only reduced distributed parameter transient responses in steady-state $\{\mathcal{H}HR_i(x,\infty)\}_i$ are considered for the solution of the approximation tasks in the block SS of the scheme in Fig. 14. along with robustification of controllers $\{R_i(z)\}_i$.
For simplicity problems of DPS control have been formulated here for the distributed desired quantity $W(x,\infty)$. In case of $W(x,k)$ is assumed, the control synthesis is realized similarly:
- *In Space Domain* - as problem of approximation in particular sampling intervals
- *In Time Domain* - as control synthesis in lumped parameter control loops, closed throughout structures of the distributed parameter control loop.

The solution of the presented problems of control synthesis an assumption is used, that in the framework of the chosen control systems the prescribed control quality can be reached both in the in space and time domain. However in the design of actual control systems for the given distributed parameter systems, usually the

- optimization of the number and layout of actuators
- optimization of dynamical characteristics of lumped/distributed parameter actuators
- optimization of dynamical characteristics of lumped parameter control loops

is required and necessary.

5. Distributed Parameter Systems Blockset for MATLAB & Simulink

As a software support for DPS modelling, control and design of problems in MATLAB & Simulink the programming environment **Distributed Parameter Systems Blockset for MATLAB & Simulink (DPS Blockset)** - a Third-Party Product of The MathWorks www.mathworks.com/products/connections/ – Fig. 15., has been developed within the program CONNECTIONS of The MathWorks Corporation by the Institute of Automation, Measurement and Applied Informatics of Mechanical Engineering Faculty, Slovak University of Technology in Bratislava (IAMAI-MEF-STU) (Hulkó et al., 2003-2010). Fig. 16. shows The library of **DPS Blockset**. The **HLDS** and **RHLDS** blocks model controlled DPS dynamics described by numerical structures as LDS with zero-order hold units - H. **DPS Control Synthesis** provides feedback to distributed parameter controlled systems in control loops with blocks for discrete-time **PID, Algebraic, State-Space and Robust Synthesis**. The block **DPS Input** generates distributed quantities, which can be used as distributed reference quantities or distributed disturbances, etc. **DPS Display** presents distributed quantities with many options including export to AVI files. The block **DPS Space Synthesis** performs space synthesis as an approximation problem.
As a demonstration, some results of the discrete-time PID control of complex-shape metal body heating by the **DPS Blockset** are shown in Fig. 17.-19., where the heating process was modelled by finite element method in the COMSOL Multiphysics virtual software environment - www.comsol.com.

The block **Tutorial** presents methodological framework for formulation and solution of control problems for DPS. The block **Show** contains motivation examples such as: *Control of temperature field of 3D metal body* (the controlled system was modelled in the virtual software environment COMSOL Multiphysics); *Control of 3D beam of „smart" structure* (the controlled system was modelled in the virtual software environment ANSYS); *Adaptive control of glass furnace* (the controlled system was modelled by Partial Differential Equations Toolbox of the MATLAB), and *Groundwater remediation control* (the controlled system was modelled in the virtual software environment MODFLOW). The block **Demos** contains examples oriented at the methodology of modelling and control synthesis. The **DPS Wizard** gives an automatized guide for arrangement and setting distributed parameter control loops in step-by-step operation.

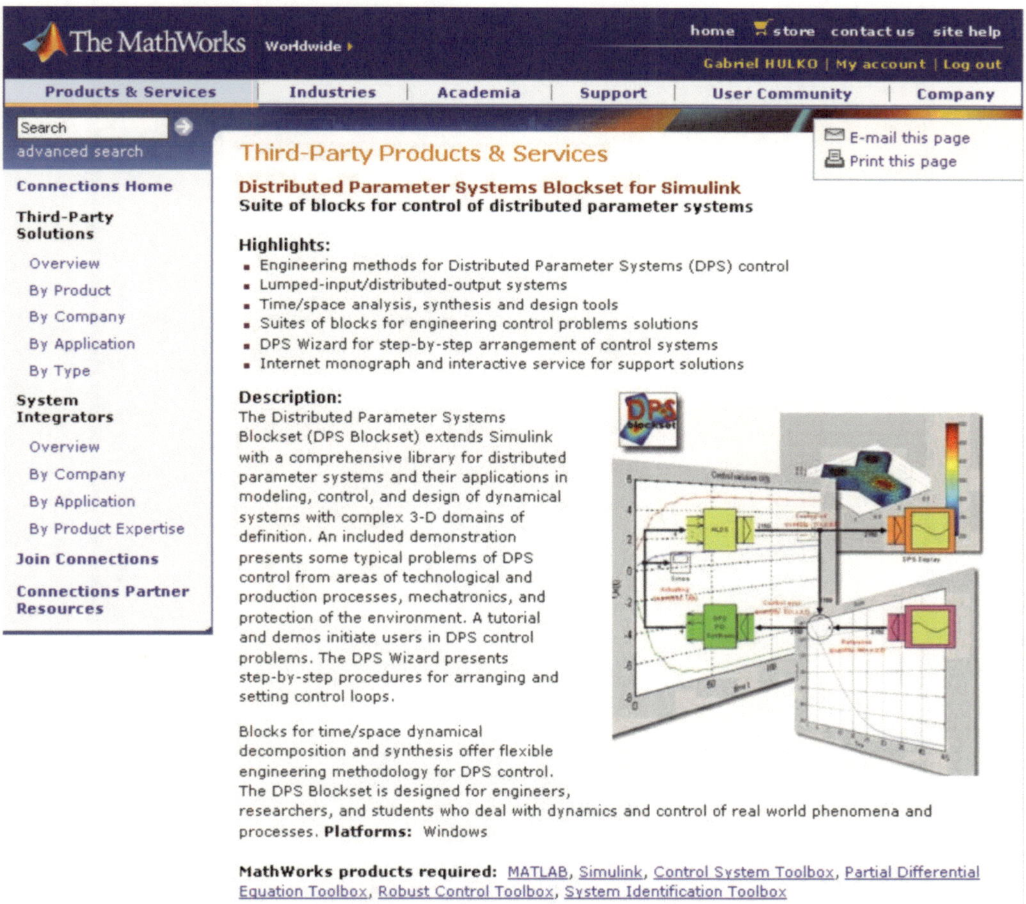

Fig. 15. Distributed Parameter Systems Blockset on the web portal of The MathWorks Corporation

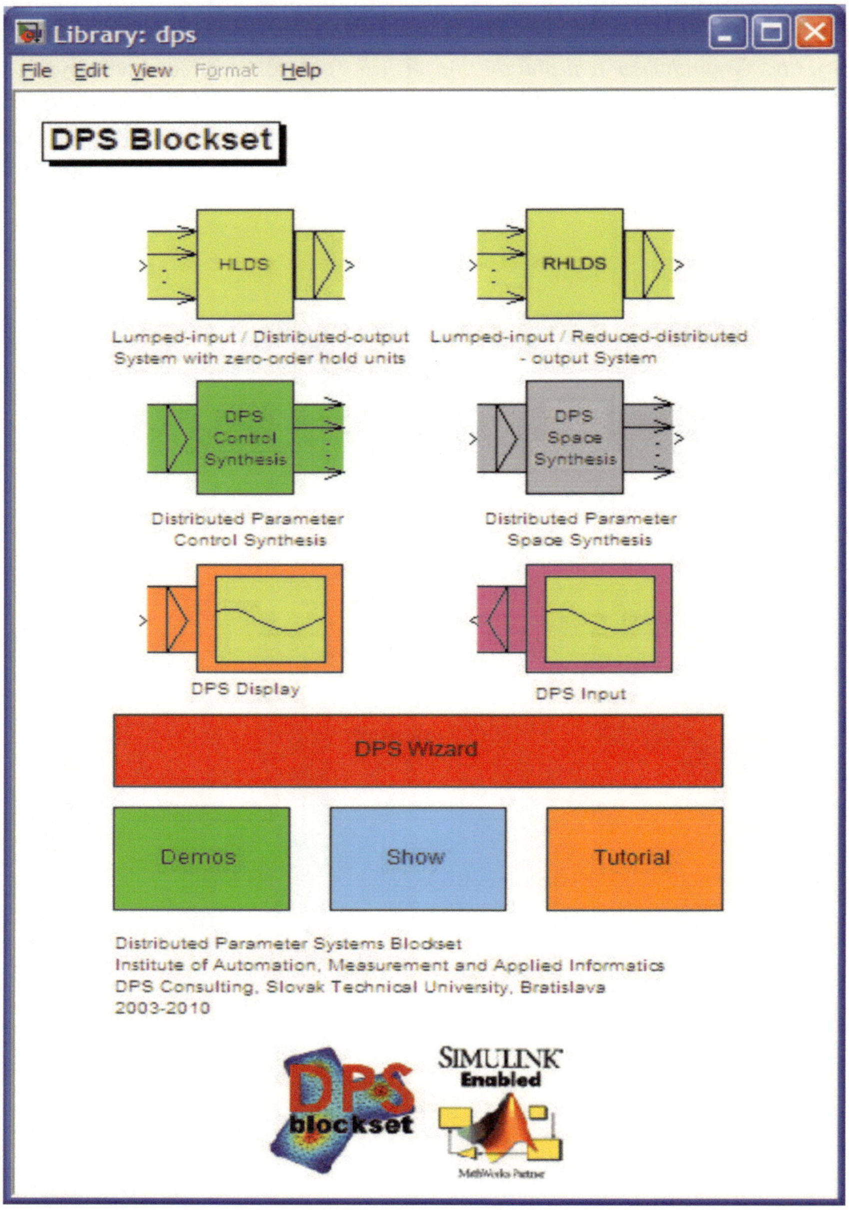

Fig. 16. The library of Distributed Parameter Systems Blockset for MATLAB & Simulink - Third-Party Product of The MathWorks

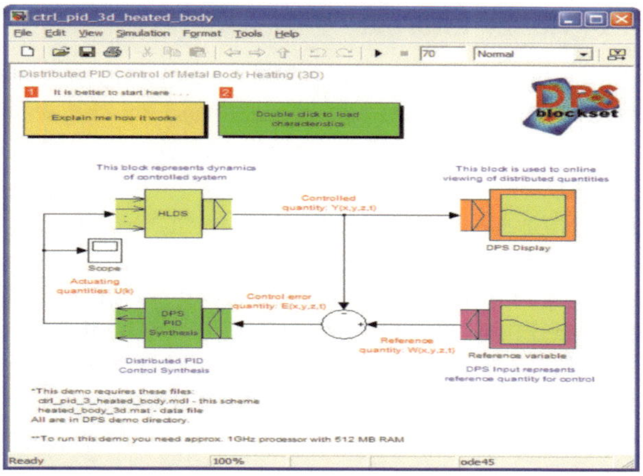

Fig. 17. Distributed parameter control loop for discrete-time PID control of heating of metal body in DPS Blockset environment

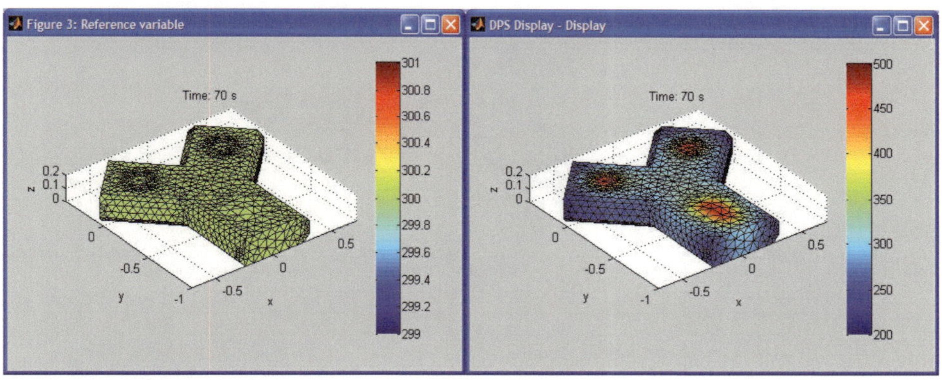

Fig. 18. Distributed reference and controlled quantities of metal body heating over the numerical net

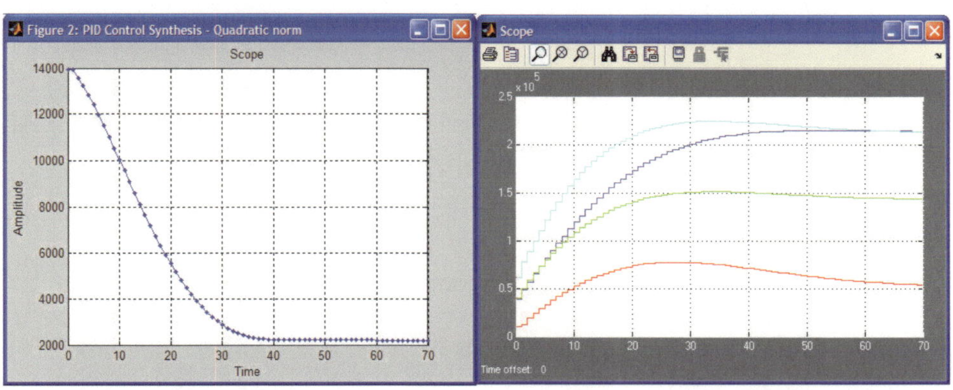

Fig. 19. Quadratic norm of distributed control error and discrete lumped actuating quantities at discrete-time PID control of heating of metal body in DPS Blockset environment

6. Interactive control via the Internet

For the interactive formulation and solution of DPS demonstration control problems via the Internet, an **Interactive Control** service has been started on the web portal **Distributed Parameter Systems Control -** www.dpscontrol.sk of the IAMAI-MEF-STU (Hulkó, 2003-2010) - see Fig. 20. for a screenshot of the site. In the framework of the problem formulation, first the computational geometry and mesh are chosen in the complex 3D shape definition domain, then DT distributed transient responses are computed in virtual software environments for numerical dynamical analysis of machines and processes. Finally, the distributed reference quantity is specified in points of the computational mesh - Fig. 18. Representing the solution to those interested animated results of actuating quantities, quadratic norm of control error, distributed reference and controlled quantity are sent in the form of **DPS Blockset** outputs - see Fig. 17-19. for illustration.

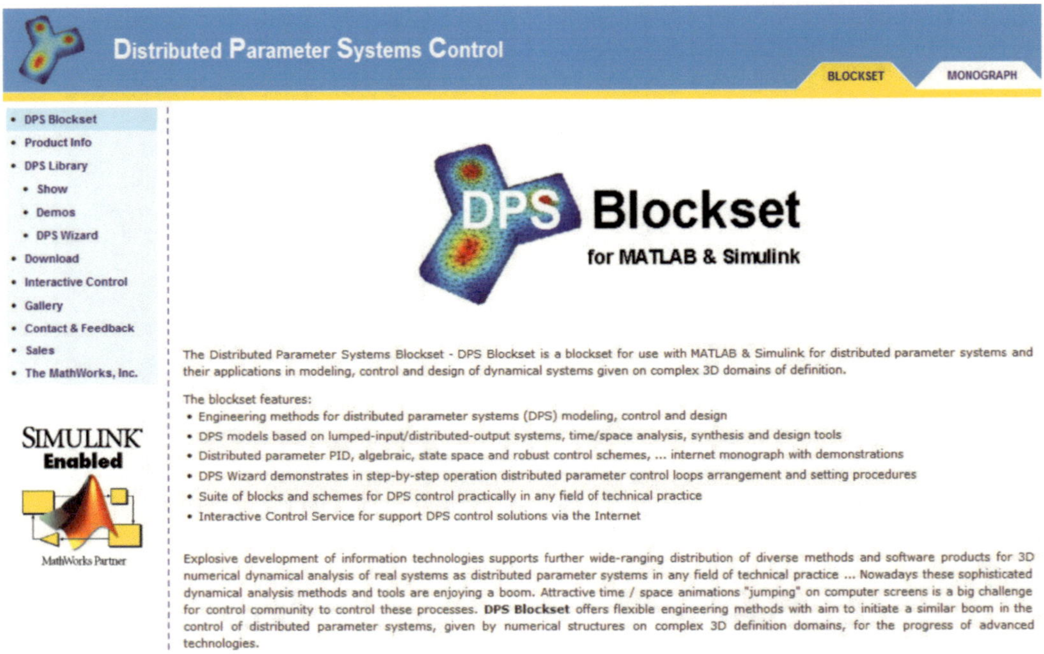

Fig. 20. Web portal Distributed Parameter Systems Control with monograph Modeling, Control and Design of Distributed Parameter Systems with Demonstrations in MATLAB and service Interactive Control

7. Conclusion

The aim of this chapter is to present a philosophy of the engineering approach for the control of DPS - given by numerical structures, which opens a wide space for novel applications of the toolboxes and blocksets of the MATLAB & Simulink software environment. This approach is based on the general decomposition into time and space components of controlled DPS dynamics represented by numerically computed distributed parameter transient and impulse characteristics, given on complex shape definition domains in 3D. Starting out from this dynamics decomposition a methodical framework is presented for the analogous decomposition of control synthesis into the space and time subtasks. In space domain approximation problems are solved, while in the time domain control synthesis is realized by lumped parameter SISO control loops (Hulkó et al., 1981-2010). Based on these decomposition a software product named **Distributed Parameter Systems Blockset for MATLAB & Simulink** - a Third-Party software product of The MathWorks - www.mathworks.com/products/connections/ has been developed within the program CONNECTIONS of The MathWorks Corporation, (Hulkó et al., 2003-2010), where time domain toolboxes and blocksets of software environment MATLAB & Simulink as Control Systems Toolbox, Simulink Control Design, System Identification Toolbox,... are made use of. In the space domain approximation problems are solved as optimization problems by means of the Optimization Toolbox.

For the further support of research in this area a web portal named **Distributed Parameter Systems Control** - www.dpscontrol.sk was realized (Hulkó et al., 2003-2010), see Fig. 20. for an illustration. On the above mentioned web portal, the online version of the monograph titled **Modeling, Control and Design of Distributed Parameter Systems with Demonstrations in MATLAB** - www.mathworks.com/support/books/ (Hulkó et al., 1998), is presented along with application examples from different disciplines such as: control of technological and production processes, control and design of mechatronic structures, groundwater remediation control, etc. This web portal also offers for those interested the download of the demo version of the **Distributed Parameter Systems Blockset for MATLAB & Simulink** with **Tutorial** , **Show** , **Demos** and **DPS Wizard**. This portal also offers the **Interactive Control** service for interactive solution of model control problems of DPS via the Internet.

8. Acknowledgment

This work was supported by the Slovak Scientific Grant Agency VEGA under the contract No. 1/0138/11 for project *„Control of dynamical systems given by numerical structures as distributed parameter systems"* and the Slovak Research and Development Agency under the contract No. APVV-0160-07 for project *„Advanced Methods for Modeling, Control and Design of Mechatronical Systems as Lumped-input and Distributed-output Systems"* also the project No. APVV-0131-10 *„High-tech solutions for technological processes and mechatronic components as controlled distributed parameter systems"*.

9. References

Butkovskij, A. G. (1965). *Optimal control of distributed parameter systems.* Nauka, Moscow (in Russian)

Hulkó, G. et al. (1981). On Adaptive Control of Distributed Parameter Systems, *Proceedings of 8-th World Congress of IFAC,* Kyoto, 1981

Hulkó, G. et al. (1987). Control of Distributed Parameter Systems by means of Multi-Input and Multi-Distributed-Output Systems, *Proceedings of 10-th World Congress of IFAC,* Munich, 1987

Hulkó, G. (1989). Identification of Lumped Input and Distributed Output Systems, *Proceedings of 5-th IFAC / IMACS / IFIP Symposium on Control of Distributed Parameter Systems,* Perpignan, 1989

Hulkó, G. et al. (1990). Computer Aided Design of Distributed Parameter Systems of Control, *Proceedings of 11-th World Congress of IFAC,* Tallin, 1990

Hulkó G. (1991). Lumped Input and Distributed Ouptut Systems at the Control of Distributed Parameter Systems. *Problems of Control and Information Theory,* Vol. 20, No. 2, pp. 113-128, Pergamon Press, Oxford

Hulkó, G. et al. (1998). *Modeling, Control and Design of Distributed Parameter Systems with Demonstrations in MATLAB,* Publishing House STU, ISBN 80-227-1083-0, Bratislava

Hulkó, G. et al. (2005). Web-based control design environment for distributed parameter systems control education, *Proceedings of 16-th World Congress of IFAC,* Prague, 2005

Hulkó, G. et al. (2003-2010). *Distributed Parameter Systems Control.* Web portal, Available from: www.dpscontrol.sk

Hulkó, G. et al. (2003-2010). *Distributed Parameter Systems Blockset for MATLAB & Simulink,* www.mathworks.com/products/connections/ - Third-Party Product of The MathWorks, Bratislava-Natick, Available from: www.dpscontrol.sk

Hulkó, G. et al. (2009). Engineering Methods and Software Support for Modeling and Design of Discrete-time Control of Distributed Parameter Systems, *Mini-tutorial, Proceedings of European Control Conference 2009,* Budapest, 2009

Hulkó, G. et al. (2009). Engineering Methods and Software Support for Modelling and Design of Discrete-time Control of Distributed Parameter Systems. *European Journal of Control,* Vol. 15, No. Iss. 3-4, *Fundamental Issues in Control,* (May-August 2009), pp. 407-417, ISSN 0947-3580

Hulkó, G. et. al (2010). Control of Technological Processes Modelled in COMSOL Multiphysics as Distributed Parameter Systems, *Proceedings of Asian COMSOL Conference,* Bangalore, 2010

Lasiecka, I., Triggiani, R. (2000). *Control Theory for Partial Differential Equations* (Encyclopedia of Mathematics and Its Applications 74), Cambridge U. Press, Cambridge, UK

Lions, J. L. (1971). *Optimal control of systems governed by partial differential equations,* Springer-Verlag, Berlin - Heidelberg - New York

Shadrin, A. (2005). *Approximation theory.* DAMTP University of Cambridge, Cambridge UK, Available from: www.damtp.cam.ac.uk

Wang, P. K. C. (1964). *Control of distributed parameter systems* (Advances in Control Systems: Theory and Applications, 1.), Academic Press, New York

3

Numerical Inverse Laplace Transforms for Electrical Engineering Simulation

Lubomír Brančík
Brno University of Technology
Czech Republic

1. Introduction

Numerical inverse Laplace transform (NILT) methods are widely used in various scientific areas, especially for a solution of respective differential equations. In field of an electrical engineering many various approaches have been considered so far, but mostly for a single variable (1D NILT), see at least (Brančík, 1999, 2007b; Cohen, 2007; Valsa & Brančík, 1998; Wu at al., 2001) from plenty of papers. Much less attention was paid to multidimensional variable (*n*D NILT) methods, see e.g. (Hwang at al., 1983; Singhal at al., 1975), useful rather for more complicated electromagnetic systems. The 2D NILT methods, see e.g. (Brančík, 2005, 2007a, 2007b; Hwang & Lu, 1999), can be applied for a transmission line analysis, or *n*D NILT methods, $n \geq 2$, for a nonlinear circuits analysis, if relevant Laplace transforms are developed through a Volterra series expansion, see e.g. (Brančík, 2010a, 2010b, Karmakar, 1980; Schetzen, 2006), to highlight at least a few applications. This paper is focused on the class of NILT methods based on complex Fourier series approximation, their error analysis, their effective algorithms development in a Matlab language, and after all, on their selected applications in field of electrical engineering to show practical usefulness of the algorithms.

2. Multidimensional numerical inverse Laplace transform

An *n*-dimensional Laplace transform of a real function $f(\boldsymbol{t})$, with $\boldsymbol{t} = (t_1,...,t_n)$ as a row vector of *n* real variables, is defined as (Hwang at al., 1983)

$$F(\boldsymbol{s}) = \underbrace{\int_0^\infty \cdots \int_0^\infty}_{n\text{-}fold} f(\boldsymbol{t})\exp(-\boldsymbol{s}\boldsymbol{t}^T)\prod_{i=1}^{n} dt_i \,, \tag{1}$$

where $\boldsymbol{s} = (s_1,...,s_n)$ and T means a transposition. Under an assumption $|f(\boldsymbol{t})| < M\exp(\boldsymbol{\alpha}\boldsymbol{t}^T)$, with M real positive and $\boldsymbol{\alpha} = (\alpha_1,...,\alpha_n)$ being a minimal abscissa of convergence, and the *n*D Laplace transform $F(\boldsymbol{s})$ defined on a region $\{\boldsymbol{s} \in C^n: \text{Re}[\boldsymbol{s}] > \boldsymbol{\alpha}\}$, with $\mathbf{c} = (c_1,...,c_n)$ as an abscissa of convergence, and the inequality taken componentwise, the original function is given by an *n*-fold Bromwich integral

$$f(\boldsymbol{t}) = \frac{1}{(2\pi j)^n} \int_{c_1-j\infty}^{c_1+j\infty} \cdots \int_{c_n-j\infty}^{c_n+j\infty} F(\boldsymbol{s})\exp(\boldsymbol{s}\boldsymbol{t}^T)\prod_{i=1}^{n} dt_i \,. \tag{2}$$

In the papers (Brančík, 2007a, 2007b, 2010b), it was shown for the 1D, 2D, and 3D cases, the rectangular method of a numerical integration leads to an approximate formula whose a relative error is adjustable, and corresponds to the complex Fourier series approximation of a respective dimension. The method has been generalized for an arbitrary dimension n in the recent work (Brančík, 2011).

2.1 Complex Fourier series approximation and limiting relative error

Substituting $s_i = c_i + j\omega_i$ into (2), and using a rectangular rule of the integration, namely $\omega_i = m_i\Omega_i$, and $\Omega_i = 2\pi/\tau_i$ as generalized frequency steps, with τ_i forming a region of the solution $t \in [0,\tau_1) \times ... \times [0,\tau_n)$, an approximate formula is

$$\tilde{f}(t) = \exp(ct^T)\left(\prod_{i=1}^{n}\tau_i^{-1}\right)\sum_{m_1=-\infty}^{\infty}\cdots\sum_{m_n=-\infty}^{\infty} F(s)\exp\left(j\sum_{i=1}^{n} m_i\Omega_i t_i\right), \tag{3}$$

with $s_i = c_i + jm_i\Omega_i$, $\forall i$. As is shown in (Brančík, 2011), a limiting relative error δ_M of (3) can be controlled by setting $\mathbf{c} = (c_1,...,c_n)$, defining paths of the integration in (2), namely

$$c_i = \alpha_i - \frac{1}{\tau_i}\ln\left(1 - \frac{1}{\sqrt[n]{1+\delta_M}}\right) \approx \alpha_i - \frac{1}{\tau_i}\ln\frac{\delta_M}{n}, \tag{4}$$

for $i = 1,\ldots,n$, and while keeping the equalities $\tau_1(c_1 - \alpha_1) = ... = \tau_n(c_n - \alpha_n)$. The simplification in (4) is enabled due to small values δ_M considered in practice. The last equation is used for setting up parameters of the nD NILT method relating them to a limiting relative error δ_M required for practical computations.

2.2 Practical computational methods

It should be highlighted that the formula (4) is valid, and a relative error supposed is really achievable by the nD NILT (3), if infinite numbers of terms are used in the series. In practice, it cannot sure be fulfilled, but a suitable technique for accelerating a convergence of infinite series is usable, as is e.g. a quotient-difference (q-d) algorithm (Rutishauser, 1957). Besides, as has been already successfully used for cases of $n \le 3$, the formula (3) can be rearranged to enable using FFT & IFFT algorithms for an effective computation.

2.2.1 Partial ILTs evaluation technique

The technique of practical evaluation of the n-fold infinite sum (3) follows the properties of the n-fold Bromwich integral (2), namely we can rearrange it into the form

$$f(t_1,t_2,\ldots,t_n) = \frac{1}{2\pi j}\int_{c_1-j\infty}^{c_1+j\infty}\left(\frac{1}{2\pi j}\int_{c_2-j\infty}^{c_2+j\infty}\left(\cdots\frac{1}{2\pi j}\int_{c_n-j\infty}^{c_n+j\infty} F(s_1,s_2,\ldots,s_n)e^{s_n t_n}ds_n\cdots\right)e^{s_2 t_2}ds_2\right)e^{s_1 t_1}ds_1, \tag{5}$$

or shortly

$$f(t_1,t_2,\ldots,t_n) = \mathbb{L}_1^{-1}\left[\mathbb{L}_2^{-1}\left[\cdots\mathbb{L}_n^{-1}\left[F(s_1,s_2,\ldots,s_n)\right]\cdots\right]\right]. \tag{6}$$

Although the order of the integration may be arbitrary on principle, here the above one will be used for an explanation. Similarly, (3) can be rewritten as

$$\tilde{f}(t_1,t_2,\dots,t_n)=\frac{e^{c_1t_1}}{\tau_1}\sum_{m_1=-\infty}^{\infty}\left(\frac{e^{c_2t_2}}{\tau_2}\sum_{m_2=-\infty}^{\infty}\left(\cdots\frac{e^{c_nt_n}}{\tau_n}\sum_{m_n=-\infty}^{\infty}F(s_1,s_2,\dots,s_n)e^{jm_n\Omega_nt_n}\cdots\right)e^{jm_2\Omega_2t_2}\right)e^{jm_1\Omega_1t_1}\,,\quad(7)$$

with $s_i = c_i + jm_i\Omega_i$. If we define $F_n \equiv F(s_1,\dots,s_{n-1},s_n)$ and $F_0 \equiv f(t_1,\dots,t_{n-1},t_n)$, then n consequential partial inversions are performed as

$$\begin{aligned}\mathbb{L}_n^{-1}\{F_n\}&=F_{n-1}(s_1,\dots,s_{n-1},t_n)\,,\\ \mathbb{L}_{n-1}^{-1}\{F_{n-1}\}&=F_{n-2}(s_1,\dots,t_{n-1},t_n)\,,\\ &\vdots\\ \mathbb{L}_1^{-1}\{F_1\}&=f(t_1,\dots,t_{n-1},t_n)\,.\end{aligned}\quad(8)$$

As is obvious we need to use a procedure able to make the inversion of Laplace transforms dependent on another n-1 parameters, complex in general. Let us denote arguments in (8) by $\boldsymbol{p}_i = (p_1,\dots,p_{n-1},p_n)$. Then the ILT of the type

$$F_{i-1}(\boldsymbol{p}_{i-1})=\mathbb{L}_i^{-1}\{F_i(\boldsymbol{p}_i)\}=\frac{1}{2\pi j}\int_{c_i-j\infty}^{c_i+j\infty}F_i(\boldsymbol{p}_i)e^{s_it_i}ds_i \quad(9)$$

can be used n times, $i = n,n$-1...,1, to evaluate (8), with $p_n = (s_1,\dots,s_{n-1},s_n)$, $p_{n-1} = (s_1,\dots,s_{n-1},t_n),\dots,$ $p_1 = (s_1,\dots,t_{n-1},t_n)$, and $p_0 = (t_1,\dots,t_{n-1},t_n)$, while $p_j = s_j$ for $j \le i$, and $p_j = t_j$ otherwise. A further technique is based on demand to find the solution on a whole region of discrete points. Then, taking into account $t_{ik} = kT_i$ in (9), with T_i as the sampling periods in the original domain, we can write an approximate formula

$$\tilde{F}_{i-1}(\boldsymbol{p}_{i-1})=\frac{e^{c_ikT_i}}{\tau_i}\sum_{m=-\infty}^{\infty}\tilde{F}_i(\boldsymbol{p}_i)e^{j2\pi mkT_i/\tau_i}\,,\quad(10)$$

$i = n,n$-1...,1, and with $\Omega_i = 2\pi/\tau_i$ substituted. As follows from the error analysis (Brančík, 2011) a relative error is predictable on the region $O_{err} = [0,\tau_1) \times\dots\times [0,\tau_n)$. For $k = 0,1,\dots,M_i$-1, $i = 1,\dots,n$, a maximum reachable region is $O_{max} = [0,(M_1\text{-}1)T_1] \times\dots\times [0,(M_n\text{-}1)T_n]$. Thus, to meet the necessary condition $O_{max} \subset O_{err}$, we can set up fittingly $\tau_i = M_iT_i$, $i = 1,\dots,n$. In practice, a region of the calculation is chosen to be $O_{cal} = [0,t_{1cal}] \times\dots\times [0,t_{ncal}]$, with $t_{ical} = (M_i/2\text{–}1)T_i$, $i = 1,\dots,n$, to provide certain margins.

2.2.2 FFT, IFFT, and quotient-difference algorithms utilization

As is shown in (Brančík, 2007a, 2010c), the discretized formula (10) can be evaluated by the FFT and IFFT algorithms, in conjunction with the quotient-difference (q-d) algorithm for accelerating convergence of the residual infinite series, see following procedures.

To explain it in more detail, let us consider an r-th cycle in gaining the original function via (9), i.e. $F_{r-1}(\boldsymbol{p}_{r-1})=\mathbb{L}_r^{-1}\{F_r(\boldsymbol{p}_r)\}$. For its discretized version (10) we have

$$\tilde{F}_{r-1}(s_1,\dots,kT_r,\dots,t_n)=\frac{e^{c_rkT_r}}{\tau_r}\sum_{m=-\infty}^{\infty}\tilde{F}_r(s_1,\dots,c_r+jm\frac{2\pi}{\tau_r},\dots,t_n)e^{j2\pi mkT_r/\tau_r}\,.\quad(11)$$

The above stated formula can be decomposed and expressed also as

$$\tilde{F}_{r-1}(s_1,\ldots,kT_r,\ldots,t_n) = \frac{e^{c_r kT_r}}{\tau_r}\left[\sum_{m=0}^{M_r-1} \tilde{F}_r^{(-m)} z_{-k}^m + \sum_{m=0}^{\infty} \tilde{G}_r^{(-m)} z_{-k}^m + \sum_{m=0}^{M_r-1} \tilde{F}_r^{(m)} z_k^m + \sum_{m=0}^{\infty} \tilde{G}_r^{(m)} z_k^m - \tilde{F}_r^{(0)}\right], \quad (12)$$

where individual terms are defined as

$$\begin{aligned} M_r &= 2^{K_r}, K_r \text{ integer}, \\ \tilde{F}_r^{(\pm m)} &= \tilde{F}_r(s_1,\ldots,c_r \pm jm2\pi/\tau_r,\ldots,t_n), \\ \tilde{G}_r^{(\pm m)} &= \tilde{F}_r^{(\pm M_r \pm m)}, \\ z_{\pm k} &= \exp(\pm j2\pi kT_r/\tau_r), \end{aligned} \quad (13)$$

when $z_{\pm k}^{M_r} = e^{\pm j2\pi k} = 1$, $\forall k$, has been considered, and $\tau_r = M_r T_r$.
As is evident the first and the third finite sum of (12) can be evaluated via the FFT and IFFT algorithms, respectively, while $2P+1$ terms from the infinite sums are used as the input data in the quotient-difference algorithm (Macdonald, 1964; McCabe, 1983; Rutishauser, 1957). We can replace the above infinite power series by a continued fraction as

$$\sum_{m=0}^{\infty} \tilde{G}_r^{(\pm m)} z_{\pm k}^m \approx d_0/(1 + d_1 z_{\pm k}/(1 + \cdots + d_{2P} z_{\pm k})), \forall k, \quad (14)$$

which gives much more accurate result than the original sum truncated on $2P+1$ terms only. The q-d algorithm process can be explained based on a lozenge diagram shown in Fig. 1.

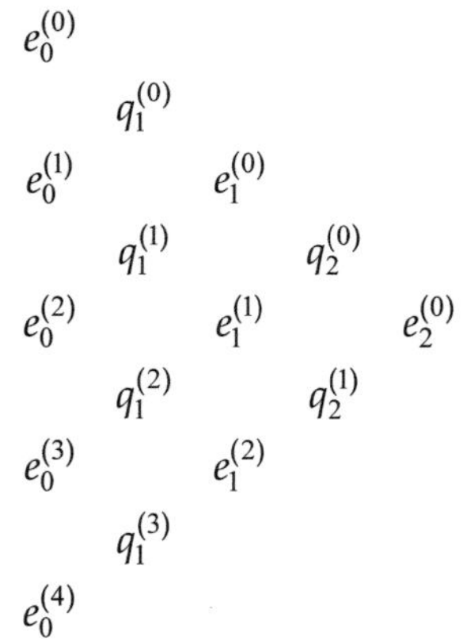

Fig. 1. Quotient-difference algorithm lozenge diagram

The first two columns are formed as

$$\begin{aligned} e_0^{(i)} &= 0, & i &= 0,\ldots,2P, \\ q_1^{(i)} &= \tilde{G}_r^{\pm(i+1)}/\tilde{G}_r^{\pm i}, & i &= 0,\ldots,2P-1, \end{aligned} \quad (15)$$

while the successive columns are given by the rules

$$\begin{aligned} e_j^{(i)} &= q_j^{(i+1)} - q_j^{(i)} + e_{j-1}^{(i+1)}, & i &= 0,\cdots,2P-2j, & \text{for } j &= 1,\ldots,P, \\ q_j^{(i)} &= q_{j-1}^{(i+1)} e_{j-1}^{(i+1)}/e_{j-1}^{(i)}, & i &= 0,\cdots,2P-2j-1, & \text{for } j &= 2,\ldots,P. \end{aligned} \quad (16)$$

Then, the coefficients d_m, $m = 0,...,2P$, in (14) are given by

$$d_0 = \tilde{G}_r^{(0)}\,,\ d_{2j-1} = -q_j^{(0)}\,,\ d_{2j} = -e_j^{(0)}\,,\quad j = 1,\dots,P\,. \tag{17}$$

For practical computations, however, the recursive formulae stated below are more effective to be used (DeHoog et al., 1982). They are of the forms

$$A_m(z_{\pm k}) = A_{m-1}(z_{\pm k}) + d_m z_{\pm k} A_{m-2}(z_{\pm k})\,,\ B_m(z_{\pm k}) = B_{m-1}(z_{\pm k}) + d_m z_{\pm k} B_{m-2}(z_{\pm k})\,, \tag{18}$$

for $m = 1,...,2P$, $\forall k$, with the initial values $A_{-1} = 0$, $B_{-1} = 1$, $A_0 = d_0$, and $B_0 = 1$. Then, instead of the continued fraction (14), we can write

$$\sum_{m=0}^{\infty} \tilde{G}_r^{(\pm m)} z_{\pm k}^m \approx A_{2P}(z_{\pm k})/B_{2P}(z_{\pm k})\,,\ \forall k\,. \tag{19}$$

The q-d algorithm is a very efficient tool just for a power series convergence acceleration, here enabling (7) to achieve a relative error near its theoretical value defined by (4), see the following examples.

2.3 Matlab listings and experimental errors evaluation

In this part experimental verifications of the nD NILT theory above will first be presented, for one to three dimensional cases, i.e. $n \le 3$. For such dimensions the Matlab functions have been developed and errors stated on a basis of some sample images with known originals. The Matlab listings of basic versions of the NILT functions are provided, together with examples of their right calling. Another Matlab listings will be discussed in more detail later, in the chapter with practical applications.

2.3.1 One-dimensional NILT

In case of the 1D inverse LT, a well-known Bromwich integral results from (2), namely

$$f(t) = \frac{1}{2\pi j} \int_{c-j\infty}^{c+j\infty} F(s) e^{st} dt\,, \tag{20}$$

where indexes 1 were omitted. By using the theory above a path of the numerical integration is stated according to (4), leading to

$$c = \alpha - \frac{1}{\tau} \ln\left(1 - \frac{1}{1+\delta_M}\right) = \alpha + \frac{1}{\tau} \ln\left(1 + \frac{1}{\delta_M}\right) \approx \alpha - \frac{1}{\tau} \ln \delta_M\,. \tag{21}$$

In contrast to most other approaches, the 1D NILT method described here enables to treat complex images resulting in complex originals as no real or imaginary parts are extracted during an evaluation process. It can be useful in some special applications, not only in the electrical engineering. We can show it on a simple transform pair

$$F(s) = \frac{1}{s - j\omega} = \frac{s}{s^2 + \omega^2} + j\frac{\omega}{s^2 + \omega^2} \quad \mapsto \quad f(t) = e^{j\omega t} = \cos \omega t + j \sin \omega t\,. \tag{22}$$

Of course, when preprocessing the transform to arrange it to a Cartesian form, as is shown on the right sides in (22), the result could by get by inverting the real and imaginary parts separately, by using an arbitrary NILT method. Here, however, no symbolic manipulations are needed in advance, and $F(s)$ enters the NILT function in its basic form as a whole.
A Matlab language listing is shown in Tab. 1, where the relative error needed is marked by `Er` and is subject to a change if necessary, similarly as the minimal abscissa of convergence (exponential order) α, `alfa`, numbers of points for the resultant solution, `M`, and for the q-d algorithm, `P`. If only real transforms $F(s)$ are considered the bottom line in the listing can be inactivated. The NILT function is called from a command line as follows: `niltc('F',tm);` where `F` is a name of another function in which the $F(s)$ is defined, and `tm` marks an upper limit of the original variable t. In our case, and for $\omega = 2\pi$, this function can have a form

```
function f=expc(s)
f=1./(s-2*pi*j);
```

```
% ------ 1D NILT for complex arguments - basic version -------
% ----------- based on FFT/IFFT/q-d, by L. Brančík -----------
function [ft,t]=niltc(F,tm);
alfa=0; M=256; P=3; Er=1e-10;                          % adjustable
N=2*M; qd=2*P+1;
t=linspace(0,tm,M); NT=2*tm*N/(N-2); omega=2*pi/NT;
c=alfa+log(1+1/Er)/NT; s=c-i*omega*(0:N+qd-1);
Fs(1,:)=feval(F,s); Fs(2,:)=feval(F,conj(s));
ft(1,:)=fft(Fs(1,1:N)); ft(2,:)=N*ifft(Fs(2,1:N));
ft=ft(:,1:M); D=zeros(2,qd); E=D;
Q=Fs(:,N+2:N+qd)./Fs(:,N+1:N+qd-1);
D(:,1)=Fs(:,N+1); D(:,2)=-Q(:,1);
for r=2:2:qd-1
    w=qd-r;
    E(:,1:w)=Q(:,2:w+1)-Q(:,1:w)+E(:,2:w+1); D(:,r+1)=-E(:,1);
    if r>2
        Q(:,1:w-1)=Q(:,2:w).*E(:,2:w)./E(:,1:w-1);
        D(:,r)=-Q(:,1);
    end
end
A2=zeros(2,M); B2=ones(2,M); A1=repmat(D(:,1),[1,M]); B1=B2;
z1=exp(-i*omega*t); z=[z1;conj(z1)];
for n=2:qd
    Dn=repmat(D(:,n),[1,M]);
    A=A1+Dn.*z.*A2; B=B1+Dn.*z.*B2; A2=A1; B2=B1; A1=A; B1=B;
end
ft=ft+A./B; ft=sum(ft)-Fs(2,1); ft=exp(c*t)/NT.*ft;
ft(1)=2*ft(1);
figure; plot(t,real(ft));
figure; plot(t,imag(ft));                              % optional
```

Table 1. Matlab listing of 1D NILT method accepting complex arguments

As is obvious, the Laplace transform must be defined to enable Matlab array processing, i.e. element-by-element array operators have to be used. Thus, the calling our function can look like `niltc('expc',4);` if the function is saved under the same name, `expc`, or it is placed inside the M-file with own NILT function (Tab. 1), following always its body. Alternatively, the calling can look like `[ft,t]=niltc('F',tm);` if respective variables in the brackets are to be saved in the memory after the function finishes.

Graphical results and corresponding errors are shown in Fig. 2. Because the originals are bounded by values ±1, and $\alpha = 0$, we can see the errors satisfy (21) very well ($\delta_M = 10^{-10}$ was considered), excluding only beginning of the interval.

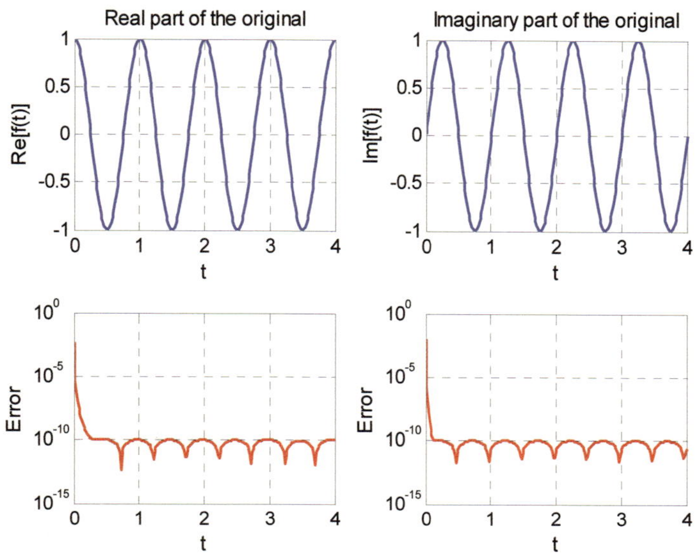

Fig. 2. Numerical inversion leading to complex original $f(t) = \exp(j\omega t)$

Another test functions are considered in Tab. 2, with numerical results shown in Fig. 3. As is again obvious from Fig. 3 the relative errors satisfy theoretical expectations, with an exception of vicinities of discontinuities.

i	1	2	3	4	5	6
$F_i(s)$	$\frac{1}{s+1}$	$\frac{1}{(s+1)^2}$	$\frac{2\pi}{s^2+4\pi^2}$	$\frac{1}{\sqrt{s^2+1}}$	$\frac{e^{-\sqrt{s}}}{s}$	$\frac{e^{-s}}{s}$
$f_i(t)$	e^{-t}	te^{-t}	$\sin(2\pi t)$	$J_0(t)$	$\mathrm{erfc}\left(\frac{1}{2\sqrt{t}}\right)$	$\underline{1}(t-1)$

Table 2. Test Laplace transforms for errors evaluation

2.3.2 Two-dimensional NILT

In case of the 2D inverse LT, a two-fold Bromwich integral results from (2), namely

$$f(t_1,t_2) = -\frac{1}{4\pi^2}\int_{c_1-j\infty}^{c_1+j\infty}\int_{c_2-j\infty}^{c_2+j\infty} F(s_1,s_2)e^{s_1t_1+s_2t_2}ds_1ds_2\,, \tag{23}$$

and by using the theory above the paths of numerical integrations are stated based on (4) as

$$c_i = \alpha_i - \frac{1}{\tau_i}\ln\left(1-\frac{1}{\sqrt{1+\delta_M}}\right) \approx \alpha_i - \frac{1}{\tau_i}\ln\frac{\delta_M}{2}, \quad i=1,2\,. \tag{24}$$

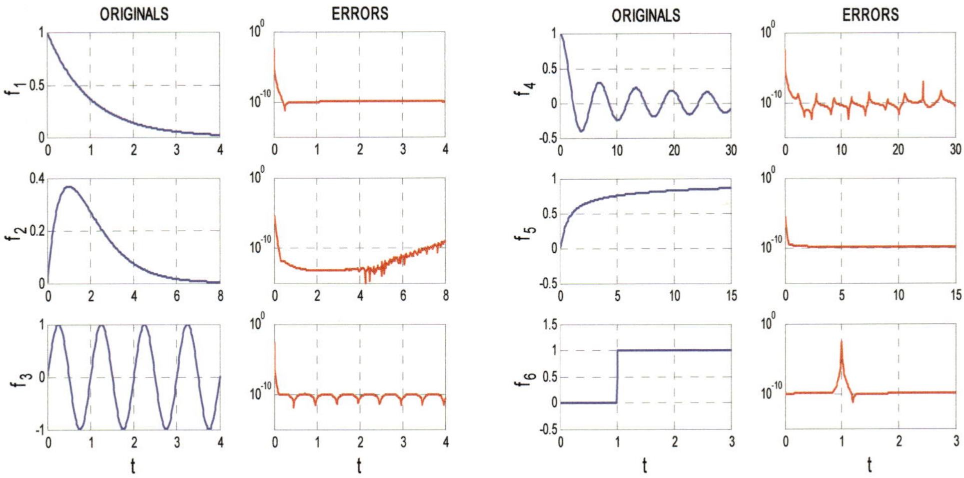

Fig. 3. Computed originals and errors for test Laplace transforms in Tab. 2

A Matlab language listing is shown in Tab. 3, with all the parameters denoted by similar way as in the previous case.
Nevertheless, the Laplace transform variables and the original variables have changed in this listing as $s_1 \to p$, $s_2 \to q$, and $t_1 \to x$, $t_2 \to y$, respectively, which simplified a writing. The parameters are then indexed in compliance with these new notations. Besides, numbers of points used to plot three-dimensional graphical results are set by `xpl` and `ypl`.
For the same reasons as at the 1D NILT, the 2D NILT method discussed here enables to treat complex images of two variables resulting in complex originals. We will show it on a simple transform pair

$$F(s_1,s_2)=\frac{1}{(s_1-j\omega_1)(s_2-j\omega_2)} \quad \mapsto \quad f(t_1,t_2)=e^{j(\omega_1 t_1+\omega_2 t_2)}. \tag{25}$$

After rearranging the above equation, we can also write

$$\begin{gathered} F(s_1,s_2)=\frac{s_1 s_2-\omega_1\omega_2}{(s_1^2+\omega_1^2)(s_2^2+\omega_2^2)}+j\frac{\omega_2 s_1+\omega_1 s_2}{(s_1^2+\omega_1^2)(s_2^2+\omega_2^2)} \quad \mapsto \\ f(t_1,t_2)=\cos(\omega_1 t_1+\omega_2 t_2)+j\sin(\omega_1 t_1+\omega_2 t_2) \end{gathered}. \tag{26}$$

The 2D NILT function is called from a command line as follows: `nilt2c('F',xm,ym);` where `F` is a name of another function in which the $F(p,q)$ is defined, and `xm` and `ym` mark upper limits of the original variables x and y. In our case, and for $\omega_1 = \omega_2 = 2\pi$, this function can have a form

```
function f=exp2c(p,q)
f=1./(p-2*pi*j)./(q-2*pi*j);
```

and its calling can look like `nilt2c('exp2c',3,3);` with graphical results in Fig. 4. As the originals are bounded by values ±1, and $\alpha_1 = \alpha_2 = 0$, we can see the errors satisfy (21) very well ($\delta_M = 10^{-8}$ was considered), excluding beginnings of the 2D region.

```
% ----- 2D NILT based on partial inversions, by L. Brančík -----
function fxy=nilt2c(F,xm,ym);
alfax=0; alfay=0; Mx=256; My=256; P=3; Er=1e-8;      % adjustable
xpl=64; ypl=64;                                       % adjustable
Nx=2*Mx; Ny=2*My; qd=2*P+1; Ke=log(1-1/sqrt(1+Er));
nx=2*xm*Nx/(Nx-2); ny=2*ym*Ny/(Ny-2);
omegax=2*pi/nx; omegay=2*pi/ny; sigx=alfax-Ke/nx;
sigy=alfay-Ke/ny; qd1=qd-1; Nxw=Nx+qd1; Nyw=Ny+qd1;
Asigx=sigx-i*omegax*(0:Nxw); Asigy=sigy-i*omegay*(0:Nyw);
Asigx2=cat(2,Asigx,conj(Asigx));
rx=[1:Mx/xpl:Mx,Mx]; ry=[1:My/ypl:My,My];
x=linspace(0,xm,Mx); y=linspace(0,ym,My); x=x(rx); y=y(ry);
[q,p]=meshgrid(Asigy,Asigx2); Fpq(:,:,1)=feval(F,p,q);
[q,p]=meshgrid(conj(Asigy),Asigx2); Fpq(:,:,2)=feval(F,p,q);
Fpyp=Pnilt(Fpq,Ny,ry,qd,y,ny,omegay,sigy); % Pnilt to get F(p,y)
Fpy(:,:,1)=Fpyp(1:Nxw+1,:).';
Fpy(:,:,2)=Fpyp(Nxw+2:2*Nxw+2,:).';
fxy=Pnilt(Fpy,Nx,rx,qd,x,nx,omegax,sigx);  % Pnilt to get f(x,y)
figure; mesh(x,y,real(fxy));
figure; mesh(x,y,imag(fxy));                          % optional
% ------ PARTIAL NILT based on FFT/IFFT/Q-D, by L.Brančík ------
function fx=Pnilt(Fq,N,grid,qd,xy,nxy,omega,c);
fx(:,:,1)=fft(Fq(:,:,1),N,2); fx(:,:,2)=N*ifft(Fq(:,:,2),N,2);
fx=fx(:,grid,:); delv=size(Fq,1); delxy=length(xy);
d=zeros(delv,qd,2); e=d; q=Fq(:,N+2:N+qd,:)./Fq(:,N+1:N+qd-1,:);
d(:,1,:)=Fq(:,N+1,:); d(:,2,:)=-q(:,1,:);
for r=2:2:qd-1
    w=qd-r; e(:,1:w,:)=q(:,2:w+1,:)-q(:,1:w,:)+e(:,2:w+1,:);
    d(:,r+1,:)=-e(:,1,:);
    if r>2
        q(:,1:w-1,:)=q(:,2:w,:).*e(:,2:w,:)./e(:,1:w-1,:);
        d(:,r,:)=-q(:,1,:);
    end
end
A2=zeros(delv,delxy,2); B2=ones(delv,delxy,2);
A1=repmat(d(:,1,:),[1,delxy,1]); B1=B2;
z1(1,:,1)=exp(-i*omega*xy); z1(1,:,2)=conj(z1(1,:,1));
z=repmat(z1,[delv,1]);
for n=2:qd
    Dn=repmat(d(:,n,:),[1,delxy,1]);
    A=A1+Dn.*z.*A2; B=B1+Dn.*z.*B2; A2=A1; B2=B1; A1=A; B1=B;
end
fx=fx+A./B; fx=sum(fx,3)-repmat(Fq(:,1),[1,delxy]);
fx=repmat(exp(c*xy)/nxy,[delv,1]).*fx; fx(:,1)=2*fx(:,1);
```

Table 3. Matlab listing of 2D NILT based on partial inversions

Another simple example shows a shifted 2D unit step, with different shifts along the axis. A corresponding transform pair is

$$F(s_1,s_2)=\frac{\exp(-2s_1-s_2)}{s_1 s_2} \quad \mapsto \quad f(t_1,t_2)=\underline{1}(t_1-2,t_2-1)\,. \tag{27}$$

In this case, a displaying imaginary part gives a zero plane, and the respective line in the 2D NILT function can be inactivated. The graphical results are depicted in Fig. 5, including an absolute error. The respective Matlab function can be of a form

```
function f=step2(p,q)
f=exp(-2*p-q)./p./q;
```

and called as `nilt2c('step2',4,4);`, with the results theoretically expected.

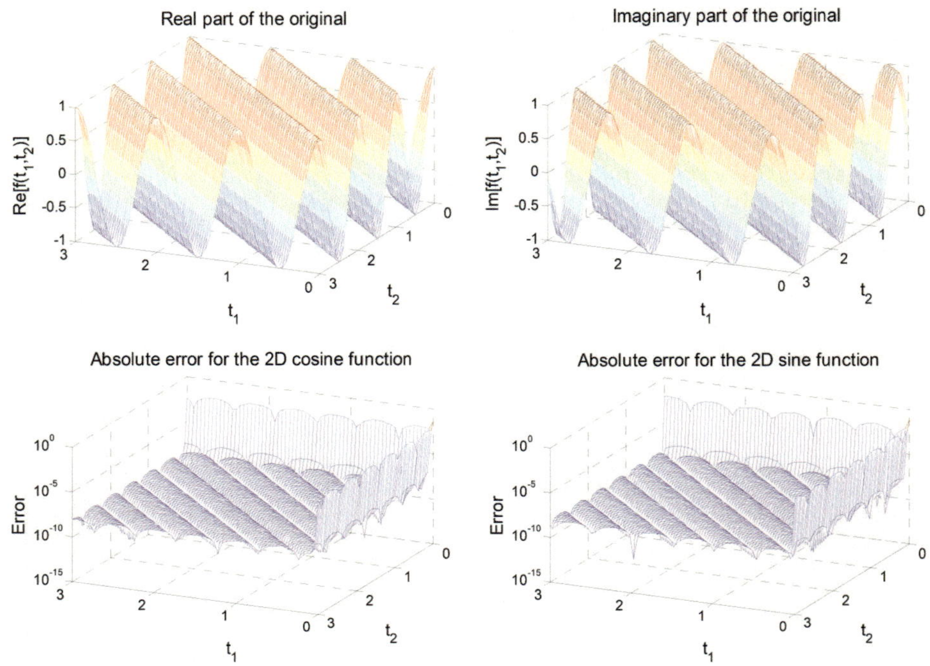

Fig. 4. Numerical inversion leading to complex original $f(t_1,t_2) = \exp(j\omega(t_1+t_2))$

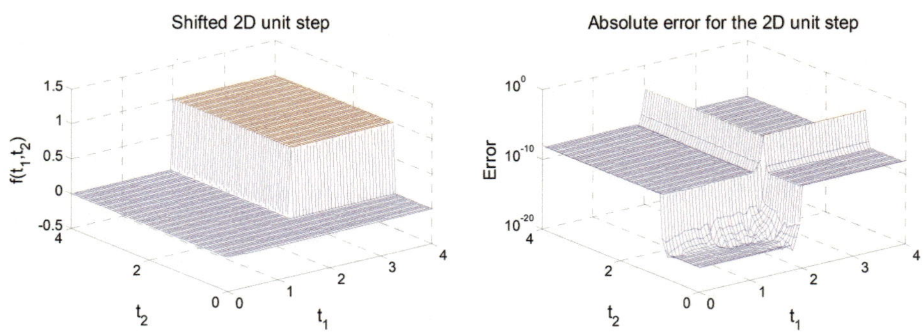

Fig. 5. Numerical inversion leading to shifted 2D unit step $f(t_1,t_2) = \underline{1}(t_1-2,t_2-1)$

2.3.3 Three-dimensional NILT

In case of the 3D inverse LT, a three-fold Bromwich integral results from (2), namely

$$f(t_1,t_2,t_3) = \frac{j}{8\pi^3} \int_{c_1-j\infty}^{c_1+j\infty} \int_{c_2-j\infty}^{c_2+j\infty} \int_{c_3-j\infty}^{c_3+j\infty} F(s_1,s_2,s_3) e^{s_1t_1+s_2t_2+s_3t_3} ds_1 ds_2 ds_3 \,, \tag{28}$$

and by using the theory above the paths of numerical integrations are stated based on (4) as

$$c_i = \alpha_i - \frac{1}{\tau_i}\ln\left(1 - \frac{1}{\sqrt[3]{1+\delta_M}}\right) \approx \alpha_i - \frac{1}{\tau_i}\ln\frac{\delta_M}{3}, \quad i = 1,2,3\,. \tag{29}$$

Here only experimental results will be shown to verify an accuracy of the method. A Matlab language listing looks similarly like for the 2D NILT case, but the partial NILT subfunction is called once more, and respective arrays dimensions are enlarged. Original functions corresponding to 3D Laplace transforms cannot be displayed graphically as a whole, of course. However, for one variable chosen as constant, it is posssible to display three respective two-dimensional cuts. It will be demonstrated on the example of 3D shifted unit step, with a Laplace transform pair

$$\frac{\exp(-s_1 - 2s_2 - 3s_3)}{s_1 s_2 s_3} \quad \mapsto \quad \underline{1}(t_1 - 1, t_2 - 2, t_2 - 3)\,, \tag{30}$$

with different values of shifts along respective coordinates so that correctness of results can easily be identified, see Fig. 6. Errors again correspond to theoretically expected ones.

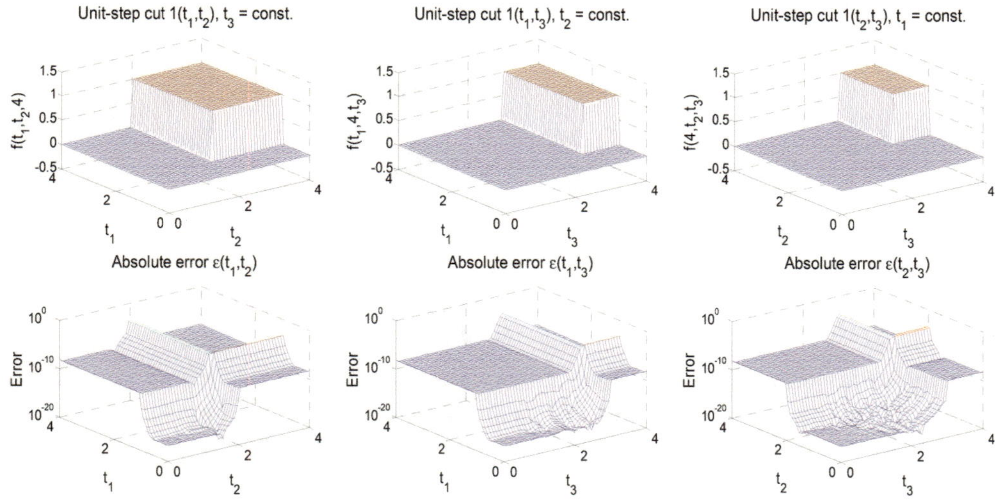

Fig. 6. Numerical inversion leading to shifted 3D unit step $f(t_1,t_2,t_3) = \underline{1}(t_1-1,t_2-2,t_3-3)$

3. Application of NILT algorithms to electrical engineering simulation

In this chapter some examples of the application of the NILT algorithms developed relating to problems of electrical engineering simulation are presented. First, the 1D NILT method is applied for the solution of transient phenomena in linear electrical circuits with both lumped and distributed parameters. This well-known approach is usable wherever linear ordinary differential equations (ODE) are transformed into algebraic ones so that an inverse Laplace transform can be considered. Then the 2D NILT method is utilized to solve transient phenomena on transmission lines (TL) after relevant telegraphic equations (a type of partial differential equations (PDE)) are transformed into algebraic ones by a 2D Laplace transform. In this way voltage and/or current distributions along the TL wires can be determined in a single calculation step. Finally, the utilization of the 1D to 3D NILTs to weakly nonlinear electrical circuits solution is discussed. In this case the relevant nonlinear ODEs describing the circuit are expanded into Volterra series which respective NILTs are applied on.

3.1 One-dimensional NILT algorithm application

3.1.1 Preliminary example based on lumped parameter circuit

A simple example demonstrating the application of the basic 1D NILT algorithm in Tab. 1 is shown in Fig. 7. This really initiatory linear electrical circuit was chosen with an intention to be also considered later, in chapter 3.3.1, as a nonlinear circuit, with G_2 being a nonlinear element. In this way one will be able to compare results and make some conclusions.

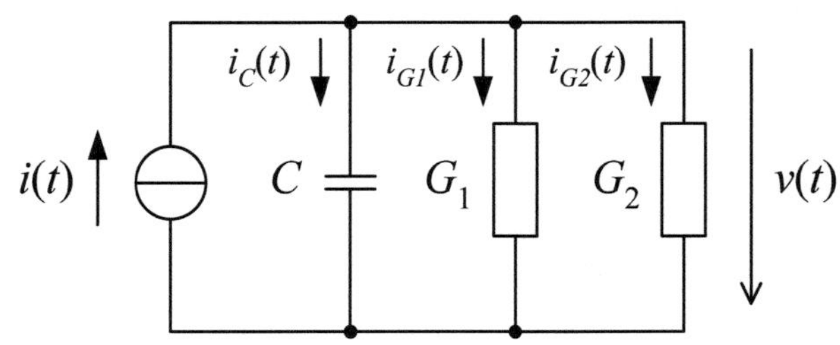

Fig. 7. Linear reactive electrical circuit of the 1st order

Denoting $G = G_1 + G_2$, the 1st-order linear ODE has a form

$$C\frac{dv(t)}{dt} + Gv(t) = i(t)\,, \tag{31}$$

with a Laplace-domain solution

$$V(s) = \frac{I(s) + Cv(0)}{G + sC}\,, \tag{32}$$

with an initial condition $v(0)$. Even if the above circuit is very simple a finding time-domain solution could be rather work-intensive if the circuit is excited from some non-trivial input current waveform. A few basic examples are given in Tab. 4, specially the first one results in a transient characteristic of the circuit.

k	1	2	3	4
$i_k(t)$	$I_0\underline{1}(t)$	$I_0 e^{-5t}\underline{1}(t)$	$I_0\sin(2\pi t)\underline{1}(t)$	$I_0\cos(2\pi t)\underline{1}(t)$
$I_k(s)$	$\frac{I_0}{s}$	$\frac{I_0}{s+5}$	$\frac{2\pi I_0}{s^2+4\pi^2}$	$\frac{sI_0}{s^2+4\pi^2}$

Table 4. Exciting current source waveforms and their Laplace transforms

For the above examples, of course, time-domain analytical solutions can be found e.g. based on a Heaviside formula. The 1D NILT function graphical results, under a condition $v(0) = 0$, and considering values $C = 1\text{mF}$, $G_1 = G_2 = 10\text{mS}$, and $I_0 = 1\text{mA}$, are shown in Fig. 8.
The above waveforms can be got by either successive application of a basic version of the 1D NILT method according to Tab. 1, or a generalized 1D NILT function, its vector version, can be used to process all the computations in parallel. This function is shown in Tab. 5.

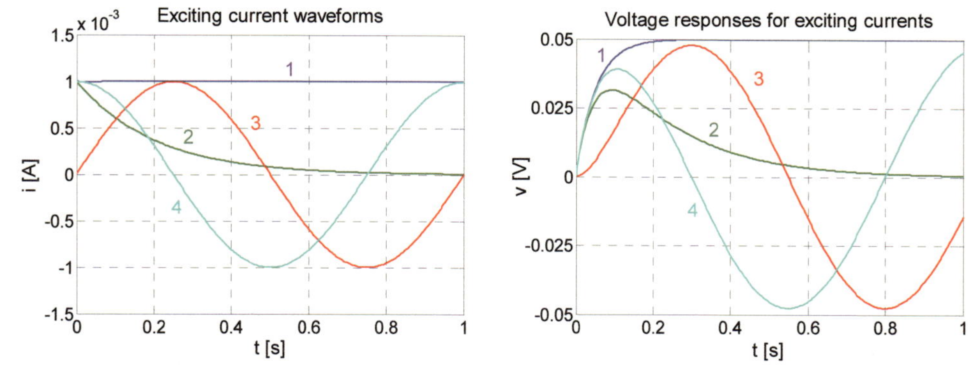

Fig. 8. Numerically computed exciting current and voltage responses waveforms

```
% ------ 1D NILT for complex arguments - vector version ------- %
% ----------- based on FFT/IFFT/q-d, by L. Brančík ------------ %
function [ft,t]=niltcv(F,tm,depict);
alfa=0; M=256; P=3; Er=1e-10;                          % adjustable
N=2*M; qd=2*P+1; t=linspace(0,tm,M); NT=2*tm*N/(N-2);
omega=2*pi/NT;
c=alfa+log(1+1/Er)/NT; s=c-i*omega*(0:N+qd-1);
Fs(:,:,1)=feval(F,s); Fs(:,:,2)=feval(F,conj(s)); lv=size(Fs,1);
ft(:,:,1)=fft(Fs(:,:,1),N,2); ft(:,:,2)=N*ifft(Fs(:,:,2),N,2);
ft=ft(:,1:M,:);
D=zeros(lv,qd,2); E=D; Q=Fs(:,N+2:N+qd,:)./Fs(:,N+1:N+qd-1,:);
D(:,1,:)=Fs(:,N+1,:); D(:,2,:)=-Q(:,1,:);
for r=2:2:qd-1
    w=qd-r;
    E(:,1:w,:)=Q(:,2:w+1,:)-Q(:,1:w,:)+E(:,2:w+1,:);
    D(:,r+1,:)=-E(:,1,:);
    if r>2
    Q(:,1:w-1,:)=Q(:,2:w,:).*E(:,2:w,:)./E(:,1:w-1,:);
    D(:,r,:)=-Q(:,1,:);
    end
end
A2=zeros(lv,M,2); B2=ones(lv,M,2); A1=repmat(D(:,1,:),[1,M,1]);
B1=B2; z1=repmat(exp(-i*omega*t),[lv,1]); z=cat(3,z1,conj(z1));
for n=2:qd
    Dn=repmat(D(:,n,:),[1,M,1]);
    A=A1+Dn.*z.*A2; B=B1+Dn.*z.*B2; A2=A1; B2=B1; A1=A; B1=B;
end
ft=ft+A./B; ft=sum(ft,3)-repmat(Fs(:,1,2),[1,M,1]);
ft=repmat(exp(c*t)/NT,[lv,1]).*ft; ft(:,1)=2*ft(:,1);
switch depict
    case 'p1', plott1(t,ft); case 'p2', plott2(t,ft);
    case 'p3', plott3(t,ft); otherwise display('Invalid Plot');
end
```

Table 5. Matlab listing of vector version of 1D NILT method

Here one more parameter `depict` is used to define a method of plotting individual items from a set of originals. The 1D NILT function is called as `niltcv('F',tm,'depict');` where `'depict'` is a text string `'p1'`, `'p2'`, or `'p3'`, see Tab. 6 for more details.

```
% --- Plotting functions called by 1D NILT, vector version ----
%----------- Multiple plotting into single figure -------------
function plott1(t,ft)
figure; plot(t,real(ft)); grid on;
figure; plot(t,imag(ft)); grid on;                  % optional
% ------------- Plotting into separate figures ----------------
function plott2(t,ft)
for k=1:size(ft,1)
    figure; plot(t,real(ft(k,:))); grid on;
    figure; plot(t,imag(ft(k,:))); grid on;         % optional
end
% ------------------ Plotting into 3D graphs ------------------
function plott3(t,ft)
global x;                                % x must be global in F
    m=length(t); tgr=[1:m/64:m,m];       % 65 time points chosen
    figure; mesh(t(tgr),x,real(ft(:,tgr)));
    figure; mesh(t(tgr),x,imag(ft(:,tgr)));          % optional
```

Table 6. Matlab listing of plotting functions for vector version of 1D NILT method

To get e.g. the right part of Fig. 8, that is the voltage responses of the circuit in Fig. 7, the calling the 1D NILT function looks like `niltcv('V4',1,'p1');` where `V4` denotes a name of the function defining individual responses as follows:

```
function f=V4(s)
I0=1e-3; C=1e-3; G=2e-2;
f(1,:)=I0./s./(G+s*C);
f(2,:)=I0./(s+5)./(G+s*C);
f(3,:)=2*pi*I0./(s.^2+4*pi^2)./(G+s*C);
f(4,:)=s.*I0./(s.^2+4*pi^2)./(G+s*C);
```

In this case the lines causing the imaginary parts plotting can be inactivated. The remaining plotting functions will be explained in the next chapter.

3.1.2 Application for transmission line simulation

Here, the 1D NILT algorithms will be used to simulate voltage and/or current distributions along transmission lines (TL), as shown on a Laplace-domain TL model in Fig. 9. As is well known, this model results from the application of a Laplace transform, with respect to time, on a pair of partial differential equations (telegraphic) of the form

$$-\frac{\partial v(t,x)}{\partial x} = R_0 i(t,x) + L_0 \frac{\partial i(t,x)}{\partial t}, \quad -\frac{\partial i(t,x)}{\partial x} = G_0 v(t,x) + C_0 \frac{\partial v(t,x)}{\partial t}, \tag{33}$$

with R_0, L_0, G_0, and C_0 as per-unit-length (p.-u.-l.) parameters, being constant for uniform TLs, and with a length l.

When considering zero initial voltage and current distributions, $v(0,x) = 0$ and $i(0,x) = 0$, and incorporating boundary conditions, we get the Laplace-domain solution in the forms

$$V(s,x) = V_i(s)\frac{Z_c(s)}{Z_i(s)+Z_c(s)} \cdot \frac{e^{-\gamma(s)x} + \rho_2(s)e^{-\gamma(s)[2l-x]}}{1-\rho_1(s)\rho_2(s)e^{-2\gamma(s)l}}, \tag{34}$$

$$I(s,x) = V_i(s)\frac{1}{Z_i(s)+Z_c(s)} \cdot \frac{e^{-\gamma(s)x} - \rho_2(s)e^{-\gamma(s)[2l-x]}}{1-\rho_1(s)\rho_2(s)e^{-2\gamma(s)l}}, \tag{35}$$

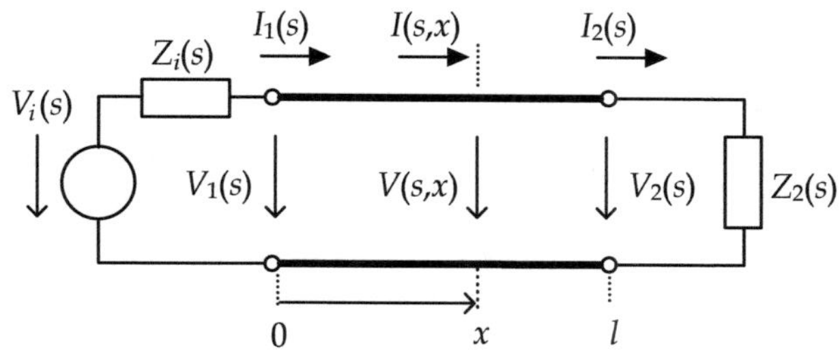

Fig. 9. Laplace-domain model of transmission line with linear terminations

where $Z_c(s)$ and $\gamma(s)$ are a characteristic impedance and a propagation constant, respectively,

$$Z_c(s) = \sqrt{\frac{R_0 + sL_0}{G_0 + sC_0}} \ , \quad \gamma(s) = \sqrt{(R_0 + sL_0)(G_0 + sC_0)} \ , \tag{36}$$

and $\rho_1(s)$ and $\rho_2(s)$ are reflection coefficients at the TL beginning and end, respectively,

$$\rho_1(s) = \frac{Z_i(s) - Z_c(s)}{Z_i(s) + Z_c(s)} \ , \quad \rho_2(s) = \frac{Z_2(s) - Z_c(s)}{Z_2(s) + Z_c(s)} \ . \tag{37}$$

In a general case of lossy TLs, the time-domain solutions cannot be found by an analytical method, thus the only way is to use some numerical technique.

As an example, let us consider the TL of a length l = 1m, with p.-u.-l. parameters R_0 = 1mΩ, L_0 = 600nH, G_0 = 2mS, and C_0 = 80pF, terminated by resistive elements Z_i = 10Ω, Z_2 = 1kΩ, and excited by the voltage source waveform $v_i(t) = \sin^2(\pi t/2\cdot 10^{-9})$, $0 \le t \le 2\cdot 10^{-9}$, and $v_i(t) = 0$, otherwise, with the Laplace transform

$$V_i(s) = \frac{2\pi^2\left[1 - \exp(-2\cdot 10^{-9} s)\right]}{s\left[(2\cdot 10^{-9} s)^2 + 4\pi^2\right]} \ . \tag{38}$$

The Fig. 10 shows time dependences at the beginning, the centre, and the end of the TL, while the 1D NILT is called as `niltcv('Vs',4e-8,'p1');` where the function `Vs` is defined as

```
function f=Vs(s)
l=1; x=[0,l/2,l];
Ro=1e-3; Lo=600e-9; Go=2e-3; Co=80e-12;
Zi=10; Z2=1e3;
Vi=2*pi^2*(1-exp(-2e-9*s))./s./((2e-9*s).^2+4*pi^2);
Z=Ro+s*Lo; Y=Go+s*Co; Zc=sqrt(Z./Y); gam=sqrt(Z.*Y);
ro1=(Zi-Zc)./(Zi+Zc); ro2=(Z2-Zc)./(Z2+Zc);
Ks=Vi./(Zi+Zc)./(1-ro1.*ro2.*exp(-2*gam*l));
for k=1:length(x)
    f(k,:)=Ks.*Zc.*(exp(-gam*x(k))+ro2.*exp(-gam*(2*l-x(k))));
end
```

Similarly, current waveforms can be computed by the above function slightly modified according to (35). Both waveforms are depicted in Fig. 10.

Finally, it will be shown, how to obtain three-dimensional graphical results representing voltage and current distributions along the TL. Besides a possibitity to use the `for` cycle, as shown in the function `Vs` above, another method based on 3D arrays will be applied, see the function `Vsx` below:

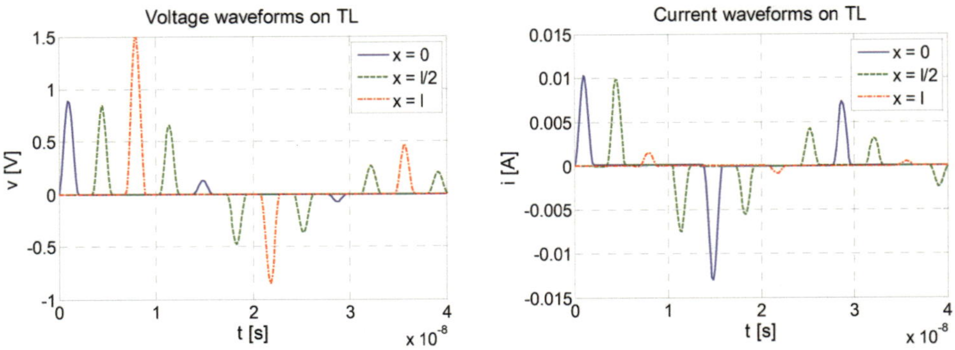

Fig. 10. Numerically computed TL voltage and current waveforms

```
function f=Vsx(s)
global x;
l=1;
Ro=1e-3; Lo=600e-9; Go=2e-3; Co=80e-12;
Zi=10; Z2=1e3;
x=linspace(0,l,65);          % 65 points along TL chosen
[S,X]=meshgrid(s,x);
Vi=2*pi^2*(1-exp(-2e-9*S))./S./((2e-9*S).^2+4*pi^2);
Z=Ro+S*Lo; Y=Go+S*Co; Zc=sqrt(Z./Y); gam=sqrt(Z.*Y);
ro1=(Zi-Zc)./(Zi+Zc); ro2=(Z2-Zc)./(Z2+Zc);
Ks=Vi./(Zi+Zc)./(1-ro1.*ro2.*exp(-2*gam*l));
f=Ks.*Zc.*(exp(-gam.*X)+ro2.*exp(-gam.*(2*l-X)));
```

In this case, the 1D NILT algorithm in Tab. 5 is called as `niltcv('Vsx',2e-8,'p3');` that is the `plott3` function is used for the plotting, see Tab. 6, and a time limit is half of that in Fig. 10 to get well-observable results. Again, the current distributions can be gained via the above function slightly modified according to (35). Both 3D graphs are depicted in Fig. 11.

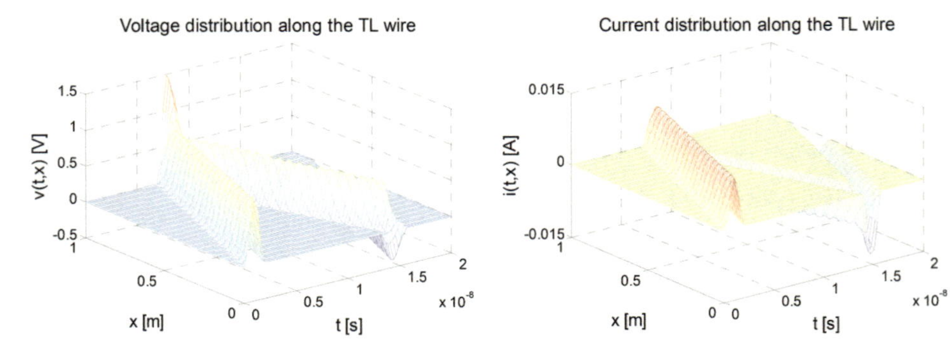

Fig. 11. Numerically computed TL voltage and current distributions

3.2 Two-dimensional NILT algorithm application

A two-dimensional Laplace transform can generally be used for the solution of linear partial differencial equations with two variables. The advantage is that we get completely algebraic equations leading to much easier solution in the Laplace domain. A final step in the solution is then the utilization of the 2D NILT algorithm to get results in the original domain. Such a possibility will be shown on the example of telegraphic equations describing transmission lines, and results will be compared with the 1D NILT approach.

3.2.1 Application for transmission line simulation

Herein, rather less conventional approach for the simulation of voltage and/or current distributions along the TLs will be discussed. As is obvious from the telegraphic equations (33) they can be transformed not only with respect to the time t, which was matter of the previous paragraph, but also with respect to the geometrical coordinate x to get completely algebraic equations. After performing such the Laplace transforms, incorporating boundary conditions given by the terminating circuits, and considering again zero initial voltage and current distributions, $v(0,x) = 0$ and $i(0,x) = 0$, we get (Valsa & Brančík, 1998b)

$$V(s,q) = \frac{qV_1(s) - \gamma(s)Z_c(s)I_1(s)}{q^2 - \gamma^2(s)}, \tag{39}$$

$$I(s,q) = \frac{qI_1(s) - \frac{\gamma(s)}{Z_c(s)}V_1(s)}{q^2 - \gamma^2(s)}, \tag{40}$$

where $V_1(s) = V(s,0)$ and $I_1(s) = I(s,0)$ are given by (34) and (35), respectively, see also Fig. 9. Thus the 2D NILT function according to Tab. 3 can be called as `nilt2c('Vsq',2e-8,1);` leading to the same graphical results as are shown in Fig. 11. The function `Vsq` can be of the form as stated below. The current distribution is obtained via the same function slightly modified according to (40).

```
function f=Vsq(s,q)
l=1; Zi=10; Z2=1e3;
Ro=1e-3; Lo=600e-9; Go=2e-3; Co=80e-12;
Vi=2*pi^2*(1-exp(-2e-9*s))./s./((2e-9*s).^2+4*pi^2);
Z=Ro+s*Lo; Y=Go+s*Co; Zc=sqrt(Z./Y); gam=sqrt(Z.*Y);
ro1=(Zi-Zc)./(Zi+Zc); ro2=(Z2-Zc)./(Z2+Zc);
Ks=Vi./(Zi+Zc)./(1-ro1.*ro2.*exp(-2*gam*l));
V1=Ks.*Zc.*(1+ro2.*exp(-2*gam*l));
I1=Ks.*(1-ro2.*exp(-2*gam*l));
f=(q.*V1-Zc.*gam.*I1)./(q.^2-gam.^2);
```

One can notice an interesting thing, namely getting both voltage and current graphs by a single computation step. It is enabled by putting together the voltage and current transforms forming respectively real and imaginary parts of an artificial complex transform, and letting active the program command for the plotting the imaginary part of the original function, see Tab. 3. In our example, if the bottom line in the `Vsq` function is changed to

```
f=((q.*V1-Zc.*gam.*I1)+j*(q.*I1-gam./Zc.*V1))./(q.^2-gam.^2);
```

then both graphs in Fig. 11 are obtained simultaneously. The same possibility exists for the 1D NILT functions discussed earlier. There is no obvious physical meaning of such artificial complex transfoms, it is only a formal tool for inverting two transforms in parallel instead.

3.3 Multidimensional LT in nonlinear electrical circuits simulation

As is known some classes of nonlinear systems can be described through a Volterra series expansion, accurately enough from the practical point of view, when a response $v(t)$ to a stimulus $i(t)$ has a form (Schetzen, 2006)

$$v(t) = \sum_{n=1}^{\infty} v_n(t) , \tag{41}$$

where the terms of the infinite sum are

$$v_n(t) = \underbrace{\int_{-\infty}^{\infty} \cdots \int_{-\infty}^{\infty}}_{n-fold} h_n(\tau_1,\tau_2,\ldots,\tau_n)\prod_{k=1}^{n} i(t-\tau_k)d\tau_k , \tag{42}$$

with $h_n(\tau_1,\tau_2,\ldots,\tau_n)$ as an n-th order Volterra kernel, called as a nonlinear impulse response as well. The Fig. 12 shows these equations in their graphical form.
By introducing new variables, $t_1 = t_2 =\ldots= t_n = t$, and by using the n-dimensional Laplace transform (1), the n-fold convolution integral (42) leads to a Laplace domain response

$$V_n(s_1,s_2,\cdots,s_n) = H_n(s_1,s_2,\cdots,s_n)\prod_{k=1}^{n} I(s_k) , \tag{43}$$

with $H_n(s_1,s_2,\ldots,s_n)$ as a nonlinear transfer function.

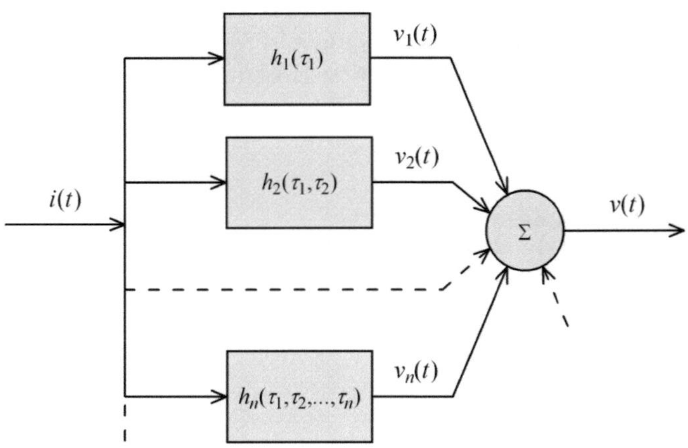

Fig. 12. Nonlinear system response via Volterra series expansion

A few methods are at disposal to find the transfer function for a given nonlinear system, like a harmonic input method, e.g. (Bussgang at al., 1974; Karmakar, 1980). Further procedure is usually based on the association of variables, (J. Debnath & N.C. Debnath, 1991; Reddy & Jagan, 1971), transforming $V_n(s_1,s_2,\ldots,s_n)$ into the function of a single variable $V_n(s)$, and enabling to use a one-dimensional ILT to get the required terms $v_n(t)$ in (41). In contrast to this procedure, it is also possible to determine the terms $v_n(t_1,t_2,\ldots,t_n)$ by the use of the n-dimensional ILT, considering $t_1 = t_2 = \ldots= t_n = t$ in the result as a final step. That is why the above NILT procedures can be adapted in this respect being able to serve as a tool for the nonlinear circuits transient simulation.

3.3.1 Utilization of 1D to 3D NILTs for nearly nonlinear circuits

The utilization of the NILT methods developed, up to three-dimensional case, will be shown on the solution of a nearly nonlinear circuit in Fig. 13. As can be observed this is just Fig. 7 modified to introduce a nonlinearity via G_2 conductance.

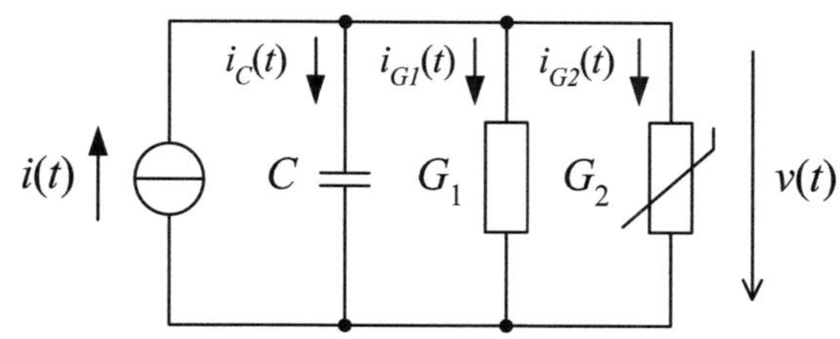

Fig. 13. Electrical circuit with nonlinear resistive element G_2

Assuming a square nonlinearity, a circuit equation is

$$C\frac{dv(t)}{dt}+G_1v(t)+G_2v^2(t)=i(t)\,. \tag{44}$$

By using the harmonic input method, and limiting the solution on the first three terms only, we get the nonlinear transfer functions for (43) as

$$H_1(s_1)=(s_1C+G_1)^{-1}, \tag{45}$$

$$H_2(s_1,s_2)=-G_2H_1(s_1)H_1(s_2)H_1(s_1+s_2), \tag{46}$$

$$H_3(s_1,s_2,s_3)=-\frac{G_2}{3}[H_1(s_1)H_2(s_2,s_3)+H_1(s_2)H_2(s_1,s_3)+H_1(s_3)H_2(s_1,s_2)]H_1(s_1+s_2+s_3)\,. \tag{47}$$

Let us use an exciting current and its Laplace transform as

$$i(t)=I_0e^{-at}\underline{1}(t)\quad\mapsto\quad I(s)=\frac{I_0}{s+a}, \tag{48}$$

$a\geq 0$. The substitution (45) - (48) into (43) gives us respective Laplace-domain responses which will undergo the 1D, 2D and 3D NILT algorithms, respectively. We can write

$$\begin{aligned}v(t)&=v_1(t)+v_2(t)+v_3(t)=v_1(t_1)\big|_{t_1=t}+v_2(t_1,t_2)\big|_{t_1=t_2=t}+v_3(t_1,t_2,t_3)\big|_{t_1=t_2=t_3=t}=\\&=\mathbb{L}_1^{-1}[V_1(s_1)]\Big|_{t_1=t}+\mathbb{L}_2^{-1}[V_2(s_1,s_2)]\Big|_{t_1=t_2=t}+\mathbb{L}_3^{-1}[V_3(s_1,s_2,s_3)]\Big|_{t_1=t_2=t_3=t}\end{aligned}, \tag{49}$$

with $\mathbb{L}_k^{-1}[.]$ as a k-dimensional ILT. Thereby, a time-consuming association of variables can be omitted, e.g. (Wambacq & Sansen, 2010). Individual terms $v_k(t)$ are depicted in Fig. 14, for values agreeing with the linear circuit version in Fig. 7. The current $i(t)$ is defined by $a = 0$ (a unit step), and $a = 5$ (an exponential impuls), compare the first two columns in Tab. 4.

The resultant voltage responses computed according to (49) are shown in Fig. 15, including relative errors, where also dependences on Volterra series orders are presented.

The relative errors above were computed via a Matlab ODE45 Runge-Kutta function applied directly to the nonlinear ODE (44). As expected, more Volterra terms lead to more accurate results, see also (Brančík, 2009) where up to 2nd-order terms were considered, and respective Matlab listings are presented.

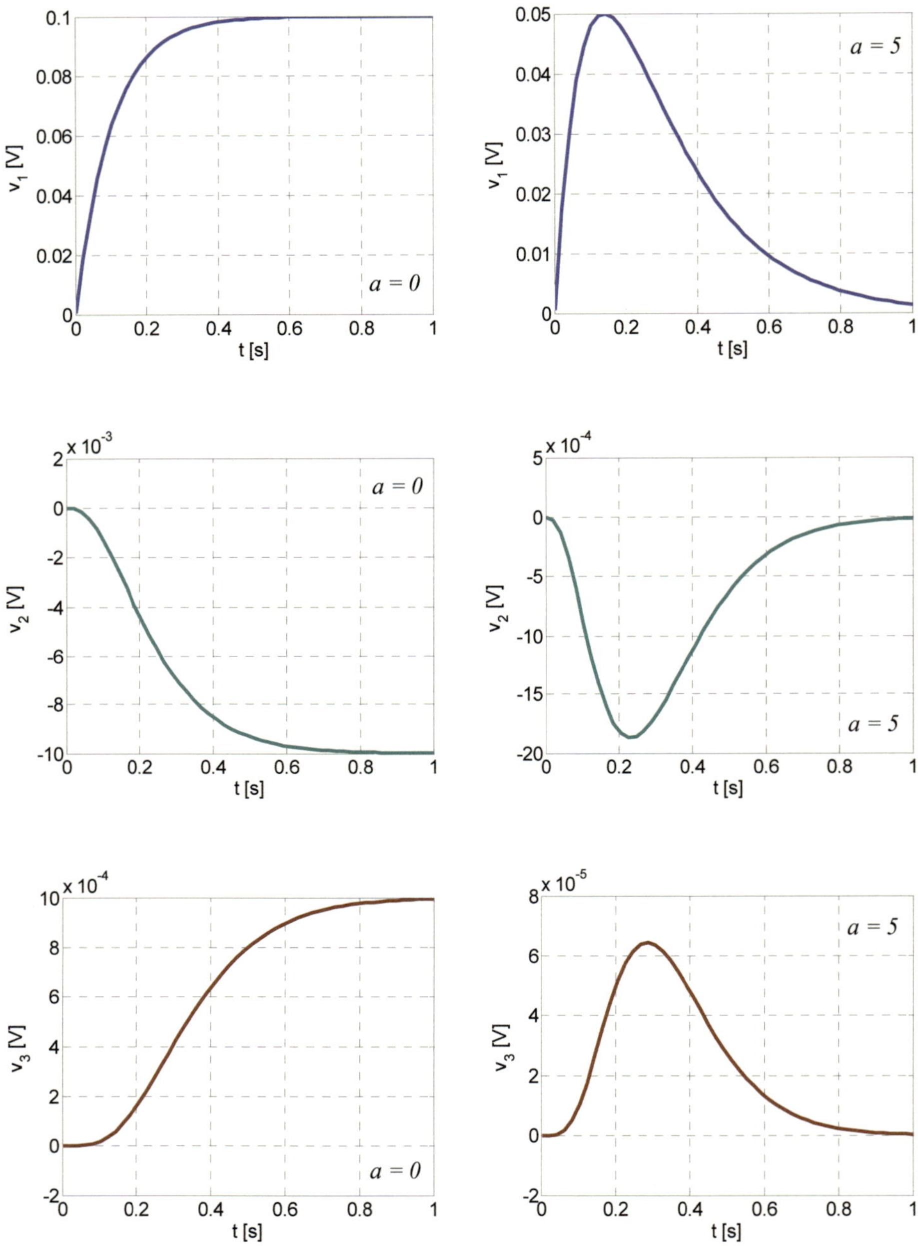

Fig. 14. Numerical inversions leading to voltage response Volterra series terms

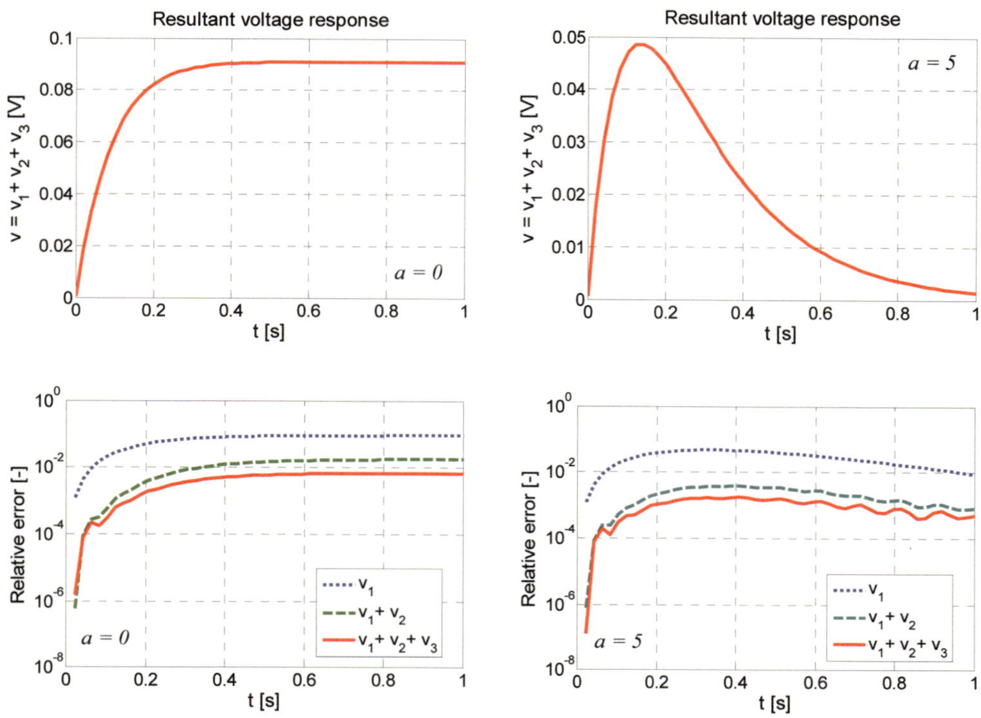

Fig. 15. Resultant voltage responses and relative errors

4. Conclusion

The paper dealt with a specific class of techniques for the numerical inversion of Laplace transforms, namely based on a complex Fourier series approximation, and connected with a quotient-difference algorithm to accelerate the convergence of infinite series arising in the approximate formulae. The 1D to 3D NILT techniques have been programmed in the Matlab language (R2007b), and most important ones provided as the Matlab function listings. To guide readers all the algorithms were explained on selected examples from field of electrical engineering, including right callings of the functions. In contrast to most others the NILT methods here developed are utilizable to numerically invert complex Laplace transforms, leading to complex originals, which can be useful for some special purposes. As has resulted from error analyses the accuracies range relative errors from 10^{-8} to 10^{-10} without difficulties which is acceptable for most of practical needs. Based on Matlab functions presented, one could further generalize a vector version of the 1D NILT function towards a matrix one, enabling e.g. to simulate multiconductor transmission line systems, as is shown in (Brančík, 1999), where, however, an alternative technique, so-called ε algorithm, has been applied to accelerate the convergence of infinite series. According to the author's knowledge, the paper presented ranks among few summary works describing multidimensional NILT techniques, covering Matlab listings beyond, based just on a complex Fourier series approximation, and in conjunction with the quotient-difference algorithm, which seems to be more numerically stable compared to the ε algorithm mentioned above.

5. Acknowledgment

Research described in this paper was supported by the Czech Ministry of Education under the MSM 0021630503 research project MIKROSYN, the European Community's Seventh Framework Programme under grant agreement no. 230126, and the project CZ.1.07/2.3.00/20.0007 WICOMT of the operational program Education for competitiveness.

6. References

Brančík, L. (1999). Programs for fast numerical inversion of Laplace transforms in Matlab language environment. *Proceedings of 7th Conference MATLAB'99,* pp. 27-39, ISBN 80-7080-354-1, Prague, Czech Republic, November 3, 1999

Brančík, L. (2005). Elaboration of FFT-based 2D-NILT methods in terms of accuracy and numerical stability. *Przeglad Elektrotechniczny,* Vol. 81, No. 2, (February 2005), pp. 84-89, ISSN 0033-2097

Brančík, L. (2007a). Numerical Inversion of two-dimensional Laplace transforms based on partial inversions. *Proceedings of 17th International Conference Radioelektronika 2007,* pp. 451-454, ISBN 1-4244-0821-0, Brno, Czech Republic, April 24-25, 2007

Brančík, L. (2007b). Modified technique of FFT-based numerical inversion of Laplace transforms with applications. *Przegląd Elektrotechniczny,* Vol. 83, No. 11, (November 2007), pp. 53-56, ISSN 0033-2097

Brančík, L. (2009). Numerical ILTs applied to weakly nonlinear systems described by second-order Volterra series. *ElectroScope,* [online], Special Issue on Conference EDS 2009, 4 pages, Available from http://electroscope.zcu.cz, ISSN 1802-4564

Brančík, L. (2010a). Utilization of NILTs in simulation of nonlinear systems described by Volterra series. *Przeglad Elektrotechniczny,* Vol. 86, No. 1, (January 2010), pp. 68-70, ISSN 0033-2097

Brančík, L. (2010b). Numerical inversion of 3D Laplace transforms for weakly nonlinear systems solution. *Proceedings of 20th International Conference Radioelektronika 2010,* pp. 221-224, ISBN 978-1-4244-6319-0, Brno, Czech Republic, April 19-21, 2010

Brančík, L. (2010c). Technique of 3D NILT based on complex Fourier series and quotient-difference algorithm. *Proceedings of 2010 IEEE International Conference on Electronics, Circuits, and Systems ICECS2010,* pp. 207-210, ISBN 978-1-4244-8156-9, Athens, Greece, December 12-15, 2010

Brančík, L. (2011). Error analysis at numerical inversion of multidimensional Laplace transforms based on complex Fourier series approximation. *IEICE Transactions on Fundamentals of Electronics, Communications and Computer Sciences,* Vol. E94-A, No. 3, (March 2011), p. 999-1001, ISSN 0916- 8508

Bussgang, J.J.; Ehrman, L. & Graham, J.W. (1974). Analysis of nonlinear systems with multiple inputs. *Proceedings of the IEEE,* Vol. 62, No. 8, (August 1974), pp. 1088-1119, ISSN 0018-9219

Cohen, A.M. (2007). *Numerical methods for Laplace transform inversion.* Springer Science, ISBN 978-0-387-28261-9, New York, U.S.A

Debnath, J. & Debnath, N.C. (1991). Associated transforms for solution of nonlinear equations. *International Journal of Mathematics and Mathematical Sciences,* Vol. 14, No. 1, (January 1991), pp. 177-190, ISSN 0161-1712

DeHoog, F.R.; Knight, J.H. & Stokes, A.N. (1982). An improved method for numerical inversion of Laplace transforms. *SIAM Journal on Scientific and Statistical Computing,* Vol. 3, No. 3, (September 1982), pp. 357-366, ISSN 0196-5204

Hwang, C.; Guo, T.-Y. & Shih, Y.-P. (1983). Numerical inversion of multidimensional Laplace transforms via block-pulse functions. *IEE Proceedings D - Control Theory & Applications,* Vol. 130, No. 5, (September 1983), pp. 250-254, ISSN 0143-7054

Hwang, C. & Lu, M.-J. (1999). Numerical inversion of 2-D Laplace transforms by fast Hartley transform computations. *Journal of the Franklin Institute,* Vol. 336, No. 6, (August 1999), pp. 955-972, ISSN 0016-0032

Karmakar, S.B. (1980). Laplace transform solution of nonlinear differential equations. *Indian Journal of Pure & Applied Mathematics,* Vol. 11, No. 4, (April 1980), pp. 407-412, ISSN 0019-5588

Macdonald, J.R. (1964). Accelerated convergence, divergence, iteration, extrapolation, and curve fitting, *Journal of Applied Physics,* Vol. 35, No. 10, (February 1964), pp. 3034-3041, ISSN 0021-8979

McCabe, J.H. (1983). The quotient-difference algorithm and the Padé table: An alternative form and a general continued fraction. *Mathematics of Computation,* Vol. 41, No. 163, (July 1983), pp. 183-197, ISSN 0025-5718

Reddy, D.C. & Jagan, N.C. (1971). Multidimensional transforms: new technique for the association of varieblες. *Electronics Letters,* Vol. 7, No. 10, (May 1971), pp. 278 - 279, ISSN 0013-5194

Rutishauser, H. (1957). *Der quotienten-differenzen-algorithmus.* Birkhäuser Verlag, Basel, Schweiz

Schetzen, M. (2006). *The Volterra and Wiener theories of nonlinear systems.* Krieger Publishing, ISBN 978-1-575-24283-5, Melbourne, Florida, U.S.A

Singhal, K.; Vlach, J. & Vlach, M. (1975). Numerical inversion of multidimensional Laplace transform. *Proceedings of the IEEE,* Vol. 63, No. 11, (November 1975), pp. 1627-1628, ISSN 0018-9219

Valsa, J. & Brančík, L. (1998a). Approximate formulae for numerical inversion of Laplace transforms. *International Journal of Numerical Modelling: Electronic Networks, Devices and Fields,* Vol. 11, No. 3, (May-June 1998), pp. 153-166, ISSN 0894-3370

Valsa, J. & Brančík, L. (1998b). Time-domain simulation of lossy transmission lines with arbitrary initial conditions. *Proceedings of Advances in Systems, Signals, Control and Computers,* Vol. III, pp. 305-307, ISBN 0-620-23136-X, Durban, South Africa, September 22-24, 1998

Wambacq, P. & Sansen, W.M.C. (2010). *Distortion analysis of analog integrated circuits.* Kluwer Academic Publishers, ISBN 978-1-4419-5044-4, Boston, U.S.A

Wu, J.L.; Chen, C.H. & Chen, C.F. (2001). Numerical inversion of Laplace transform using Haar wavelet operational matrices. *IEEE Transactions on Circuits and Systems – I: Fundamental Theory and Applications,* Vol. 48, No. 1, (January 2001), pp. 120-122, ISSN 1057-7122

4

Linear Variable Differential Transformer Design and Verification Using MATLAB and Finite Element Analysis

Lutfi Al-Sharif, Mohammad Kilani, Sinan Taifour, Abdullah Jamal Issa, Eyas Al-Qaisi, Fadi Awni Eleiwi and Omar Nabil Kamal
Mechatronics Engineering Department, University of Jordan
Jordan

1. Introduction

The linear variable differential transformer is one of the most widely used transducers for measuring linear displacement. It offers many advantages over potentio-metric linear transducers such as frictionless measurement, infinite mechanical life, excellent resolution and good repeatability (Herceg, 1972). Its main disadvantages are its dynamic response and the effects of the exciting frequency. General guidelines regarding the selection of an LVDT for a certain application can be found in (Herceg, 2006).

The LVDT is also used as a secondary transducer in various measurement systems. A primary transducer is used to convert the measurand into a displacement. The LVDT is then used to measure that displacement. Examples are:

1. Pressure measurement whereby the displacement of a diaphragm or Bourdon tube is detected by the LVDT (e.g., diaphragm type pressure transducer, (Daly *et al.*, 1984)).
2. Acceleration measurement whereby the displacement of a mass is measured by the LVDT (e.g., LVDT used within an accelerometer, (Morris, 2001).
3. Force measurement whereby the displacement of an elastic element subjected to the force is measured by the LVDT (e.g., ring type load cell, (Daly *et al.*, 1984)).

The classical method of LVDT analysis and design is based on the use of approximate equations as shown in (Herceg, 1972) and (Popovic *et al.*, 1999). These equations suffer from inaccuracy especially from end effects. More novel methods for design employ finite element methods (Syulski *et al.*, 1992), artificial neural networks (Mishra *et al.*, 2006) and (Mishra *et al.*, 2005). The dynamic response of the LVDT is discussed in (Doebelin, 2003). The LVDT has also been integrated into linear actuators (Wu *et al.*, 2008).

2. General overview

A diagram showing the dimensional parameters of the LVDT is shown in Figure 1 below. The important parameters that are taken into consideration in the design of the LVDT are listed below.

1. The length of the primary coil, l_p.
2. The length of the secondary coil, l_s. It is assumed that both secondaries have the same length.

3. The length of the core, l_c.
4. The diameter of the core r_c.
5. The inner diameter of the coils, r_i. It is assumed that the primary and both secondaries have the same inner radius.
6. The outer diameter of the coils, r_o. It is assumed that the primary and both secondaries have the same outer diameter.
7. The separation of the wires (centre to centre), w_S. It is important to note that the diameter of the wire itself is not taken into consideration and is assumed to be less than the separation (centre to centre). This is the best arrangement as it makes an allowance for the insulation of the wire. The diameter of the wire affects the effective overall resistance of the coil. As shown in Figure 1, it can be seen that the wires are assumed to be arranged in rows and columns.
8. The excitation frequency, f.
9. The primary current peak value, I. A sinusoidal waveform is applied to the primary in order to achieve a peak value of current I.
10. The separation between the coils, c_S. This parameter is important, as the former (spindle) on which the three coils are wound must have some thickness to retain its structural integrity.
11. The material of the rod has been assumed to be pure iron with a relative permeability μ_r of 14 000.

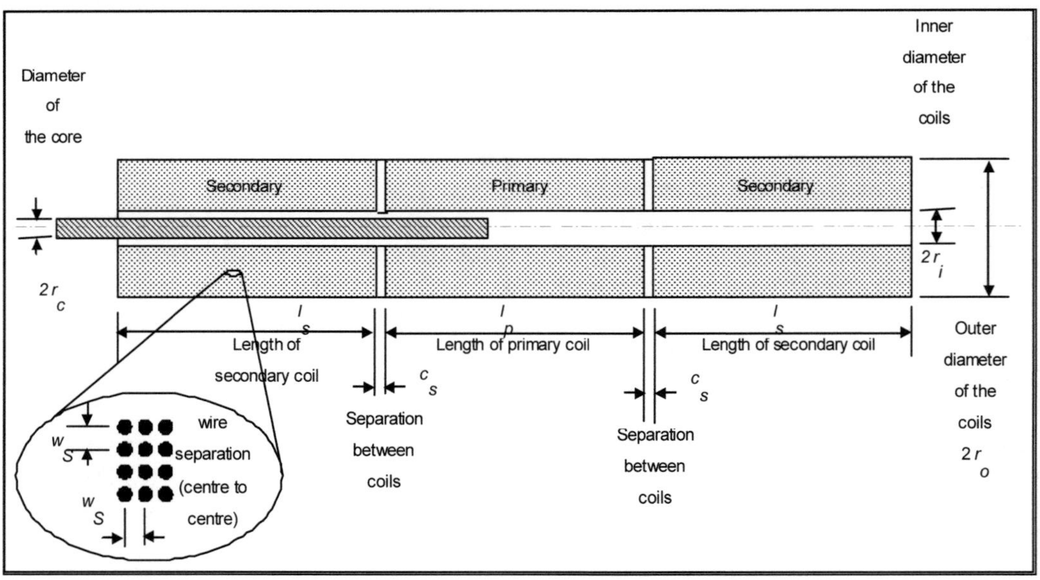

Fig. 1. Diagram showing the critical dimensions of the LVDT model

3. Objectives and methodology

The main objective of this piece of work is to develop a methodology for the design and verification of the linear variable differential transformer, using MATLAB to control and communicate with a magnetic finite element analysis tool. The methodology involves the following elements:

1. The capturing and coding of a number of rules of thumb that are used to find initial suitable values for the primary, secondaries and core length in relationship to the required stroke. These rules of thumb have been based on industrial experience.
2. The use of a finite element model (finite element magnetic tool) that is used to find the total flux linkage between the primary and the two secondaries based on a certain position of the core.
3. The use of MATLAB as a control tool to call the finite element modeling tool in order to find the output voltage of the two seconardies at each core position. MATLAB is then used to repeat this process until the full curve is produced.
4. A MATLAB based graphical user interface (GUI) has also been developed to act as a user friendly platform allowing the user to enter the required specification and to derive the output voltage characteristics.
5. Theoretical verification has been carried out, whereby the equation for the total flux linkage between two loops has been developed and then checked against the output of the finite element model to ensure that it is producing correct results.
6. In order to provide practical verification, an LVDT has then been built and the output measured and compared with the theoretical finite element outputs.

4. FEMM based model

The aim of the modeling methodology is to derive the transfer characteristic of an LVDT with certain dimensions and parameters. The transfer characteristic (or output characteristic) is a relationship between the displacement of the core and the output resultant dc voltage. It is assumed that the two ac signals from the two secondaries are processed by full wave rectifying them, smoothing the signals and then subtracting them.

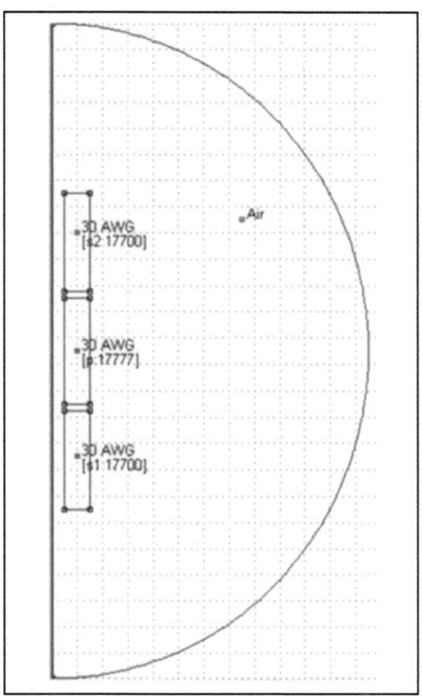

Fig. 2. Use of FEMM for LVDT modelling.

The FEMM (Finite Element Method, Magnetic) software is used to model the LVDT and find the total coupling flux from the primary to each of the secondaries at each position of the core. The total coupled flux is then divided by the primary core current to find the mutual inductance at this specific core position. By knowing the mutual inductance between the primary and each of the secondaries at a certain core position, the two output ac voltages can be found and hence the dc output voltage could be found. This process is then repeated for many other positions of the core, and the total transfer characteristic is then plotted.
The MATLAB software controls the whole process. It acts as the main controller to call the finite element magnetic tool and generate a point by point plot of the secondary output voltage at each point that corresponds to the position of the rod. Figure 2 shows the model of an LVDT within FEMM. It only shows half of the LVDT assuming symmetry between the two halves (left and right).
Using the FEMM software a large number of runs is carried out. These runs are automated using MATLAB. Starting values for all the parameters are used and these are referred to as the default parameters. Then one of the variable parameters is varied while all of the other parameters are kept constant.

Symbol	**Description**	**Default value**	**variable/fixed**	**Range**
l_p	length of the primary coil	80 mm	variable	26 to 133 mm (10 values)
l_s	length of the secondary coil	75 mm	variable	36 to 125 mm (9 values)
l_c	The length of the core	130 mm	variable	62 to 216 mm (9 values)
r_c	The radius of the core	4.5 mm	variable	2.1 to 7.5 mm (9 values)
r_i	The inner radius of the coils	10 mm	variable	4.8 to 16.7 mm (9 values)
r_o	The outer radius of the coils	35 mm	variable	16.8 to 58.3 mm (9 values)
w_s	The separation of the wires (centre to centre)	0.3 mm	variable	0.14 to 0.50 mm (9 values)
f	The excitation frequency	50 Hz	fixed	Not applicable
I	The primary current peak value	50 mA	fixed	Not applicable
c_s	The separation between the coils	5 mm	fixed	Not applicable
μ_r	Relative permeability of the core	14 000	fixed	Not applicable

Table 1. Parameters of the LVDT modelling.

4.1 Generation of a set of curves

In order to generate a set of curves that show the change of the output characteristic with the change of certain design parameters, a number of curves have been generated as follows.

Each variable is changed 9 times within the range, while keeping all other parameters fixed. Figure 3, Figure 4, Figure 5, Figure 6, Figure 7, Figure 8 and Figure 9 show the effect on the transfer characteristic of changing the primary length, secondary length, core length, core radius, coil inner radius, coil outer radius and wire separation respectively.

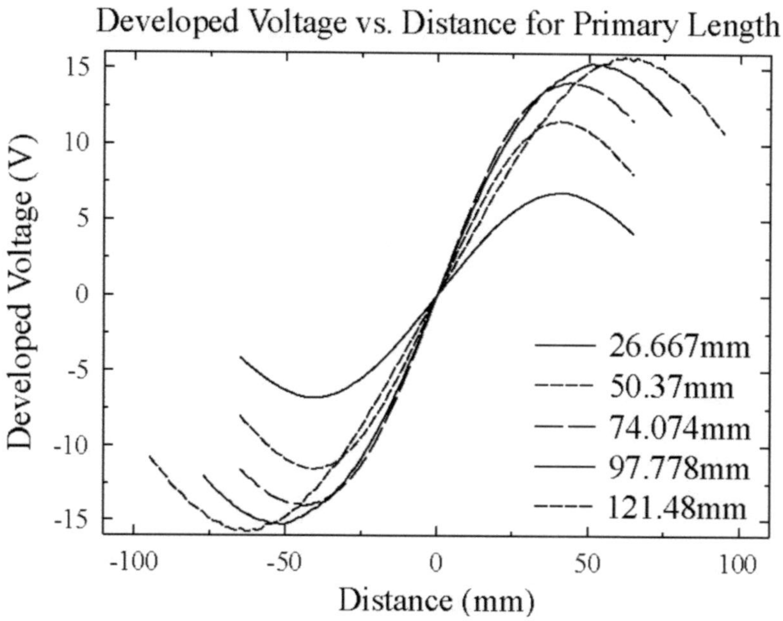

Fig. 3. Effect of the length of the primary coil on the transfer characteristic.

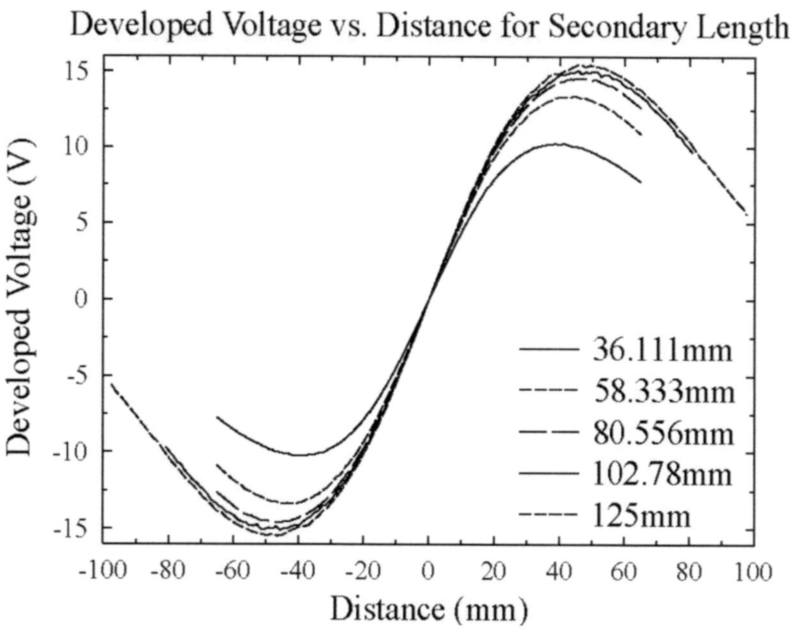

Fig. 4. Effect of the length of the secondary coil on the transfer characteristic.

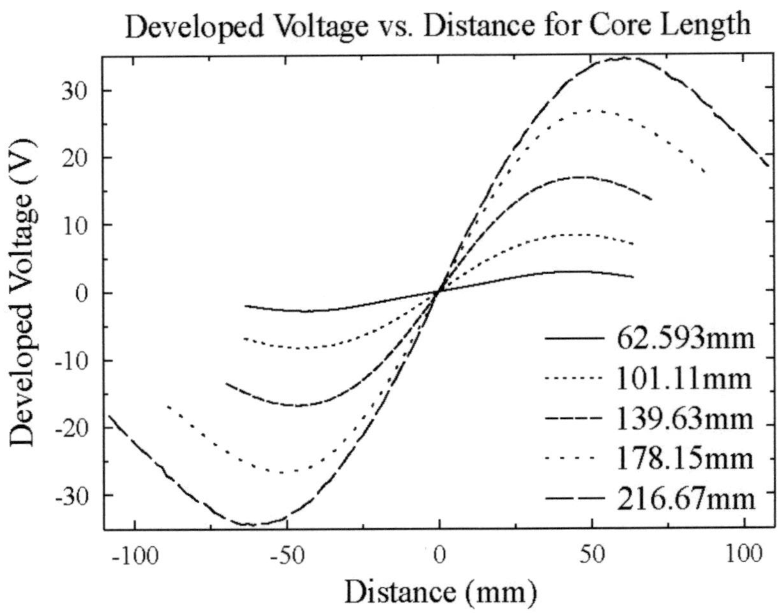

Fig. 5. Effect of the length of the core on the transfer characteristic.

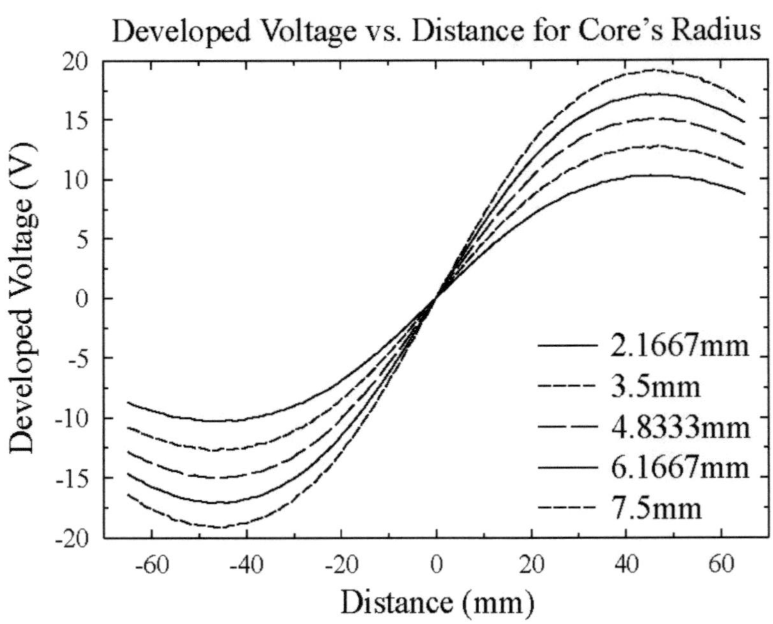

Fig. 6. Effect of the radius of the core on the transfer characteristic.

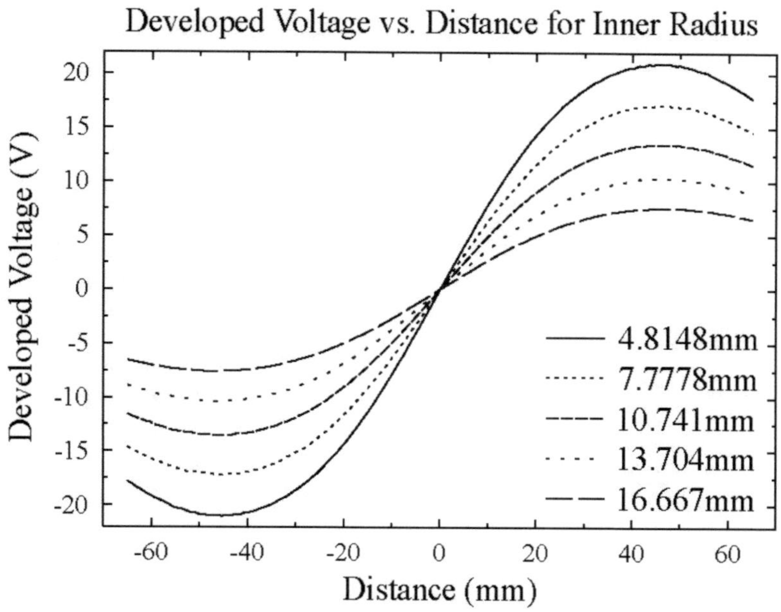

Fig. 7. Effect of the inner radius of the coils on the transfer characteristic.

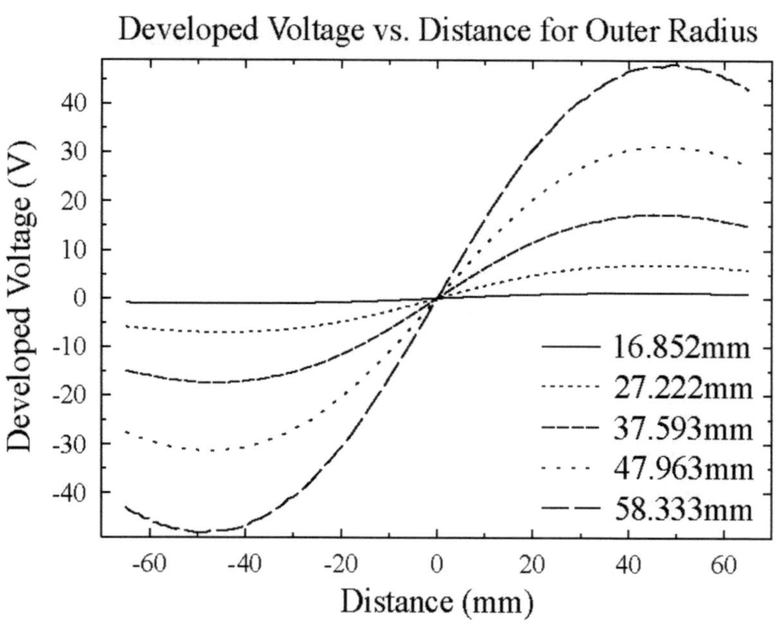

Fig. 8. Effect of the outer radius of the coils on the transfer characteristic.

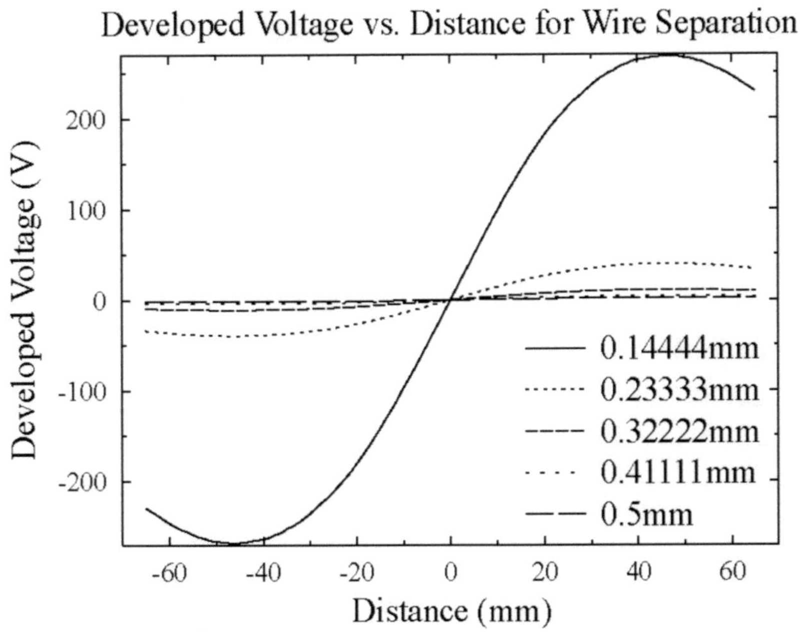

Fig. 9. Effect of the wire separation on the transfer characteristic.

MATLAB code has been used to automate the process of varying the parameters and to call the finite element modeling magnetic software. A parameter that is specific to the finite element software used is the so-called coarseness factor (c_f). Larger values of this variable result in finer graining. This is set to 18.
The two main characteristics of the LVDT that can be drawn from the graphs above are the sensitivity (mV/mm/V) and the stroke (mm). These are discussed in the next section.

4.2 Effect of parameters on stroke and sensitivity

The information gathered in the graphs generated in the last sub-section can be used to draw some general conclusions regarding the stroke and the sensitivity. The stroke is expressed in mm and the sensitivity is expressed in units of mV/mm/V (i.e., mV output volts dc for every mm core displacement for every voltage of excitation on the primary).
The effects of the primary length, secondary length, core length and outer coil radius on the stroke are shown in Figure 10, Figure 11, Figure 12 and Figure 13 respectively. It can be seen that the stroke increases with the length of the all of the four parameters, although it does flatten off in case of the secondary length.
The effects of the primary length, secondary length, core length and outer coil radius on the sensitivity have been shown in Figure 14, Figure 15, Figure 16 and Figure 17 respectively. The sensitivity is measured as the slope of the transfer characteristic at the null point.
It can seen that the sensitivity increases with the secondary length and the core length and decreases with the primary length and the outer radius of the coils.

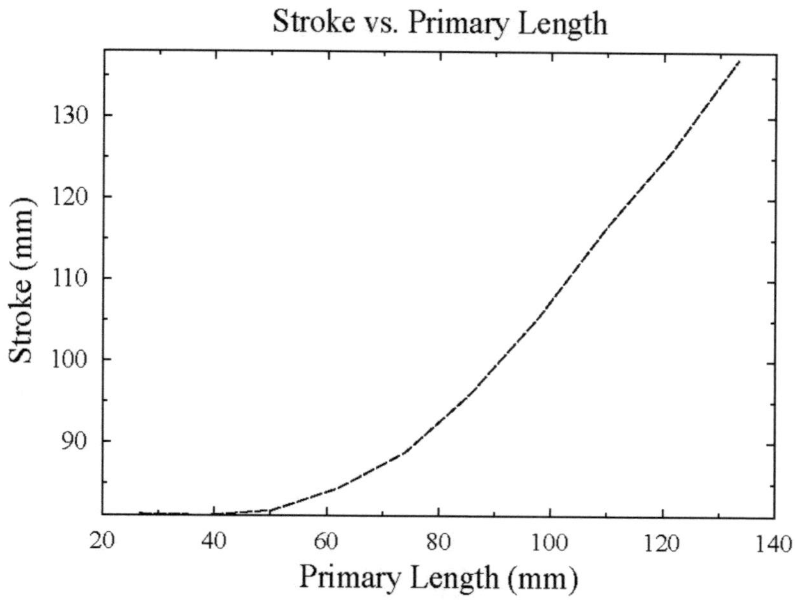

Fig. 10. Effect of the length of the primary coil on the stroke.

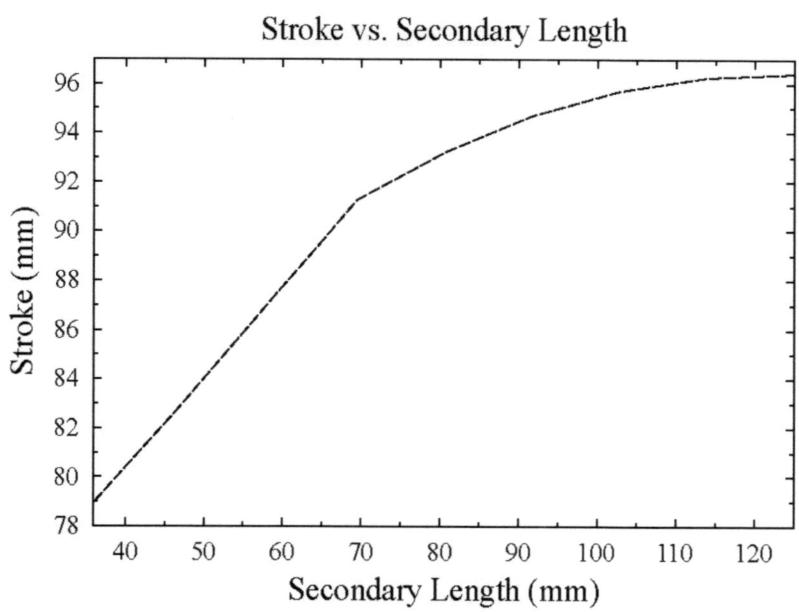

Fig. 11. Effect of the length of the secondary coil on the stroke.

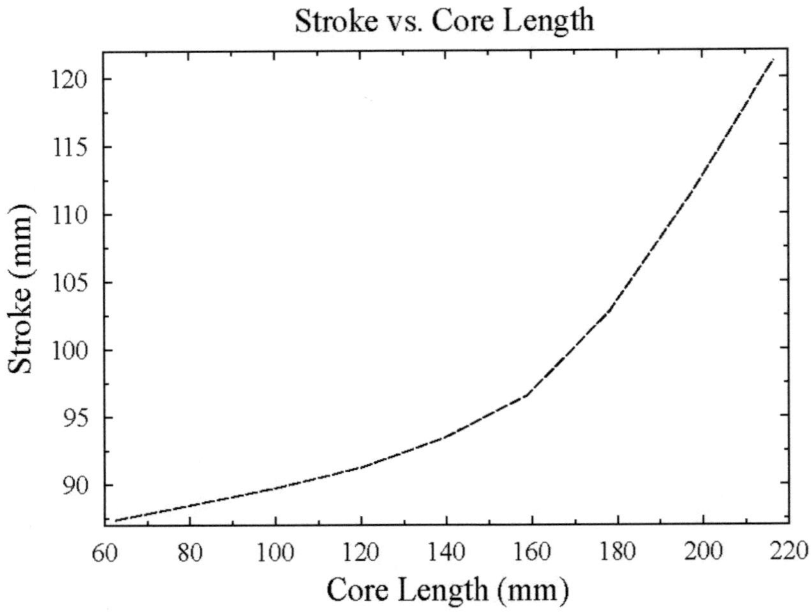

Fig. 12. Effect of the length of the core on the stroke.

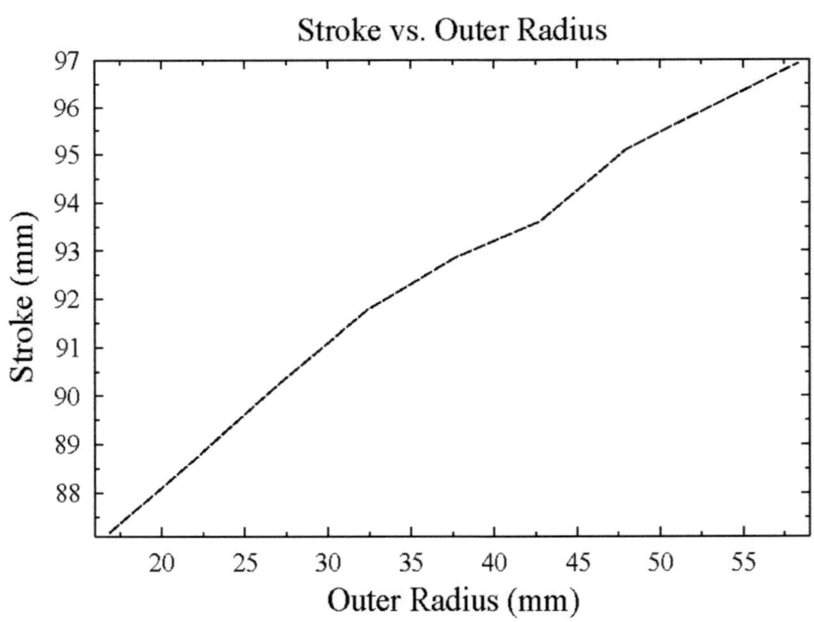

Fig. 13. Effect of the outer radius of the coils on the stroke.

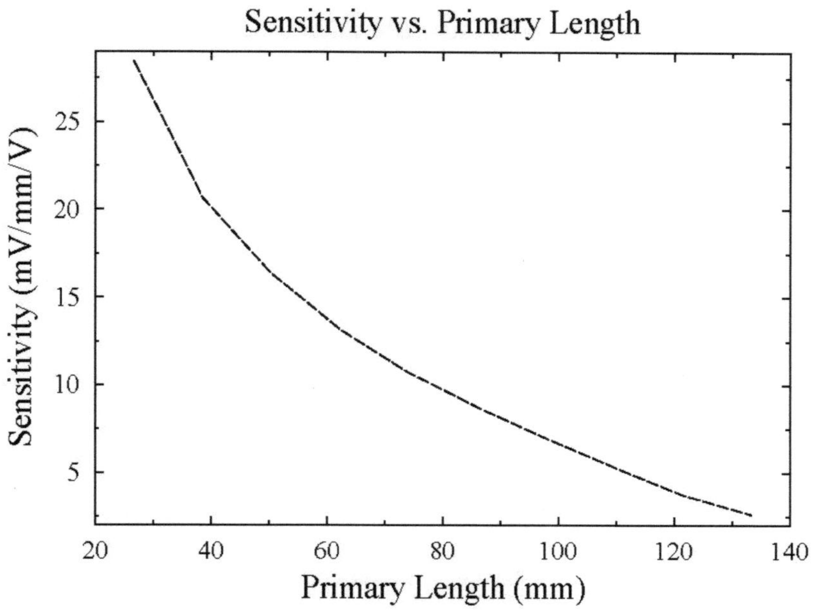

Fig. 14. Effect of the length of the primary coil on the sensitivity.

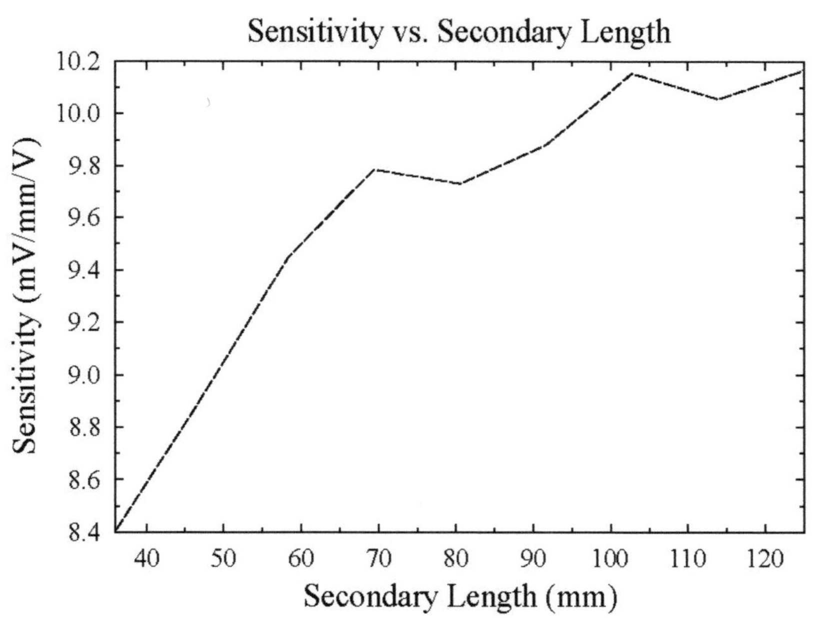

Fig. 15. Effect of the length of the secondary coil on the sensitivity.

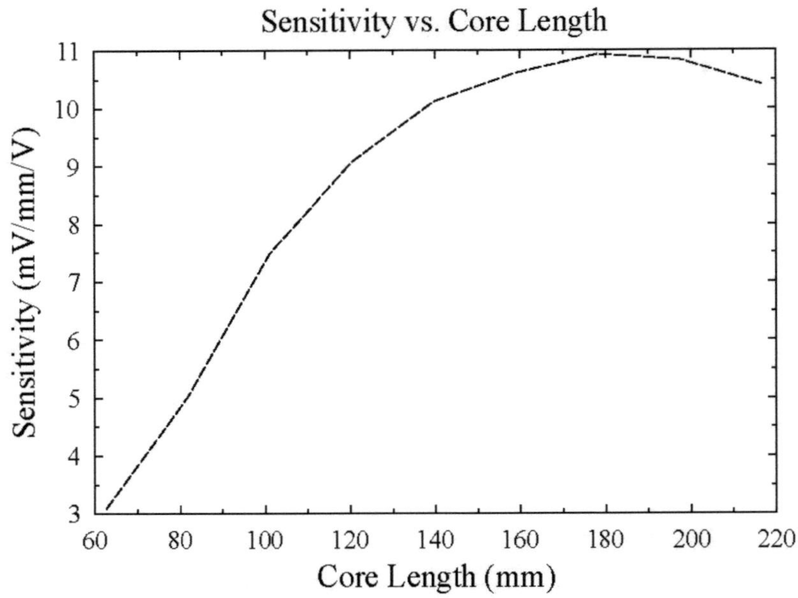

Fig. 16. Effect of the length of the core on the sensitivity.

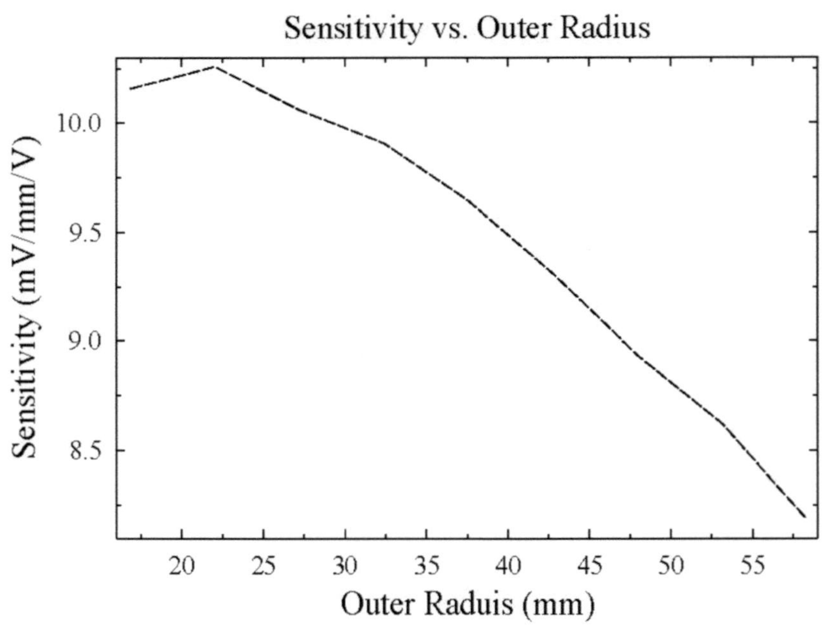

Fig. 17. Effect of the outer radius of the coils on the sensitivity.

5. Matlab GUI as a LVDT design tool

In order to automate the design process, a MATLAB graphical user interface (GUI) has been developed in order to provide a user friendly platform that allows the user to enter all the required parameters and run the LVDT. The software behind the GUI includes the rules of thumb, as well as suggested default values to the user. The output generated by the GUI is the output voltage curve plotted against the position of the rod. An example of a GUI screen is shown below.

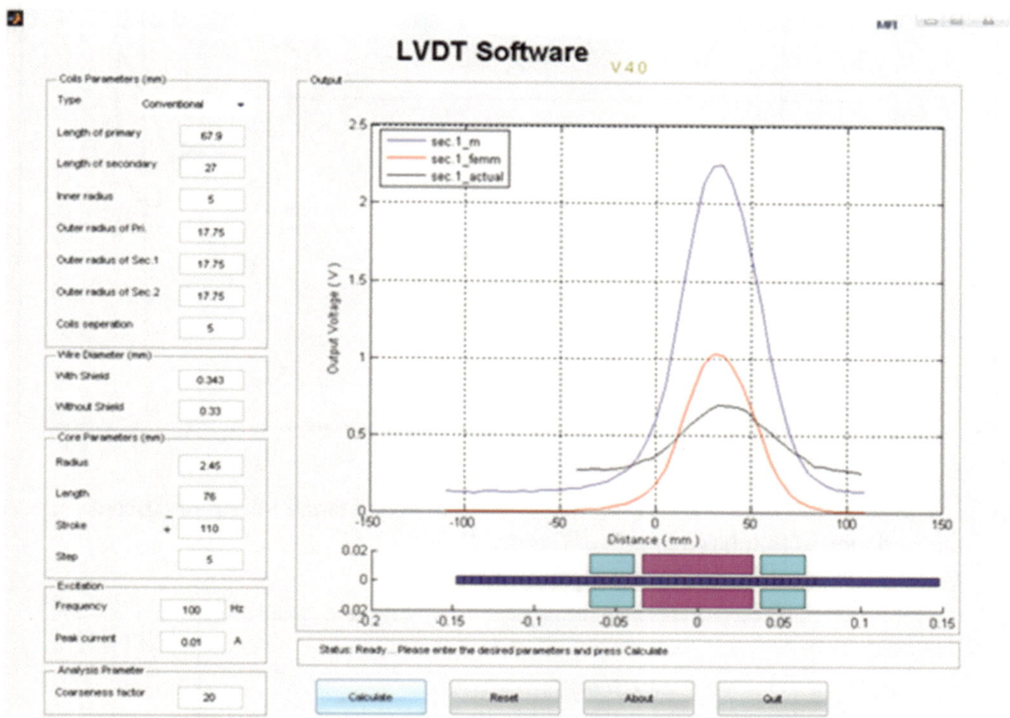

Fig. 18. Graphical User Interface.

6. Formulae for the flux linkage between two loops

In order to carry out a partial verification of the MATLAB/FEA model, an analytical method has been developed in order to find the expected output of each secondary based on the dimensions of the LVDT and the current in the primary. The basic model uses two concentric loops as shown Figure 19. One loop carries a certain current, and the flux linking the other loop is required. The aim is to find the total flux linked from one loop to another loop.

Let it be assumed that:

1. The radius of the first loop is A
2. The radius of the second loop is B
3. The current in the first loop is i
4. The two loops are concentric and separated by a distance h
5. The permittivity of the medium separating them is μ

The two loops lie in two parallel planes and are concentric as shown in Figure 19 below.

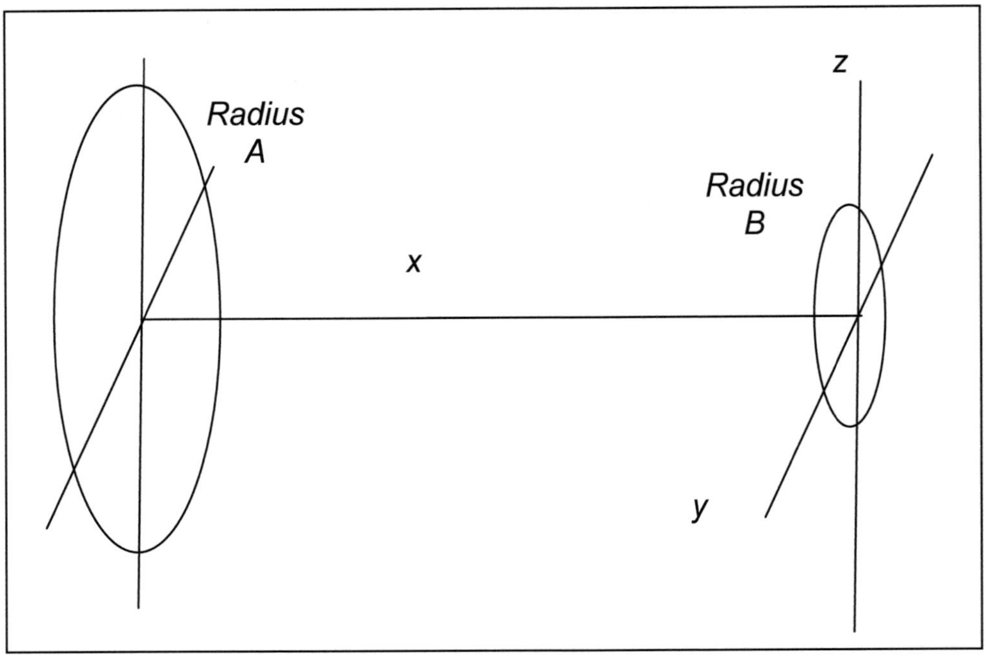

Fig. 19. General layout for the two loops.

Let us assume that loop A carries a current *i*. We will take a small length of current carrying conductor on loop A that has a length *dl* (Figure 21).

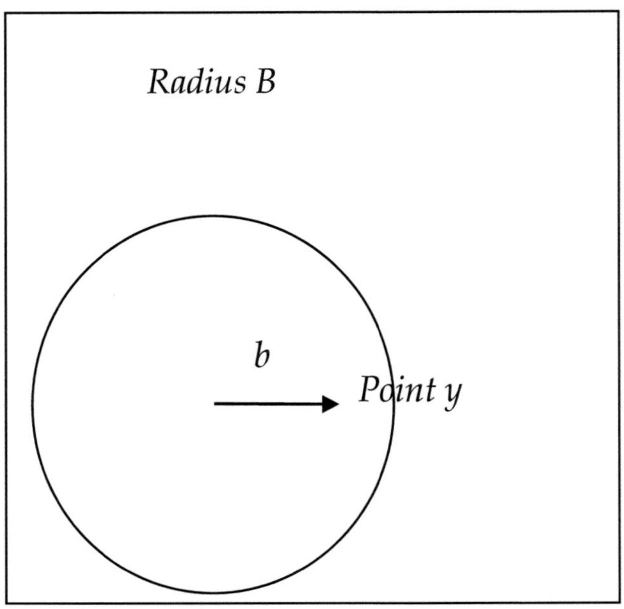

Fig. 20. Loop B

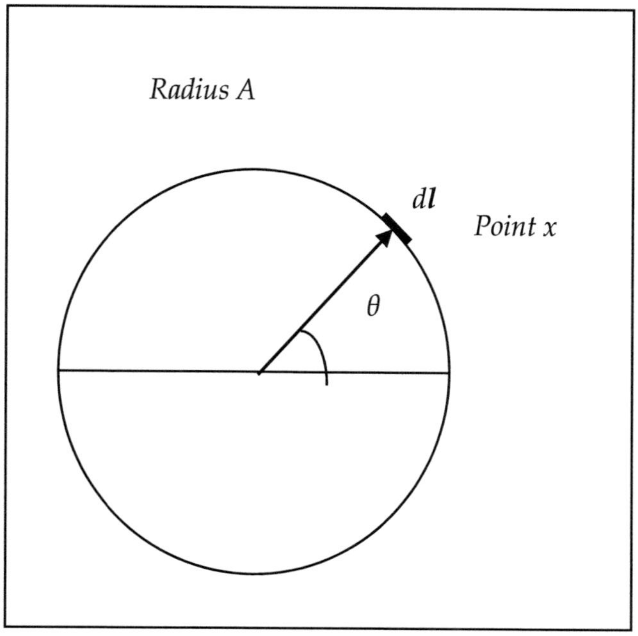

Fig. 21. Loop A.

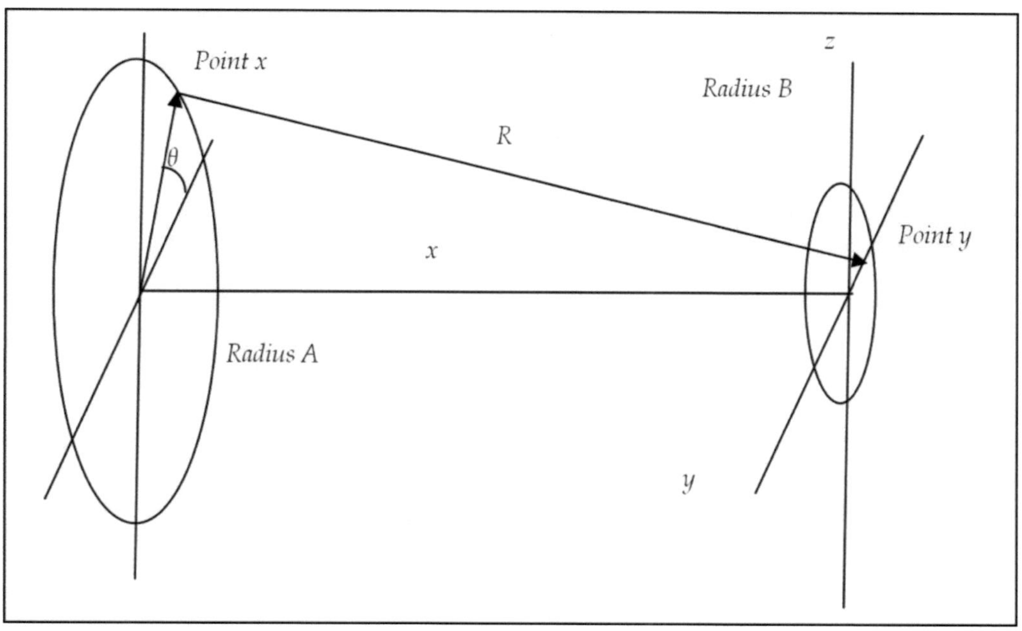

Fig. 22. General layout for the Biot-Savart Law.

We shall take a small section of the large loop, denoted as *dl* (vector) that carries a current *i*. The first step is to find the resultant magnetic flux density caused by a small section of the large loop dl (located at point *x*) at a point inside the smaller loop, denoted as point *y* (Figure 20). The point y has been taken inside the smaller loop on the y axis (without any

loss of generality) at a distance b from the centre of the loop. The vector connecting points x and y represents the direction of the resultant magnetic flux density (Figure 22).
We shall denote the vector that connects points x to y as ***R***. Using Biot-savart law gives:

$$\vec{dB} = \frac{\mu \cdot i \cdot \vec{dl} \times \vec{R}}{4 \cdot \pi \cdot R^3} \tag{1}$$

The coordinates of point x are:

$$(0, A \cdot \cos\theta, A \cdot \sin\theta) \tag{2}$$

The coordinates of point y are:

$$(h, b, 0) \tag{3}$$

The magnitude of R can be calculated as follows:

$$|R| = \sqrt{h^2 + (A \cdot \cos\theta - b)^2 + (A \cdot \sin\theta)^2} \tag{4}$$

$$\begin{aligned} |R| &= \sqrt{h^2 + A^2 \cdot \cos^2\theta - 2bA \cdot \cos\theta + b^2 + A^2 \cdot \sin^2\theta} \\ &= \sqrt{h^2 + A^2 + b^2 - 2bA \cdot \cos\theta} \end{aligned} \tag{5}$$

This gives us the magnitude of R. We next find the components of the two vectors, ***R*** and ***dl***:

$$\vec{R} = [h \quad b - A \cdot \cos\theta \quad -A \cdot \sin\theta] \tag{6}$$

$$\vec{dl} = [0 \quad -A \cdot \sin\theta \cdot d\theta \quad A \cdot \cos\theta \cdot d\theta] \tag{7}$$

We now turn to find the cross product of these two elements (note that we will only evaluate the x component as this is the component that is of interest to us).

$$\vec{dB_i} = \frac{\mu \cdot i \cdot d\theta \cdot \left(A^2 - A \cdot b \cdot \cos\theta\right)\vec{i}}{4 \cdot \pi \cdot \left(h^2 + A^2 + b^2 - 2 \cdot A \cdot b \cdot \cos\theta\right)^{\frac{3}{2}}} \tag{8}$$

We have taken the x direction only as this is the direction that is perpendicular to the area of the smaller loop.
This effect is only caused by a small strip dl of the larger loop. In order to find the effect of the whole larger loop on the point y, we need to integrate around the larger loop. This is done as follows:

$$\vec{dB_{iloop}} = \int_0^{2\pi} \frac{\mu \cdot i \cdot \left(A^2 - A \cdot b \cdot \cos\theta\right)}{4 \cdot \pi \cdot \left(h^2 + A^2 + b^2 - 2 \cdot A \cdot b \cdot \cos\theta\right)^{\frac{3}{2}}} d\theta \, \vec{i} \tag{9}$$

If we now take an annulus of radius b inside the smaller loop, we can see that by symmetry, the value of the magnetic flux density component that is perpendicular to the area of the loop is constant everywhere on the annulus (Figure 23). We can now calculate the total flux that is passing through this annulus caused by the current i in the large loop. We shall set the width of this annulus as db and its radius as b.

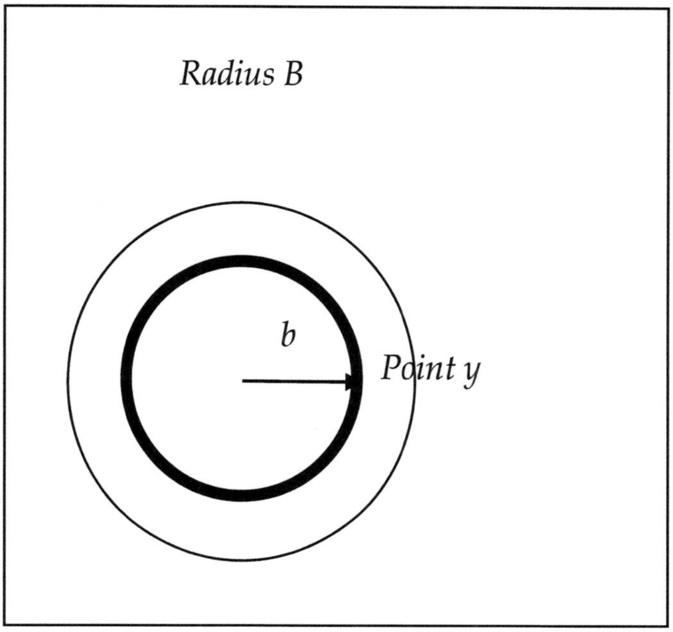

Fig. 23. Annulus in loop B.

So the total flux through the annulus can be found by multiplying the value of the magnetic flux density by the area of the annulus:

$$d\Phi_{annulus} = 2\cdot\pi\cdot b\cdot\left(\int_0^{2\pi}\frac{\mu\cdot i\cdot\left(A^2 - A\cdot b\cdot\cos\theta\right)}{4\cdot\pi\cdot\left(h^2 + A^2 + b^2 - 2\cdot A\cdot b\cdot\cos\theta\right)^{\frac{3}{2}}}d\theta\right)db \tag{10}$$

So the total flux in the smaller loop can now be found by integrating over b from the value of b equal to 0 up to the radius of the smaller loop B.

$$\Phi = \int_0^B 2\cdot\pi\cdot b\left(\int_0^{2\pi}\frac{\mu\cdot i\cdot\left(A^2 - A\cdot b\cdot\cos\theta\right)}{4\cdot\pi\cdot\left(h^2 + A^2 + b^2 - 2\cdot A\cdot b\cdot\cos\theta\right)^{\frac{3}{2}}}d\theta\right)db \tag{11}$$

$$\Phi = \int_0^B\left(\int_0^{2\pi}\frac{2\cdot\pi\cdot\mu\cdot i\cdot b\cdot\left(A^2 - A\cdot b\cdot\cos\theta\right)}{4\cdot\pi\cdot\left(h^2 + A^2 + b^2 - 2\cdot A\cdot b\cdot\cos\theta\right)^{\frac{3}{2}}}d\theta\right)db \tag{12}$$

Simplifying gives the final result:

$$\Phi = \int_{0}^{B} \left(\int_{0}^{2\pi} \frac{\mu \cdot i \cdot b \cdot \left(A^2 - A \cdot b \cdot \cos\theta\right)}{2 \cdot \left(h^2 + A^2 + b^2 - 2 \cdot A \cdot b \cdot \cos\theta\right)^{\frac{3}{2}}} d\theta \right) db \tag{13}$$

The formula shown above cannot be solved analytically. MATLAB is used to evaluate the double integral.

Verification was carried out between the formula above implemented in MATLAB for a primary and a secondary without an inserted core and the output of FEMM. A numerical example is shown below. It shows excellent agreement between the analytical formula used in (13) and the output of the FEMM.

The parameters and results of the numerical example are as follows:

Primary excitation current	30 mA
Radius of primary loop	25 mm
Radius of secondary loop	15 mm
Distance between loops	80 mm
Flux linkage	
FEMM	1.37551e-11 Wb
MATLAB (double integration equation)	1.3558e-11 Wb

7. Practical verification

A practical verification of the results from the MATLAB/FEA model and the analytical equation within MATLAB was then carried out. A model of the LVDT is built and tested. The results are compared and verified with outputs from the models.

Figure 24 shows the output voltage as a function of the displacement of the core. This has been carried out at an excitation frequency of 100 Hz. As the frequency is increased it is noted that a larger discrepancy between the expected and actual outputs exists. The explanation for this discrepancy is the eddy current losses with the core (which is a conducting material as well as being ferromagnetic). Eddy current losses are not currently modeled and this will be necessary in order to fully quantify the expected eddy current losses.

8. Conclusions

A methodology has been developed that allows the user to design and verify the output of an LVDT. A finite element magnetic model in conjunction with MATLAB has been developed that allows the user to design an LVDT and produce the expected output characteristics. A graphical user interface has been added to the software to facilitate data entry and design visualization.

Analytical and practical verification has been carried out. Good agreement has been achieved via the analytical verification. However, a discrepancy has been noted in the practical verification caused by the Eddy current losses (as it seems to increase with the frequency). This requires further investigation and modeling.

Sensitivity analysis has been carried out on some of the design parameters. General conclusions have been drawn showing the effect of the primary coil length, secondary coil

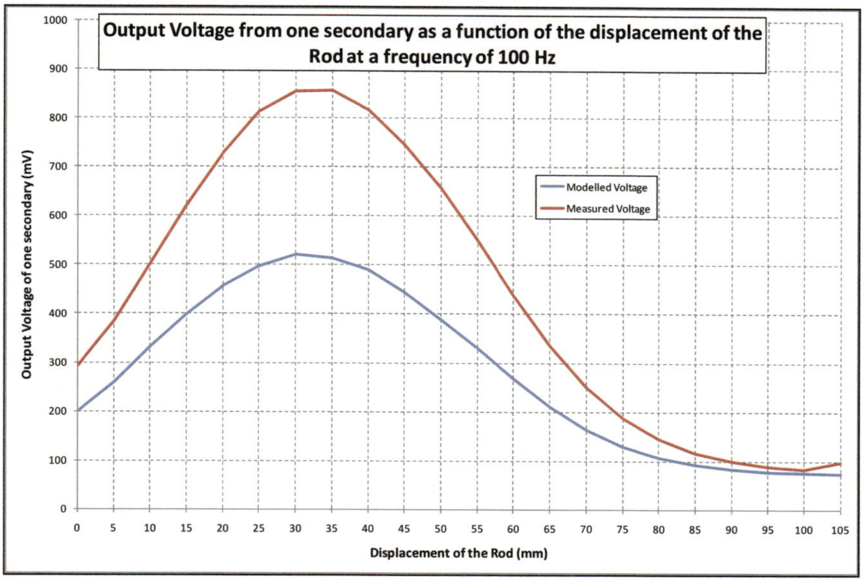

Fig. 24. Output voltage from one secondary as the core is displaced.

length, core length and outer radius of the coils on both the stroke and the sensitivity of the LVDT

9. Further work

Further work is still needed in the following areas:

1. The seven variables that are varied are varied one at a time, keeping all the other parameters fixed. It is now the intention to vary all parameters at the same time to see the overall effect on the transfer characteristic.
2. Four of the parameters are kept constant. Further work is needed to understand the effect of varying them on the transfer characteristic. Of particular importance is the effect of the frequency on the design (Herceg, 2006).
3. The range of variation of the variables was restricted. More readings are needed outside the range used in order to draw more general conclusions.
4. Variation of the variables is needed in pairs to see the relative importance of these variables. For example, the length of the core in relation to the primary as a ratio could be more important than the absolute values of the two variables.
5. Further experimental verification is required. Moreover, modeling of the Eddy current losses is required in order to quantify the effect of the excitation frequency on the discrepancy between the expected output voltage and the measured output voltage.
6. Further investigation is required into the possibility of combining a linear electromagnetic actuator with an LVDT in the same hardware as discussed in (Wu *et al.*, 1999). This offers a very compact closed loop linear electromagnetic actuator.

10. Acknowledgement

The practical verification and the analytical numerical example shown in this piece of work have been based on the graduation project work by a group of Mechatronics Enginering students at the University of Jordan. The members of the group are:

- "Mohammad Hussam ALDein" Omar Ali Bolad
- Anas Imad Ahmad Farouqa
- Anas Abdullah Ahmad Al-shoubaki
- Baha' Abd-Elrazzaq Ahmad Alsuradi
- Yazan Khalid Talib Al-diqs

11. References

Beckwith, Buck & Marangoni, (1982), Mechanical Measurements, Third Edition, 1982.

Daly, James; Riley, William; McConnell, Kennet, (1984), Instrumentation for Engineering Measurements, 2nd Edition, 1984, John Wiley & Sons.

Doebelin, E., (2003), Meaurement Systems: Application and Design, 5th Edition, McGraw Hill, 2003.

Herceg, Ed, (2006), Factors to Consider in Selecting and Specifying LVDT for applications, Nikkei Electronics Asia, March 2006.

Herceg, Edward, (1972), Handbook of Measurement and Control: An authoritative treatise on the theory and application of the LVDT, Schaevitz Engineering, 1972.

Mishra, SK & Panda, G, (2006), A novel method for designing LVDT and its comparison with conventional design, Proceedings of the 2006 IEEE Sensors Applications Symposium, pages: 129-134, 2006.

Mishra, SK; Panda, G; Das, DP; Pattanaik, SK & Meher, MR, (2005), A novel method of designing LVDT using artificial neural network, 2005 International Conference on Intelligent Sensing and Information Processing Proceedings, page 223-227, 2005.

Morris, Alan S., (2001), Measurement & Instrumentation Principles, Elsevier Butterworth Heinemann, 2001.

Popović, Dobrivoje; Vlacic, Ljubo, (1999), Mechatronics in Engineering Design and Product Development, CRC Press, 1999.

Syulski, J.K., Sykulska, E. and Hughes, S.T., (1992), Applications of Finite Element Modelling in LVDT Design, The International Journal for Computation and Mathematics in Electrical and Electronic Engineering, Vol. 11, No. 1, 73-76, James & James Science Publishers Ltd.

Wu, Shang-The; Mo, Szu-Chieh; Wu, Bo-Siou, (2008), An LVDT-based self-actuating displacement transducer, Science Direct, Sensors and Actuators A 141 (2008) 558–564.

Part 2

Hardware and Photonics Applications

5

Computational Models Designed in MATLAB to Improve Parameters and Cost of Modern Chips

Peter Malík
Institute of Informatics, Slovak Academy of Sciences
Slovak Republic

1. Introduction

Methods and techniques to design integrated circuits made a huge progress since German engineer Werner Jacobi filed a first patent for an integrated-circuit-like semiconductor amplifying device in 1949 or since Jack Kilby successfully demonstrated the first working integrated circuit on September 12, 1958. The first integrated circuits were composed of a small number of transistors and their functionality was very limited. They were designed manually without any effective calculation tools and therefore the developing phase took long time. Each design error was difficult to discover and the whole process had to be repeated when uncovered during physical prototype testing. This further increased time necessary to develop a working chip. An important milestone in integrated circuits design is the first microprocessor Intel 4004 produced in April 1971. The significance lies in the beginning of mutual bond between produced microprocessors and methods to design them. It was discovered very soon that the high computation power of microprocessors can be utilized directly by the design process to improve future microprocessors. High performance microprocessors started to be used for calculations of an estimated behavior of future prototypes and their parameters. The simple models were transformed to more complex models that closer represented the reality. More precise models increased a chance to uncover a design error in early design phases and accelerated its correction. The continual upgrading process of design methods and tools matures into computer aided design (CAD) software platforms that are able to carry out many tasks automatically which had to be done manually in the past.

Constant refinement of design methods, tools and technology secured the steady grow of integrated circuits internal complexity. Intel co-founder Gordon E. Moore described the trend in his 1965 paper that the number of components in integrated circuits had doubled every year from the invention of the integrated circuit in 1958 until 1965. He predicted that the trend would continue for at least ten years Moore (1965). His prediction has proved to be uncannily accurate and is now used in semiconductor industry to guide long-term planning and to set targets for research and development ITRS (2009). This long-term trend is also known as Moore's law.

The digital design process uses highly automated CAD tools that significantly reduce the time necessary to design a prototype when the design is closely specified by full set of parameters. The original specification is usually general and many parameters have to be defined later. The process specifying missing parameters is an inseparable part of feasibility study or the first design phases. It is very important to set suitable parameters because they determine the resulting prototype. More complex integrated circuits require more parameters to be defined

and therefore more analysis and simulation work is necessary. Usually this process requires more time in comparison to the physical design that is mostly done by modern CAD tools.
The modern CAD tools include models that closely represent the resulting prototype; however, their calculation is too much time consuming. The feasibility study and first design stages require different models. The models have to be relatively simple with the acceptable correlation to reality. An excellent software environment to create and evaluate these models is MATLAB.
Users can create new functions and procedures in MATLAB similarly as in a common programing language environment. An advantage is that MATLAB has a more simple and intuitive syntax and thorough help with many practical examples. Additionally, it has an extensive database of internal functions that can be used directly in the source code of new functions. Models usually describe a simulated behavior by mathematical equations or some iterative process. Both types of model description can be written in MATLAB intuitively with the short source code. However, the biggest advantage is very fast and simple work with calculated results and the ability to visualize the resulted data with internal MATLAB functions.
A hardware implementation of an algorithm or computation scheme implies new challenges that have to be overcome. The general aim is to design an integrated circuit with minimal area that produces results with a pre-specified overall precision. Deep analysis and lot of simulations are needed to attain this. MATLAB can be used as a part of this optimization process. The advantages are extensive mathematical support with the option to create own optimization code and easy way to sort and evaluate excessive calculated results. A simple software computational model can be created in MATLAB and later used within optimization routines. An example of this optimization process is presented in the following sections with an integrated circuit for acceleration of time consuming computations of forward and backward modified discrete cosine transform (MDCT) that is used in audio compression and coding. MDCT is used in many audio coding standards for time-to-frequency transformation of digital signals. It is perfect reconstruction cosine-modulated filter bank based on the concept of time domain aliasing cancellation Princen et al. (1987). MDCT is the basic processing block for high-quality audio compression in the international audio coding standards and commercial audio compression algorithms in consumers electronics Bosi & Goldberg (2003); Spanias et al. (2007). Forward and backward MDCT computations are the most computationally intensive operations in the well-known audio coding standards. Thus, an efficient implementation of the MDCT has become the key technology to realize real-time and low-cost audio decoders.

2. Computational models in digital design process

A computational model is a set of equations that describe some selected attribute or feature in a more simplified way compared to its true physical nature. The idea behind creating a computational model is to be able to run complex analyses and simulations of specific scenarios on PC. The fast computational speed and the ability to calculate with a wide spectrum of input data variations is very important. A computation power of common PC has been increased significantly in recent years, which enabled to run usual simulations on ordinary PC that required big server clusters in the past. The ability to create a computational model easily and in short time accelerates the design process in general. The result is that a designer can verify his/her designs in early developing phases and use the saved time to further improvements.

Digital circuit design is composed of many steps that continually shape the final integrated circuit. The technology advancement paved the road to very complex integrated circuits called system on a chip (SoC). The more complex the chip is the more design steps it requires. Considerable interest has been oriented toward computational models with lower abstraction levels. This resulted in the development of precise computational models that are integrated in modern professional design tools. Easy access to these models is a great advantage. They are utilized mostly during moderate and finalizing design steps. This chapter is oriented to computational models on higher abstraction levels that are used in feasibility studies and first design steps.

At the beginning of design process, the computational models depend considerably on a selection of design characteristics. In this design phase, the designers create more detailed specifications and develop the guidelines to reach them. The original specification is usually too general and its parametric goals can be reached by different means. Each selected solution has to be analyzed and evaluated. Simple computational models are very important in this process. These models can differ from each other significantly. They use limited amount of parameters and many unnecessary features are omitted. Models are used in many situations, e.g., a comparison analysis of hardware implementation with software solution, analysis of different algorithms, evaluation of different hardware architectures or components. These are few examples with the most significant influence on the following design steps.

Each hardware implementation performs one or several algorithms. An algorithm is evaluated by a number of operations that has to be carried out to produce a set of output data. Long computation process can produce a significant computation error that distorts the results. Each algorithm has different sensitivity to accumulation of errors. Therefore, an analysis of computation errors by models is very important and the results usually dictate minimal precision requirements of hardware components. These models are usually very simple with minimal utilization of hardware parameters. In general, all operations are transformed to basic mathematical operations that the selected hardware is capable to perform. Each transformed operation uses rounding or truncating operation to model limited precision of hardware components.

Mathematical operations can be performed with data in different data representations. Selecting an appropriate data representation can improve the resulted parameters. This effect can be modeled and analyzed. Data can be represented by floating point or fixed point. Fixed point representations are also called integer representations. Floating point has better precision for wide data intervals but if data variations are small an integer is a better solution Inacio & Ombres (1996). An integer does not contain information about decimal point placement and therefore it has to be managed externally. Floating point computation components are more complex and thus larger area of a final chip is taken Kwon et al. (2005). The increased area means higher cost of integrated circuits; hence, integer components utilization can reduce the price of a final chip. These are universal guidelines but the optimal results can be achieved only by deep analyses.

Models that analyze data variations are the good starting point to decide between floating point and integer. The level of specialization is the key information in the decision process. More universal applications usually use floating point due to more difficult estimation of data variations. In highly specialized applications integer can be a better solution because internal data structure can be highly optimized. The optimization results depend considerably on the quality of used models and on the optimization extent.

Integer is more susceptible to data overflow than floating point Beauchamp et al. (2008). Data overflow significantly distorts actual values and therefore digital designs have to include some form of protection mechanism. Before it can be designed, the knowledge where and when the data overflow happens is necessary. This is usually analyzed with simple models that work with wide data intervals and the point of interest is oriented to data that produce highest peak values. It is also important to monitor the highest negative peaks, because they can cause data underflow which has similar effect as data overflow. The data producing these peaks are later used as test vectors for verifications of created designs.

An important part of modern integrated circuit is memory and memory controller. The cost of memory has been falling in last years, which changed the focus from memory size to memory controller bandwidth. The bandwidth depends on the speed of access to memory, on memory delays and on memory interface bit-width. Access to memory can be improved by rearranging of data in the memory. Reading data from memory that are placed next to each other is much faster than reading data that are randomly distributed through the whole memory. Grouping data that are often accessed at the same time and placing them in the shared memory block as close as possible can significantly reduce the access time and increase the bandwidth. Optimal data rearranging can be modeled and analyzed.

Another improvement of the memory bandwidth can be achieved by analysis of data values. If the data values are from a narrow data range, the universal exponent can be transferred separately and following data are represented only with a mantissa. This methodology is mostly used in serial data transfers and with integer representations. In this case, the better bandwidth utilization is increasing complexity of memory controller and therefore it has to be evaluated more thoroughly. A similar principle can be applied to optimization of integer representation itself.

Modern algorithms often require large memory. Lot of data are stored for a short time only. If these time periods are not overlapped, the data can be rewritten and memory size can be reduced. In many cases, the time periods are overlapped only partially and small changes within an order of operations can eliminate overlapping. Of course, this requires more complex models and deeper analysis. The result is represented by a significant reduction of memory size.

Digital designs can utilize different computation flows. A design with few universal computation blocks depends more on a memory subsystem. The advantage is a simple design and support for many different algorithms. The optimization objectives are mostly oriented to a memory subsystem and to the number of universal computational blocks. Deeper analysis can evaluate the necessary complexity level of used computational blocks. An exchange of several computational blocks with simplified blocks can reduce the final area of a chip.

A highly specialized digital design has usually a custom hardware architecture that gone through a long optimization process. Its significant part is done at a higher abstraction level. The important subject of analysis is the effect of increased parallel structures or utilization of computational pipeline. Precision and overflow analysis is more the necessity than an option. Each computational block can use unique interconnection, special features and attached latch or register. The aim is to utilize these options efficiently. Then, the resulting design has excellent parameters. The time consuming optimizations are costly and still economical in large production quantities.

During the computational model design, it is important to select an area of interest and to be able to verify precision of results. A model that produces results that differ from reality too significantly has to be corrected immediately. In many situations, the simple model composed of few mathematical equations can be sufficient, e.g., to verify an algorithm or some independent feature. Mutually dependent features have to be modeled by more robust models. The models that mimic hardware architectures with high precision give designers a chance to analyze the hardware behavior before it is actually produced. This saves time and reduces the overall cost.

The simple model is an advantage when used under optimization routines with many computation loops. Many mutually dependent parameters can easily rise the number of optimization cycles over the acceptable level. In these cases, the very simple models can produce more data on parameters' dependency that is later used to reduce the number of optimization dimensions and widths of input data intervals. This procedure can be repeated later with more robust and more precise models.

3. MDCT computational models in MATLAB

Hardware implementation has special preferences for computational algorithms. The number and complexity of computation operations are most important. An algorithm with smaller number of operations computes results in shorter time which represents improved computational speed. The number of computation operations reduced only by single operation can significantly improve overall performance if the computation is run many times under a loop or in more complex algorithm. Not all operations are equal. Addition and subtraction operations are similar in their complexity. Multiplication operation is much more complex and therefore consumes much more area on a chip. There is an exception. Multiplication by a constant that equals to power of 2 (2, 4, 8, 16, 32, 64, ...) is the same as shifting the original binary number to the left by the number of bits that equals to base 2 logarithm of the constant. It is similar to a constant that equals to negative power of 2 (1/2, 1/4, 1/8, ...) with the difference that shifting is to the right. Hence, one removed multiplication is more significant than a removed addition or subtraction, and multiplication by power of 2 can be neglected.
The algorithm selected for hardware implementation is presented in Britanak & Rao (2002). The algorithm computes MDCT that is used in audio compression. It has low number of mathematical operations. Additionally, it has a symmetric computational structure that is an advantage in digital design. The symmetric structure can be implemented more efficiently. The resulting hardware is dedicated to accelerate the time consuming MDCT computations in audio compression.
Correct verifications during the whole design process save time. Frequent verifications facilitate a process of locating errors, because only few modifications were made between two following inspections. An algorithm verification can be done by another algorithm that is widely accepted and well proven. The best choice for verification of MDCT algorithm is the original MDCT algorithm Princen & Bradley (1986). Its mathematical equations are:

$$c_k = \sum_{n=0}^{N-1} x_n cos\left[\frac{\pi}{2N}\left(2n+1+\frac{N}{2}\right)(2k+1)\right], \quad k = 0,1,\ldots,\frac{N}{2}-1, \tag{1}$$

$$\hat{x}_n = \frac{2}{N}\sum_{k=0}^{\frac{N}{2}-1} c_k cos\left[\frac{\pi}{2N}\left(2n+1+\frac{N}{2}\right)(2k+1)\right], \quad n = 0,1,\ldots,N-1, \tag{2}$$

where $\{c_k\}$ are MDCT coefficients and $\{\hat{x}_n\}$ represents the time domain aliased data sequence recovered by backward MDCT. The verification model was designed straightforward by simple computation loops. The source code is shown in the following MATLAB example.

```
function Z = MDCT_analytic(X, N)
Z = zeros(1, N/2);
for k = 0:((N/2) - 1)
    sum = 0.0;
    for n = 0:(N - 1)
```

```
        arg = pi / (2 * N) * ((2 * n + 1 + N/2) * (2 * k + 1));
        sum = sum + (X(n + 1) * cos(arg));
    end
Z(k + 1) = sum;
```

Complete formulas constituting the selected MDCT algorithm are as follows:

$$z_{2k} = (-1)^k \frac{\sqrt{2}}{2} \sum_{n=0}^{\frac{N}{4}-1} \left(a_n cos\left[\frac{\pi(2n+1)k}{2(N/4)}\right] - b_n sin\left[\frac{\pi(2n+1)k}{2(N/4)}\right] \right),$$
$$z_{2k+\frac{N}{2}} = (-1)^{k+\frac{N}{4}} \frac{\sqrt{2}}{2} \sum_{n=0}^{\frac{N}{4}-1} (-1)^{n+1} \left(a_n sin\left[\frac{\pi(2n+1)k}{2(N/4)}\right] + b_n cos\left[\frac{\pi(2n+1)k}{2(N/4)}\right] \right),$$
$$k = 0, 1, \ldots, \frac{N}{4} - 1, \tag{3}$$

where

$$a_n = \left(x_n^{'} - x_{\frac{N}{2}-1-n}^{''}\right) cos\frac{\pi(2n+1)}{2N} - \left(x_n^{''} - x_{\frac{N}{2}-1-n}^{'}\right) sin\frac{\pi(2n+1)}{2N},$$
$$b_n = \left(x_n^{'} - x_{\frac{N}{2}-1-n}^{''}\right) sin\frac{\pi(2n+1)}{2N} + \left(x_n^{''} - x_{\frac{N}{2}-1-n}^{'}\right) cos\frac{\pi(2n+1)}{2N}, \quad n = 0, 1, \ldots, \frac{N}{4} - 1, \tag{4}$$

and

$$x_n^{'} = x_n - x_{N-1-n}, \quad x_n^{''} = x_n + x_{N-1-n}, \quad n = 0, 1, \ldots, \frac{N}{2} - 1. \tag{5}$$

Final MDCT coefficients are obtained as

$$c_{2k} = z_{2k}, \quad c_{2k+1} = -z_{N-2-2k}, \quad k = 0, 1, \ldots, \frac{N}{4} - 1. \tag{6}$$

The model of selected algorithm is used for verification and optimization of an internal computational structure and it is also used under optimization routines with many loops. Therefore, the model has to be designed more efficiently in comparison to the algorithm verification model. MATLAB can calculate matrix equations more efficiently than equations written in linear code. A model described by matrix equations can reduce computation time significantly. This is very important when the model is a part of optimization process with many loops, because the saved computation time is multiplied by a number of loops.
Equations (5) can be transformed to matrix form

$$\mathbf{x}^{'} = \mathbf{X}_{N/2\times N}^{'}\mathbf{x}, \quad \mathbf{x}^{''} = \mathbf{X}_{N/2\times N}^{''}\mathbf{x}, \tag{7}$$

where matrices $\mathbf{X}_{N/2\times N}^{'}$ and $\mathbf{X}_{N/2\times N}^{''}$ are spare matrices that compute addition or subtraction of two input data. They can be merged to single matrix $\mathbf{X1}_{N\times N}$. These matrices model a set of adders and subtracters and can be used as a part of hardware architecture model. They are given by

$$\mathbf{X}_{N/2\times N}^{'} = \left[\mathbf{I}_{N/2}\ -\mathbf{J}_{N/2}\right], \quad \mathbf{X}_{N/2\times N}^{''} = \left[\mathbf{I}_{N/2}\ \mathbf{J}_{N/2}\right], \quad \mathbf{X1}_{N\times N} = \begin{bmatrix} \mathbf{I}_{N/2} & \mathbf{J}_{N/2} \\ \mathbf{J}_{N/2} & -\mathbf{I}_{N/2} \end{bmatrix}, \tag{8}$$

where $\mathbf{I}_{N/2}$ is the identity matrix, $\mathbf{J}_{N/2}$ is the reflection matrix, all of order $N/2$. The matrix $\mathbf{X1}_{N\times N}$ written in MATLAB is shown in the following example.

```
X1 = [    eye(N/2)        fliplr(eye(N/2));
       fliplr(eye(N/2))        -eye(N/2)   ];
```

Equation (4) can be decomposed into several stand-alone operations that are easily transformed to spare matrices. The first matrix $\mathbf{X2}_{N/2\times N}$ represents subtraction in the brackets of equation (4). The second matrix $\mathbf{G}_{N\times N/2}$ represents multiplication by cosines and sines constants. The third matrix $\mathbf{G2}_{N/2\times N}$ represents the remaining subtraction and addition. The matrix $\mathbf{X2}_{N/2\times N}$ models a set of subtracters, matrix $\mathbf{G}_{N\times N/2}$ models a set of multipliers and $\mathbf{G2}_{N/2\times N}$ models a set of adders and subtracters. They are given by

$$\mathbf{X2}_{N/2\times N} = \begin{bmatrix} \mathbf{0}_{N/4} & -\mathbf{I}_{N/4} & \mathbf{0}_{N/4} & \mathbf{I}_{N/4} \\ \mathbf{I}_{N/4} & \mathbf{0}_{N/4} & -\mathbf{I}_{N/4} & \mathbf{0}_{N/4} \end{bmatrix}, \quad \mathbf{G2}_{N/2\times N} = \begin{bmatrix} \mathbf{I}_{N/4} & \mathbf{0}_{N/4} & -\mathbf{I}_{N/4} & \mathbf{0}_{N/4} \\ \mathbf{0}_{N/4} & \mathbf{I}_{N/4} & \mathbf{0}_{N/4} & \mathbf{I}_{N/4} \end{bmatrix}, \tag{9}$$

$$\mathbf{G}_{N\times N/2} = \begin{bmatrix} cos\frac{(N/2-1)\pi}{2N} & & & & & & & \\ & \ddots & & & & & & \\ & & cos\frac{3\pi}{2N} & & & & & \\ & & & cos\frac{\pi}{2N} & & & & \\ & & & & cos\frac{\pi}{2N} & & & \\ & & & & & cos\frac{3\pi}{2N} & & \\ & & & & & & \ddots & \\ & & & & & & & cos\frac{(N/2-1)\pi}{2N} \\ & & & & & & & sin\frac{(N/2-1)\pi}{2N} \\ & & & & & & \therefore & \\ & & & & & sin\frac{3\pi}{2N} & & \\ & & & & sin\frac{\pi}{2N} & & & \\ & & & sin\frac{\pi}{2N} & & & & \\ & & sin\frac{3\pi}{2N} & & & & & \\ & \therefore & & & & & & \\ sin\frac{(N/2-1)\pi}{2N} & & & & & & & \end{bmatrix}, \tag{10}$$

where $\mathbf{0}_{N/4}$ is the zero matrix, $\mathbf{I}_{N/4}$ is the identity matrix, $\mathbf{J}_{N/4}$ is the reflection matrix, all of order $N/4$. The matrices $\mathbf{X2}_{N/2\times N}$, $\mathbf{G}_{N\times N/2}$ and $\mathbf{G2}_{N/2\times N}$ written in MATLAB are shown in the following example.

```
X2 = [zeros(N/4) -eye(N/4)   zeros(N/4)    eye(N/4);
       eye(N/4)   zeros(N/4)   -eye(N/4)   zeros(N/4)];
G = [    diag(cos((((N/2)-(1:2:N/2))*pi)/(2*N)))         zeros(N/4);
      zeros(N/4)      diag(fliplr(cos((((N/2)-(1:2:N/2))*pi)/(2*N))));
      zeros(N/4)      fliplr(diag(sin((((N/2)-(1:2:N/2))*pi)/(2*N))));
     flipud(diag(sin((((N/2)-(1:2:N/2))*pi)/(2*N))))    zeros(N/4) ];
G2 = [ eye(N/4)   zeros(N/4) -eye(N/4)   zeros(N/4);
      zeros(N/4)   eye(N/4)   zeros(N/4)   eye(N/4) ];
```

Equation (6) represents permutation operations that change signs and order of data. It can be transformed to the matrix form. The source code of the resulting matrix $\mathbf{Q}_{N/2\times N/2}$ is shown in the following MATLAB example.

```
function Q = permatrix(N);
Q = zeros(N/2);
for k = 1:(N/4)
Q(2*k-1, k) = 1;
Q(2*k, N/2-k+1) = -1;
end
```

The most complex part of the selected algorithm is equation (3). It represents N/4-point DCT-II and N/4-point DST-II combined by a butterfly operation Britanak & Rao (2002). DCT-II and DST-II can be represented by a matrix but it cannot be generated universally for any N/4 due to their not symmetrical internal computational structure. The MDCT computational model is optimized for audio standard MP3 that uses 36-point MDCT for slowly changing audio signal and 12-point MDCT for rapidly changing audio signal. Hence, the model requires 9-point DCT-II/DST-II and 3-point DCT-II/DST-II matrices. The matrices DCT-II and DST-II are similar and it is possible to transform one to the other with simple modifications. The procedure to transforming DST-II to DCT-II is described in Britanak (2002). The transformation is composed of extra operations that invert each odd input data and reverse order of all input data. It results in one DCT-II that is used two times with different sets of data. This is advantageous when dedicated hardware architecture is to be designed. The single hardware block can be optimized within shorter time and overall hardware architecture can be reduced easily by multiplexing input data from two datasets to single hardware block. The 9-point DCT-II matrix can be derived directly from the mathematic equation. The result is a matrix that represents many operations of addition and multiplication. The number of these operations can be reduced significantly by matrix decomposition to several spare matrices or by optimized linear code. The both principles utilize computation with partial results that influence several output data. It is more efficient to use already computed partial results during the following computations than to calculate all results from input data only. The 9-point DCT-II matrix $\mathbf{DC}_{9\times 9}$ written in MATLAB is shown in the following example.

```
u = 2 * pi / 9;
d1 = sqrt(3)/2;
d2 = 0.5;
d3 = cos(4*u);
d4 = cos(2*u);
d5 = cos(u);
d6 = sin(4*u);
d7 = sin(2*u);
d8 = sin(u);
DC = [ 1        1    1        1        1   1        1        1    1;
       d7       d1   d8       (d7-d8)  0   (d8-d7)  -d8      -d1  -d7;
       -d3      d2   (d3+d5)  -d5      -1  -d5      (d3+d5)  d2   -d3;
       d1       0    -d1      -d1      0   d1       d1       0    -d1;
   -(d3+d4)     -d2  d3       d4       1   d4       d3       -d2  -(d3+d4);
     (d7-d6)    -d1  -d6      d7       0   -d7      d6       d1   (d6-d7);
       d2       -1   d2       d2       -1  d2       d2       -1   d2;
       d6       -d1  (d6+d8)  -d8      0   d8       -(d6+d8) d1   -d6;
```

```
d4    -d2   d5    -(d4+d5) 1  -(d4+d5)   d5   -d2      d4];
```

It can be seen from the 9-point DCT-II example that the matrix $\mathbf{DC}_{9\times9}$ is not a spare matrix. It is composed of many nonzero constants. Most of them are not equal to power of 2; hence, shift operations are used rarely. When the computation of this matrix is carried out directly, the number of multiplications is equal to the number of matrix elements that are not equal to ±1 or 0. The number of multiplications is equal to 60. 12 of them are multiplication by 0.5 and therefore the number of nontrivial multiplication is 48.

Many scientific papers oriented to reduction of mathematical operations within specific algorithms were published. The research in this area of interest is highly valued. The paper Britanak & Rao (2001) presents linear code that requires 10 multiplications for a computation of 9-point DCT-II and 2 of them are multiplication by 0.5. The optimized linear code needs 6-times less multiplications. This code can be transformed to a set of spare matrices that calculate results with minimized number of mathematical operations when multiplied in correct order. One version of these spare matrices is shown in the following MATLAB example.

```
DC1 = [  0  0  0  1  0  1  0  0  0;
         0  0  0  1  0 -1  0  0  0;
         0  0  1  0  0  0  1  0  0;
         0  0 -1  0  0  0  1  0  0;
         0  1  0  0  0  0  0  1  0;
         0  1  0  0  0  0  0 -1  0;
         1  0  0  0  0  0  0  0  1;
        -1  0  0  0  0  0  0  0  1;
         0  0  0  0  1  0  0  0  0];

DC2 = [  0   0   0   0   1   0   0   0   1;
         1   0   1   0   0   0   0   0   0;
         0   0   1   0   0   0  -1   0   0;
         1   0   0   0   0   0  -1   0   0;
         1   0  -1   0   0   0   0   0   0;
         0   1   0  -1   0   0   0   0   0;
         0   0   0   1   0   0   0   1   0;
         0   1   0   0   0   0   0  -1   0;
         0   1   0   1   0   0   0   0   0;
         0   0   0   0   0  -d1  0   0   0;
         0   0   0   0  d2   0   0   0   0;
         0   0   0   0   0   0   1   0   0;
         0   0   0   0   0   0   0   1   0;
         0   0   0   0   0   0   0   0   1];

DC3 = [  0  1  0  0  0  0  0  0  0  0  0  1  0  0;
         0  0  0  0  0  1  0  0  0  0  0  0  1  0;
         0  0 -d3 0  0  0  0  0  0  0  0  0  0  0;
         0  0  0 -d4 0  0  0  0  0  0  0  0  0  0;
         0  0  0  0 -d5 0  0  0  0  0  0  0  0  0;
         0  0  0  0  0  0 -d6 0  0  0  0  0  0  0;
         0  0  0  0  0  0  0 -d7 0  0  0  0  0  0;
         0  0  0  0  0  0  0  0 -d8 0  0  0  0  0;
```

```
          0  0  0  0  0  0  0  0  0  0 -1  0  0  1;
          1  0  0  0  0  0  0  0  0  0  0  0  0  0;
          0  0  0  0  0  0  0  0  0  1  0  0  0  0];

DC4 = [ d2 0  0  0  0  0  0  0  0  0  0;
        0 -d1 0  0  0  0  0  0  0  0  0;
        0  0  1  0  0  0  0  0  1  0  0;
        0  0 -1  0  0  0  0  0  1  0  0;
        0  0  0  1  0  0  0  0  1  0  0;
        0  0  0  0  0  1  0  0  0  0  1;
        0  0  0  0  0 -1  0  0  0  0  1;
        0  0  0  0  0  0  1  0  0  0  1;
        1  0  0  0  0  0  0  0  0  1  0;
        0  0  0  0  0  0  0  0  0  1  0;
        0  0  0  1  0  0  0  0  0  0  0;
        0  0  0  0  1  0  0  0  0  0  0;
        0  0  0  0  0  0  1  0  0  0  0;
        0  0  0  0  0  0  0  1  0  0  0];

DC5 = [ 0  0  0  0  0  0  0  0  1  0  0  0  0  0;
        0  0  0  0  0  0  0 -1  0  0  0  0  0  1;
        0  0 -1  0  0  0  0  0  0  0  0  1  0  0;
        0  1  0  0  0  0  0  0  0  0  0  0  0  0;
        0  0  0  1  0  0  0  0  0  0 -1  0  0  0;
        0  0  0  0  0  0  1  0  0  0  0  0 -1  0;
        1  0  0  0  0  0  0  0  0 -1  0  0  0  0;
        0  0  0  0  0  1  0  0  0  0  0  0  0  1;
        0  0  0  0  1  0  0  0  0  0  0  1  0  0];
```

The matrices $\mathbf{DC1}_{9\times9}$, $\mathbf{DC2}_{14\times9}$, $\mathbf{DC3}_{11\times14}$, $\mathbf{DC4}_{14\times11}$ and $\mathbf{DC5}_{9\times14}$ use the same constants as the matrix $\mathbf{DC}_{9\times9}$ from the previous example. They are designed to model hardware architecture. Addition or subtraction operations have only two inputs which is characteristic for hardware implementations. Mutual addition of more input data is distributed through several matrices. The last few lines of the several matrices perform no mathematical operation. These lines provide access to input data or partial results for the following matrices.

Computation of 9-point DST-II with 9-point DCT-II requires two small modifications. Inversion of odd input data can be modeled by a modified identity matrix that has all odd diagonal elements equal to -1. Reverse order of input data can be modeled by a reflection matrix. These two matrices are used together with $\mathbf{DC1}_{9\times9}$ during computation of 9-point DST-II. The computations of 9-point DCT-II and 9-point DST-II are done independently with clearly separated input data and results. The model with both 9-point DCT-II and 9-point DST-II is shown in the following MATLAB example.

```
M1 = [ fliplr(eye(9)), zeros(9);
              zeros(9),     eye(9)];
M2 = diag([ones(1,9), repmat([1 -1],1,4), 1 ]);
DCC1 = [ DC1     zeros(9);
        zeros(9)   DC1    ];
DCS1 = DCC1*M2*M1;
DCS2 = [      DC2     zeros(14,9);
```

```
         zeros(14,9)       DC2     ];
DCS3  =  [      DC3     zeros(11,14);
         zeros(11,14)      DC3     ];
DCS4  =  [      DC4     zeros(14,11);
         zeros(14,11)      DC4     ];
DCS5  =  [      DC5     zeros(9,14);
         zeros(9,14)      DC5      ];
```

The results from DCT-II and DST-II are combined by a butterfly operation. It is a symmetrical operation and therefore can be described universally for any $N/4$ by a matrix $\mathbf{D}_{N/2\times N/2}$. The matrix written in MATLAB is shown in the following example.

```
D = [        1,                          zeros(1,N/2-1);
    zeros(N/4-1,1)  eye(N/4-1)  zeros(N/4-1,1) -fliplr(eye(N/4-1));
                    zeros(1,N/4)               -1      zeros(1,N/4-1);
    zeros(N/4-1,1) -fliplr(eye(N/4-1)) zeros(N/4-1,1) -eye(N/4-1)];
```

The presented matrices are the main elements of the MDCT model. The model computation core is composed of multiplications of these matrices in a correct order. The MDCT model is shown in the following MATLAB example.

```
function C = MDCT36(x);
N = 36;
nc = sqrt(2)/2;
u = 2 * pi / 9;
d1 = sqrt(3)/2;
d2 = 0.5;
d3 = cos(4*u);
d4 = cos(2*u);
d5 = cos(u);
d6 = sin(4*u);
d7 = sin(2*u);
d8 = sin(u);
C = nc*Q*D*DCS5*DCS4*DCS3*DCS2*DCS1*G2*G*X2*X1*x;
```

All matrices used in the model are spare matrices with low number of mathematical operations which increases computational speed in MATLAB. They also correspond to basic hardware computational blocks as an adder, subtracter or multiplier. Further optimization of these matrices also improves the resulting hardware architecture.

The MDCT computational model is created. The next step is analysis of data variations. Its results represent actual intervals of data inside the modeled computational structure. The positive and negative extreme input values can cause data overflow or data underflow and therefore it is important to understand how the extreme values are propagated through the computational structure. This knowledge facilitates a selection of appropriate data representations and is necessary when integer representations are selected. Extreme values of partial results can be paired with input data that caused them. These input data can be included into a verification data set and used later to test if overflowing or underflowing can happen. A computational model described by a matrix equation simplifies the analysis process which is based on solving these mathematical equations. The equation

$$\mathbf{y}^{X1} = \mathbf{X1}_{N\times N}\mathbf{x}, \tag{11}$$

can be transformed to a set of equations

$$
\begin{aligned}
y_1^{X1} &= \mathbf{X1}(1,:)\mathbf{x} = \mathbf{X1}(1,1)x_1 + \mathbf{X1}(1,2)x_2 + \ldots \mathbf{X1}(1,N)x_N, \\
y_2^{X1} &= \mathbf{X1}(2,:)\mathbf{x} = \mathbf{X1}(2,1)x_1 + \mathbf{X1}(2,2)x_2 + \ldots \mathbf{X1}(2,N)x_N, \\
&\vdots \\
y_N^{X1} &= \mathbf{X1}(N,:)\mathbf{x} = \mathbf{X1}(N,1)x_1 + \mathbf{X1}(N,2)x_2 + \ldots \mathbf{X1}(N,N)x_N,
\end{aligned}
\tag{12}
$$

where $\mathbf{X1}(i,:)$ is the i-th line of the matrix $\mathbf{X1}_{N\times N}$. The positive extreme value of y_i^{X1} is produced by addition of partial results $\mathbf{X1}(i,j)x_i$ with maximal values that are all positive. This means that if $\mathbf{X1}(i,j)$ is positive then x_i should be maximal value within the interval of input data. If it is negative then x_i should be maximal negative value within the interval of input data. Similarly, the negative extreme value of y_i^{X1} is produced by addition of partial results $\mathbf{X1}(i,j)x_i$ with maximal values that are all negative. The matrix $\mathbf{X1}_{N\times N}$ is very simple with only additions and subtractions and therefore it is intuitive that maximal value of results is double the maximal input value. This simple conclusion is valid only at the beginning of computation. In the middle, it is influenced by the internal constants and computational structure.

The computation of extreme values that are produced by other matrices is done by the same principle. The matrix $\mathbf{X1}_{N\times N}$ in equation (11) is substituted by product of the matrix under investigation and other matrices that precede it. This principle is shown in equation (13). The product of necessary matrices can be calculated easily in MATLAB. The whole process can be also automated by new function created in MATLAB.

$$
\begin{aligned}
\mathbf{y}^{X1} &= \mathbf{MX2} = \mathbf{X2} * \mathbf{X1} * \mathbf{x} \\
\mathbf{y}^{G} &= \mathbf{MG} = \mathbf{G} * \mathbf{X2} * \mathbf{X1} * \mathbf{x} \\
\mathbf{y}^{G2} &= \mathbf{MG2} = \mathbf{G2} * \mathbf{G} * \mathbf{X2} * \mathbf{X1} * \mathbf{x} \\
\mathbf{y}^{DCS1} &= \mathbf{MDCS1} = \mathbf{DCS1} * \mathbf{G2} * \mathbf{G} * \mathbf{X2} * \mathbf{X1} * \mathbf{x} \\
\mathbf{y}^{DCS2} &= \mathbf{MDCS2} = \mathbf{DCS2} * \mathbf{DCS1} * \mathbf{G2} * \mathbf{G} * \mathbf{X2} * \mathbf{X1} * \mathbf{x} \\
\mathbf{y}^{DCS3} &= \mathbf{MDCS3} = \mathbf{DCS3} * \mathbf{DCS2} * \mathbf{DCS1} * \mathbf{G2} * \mathbf{G} * \mathbf{X2} * \mathbf{X1} * \mathbf{x} \\
\mathbf{y}^{DCS4} &= \mathbf{MDCS4} = \mathbf{DCS4} * \mathbf{DCS3} * \mathbf{DCS2} * \mathbf{DCS1} * \mathbf{G2} * \mathbf{G} * \mathbf{X2} * \mathbf{X1} * \mathbf{x} \\
\mathbf{y}^{DCS5} &= \mathbf{MDCS5} = \mathbf{DCS5} * \mathbf{DCS4} * \mathbf{DCS3} * \mathbf{DCS2} * \mathbf{DCS1} * \mathbf{G2} * \mathbf{G} * \mathbf{X2} * \mathbf{X1} * \mathbf{x} \\
\mathbf{y}^{D} &= \mathbf{MD} = \mathbf{D} * \mathbf{DCS5} * \mathbf{DCS4} * \mathbf{DCS3} * \mathbf{DCS2} * \mathbf{DCS1} * \mathbf{G2} * \mathbf{G} * \mathbf{X2} * \mathbf{X1} * \mathbf{x} \\
\mathbf{y}^{Q} &= \mathbf{MQ} = \mathbf{Q} * \mathbf{D} * \mathbf{DCS5} * \mathbf{DCS4} * \mathbf{DCS3} * \mathbf{DCS2} * \mathbf{DCS1} * \mathbf{G2} * \mathbf{G} * \mathbf{X2} * \mathbf{X1} * \mathbf{x}
\end{aligned}
\tag{13}
$$

The next step is optimization of all data representations within the whole computational structure. Integer representations are selected for the MDCT model. The extreme values are known, therefore data overflow is no longer a problem. The aim of the following optimization is to set an optimal ratio between overall computation error, input data precision and output data precision. The MDCT algorithm is composed of many mathematical operations and most of them increase the interval of their results. This means widening of integer interface. An addition usually increases the interface by one bit and a multiplication increases it to double.

The value of the least significant bit (LSB) decreases exponentially with linear increasing of integer interface bit-width. When the LSB value is too small the information that it carries can be discarded without increasing the overall computation error. This can be modeled by introduction of rounding or truncating operations into the model. MATLAB contains internal functions that transform data to binary integer and back. This is shown in the following MATLAB example where b1 is an integer variable and a2 is recovered value of a1 with finite precision set by q.

```
q = quantizer([16,15]);
a1 = 0.54321;
b1 = num2bin(q, a1);
a2 = bin2num(q, b1);
```

The functions used in the previous example take too much time to compute. A faster method to model finite precision of data is the utilization of truncating operations that directly represents discarding of several LSBs. The rounding operation is more complex and requires additional computations. The rounding operation is usually transformed to a combination of addition and truncating operation where the added value is equal to the half of new LSB after rounding. Data in hardware are usually represented in two's-complement arithmetic and discarding of several LSBs in this system represents rounding toward zero. The function that performs rounding toward zero in MATLAB is called **fix()**. The operation of the **fix()** function is confined to the placement of decimal point. The shift of decimal point modifies the amount of data that is going to be discarded. The new data has to be in original form and this implies a second shift of the decimal point in opposite direction. The combination of shift, rounding toward zero and opposite shift can model the truncating operation in hardware. A shift is represented by multiplication of a constant. A constant in the binary shift is equal to power of 2. The positive power represents data shift to the left and negative power stands for data shift to the right. This is shown in the following MATLAB example that is a modification of the MDCT computational model.

```
yX1 = X1*x;
fyX1 = fix(2^s1 * yX1) * 2^(-s1);
yX2 = X2*fyX1;
fyX2 = fix(2^s2 * yX2) * 2^(-s2);
yG = G*fyX2;
fyG = fix(2^s3 * yG) * 2^(-s3);
yG2 = G2*fyG;
fyG2 = fix(2^s4 * yG2) * 2^(-s4);
yDCS1 = DCS1*fyG2;
fyDCS1 = fix(2^s5 * yDCS1) * 2^(-s5);
yDCS2 = DCS2*fyDCS1;
fyDCS2 = fix(2^s6 * yDCS2) * 2^(-s6);
yDCS3 = DCS3*fyDCS2;
fyDCS3 = fix(2^s7 * yDCS3) * 2^(-s7);
yDCS4 = DCS4*fyDCS3;
fyDCS4 = fix(2^s8 * yDCS4) * 2^(-s8);
yDCS5 = DCS5*fyDCS4;
fyDCS5 = fix(2^s9 * yDCS5) * 2^(-s9);
yD = D*fyDCS5;
fyD = fix(2^s10 * yD) * 2^(-s10);
```

```
yQ = Q*fyD;
fyQ = fix(2^s11 * yQ) * 2^(-s11);
C = nc*fyQ;
```

The variables s1, s2, ..., s11 from the previous example represent the precision of partial results. The values of variables are natural numbers and they depend on the input data precision, input data interval and intervals of partial results. They all can be used as inputs of an optimization process where low values of the variables mean low overall computation precision and high values of the variables imply large area of a resulted hardware implementation. Some of them are more important than others. Multiplication doubles the output precision. It means that a multiplier output has two time more bits in comparison to a single multiplier input and therefore the precision of multiplication results has to be modified. Overall computation precision is influenced significantly by precision of internal constants. The MDCT algorithm uses constants three times during the whole computation. The first set of constants is represented by the matrix $\mathbf{G}_{N \times N/2}$. The second set of constants is used during computation of DCT-II and DST-II and the last multiplications by constant represent the normalization of all results by the scaling constant nc. Precision of the internal constants can be optimized together with other variables.

Suitable values of the variables and precision of constants can be set by a simple analysis. Several variables can be set intuitively. One of them is s1 that stands for the precision of matrix $\mathbf{X1}_{N \times N}$. This matrix performs addition and subtraction operations and adding one extra bit is required. The truncating operation at the beginning of computation affects overall computation error more significantly. This truncating operation can be omitted. A similar principle can be done also for matrix $\mathbf{X2}_{N/2 \times N}$. The other variables can be set to the output precision that is increased by one or two bits. The effect of higher precision can be easily visualized up to three dimensions in MATLAB. In direct approach, more dimensions are not possible to show clearly. Therefore, it is useful to modify only two variables at a time when the visualization is the main optimization tool. An example of the described visualization is shown in Figures 1 and 2. As can be seen, the multiplication results with bit-width wider than 20 bits does not improve overall precision in the specific situation shown in Figures 1 and 2. The combination of visualizations and intuitive approach usually result in a set of suitable variable and parameter values within short time. However, complex optimization routines are necessary to calculate the best set of variables and parameters.

4. Refinement of computational models and their application

Computational models are used in analyses, simulations and optimization processes. They are the key elements to further improve the parameters of future products. Optimized computational models represent hardware architectures that are later implemented as hardware prototypes. Verification of hardware prototypes and their following modifications are necessary. Hardware prototypes are designed in different platforms; therefore, direct verification is not possible. Verification models have been created to test designed computational models. The mechanism to generate input stimuli and pair them with correct results can be utilized. The necessary modifications have to be made to transform generated data to the specific data representations that are used in hardware prototypes. The models can be upgraded to write the transformed data to an external file that is directly used as input of a verification process. The modification of the final computational model allows to include not only input output pairs but also data that represent partial results of the internal computational structure.

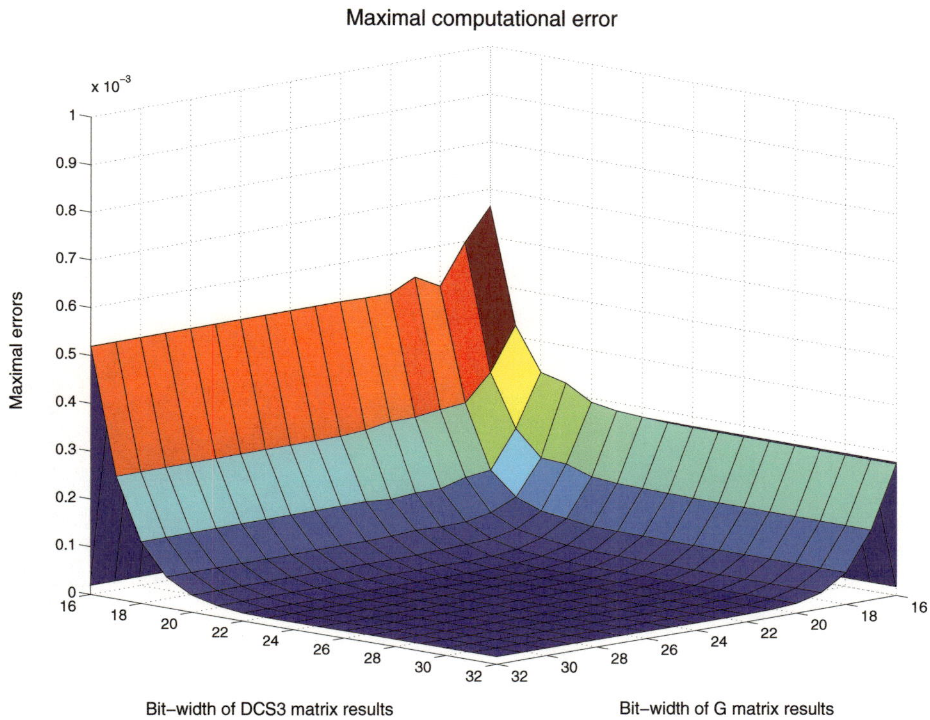

Fig. 1. Maximal computational error dependence on the bit-width of multiplication results.

The most important parameters of the hardware chip are the area, speed or frequency and delay. These parameters depend significantly on implementation technology. They cannot be calculated directly or at least without extremely complex models. Low abstraction level models are capable to compute them with high precision but they are too time demanding. They are used usually only for verification or fine-tuning during the final steps of the design process. The problem is that these parameters are necessary within the optimization process. They are important factors of final product specification. At the same time, they represent feasibility boundaries. The chip with the area larger than few hundreds square millimeters is not possible to produce and it is the same with too high frequency. Many other parameters influence their values, e.g., higher precision stands for larger area. Precision can be easily modeled and accurately calculated. However, this is not true for the area. An optimization process has to be able to evaluate the effect of increased precision to the area. Otherwise, a cost of increased precision cannot be assessed.

Time consuming calculations can be replaced by an estimation. The advantage is in significantly reduced computation complexity. This allows to use an estimation as a part of the optimization process and to optimize other parameters more efficiently. A disadvantage is in limited accuracy. In general, estimation of some complex parameter, e.g., the area, can be implemented into computational models with any abstraction levels. Estimation capabilities of higher abstraction models produce more coarse results. However, the accuracy can be improved by increasing the amount of data that the estimation is based on. The estimation data can be taken from many diverse situations and can be represented by many different forms. The most common procedure is to take data from well known previous situations or

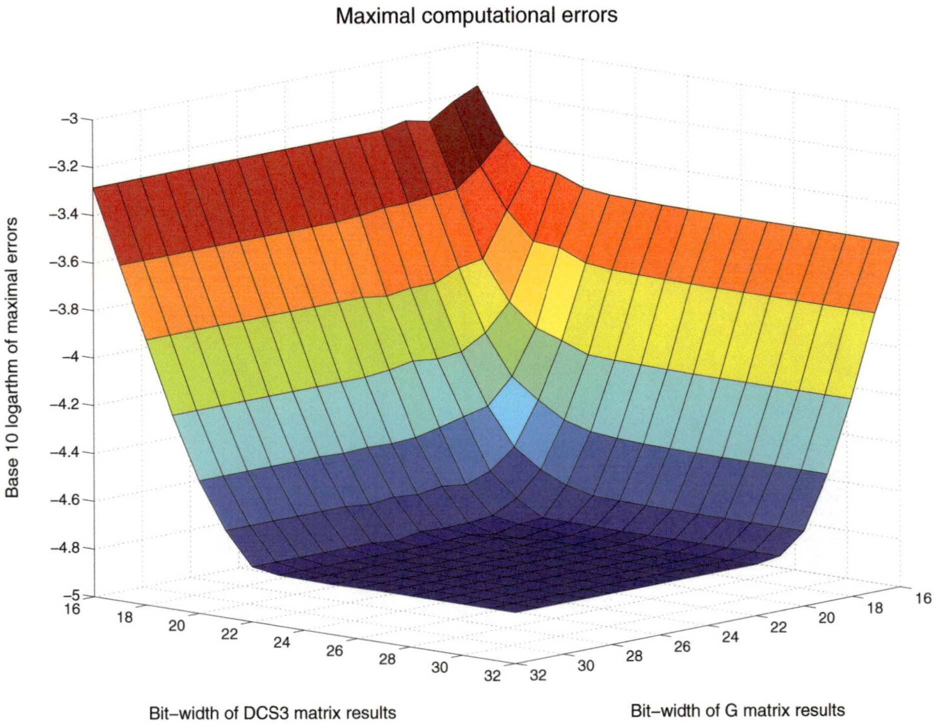

Fig. 2. Maximal computational error dependence on the bit-width of multiplication results displayed in base 10 logarithmic scale.

product versions and to interpolate between them. Higher number of situations or different versions imply a better interpolation and also more accurate estimation.

An estimated parameter is dependent on many other parameters. Each parameter included into estimation function increases the number of dimensions that the interpolation has to work with. An estimation can be simplified by reducing this number with selecting only the most important parameters. A simplified estimation can be used at the beginning of optimization process together with higher abstraction computational models. When more data are accumulated, additional parameters can be used to increase accuracy. Later, the new data can be taken from early prototypes which further improves accuracy.

More refined computational models can be transformed to independent applications. This can be useful when a product is a part of a more complex unit. Teams that design other parts can test mutual features and integration capability much sooner. Another example is the hardware-software co-design. The created applications can allow to test new software before the hardware is actually produced. Computational models with improved estimation capabilities can be transformed to applications that are offered together with final products as an extra tool. This is useful for universal products with several setting values or many parameters that can be modified by customers.

An independent application requires to design an input/output interface for users. The best choice is a graphical interface that is easy to understand and can be operated intuitively. MATLAB is a great tool to design computational models. The models can also be upgraded with a new graphical interface. MATLAB is also able to transform their source code to independent application that can be run on a common PC.

5. Modifications of the MDCT computational model to improve hardware architecture parameters

The most important goal of computational models is to improve the resulting hardware implementation or some parameters of final chip. The original MDCT computational model had been continually upgraded. Modifications were oriented to simplify the computational structure, reduce mathematical operations and improve generality. Changes were done to the algorithm, order, type and number of mathematical operations, computational pipeline and level of parallel computations.

The first major modification is oriented to a simplification of the computational structure located between inputs and first multiplications. This part is described by mathematical equations (4) and (5) or by matrices $\mathbf{X1}_{N\times N}$, $\mathbf{X2}_{N/2\times N}$, $\mathbf{G}_{N\times N/2}$, $\mathbf{G2}_{N/2\times N}$ of the MDCT computational model. Basic algebraic manipulations applied to these equations transform several additions of input data to additions of internal constants. The constants are not changed during the whole computation process and therefore the addition of internal constants can be calculated in advance. This produces new constants that are used as replacement of the original constants and the overall number of addition operations is reduced. This process is presented in Šimlaštík et al. (2006).

Another modification is associated with a scaling factor. The MDCT algorithm uses the scaling constant nc that is applied to all results. Algebraic manipulation can change the position of this multiplication and combine it with any matrix of the MDCT computational model. The matrix $\mathbf{DCS3}_{22\times 28}$ represents multiplication by constants; however, few of them are equal to ± 0.5 that can be implemented by shift operations. Combination of the scaling factor with these constants nullifies this advantage and then a standard multiplier has to be used. The best option is to use the matrix $\mathbf{G}_{N\times N/2}$ again. In this situation, the new constants are calculated as a product of scaling factor and original constants. This results in a reduced number of multipliers used within MDCT computational structure Malík et al. (2006).

The original MDCT computational structure does not differentiate between addition of both positive, combination of positive and negative and both negative input variables. Addition of both positive input variables is implemented by an adder. Addition of one positive and one negative is implemented by a subtracter. Addition of two negative input variables is implemented by a combination of inverter and subtracter. The inverter changes the sign of the first input and then the subtracter calculates the result. The problem is that this operation is not usually implemented into standard computation blocks and extra inverters increase the final area. The solution lies in further optimization of the MDCT computational structure. The inversion can be separated from the subtraction and combined with preceding mathematical operations by applying basic algebraic manipulations. The separated operation of inversion can be completely absorbed and then the extra inverter is omitted. An example of this situation is described by equations (14) and (15).

$$e = a - b, \quad f = c + d, \quad g = -e - f, \tag{14}$$

$$e = -(a - b) = -a + b = b - a, \quad f = c + d, \quad g = e - f. \tag{15}$$

The sign change of the variable e in equation (15) is done by exchanging the input variables a and b before the variable e is calculated. Internal constants can also be used to completely absorbed extra inversions. In this case, new constants are equal to product of -1 and original constants which is the same as inversion of the original constants. The MDCT computational model described by matrix equations is a great advantage, because the inversion separation can be written by matrix decomposition. The new matrix that depicts separated inversions is spare diagonal matrix with most diagonal elements equal to 1 and only the elements that represent inversions under investigation equal to -1. MATLAB can easily calculate the product of this matrix with a preceding matrix. If the result does not represent a situation when extra inversion can be absorbed completely, MATLAB can calculate new matrix decomposition and then the process is repeated. Optimized MDCT hardware architecture with reduced extra inverters is presented in Malík et al. (2006).

The next major modification allows computation of backward MDCT by the computational structure optimized for forward MDCT. This means that computation of forward and backward MDCT can be calculated by the same MDCT kernel. Complexity of the required changes within MDCT computational structure is not high which was presented in Cho et al. (2004) with a different MDCT algorithm. The changes are related to the inversion of several signals and modification of the input and output parts of the MDCT computational structure. Backward MDCT has twice as many outputs than inputs which is exactly opposite in comparison to forward MDCT. The matrices at the beginning and at the end of the MDCT computational structure were modified to include this. Backward MDCT uses extra scaling factor equal to $2/N$ that was absorbed to internal constants. Modified MDCT computational structure and resulted hardware architecture is presented in Malík (2007).

The MDCT computational structure is composed of many mathematical operations. When they are implemented directly the resulted hardware consumes a large area. The advantage is in high computational speed. However, higher computational speed can be achieved by increasing operational frequency and therefore the large area is a disadvantage. The area can be scaled down by separating mathematical operations to different time periods. It is actually a reduction of parallel computational level. This process requires to add memory elements into architecture to store partial results and to keep them unchanged for several computational cycles. The symmetrical computational structure, e.g., the butterfly structure, can be scaled down intuitively. In this case, all results are described by the same equation with different input variables. This means that computational structure of a single result is able to compute other results if a mechanism that selects different input variables is attached to it. The situation is more difficult when a computational structure is not symmetrical, because the universal computational structure dedicated for several results has to be designed manually. This is usually a challenging and time consuming process.

The memory elements added into computational structure can be used to introduce a pipeline computation. A pipelined computational structure represents a computational structure that is divided into several parts and all these parts compute their partial results at the same time. The aim is to design these parts so the whole computation process is continual and none part has to wait for its input data. This results in significantly increased computational speed without increasing operational frequency. A minor disadvantage is in induced computational delay. The MDCT computational structure with reduced parallel computational level and pipelined computation is presented in Malík (2007).

The MDCT computational model was upgraded with estimation capabilities. The estimated parameter is the area described in 4-input Look-Up Tables (LUTs) which are basic computational blocks used in FPGA technology. The FPGA chips were used for hardware prototyping. Estimation data were taken from elementary prototypes. The estimation uses a linear interpolation to calculate estimated results. The estimated results of this simple model had been used within the optimization process. However, later evaluation showed that the

Complete	Computation	4-input LUTs	Flip flops	Frequency	Latency
No optimization	MDCT	18661	8174	32.26 MHz	341 ns
After optimization	MDCT / IMDCT	15536	1269	41.67 MHz	192 ns

Table 1. 36-point MDCT prototypes implemented into FPGA

Complete	4-input LUTs	Flip flops	Frequency	Latency
No optimization	100 %	100 %	100 %	100 %
After optimization	83.3 %	15.5 %	129.2 %	56.3 %
Difference	-16.7 %	-84.5 %	29.2 %	-43.7 %

Table 2. Comparison of 36-point MDCT prototypes implemented into FPGA

estimated results were significantly different in comparison to prototypes. A further analysis showed that the generated set of input parameters represents hardware architecture with acceptable overall parameters and the estimation was not upgraded further.
The MDCT computational model was used to calculate optimal input parameters. These parameters represent the precision of internal constants and several partial results. The necessary input variables are input precision and overall computation precision. The optimization process is presented in Malík et al. (2006).

6. Evaluation of the optimization process

Several hardware prototypes were implemented into FPGA technology. The first prototype represents implementation of MDCT hardware architecture without any optimization. It is implementation of a complete MDCT computational structure based on the selected MDCT algorithm. The resulted parameters are shown in the first line of Table 1.
The second line of Table 1 represents parameters of the optimized MDCT computational structure with no reduction of parallel computational level. This prototype is able to calculate both forward and backward MDCT. The comparison of these two prototypes from Table 1 is shown in Table 2.
As can be seen in Table 2, all parameters were improved. The highest improvement is in reduction of internal memory elements, represented by flip flops, which are reduced by nearly 85 %. The latency is reduced by 44 % which is also induced by operational frequency increased by 29 %. The area of the combination logic, represented by 4-input LUTs, was reduced by nearly 17 %.
The MDCT implementations with a complete computational structure consume too large area and therefore several prototypes with a reduced level of parallel computation were implemented. The parameters of two such prototypes are shown in Table 3 and Table 4.
The first lines of Table 3 and Table 4 represent parameters of the first reduced MDCT computational structure that was designed directly from the complete MDCT computational structure shown in the first line of Table 1. The reduced implementation prototype has only minimal extra optimizations. The second lines of Table 3 and Table 4 represent parameters of the reduced MDCT computational structure that was designed from the optimized MDCT computational structure with no reduction of parallel computational level shown in the

Reduced	Computation	4-input LUTs	Flip flops	TBUFs	Block RAM
No optimization	MDCT	5472	2467	2070	0
After optimization	MDCT / IMDCT	3275	1752	0	0

Table 3. 36-point MDCT prototypes with reduced level of parallel computation implemented into FPGA

Reduced	Frequency	Clock period	Computation	Latency	Latency
No optimization	18.52 MHz	54 ns	18 x CLK	26 x CLK	1 404 ns
After optimization	35.71 MHz	28 ns	18 x CLK	42 x CLK	1 176 ns

Table 4. 36-point MDCT prototypes with reduced level of parallel computation implemented into FPGA

Reduced	4-input LUTs	Flip flops	TBUFs	Frequency	Latency
No optimization	100 %	100 %	100 %	100 %	100 %
After optimization	59.9 %	71.0 %	0.0 %	192.9 %	83.8 %
Difference	-40.1 %	-29.0 %	-100 %	92.9 %	-16.2 %

Table 5. Comparison of 36-point MDCT prototypes with reduced level of parallel computation implemented into FPGA

second line of Table 1. The comparison of the two implemented prototypes with a reduced level of parallel computation is shown in Table 5.

As can be seen in Table 5, all parameters were improved. The highest improvement is in increasing operational frequency by nearly 93 %. This is partially caused by introducing a computational pipeline with 3 stages. As a result the latency is reduced by 16 % even though the number of clock cycles that represent latency is increased (see the fifth column of Table 4). Internal memory elements are reduced by 29 %. The area of the combinational logic is reduced by 40 % and additionally no tree-state buffers (TBUFs) were used. The optimized reduced prototype is able to calculate both forward and backward MDCT.

The MDCT hardware prototypes were also implemented into two ASIC technologies. Comparison between implementation into AMS 350nm CMOS standard cell library and implementation into UMC 90nm CMOS low power digital library technology with clock gating technique is presented in Malík et al. (2009).

The all MDCT computational models were designed in MATLAB. Most optimization work and time consuming calculations were also done in MATLAB, which substantially contributed to overall improvements. Additionally, many internal MATLAB functions were used to generate random input values and to visualize results, which accelerated the whole optimization process significantly.

7. Conclusion

The technology of integrated circuit production has been significantly improved which resulted in very high integration of currently produced chips. The advantage is in lower cost and higher computational speed of produced chips. Higher functionality represents increased complexity of the internal computational structure that has to be designed. The designed hardware architecture has to be optimized. Each small improvement that reduces the chip final area, represents lower cost of the produced chips. This is very important in high volume productions where the savings can grow to high values. Computer aided design systems represent powerful tools that facilitate and speed up the design process. Most of these tools include complex low abstraction level models that are able to optimize parameters of the final chip. However, they are not suitable for a general optimization, because they are too computation power demanding. An increase of modern chip complexity resulted in more optimization steps that use models with higher abstraction level. MATLAB is an excellent software platform that can be used to design, verify and highly optimize these computational models. The optimization with higher abstraction level models is faster and therefore wider intervals of input parameters and more suitable solutions can be evaluated. This implies the final chip with better parameters and lower cost.

Many computational models have to be created during the whole design process. The feasibility study and early design steps are examples where the computational models are created anew. MATLAB includes extensive database of internal functions that can be directly used into computational models which reduces the time necessary to design them. The created models have to be verified and therefore the ability to generate input test data and to analyze and visualize the calculated results is necessary. This is supported by embedded MATLAB functions and the representing functions are easy to use. Additional manipulation with calculated data further improves the effect of visualizations.

The design process of computational models created in MATLAB was presented by MDCT computational models. The presented models are oriented to different tasks with a common goal to improve parameters of the resulting hardware architecture and its implementation to a chip. The effect of the optimization process was shown by the comparison of several hardware prototypes implemented into FPGA technology during different optimization phase. The parameters of the optimized prototypes are significantly improved. The improvements range from 17 % to 93 %.

8. References

Beauchamp, M. J., Hauck, S., Underwood, K. D. & Hemmert, K. S. (2008). Architectural Modifications to Enhance the Floating-Point Performance of FPGAs, *IEEE Transactions on Very Large Scale Integration (VLSI) Systems* 16(2): 177–187.

Bosi, M. & Goldberg, R. E. (2003). *Introduction to Digital Audio Coding and Standards*, Springer Science + Business Media, Inc., New York, NY.

Britanak, V. (2002). The refined efficient implementation of the mdct in mp3 and comparison with other methods, *Technical Report IISAS-2002-2*, Institute of Informatics SAS, Bratislava.

Britanak, V. & Rao, K. (2002). A New Fast Algorithm for the Unified Forward and Inverse MDCT/MDST Computation, *Signal Processing* 82(3): 433–459.

Britanak, V. & Rao, K. R. (2001). An Efficient Implementation of the Forward and Inverse MDCT in MPEG Audio Coding, *IEEE Signal Processing Letters* 8(2): 48–51. Erratum: IEEE Signal Processing Letters, Vol. 8, No. 10, Oct. 2001, p. 279.

Cho, Y.-K., Song, T.-H. & Kim, H.-S. (2004). An optimized algorithm for computing the modified discrete cosine transform and its inverse transform, *Proc. of the IEEE Region 10 International Conference on Analog and Digital Techniques in Electrical Engineering*, Vol. A, Chiang Mai, Thailand, pp. 626–628.

Inacio, C. & Ombres, D. (1996). The DSP Decision fixed point or Floating?, *IEEE Spectrum Magazine of Technology Insiders* 33(9): 72–74.

ITRS (2009). International technology roadmap for semiconductors, 2009 edition executive summary, *Technical report*. `http://www.itrs.net/Links/2009ITRS/2009Chapters_2009Tables/2009_ExecSum.pdf` [Accessed: April 2011].

Kwon, T. J., Sondeen, J. & Draper, J. (2005). Design Trade-Offs in Floating-Point Unit Implementation for Embedded and Processing-In-Memory Systems, *Proc. of the IEEE Circuits and Systems*, USC Inf. Sci. Inst., Marina del Rey, CA, pp. 3331–3334.

Malík, P. (2007). A generic IP Core of Indetical Forward and Inverse 12/36 Point MDCT Architecture and an Architectural Model Simulation Toolbox, *Proc. of. the 14th IEEE International Conference on Electronics, Cirsuits and Systems*, Marrakech, Maroko.

Malík, P., Baláž, M., Pikula, T. & Šimlaštík, M. (2006). MDCT IP Core Generator with Architectural Model Simulation, *Proc. of the IFIP International Conference on Very Large Scale Integration*, Nice, France, pp. 18–23.

Malík, P., Ufnal, M., Łuczyk, A. W., Baláž, M. & Pleskacz, W. (2009). MDCT / IMDCT Low Power Implementations in 90 nm CMOS Technology for MP3 Audio, *Proc. of the IEEE Symposium on Design and Diagnostics of Electronic Circuits and Systems*, Liberec, Czech Republic, pp. 144–147.

Moore, G. E. (1965). Cramming more components onto integrated circuits, *Electronics* 38(8): 114–117.

Princen, J. P. & Bradley, A. B. (1986). Analysis/Synthesis Filter Bank Design Based on Time Domain Aliasing Cancellation, *IEEE Transaction on Acoustic, Speech and Signal Processing* 34(5): 1153–1161.

Princen, J. P., Johnson, A. W. & Bradley, A. B. (1987). Sub-band/transform coding using filter bank designs based on time-domain aliasing cancellation, *Proc. of the IEEE ICASSP'87*, Dallas, TX, pp. 2161–2164.

Spanias, A., Painer, T. & Atti, V. (2007). *Audio Signal Processing and Coding*, John Wiley & Sons, Inc., Hoboken, NJ.

Šimlaštík, M., Malík, P., Pikula, T. & Baláž, M. (2006). FPGA Implementation of a Fast MDCT Algorithm, *Proc. Of the IEEE Workshop on Design and Diagnostics of Electronic Circuits and Systems*, Praha, Czech Technical University Publishing House, pp. 228–233.

6

Results Processing in MATLAB for Photonics Applications

I.V. Guryev, I.A. Sukhoivanov, N.S. Gurieva, J.A. Andrade Lucio and O. Ibarra-Manzano
University of Guanajuato, Campus Irapuato-Salamanca, Division of Engineering
Mexico

1. Introduction

The chapter is intended to provide the reader with powerful and flexible tools based on MATLAB and its open-source analogs for the processing and analyzing the results obtained by means of highly specialized software.

Particularly, in the chapter we give a brief overview of free and open-source as well as shareware software for computation of the photonic crystals characteristics. We concentrate attention mostly to their advantages and drawbacks and give short description of the data files they give results in.

The next parts of the chapter are dedicated to processing of the results obtained within the specific software.

Firstly, we consider the most basic case of plane results represented by a functional dependences. In this part, we are talking about the plane data interpolation, approximation and representation.

Data interpolation may be used as a tool intended to avoid high resolution computation (when scanning, say, through the wavelength or frequency) and, therefore, to reduce computation time which may achieve weeks in the modern numerical problems.

Data approximation allows highly efficient data analysis by means of finding the parameters of the target function. For this reason, the numerically obtained data is approximated (within the certain accuracy) by the analytical functions including variable coefficients which are usually posses physical meaning. As a result of the approximation, the unknown coefficients are found.

Correct and obvious data representation is very important when writing the scientific paper. Therefore, in the end of current part we give an idea of figure formatting.

The next part of the chapter shows reader how to process and represent three-dimensional and multi-dimensional data. Basically, the operations described for plane data is extrapolated to multidimensional data arrays.

In many cases, the results of the complex numerical research is represented in the form of multiple files with similar format. In the next part of the chapter we show how to use MATLAB for merging the data into a single multidimensional array and for representing it in convenient form.

The last part of the chapter is dedicated to the animations creation out of multiple instant data shots. Such form of the data representation is useful when representing time-dependent results as well as multidimensional data arrays.
During all the chapter, we provide reader with working MATLAB codes as well as figures illustrating the programs results. We believe this information together with learning of MATLAB fundamentals *MATLAB manual* (2011) will help young scientists, master and PhD students especially in the area of opto-electronics and photonics to analyze and represent their computation results in the most effective way.

2. Brief review of the Photonic crystals modeling software

Photonic crystals are optical media possessing the periodic modulation of the refractive index. Due to this, the light behavior inside such structures is similar to the one of the electrons in the atomic structures (this gives them the name "Photonic crystals"). Main property the PhCs possesses is the photonic band gap (PBG) which is an optical analog of the electronic band gap in semiconductor materials.
Depending on the geometrical peculiarities, the PhCs are subdivided to several categories. Particularly, there are wide classes of 1D, 2D and 3D PhCs classified by number of dimensions where the variations of the refractive index appear. These classes, in turn, are divided according to the lattice type, existence or absence of the PBG, etc.
The physical principles of the PhCs are well-known and are considered in numerous articles and books Joannopoulos et al. (1995), Lourtioz et al. (2005), Sakoda (2001). There exist numerous methods for modeling the PhC characteristics, which are well described Sakoda (2001), Taflove & Hagness (2005) and are implemented in a numerous software products. This chapter is considered by us as a natural addition to the book Sukhoivanov & Guryev (2009) which describes computation methods of the PhCs characteristics. It is intended to extend and improve the efficiency of the results representation.
Particularly, this section is dedicated to brief introduction into freeware and shareware software for PhC and PhC-based devices basic modeling.
Since the PhC-based devices are investigated intensively today, the crucial moment is the right choice of the computational methods which are implemented in a number of software.
Particularly, the development of the PhC devices require detailed analysis of the PhC eigenstates (or resonant frequencies) as a dependence of the direction of the light propagation. This kind of tasks may be done by means of different methods like analytical one (however, for 1D PhC only), finite differences time domain (FDTD) method, finite elements method (FEM), plane wave expansion method (PWE). Each method has its advantages and drawbacks, they all require different computation time and accuracy and are implemented in a different kinds of software.
The other important problem for PhC investigation is the computation of the field distribution inside the defined structure. Again, in the simplest cases (particularly, in case of 1D PhC with passive optical materials) the field distribution can be found analytically. However, in the most cases the numerical methods are required such as FDTD, FEM, PWE, etc.
Most of the software (especially, free ones) are intended to implement all the aspects of a single methods. However, professional shareware soft implements several different methods allowing the user to investigate the device from different points of view.

2.1 Free and open-source software

Within all the variety of the scientific software available, the developers are allowed to choose between low price and friendly interface. The friendly interface provides the user with a lot of default settings and saves a lot of time which may be spent to the research problems. On the other hand, being more complicated for user, free software requires deep knowledge of physical and mathematical aspects of the investigated area (which is considered by authors as an advantage of free software). Particularly, the scientist intended to investigate the optical properties of the periodic structures has to be well-educated in the fields of solid-state physics, electromagnetism, numerical methods, etc. Having these knowledge, the user may define the problem more precisely and carry out the research at higher level with deeper understanding of the matter of the problem.

Therefore, this part of our review is dedicated to the software which is available online and may be easily tested and learned by reader.

2.1.1 MPB

The MIT Photonic Bands (MPB) *MPB* (2011) software is one of the most powerful tools available freeware which is intended to compute the eigenstates of the photonic crystal of different configurations by means of PWE method. It is written by developers of the PhC theory whose investment into the physics of PhC devices was critical. Therefore, the MPB solves the problems in a most suitable way for the scientists.

However, since MBP runs script files with detailed description of the structure and computation conditions, using of the MBP requires from user high skills, particularly, in solid-state physics and turns computation of even the simplest case into a serious programming task. Several examples provided with the installation help to understand the principles of the structure setup and they may be used as a default structures which is easy to modify and use for other structures.

The program outputs results into console which allows to read them but not analyze. Therefore, file output should be used. Particularly, the field distribution is being output into HDF5 format which is supported by visualization tools like h5utils. However, even for simple analysis, approximation and decoration the user has to use additional software such as MATLAB.

2.1.2 MEEP

Meep (or MEEP) *MEEP* (2011) is a free finite-difference time-domain (FDTD) simulation software package developed at MIT to model electromagnetic systems.

It can be used to successfully compute electromagnetic field distribution inside the PhC-devices made either of linear or nonlinear materials (possessing Kerr of Pockels nonlinearities).

2.2 Shareware software

In contrast to free software, the shareware ones have, in most cases, highly advanced user interface which helps novice to study the new soft and, on the other hand, saves professionals' time keeping them from the necessity of learning side skills such as programming.

As for the PhC modeling, the most advanced computation tools available on the markets are RSoft (namely, BandSolve and FullWave) and Comsol Multiphysics (namely, RF module).

2.2.1 RSoft

RSoft *RSoft* (2011) being developed by the RSoft-group for many years and it have come a long way since its earlier versions to its modern view.
Though its interface has been changed from version to version, it uses the same methods for computation of the PhC characteristics. Namely, BanSolve module allows one to compute the band structures of the PhC as well as its modes' field distribution by means of PWE method while FullWave implements FDTD method applying it to the field distribution computation inside the arbitrary structures and, in special case, the band structure.
The RSoft interface provides user with many useful models generated with default parameters. Moreover, wise linking to the variables allows flexible modifications of the default structures. This allows you to create the simple structure in a several mouse clicks and more advanced structures in several minutes. Among the drawbacks of the interface it should be mentioned too simple 3D structure definition which does not allow visual representation of the structure. To do this, additional software such as MayaVi should be used.
Except the possibility of modifying the structure with variables, RSoft's dialog boxes provide dozens of visual controls allowing definition of an arbitrary structure, computation conditions and the output information.
It should also be mentioned the graphic output of the RSoft. Although it allows analyze the computation results, their quality is unsatisfactory and one have to use additional software to make results representation suitable for publications. Moreover, in case of FullWave module, continuous graphic output essentially slows down the computation process.
In general, the RSoft is a powerful PhC modeling tool which allows solution of wide range of problems. However, results output is performed into the data files only and requires additional postprocessing, particularly, with Matlab.

2.2.2 Comsol Multiphysics

The Comsol Multiphysics *COMSOL* (2011) (previously known as Femlab) allows solving wide variety of problems defined by the partial differential equations in a number of fields of Physics by means of FEM. Particularly, in the area of PhC devices it allows to solve the Helmholtz equation with certain kinds of boundary conditions, thus, giving as a result the electromagnetic field distribution inside the device.
The structure definition as well as setting the properties of the structure, boundary conditions and node conditions are highly visualized and it makes no difficulties in creating computation model.
As for results representation, Comsol Multiphysics provides a lot of different visualization modes in form of 2D, 3D, contour, etc., thus, making for user unnecessary to deal with visualization of quite complicated data structures.
However, field distribution and basic data analysis is not always enough for serious scientific research. In case the PhC device has complex structure and requires detailed analysis of the field distribution (like confinement factor of the waveguide), the output files data should be investigated separately.
Therefore, independent on the convenience of the software itself, the problem of the output data processing is always arising and the best way to carry this out is by means of MATLAB.

3. Data files formats

As a result of computation of any PhC characteristic such as band structure, field distribution, temporal response, etc., the data is alway represented in some special format which can be read and processed with MATLAB.
With simulation software you may obtain several different kinds of data files, namely, the plane data (two-coordinate dependence), 3D data (tree-coordinate dependence), random data (where data points are linked to the mesh nodes), structured data (the data is represented in the form of known structures), multiple files data (usually, the parametric data where each file corresponds to the solution with a single value of the parameter).

3.1 Reading plane data

The data represented in a plane form usually represents the tabulated function of one variable and is really the simplest data format. In many cases, the computational programs output the data in a form of two rows as presented in figure 1

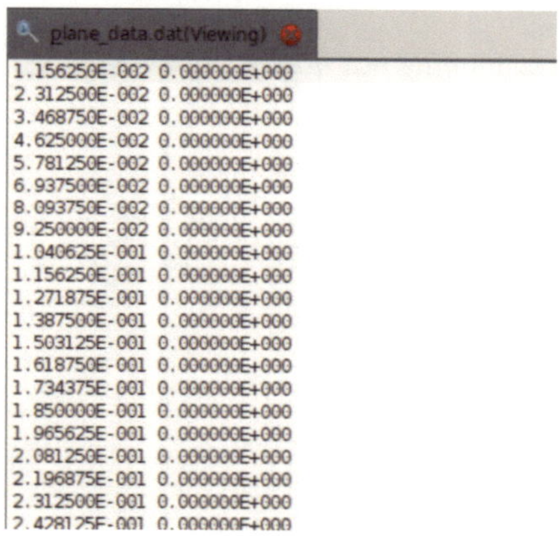
plane_data.dat(Viewing)

```
1.156250E-002 0.000000E+000
2.312500E-002 0.000000E+000
3.468750E-002 0.000000E+000
4.625000E-002 0.000000E+000
5.781250E-002 0.000000E+000
6.937500E-002 0.000000E+000
8.093750E-002 0.000000E+000
9.250000E-002 0.000000E+000
1.040625E-001 0.000000E+000
1.156250E-001 0.000000E+000
1.271875E-001 0.000000E+000
1.387500E-001 0.000000E+000
1.503125E-001 0.000000E+000
1.618750E-001 0.000000E+000
1.734375E-001 0.000000E+000
1.850000E-001 0.000000E+000
1.965625E-001 0.000000E+000
2.081250E-001 0.000000E+000
2.196875E-001 0.000000E+000
2.312500E-001 0.000000E+000
2.428125E-001 0.000000E+000
```

Fig. 1. The example of the plane data file

In the one wants to plot or process this kind of data, then it can be easily read by MATLAB script using a single command:

varName=load(fileName, '-ASCII')

After this, the variable varName contains an array Nx2.
However, in some cases, the plane data file has the text header before the data itself (see figure 2 which demonstrates the data where the first line is a text header). This causes the problem since the data cannot be read with load command from the MATLAB. One of the solution is to use the Import Data dialog (Menu File/Import Data...) which performs smart data analysis and separates the numerical data from the text one.
On the other hand, it is more suitable to integrate the data import procedure into the script in order to avoid manual operations and, to be able to perform multiple import operations when processing multiple data files. For this reason, we have to use standard data reading operations to analyze file. The drawback of this method is necessity to know exactly the file structure, namely, how many strings takes the text header. Here is the simple example of opening the file generated by RSoft and having the text header.

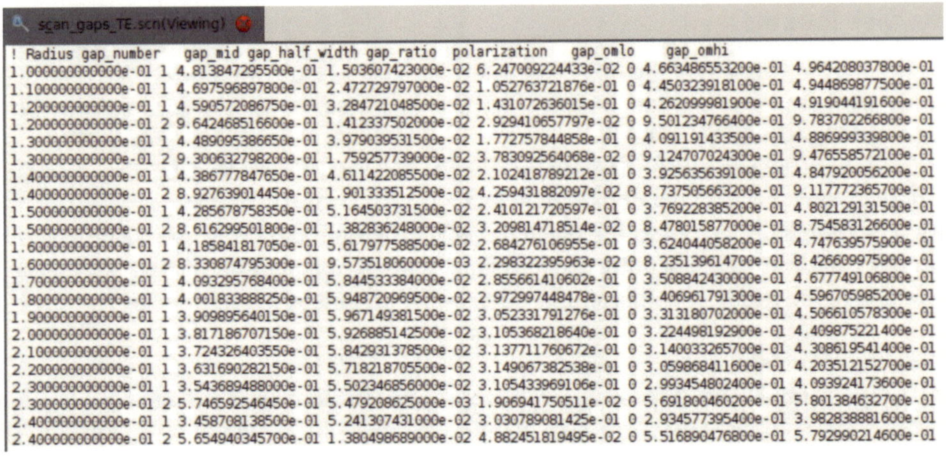


```
! Radius gap_number   gap_mid gap_half_width gap_ratio  polarization   gap_omlo    gap_omhi
1.000000000000e-01 1 4.813847295500e-01 1.503607423000e-02 6.247009224433e-02 0 4.663486553200e-01 4.964208037800e-01
1.100000000000e-01 1 4.697596897800e-01 2.472729797000e-02 1.052763721876e-01 0 4.450323918100e-01 4.944869877500e-01
1.200000000000e-01 1 4.590572086750e-01 3.284721048500e-02 1.431072636015e-01 0 4.262099981900e-01 4.919044191600e-01
1.200000000000e-01 2 9.642468516600e-01 1.412337502000e-02 2.929410657797e-02 0 9.501234766400e-01 9.783702266800e-01
1.300000000000e-01 1 4.489095386650e-01 3.979039531500e-02 1.772757844858e-01 0 4.091191433500e-01 4.886999339800e-01
1.300000000000e-01 2 9.300632798200e-01 1.759257739000e-02 3.783092564068e-02 0 9.124707024300e-01 9.476558572100e-01
1.400000000000e-01 1 4.386777847650e-01 4.611422085500e-02 2.102418789212e-01 0 3.925635639100e-01 4.847920056200e-01
1.400000000000e-01 2 8.927639014450e-01 1.901333512500e-02 4.259431882097e-02 0 8.737505663200e-01 9.117772365700e-01
1.500000000000e-01 1 4.285678758350e-01 5.164503731500e-02 2.410121720597e-01 0 3.769228385200e-01 4.802129131500e-01
1.500000000000e-01 2 8.616299501800e-01 1.382836248000e-02 3.209814718514e-02 0 8.478015877000e-01 8.754583126600e-01
1.600000000000e-01 1 4.185841817050e-01 5.617977588500e-02 2.684276106955e-01 0 3.624044058200e-01 4.747639575900e-01
1.600000000000e-01 2 8.330874795300e-01 9.573518060000e-03 2.298322395963e-02 0 8.235139614700e-01 8.426609975900e-01
1.700000000000e-01 1 4.093295768400e-01 5.844533384000e-02 2.855661410602e-01 0 3.508842430000e-01 4.677749106800e-01
1.800000000000e-01 1 4.001833888250e-01 5.948720969500e-02 2.972997448478e-01 0 3.406961791300e-01 4.596705985200e-01
1.900000000000e-01 1 3.909895640150e-01 5.967149381500e-02 3.052331791276e-01 0 3.313180702000e-01 4.506610578300e-01
2.000000000000e-01 1 3.817186707150e-01 5.926885142500e-02 3.105368218640e-01 0 3.224498192900e-01 4.409875221400e-01
2.100000000000e-01 1 3.724326403550e-01 5.842931378500e-02 3.137711760672e-01 0 3.140033265700e-01 4.308619541400e-01
2.200000000000e-01 1 3.631690282150e-01 5.718218705500e-02 3.149067382538e-01 0 3.059868411600e-01 4.203512152700e-01
2.300000000000e-01 1 3.543689488000e-01 5.502346856000e-02 3.105433969106e-01 0 2.993454802400e-01 4.093924173600e-01
2.300000000000e-01 2 5.746592546450e-01 5.479208625000e-03 1.906941750511e-02 0 5.691800460200e-01 5.801384632700e-01
2.400000000000e-01 1 3.458708138500e-01 5.241307431000e-02 3.030789081425e-01 0 2.934577395400e-01 3.982838881600e-01
2.400000000000e-01 2 5.654940345700e-01 1.380498689000e-02 4.882451819495e-02 0 5.516890476800e-01 5.792990214600e-01
```

Fig. 2. The example of the data file containing text header

```
%Code for reading the data file containing text header

%opening the file
file=fopen('scan_gaps_TE.scn');

%skipping the file header (this part should be modified according
%to the specific file format)
fscanf(file,'%s',9);

%Reading the first line of the data.
%variable 'read' contains the data from the read string,
%variable 'num' contains the number of variables actually read.
%the length of the array to read to should be selected according
%to the dimensions of the data in the file
[read, num]=fscanf(file,'%f',[1,8]);

%Resetting the counter to write into the data array
counter=1;

%main reading cycle. Executes while the data read from the file
%contains actual data (num>0)
while(num)
  %copying the data from temporary variable into the data
  %variable
  data(counter,:)=read;

  %increasing the counter value
  counter=counter+1;

  %reading the next line from the file
  [read, num]=fscanf(file,'%f',[1,8]);
```

end

%closing the data file
fclose(file);

This code opens the data file as a regular file and then uses the function scanf() to read the data of the certain format. Particularly, for the file presented in the figure 2 it first reads 9 strings separated by the whitespaces and then reads each line containing 8 numbers into an array 1x8. Then in the cycle it copies each row into the resulting 2D array.
In case of plane data, each column has its meaning and have to be treated by the program accordingly. For instance, in case of the RSoft file generated by the scanning the full photonic band gaps (PBG) over some parameter, the first row indicates the value of the parameter, the second one is for the number of the PBG starting from the one with the lowest frequency, the third is for the central frequency of the PBG and so on. Detailed information on the specific files formats is usually contained in the manual for the specific software.

3.2 Reading 3D data

3D data is represented in the file in form of 2D array. In this case, each dimension of the array corresponds to the space dimension and, therefore, each number placed in the position (X,Y) in the file is treated as an altitude of the point with coordinates (X*scale,Y*scale). The value of the variable 'scale' depends on the physical dimensions of the structure.
Usually, reading of the 3D data does not differ from reading the plane data. In case of files without headers, the data is read by a simple load() function of the MATLAB. The scale of the structure should be known in this case to be able to assign physical coordinates to the positions in the array.
However, in case of the header presence, we have to use the method described in the subsection 3.1 for plane data. In this case the header may contain useful information such as linking to the physical dimensions, position of the structure, etc (see figure 3).

```
field_high_state.fld(Viewing)
/rn,a,b/nx0/ls1
/r,qa,qb
166 -1.90875 1.906875 148.7053125 OUTPUT_REAL_3D
227 -2.263032633 2.263032633
 0.00000E+000  0.00000E+000  0.00000E+000  0.00000E+000  0.00000E+000  0.00000E+000  0.00000E+000  0.0000
 0.00000E+000  1.16011E-007  2.13808E-007  1.47766E-007  1.45550E-007  1.58532E-006  4.46571E-006  8.7482
 0.00000E+000  3.27156E-007  5.81678E-007  5.07427E-007  7.15404E-007  3.97621E-006  9.73524E-006  2.0548
 0.00000E+000  6.41676E-007  1.12300E-006  1.21800E-006  2.26615E-006  8.41034E-006  1.73899E-005  4.6503
 0.00000E+000  7.75648E-007  1.47682E-006  2.28475E-006  5.69845E-006  1.66589E-005  2.88089E-005  8.2279
 0.00000E+000  3.66530E-007  1.37129E-006  4.07708E-006  1.19842E-005  2.87590E-005  4.05819E-005  6.3685
 0.00000E+000 -3.34949E-007  1.13705E-006  6.07101E-006  1.74831E-005  3.49638E-005  3.66188E-005 -1.6786
 0.00000E+000 -2.60464E-006 -3.42205E-006 -1.52714E-006  4.66920E-006  1.11725E-005 -6.96961E-006 -7.5728
 0.00000E+000 -1.40709E-005 -2.72479E-005 -3.85360E-005 -4.51006E-005 -5.18796E-005 -8.33064E-005 -1.4873
 0.00000E+000 -3.75397E-005 -6.99168E-005 -9.20646E-005 -1.00174E-004 -1.06144E-004 -1.38601E-004 -2.0108
 0.00000E+000 -4.23924E-005 -7.17707E-005 -8.31548E-005 -8.48550E-005 -1.07436E-004 -1.88406E-004 -3.3546
 0.00000E+000  8.26309E-006  1.89409E-005  1.96574E-005 -1.97545E-005 -1.39786E-004 -3.63653E-004 -6.5356
 0.00000E+000  6.84080E-005  1.05202E-004  7.88253E-005 -3.98659E-005 -2.58448E-004 -5.28568E-004 -7.3286
 0.00000E+000  6.18233E-005  7.99362E-005  3.46772E-005 -6.85105E-005 -1.81031E-004 -2.07156E-004 -1.0833
 0.00000E+000  7.16924E-005  1.25013E-004  1.63260E-004  2.12892E-004  3.27253E-004  5.15498E-004  6.1250
 0.00000E+000  2.04935E-004  3.84433E-004  5.37259E-004  6.78600E-004  7.99489E-004  7.85964E-004  4.7448
 0.00000E+000  2.56954E-004  4.55402E-004  5.79582E-004  6.18078E-004  5.36540E-004  3.05633E-004  4.8510
 0.00000E+000  2.20070E-005  1.04412E-005 -3.18961E-005 -7.31545E-005 -5.18419E-005  8.41416E-005  3.9649
 0.00000E+000 -2.40608E-004 -4.23292E-004 -4.78464E-004 -3.42779E-004 -2.78389E-005  4.03745E-004  1.0637
 0.00000E+000 -1.90544E-004 -2.76099E-004 -2.17651E-004 -4.48200E-005  1.91901E-004  5.26116E-004  1.0124
```

Fig. 3. The 3D data file with header

In this case, instead of just skipping the header block, we can extract useful information from it. The following code demonstrates how to read and analyze the header info when drawing the field distribution computed by RSoft:

```
%Opening the data file
fff=fopen('field.fld');

%Skipping two lines containing picture formatting info
%(namely, two strings separated by the <CR>)
fscanf(fff,'%s',2);

%Reading contents of the numerical part of the header into
%variable 'field_info'
field_info=fscanf(fff,'%i %f %f %f OUTPUT_REAL_3D\n %i %f %f\n',7);

%using the variable 'field_info' to read properly formatted
%data on the field distribution
field=fscanf(fff, '%f', [field_info(5), field_info(1)]);
```

Here, after opening the file, we are skipping two strings which mean nothing for us. Then we read all the numerical values into the array and can use this variable to determine the dimension of the array, the physical size of the computation region, etc.

3.3 Reading the random data

Using the header to define the parameters of the figure is not always enough. Particularly, it works for the uniformly distributed data points such as in FDTD method. However, if you use FEM, for example, Comsol Multiphysics, you will deal with non-uniform triangular mesh. In this case, the data is organized into structured. Each unit contains X and Y coordinate (in case of 2D model) or X, Y and Z coordinate (in case of 3D physical model) and the value of the field intensity corresponding to this point (see figure 4).

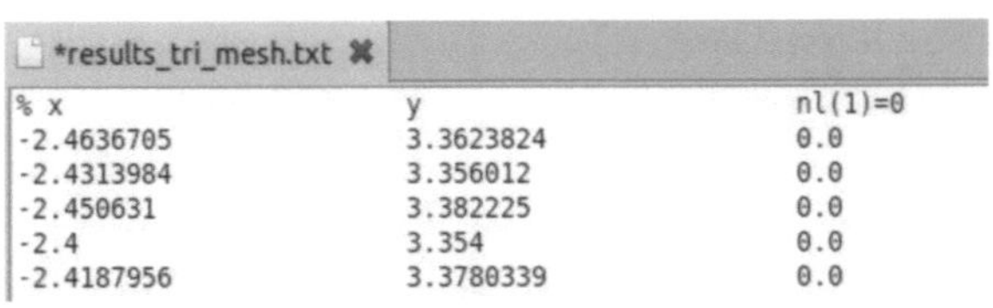
*results_tri_mesh.txt

% x	y	nl(1)=0
-2.4636705	3.3623824	0.0
-2.4313984	3.356012	0.0
-2.450631	3.382225	0.0
-2.4	3.354	0.0
-2.4187956	3.3780339	0.0

Fig. 4. The file containing random data linked to the specific points of the mesh

Reading of the date in this case is performed just as in case of the plane data, however, one have to fill two or three coordinate arrays X, Y and possibly Z, and the array of corresponding values of the field intensity.

It is also possible to convert this data into a regular mesh data which will be described in following section.

3.4 Reading structured data

In case of MPB and MEEP software, the field distribution is being output in so-called HDF5 format which is supported by many visualization tools as well as programming languages.

Particularly, in MATLAB there is a set of functions providing correct work with the HDF5. The MATLAB command HDF5Read(...) reads the contents of the file into the structure from where it can be easily extracted by standard structure addressing command (in case of MATLAB it is the dot operator). Here is simple MATLAB program which reads results computed by MEEP from HDF5 file and analyzes parameters of the results.

```
%Program allows reading from the the .h5 file containing the results of the
%field distribution computed with MEEP

clear all

%The function hdf5info allows obtatining the information from the .h5 file
%required to read the actual data
hinfo=hdf5info('/home/igor/temp/wg_bend-ez.h5');

%Then we are reading the information using the query string from the hinfo
%structure
res=hdf5read(hinfo.GroupHierarchy.Datasets(1));

%In this particular case, the computation results contain several frames
%with field distribution at different moments of time. The cycle reads them
%from the data structure and then draws.
for i=1:(size(res))(1)
  %Copying the frame into a separate 2D array
  drawres(:,:)=res(i,:,:);

  %Drawing the frame
  image(drawres*1000);
  colormap('gray');

  %Drawing immediately
  drawnow;
end
```

However, as it have been described in the previous section, the data in the files may be represented in the forms of an arbitrary structures which requires a lot of work to dig in and to write corresponding unique decoders.

3.5 Reading multiple files data

In many cases, when you perform the parametric computations, the results have form of multiple files. Each file corresponds to a single value of the parameter and may have one of the formats described earlier.

The main problem in this case is to gather the data from all the files into a single data structure. This problem will be discussed in the following section. Here we will focus on how to open multiple files. The following piece of code shows how to open the files which have similar names with a counter attached to them:

```
%Scanning over all the numbers of the files
for num=0:90

  name=strcat(path,'metadata',num2str(num,'%02i'),'.dat')


  clear temporal_response;
  temporal_response=load(name, '-ASCII');

%Here performing all the operations we need
... ...

end
```

We presume to have file names in the following form: "metadata00.dat", "metadata01.dat", "metadata02.dat",...,"metadata90.dat". In this code, the outer loop scans over all the numbers from 0 to 90. The function strcat() allows concatenating several strings into one and generate the name. Using the function num2str() we convert the numerical type into a string.

The problem, may appear with the filenames since for the numbers lower than 10 we have zero-filler in the name. We can fix the problem in two different ways. The first one is just to compare the variable 'num' with 10 and if it's lower than 10, just to add '0' to the string manually. However, this is a solution only in particular cases. Suppose, you have numbers from 0 to 100000. In this case, you will have to make 5 different comparisons each for one digit ($num < 10$, $num < 100$, $num < 1000$, $num < 10000$, $num < 100000$). This is already a sort of annoying and far from elegance.

The second possible solution is to use formatted conversion of the number. In this case we just have to use format string "%02i" to fill the spaces before the number with zeros. Here the symbol of "%" tells MATLAB about the beginning of the format string, following "0" makes MATLAB to fill the spaces with zeros, "2" tells exactly how many digits it is suppose to be in the number and "i" indicates integer data type. Detailed information about the string formatting can be found in the MATLAB documentation in the section of the function fprintf().

4. Processing plane data

The plane numerical data is represented by two arrays, one of which contains values along one coordinate axis while another one corresponds to another axis. This simplest form of the data representation is actually the most clear and understandable when you want to present your results.

However, in some cases direct plotting of the data is not really representable. Particularly, when you make an expensive experimental research like temporal response measurement of the nonlinear PhC using ultra-short pulses, or when you perform the computation which is so time- and resource-consuming that you are unable to obtain sufficient number of data points like, for instance, computation of the photonic band gap maps. In these cases, before to create the data output, you have to convert it, improve it or make some other handling. This section is dedicated to the manipulations on the data which allow to improve its representation.

4.1 Data interpolation

The interpolation is the most useful operation on the data obtained during the experimental research on numerical computation. In the mathematical subfield of numerical analysis, interpolation is a method of constructing new data points within the range of a discrete set of known data points. There are a lot of different ways to interpolate the data like linear interpolation, polynomial interpolation, spline interpolation, etc. We will not consider mathematical side of the interpolation process concentrating on the implementation of this operation in MATLAB.

For the interpolation of the plane data, MATLAB uses the function interp1(). As an input arguments, the function has initial X and Y values of the data as well as new values of X at which you want to obtain the new values. It is also possible to select the interpolation method. As an output, this function returns the new values of Y found by interpolation process.

Here is the simple example of the data interpolation. In this example, we have the dependence of the photonic band gap width of the 1D PhC on the layer width. The data points are calculated for the limited number of values of the witdh. However, due to interpolation, we have smooth curve which looks much nicer.

```
%The program demonstrates different interpolation techniques
%performed by MATLAB. The interpolation is applied
%to the dependence of the photonic band gap width of 1D PhC on the
%layers witdh

%Loading the information on the PBG width from the file
data=load('pbg_width.dat','-ASCII');

%Getting the values of X from the data array
x=data(:,1)';

%Getting the values of Y for the second band (third column)
%in the datafile
y=data(:,5)';

%Creating the mesh 10 times more dense which is required
%for interpolation
x1=interp1(1:length(x),x,1:0.1:length(x));

%Creating new figurefigure;
%Drawing at the same figure
hold on;
%Using the function interp1, interpolating the data with nearest values
y1=interp1(x,y,x1,'nearest');
%Plotting the initial data with blue round markers
plot(x,y, 'bo', 'LineWidth',2);
%Plotting the interpolated data with grin solid line
plot(x1,y1, 'g', 'LineWidth',2);

%Doing the same with linear interpolation
```

```
figure;
hold on
y1=interp1(x,y,x1,'linear');
plot(x,y, 'bo', 'LineWidth',2);
plot(x1,y1, 'g', 'LineWidth',2);

%Doing the same with spline interpolation
figure;
hold on;
y1=interp1(x,y,x1,'spline');
plot(x,y, 'bo', 'LineWidth',2);
plot(x1,y1, 'g', 'LineWidth',2);

%Doing the same with cubic interpolation
figure;
hold on;
y1=interp1(x,y,x1,'cubic');
plot(x,y, 'bo', 'LineWidth',2);
plot(x1,y1, 'g', 'LineWidth',2);
```

As a result of the program we obtain four figures each for one interpolation type.

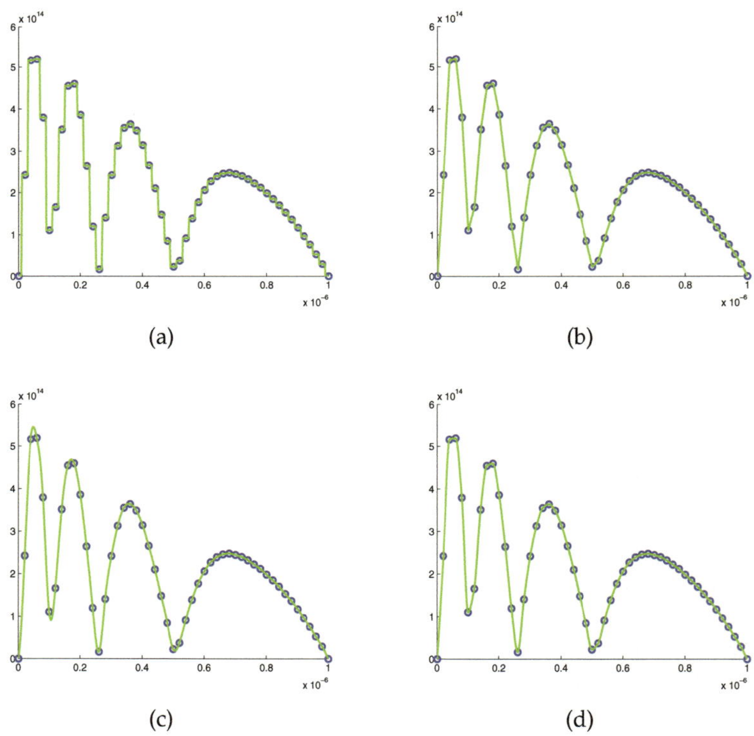

Fig. 5. Examples of basic interpolation. a) Nearest, b) linear, c)spline and d) cubic

In the program, the interpolation is performed in four different ways provided by MATLAB (actually, there are also "pchip" and "v5cubic" types. However, pchip is similar to cubic and v5cubic is just an old version of cubic). From the results, it is seen that for the selected curve the best interpolation technique is a spline interpolation.

4.2 Data approximation

Data approximation is an operation which allows to describe (approximate) the tabulated data by an analytical function.

The approximation is always used when the general view of the analytical dependence can be predicted, however, the coefficients still remain unknown. This is usually happens in the experimental researches when it is necessary to determine the parameters of the analytical dependence. Particularly, when the experiment is intent to determine the effective refractive index of the PhC by measuring the radiation deviation at different wavelength. After the experiment, the data is approximated by parametric analytical function where the parameter is the effective refractive index. The best approximation result gives the value of the mentioned parameter.

In MATLAB there is a separate toolbox providing the approximation of the tabulated data, namely, the Curve Fitting Toolbox. And again, using of the toolbox is possible in a single case only. However, using the toolbox requires definite time and when you need to perform multiple operations, this turns into a mess.

In this section we describe how to approximate the data in MATLAB without using the toolbox. The following program generates randomly five points and then approximates them with polynomial function of the fourth order.

```
%This function approximates five random points with 4-th order
%polynomial function. Since 4-th order polynom allows exact approximation,
%the error should be absent.

function approximation_plane
%Creating five X values
x=1:5;

%Randomly generating 5 Y values
y=rand(1,5)*10;

%Creating the initial values for approximation process
start=[1 1 1 1 1];

%Starting five minimization interations
for i=1:5
   %Using the function fminsearch() to optimize the 'coefs' a the selected
   %points (X, Y)
   estimated_coefs = (fminsearch(@(coefs)fitfun(coefs,x,y),start));

   %changing the starting values to the optimized ones and then starting
   %over
   start=estimated_coefs;
```

```
end

%Building the smooth analytical function with coefficients obtained during
%optimization process
x1=0:0.1:6;
y1=analyt_fn(estimated_coefs,x1);

%Creating the figure
figure;
hold on;
%Plotting the initial points
plot(x,y,'bo','LineWidth',2);
%and the smooth analytical function
plot(x1,y1,'g','LineWidth',2);

%In the title writing the final polynom
title(strcat('y=',num2str(estimated_coefs(1)),'\cdotx^4+(',...
  num2str(estimated_coefs(2)),')\cdotx^3+(',...
  num2str(estimated_coefs(3)),')\cdotx^2+(',...
  num2str(estimated_coefs(4)),')\cdotx+(',...
  num2str(estimated_coefs(1)),')'),'FontSize',16);


%Function for optimization
function err=fitfun(coefs,x,y)
  %The function returns the difference between the analytical function
  %with coefficients 'coefs' at points X and the actual values of Y
  err=norm(analyt_fn(coefs,x)-y);
end

%Analytical parametric function to be optimized
function analyt_fn=analyt_fn(coefs,x)
  analyt_fn=coefs(1)*x.^4+coefs(2)*x.^3+coefs(3)*x.^2+coefs(4)*x+coefs(5);
end
end
```

The result of the function work is presented in figure 6. It can bee seen that approximation is quite accurate.

For the optimization procedure, MATLAB uses simplex search method which is implemented in the form of function fminsearch(). As an input parameters it has a pointer to a function to be minimized and the initial values of the parameter. In our case, the function to minimize returns the difference between actual points and the analytical function which, in turn, is defined in the function analyt_fn().

It should be paid attention to the fact that in current example the polynomial function of the fourth power approximates five data points. In this case, there is only one strict solution. However, in most cases, the approximation is made with certain accuracy which should be properly estimated. The best way to estimate the accuracy is to measure minimum, maximum and avarage deviation.

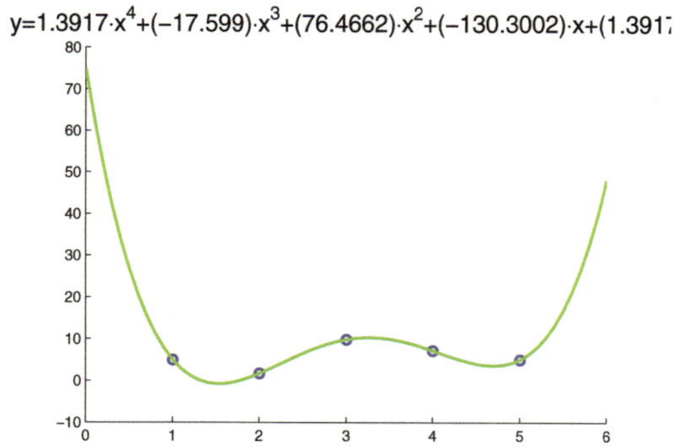

Fig. 6. Result of approximation of the data by the polynomial function

As an example, we give the code which approximates the dependence of central frequency of the photonic band gap of 1D PhC on the layer width, with hyperbolic function and estimates the approximation error. The data is obtained by means of plane wave expansion method Sukhoivanov & Guryev (2009) with low accuracy. With approximation it is possible to determine the analytic function describing such a dependence.
Consider the following code:

```
%This function approximates the dependence of the central
%wavelength of the photonic band gap of 1D PhC on the layer
%width with hyperbolic function.
%It also performs the error estimation.


function approximation_plane_err_estimation
%Loading information about the central frequency of the
%bandgap of 1D PhC from the file
data=load('pbg_center.dat','-ASCII');

%Getting the values of X from the data array
x=data(:,1)';

%Getting the values of Y for the second band (third column)
%in the datafile
y=data(:,3)';

%Creating the initial values for approximation process
%Now there's only four values since we use 3-rd order polynom
start=[1e14 0];



%Using the function fminsearch() to optimize the 'coefs' a the selected
%points (X, Y)
estimated_coefs = (fminsearch(@(coefs)fitfun(coefs,x,y),start));
```

```
%Building the smooth analytical function with coefficients obtained during
%optimization process
x1=interp1(1:length(data(:,1)),data(:,1),1:0.1:length(data(:,1)));
y1=analyt_fn(estimated_coefs,x1);

%using the function 'find' searching for indices of the refined X values
%which are equal to the initial ones
[row est_ind]=find(meshgrid(x1,x)–meshgrid(x,x1)' == 0);

%Searching for minimum deviation of the analytical function from the initial
%data (using est_index to compare corresponding points)
minerr=min(abs(y1(est_ind)–y));

%In the same manner, searching for maximum deviation
maxerr=max(abs(y1(est_ind)–y));

%Calculating avarage error
avgerr=sum(abs(y1(est_ind)–y))/length(y)


%Creating the figure
figure;
hold on;

%plotting the solution
plot(x,y,'bo','LineWidth',2);
%and the smooth analytical function
plot(x1,y1,'g','LineWidth',2);


%Writing the error values at the figure
text(min(x1),min(y1)+(max(y1)–min(y1))/10,...
   strcat('Minimum error = ',num2str(minerr,'%.2e')),'FontSize',14);
text(min(x1),min(y1)+(max(y1)–min(y1))/10*2,...
   strcat('Maximum error = ',num2str(maxerr,'%.2e')),'FontSize',14);
text(min(x1),min(y1)+(max(y1)–min(y1))/10*3,...
   strcat('Avarage error = ',num2str(avgerr,'%.2e')),'FontSize',14);

%Creating the title to the figure
title(strcat('y=',num2str(estimated_coefs(1),'%.2e'),'/(x+',...
   num2str(estimated_coefs(2),'%.2e'),')'),'FontSize',16);


%Function for optimization
function err=fitfun(coefs,x,y)
```

```
    %The function returns the difference between the analytical function
    %with coefficients 'coefs' at points X and the actual values of Y
    err=norm(analyt_fn(coefs,x)-y);
end

%Analytical parametric function to be optimized
function analyt_fn=analyt_fn(coefs,x)
    analyt_fn=coefs(1)./(x+coefs(2));
end
end
```

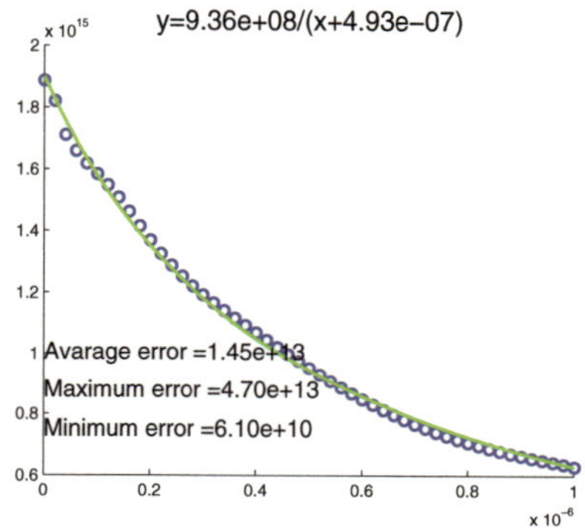

Fig. 7. Displaying the approximation accuracy information

Now the result is represented in the form shown in the figure 7. We currently used the hyperbolic function which gave good agreement with numerical results. In this case, not all the points (in general case, neither of them) are fall at the analytical curve. Thus, estimating the error, we are able to confirm the validity of the approximation. In case of large error value, the function is unable to approximate the data at any conditions. This may happen when you have selected wrong kind of approximating function or, in case of too complex function, have selected wrong values of the initial parameters.

4.3 Data representation

In the scientific publication the data representation plays main role when it comes to correct understanding of the computation or experimental results. In two previous subsections we have described the way for data interpolation and approximation which helps to perform the data analysis as well as smooth the data. However, the data presentation is also important. Some basic techniques have already been used earlier without explanation such as manipulation of the figure's and plot's parameters. In this subsection we will try to describe and explain the most useful of them.

First thing which should be known about MATLAB, it is the object-oriented environment. This means that after creating some object such as plot, text, line, etc., they can be modified and their properties can be easily changed.

As always, the most simple way to manipulate the objects parameters is to use visual environment provided by MATLAB. For this reason, it is enough just to double-click at some object while editing mode is active (for this, you have to press the mouse pointer icon at the

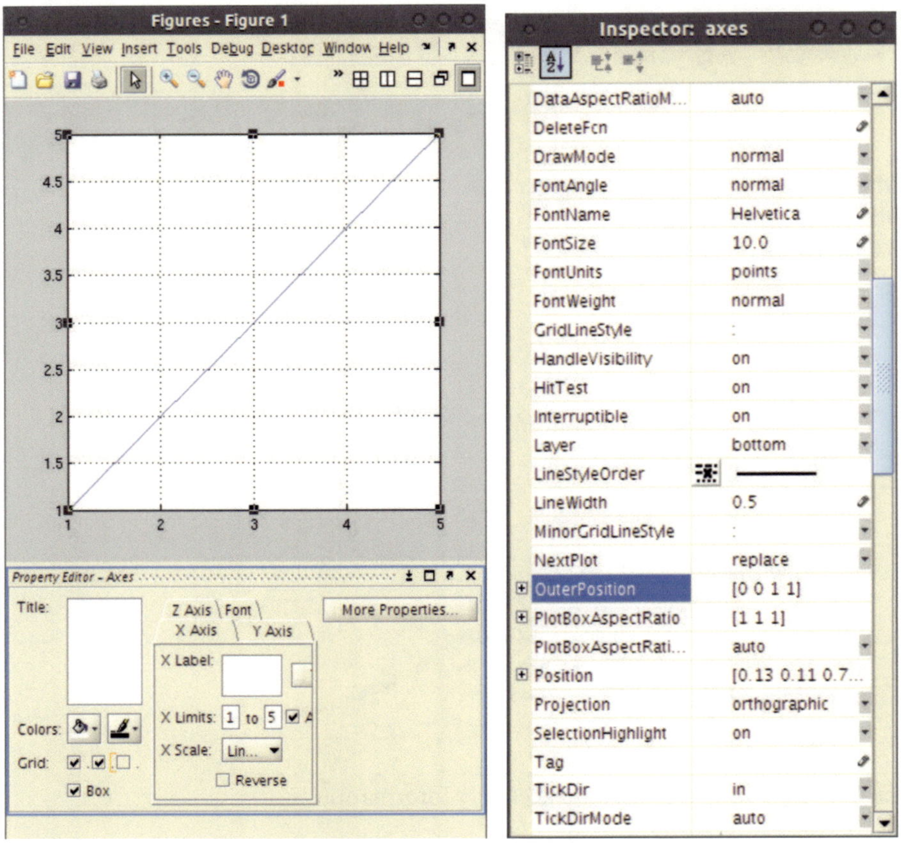

(a) (b)

Fig. 8. Visual editing of the object's properties

tool panel). After this, you will see the editing panel which allows editing some parameters of the selected object (see figure 8(a)).

Deeper understanding of the parameters of the objects can be achieved when opening additional parameters panel or properties inspector (see figure 8(b)). Here you can see and edit all the parameters available for the object.

However, editing parameters inside your script is the most fast and productive way to change the figure appearance (imagine that you have to redraw the figure over and over and modify dozens of parameters manually).

There are two ways to set up the parameters of the objects. The first one is to set them on the stage of their creation. And the second one is modify them after the object is created with default properties.

In the first method, the parameters are transfered as arguments to the function which creates an objects like in following code:

```
%Approximation process
...
...
...
```

```
%Plotting the initial data
plot(x,y, 'LineWidth',2, 'LineStyle','none','Marker','o','Color','k');
%Plotting the approximated data
plot(x1,y1,'LineWidth',2, 'LineStyle','--','Color',[0 0.3 1]);

%Adding the text marks
text(min(x1)+0.1,min(y1)+(max(y1)-min(y1))/10,...
  strcat('Minimum error = ',num2str(minerr)),'FontSize',14);
text(min(x1)+0.1,min(y1)+(max(y1)-min(y1))/10*2,...
  strcat('Maximum error = ',num2str(maxerr)),'FontSize',14);
text(min(x1)+0.1,min(y1)+(max(y1)-min(y1))/10*3,...
  strcat('Avarage error = ',num2str(avgerr)),'FontSize',14);
```

Here we show more advanced plotting from the approximation example. Pay attention that after plotting the data (X-values and Y-values), we place a lot of textual and numerical parameters. Parameters are usually defined by a pair name-value. The value can be a string, a number or an array depending on the parameter's requirements.
Particularly, the first plot function will draw the data with the LineWidth=2 (initially its 0.5), without the lines connecting the data points (LineStyle=none), but with circular markers (Marker=o) drawn with black color (Color=k).
The second plot draws the approximated data with LineWidth=2, with dashed line (LineStyle='–') and with color defined by three RGB values (each value varies from 0 to 1).
The text marks have only the parameters Fontsize=14.
As we have mentioned previously, there is another way to change the parameters of the objects using the object identifier. Note that each function which creates an objects, also returns an object identifier which can be stored into a variable and used lately to manipulate the object. Particularly, the properties of the object can be easily changed using the function set() which has as a parameters the object identifier and the set of object's properties. Consider this simple example which makes the same as previous one but modifying the properties after the object is created:

```
%Approximation process
...
...
...

%Plotting the initial data
p1=plot(x,y);
set(p1, 'LineWidth',2, 'LineStyle','none','Marker','o','Color','k');

%Plotting the approximated data
p2=plot(x1,y1);
set(p2,'LineWidth',2, 'LineStyle','--','Color',[0 0.3 1]);

%Adding the text marks
t1=text();
set(t1, 'Position',[min(x1)+0.1,min(y1)+(max(y1)-min(y1))/10,0],...
```

```
    'String',strcat('Minimum error = ',num2str(minerr)),...
    'FontSize',14);
t2=text();
set(t2, 'Position',[min(x1)+0.1,min(y1)+(max(y1)-min(y1))/10*2,0],...
    'String',strcat('Maximum error = ',num2str(maxerr)),...
    'FontSize',14);
t3=text();
set(t3, 'Position',[min(x1)+0.1,min(y1)+(max(y1)-min(y1))/10*3,0],...
    'String',strcat('Maximum error = ',num2str(avgerr)),...
    'FontSize',14);
```

This code does exactly the same as previous one, however with significant difference. When the function creating the object is called, the object identifier is stored into a corresponding variable. After this, the function set() is called to modify the objects properties. Pay attention, in case of text labels, the object is created with default properties. All the properties including the text strings are set later using the identifiers.
This code seems to be unnecessarily more awkward then the previous one but actually, it has one great advantage. After you stored the variable identifier, you are able to manipulate the object in any way you want. Particularly, you can easily create an animation by varying the parameters of the object (such as camera view) in a loop and saving each frame (for information about animations see the last section).

5. Simple 3D data processing

Operating with 3D data is more complicated than with plane one. Particularly, the most simple data to be work with is data organized into a regular 2D mesh such as results of FDTD computation. However, in some cases it is important to perform the data interpolation.

5.1 Data on rectangular mesh

The most frequently, the data organized into a rectangular mesh may be found in the field distribution output of the software implementing the FDTD method. However, each of the programs creates its own data format and, therefore, should be treated individually. Here as an example, we will give the programs reading the data from RSoft and MEEP.

5.1.1 Processing the data from RSoft

When the RSoft outputs the field distribution, it usually created two different files. The first one contains the field distribution and the second one contains the information about the structure boundaries. Therefore, it is necessary to read both files for correct representation the computed data.
Consider the following code for reading the RSoft field output:

```
%The program draws the field distribution computed by RSoft
%Over the field distribution it draws the structure which is
%read from the file generated by RSoft

clear all
```

```
%The variable 'name' contains filename without the extension
name='field_high_state'

%Opening the file containing the field info
fff=fopen(strcat(name,'.fld'));

%Skipping the inforation about the plotting
%which is unuseful for us
fscanf(fff,'%s',2);

%Into the variable 'field_info' reading useful information
field_info=fscanf(fff,'%i %f %f %f OUTPUT_REAL_3D\n %i %f %f\n',7);

%Reading the data points into 2D array. The dimensions of the
%array are taken from the variable 'field_info'
field=fscanf(fff, '%f', [field_info(5), field_info(1)]);

%Plotting the field with filled contour plot
figure;

%Again, the information about absolute coordinates is taken from the
%variable 'field_info'
contourf(field_info(2)*1e-6:...                  %from minimum X

    %with the step computed from the number of points over X
    ((field_info(3)*1e-6)-field_info(2)*1e-6)/(field_info(1)-1):

    field_info(3)*1e-6,... %to maximum X

    field_info(6)*1e-6:... %from minimum Y

    %with the step computed from the number of points over Y
    ((field_info(7)*1e-6)-field_info(6)*1e-6)/(field_info(5)-1):...

    field_info(7)*1e-6,... %to maximum Y

    %plotting the field data points without contour lines
    field, 'LineStyle','none');

%Setting the color map
colormap('copper');

%Making MATLAB to draw at the same plot
hold on;

%Opening the file with the structure boundaries
fff=fopen(strcat(name,'.pdo'));
```

```
%Reading header with useful information about filling
[isfill count]=fscanf(fff,'fill %i\n');
[color count] =fscanf(fff,'color %i\n');
num_points=fscanf(fff,'polygon %i\n',1);
while(num_points)

        str=(fscanf(fff,'%f ',[2 num_points]))'*1e-6;
        fscanf(fff, 'end polygon\n',1);
        patch(str(:,1),str(:,2),zeros(num_points,1),'FaceColor',[1 1 1],...
              'EdgeColor',[1 1 1],'LineWidth',2);
        num_points=fscanf(fff,'polygon %i\n',1)
end
fclose(fff);
```

In this case, the first file "field_high_state.fld" is a simple 3D data with header containing information linking to the field distribution to real coordinate system, some auxiliary information about the number of data points, etc. Before writing the program reading and displaying such kind of data, it is useful to consult with the software manual and, which is very important, to open the file with text editor and check the header and data formats manually.
The second file "field_high_state.pdo" which contains information about the optical structure, contains structured data and should be read accordingly. Namely, each of the boundaries of the structure is stored in the form of polygon. The information about the polygon size is contained in the polygon's header. Before working with this file, it is also useful to take a look with a simple text editor.

5.2 3D data visualization

Unlike 2D data containing only two independent coordinates, the 3D data may be visualized in a variety of different ways. Depending on convenience, the following visualizing functions are most frequently used:

- surf()
- mesh()
- contour()
- contourf()
- image()

All the function actually take the same parameters, namely, X, Y arrays containing coordinates and Z 2D-array containing actual data.
Such kinds of visualization possess different functionality and speed which condition their usage. Particularly, if you need to express the intensity levels, the "contour()" function is the right choice. However, this function is too slow and trying to make animation with it requires a lot of time. The best choice for the animation is the function "image()".

6. Random data processing

In several cases, such as computation of the electromagnetic field distribution inside the PhC by means of FEM, the results appear within the nodes of irregular mesh. In this case it is impossible to perform the interpolation or other regular operation by means of standard MATLAB functions. In a professional software such as Comsol Multiphysics, this problem is overcome and now it is possible to export the results linked to a regular or user-defined mesh.
However, for example, in case of PDE Toolbox available in MATLAB, the results are exported in a form of random data where the specific value correspond to a node of triangular mesh. Dealing with this kind of data becomes a total mess.

6.1 Processing data on triangular mesh

In many cases, it is not necessary to output the data but we need to obtain some information from it. For instance, when one investigates the transmission characteristics of the microstructure, it is necessary to analyze the field distribution before the structure and after the structure. Namely, one knows exactly the regions of space where the field intensity should be found. In case of triangular mesh, the simplest way to do this is to find all the points within each region, the intensity in each point and then divide it by the number of points in the region. Consider the following code which finds average intensity within the region in space using the results exported from Comsol Multiphysics:

```
%Function for computation of the transmittance of the nonlinear
%photonic crystal from the field distribution computed in Comsol

clear all

%Loading the file with random data containing the field distribution
%inside the investigated structure
field=load('results_tri_mesh.txt','ASCII');

%Determining maximum and minimum values of coordinates
%Considering y-coordinate only since we are interested in
%the whole width of the structure
ymax=max(field(:,2));
ymin=min(field(:,2));

%Defining the limits for optical intensity calculation. Namely,
%from the bottom
y00=ymin;
%to bottom+3 microns
y01=ymin+3;
%from the top-3 microns
y10=ymax-3;
%to the top
y11=ymax;

%Counter of nodes in the bottom region (corresponding to reflection)
```

```
count_reflect=1;

%Counter of nodes in the top region (corresponding to transmission)
count_transmit=1;

%Determinig the length of the field structure
len=length(field);

%Counter for different intensity values
count_intensity=1;

%The cycle for the intensity
for intensity=0:0.01:0.5
  %The variable to sum the field intensity in all the points of
  %the bottom region
  reflect_total=0;

  %The variable to sum the field intensity in all the points of
  %the top region
  transmit_total=0;

  %The cycle for all the points in the mesh
  for iii=1:len

    %If the point is inside the bottom region,
    if (field(iii,2)>y00)&&(field(iii,2)<y01)
      %and if it is not NaN value
      if(abs(field(iii,3))>=0)
        %Adding its absolute value to the total reflected field
        reflect_total=reflect_total+(abs(field(iii,2+count_intensity)));
        count_reflect=count_reflect+1;
      end
    end

    %If the point is inside the bottom region,
    if (field(iii,2)>y10)&&(field(iii,2)<y11)
      %and if it is not NaN value
      if(abs(field(iii,3))>=0)
        %Adding its absolute value to the total transmitted field
        transmit_total=transmit_total+(abs(field(iii,2+count_intensity)));
        count_transmit=count_transmit+1;
      end
    end
  end


  %Normalizing the field intensities by the number of
```

```
    %points
    reflect=reflect_total/count_reflect;
    transmit=transmit_total/count_transmit;

    %Assuming the total field intensity as a sum of reflectance
    %and transmittance, calculating the reflectance of the structure
    reflectance(count_intensity)=reflect/(reflect+transmit);
    intensities(count_intensity)=intensity;
    count_intensity=count_intensity+1;

end

%Plotting the result and formatting the plot
figure;
plot(intensities,reflectance, 'LineWidth',2);
xlabel('Radiation intensity','FontSize',14, 'FontWeight','bold');
ylabel('Transmittance','FontSize',14, 'FontWeight','bold');
set(gca, 'FontSize',12)
grid on;
```

The program, in general, is quite simple. The triangular mesh is written into a file as a number of point coordinates with corresponding field intensity. It is just necessary to find all the points falling at the region required and sum all the intensities within the region.

6.2 Converting into a regular mesh

To improve the data quality and perform regional analysis of the field distribution, it is more convenient to use the regular data array instead of random data. Therefore, in this section, we provide reader with useful program able to convert the triangular mesh into a regular mesh by performing simple linear 3D interpolation.

In PDE Toolbox, the data is always exported as one-dimensional or two-dimensional array (depending on the specific task). In case of two-dimensional array, each column corresponds to a single solution. It is also can be exported the mesh information. Particularly, we are interested in nodes coordinates and also particular interest represents the information about nodes which form the triangles. By default, this information is contained in the variables named "u" (the solution), "p" (coordinates of the nodes) and "t" (information about triangles formation) respectively. The information about the triangles is contained in the array "t" in a form of indices of the coordinate points stored in the array "p".

After exporting this information, we can now start converting the mesh using the following code:

```
%The program converts the data on triangular mesh
%obtained in PDE Tool of the MATLAB into a data on square mesh
%The data from PDE Tool, namely, array of data points 'u',
%Data of the triangles of the mesh 't' and the array of
%coordinates 'p' should be previously exported to MATLAB workspace

clear data
```

```
clear datanew

%For convenience, we will use the 2D array to store the coordinates
%and corresponding data values
%First writing the coordinates of the points
data=p';

%and then, the values computed by PDE Toolbox in these points
data(:,3)=u(:,3)';

%Finding minimum and maximum values of the cooerditates
xmin=min(data(:,1));
xmax=max(data(:,1));

ymin=min(data(:,2));
ymax=max(data(:,2));

%Defining the number of square mesh nodes in both dimensions
%Pay attention that the best way is to sellect the number of
%points in correspondence with the size on the structure in
%each dimension
xnpoints=50;
ynpoints=50;

%Generating coordinated of the rectangular mesh
xnew=xmin:(xmax-xmin)/xnpoints:xmax;
ynew=ymin:(ymax-ymin)/ynpoints:ymax;

%Now we have to find the data value in each of the points of the mesh
for xc=1:length(xnew)
  for yc=1:length(ynew)

          %To determine the point of the triangular mesh which is the closest
          %one to the current point of rectangular mesh, we compute the
          %Cartesian distances between them.
    len=(sqrt((data(:,1)-xnew(xc)).^2+(data(:,2)-ynew(yc)).^2));

          %Using the fucntion find(), we are searching for the minimum distance.
    i1=find(len==min(len), 1, 'first');
    if(len(i1)==0)
      datanew(yc,xc)=data(i1,3);
      continue;
    end

          %Now we are searching for all the triangles containing the point found

    [row, triangles]=find(t==i1);
```

```
    num_t=-1;

  %Then checking if any of the triangles contains the point of the
  %rectangular mesh
    for tc=1:length(triangles)
      %For this reason, calculating the area of the triangle
      area_mesh=abs(tri_area([p(1,t(1,triangles(tc)))...
                        p(2,t(1,triangles(tc)))], ...
                       [p(1,t(2,triangles(tc)))...
                        p(2,t(2,triangles(tc)))],...
                       [p(1,t(3,triangles(tc)))...
                        p(2,t(3,triangles(tc)))]));

      %and the sum of areas of three triangles formed by the
      %point of the square mesh and each two points of the
      %triangular mesh element
      area_sum=abs(tri_area([xnew(xc) ynew(yc)],...
                       [p(1,t(2,triangles(tc)))...
                        p(2,t(2,triangles(tc)))],...
                       [p(1,t(3,triangles(tc)))...
                        p(2,t(3,triangles(tc)))]))+...
          abs(tri_area([p(1,t(1,triangles(tc)))...
                        p(2,t(1,triangles(tc)))],...
                       [xnew(xc) ynew(yc)],...
                       [p(1,t(3,triangles(tc)))...
                        p(2,t(3,triangles(tc)))]))+...
          abs(tri_area([p(1,t(1,triangles(tc)))...
                        p(2,t(1,triangles(tc)))],...
                       [p(1,t(2,triangles(tc)))...
                        p(2,t(2,triangles(tc)))],...
                       [xnew(xc) ynew(yc)]));
   %The points is inside the triangular element if the sum of
   %the areas of three triangles is less or equivalent to the
   %one of the triangluar element
      if(abs(area_mesh-area_sum)<=0)
        %writing the number of the triangle
        num_t=triangles(tc);
        %and finising the cycle
        break;
      end
    end
    %if the trianle not found then the requested point is outside
    %the compoutation area
    if(num_t==-1)
      datanew(yc,xc)=NaN;
      continue;
```

```
        end

        %otherwise, reading the coordinate points and
        %the field values within these points
        x1=data(t(1, num_t),1);
        y1=data(t(1, num_t),2);
        z1=data(t(1, num_t),3);

        x2=data(t(2, num_t),1);
        y2=data(t(2, num_t),2);
        z2=data(t(2, num_t),3);

        x3=data(t(3, num_t),1);
        y3=data(t(3, num_t),2);
        z3=data(t(3, num_t),3);

        %Building the equation of the plane using vector
        %cross-product
        n=cross([x1-x2 y1-y2 z1-z2], [x3-x2 y3-y2 z3-z2]);
        A=n(1);
        B=n(2);
        C=n(3);
        D=-n(1)*x1-n(2)*y1-n(3)*z1;
        %and from the plane equation finding new value of the
        %field intensity within the point of square mesh
        datanew(yc,xc)=(-D-A*xnew(xc)-B*ynew(yc))/C;

    end
end

%Refining the mesh using the interp2() function
[xrefined yrefined]=meshgrid(xmin:(xmax-xmin)/ynpoints/10:xmax,...
                     ymin:(ymax-ymin)/ynpoints/10:ymax);
datanew_interp=interp2(xnew, ynew, datanew, xrefined, yrefined);

%And plotting the resulting field distribution
surfc(datanew_interp,'LineStyle','none');figure(gcf)

function tri_area=tri_area(p1,p2,p3)
  tri_area=0.5*(p1(1)*p2(2) + p1(2)*p3(1) + p3(2)*p2(1) - p3(1)*p2(2) -...
                          p3(2)*p1(1) - p2(1)*p1(2));
end
```

Here in this program we are using the PDE Toolbox data structures to demonstrate the mesh conversion technique. In case of using other computation software, the results output may differ from the one shown here.

In this case, the program generates the regular square mesh. Then it scans over all the points in the mesh and for each point searches the closest one of the initial triangular mesh. After

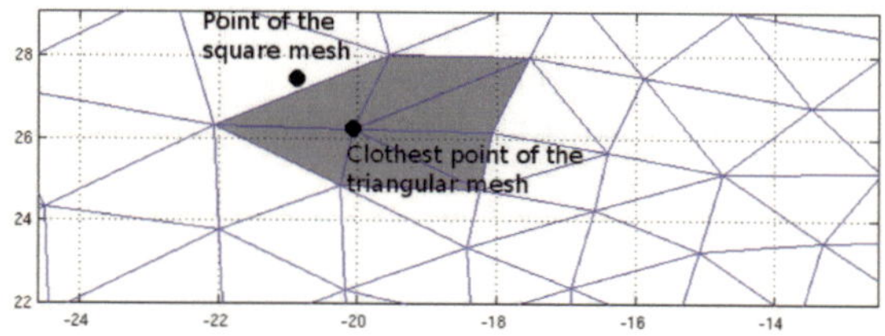

(a)

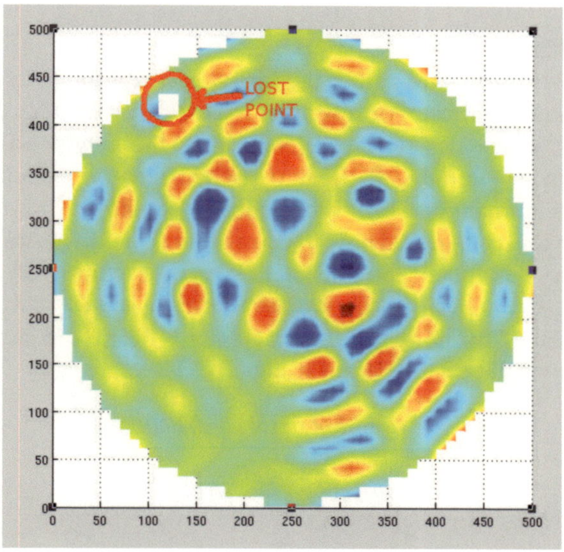

(b)

Fig. 9. Field distribution of the leaky mode of the PhC fiber containing the defect of triangular to rectangular mesh conversion

it finds the closest point, it uses the array "t" to find all the triangles containing this point. Then it checks which triangle contains current point of the rectangular mesh. For this reason it uses the method of the areas summation. If the one is not found, the point is outside the computation area and NaN is written into a resulting array. Otherwise, it builds the equation of the plane using the normal vector and one point. Then, using this equation, it calculates the value of the data at the required point.

The conversion of from the triangular mesh into a rectangular one has one serious drawback. Since, triangular mesh may be highly non-uniform, it is possible to lost some points independently on the meshes resolution. Consider situation presented in figure 9(a)

Here, two points mark the node of the rectangular mesh and the closest point of the triangular mesh. The grayed triangles are the ones containing the closest point. Pay attention that the node of the rectangular mesh does not belong to any of the triangles. In this case, the program puts NaN into this node, thus creating the hole in the resulting field distribution (see figure 9(b)).

This drawback, while being almost unessential for analysis, makes the method useless for data representation. In this case, the bes solution is to use something like neural networks interpolation which are presented in the following section.

7. Multiple files data processing

In most cases, you have the results in a form of a multiple files. For instance, when you computing the characteristics for the structure which parameters are varied during the computation process. In this case, each file corresponds to the specific value of the parameter.

7.1 Gathering the multiple files with MATLAB

The main problem in this case is to gather the files in a single data structure. This particular task depends on the kind of data. For example, in case of plane data you may want to plot the surface. However, when each file contains 3D data, the only possibility to visualize it is to make slices or animate the data. Particularly, when time-dependent field distribution is computed, it is wise to animate the results for better presentation.
In the first section we have considered how to open several files in a row. Here is the MATLAB program which gathers the data of the PhC band structures computed by RSoft into a single 3D array and plots the surfaces each one of which corresponds to a single PhC band. At this, the band structures of the PhC having different elements radius are suppose to be saved is a separate files with names like "bs_separate00_eigs_TE.dat".

```
%The program opens the files with the results of the band structure
%computation as a function of the refractive index
%obtained by RSoft and merges them into a single data structure.
%Then each band is displayed as a single surface

clear all;

%Parts of the filename
name='bs_single';
name_fin='_eigs_TE.dat';

%Cycle for the numbers of files
for nc=0:50

  %Forming the name
  full_name=strcat(name, num2str(nc,'%02i'), name_fin);

  %Opening the file
  f=fopen(full_name,'r');

  %Skipping the header
  skip=fscanf(f,'%s\n',5);

  %Reading the data from file into a 2D array
  data=fscanf(f,'%f ',[9 16]);
```

```
    %Closing the file
    fclose(f);

    %The first raw of the data corresponds to the X-values and is copied
    %Into array data_x
    data_x(1,:)=data(1,:);

    %the array data_y is formed automatically from number of file
    data_y(nc+1)=nc*0.01;

    %The actual 3D data is contained within the raws from 2 to 9 and
    %is being copied into corresponding 3D array
    data_z(nc+1,:,:)=data(2:9,:);
end

%Creating the figure
figure;

%Making MATLAB to add new plot to the existing figure
hold on;

%The cycle for the number of levels now nl scans over another dimension
%of the array (namely, to a band number).
for nl=1:8
    %Copying the data for a single band into a temporal 2D array
    draw_data(:,:)=data_z(:,nl,:);

    %Plotting the surface
    surf(data_x, data_y, draw_data,'MeshStyle','row');
end

%Creating the labels and decorating the plot
xlabel('Wave vector','FontSize',14, 'FontWeight','bold');
ylabel('Radius r/a','FontSize',14, 'FontWeight','bold');
zlabel('Frequency, \omegaa/2\pic','FontSize',14, 'FontWeight','bold');
set(gca,'XGrid','on','YGrid','on','ZGrid','on',...
                'CameraPosition',[7.9 -2.89 4.6]);
ylim([0 0.5]);
colormap('gray');
```

The function simply merges the multiple files into a single data structure and then plots separately each surface corresponding to each PhC band.

8. Building animations

Animations may become important when you are creating the presentation. In this case, dynamic representation of the results gives listener deep understanding of the problem.

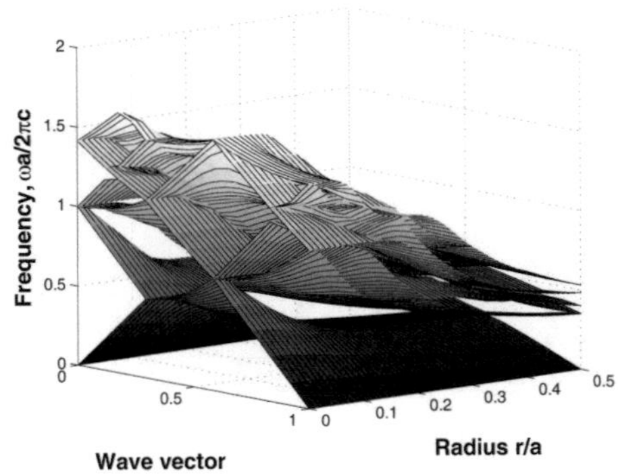

Fig. 10. The result of merging the data from multiple files

MATLAB provides users with methods for creating basic animations capturing frame by frame from a graph area. To record an animation, you first have to perform the graphic output of the results. To output the data in the real time, the function "drawnow" is required. Then, using the function "getframe" each frame is saved into an array which then can be animated in MATLAB or stored into a file to insert into the presentation.
As an example, we will consider previous case with the band structure computation and will animate the band structure in time instead of representing it in a form of surfaces. Consider the following program:

```
%The program reads the series of files from the specific location
%and builds the animation which is then written into a file

%Clearing the workspace
clear all;

%The first and the last constant parts of the name
name='bs_single';
name_fin='_eigs_TE.dat';
figure;

%The cycle through all the file numbers
for nc=0:50
   %Forming the filename
   full_name=strcat(name, num2str(nc,'%02i'), name_fin);
   %Reading the current file data
   f=fopen(full_name,'r');
   skip=fscanf(f,'%s\n',5);
   data=fscanf(f,'%f ',[9 16]);
   fclose(f);

   %Extracting the X data
   data_x(1,:)=data(1,:);

   %Extracting the Y datafor 8 bands
```

```
    data_y=data(2:9,:);

    %Drawing the bands
    for nl=1:8
      plot(data_x, data_y(nl,:),'k','LineWidth',2);
      hold on;
    end

    %Setting up the parameters of the plot
    ylim([0 1.5]);
    xlabel('Wave vector','FontSize',14,'FontWeight','bold');
    ylabel('Frequency, \omegaa/2\pic','FontSize',14,'FontWeight','bold');
    set(gca,'XGrid','on','YGrid','on');

    %Making MATLAB to display the plot immidiately
    drawnow;

    %Saving current figure as a frame
    ani(nc+1)=getframe(gcf);
    hold off;

end

%Playing back all the array of frames
movie(ani);

%Saving the animation into a video file
movie2avi(ani,'bs_on_radius');
```

Here in this program, three different kinds of animations in MATLAB are represented. Namely, using the command "drawnow", the animation is performed in the first time. Then, after it have been stored into an array "ani", the animation is played by the command "movie" which makes nothing more but displaying frame by frame the array. After this, the animation is stored into a ".avi" file which can be played separately in a video player or can be inserted into a presentation.

9. Conclusion

In this chapter, we have shared the experience of using the MATLAB for the photonic crystals modeling. Computation techniques considered in this chapter represent the examples aplicable to different fields of physics and electronics. The codes demonstrating the PhC computations, have been selected by authors following their experience and represent particular problems being solved during their investigation in the PhC field.
Particularly, there have been given the brief review of several well-knows software projects for PhC devices investigation, presented the techniques for working with different useful data formats for different kinds of the data representation; presented several working codes for reading and analyzing the data from RSoft, COMSOL multiphysics, MPB and MEEP;

processing data represented in different forms such as plane data, 3D (rectangular and triangular mesh) data, the data represented by several files.
The examples of working codes given in the chapter allow wide range of investigators and, in the first place, PhD and master students, to start quickly the solution of their own original problems.

10. References

COMSOL (2011).
URL: *http://www.comsol.com*

Joannopoulos, J., Meade, R. & Winn, J. (1995). *Photonic Crystals: Molding the Flow of Light*, Princeton University Press, Princeton.

Lourtioz, J.-M., Benisty, H. & Berger, V. (2005). *Photonic Crystals, Towards Nanoscale Photonic Devices*, Springer-Verlag.

MATLAB manual (2011).
URL: *http://www.mathworks.com/help/techdoc/*

MEEP (2011).
URL: *http://ab-initio.mit.edu/wiki/index.php/Meep_manual*

MPB (2011).
URL: *http://ab-initio.mit.edu/wiki/index.php/MPB_manual*

RSoft (2011).
URL: *http://www.rsoftdesign.com/*

Sakoda, K. (2001). *Optical Properties of Photonic Crystals*, Springer-Verlag.

Sukhoivanov, I. & Guryev, I. (2009). *Photonic crystals – physics and practical modeling*, Optical sciences, 1 edn, Springer, Berlin.

Taflove, A. & Hagness, S. (2005). *Computational Electrodynamics: The Finite-Difference Time-Domain Method*, 3 edn, Artech House, Norwood, MA.

Part 3

Power Systems Applications

7

MATLAB Co-Simulation Tools for Power Supply Systems Design

Valeria Boscaino and Giuseppe Capponi
University of Palermo
Italy

1. Introduction

Modern electronic devices could be thought as the collection of elementary subsystems, each one requiring a regulated supply voltage in order to perform the desired function. Actually, in a system board you can find as many as ten separate voltage rails, each one rated for a maximum current and current slew-rate. If the available energy source is not suitable for the specific application, a power supply system is required to convert energy from the available input form to the desired output. Since power-up, power-down sequences and recovery from multiple fault conditions are usually offered, monitoring and sequencing the voltage rails is quite complex and a central power management controller is used. The design of the power management system is a key step for a successful conclusion of the overall design. The cost, size and volume of the electronic device are heavily affected by the power supply performances. The proliferation of switching converters throughout the electronic industry is a matter of fact. Unlike linear regulators, switching converters are suitable for both reducing and increasing the unregulated input voltage and efficiency can be as high as 97%. Classification of switching power supplies is mainly based on the available input energy form and the desired output: AC-AC cycle conversion: alternate input, alternate output; AC-DC rectification: alternate input, continuous output; DC-AC inversion: continuous input, alternate output; DC-DC conversion: continuous input, continuous output. Several topologies are well suited to perform the required conversion (Erikson et al., 2001; Pressman et al., 2009). Independently of the specific topology, the architecture of a power supply system can be generalized as shown in Fig.1. A power section and a control section are highlighted. The switching converter is included in the power section while the feedback network and protection circuits for safe operation are collected in the control system. Mainly because of the growing interest in digital controllers, a power supply system can be modelled as a complex system, quite often involving both digital and analog subsystems. If compared to their analog counterparts, digital controllers offer lower power consumption, higher immunity to components aging and higher and higher design flexibility. The control algorithm is often described at a functional level using hardware description language, as VHDL or Verilog. ASICs or FPGA based controllers are usually integrated by the means of sophisticated simulation, synthesis and verification tools. Time to market is heavily reduced by the means of powerful simulation environments and accurate system modelling. Achieving high accuracy models for mixed-mode systems is quite difficult. Specific simulation tools are available on the market, each one oriented to a specific abstraction level. Circuit simulation software as *Powersim PSIM* and *Orcad Pspice* are the most common choice for circuit modelling. In (Basso, 2008), the design and simulation of switch-mode power supplies is deeply analyzed and simulation tips in several environments are proposed. ASIC simulation and verification tools as Xilinx ISE/Modelsim or Aldec Active-HDL are available to implement the digital controller by the VHDL or VERILOG source code. Since the interaction between subsystems is the most common source of faults, testing separately analog and digital subsystems by the means of different verification tools is a severe mistake. Matlab is a powerful simulation environment for mixed-mode systems modelling and simulation, providing several tools for system co-simulation (Pop, 2010; Kaichun et al., 2010). The Matlab suite offers co-simulation tools for *PSIM, Modelsim* and *Active-HDL* simulation environments. Ideally, modelling the power converter by a circuit implementation in PSIM environment and the digital controller by the VHDL code in *Xilinx ISE* or *Active-HDL* environment allows the designer to test the composite system in Matlab environment using co-simulation procedures. Unfortunately, the use of several co-simulation tools in the same Simulink model heavily reduces the processing speed. As an example, in this chapter the Simulink model of a multiphase dc-dc converter for VRMs applications is described. The control system is described by VHDL language and the controller model is implemented in *Active-HDL* environment. For the highest processing speed, an alternative modelling technique for the power section is proposed by the means of elementary library blocks, avoiding *PSIM* co-simulation and not affecting the accuracy of behavioural simulations. As shown by simulation results, the high accuracy relies in the opportunity to match the system behaviour both within the switching event and during long-time events such as load transients and start-up. The great potential of the co-simulation procedure for mixed-mode systems is highlighted by the comparison between simulation and experimental results.

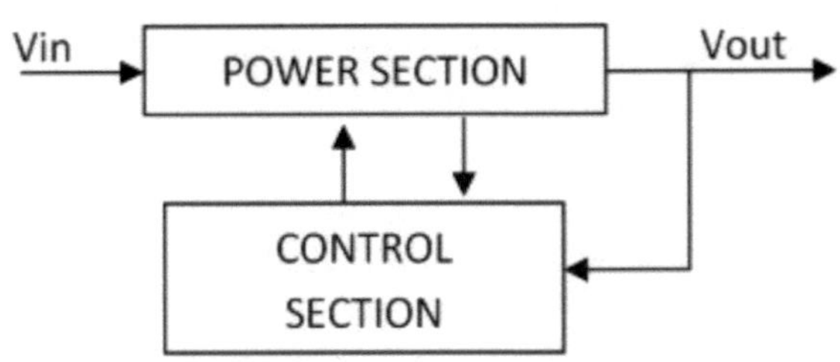

Fig. 1. Power supply system architecture.

2. Multiphase dc-dc converters for VRM applications

The evolution in microprocessor technology poses new challenges for power supply design. The end of 2009 marked the birth of 32nm technology for semiconductor devices, and 22nm is expected to be reached in the 2011-2012 timeframe. The next generation of computer microprocessors will operate at significantly lower voltages and higher currents than today's generation in order to decrease the power consumption and increase the processing speed. Within several years, Intel cores are expected to operate on a 0.8V supply voltage. High-quality power is delivered to the microprocessor by a point-of-load (POL) converter, also known as voltage regulator module (VRM), which is located on the motherboard next to the load. Embedded POL converters are designed to supply a tight regulated output voltage in the 0.8 - 1.2V range. Due to integration advances and increasing clock frequencies, high current

values, often higher than 100A, are required. VRMs supply highly dynamic loads exhibiting current slew rates as high as 1000A/µs. Today, in distributed power architectures, individual POL converters usually draw power from a 12V intermediate power bus. Lowering the core voltage results in a very narrow duty cycle of the 12V-input converter, worsening the converter efficiency and load transient response. The best topology for VRM applications features tight voltage regulation, very fast transient response, high-current handling capabilities and high efficiency. Modern technology advances constantly prompt electronics researchers to meet all requirements investigating innovative solutions. The evolution from a classical buck topology to multiphase architectures is described to better understand the great advantages brought by multiphase architectures.
The buck topology and the MOSFET gate drive signal are shown in Fig.2. The gate signal period is always referred to as the converter switching period T. The duty-cycle D is defined as the ratio between the MOSFET on-time and the switching period. Since one terminal of the power MOSFET is tied to the high-side of the input voltage rail, the MOSFET is also called high-side MOSFET. The steady-state analysis is here performed assuming constant the input voltage and the output voltage during a switching period.

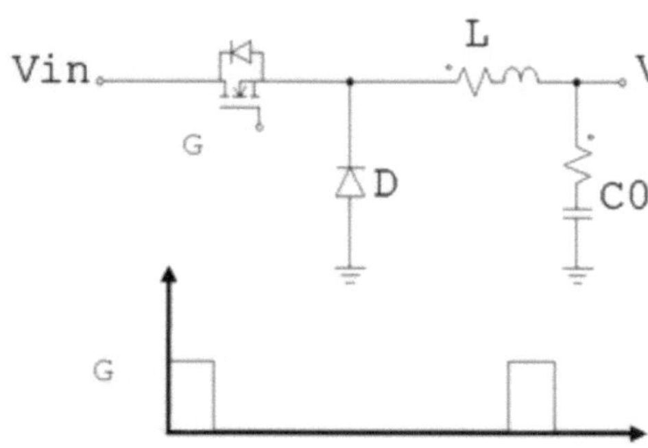

Fig. 2. The buck converter topology and gate drive signal.

On the rising edge of the gate drive signal, the high-side MOSFET is turned on. The inductor is now series connected between the input and output rails and the diode is reverse biased. During the MOSFET on-time, the inductor current slope is constant and it can be expressed as:

$$s_{on} = \frac{Vin - Vout}{L} \tag{1}$$

On the falling edge of the gate drive signal, the MOSFET is turned off. The inductor opposes the current break trying to maintain the previously established current. The voltage polarity across it immediately reverses. Since the right terminal of the inductor is tied to the output rail, the cathode voltage of the diode D is driven toward negative values. When zero crossing occurs, the diode D is forced into conduction clamping the cathode node to ground. The inductor voltage is now reversed and full inductor current flows through the diode D.
The inductor is now connected in parallel to the output voltage rail. During the OFF-time, the slope of the inductor current is given by:

$$s_{off} = \frac{-Vout}{L} \tag{2}$$

Under steady-state conditions, the average inductor voltage over a switching period is zero, resulting in the expression:

$$(Vin - Vout) \cdot T_{on} = -Vout \cdot T_{off} \tag{3}$$

Or

$$Vout = Vin \cdot \frac{T_{on}}{T_{on} + T_{off}} \tag{4}$$

where Ton is the MOSFET conduction time and Toff the MOSFET off-time.
As shown in Fig.3 the inductor undergoes a magnetizing cycle over the entire switching period. The inductor current ripple could be expressed as:

$$\Delta I_L = \frac{Vin - Vout}{L} \cdot T_{on} = \frac{-Vout}{L} \cdot T_{off} = \frac{Vin(1-D)D}{L} T \tag{5}$$

where D is the duty cycle and T the switching period.

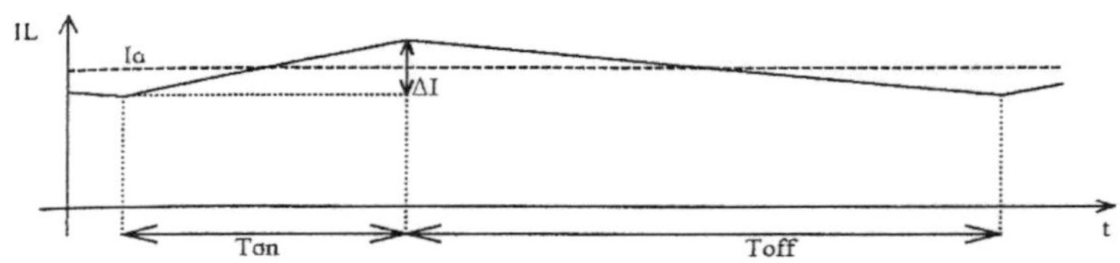

Fig. 3. The inductor current waveform over the switching period under steady-state conditions.

Since at steady-state the average capacitor current is null, the average inductor current is equal to the load current. The ac component of the inductor current flows through the parallel connection between load and capacitor. Commonly, the capacitor is large enough to assume that its impedance at the switching frequency is much smaller than the load resistance. Hence nearly all the inductor current ripple flows through the capacitor. The ac current flowing into the load could be reasonably neglected. A continuous conduction mode is assumed. The inductor is sufficiently large to assume:

$$\frac{\Delta IL}{2} \ll I_{out} \tag{6}$$

The inductor current never crosses zero during the switching period. A continuous conduction mode is preferred in high-current applications since lower and lower conduction power losses are involved.
The capacitor current waveform is shown in Fig.4. When the capacitor current is positive, the stored charge as well as the capacitor voltage will increase. Vice versa, when the capacitor current goes negative, stored charge will be released and the output voltage will decrease as well.
The total voltage change occurs between two consecutive zero-crossings of the capacitor current. Evaluating the total charge q as the grey-coloured area in Fig.4 yields:

$$q = \frac{1}{2} \frac{\Delta I_L}{2} \frac{T}{2} \tag{7}$$

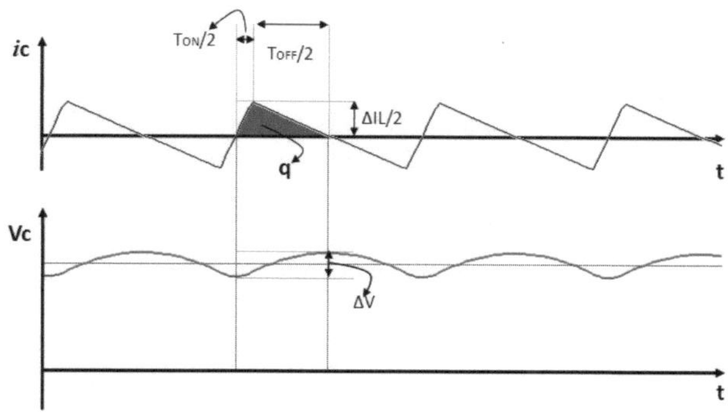

Fig. 4. At the top, the output capacitor current. At the bottom, the output voltage.

The voltage ripple across the output capacitor is given by:

$$\Delta V = \frac{q}{C} = \frac{\Delta I_L T}{8C} \tag{8}$$

Increasing the output capacitor value or the switching frequency directly improves the output voltage regulation. If a larger inductor is selected, the ripple current would decrease as well as the output voltage ripple. Yet, by increasing the inductor value the load transient response is worsened. A load transient could be modelled by the equivalent circuit shown in Fig.5.

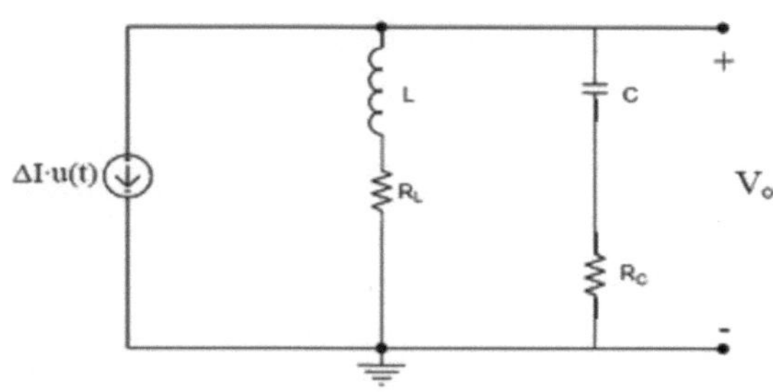

Fig. 5. The equivalent circuit under large-signal load transients.

The load transient is modelled as an ideal current step. Since the input voltage is assumed constant, the switching node is dynamically tied to ground. The inductor is thus parallel connected to the output capacitor filter. If the loop response is sluggish, the peak output voltage deviation $\Delta V_{out,max}$ tends to approach the open-loop value which is given by:

$$\Delta V_{out,max} = \Delta I \cdot \sqrt{\frac{L}{C}} + Rc \cdot \Delta I \tag{9}$$

where ΔI is the current step width and Rc the equivalent series resistor of the output capacitor.

In Fig.6 the load current *Iload*, the inductor current *IL*, the capacitor current *Ic* and the output voltage V*out* under a load transient are shown. By increasing the output capacitor value, the dynamic response could be further improved. Yet, in high-current applications a too large capacitance will be obtained affecting the system cost and size.

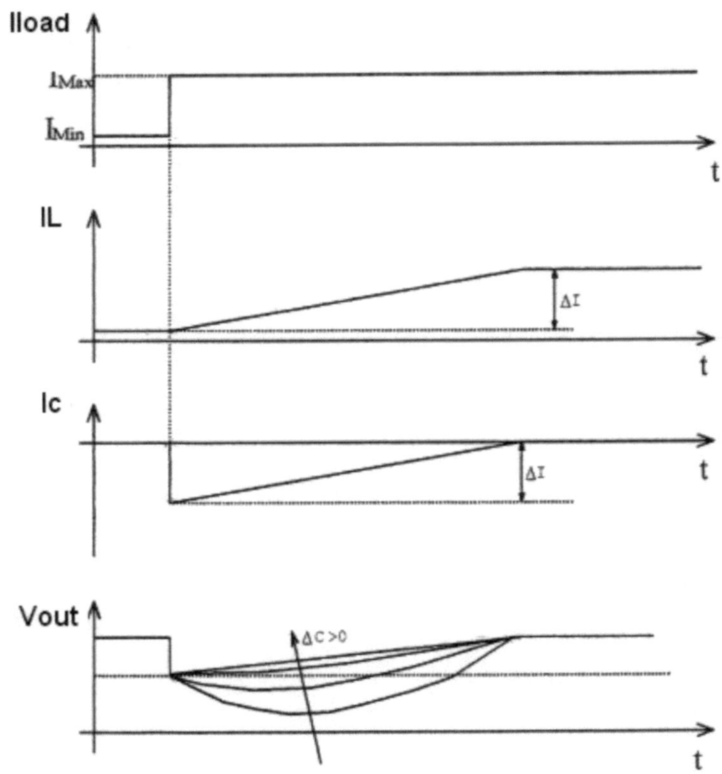

Fig. 6. The converter waveforms under a large-signal transient.

The optimization of steady-state and dynamic performances leads to a trade-off in the choice of the inductor value. As will be further discussed, the inductor value is usually chosen to meet steady-state requirements and dynamic performances are improved by the control algorithm.

As shown by (4), the buck converter reduces the dc input voltage by the means of switching elements. Power loss due to switches is ideally zero. Yet, switches are not ideal. Further, switching losses cannot be neglected. The inductor current flows through the MOSFET during the on-time and through the diode during the OFF time. Conduction losses are proportional to the forward voltage drop across the active elements. The MOSFET forward voltage drop is lower than the diode threshold voltage. In a buck converter, conduction losses are mainly due to the freewheeling diode.

In high-current low-voltage applications, synchronous rectification is widely used to improve efficiency. As shown in Fig.7, the diode D is replaced by a MOSFET featuring a very low forward voltage drop. The rectification function, typically performed by diodes, is now achieved by the means of a MOSFET which is driven synchronously with the high-side MOSFET. For this reason, the added MOSFET is sometimes referred to as the synchronous rectifier MOSFET. Since the rectifier MOSFET source terminal is tied to the low-side of the input voltage rail, the MOSFET is also called low-side MOSFET. If compared with classical topology, synchronous rectification heavily reduces conduction losses improving efficiency. During the conduction time of the high-side (on time) the low-side is off and vice versa.

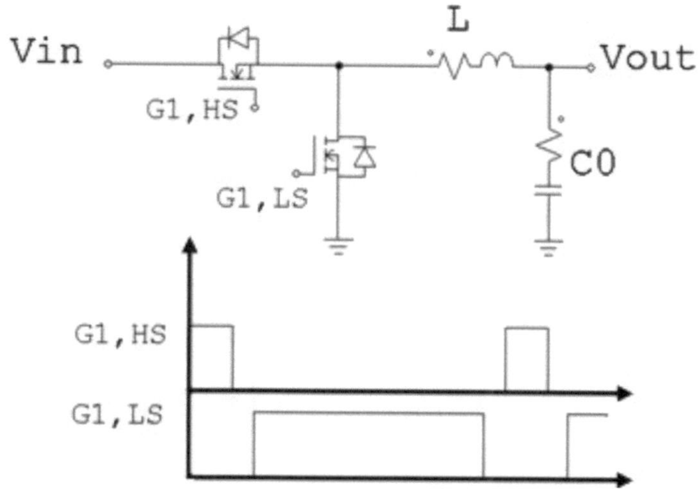

Fig. 7. The synchronous buck topology and MOSFETs gate drive signals.

A dead-time is required to avoid the simultaneous conduction of high-side and low-side MOSFETs. During the dead time, neither the low-side nor the high side MOSFET is on. When the high-side MOSFET is turned off, the inductor opposes the current break forcing the low-side MOSFET body-diode into conduction. Over the entire dead time the full inductor current flows through the body diode itself. At the end of the dead time, the low-side MOSFET is turned on, the body diode is bypassed by the active MOSFET channel and the inductor current flows through the low-side MOSFET channel. During the dead time, classical and synchronous topologies are exactly alike. It would be advisable a further reduction of both the diode threshold voltage and the dead time in order to limit power losses. A Schottky diode is often integrated in parallel to power MOSFET: the body diode will be bypassed by the Schottky diode over the entire dead time lowering the effective threshold voltage. A minimization of the low-side body-diode conduction time is required to take advantage from synchronous rectification. Sophisticated dead-time control algorithms are usually implemented by synchronous MOSFET drivers. If a single buck converter topology were employed in high-current applications, a large amount of output-filter and on-board decoupling capacitance would be required to achieve the expected transient response. The size and cost of the voltage regulator would increase as well. Multi-phase converters are widely used. Ripple cancellation and improved transient response are only a few advantages of multi-phase architectures. A detailed analysis of multiphase converters is reported in (Miftakhutdinov, 2001). In N-modules architecture, N identical buck converters are connected in parallel to the load resulting in a heavy reduction of the output ripple. Smaller inductances are allowed thus improving the transient response. Note that increasing the number of modules emphasizes the advantages of a multiphase architecture. Gate drive signals are interleaved to take full advantage from the multiphase architecture. Assume that each channel operates at a switching frequency f_{sw}. Under steady-state conditions, the phase shift between gate drive signals of each module depend on the number of interleaved channels. If an N-channels architecture is considered, assume that the control signal sequence is Phase 1, 2,.., N. The interleaved technique requires a 360°/N phase shift between two following channels. The maximum number of channel is limited by the relationship:

$$(1 - D) > N \cdot D \tag{10}$$

where N is the number of channel and D is the duty-cycle. A key feature of multiphase architecture is now highlighted: the ripple frequency of the output voltage is N-times the switching frequency of each power module. The equivalent switching frequency is higher and higher than the effective switching frequency of each module. The designed multiphase converter features a 4-modules architecture, as shown in Fig.8. Inductors and capacitors are modelled including the parasitic equivalent series resistance. Assume that the control sequence is Phase 1,2,3,4. Interleaved gate drive signals are shown in Fig.9. Fig.10 shows the inductor current waveforms for each buck channel. As shown in Fig.11, the equivalent current is defined as:

$$IL_{eq} = \sum_{i=1}^{n} IL_i = IL_1 + IL_2 + IL_3 + IL_4 \tag{11}$$

Ripple cancellation derives from the interleaving technique. The steady-state analysis is carried on within a fundamental Tsw/4 time interval. Within a Tsw/4 period, only one module could be driven in the ON state, the others are constantly OFF. For example, from 0 to Tsw/4 modules 2, 3 and 4 are constantly OFF while the first module (phase 1) is driven in the ON state during the subinterval [0, DTsw/4]. No matter which phase is active in the ON state, the fundamental period of the output waveforms is Tsw/4 since we have assumed identical modules.

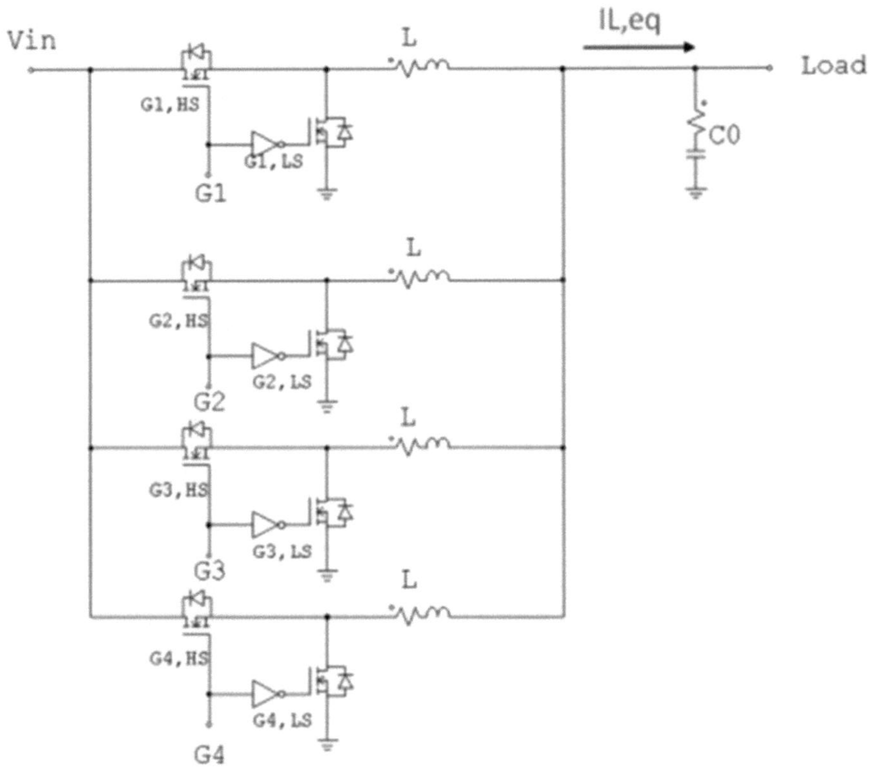

Fig. 8. Multiphase architecture.

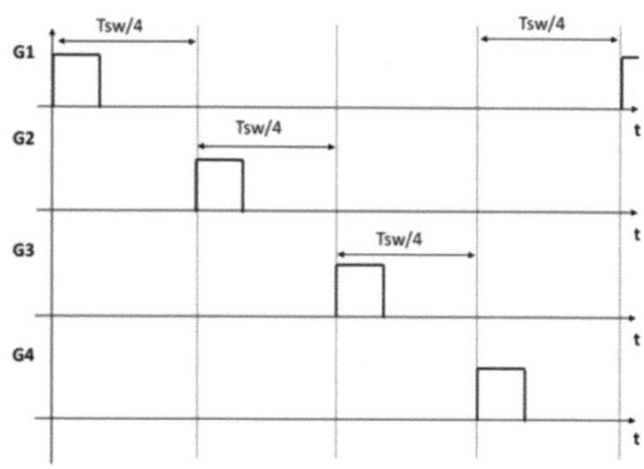

Fig. 9. High-side MOSFETs gate drive signals.

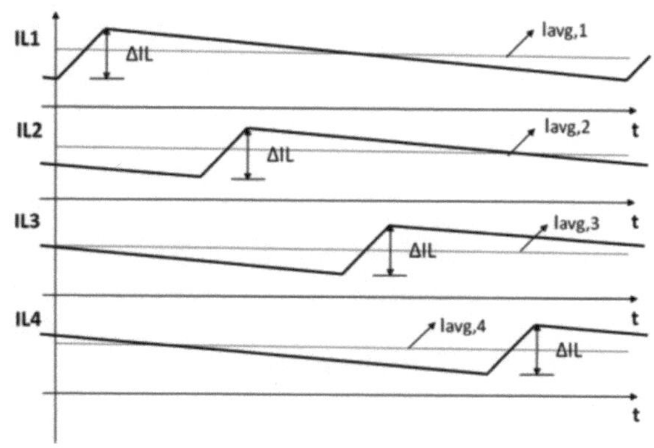

Fig. 10. Inductor current waveforms under steady-state conditions.

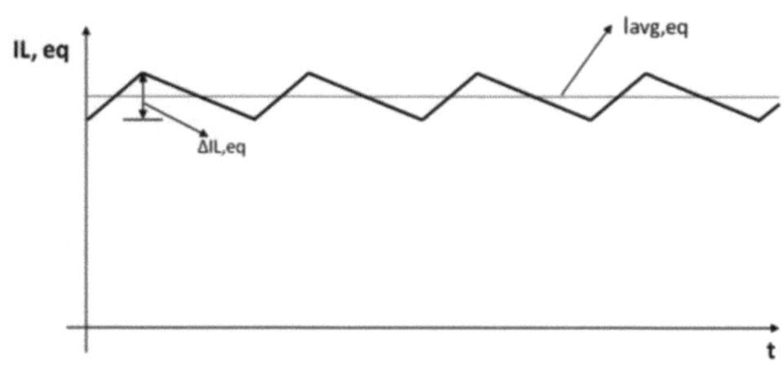

Fig. 11. Equivalent inductor current under steady-state conditions.

Within the time interval [0, DTsw/4] the slope of the equivalent current is given by:

$$s_{eq,on} = \frac{Vin - Vout}{L} - (N-1)\frac{Vout}{L} = \frac{Vin(1-ND)}{L} \quad (12)$$

The equivalent slope is positive during the first subinterval. During the second subinterval [DTsw/4,Tsw/4] all modules are driven OFF. The equivalent current slope is negative according to the equation:

$$s_{eq,off} = -N\frac{Vout}{L} \tag{13}$$

The equivalent current ripple is given by:

$$\Delta I_{L,eq} = \frac{Vin(1-ND)D}{L}T_{sw} = \frac{\Delta IL\,(1-ND)}{(1-D)} \tag{14}$$

As (14) states, in a multiphase architecture the current ripple is cancelled. If compared with classical buck converters, the current ripple is reduced by (1-ND)/(1-D). Moreover, the equivalent switching frequency as seen by the power load is N times the operating switching frequency of each power module.
Note that (14) could be expressed as:

$$\Delta I_{L,eq} = \frac{Vin(1-ND)D}{L}T_{sw} = \frac{Vin(1-ND)DN\cdot N}{N\cdot N\,L}T_{sw} = \frac{Vin,eq(1-Deq)Deq}{Leq}T_{sw,eq} \tag{15}$$

where N is the number of modules and $Deq = N\cdot D,\ fsw,eq = N\cdot fsw,\ Leq = \frac{L}{N}, Vin,eq = \frac{Vin}{N}$.
By comparing (15) and (5), conclusions are drawn: a N-modules architecture is equivalent to a buck converter operating at $f_{sw,eq}$ switching frequency, D_{eq} duty-cycle, supplied by $V_{in,eq}$ input voltage and featuring L_{eq} inductance. Then, if compared with a buck converter fed by the same input voltage rail and supplying the same voltage bus, the multiphase architecture features higher switching frequency, higher duty-cycle and lower inductance. Both steady-state and dynamic performances of the switching regulator take a great advantage from these interesting properties. With regards to steady-state performances, tight voltage regulation could be achieved thanks to the ripple cancellation effect. Dynamic performances are greatly improved by the reduction of the equivalent inductor under load transients. The steady-state and dynamic performances of multiphase converters are affected by the duty cycle value. A narrow duty cycle results in a poor ripple cancellation. Hence, a larger inductance should be selected to keep tight voltage regulation worsening the transient response. If a wide input-output voltage range is considered, a proper design of passive components is not yet suitable for speeding up the system performances. Multiphase architectures achieving a duty cycle extension by the means of coupled inductors are frequently proposed in literature.
Otherwise, unconventional control algorithms are proposed to speed up the transient response not affecting the passive components design.

3. The control system

A survey of the control algorithm is given to highlight the system complexity and high accuracy of simulation results. Authors suggest (Boscaino et al., 2009) for further details. A linear-non-linear digital controller oriented to IC implementation, improving both steady-state and transient response is presented. A schematic block diagram of the linear loop is shown in Fig.12.
A Pulse Width Modulation (PWM) current-mode control is implemented. Two 10 bits/2V ADCs and a 12 bits /5V DAC are included in the analog-digital interface. The output voltage is converted to digital and compared to a reference voltage V_{ref}. The error signal

COMP_OUT is generated by the error amplifier which includes the adder and the *COMP* block. A type-2 compensation action is digitally implemented to ensure system stability. The error signal is then converted to analog and compared to the current sense signal of each power module Vc2,i.

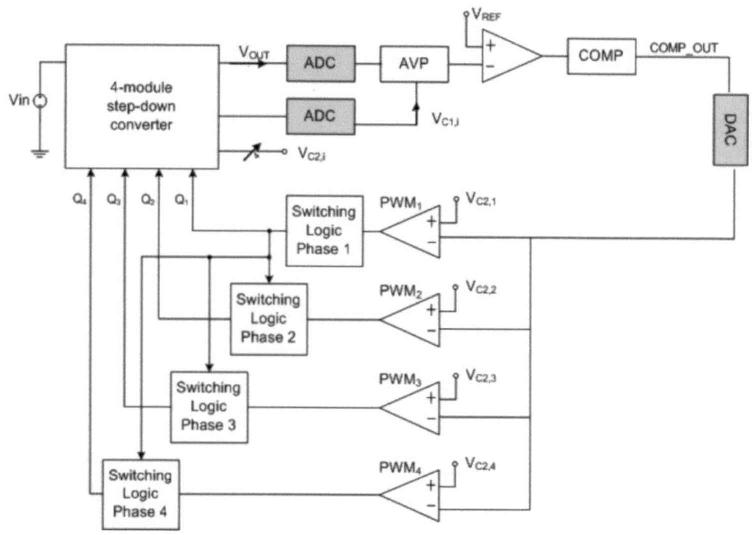

Fig. 12. Schematic block diagram of the linear controller.

The gate drive interleaved technique is digitally implemented by the *Switching logic* subsystems. The master module is the Phase 1, the others slave. Fig.13 shows the switching logic algorithm for the master power module. A clock signal at the switching frequency is synchronously derived from the system clock. The switch-on of the high-side MOSFET is triggered by the rising-edge of the switching clock Ck1. The high-side MOSFET switch-off is triggered by the rising-edge of the corresponding PWM signal.

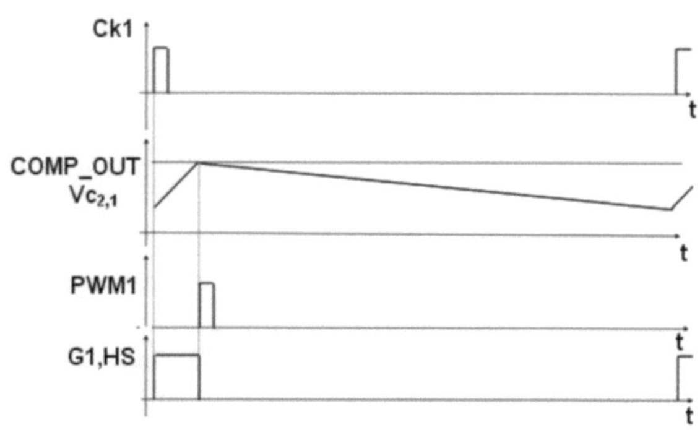

Fig. 13. Switching logic for the master module.

A digital counter generates a switching clock for each slave module which is synchronous with the master switching clock and phase-shifted according to the interleaved technique.
The sense signal $V_{c2,i}$ reproduces the instantaneous inductor current of the *i-th* power module. RC networks are used to sense the instantaneous inductor current of each power

module. As shown in Fig.14, a RC filter is connected across the low-side MOSFET of each power module. The capacitor voltage V_{c2} is the sense signal for current-mode control implementation.

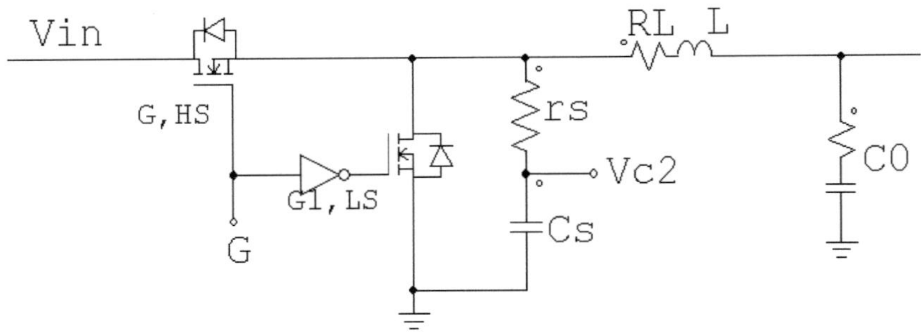

Fig. 14. Current sense network.

The period $T=r_sC_s$ is fixed according to the equation:

$$D_{max}T_{sw} \ll T \tag{16}$$

where T_{sw} is the switching period and D_{max} the maximum operating duty-cycle. The charge and discharge of the capacitor C_2 within the switching period reproduces the charge and discharge of the inductor L. The average value of the sense signal is given by:

$$\overline{V_{c2}} = Vout + \overline{I_L}R_L \tag{17}$$

where $\overline{I_L}$ is the average inductor current and R_L the ESR of the inductor L.
The superimposed ripple is given by:

$$\Delta V_{c2} = R_v \Delta I_L \tag{18}$$

where ΔI_L is the inductor current ripple and R_v the virtual sensing resistor which is given by:

$$R_v = \frac{L}{r_s C_s} \tag{19}$$

The current-mode control is implemented by the Vc2 sense signal. A detailed analysis of the proposed current-sensing technique, including design guidelines is reported in (Boscaino et al., 2008).
Another RC network featuring a lower cut-off frequency is connected across the switching node of the master phase. The sense capacitor voltage V_{c1} reproduces the average inductor current. V_{c1} is converted to digital and feeds the *AVP* subsystem which implements the well-known Adaptive Voltage Positioning (AVP) technique. Fig.15 shows the output voltage and the load current waveforms under a load current step without AVP. The maximum tolerance window on the output voltage is given by:

$$\Delta V_{out,max} = 2 \cdot \Delta I_{o,max} Rc \tag{20}$$

With the AVP technique, the reference voltage becomes a function of the load current according to the following equation.

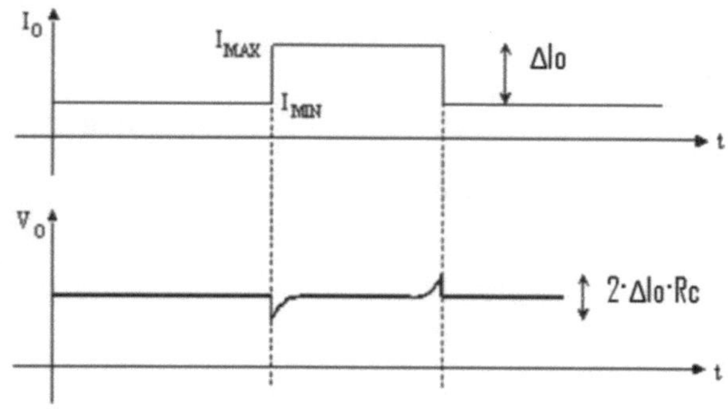

Fig. 15. Dynamic response under load transients. At the top the load current step, at the bottom, the output voltage waveforms are shown.

$$v'_{ref} = V_{ref} - I_o Rc \quad (21)$$

where, v'_{ref} is the variable reference voltage, V_{ref} is a fixed reference voltage, I_o is the load current and R_c is the equivalent series resistor of the output capacitor. The DC set point of the output voltage changes accordingly to the output current, as shown in Fig.16. At steady-state, the output voltage is forced by the AVP technique to the variable reference voltage, instead of a fixed value V_{ref} . Under high-load conditions, the DC set point drops in the lower part of the allowable tolerance window. The maximum tolerance window is now given by:

$$\Delta V_{out,max} = \Delta I_{o,max} Rc \quad (22)$$

The technique results in added margin to handle load transients. Since the load current is equal to the average inductor current, the AVP technique is implemented by sensing the average inductor current of the master phase.

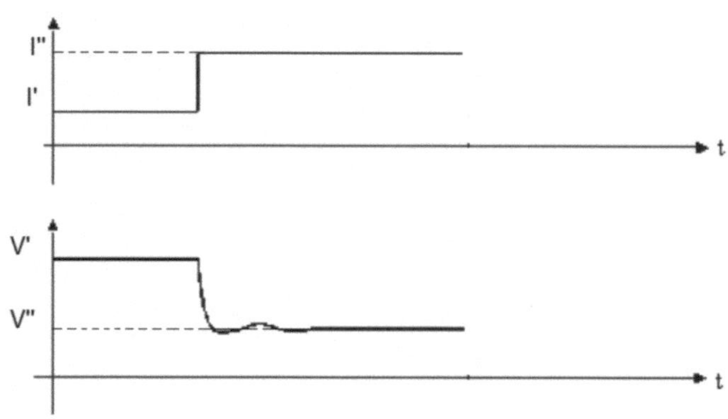

Fig. 16. The dynamic response to a load current step with Adaptive Voltage Positioning.

A non-linear control is introduced to speed-up the transient response not affecting steady-state performances. During transients, the non-linear control modifies a few linear loop parameters, as the reference voltage or the duty-cycle. Since the converter output voltage is the only non-linear loop input, the proposed technique can be efficiently applied to each power supply system independently of the specific converter topology and linear loop architecture. Thanks to the AVP technique, load transients are detected by an instantaneous drop of the output voltage, and the increasing or decreasing load current transient is detected by monitoring the output voltage drop in terms of sign and width. Two different non-linear control actions are implemented: under a load current increase (*case a*) or decrease (*case b*). The reference voltage (*case a*) or the duty-cycle (*case b*) is modified by the non-linear control loop. Under increasing load current steps, the non-linear control loop acts on the reference voltage advancing the linear loop action. Two auxiliary signals, V_{VAR} and V_{LOOP}, are defined: V_{VAR} is the output voltage value related to the new steady-state condition while V_{LOOP} is the output voltage ripple during transient referred to V_{VAR} value, as shown in Fig.17.

$$V_{LOOP} = Vout - V_{VAR} \tag{23}$$

$$v'_{ref} = V_{ref} - V_{LOOP} \tag{24}$$

In order to achieve the fastest transient response, the gain factor K_{NL} is introduced. Hence, v'_{REF} is given by:

$$v'_{ref} = V_{ref} - K_{NL}V_{LOOP} \tag{25}$$

The K_{NL} value is designed by the frequency response analysis to ensure the fastest effective gain under transients avoiding loop instabilities. Under transients, the difference between the output voltage and V_{VAR} is monitored and compared with the maximum steady-state output voltage ripple V_{OUT_STEADY}. If the condition (26) is continuously verified over T_{STEADY} time, the non-linear control action ends.

$$Vout - V_{VAR} < \Delta V_{OUT\_STEADY} \tag{26}$$

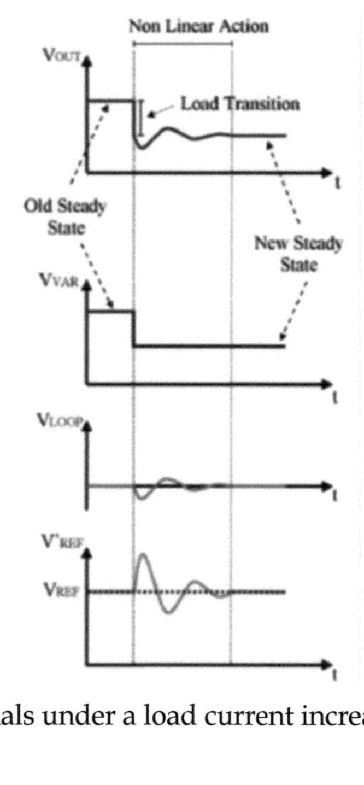

Fig. 17. Non linear control signals under a load current increase.

Under a load current decrease, the non-linear control loop modifies the duty-cycle signal, as shown in Fig.18. All modules are simultaneously turned off to allow the inductor current to decrease as fast as possible. Turning off all modules allows the fastest transient response. Unfortunately, the system is driven towards a loop upsetting and thus to an increase, instead of a reduction, of the output voltage over-and-under shoots. Then, a fixed duty-cycle is forced to all modules according to the interleaved technique. Known the V_{VAR} value, the new steady-state duty-cycle is evaluated and forced by the non-linear subsystem to maintain a regulated output voltage during linear loop resettling. The false steady-state period is a tunable parameter to achieve high design flexibility.

$$D_{NL} = \frac{Vout + \overline{I_L} R_L}{Vin} \tag{27}$$

where Vout is the regulated output voltage, $\overline{I_L}$ is the average inductor current of a single module, R_L the inductor parasitic resistance and Vin the converter input voltage.
From (27), defining the K_R constant as:

$$K_R = \frac{4R_L}{Rc} \tag{28}$$

the forced D_{NL} value is obtained:

$$D_{NL} = \frac{V_{VAR} + (Vout_{I=0} - V_{VAR})K_R}{Vin} \tag{29}$$

The duty-cycle value is evaluated by the non linear controller by the means of fixed parameters and the V_{VAR} value which is obtained by monitoring the output voltage. The difference between the output voltage and V_{VAR} is monitored and compared to the maximum steady-state output voltage ripple V_{OUT_STEADY}. If the condition (30) is continuously verified over a fixed T_{FSS} time, the non-linear control action ends.

$$Vout - V_{VAR} < \Delta V_{OUT\_STEADY} \tag{30}$$

Further design guidelines could be found in (Boscaino et al. 2009, 2010).

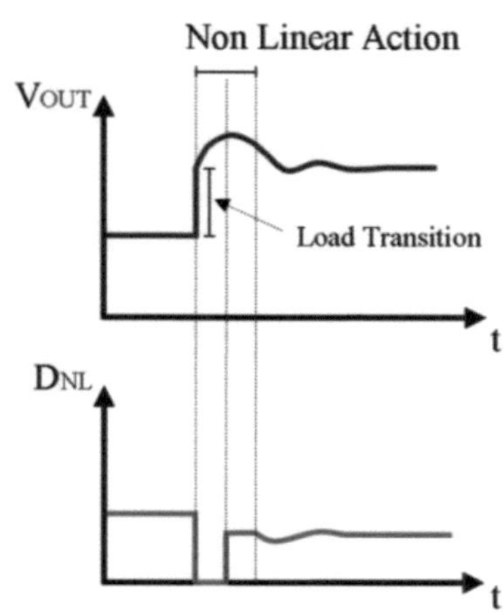

Fig. 18. The output voltage and the forced duty-cycle value under a load current decrease.

4. Co-simulation set-up

Active-HDL provides an interface to MATLAB/Simulink simulation environment which allows co-simulation of functional blocks described by using hardware description languages. The digital controller is tested on a FPGA device. A specific co-simulation procedure should be activated in order to make each VHDL design unit available in Simulink libraries. The VHDL code and signal timing are tested as well. High-accuracy simulation results are obtained heavily reducing experimental fault conditions. The co-simulation procedure features automatic data type conversion between Simulink and Active HDL and simulation results could be displayed in both simulation environments. All VHDL entities are collected in an Active HDL workspace. A MATLAB m-file is generated for each VHDL entity. By right clicking on a VHDL entity, select the option "Generate Block Description for Simulink". The procedure is repeated for each VHDL entity of current Workspace. After generating the m-files, the *Active-HDL Blockset* is available in the Simulink library browser. The *Active-HDL Co-Sim* and *HDL Black-Box* elements are used for system co-simulation. The *Active-HDL Co-Sim* element must be included in the Simulink top level model. The block allows the designer to fix co-simulation parameters. In order to simulate a VHDL entity as an integral part of the current model, a *HDL Black-Box* block should be added and associated to the corresponding m-file by the configuration box. When the model is completed, running simulation from Simulink starts the co-simulation. The connection to the Active-HDL server will be opened and all *HDL Black-Boxes* simulated with the Active-HDL simulator. Input and output waveforms can be analyzed both in Simulink and Aldec environment while internal signal waveforms can be analyzed in Aldec environment only.

5. MATLAB/Simulink model

The top level model is shown in Fig.19. The power section includes the *Multiphase converter* and the *Current-sense* subsystems. In the *A/D converter* subsystem, the Analog-to-Digital interface is modelled by Simulink library elements. The controller is modelled in Aldec Active-HDL environment and each design unit is included in the *Controller* subsystem. The *Active-HDL Co-Sim* block is added to the top level model.

5.1 The power section model

The power section includes the multiphase converter and current-sense filters. A four-module interleaved synchronous buck converter is connected to the power load. The power section is modelled by Simulink library elements in order to achieve the highest processing speed. The use of several co-simulation tools is avoided, keeping at the same time the highest accuracy. In this paragraph, the Simulink model of the multiphase converter based on a continuous-time large-signal model is described. The proposed modelling technique could be efficiently extended to each switching converter.

In Simulink environment, the State-Space block models a system by its own state-space equations:

$$\begin{aligned} \dot{x} &= \boldsymbol{Ax} + \boldsymbol{Bu} \\ y &= \boldsymbol{Cx} + \boldsymbol{Du} \end{aligned} \qquad (31)$$

where **x** is the state vector, **u** the input vector and **y** the output vector.

According to (31), the block is fed by the input vector $\boldsymbol{u}$ and the output vector $\boldsymbol{y}$ is generated. As shown in Fig.20, the designer could enter the matrix coefficients in the parameter box.

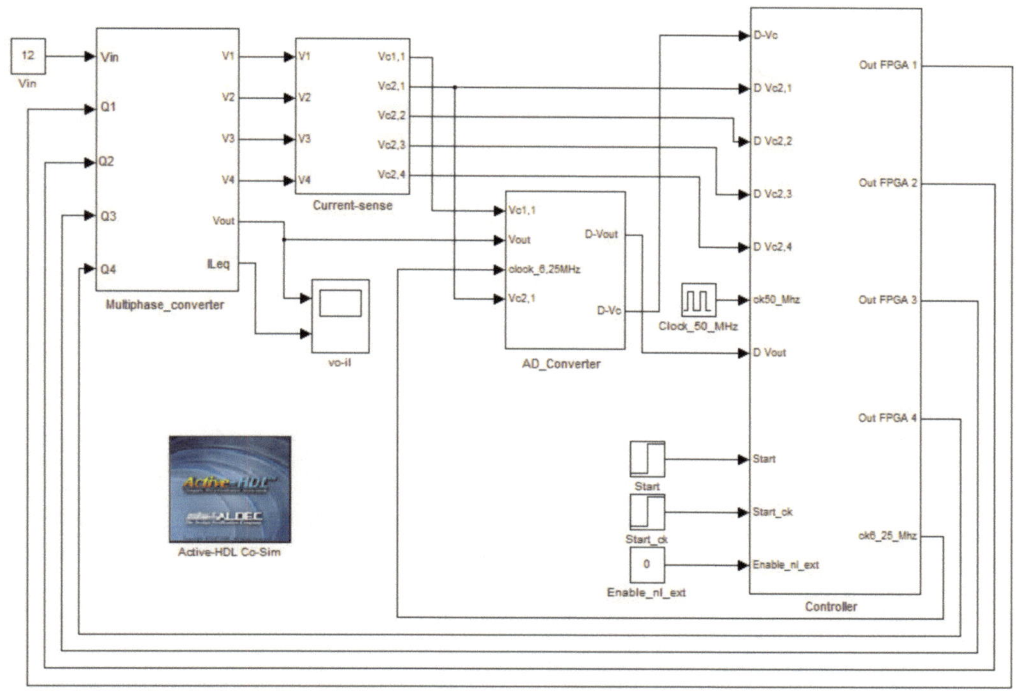

Fig. 19. Top level model

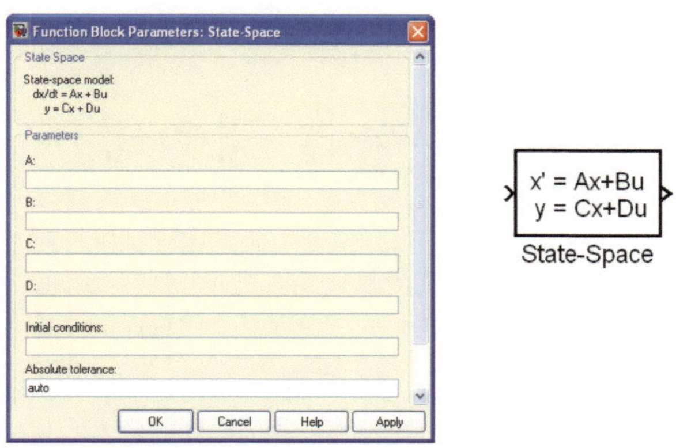

Fig. 20. The State-Space block and the parameter box.

A continuous large-signal model of the buck converter is derived and implemented by the state-space block. The Parasitic components of passive elements as the DC resistance of the inductor (DCR) and the capacitor equivalent series resistor (Rc) are included. Assuming identical MOSFETs, the model accounts for the MOSFET equivalent resistance $R_{ds,on}$. Define a state vector as:

$$\boldsymbol{x}(t) = \begin{bmatrix} x_1(t) \\ x_2(t) \end{bmatrix} = \begin{bmatrix} i_L(t) \\ v_c(t) \end{bmatrix} \tag{32}$$

where $i_L(t)$ is the inductor current and $v_c(t)$ is the voltage across the output capacitor.
In the proposed model, the output vector is defined as:

$$\boldsymbol{y}(t) = \begin{bmatrix} y_1(t) \\ y_2(t) \end{bmatrix} = \begin{bmatrix} i_L(t) \\ v_{out}(t) \end{bmatrix} \tag{33}$$

where $v_{out}(t)$ is the output voltage and $i_L(t)$ the inductor current.
During the on-time, the buck converter is equivalent to the circuit shown in Fig.21.

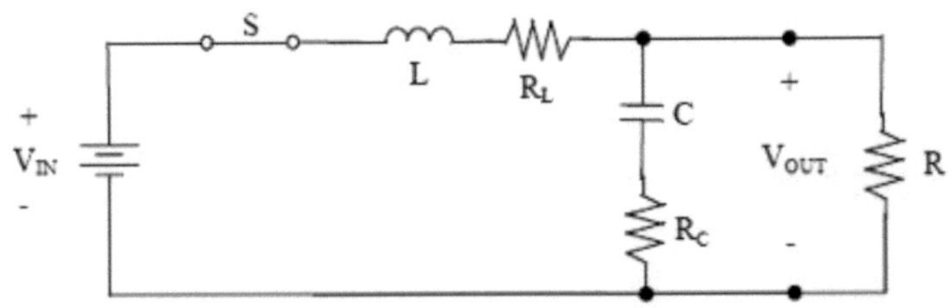

Fig. 21. On-time equivalent circuit.

Both the inductor DCR and the high-side $R_{ds,on}$ are included in the resistance R_L. The analysis of the on-time circuits yields:

$$\begin{cases} L\dot{x}_1(t) + RcC\dot{x}_2(t) = -R_L x_1(t) - x_2(t) + Vin \\ (Rc + R)C\dot{x}_2(t) = Rx_1(t) - x_2(t) \end{cases} \tag{34}$$

The corresponding matrix equation is given by:

$$\begin{bmatrix} L & RcC \\ 0 & (Rc+R)C \end{bmatrix} \dot{\boldsymbol{x}}(t) = \begin{bmatrix} R_L & -1 \\ R & -1 \end{bmatrix} \boldsymbol{x}(t) + \begin{bmatrix} 1 \\ 0 \end{bmatrix} Vin \tag{35}$$

From (35), the (36) is obtained:

$$\dot{\boldsymbol{x}}(t) = \begin{bmatrix} \dfrac{R_L Rc + R(R_L + Rc)}{(Rc+R)L} & -\dfrac{R}{(Rc+R)L} \\ \dfrac{R}{(Rc+R)C} & -\dfrac{1}{(Rc+R)C} \end{bmatrix} \boldsymbol{x}(t) + \begin{bmatrix} \frac{1}{L} \\ 0 \end{bmatrix} Vin \tag{36}$$

The OFF-time equivalent circuit is shown in Fig.22. Both inductor DCR and low-side $R_{ds,on}$ are included in R_L resistance.

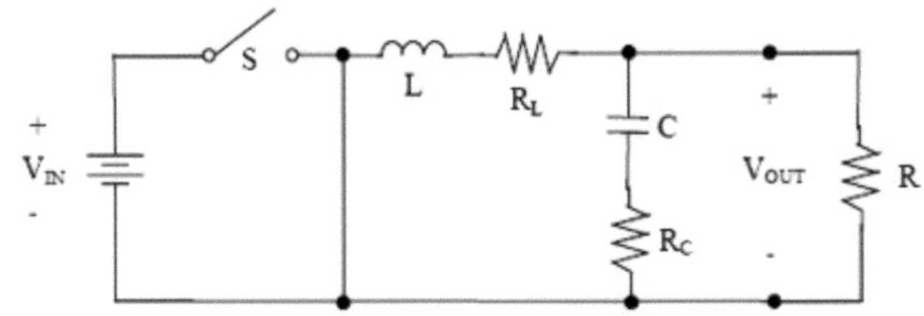

Fig. 22. OFF-time equivalent circuit

The analysis yields:

$$\begin{cases} L\dot{x}_1(t) + RcC\dot{x}_2(t) \doteq -R_L x_1(t) - x_2(t) \\ (Rc+R)C\dot{x}_2(t) = Rx_1(t) - x_2(t) \end{cases} \tag{37}$$

The corresponding matrix equation is given by:

$$\begin{bmatrix} L & RcC \\ 0 & (Rc+R)C \end{bmatrix} \dot{\boldsymbol{x}}(t) = \begin{bmatrix} R_L & -1 \\ R & -1 \end{bmatrix} \boldsymbol{x}(t) \tag{38}$$

Manipulating (38) the (39) is obtained:

$$\dot{\boldsymbol{x}}(t) = \begin{bmatrix} \dfrac{R_L Rc + R(R_L + Rc)}{(Rc+R)L} & -\dfrac{R}{(Rc+R)L} \\ \dfrac{R}{(Rc+R)C} & -\dfrac{1}{(Rc+R)C} \end{bmatrix} \boldsymbol{x}(t) \tag{39}$$

With regard to the output vector, the analysis of both circuits yields:

$$\begin{cases} y_1(t) = x_1(t) \\ y_2(t) = \dfrac{RcR}{R+Rc} x_1(t) + \dfrac{R}{R+Rc} x_2(t) \end{cases} \tag{40}$$

The corresponding matrix equation is given by:

$$\boldsymbol{y}(t) = \begin{bmatrix} 1 & 0 \\ \dfrac{RRc}{R+Rc} & \dfrac{R}{R+Rc} \end{bmatrix} \boldsymbol{x}(t) \tag{41}$$

The analysis of equivalent circuits results in two linear state-space models. During the on-time, the converter is modelled by state-space equations (42):

$$\begin{aligned} \dot{\mathbf{x}}(\mathbf{t}) &= \mathbf{A_{on}} \cdot \mathbf{x}(\mathbf{t}) + \mathbf{b_{on}} \cdot u(\mathrm{t}) \\ \mathbf{y}(\mathbf{t}) &= \mathbf{C_{on}} \cdot \dot{\mathbf{x}}(\mathbf{t}) + \mathbf{d_{on}} \cdot u(\mathrm{t}) \end{aligned} \tag{42}$$

where:

$$\boldsymbol{A}_{on} = \begin{bmatrix} \dfrac{R_L Rc + R(R_L + Rc)}{(Rc+R)L} & -\dfrac{R}{(Rc+R)L} \\ \dfrac{R}{(Rc+R)C} & -\dfrac{1}{(Rc+R)C} \end{bmatrix} \tag{43}$$

$$\mathbf{b_{on}} = \begin{bmatrix} \dfrac{1}{\mathrm{L}} \\ 0 \end{bmatrix} \tag{44}$$

$$\mathbf{C_{on}} = \begin{bmatrix} 1 & 0 \\ \dfrac{\mathrm{RRc}}{\mathrm{R+Rc}} & \dfrac{\mathrm{R}}{\mathrm{R+Rc}} \end{bmatrix} \tag{45}$$

$$\mathbf{d_{on}} = \begin{bmatrix} 0 \\ 0 \end{bmatrix} \tag{46}$$

During the OFF-time, the converter is modelled as:

$$\dot{\mathbf{x}}(\mathbf{t}) = \mathbf{A_{off}} \cdot \mathbf{x}(\mathbf{t}) + \mathbf{b_{off}} \cdot u(\mathrm{t})$$

$$\mathbf{y}(\mathbf{t}) = \mathbf{C_{off}} \cdot \mathbf{x}(\mathbf{t}) + \mathbf{d_{off}} \cdot u(\mathrm{t}) \tag{47}$$

where

$$\boldsymbol{A}_{on} = \begin{bmatrix} \frac{R_L Rc + R(R_L + Rc)}{(Rc + R)L} & -\frac{R}{(Rc + R)L} \\ \frac{R}{(Rc + R)C} & -\frac{1}{(Rc + R)C} \end{bmatrix} \tag{48}$$

$$\mathbf{b_{off}} = \begin{bmatrix} 0 \\ 0 \end{bmatrix} \tag{49}$$

$$\mathbf{C_{off}} = \begin{bmatrix} 1 & 0 \\ \frac{\mathrm{RRc}}{\mathrm{R} + \mathrm{Rc}} & \frac{\mathrm{R}}{\mathrm{R} + \mathrm{Rc}} \end{bmatrix} \tag{50}$$

$$\mathbf{d_{off}} = \begin{bmatrix} 0 \\ 0 \end{bmatrix} \tag{51}$$

Note that:

$$\mathbf{A}=\mathbf{A}_{\mathrm{ON}}=\mathbf{A}_{\mathrm{OFF}}$$

$$\mathbf{C}=\mathbf{C}_{\mathrm{ON}}=\mathbf{C}_{\mathrm{OFF}}$$

$$\mathbf{b}_{\mathrm{OFF}}=\mathbf{0}$$

$$\mathbf{d}_{\mathrm{ON}}= \mathbf{d}_{\mathrm{OFF}}=\mathbf{0} \tag{52}$$

Define the gate drive signal $q(\mathrm{t})$ as:

$$q(t) = \begin{cases} 1 \; during \; the \; ON \; time \\ 0 \; during \; the \; OFF \; time \end{cases} \tag{53}$$

With the aid of q signal, a new input signal is defined as:

$$u(t) = q(t) \cdot Vin \tag{54}$$

A unique state-space model is thus obtained:

$$\dot{\mathbf{x}}(\mathbf{t}) = \mathbf{A} \cdot \mathbf{x}(\mathbf{t}) + \mathbf{b} \cdot Vin \cdot q(t)$$

$$\mathbf{y}(\mathbf{t}) = \mathbf{C} \cdot \mathbf{x}(\mathbf{t}) \tag{55}$$

The Simulink model of the buck converter is shown in Fig.23.

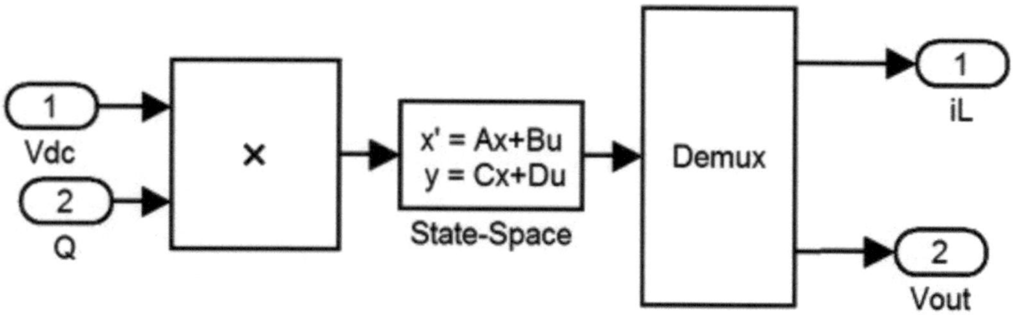

Fig. 23. The buck converter model.

In the state space block, matrix coefficients are entered. The input voltage V_{dc} and the gate drive logic signal Q are the subsystem inputs. The scalar components of the output vector are obtained by the *Demux* block.
The modelling technique is extended to the four-modules architecture which is shown in Fig.24.

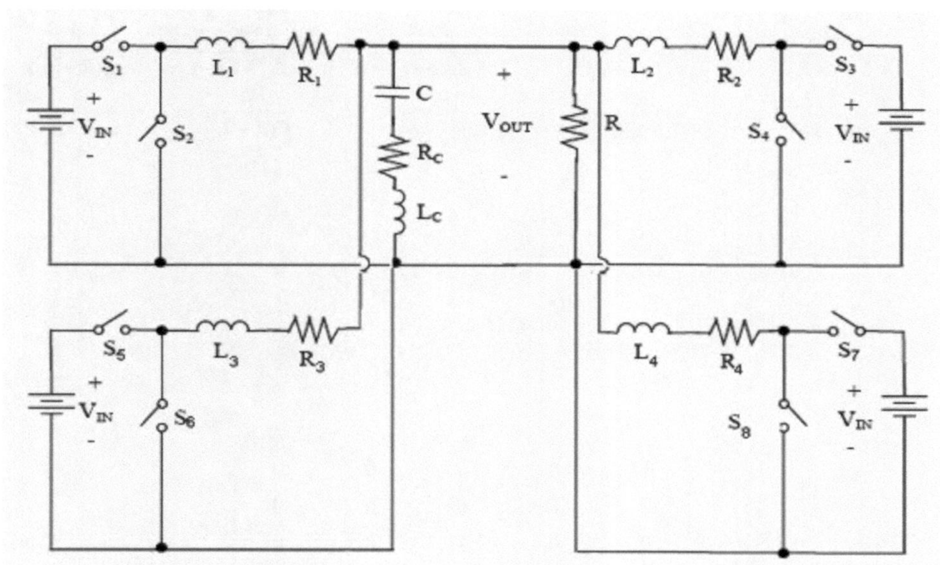

Fig. 24. A four-modules buck converter.

The state-vector is defined as:

$$x(t) = \begin{bmatrix} i_{L1}(t) \\ i_{L2}(t) \\ i_{L3}(t) \\ i_{L4}(t) \\ v_c(t) \end{bmatrix} \tag{56}$$

The output vector is defined as:

$$\mathbf{y}(t) = \begin{bmatrix} i_{L1}(t) \\ i_{L2}(t) \\ i_{L3}(t) \\ i_{L4}(t) \\ v_{out}(t) \end{bmatrix} \tag{57}$$

The state-space model is obtained:

$$\dot{\mathbf{x}}(\mathbf{t}) = \mathbf{A} \cdot \mathbf{x}(\mathbf{t}) + \mathbf{b} \cdot Vin \cdot \boldsymbol{q}(t)$$

$$\mathbf{y}(\mathbf{t}) = \mathbf{C} \cdot \mathbf{x}(\mathbf{t}) \tag{58}$$

where:

$$A = \begin{bmatrix} \frac{RR_1 + RR_C + R_C R_1}{L_1(R+R_C)} & -\frac{RR_C}{L_1(R+R_C)} & -\frac{RR_C}{L_1(R+R_C)} & -\frac{RR_C}{L_1(R+R_C)} & -\frac{R}{L_1(R+R_C)} \\ -\frac{RR_C}{L_2(R+R_C)} & -\frac{RR_2 + RR_C + R_C R_2}{L_2(R+R_C)} & -\frac{RR_C}{L_2(R+R_C)} & -\frac{RR_C}{L_2(R+R_C)} & -\frac{R}{L_2(R+R_C)} \\ -\frac{RR_C}{L_3(R+R_C)} & -\frac{RR_C}{L_3(R+R_C)} & -\frac{RR_3 + RR_C + R_C R_3}{L_3(R+R_C)} & -\frac{RR_C}{L_3(R+R_C)} & -\frac{R}{L_3(R+R_C)} \\ -\frac{RR_C}{L_4(R+R_C)} & -\frac{RR_C}{L_4(R+R_C)} & -\frac{RR_C}{L_4(R+R_C)} & -\frac{RR_4 + RR_C + R_C R_4}{L_4(R+R_C)} & -\frac{R}{L_4(R+R_C)} \\ \frac{R}{C(R+R_C)} & \frac{R}{C(R+R_C)} & \frac{R}{C(R+R_C)} & \frac{R}{C(R+R_C)} & -\frac{1}{C(R+R_C)} \end{bmatrix} \tag{59}$$

$$B = \begin{bmatrix} \frac{1}{L_1} & 0 & 0 & 0 \\ 0 & \frac{1}{L_2} & 0 & 0 \\ 0 & 0 & \frac{1}{L_3} & 0 \\ 0 & 0 & 0 & \frac{1}{L_4} \end{bmatrix} \tag{60}$$

$$C = \begin{bmatrix} 1 & 0 & 0 & 0 & 0 \\ 0 & 1 & 0 & 0 & 0 \\ 0 & 0 & 1 & 0 & 0 \\ 0 & 0 & 0 & 1 & 0 \\ \frac{RR_C}{R+R_C} & \frac{RR_C}{R+R_C} & \frac{RR_C}{R+R_C} & \frac{RR_C}{R+R_C} & \frac{R}{R+R_C} \end{bmatrix} \tag{61}$$

$$\boldsymbol{q}(t) = \begin{bmatrix} q_1(t) \\ q_2(t) \\ q_3(t) \\ q_4(t) \end{bmatrix} \tag{62}$$

Fig. 25 shows the Simulink model of the multiphase converter. The input voltage and scalar components of the q vector are the model inputs. The *Mux* block multiplexes scalar components into the input vector **u**. The *Demux* block generates the scalar components of the output vector **y**(t).

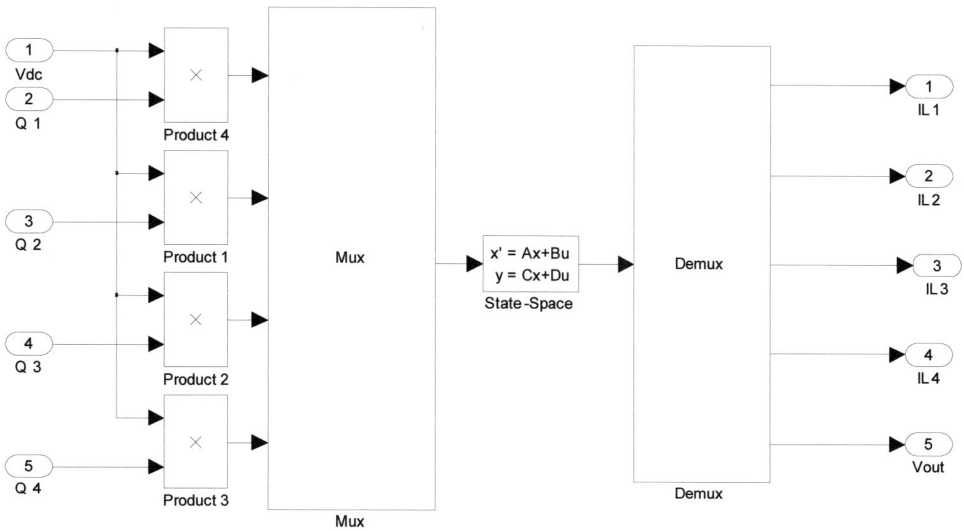

Fig. 25. Simulink model of a four-module buck converter. Inductor currents are the output vector components.

The proposed model could be adapted to the designer requirements. For example, in Fig.26 another implementation is shown. Besides the inductor current signals and the output voltage, the switching node voltages V_{sw} of each module are also included in the output vector. Further, the equivalent inductor current instead of the inductor currents as well as switching node voltages are available outside the subsystem. The equivalent current is obtained as the sum of inductor currents by the means of *Adder* blocks.

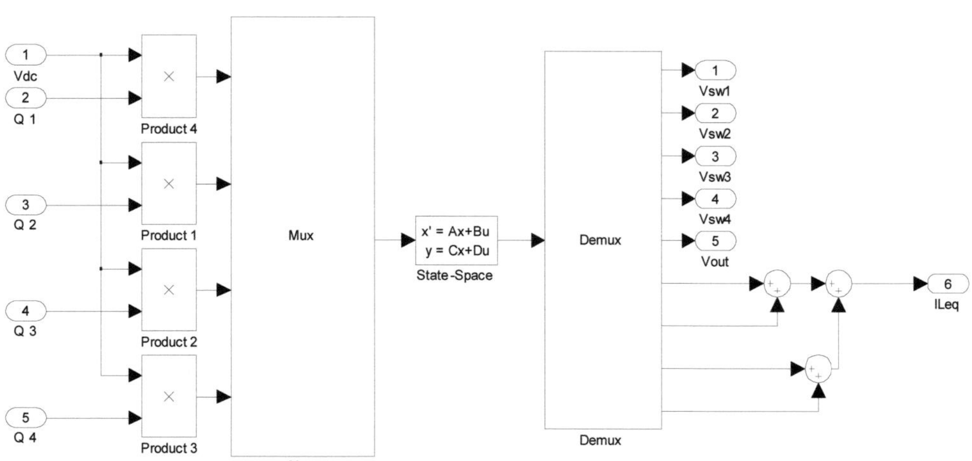

Fig. 26. Simulink model of the multiphase converter.

5.2 The sense network

Current sense filters are modelled by their own Laplace transfer function using the *Transfer Function* block. In the parameter box the coefficients of the Laplace function are entered. The *low-pass filter* subsystem of the master phase is shown in Fig.27. Low-pass filter subsystems are fed by the switching node voltage of the corresponding power module.

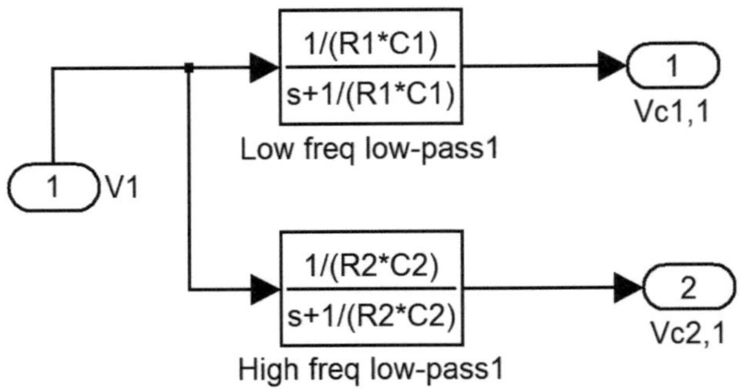

Fig. 27. Current-sense filters of the master module.

5.3 The digital controller model

The digital controller is modelled as the collection of VHDL entities, each one described by the VHDL code in Active-HDL environment. By the co-simulation procedure, each design unit is added to the Simulink model and simulated among the others. The Simulink model of the *Controller* subsystem is shown in Fig.28. Two subsystems are highlighted: the *Non_linear_controller* and the *Linear_Controller.* VHDL entities are collected in the *Controller* subsystem. The 6.25MHz system clock is derived from the 50MHz clock signal available from the FPGA device by the means of a digital clock divider, described in the *clock_div* entity. VHDL entities are linked in Simulink environment. Note that modelling the digital controller by multiple entities is a unique choice of the designer. Instead of modelling the controller by a unique VHDL entity, authors suggest a multiple entities approach to monitor internal signal of the FPGA controller in Simulink environment. The co-simulation procedure allows the designer to test the VHDL code, including timing between entities. The digital controller is thus tested as closely as possible to the effective FPGA implementation.

Each VHDL entity accomplishes a specific task of the digital controller: soft-start, protection circuits for safe operation, adaptive voltage positioning and the strictly-named controller implementing the sophisticated control algorithm, as shown in Fig.29. The co-simulation procedure as well as the proposed modelling approach allows the designer to test each available function by behavioural simulations, thus reducing the risk of experimental fault conditions.

In the *Linear Controller*, the error signal is converted to analog by the DAC subsystem and then compared to the analog saw-tooth within the PWM generator. The interleaved technique is digitally implemented. Fig.30 shows the switching logic subsystem of the master phase. The *f1_sim* VHDL entity is fed by the master phase PWM signal and non-linear control signals. The unit generates the q-signal for the master module. The digital counter which generates the switching clocks (*SwCk*) of all slave modules is modelled by the *acc_sint* VHDL unit.

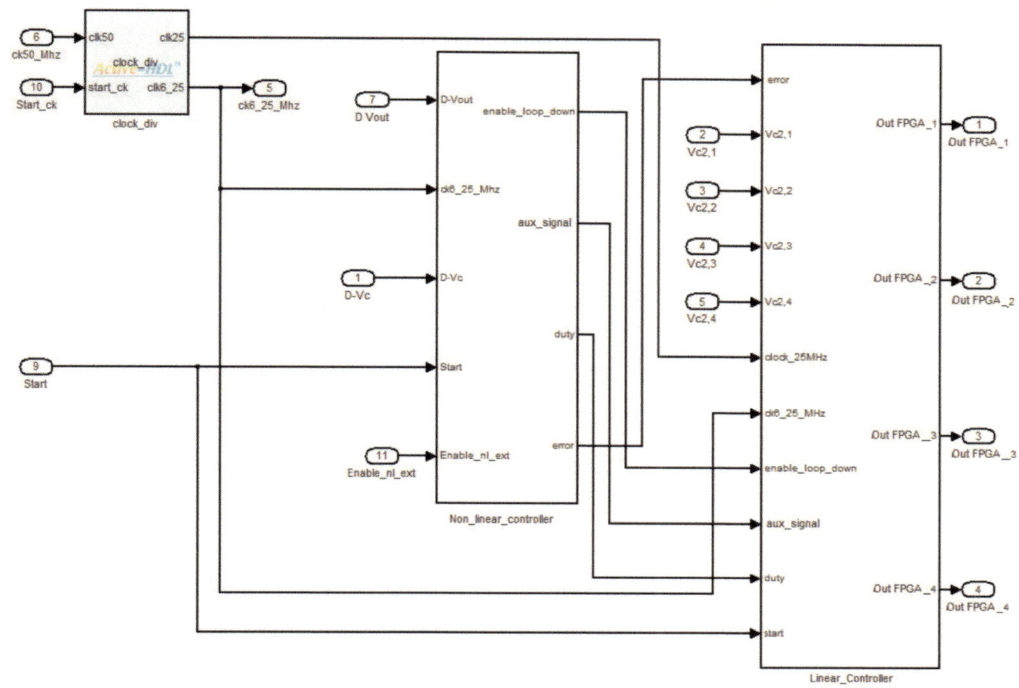

Fig. 28. The Controller subsystem.

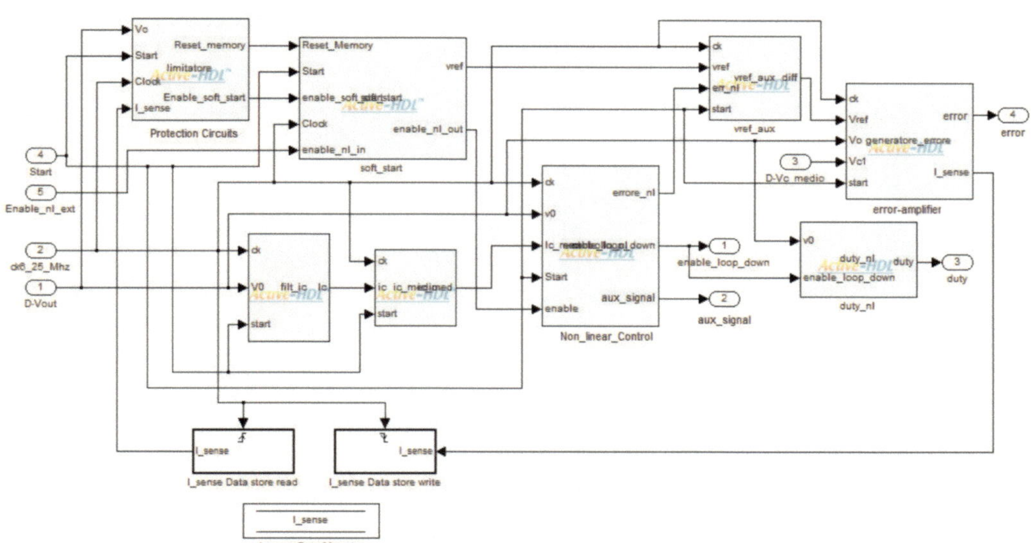

Fig. 29. The non-linear controller.

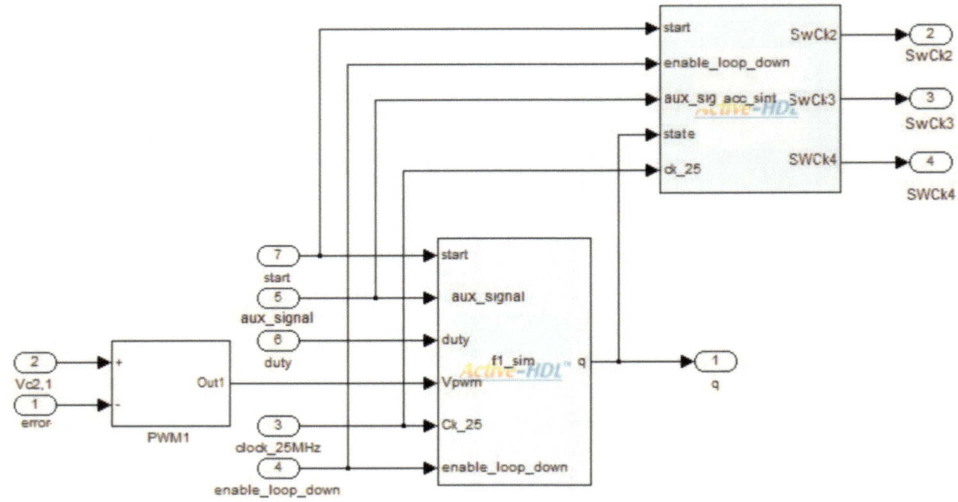

Fig. 30. The Switching Logic model of the master module.

5.4 Analog-digital interface

Co-simulation features are to be well-understood before implementing a mixed-mode model. ALDEC and Simulink automatically code common signals. In ALDEC environment signals are coded as signed binary vectors. The output of each HDL block is thus a binary vector. Simulink automatically codes binary vectors by the equivalent decimal number. HDL block inputs are Simulink signals thus coded as decimal numbers. ALDEC environment codes decimal numbers as the equivalent signed binary vector. The Simulink model should account for binary-decimal data conversion. Digital to analog converters and analog to digital converters are introduced in the Simulink model.
The A/D converter section includes two A/D converters, each modelled as shown in Fig.31 by the means of elementary blocks of Simulink libraries.

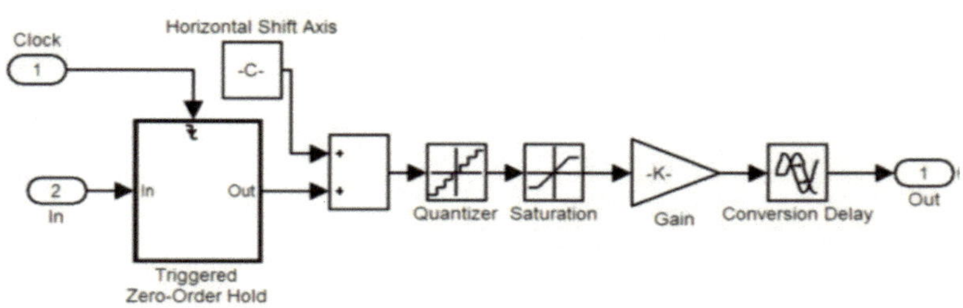

Fig. 31. The A/D converter model

The input signal is sampled at the clock frequency by the *Triggered Zero-Order Hold* block. Since in the Simulink library browser only an ideal symmetrical *Quantizer* block is provided, a non-ideal A/D converter model is achieved by adding the horizontal shift. The horizontal shift constant is given by:

$$C = \frac{FS}{2^{Nbit+1}} \tag{63}$$

where N_{bit} is the bit resolution and FS the full scale voltage.
The available *Quantizer* block allows the user to set the voltage resolution while the number of levels is yet unlimited.
The *Saturation* block is thus cascaded to the *Quantizer* in order to set the full scale range. The high-level saturation limit is given by:

$$\mathrm{High} = V_{res} \cdot N_{lev} = \frac{FS}{2^{Nbit}} \cdot (2^{Nbit} - 1) \tag{64}$$

where V_{res} is the voltage resolution and N_{lev} the number of levels. The discrete output of the *Saturation* block should be coded. In order to simulate the ADC coding, the *Gain* block is cascaded to the saturation block. The output of the ADC model is the equivalent decimal number of the binary vector. The conversion gain is given by:

$$K = \frac{FS}{2^{Nbit}} \tag{65}$$

The *Conversion Delay* block accounts for the input-output delay of the modelled A/D converter.
The Simulink model of the digital-to-analog converter is shown in Fig.32. The subsystem is fed by a digital signal and generates a discrete analog signal. The maximum value of the input signal is given by:

$$Vmax = 2^{N_{bit,dac}} - 1 \tag{66}$$

where $N_{bit,dac}$ is the converter bit resolution. The maximum value of the output voltage is equal to the DAC full scale voltage. The digital-to-analog converter is modelled by a gain factor K_{dac}:

$$K_{dac} = \frac{FS_{dac}}{2^{N_{bit,dac}}} \tag{67}$$

In order to model the full scale range of the converter, a *Saturation* block is cascaded with the gain block. Saturation levels are equal to the full scale range.

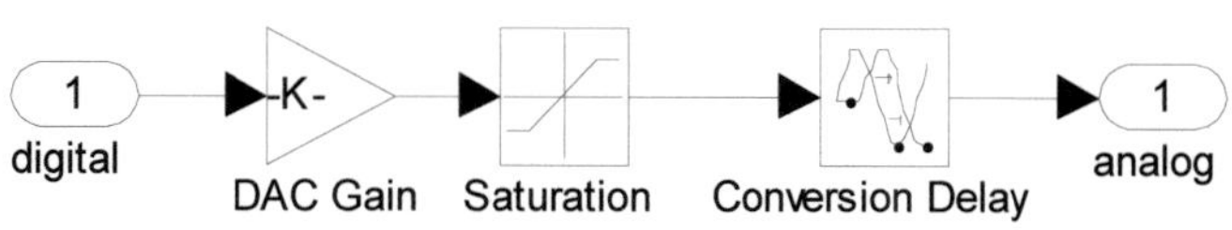

Fig. 32. The Simulink model of a digital-to-analog converter.

5.5 PWM comparator model

The PWM comparator is fed by the analog error signal and the analog current sense signal. The analog comparator model is shown in Fig.33. An adder block is used as the input stage of the comparator. The *Relay* block models the non-linearity of the comparator. The Relay block allows its output to switch between two specified values. The state of the relay is obtained by comparing the input signal to the specified thresholds, the *Switch-off point and the Switch-on point* parameters. When the relay is on, it remains on until the input drops below the value of the *Switch-off point* parameter. When the relay is off, it remains off until the input exceeds the value of the *Switch-on point* parameter. The parameter box allows the end user to set a specified value for both on and off conditions. In this model, the output value is equal to "1" in the on-state, "0" in the off-state.

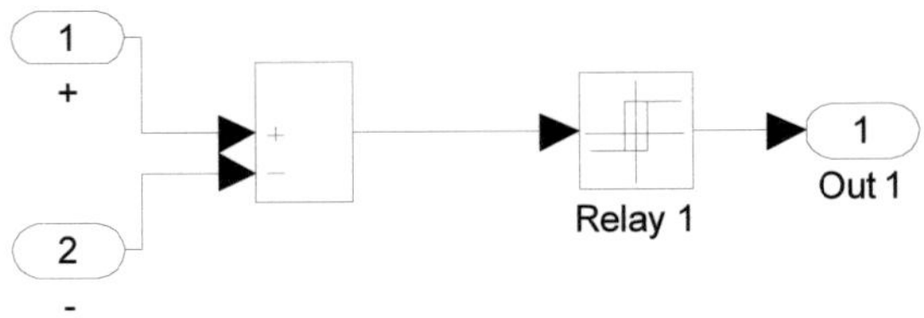

Fig. 33. The Simulink model of the PWM comparator.

6. Simulation results

A 12V/1V@120A four-module buck converter has been designed and modelled in Simulink-Aldec mixed environment. Each power module operates at 250kHz switching frequency. Simulation results are shown to highlight the high accuracy of the modelling approach. Steady-state waveforms under 1A load are shown in Fig.34. At the top the output voltage waveform, at the bottom the equivalent inductor current is shown. The proposed modelling approach allows the designer to simulate the system behaviour within the switching period achieving high accuracy results. The output voltage ripple and the current ripple are accurately modelled. The DC set point of the output voltage is fixed at the nominal value. The output voltage, at the top, and the equivalent current, at the bottom, under 115A load are shown in Fig.35. The DC set point is fixed at 0.96V at full load due to the implemented AVP technique.
The system is tested under load current transients to evaluate the non-linear control performances. Under a 0-120A load current step, if the non linear controller is disabled the system behaviour shown in Fig.36 is obtained. Under a 120A -0 load current step, if the non linear controller is disabled the system behaviour shown in Fig.37 is obtained. The output voltage, at the top, and the equivalent current, at the bottom, are shown. Note that the proposed design approach accurately models the system behaviour within the switching period as well as under large-signal transients.

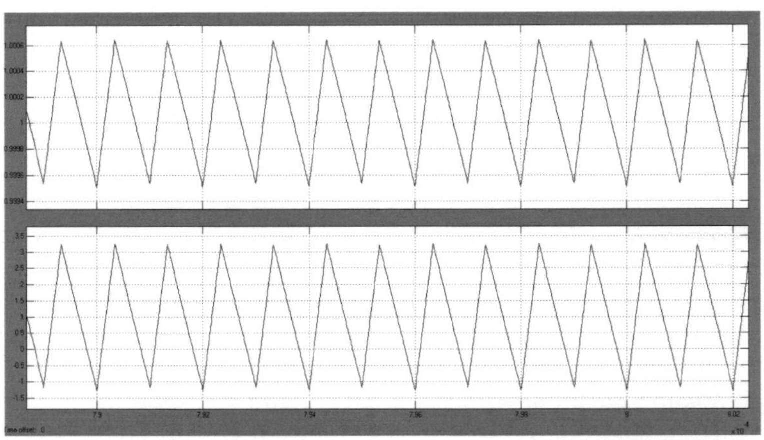

Fig. 34. Steady-state waveforms under 1A load current. At the top the output voltage, at the bottom the equivalent current waveforms are shown.

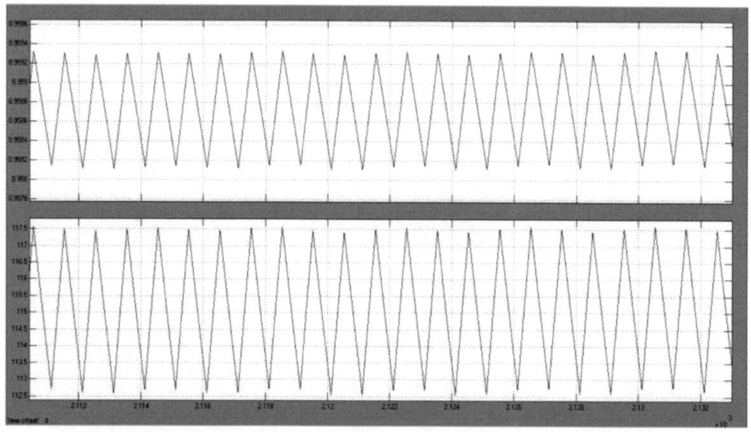

Fig. 35. Steady-state waveforms under 115A load current. At the top the output voltage, at the bottom the equivalent current waveforms are shown.

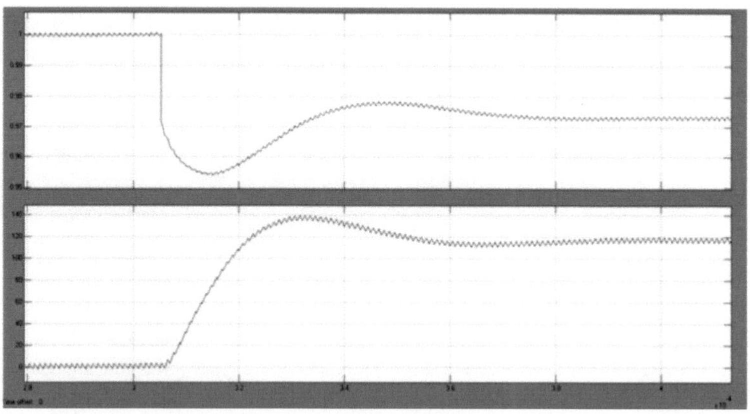

Fig. 36. Dynamic response to a 0-120A load current step without the non-linear control. At the top the output voltage, at the bottom the equivalent current waveforms are shown.

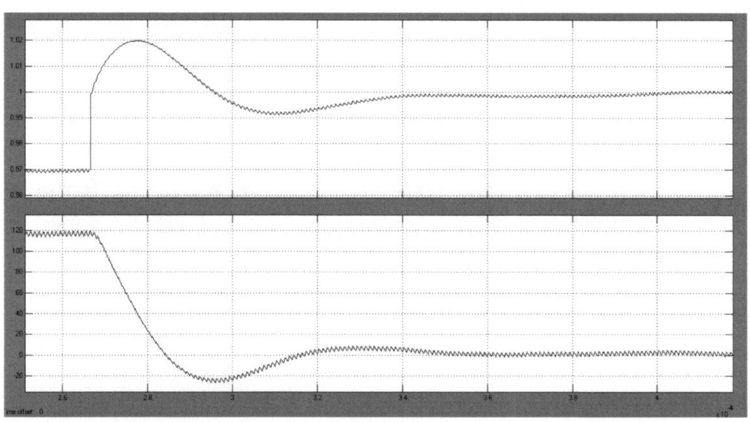

Fig. 37. Dynamic response to a 120A-0 load current step without the non-linear control. At the top the output voltage, at the bottom the equivalent current waveforms are shown.

Fig.38 and 39 show the dynamic response to a 0-120A and 120A-0 load current step, respectively, obtained by enabling the non-linear controller.

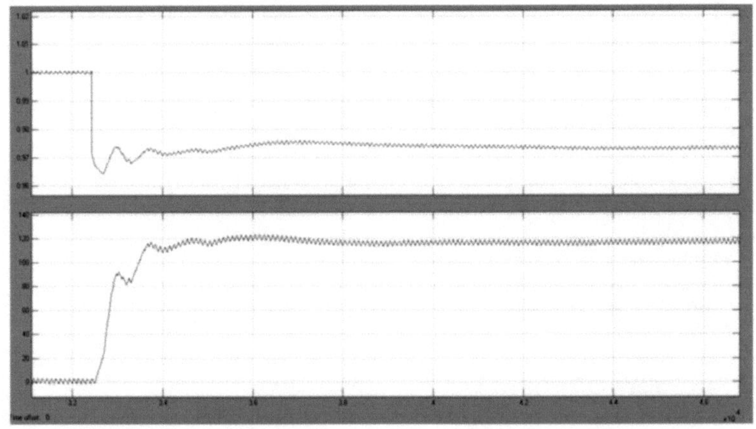

Fig. 38. Dynamic response to a 0-120A load current step with the non-linear control. At the top, the output voltage. At the top the output voltage, at the bottom the equivalent current waveforms are shown.

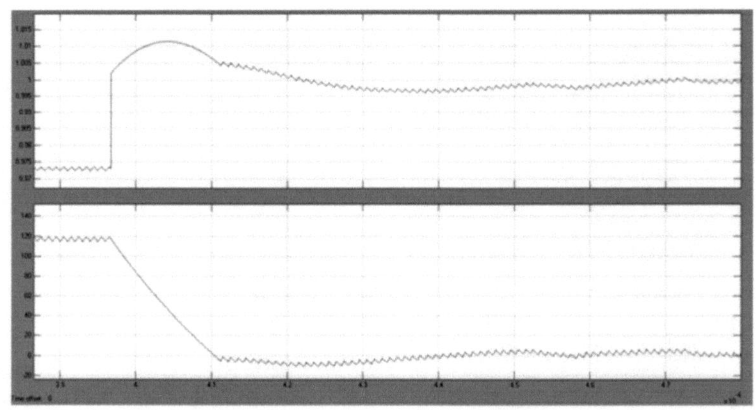

Fig. 39. Dynamic response to a 120A-0 load current step with the non-linear control. At the top the output voltage, at the bottom the equivalent current waveforms are shown.

As shown by simulation results, the non linear controller ensures a reduction of the output voltage over- and-under-shoots during large-signal transients. Under the rising edge of the load current step, the output voltage under-shoot is reduced by 22%. Under the falling edge of the load current step, the output voltage over-shoot is reduced by 26%. The recovery time is reduced by 24%. The instantaneous output voltage change due to the capacitor ESR is included. Note that the instantaneous drop is not affected by the non-linear control.

7. Experimental results

A laboratory prototype has been realized to test the efficiency of the non-linear control algorithm. Experimental validation of the non linear control algorithm has been proposed in

(Boscaino et al., 2010). The high accuracy of the proposed design approach is here discussed by the comparison of simulation and experimental results. Experimental waveforms in Fig.40 show the system behaviour under 120A load current square-wave obtained by disabling the non-linear control (a), and by enabling the non-linear control (b). Ch1 shows the output voltage (200mV/div), Ch3 shows the master module inductor current (10A/div) and Ch4 shows the load current (60A/div).

The great potential of the proposed design approach relies in the performance evaluation of the designed controller. Under load transients, the recovery time as well as the percentage of drop reduction due to the non linear control accurately matches experimental results. The system behaviour is perfectly matched by simulation results. Evaluating system performances by simulation or experimental results leads to the same conclusions. A detail of Fig.40 under the rising edge of the load current square wave is shown in Fig.41: (a) the linear controller response, (b) the non-linear controller response. As shown by experimental results, under the load current rising-edge, the under-shoot of the output voltage is reduced by 29%.

A detail of Fig.40 under the falling edge of the load current square wave is shown in Fig.42: at the left the linear controller response, at the right the non-linear controller response. By comparing experimental waveforms in Fig.42 the output voltage over-shoot under a load current falling edge is reduced by 28%. Under both transients, the recovery time is reduced by 25%.

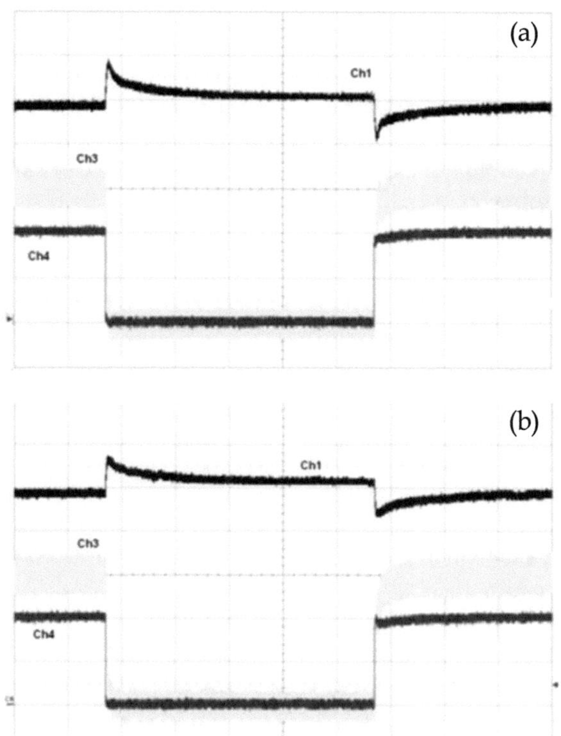

Fig. 40. System behaviour under a 115A width load current square wave. Ch1 shows the output voltage (200mV/div), Ch3 shows the master module inductor current (10A/div) and Ch4 shows the load current (60A/div). (a) The non-linear control is disabled. (b) The non-linear controller is enabled.

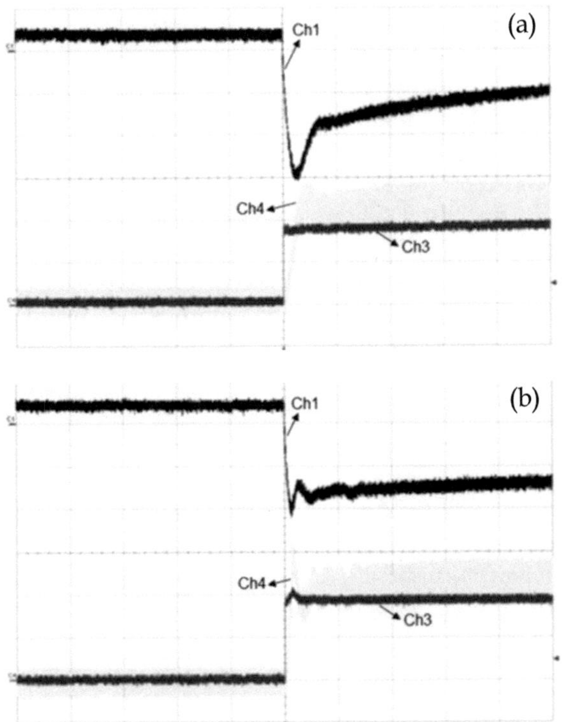

Fig. 41. System behaviour under the load current rising-edge. Ch1 shows the output voltage (50mV/div, AC coupling), Ch3 shows the master module inductor current (10A/div) and Ch4 shows the load current (60A/div). At the left, the non-linear control is disabled. At the right, the non-linear controller is enabled.

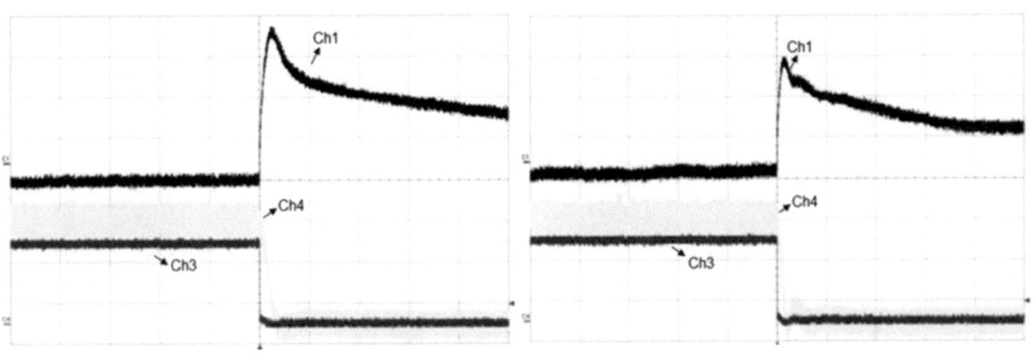

Fig. 42. System behaviour under the load current falling-edge. Ch1 shows the output voltage (50mV/div, AC coupling), Ch3 shows the master module inductor current (10A/div) and Ch4 shows the load current (60A/div). At the left, the non-linear control is disabled. At the right, the non-linear controller is enabled.

8. Conclusion

In this chapter, a high-accuracy design approach for power supply systems is proposed. Mixed-mode systems are modelled in Simulink environment using powerful co-simulation tools. For the highest processing speed, a modelling technique for the power section is proposed. The digital subsystems are described by VHDL source code and verified by Aldec/Simulink co-simulation tool, allowing the test of the VHDL code and timing between separate entities. As an application, the model of a multiphase dc-dc converter for VRM applications is described. Thanks to the available co-simulation tool, all provided functions such as soft-start, protection algorithms for safe operation and adaptive voltage positioning are accurately modelled and verified during behavioural simulations. As shown by simulation results, the proposed model matches the system behaviour both within the switching period and during load transients. The design approach allows the designer to simulate the system behaviour as closely as possible to the effective behaviour, modelling and testing the "effective" controller. The controller performances are evaluated by simulation and experimental results leading to the same conclusions. Authors suggest the co-simulation tool for mixed-mode system and complex architectures. Actually, the IC implementation of the proposed controller in BCD6S technology is carried on. A central unit for signal processing is introduced. Mathematical operations are time-multiplexed in order to speed up the input-output delay in the control loop. The co-simulation tool is already used to test the efficiency of the implemented solution.

9. Acknowledgements

Authors would like to thank ST Microelectronics for supporting this research activity.

10. References

Basso, C. (2008). *Switch-mode Power Supplies,* McGraw Hill, ISBN 978-0-07-150859-0, USA.

Boscaino, V., Livreri, P., Marino, F. & Minieri, M. (2008). Current-Sensing Technique for Current-Mode Controlled Voltage Regulator Modules. *Microelectronics Journal,* Vol.39, No. 12, (December 2008), pp. 1852-1859, ISSN:0026-2692.

Boscaino, V., Livreri, P., Marino, F. & Minieri, M. (2009). Linear-non-linear digital control for dc/dc converters with fast transient response. *International Journal of Power and Energy Systems,* Vol.29, No.1, (March, 2009), pp. 38-47, ISSN: 10783466.

Boscaino, V., Gaeta, Capponi, G. & M., Marino, F. (2010). Non-linear digital control improving transient response: Design and test on a multiphase VRM, *Proceedings of the International Symposium on Power Electronics, Electrical Drives, Automation and Motion,* ISBN: 978-142444987-3, Pisa, Italy, June 2010.

Erickson, R. & Maksimovic, D. (2001). *Fundamentals of Power Electronics (2nd ed),* Springer Science, ISBN 0-7923-7270-0, USA.

Kaichun, R. et al. (October 2010). Matlab Simulations for Power Factor Correction of Switching Power, In: *Matlab -Modelling, Programming and Simulations,* Emilson Pereira Leite, pp. 151-170, Scyio, ISBN 978-953-307-125-1, Vukovar, Croatia.

Miftakhutdinov, R. (June 2001). Optimal Design of Interleaved Synchronous Buck Converter at High Slew-Rate Load Current Transients. IEEE *Power Electronics Specialists Conference,* ISBN 0-7803-7067-8, Vancouver, BC, Canada, June 2001.

Pop, O. & Lungu, S. (October 2010). Modelling of DC-DC Converters, In: *Matlab -Modelling, Programming and Simulations,* Emilson Pereira Leite, pp. 125-150, Scyio, ISBN 978-953-307-125-1, Vukovar, Croatia.

Pressman, A. & Billings, K. (2009). *Switching Power Supply Design* (3rd *ed.*), McGraw Hill, ISBN 978-0-07-148272-1, USA.

8

High Accuracy Modelling of Hybrid Power Supplies

Valeria Boscaino and Giuseppe Capponi
University of Palermo
Italy

1. Introduction

This chapter proposes a modelling approach based on the PSIM/Simulink co-simulation toolbox for hybrid power supplies, featuring high accuracy. Hybrid source performances are fully tested during behavioural simulations. The importance of high-accuracy modelling is investigated and modelling guidelines for both power sources and load are given for further applications. The Simulink model is analyzed and the efficiency of the proposed approach is verified by the comparison between simulation and experimental results.

In the last few years, hybrid power supplies are investigated for a wide variety of application areas: two primary sources are coupled to take advantages of both, overcoming their drawbacks. The growing interest in hybrid sources is mainly due to the spread of fuel cells.

Fuel cells are renewable energy sources, fed by an external fuel and thus potentially infinite source of energy. The fuel cell supplies power until the fuel is supplied to, thus ensuring potentially infinite life cycle to each power load. Automotive, residential and portable electronics are only a few examples of fuel cells application areas. Powering a portable electronic device by a fuel cell is still a challenge for the scientific world. With the aid of fuel cells, the full portability is achieved: electronics devices could be recharged by simply replacing the fuel cartridge instead of being connected to the power grid. Further, fuel cells ensure the highest energy density allowing higher and higher device run time. Yet, portable devices feature a pulsed power consumption profile which depends on the user-selected function. The required peak power is usually higher and higher than the average power. Since the response of fuel cells to instantaneous power demands is relatively poor, innovative solutions are investigated to take full advantage from the fuel cell use. The goal is to couple the fuel cell with a high power density component. The instantaneous peak power is supplied by the high power density component while the average power is supplied by the fuel cell itself. Specific power management algorithms for active power sharing are required. Life-cycle and transient response are directly controlled thus leading to a close dependence of the power management control algorithms on the related application and power load. In the last few years, authors experienced the importance of accurate modelling of both power source and load to evaluate the system performances since the simulation step. The efficiency of power management algorithms is ensured by the high accuracy of source, power load and power management system modelling.

The choice of a powerful simulation environment is a key step for a successful conclusion of the overall design process. The power consumption profile of the specific load device should be deeply analyzed to ensure proper control algorithms. Load emulators best fit designers' requirements. During behavioural simulations, emulators allow the designer to virtually use the load device reproducing the effective power consumption profile. Hence, no assumptions are made on the load power consumption profile while designing the power management algorithms avoiding the risk of experimental failures.

Fuel cell modelling is a critical step since fuel cells are non linear devices whose performances are heavily affected by temperature, fuel pressure and voltage-current operating conditions. Since electro-chemical, physical and geometrical parameters are not readily available to applications engineers, a black-box approach is usually preferred to an analytical one. Both steady-state and dynamic behaviour should be accurately modelled in order to design an efficient power supply design. In this chapter, an accurate modelling approach is proposed.

As an application, a fuel cell – supercapacitor hybrid power supply for portable applications is designed and tested. The proposed system supplies a Digital Still Camera (DSC). Like any other portable device, the digital still camera behaviours as a pulsed load. Unlike the others, the power consumption profile features three possible standby modes (playback, photography and movie mode), each one requiring a specific average current value. The load power consumption profile is closely dependent on the user-selected function and thus unpredictable. Consequently, the DSC represents the worst-case portable device for hybrid power supply design and optimization. Note that accurate modelling is required for testing purposes only. Useful information about the DSC state is reproduced by sampling the supply voltage. The power load, a Fujifilm S5500 Digital Still Camera is modelled in Simulink environment with the aid of the *Stateflow* toolbox. A user-interactive interface is provided. During behavioural simulations, the designer is able to select a specific DSC function and the corresponding power consumption profile is emulated. The fuel cell is modelled in Simulink environment. The architecture and modelling technique is suitable for each fuel cell type and power level. The proposed fuel cell model has been implemented by authors in several simulation environments like PSIM, Simulink and PSPICE and further implementations are readily available in literature. Yet, authors suggest the Simulink implementation to achieve low-complexity, high accuracy and the highest processing speed. On the basis of the Simulink model, a FPGA-based fuel cell emulator has been realized. With the aid of the fuel cell emulator, preliminary tests could be performed saving hydrogen reserve. A circuit implementation of the analog controller in PSIM environment is proposed. PSIM by Powersim Inc. is a circuit simulation software oriented to power electronics systems. Furthermore, a Matlab/PSIM co-simulation tool allows behavioural simulation in a mixed environment. In the basic package, PSIM consists of two programs: PSIM Schematics, full-featured schematic-entry program and SIMVIEW, advanced waveforms viewer software. As soon as the PSIM schematic is built, the designer is able to start the co-simulation procedure. In PSIM Elements/Control Library, the *SimCoupler Module* is provided for Matlab/Simulink co-simulation. Simulink input and output nodes are available. The Simulink input nodes receive values from Simulink and behaviour as voltage sources while the output nodes send values to Simulink. Input and output nodes can be placed in the PSIM schematics according to co-simulation requirements. After generating the circuit netlist in PSIM environment, the PSIM procedure for system co-simulation is completed. In Simulink, the *SimCoupler* block can be added to the existing

Simulink model and linked to the PSIM netlist file by the block parameter box. The *SimCoupler* block now behaviours as a Simulink subsystem showing input and output ports as specified in the corresponding PSIM schematic: the Simulink output nodes are the subsystem input ports and the Simulink input nodes are the subsystem output ports. The PSIM schematic is simulated as an integral part of the active Simulink model. The efficiency of the Simulink-based modelling technique is shown by the comparison between simulation and experimental results.

2. Hybrid power supply architectures

Hybrid power sources have received a great deal of attention in the last few years and they are considered the most promising source of energy for portable applications. Two basic sources are coupled: a high energy density and a high power density source. The goal is to optimize the power and energy performances of the composite power source. Each basic source supplies the load current under a specific working condition, as steady-state or transient, according to its own stand-alone performances. The high energy density source, i.e. fuel cell, supplies the load current under steady-state. Simultaneously, under a load transient the high power density component, i.e. battery or supercapacitor, supplies the load with the difference between the instantaneous and the steady-state load current. The controller is accurately designed to correctly manage the power flow between primary sources and load. If properly controlled, the hybrid source is neither influenced by the transient response of the high energy density source nor by the running time of the high power density source. If compared with stand-alone basic sources, the hybrid source shows longer running time, faster transient response, higher power and energy density.

In literature, battery-ultracapacitor or fuel cell-battery power supply systems are presented (Gao &Dougal, 2003; Alotto et al., 2008). Coupling a battery and an ultracapacitor yields higher specific power than a battery-alone source and higher specific energy than an ultracapacitor-alone source. In the meantime higher running time is achieved. Research on battery/ultracapacitor hybrids has been actively carried out for electric vehicles, portable electronics, weapon systems, as well as for industrial applications.

In literature hybrids are classified in active and passive sources. Direct coupling is a passive hybrids feature while in active hybrids a DC-DC converter is interposed between the two basic sources. Several advantages are brought by the DC/DC converter. A detailed comparative analysis of a battery/supercapacitor hybrid in passive and active configuration is reported in (Gao & Dougal, 2003). The active hybrid configuration ensures an increase in power capability, a better regulation of the output voltage, a minimization of the current ripple and a reduction of the system weight and volume. If a capacitor based hybrid is considered, since the voltage of the two basic sources may be different, the capacitor array size could be designed independently of the other primary source. The DC-DC converter plays an important role in regulating the output voltage and making the voltage of the two basic sources independent of each other. The active hybrids ensure higher power capability than passive hybrids since the power sharing is directly controlled by the switching converter. Further, in active hybrids the output voltage is independent of the discharge curve of its stand-alone sources. In battery-based hybrids, the DC/DC converter can also act as a battery charger, leading to a decrease in system cost and weight.

Yet, all described hybrid systems are designed and tested with regular pulsed load, featuring a square wave current profile. The frequency and width of the current profile are usually assumed as design ratings by control algorithms, even if these assumptions are not verified by commercial devices. If tested with commercial devices, these algorithms would lead to an accidental turning-off or alternatively to a weak optimization of the hybrid power source in terms of both running time and power capability. A fuel cell/supercapacitor active hybrid system supplying a digital still camera is presented. A buck converter is interposed between the primary sources. The specific load device affects system ratings and the architecture of the hybrid source but not the control algorithm. Even under stress, an accidental turning-off is avoided. A high-accuracy model is proposed for both power sources and load. The importance of modelling is confirmed by the comparison between simulation and experimental results.

3. The importance of measurements

The importance of accurate modelling is extensively analyzed in literature. A detailed analysis of several modelling techniques is reported in (Liu, 1993). Measurement-based models are here proposed for both power source and load. Critical features are accurately highlighted and characterized by well-defined measurements. Designers accurately plan the measurement stage to achieve the best accuracy as well as the lowest complexity. Since the modelling approach can be efficiently applied to other devices, performed measurements are described for further applications. The model accuracy is closely related to the experimental setup. The goal is to minimize the difference between the experimental and simulated response to the same input which is usually referred to as the model error. The least the model error, the more efficient the model is. Under ideal conditions, the error is null and the model perfectly matches the effective behaviour of the device under test (DUT). A source of error relies in the model architecture. For example, a highly non-linear device is usually modelled by a linear model leading to an intrinsic source of error. Further, the model error is affected by the accuracy of measures since the model parameters are estimated from a finite and noisy data set. The proposed models are based on high-accuracy measurements and a non-linear model is proposed despite of the model complexity. Tunable parameters are provided for further applications.

3.1 Measurements on the load device

The digital camera behaviours as a pulsed load whose power consumption profile highlights two critical features: the power consumption profile is unpredictable since it depends on the user-selected function and the peak power is usually higher and higher than the average power drawn by the power supply. The power source life cycle and fuel consumption as well as the tolerance window on the output voltage are only a few performance indicators of the hybrid power supply. Hence, a complete analysis is performed to identify critical working conditions. The goal is to reproduce the power consumption profile of the load device and its correlation with the running function. The proposed model allows the designer to virtually use the digital camera during behavioural simulations. The designer is able to select a function obtaining the required consumption profile. The supply current of the digital camera has been monitored under function running. Experimental data are stored in look-up-tables and included in the Simulink model. Samples of measures are here discussed. The DSC features three stand-by modes of operation playback, photography and movie mode. Each mode can be maintained indefinitely active even if no function is running. The standby current is constant and closely related to the actual mode: 180mA for playback mode, 330mA for photography mode and 440mA for movie mode. Each available function requires a pulsed current over the entire function run time. The load current profile under turning-on in playback mode is shown at the left in Fig.1. At the end of function transient, the required load current is strictly constant at 180mA. Yet, during the transient, the peak current reaches 486mA and the run time is equal to 1.24s. The load current profile under the zoom function in playback mode is shown at the right in Fig.1. The transient time is equal to 88.4ms and the peak current reaches 351mA. The average current value over the function transient time is equal to 269mA. If compared with turning-on in playback mode, the transient time is quite short and the peak current value is quite similar to the average current value. Hence, the zoom function is not critical for the hybrid power supply.

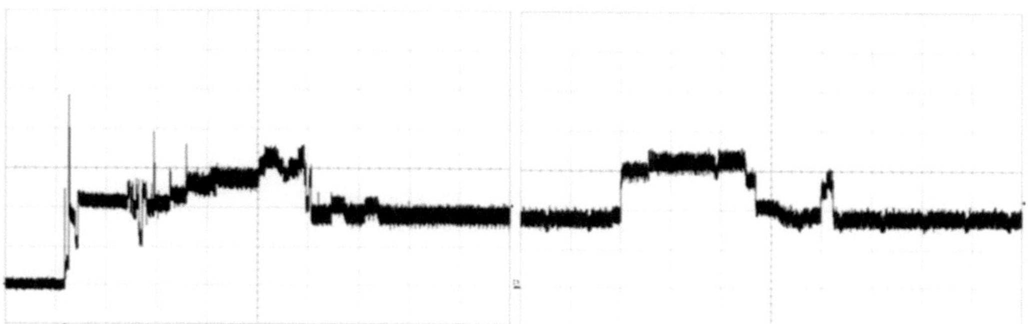

Fig. 1. At the left, the DSC current profile under turning-on in playback mode (100mA/div) is shown. Time base is set to 200ms/div. At the right, the DSC current profile under zoom function in playback mode (100mA/div) is shown. Time base is set at 20ms/div.

The load current profile under turning-on the DSC in photography mode is shown at the left in Fig.2. At the end of transient the current is constant at 330mA which is the standby current of the photography mode. Yet, under function running, the load current reaches a 611mA peak value and the transient time is equal to 4.6s. The load current profile required for taking picture without flash is shown at the right in Fig.2. The transient time is equal to 2.9s. The peak current value is equal to 716mA and the average current over the transient time is equal to 443mA. The load current under movie mode selection is shown at the left in

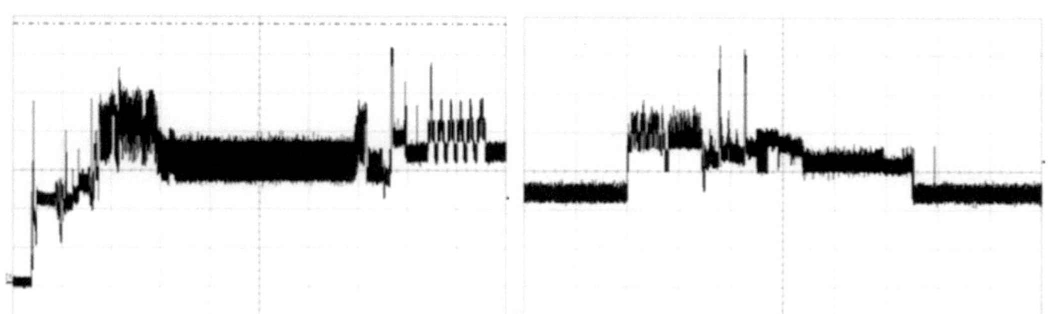

Fig. 2. At the left, the DSC current profile under turning-on in photography mode (100mA/div) is shown. Time base is set to 500ms/div. At the right, the DSC current profile under taking picture without flash (100mA/div) is shown. Time base is set at 500ms/div.

Fig.3. The peak current value is equal to 669mA and the transient time is equal to 430ms. At the right, the load current under the zoom function in movie mode is shown. The transient time is 630ms long and the current reaches a 691mA peak value. Only a few examples are shown. The load current profile of each available function is monitored and collected data are stored to be used in the DSC model. Critical functions for the hybrid power supplies are identified by the transient time and the current peak value. The worst-case function features the highest current peak value and the longest transient time. The power management system should prevent an excessive supercapacitor discharge under the worst-case.

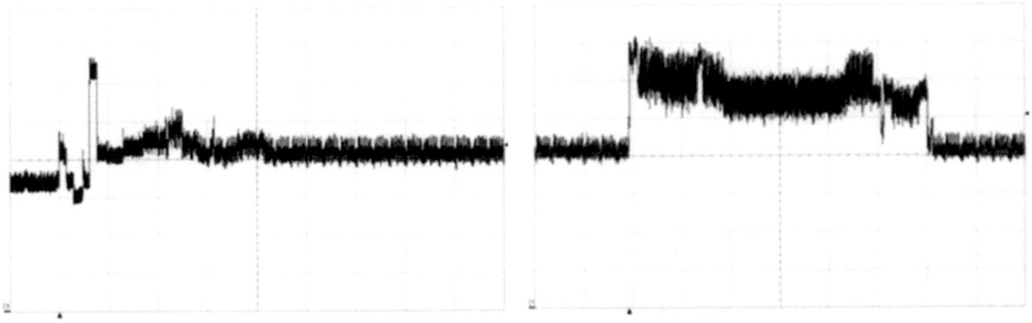

Fig. 3. At the left, the DSC current profile under the transition from photography to movie mode (100mA/div) is shown. Time base is set to 100ms/div. At the right, the DSC current profile under zoom function in movie mode (100mA/div) is shown. Time base is set at 100ms/div.

3.2 Measurements on the fuel cell

A measurement-based fuel cell model is proposed. The model matches the steady-state and dynamic behaviour of the stack under test, including temperature effects. The stack is accurately characterized to achieve high-accuracy. Even if a 10W, 9V Proton Exchange Membrane (PEM) fuel cell stack is tested, the model can be efficiently applied to each fuel cell type and power level. Steady-state measurements are performed. Iso-thermal steady-state V-I curves are measured at several temperature values ranging from 20°C to 40°C by 5°C step. Experimental data are collected and averaged over multiple measures. Average iso-thermal steady-state curves are plotted in Fig.4. A current limit is shown for each steady-state curve. If the fuel cell current overcomes the limit a flooding event occurs: hydrogen is not enough to produce the required current. Hence, water is sucked into the stack obstructing the membrane pores. A flooding event leads to an instantaneous voltage drop and the device is immediately turned-off. The limit is a function of the operating temperature since the reaction speed increase with increasing temperature. The fuel cell current is directly controlled by the power management system avoiding the flooding risk. The frequency response analysis is performed to model the dynamic behaviour of the stack under test. The impedance function is measured under linear conditions. A sinusoidal current is forced and the magnitude of the sinusoidal voltage is measured. The stack non-linearity is neglected while measuring the transfer function. Non-linear effects of operating temperature are neglected by performing measurements at a fixed temperature value of 30°C. Further, the steady-state curve non-linearity is neglected by a small-signal approximation. The average current value is fixed at 600mA and a sinusoidal signal of 200mAp-p is forced. In the fixed current region, at 30°C, the non-linearity of the steady-stare curve could be neglected. The goal is to model the impedance transfer function by a dynamic admittance which is connected in parallel with the steady-state model. The equivalent resistance of the steady-state model is then connected in parallel to the dynamic impedance. If the operating condition changes, the equivalent resistance of the steady-state model changes and the model is able to fit the dynamic behaviour of the stack under test. Experimental results validate the modelling technique. For further details, please refer to (Boscaino et al., 2009b). The Bode plot of the impedance magnitude is shown in Fig.5. On y-axis a linear scale is used. Since the system square wave response analysis shows no time constant lower than 1μsec, the magnitude of the transfer function is assumed constant for high frequency values.

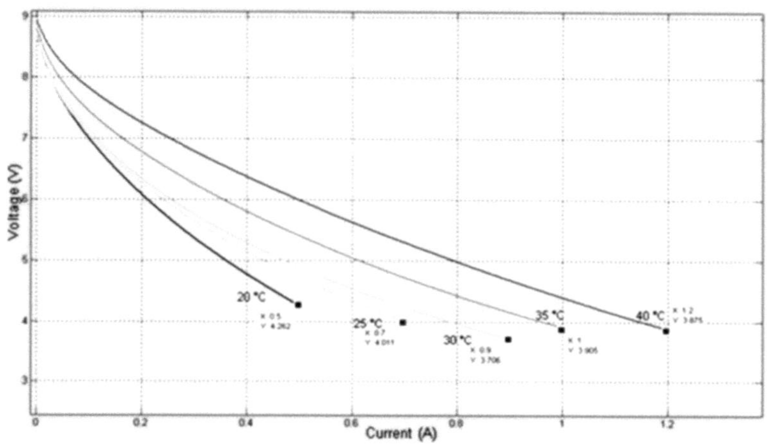

Fig. 4. Average iso-thermal steady-state curves.

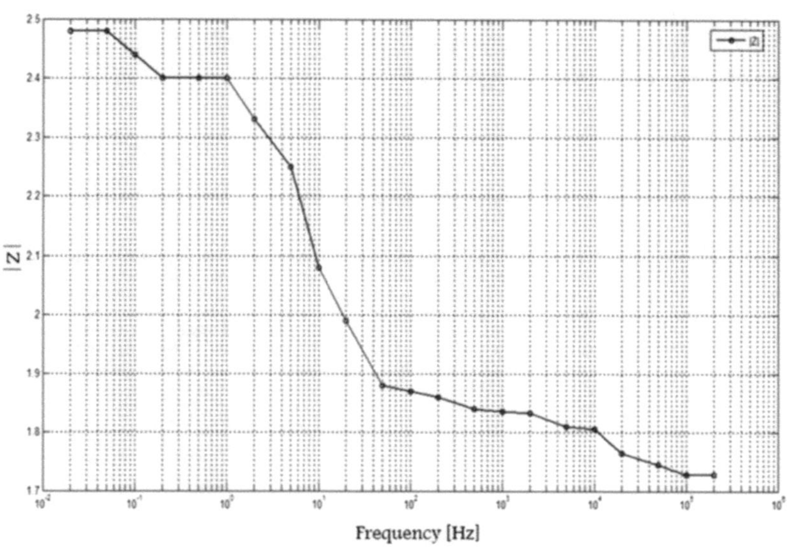

Fig. 5. Bode plot of the impedance magnitude.

Measurements are performed up to 200kHz. Temperature effects on the fuel cell performance are included in the fuel cell model. Further, the model reproduces the stack temperature as a function of the fuel cell current. The thermal response of the fuel cell is monitored as shown in Fig.6. Thermal measurements are performed by monitoring the current profile and the corresponding temperature profile.

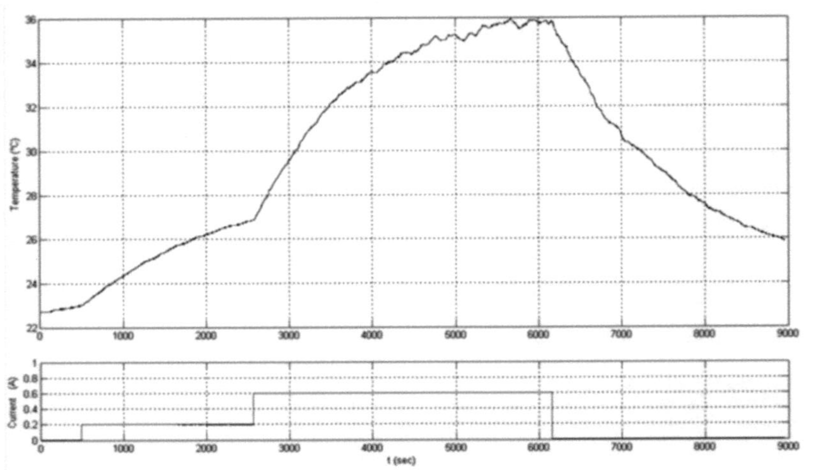

Fig. 6. At the top, the thermal response of the fuel cell stack. At the bottom, the corresponding current waveform.

4. The simulink model

A fuel cell - supercapacitor hybrid power supply is designed. The active hybrid source is modelled by a PSIM schematic as well as the power management control system. The primary source and the power load are modelled in Simulink environment. The top level model is shown in Fig.7. The *SimCoupler* block simulates the power management system implemented by a PSIM schematic which is fed by the fuel cell voltage and the load current signals and generates the output voltage of the hybrid supply.

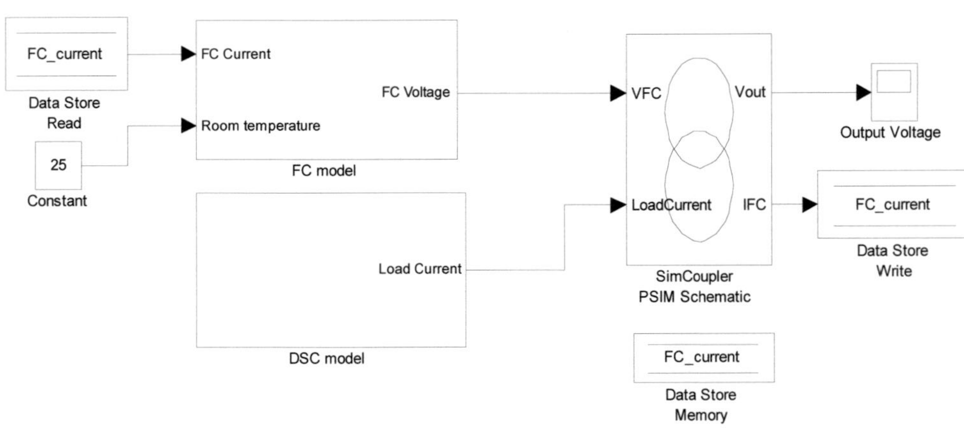

Fig. 7. Hybrid power supply model.

The fuel cell current is sensed within the PSIM schematic. The fuel cell current signal feeds the fuel cell subsystem by the means of data stores. In order to enable the signal analysis in Simulink environment too, the output voltage is considered as a Simulink Output Node.

4.1 The fuel cell model

The fuel cell model is shown in Fig.8. The stack voltage is generated as a function of the fuel cell current. The room temperature is introduced as an external parameter. The steady-state and dynamic sections are highlighted. The steady-state behaviour, including temperature effects, is modelled by the *Steady-state Section*. The dynamic section models the transient response by the means of an admittance which is connected in parallel to the steady-state model. Hence, the parallel connection is modelled by feeding the *Dynamic Section* by the output voltage and introducing a current node at the input of the *Steady-State Section*. By the means of data stores, the fuel cell voltage is stored as an output of the *Steady-State Section* and then read by the *Dynamic Section* as an input signal. The *Steady-State Current* is obtained by adding the *Dynamic Current* to the external fuel cell current.

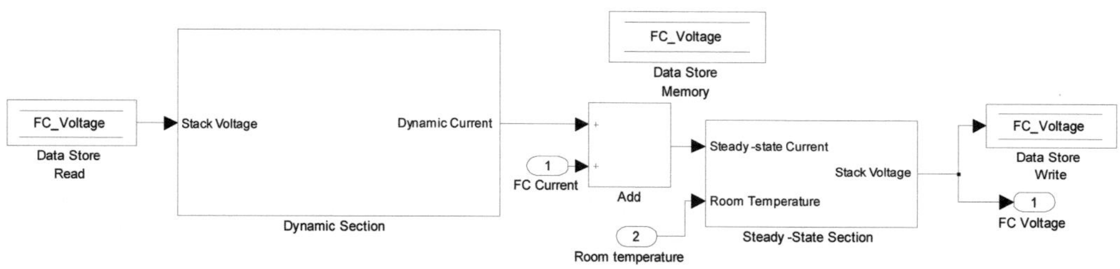

Fig. 8. The fuel cell model.

The steady-state section is modelled as shown in Fig.9. Note that the stack temperature is quite different from the room temperature. The room temperature is an external signal while the stack temperature is reproduced as a function of the fuel cell current by the temperature subsystem. The steady-state subsystem reproduces the stack voltage as a function of the fuel cell current *i* and the reconstructed temperature value *T*. The steady-state subsystem is modelled as shown in Fig.10. The steady-state voltage at a temperature *T* under a current *i* is given by:

$$V(i,T)=V(i,Tref)+c(i,T-Tref) \quad (1)$$

where *V(i,Tref)* is the steady-state voltage at a nominal temperature of 30°C under a current *i* and *c(i,T-Tref)* is the voltage correction term accounting for a temperature *T* which is different from the nominal one.

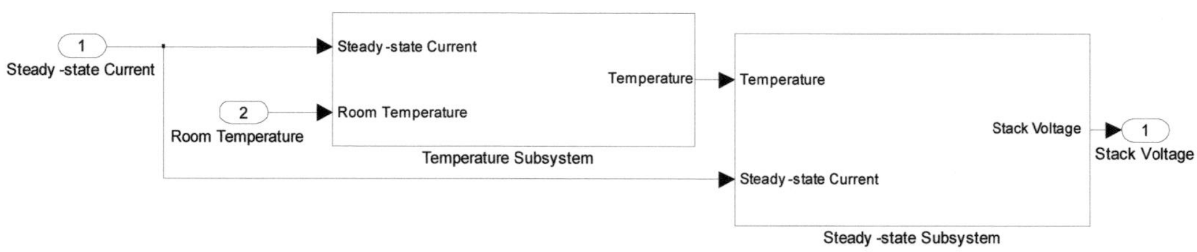

Fig. 9. The steady-state section model.

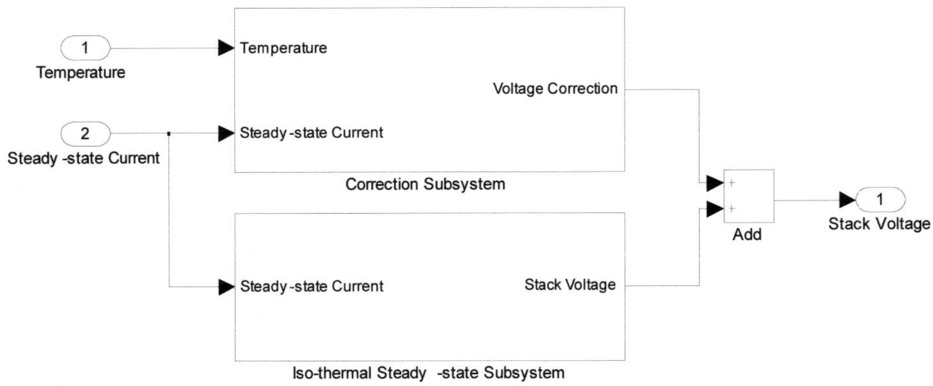

Fig. 10. The steady-state subsystem model.

The term *V(i,Tref)* is the output signal of the so-called I*so-thermal steady-state subsystem* while the correction term is generated by the *Correction subsystem*. No matter how many and which the involved physical, geometrical and chemical parameters are, the iso-thermal steady-state curve at the reference temperature is fitted by the law:

$$V(i,Tref) = A - B \cdot ln\left(1 + \frac{i}{C}\right) - D \cdot e^{\frac{i}{E}} \tag{2}$$

where A,B,C,D,E are the iso-thermal steady-state model parameters. Model parameters are obtained by fitting the experimental data with the aid of the *Curve Fitting Tool* which is available in MATLAB environment. The *Iso-thermal steady-state subsystem* is shown in Fig.11. The subsystem is fed by the Steady-state current and reproduces the stack voltage at the reference temperature of 30°C. The A parameter is modelled by the *constant* block. Exponential and logarithmic terms are generated by the subsystems shown in Fig.12. According to (2), parameters B, C, D and E are modelled by proper *Gain* blocks which are introduced in the signal chain. The gain value is entered by the parameter box. Exponential and logarithmic functions are implemented by *Math Function* blocks which are readily available in the Simulink library browser.

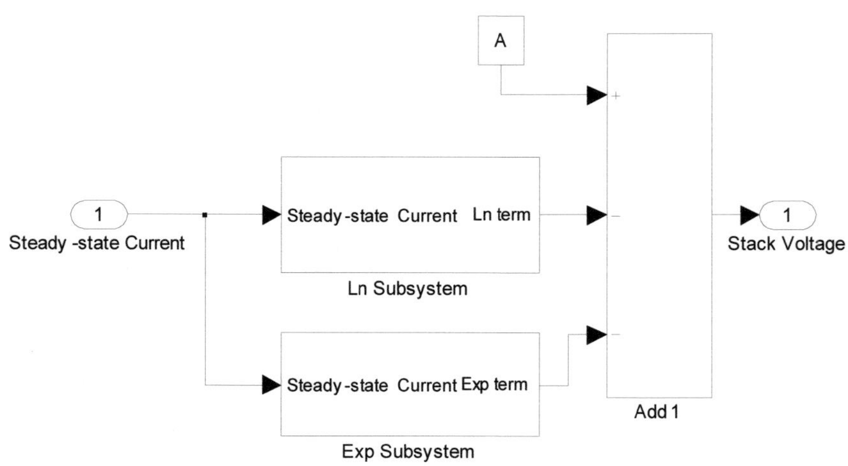

Fig. 11. The iso-thermal steady-state subsystem model.

The type of function is selected by the parameters box. The shift by 1 of the logarithmic argument is modelled by the *Bias* block. The shift constant is introduced by the block parameter box. Very complex functions, such as the logarithmic or exponential function are readily implemented by elementary blocks.

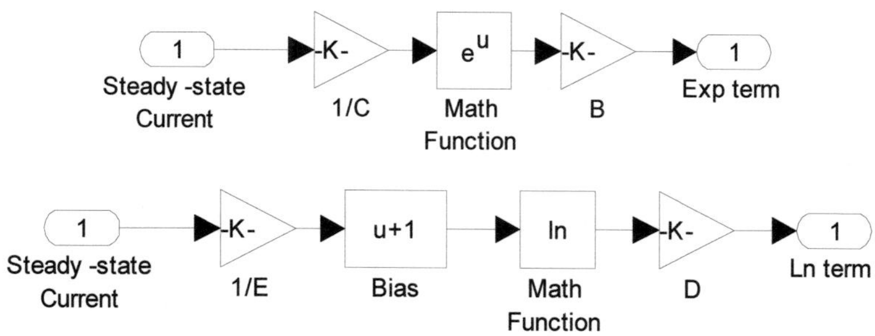

Fig. 12. The exponential and logarithmic subsystems.

The correction subsystem accounts for temperature effects. The subsystem is fed by the stack temperature and the fuel cell steady-state current, as shown in Fig.13.

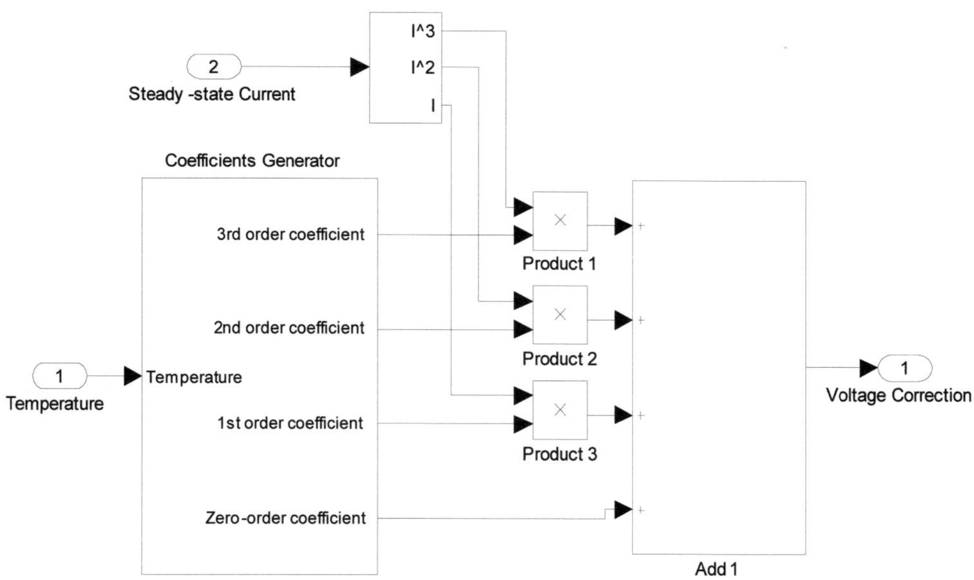

Fig. 13. The correction subsystem model.

According to (1) a set of average correction curves is obtained. If a point of the iso-thermal correction curve at the temperature T is selected, the x-axis coordinate equals the fuel cell current i and the y-axis coordinate the correction term $c(i,T\text{-}T_{ref})$. The correction subsystem is modelled by a bi-dimensional polynomial fitting of the average correction curves. A third-order polynomial is chosen for current-fitting while a fourth-order polynomial is chosen for temperature fitting. The correction curve at a temperature T_1 is fitted as a function of current by the polynomial law:

$$C(i,T_1) = C_0(T_1)\cdot i^0 + C_1(T_1)\cdot i^1 + C_2(T_1)\cdot i^2 + C_3(T_1)\cdot i^3 \tag{3}$$

where C0, C1, C2 and C_3 are the polynomial coefficients. Each coefficient of the current polynomial is given by evaluating a fourth-order polynomial at the fixed input temperature. Coefficients at a fixed temperature T_1 are given by:

$$\begin{aligned} C_0 &= C_{0,0} + C_{0,1}(T_1 - T_{ref}) + C_{0,2}(T_1 - T_{ref})^2 + C_{0,3}(T_1 - T_{ref})^3 + C_{0,4}(T_1 - T_{ref})^4 \\ C_1 &= C_{1,0} + C_{1,1}(T_1 - T_{ref}) + C_{1,2}(T_1 - T_{ref})^2 + C_{1,3}(T_1 - T_{ref})^3 + C_{1,4}(T_1 - T_{ref})^4 \\ C_2 &= C_{2,0} + C_{2,1}(T_1 - T_{ref}) + C_{2,2}(T_1 - T_{ref})^2 + C_{2,3}(T_1 - T_{ref})^3 + C_{2,4}(T_1 - T_{ref})^4 \\ C_3 &= C_{3,0} + C_{3,1}(T_1 - T_{ref}) + C_{3,2}(T_1 - T_{ref})^2 + C_{3,3}(T_1 - T_{ref})^3 + C_{3,4}(T_1 - T_{ref})^4 \end{aligned} \tag{4}$$

where Ci,j is the j-th order coefficient of the temperature polynomial which gives the Ci coefficient of the current polynomial. Fig.14 shows the iso-thermal correction curves after the fitting operation as a function of the fuel cell current.
The *Coefficients generator subsystem* is fed by the temperature signal and generates the coefficients of the current polynomial C_0, C1, C2 and C_3 corresponding to the input temperature value. Then the current polynomial is evaluated at the input current value. The subsystem is modelled by elementary blocks of Simulink libraries.

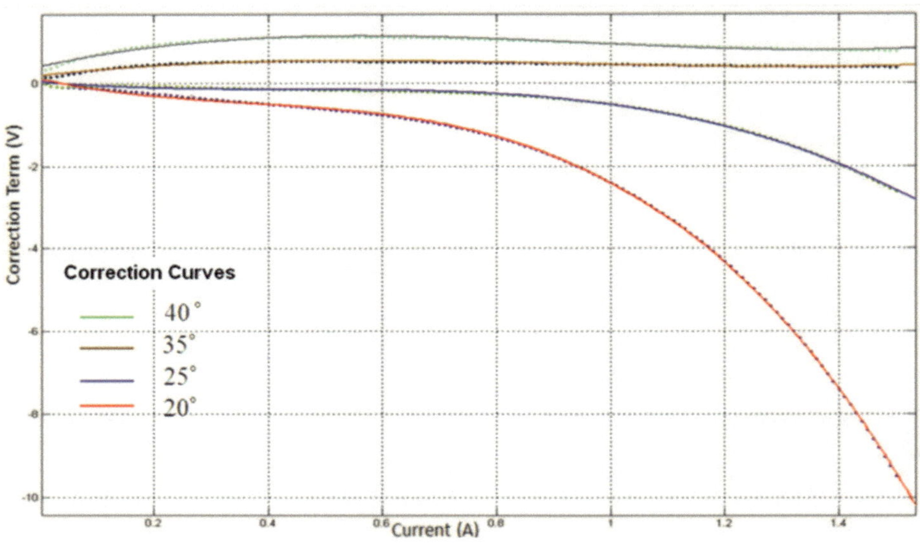

Fig. 14. Iso-thermal correction curves after current fitting procedure.

The model of the *Coefficients Generator* subsystem is shown in Fig.15. *Polyval* blocks are introduced to model a polynomial. Coefficients are set by the parameter box.
Hence, the current polynomial coefficients are evaluated by the *Coefficients Generator* subsystem which is fed by the temperature value *T*. The coefficients are applied to evaluate the current polynomial at the input current value *i*.
The thermal section is modelled by fitting the fuel cell thermal transient response by the *Parameters Estimation Toolbox* which is available in MATLAB/Simulink environment. The temperature profile is reproduced by the Temperature subsystem as a function of the fuel cell current. The thermal response of the fuel cell is modelled as:

$$a\frac{dT}{dt} = -(T - T_{room}) + g \cdot i + d \cdot i^2 \tag{5}$$

where T is the absolute stack temperature, T_{room} the ambient temperature and i the total current.

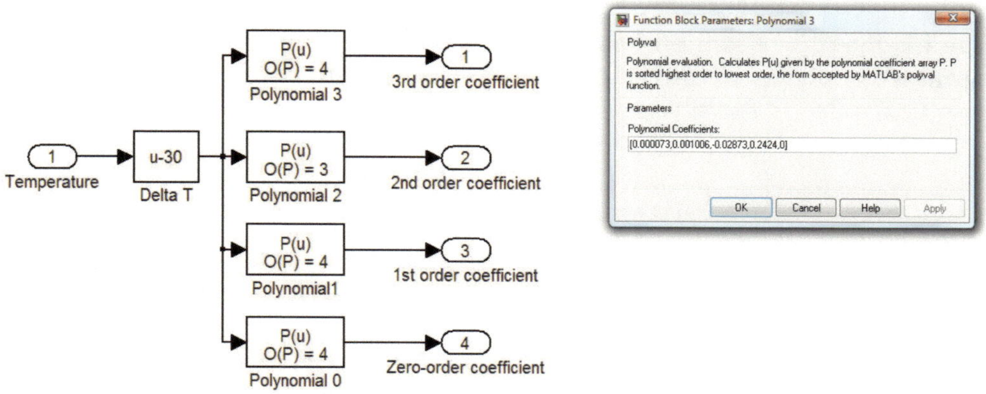

Fig. 15. The Coefficients Generator subsystem model.

The term $d\,i^2$ involves Joule heating to temperature T and the term $g\,i$ models the evolved heat, the effects of the reaction rate and lost heat. Effects of room temperature are encountered by the first term in (5). Thermal model parameters a, g, d are obtained by performed measurements with the aid of the *Parameter Estimation Toolbox*, which is available in Simulink environment. By Laplace transform, the (5) is solved as:

$$T(t) = T_0 \cdot e^{-\frac{t}{a}} + \frac{1}{a} \cdot e^{-\frac{t}{a}} \cdot \int_0^t T_{room}(t) \cdot e^{\frac{\tau}{a}} \cdot d\tau + \frac{g}{a} \cdot e^{-\frac{t}{a}} \cdot \int_0^t i(\tau) \cdot e^{\frac{\tau}{a}} \cdot d\tau +$$

$$+ \frac{d}{a} \cdot e^{-\frac{t}{a}} \cdot \int_0^t i^2(\tau) \cdot e^{\frac{\tau}{a}} \cdot d\tau \qquad (6)$$

In Fig.16 the temperature subsystem model is shown. The temperature signal is generated by adding integral and exponential terms. Each elementary term of (6) is modelled by Simulink library blocks. The *Clock* block generates the simulation time t. Exponential terms are evaluated by the means of the time t and the *Math function* block. The integral operator is modelled by the *Integrator* block.

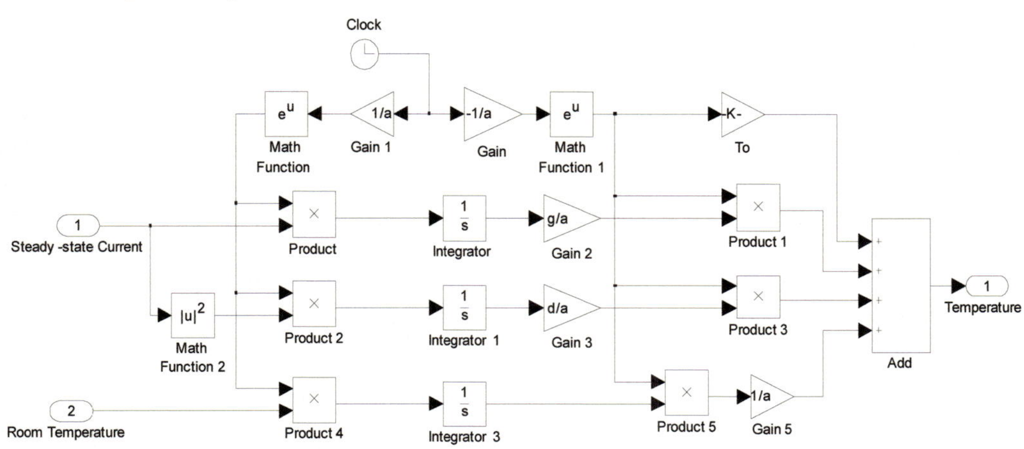

Fig. 16. The temperature subsystem.

According to (5), the thermal response to a current step is given by:

$$T(t) = T_0 + (T_{room} - T_0 + g \cdot I + d \cdot I^2)\left(1 - e^{-\frac{t}{a}}\right) \tag{7}$$

where I is the current step final value, T_{room} is the room temperature and To the initial temperature condition. A current step towards zero current leads to a thermal transient whose final value is the environment temperature T_{room}. According to (5), the thermal response to a current step towards zero current value is given by:

$$T(t) = T_0 + (T_{room} - T_0)\left(1 - e^{-\frac{t}{a}}\right) \tag{8}$$

By fitting the thermal response to a current step towards zero value, the a parameter is obtained. The thermal response to the rising and falling-edge of a current step is monitored, obtaining g and d parameters.

As discussed, the dynamic subsystem models the impedance which is dynamically connected in parallel to the steady-state model. The approximated impedance transfer function is modelled by the *Transfer Function* library block, as shown in Fig.17. The dynamic voltage is obtained by subtracting the constant term of the steady-state model to the stack voltage. The dynamic current is generated by the transfer function block Y(s). The analysis of the model accuracy yields a maximum voltage error value of 0.2V, comparable to experimental data scattering. The thermal model error is limited to 1°C. Authors suggest (Boscaino et al., 2009b) for further details.

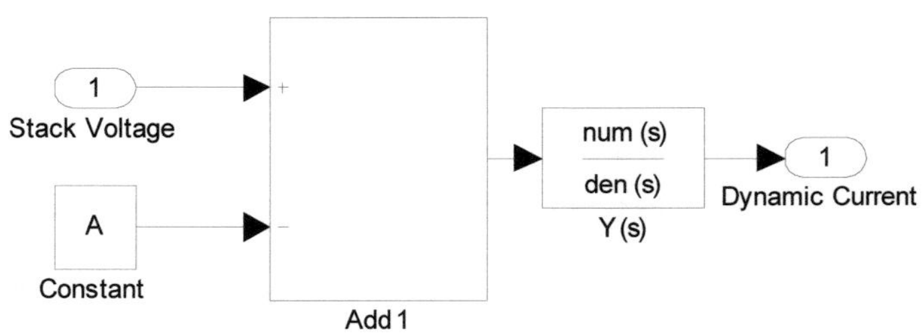

Fig. 17. The dynamic section model.

4.2 The DSC model

The load emulator is modelled in Simulink environment. Thanks to the powerful *Stateflow* toolbox a user-interactive model is implemented. During behavioural simulation, the designer is able to select a DSC function emulating the effective load device. The effective power consumption pattern corresponding to the actual user-selected function is generated by the load model. The designer is able to reproduce a random usage of the electronic load device.

No assumptions are made about the load current profile during behavioural simulations. System performances are already evaluated by computer simulations saving hydrogen reserve for preliminary tests and avoiding the risk of experimental fault conditions. The hybrid source life-cycle and fuel consumption could be tested as well as system stability and dynamic response.

The load device is modelled by a state machine: user-selections are modelled as events and the available functions are modelled as the finite states. The state-machine is implemented by the *Stateflow* toolbox which is available in Simulink library browser. The model is based on a Fujifilm S5500 digital still camera. Main sections of the DSC model are highlighted in Fig.18: *User Interface, Mux* and *DSC subsystem.* Manual switches are included in the *User Interface* section. Each manual switch is labelled by a specific DSC function. By acting on a manual switch, the designer generates events for the state-machine thus running the corresponding function. Scalar events are collected by the *Mux* subsystem into *DSC subsystem* input vector. In the *DSC subsystem,* the state-machine and the output section are modelled.

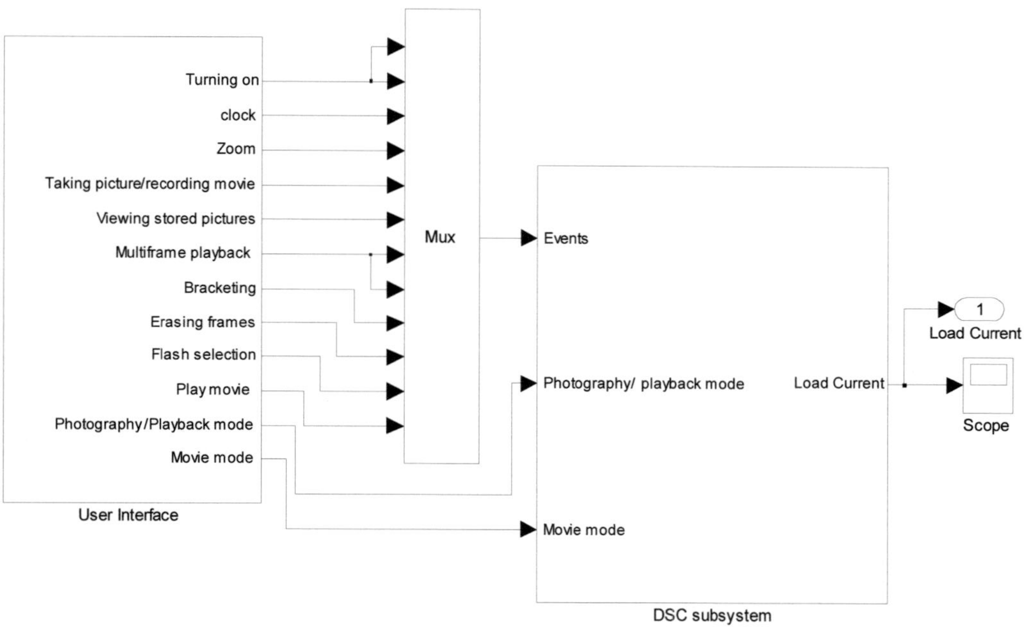

Fig. 18. MATLAB/Simulink DSC model.

The state-machine receives events and conditions. The event immediately triggers a state transition. Under the clock rising-edge conditions are verified thus enabling a state transition. Events and conditions are generated in the User-Interface subsystem as shown in Fig.19.

Manual switches are collected within the subsystems. Take a look to the *Conditions* subsystem shown in Fig.20. Photography or playback mode is selected by double-clicking on the corresponding manual switch. A condition for the state-machine is generated by the manual switch. If the condition is true, corresponding to the logic value 1, the state-machine is driven toward the Photography Mode. Otherwise, the system is driven towards the Playback Mode. Even though events are generated instead of conditions, the Events subsystem features a similar architecture, as shown in Fig.21. End-user actions on the digital camera selector switch are marked as conditions while actions on buttons are marked as events. Each manual switch within the Events subsystems emulates a physical button of the digital camera under test. As shown Fig.22, the *DSC subsystem* is modelled by a state diagram and an output section.

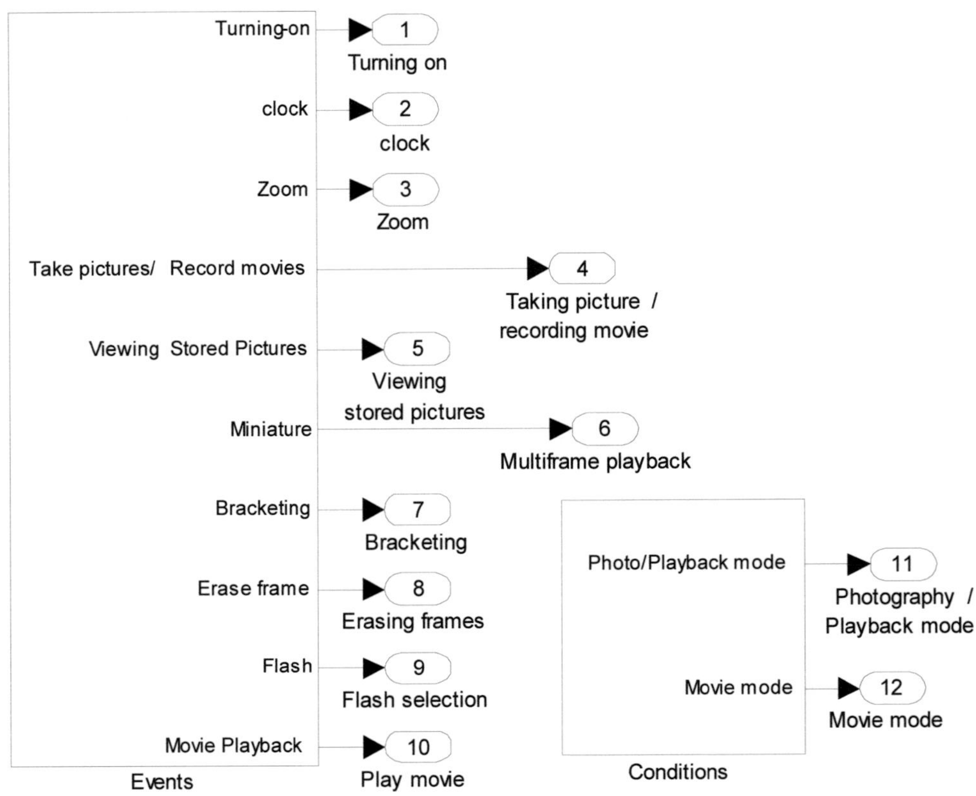

Fig. 19. The user-interface subsystem.

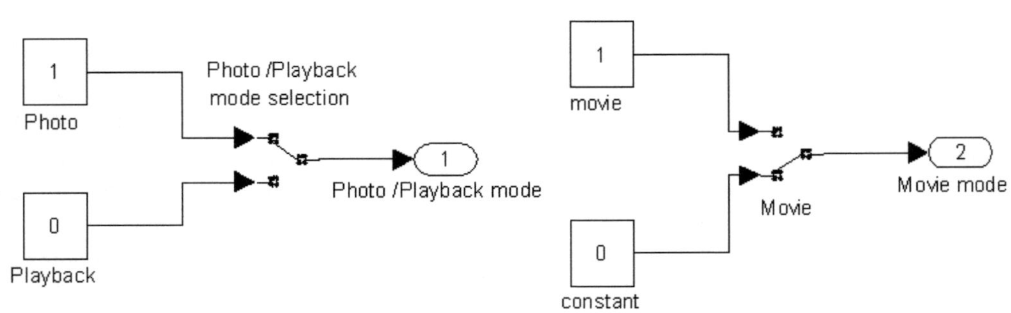

Fig. 20. Conditions.

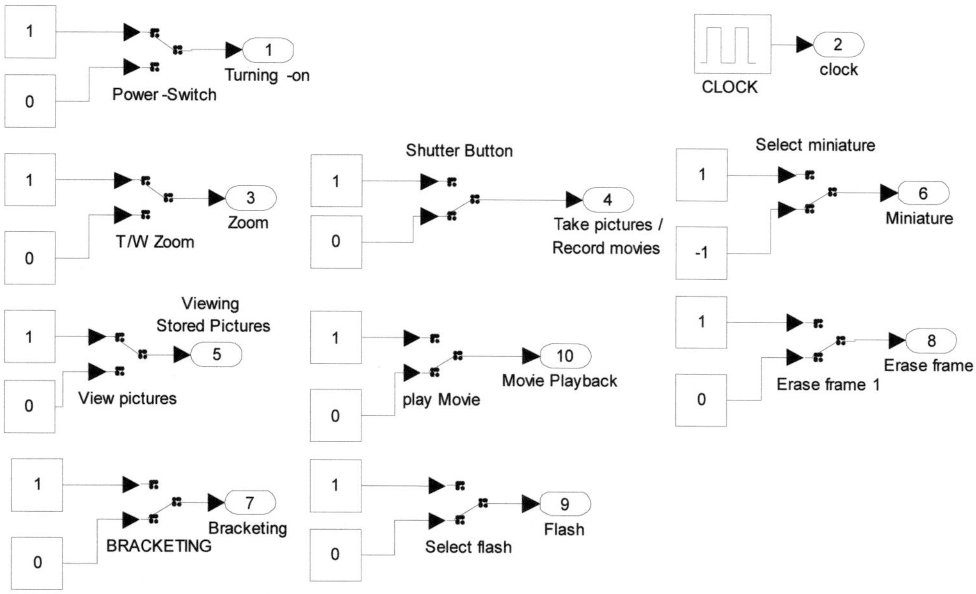

Fig. 21. Events.

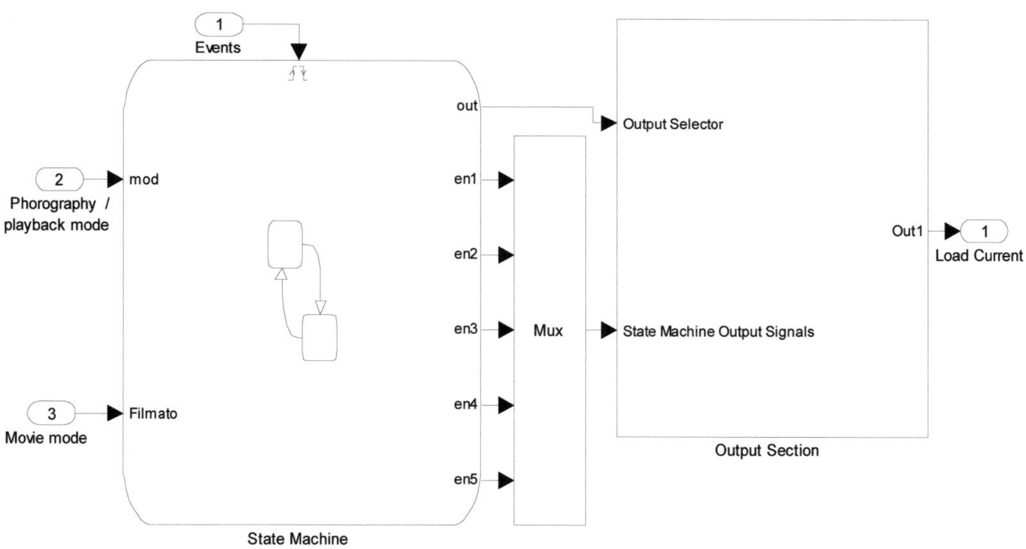

Fig. 22. The DSC subsystem.

A set of look-up tables (LUT) is included in the output section, as shown in Fig.23. Each LUT stores the current profile of a DSC function. The state diagram generates five control signals which are multiplexed in a control vector by the *Mux* block. In the output section, a decoder is fed by the control vector and generates the enable signals for LUTs. Only one enable signal at once is active. If a function is selected by user, the corresponding state in the state diagram is active and then the corresponding LUT in the output section is enabled and sequentially read. The output bus is connected to the active LUT output by the multiport switch which is driven by the output selector signal.

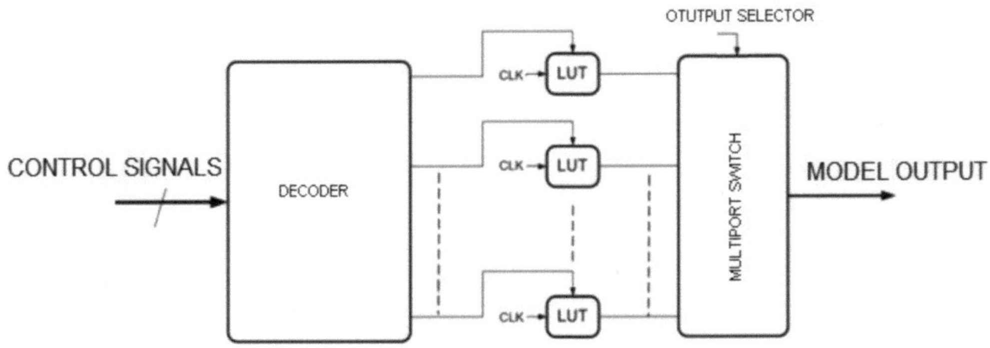

Fig. 23. The output section.

The state machine is modelled by the Stateflow toolbox. Only one state at once is enabled. Three standby modes of operation are available: playback, photography and movie mode. Each one could be maintained indefinitely active even if no function is selected by user. Each mode allows the user to select a limited number of functions. For example, under photography mode taking picture, bracketing, taking picture with flash are available while stored pictures could be viewed if the DSC is in playback mode only. Then, the state machine is intrinsically hierarchical. Fig.24 shows a schematic block diagram of the state machine. Under system start-up, the DSC is driven towards the OFF state by the default transition. No function is available in the OFF state and the output current is null. By double-clicking on the power switch button, the on_switch event is generated and the DSC is driven towards the ON state. The ON-state architecture is shown in Fig.25. Within the ON state, a decision point is set. The position of the mode selector enables playback or photography mode. Note that for the DSC under test, the movie mode is selected by acting on two manual selectors: the first is set on photography mode and the latter selects movie mode. The model reflects the operation of the DSC under test. Within each state, available functions are modelled as states. Authors suggest (Boscaino et al., 2008) for further details.

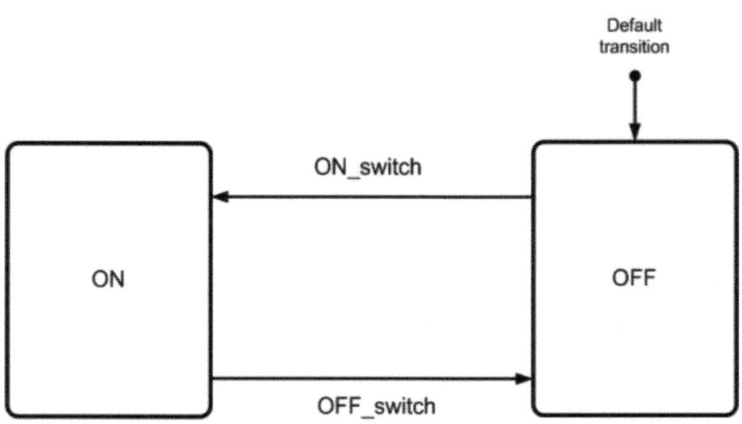

Fig. 24. A schematic block diagram of the DSC state machine.

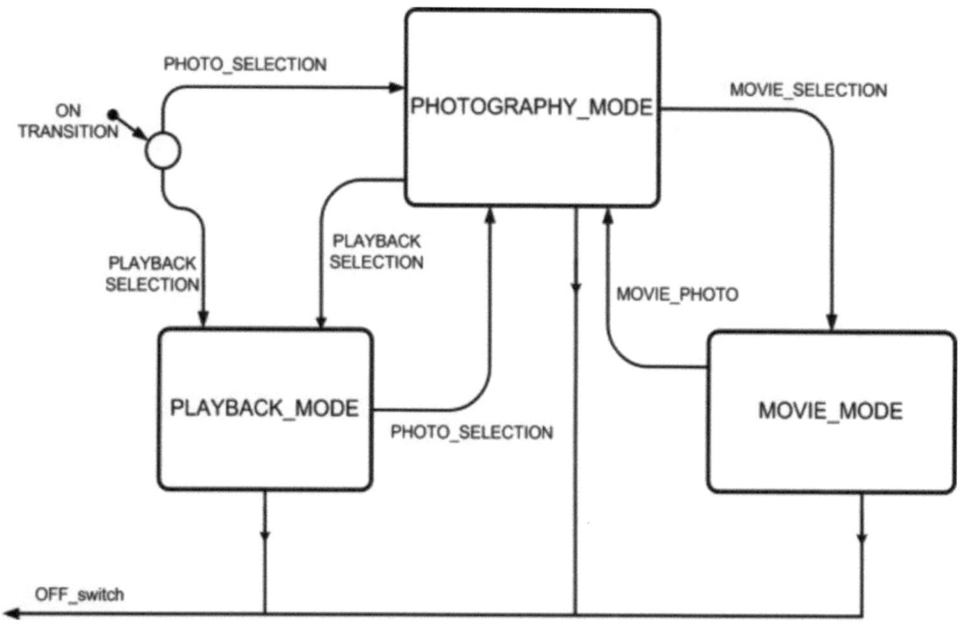

Fig. 25. The ON state architecture.

4.3 PSIM schematic

The active hybrid source and the power management system are modelled in PSIM environment. The stack current is directly controlled to improve dynamic performances. The fuel cell load is levelled by the power management system. The supercapacitor meets the load transient power demand, required for each function running while the fuel cell supplies the standby current of each available mode of the digital camera: playback, photography and movie mode. The equivalent fuel cell load is rather constant except for mode transitions of the DSC. Since the standby current required by the DSC depends on the selected mode of operation, a multiple steady-state control is applied. The fuel cell current is limited to the required stand-by current. Hence, the information about the actual DSC mode is required by the control system. The information is derived by a digital subsystem by monitoring the output voltage and comparing the last few samples.
Fig.26 shows the PSIM top level model. The DC-DC converter and supercapacitor bank are included in the *Hybrid Source* subsystem. The *Control System* is fed by the output voltage and the current sense signal. The output of the controller feeds the *Driver* subsystem which drives the synchronous buck MOSFETs. The Simulink model of the fuel cell reproduces the fuel cell voltage by sampling the fuel cell instantaneous current. In PSIM circuit, the fuel cell voltage is considered an input node from Simulink while the fuel cell current signal is an input signal for the Simulink model. Since Simulink input and output nodes behaviour as voltage sources, the fuel cell current is converted to a voltage signal by a current controlled voltage source which is included in the *Hybrid source* subsystem. The DSC model reproduces the current profile corresponding to the user-selected function. The load current signal is thus obtained by the *Load Current* Simulink input node. Since Simulink input nodes behaviour as voltage sources in PSIM schematics, the signal is converted to a current signal by the means of a voltage controlled current source.

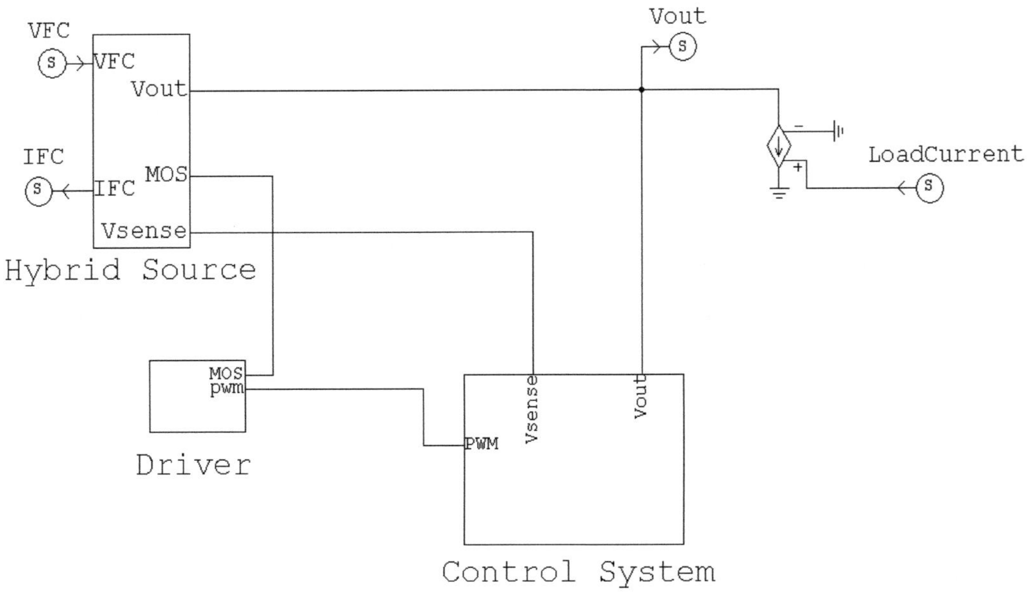

Fig. 26. The PSIM schematic.

Fig.27 shows the active hybrid source. The Fuel cell is connected in series with a buck converter and the supercapacitor bank. Even under the worst-case scenario, the supercapacitor should supply the load current under function transients avoiding any accidental turning-off of the electronic device. The supercapacitor value has been designed to ensure a negligible supercapacitor discharge under the worst-case obtaining a 4.6F value. The load nominal voltage is 6V while turning-off voltage is 4.2V. Since the maximum value of the supercapacitor voltage is 2.5V, three supercapacitors are connected in series to match the load nominal voltage. Two parallel branch of Maxwell PC5 and PC10 supercapacitors are connected. A charge balancing circuit is provided on the experimental prototype. Low ESR capacitors are necessary to limit the output voltage ripple avoiding high inductance values. A sense resistor is introduced to sense the instantaneous inductor current waveform generating the V_{sense} signal.

The control loop architecture is shown in Fig.28. The output voltage is controlled by a Pulse Width Modulation (PWM) control loop. The load levelling function is implemented by a current loop. If a DSC function is selected, the current loop limits the fuel cell current at the standby current value of the actual DSC mode of operation. For example, if bracketing is selected the DSC is in photography mode. The buck inductor current and hence the fuel cell current is limited at the photography standby current value by the current control loop. The pulsed current is supplied by the supercapacitor bank over the entire function runtime. Then, under function running the current loop is active and the current loop action must prevail over the voltage one. Further, the control loop should detect the mode of operation of the power load. The voltage reference subsystem detects the actual DSC mode generating the corresponding voltage reference of the current loop.

Error amplifiers are implemented as Transconductance Operational Amplifiers (OTA). The OTAs are modelled by elementary blocks of PSIM libraries. The differential input is modelled by an adder, the OTA gain is modelled by a multiplier and the linearity range is modelled by a signal limiter.

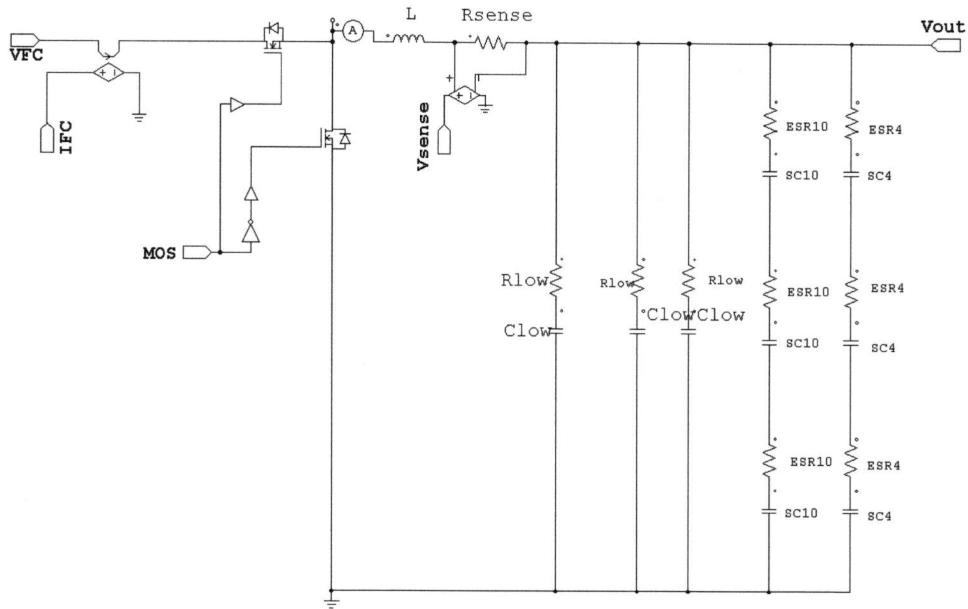

Fig. 27. The hybrid source model.

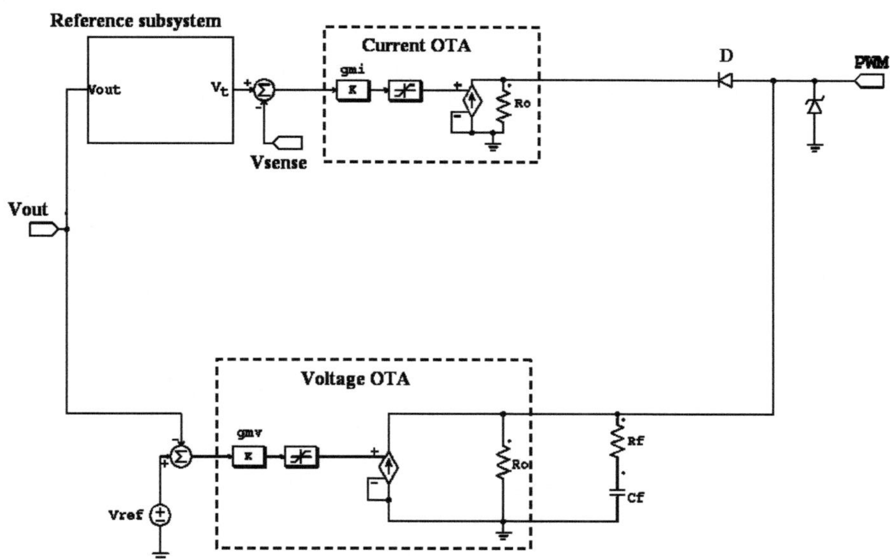

Fig. 28. The control subsystem.

The output current signal is obtained by a voltage controlled current source connected in parallel to the output resistance of the OTA. The compensation action is implemented by the RfCf network. Under steady-state condition, the inductor current is below the current limit and hence the cathode node of the diode D is tied to high-level. The diode D is turned-off. Under load transients, the inductor current tries to overcome the current limit, the cathode voltage is tied to lower level thus turning-on the diode D. By a proper design of the control loop parameters, if the diode is turned-on the current loop action prevails over the voltage one. The interface diode turns on under the condition:

$$I_I \cdot R_0 \leq R_0 \cdot I_V - V_\gamma \tag{9}$$

where $V\gamma$ is the diode threshold voltage, I_I is the current OTA output signal, Iv is the voltage OTA output signal. The turn on condition can be expressed as:

$$g_{m,I} \cdot e_I \cdot R_0 \leq g_{m,V} \cdot e_V \cdot R_0 - V_\gamma \tag{10}$$

where e_V and e_I are the voltage and current differential input signal, respectively, while $g_{m,I}$ and $g_{m,V}$ are the current and voltage OTA gains, respectively.
The current loop action should prevail over the voltage loop action even if the voltage loop is completely upset so ensuring the load levelling function. Hence, assuming the total upset of the voltage loop, the worst-case diode turning-on condition is given by:

$$g_{m,I} \cdot e_I \cdot R_0 \leq R_0 \cdot I_{LIM} - V_\gamma \tag{11}$$

where I_{LIM} is the voltage loop OTA maximum output current and e_I is the desired tolerance on current control. The tolerance is fixed at one half of the steady-state inductor current ripple to achieve a peak current control. The OTA gain of the current loop is designed to verify the (11). Under a load transient, the load current I_{LOAD} exceeds the reference value $I_{L,th}$. Hence, the inductor current is limited to $I_{L,th}$ and the current $I=I_{LOAD}-I_{L,th}$ is supplied by the supercapacitor until the end of transient. Consequently, under a load transient the fuel cell current is maintained constant for hybrid power source optimization: the fuel cell supplies a constant load except for reference value changes. The OTA gain of the voltage loop is chosen by frequency domain analysis to ensure system stability and an adequate bandwidth.
The operating mode of the power load is detected by the reference subsystem by sampling the output voltage only. The reference subsystem is able to detect mode transitions neglecting function transients. Under function transients, the reference voltage is kept constant while under mode transients the voltage reference is adapted to the new mode of operation. Unlike mode transients, function transients feature a limited run time. The subsystem clock period is longer than the highest runtime and hence the control loop is insensitive to function transients.
Fig.29 shows the reference subsystem model which is implemented by logic gates. The output voltage sample is compared with two threshold levels, which are accurately designed to prevent an excessive discharge. Information about the instantaneous charge state of the supercapacitor bank is obtained. The output voltage sample is coded by the logic signals up, mid and down: up is active if the output voltage is over both levels, mid if the sample is in the middle, down if the output voltage is lower than the lowest level. By comparing the two last samples of binary signals, the charge process is monitored and the DSC mode is detected.
Four possible steady-states, coded by s1 and s2 bits, are provided: 240mA, corresponding to DSC playback mode standby power consumption, 390mA, corresponding to DSC photography mode standby power consumption, 480mA, corresponding to DSC movie mode standby power consumption, 700mA, corresponding to a safety state. If an excessive supercapacitor discharge occurs, the safety state will prevent any accidental DSC turning-off. Four possible actions, coded by *a* and *b* bits, are provided: increase by one, increase by

two, decrease by one and keep constant the reference voltage. The subsystem decides which action should be performed on the voltage reference. The new voltage reference bits are determined by the old reference bits and by the action bits. The reference bits feed a digital-to-analog converter which outputs the analog voltage reference value. The proposed algorithm reproduces information about the DSC state by monitoring the charge and discharge profile of the supercapacitor bank. The PWM control technique is implemented within the *Driver* subsystem shown in Fig.30. The error signal is compared with the external saw-tooth voltage V_{ramp} and the PWM signal is generated. The PWM signal and the clock signal feed the D flip-flop with asynchronous reset input which generates the driver signal for both MOSFET gates of the buck converter. Authors suggest (Boscaino et al., 2009a) for further details.

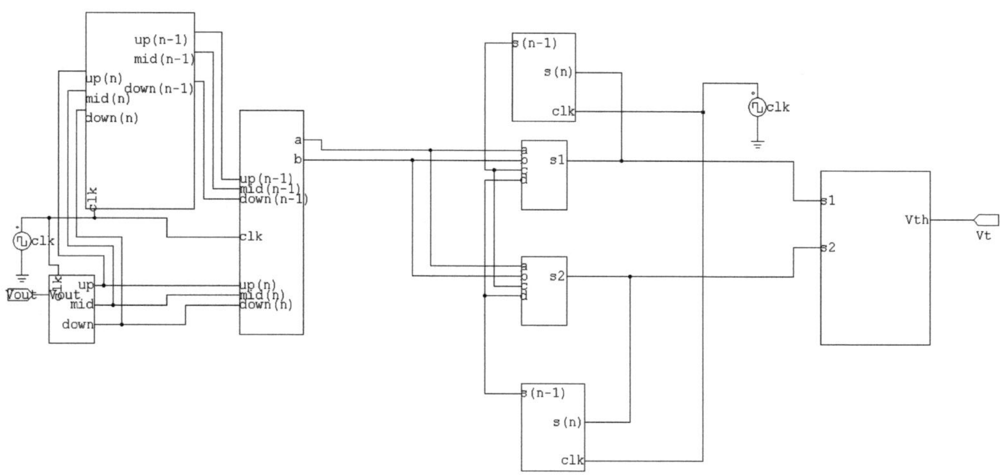

Fig. 29. The reference subsystem.

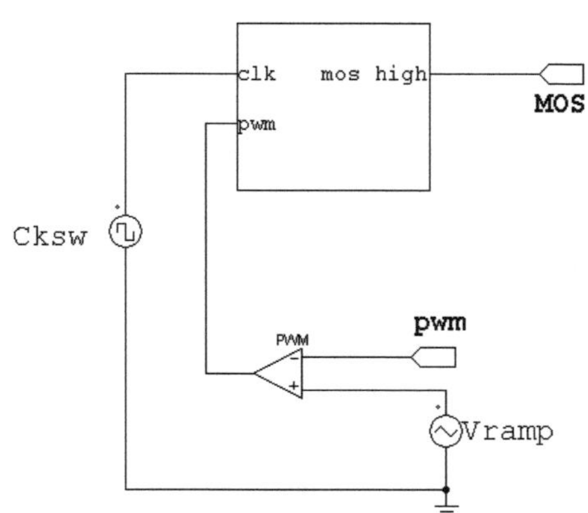

Fig. 30. The driver subsystem.

5. Simulation and experimental results

The efficiency and accuracy of the proposed simulation set-up is confirmed by the comparison between simulation and experimental results. Simulation results accurately match experimental ones. The output voltage profile depends not only on the selected function but above all on the "history" of the power supply system since the turning-on. Yet, the system is tested since the simulation step with the effective load consumption profile. Long-time simulation tests are performed to show the robustness of the power management algorithms. The system prevents any accidental turning-off of the digital still camera improving the hybrid source performances. The hybrid source features the same dynamic response of the supercapacitor bank under pulsed current profile, the life cycle is closely related to the hydrogen reserve and quite independent of the supercapacitor state of charge. After all, the hybrid source features the high power capability of the supercapacitor bank and the high energy capability of the fuel cell. The performances of the hybrid source are not affected by drawbacks of both primary sources. The inductor current and the output voltage waveforms under no-load conditions are shown in Fig.31. The output voltage is controlled by the voltage loop while the current loop is not active.

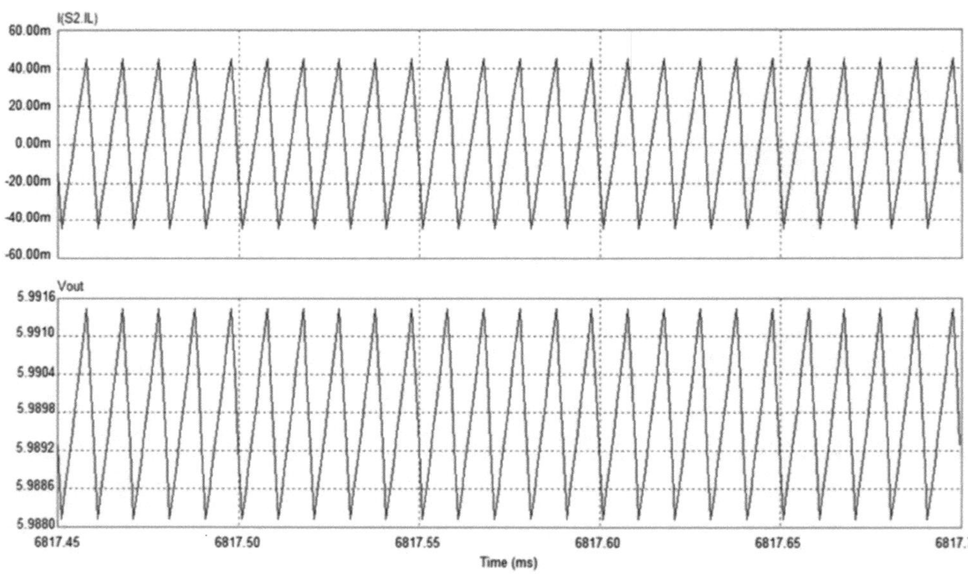

Fig. 31. At the top the inductor current, at the bottom the output voltage waveforms under no-load conditions.

The inductor current and the interface diode current waveforms under current loop limitation are shown in Fig.32 the current limit is fixed at 240mA, corresponding to the playback mode of operation. When the inductor current overcomes the 210mA limit, the interface diode is forced into conduction. The tolerance on the current control is 30mA within the tolerance window of 40mA designed by (11).

Simulation results under turning-on in photography mode are shown to better understand the efficiency of the designed control algorithm. Turning-on in photography mode is a critical transient since the transient time is quite long and peak current value is higher and higher than the average value. Figures from 33 to 36 show the system behaviour under the turning-on function. Take a look to the evolution of the system from start-up till the end of transient. At the top, the pulsed current load and the inductor current, at the bottom the output voltage waveforms are shown. Under start-up conditions, the system starts at the lowest threshold value corresponding to the playback mode (240mA). Yet, the digital camera is turned-on in photography mode corresponding to a higher current limit (390mA). The fuel cell supplies the standby current of the playback mode while the pulsed current is supplied by the supercapacitor bank, as shown in Fig.33.The turning-on function in photography mode lasts 4.6s. Until the effective mode of operation is detected, the inductor current is limited to the playback mode current threshold, as shown in Fig.33. In the intermediate part of the function transient the main peak of the load current is entirely supplied by the supercapacitor, as shown in Fig.34. The supercapacitor bank is constantly discharged. Even under stress, the output voltage does not drop below the turning-off limit, which is equal to 4.2V, thanks to an accurate design of the power stage. Fig.35 shows the system behaviour under the last part of the turning on function, corresponding to the lens movement. The inductor current is already limited at the playback mode current limit. At the end of turning-on in photography mode, the actual mode of operation is detected by the reference subsystem as shown by Fig.36. The inductor current limit is increased up to the photography mode standby current value. No function is actually selected by the end-user. The standby current of the photography mode is supplied by the fuel cell thus interrupting the supercapacitor discharge. The safety state is not reached since no excessive discharge has been detected by the reference subsystem.

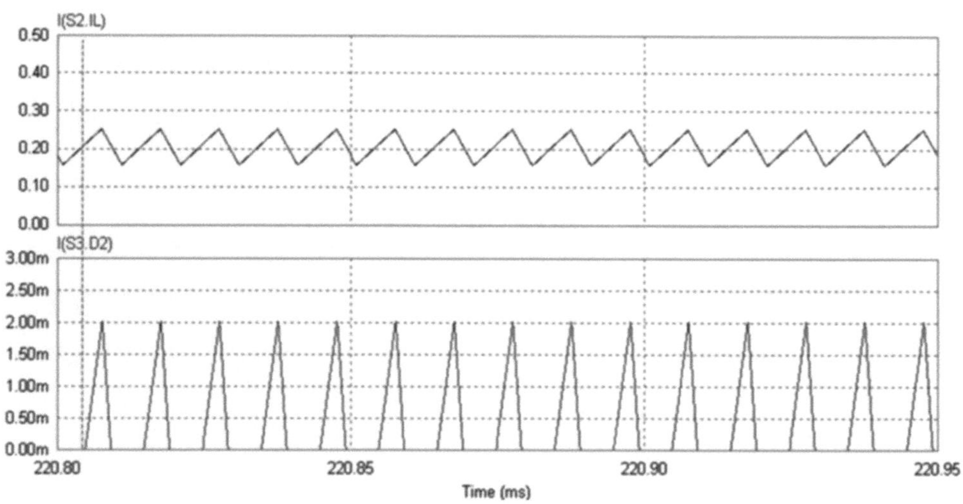

Fig. 32. At the top the inductor current, at the bottom the diode current waveforms under current limitation.

Experimental results under turning-on in photography mode are shown in Fig.37. The output voltage (C1, 1V/div), the load current (C2, 200mA/div) and the inductor current (C3, 200mA/div) are shown. Time base is fixed at 2s/div. As shown by simulation results, the system does not detect the actual mode of operation until the end of transient. Hence, the transient current is supplied by the supercapacitor bank while the standby current is supplied by the fuel cell. Then, the actual mode is detected and the current limit is increased.

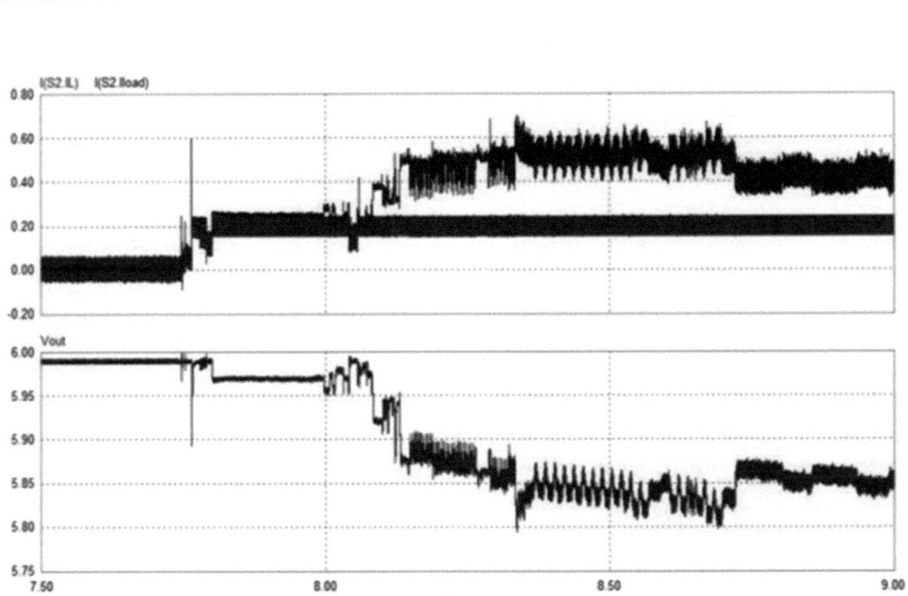

Fig. 33. Simulation results under turning-on in photography mode. At the top the pulsed load current and the inductor current, at the bottom the output voltage waveforms at the beginning of function transient are shown. The system starts at playback mode current limit and the actual state is not yet detected.

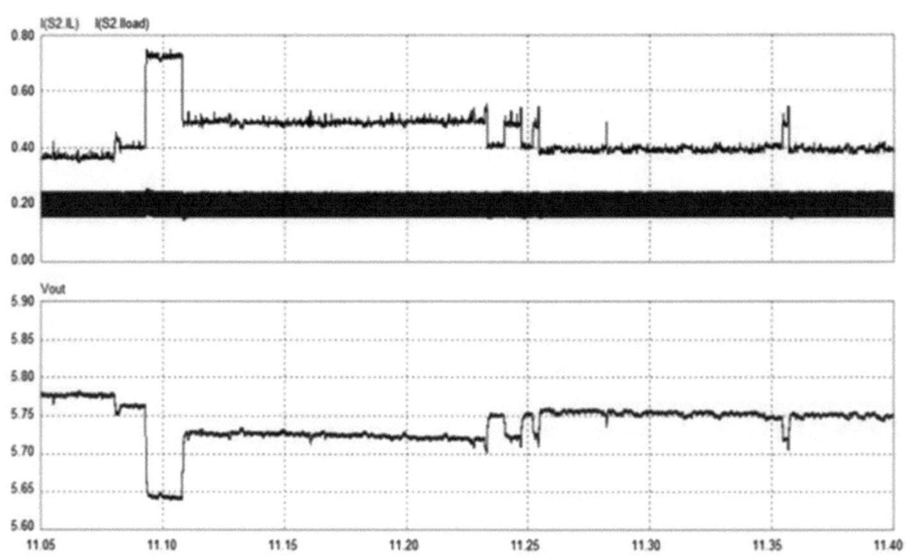

Fig. 34. Simulation results under turning-on in photography mode, intermediate part of function transient. At the top the pulsed load current and the inductor current, at the bottom the output voltage waveforms during the peak power consumption are shown. The DSC state is not yet detected.

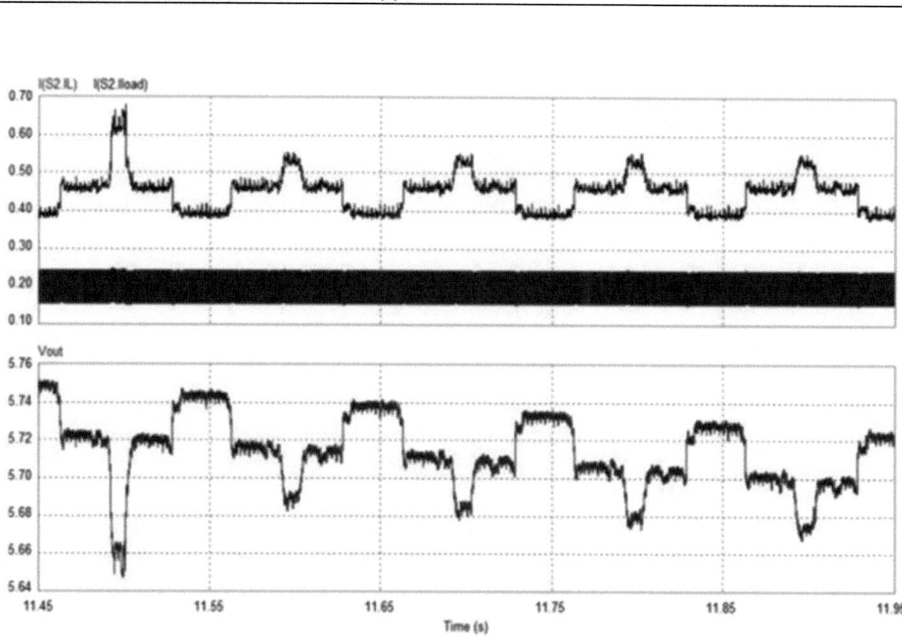

Fig. 35. Simulation results under turning-on in photography mode. At the top the pulsed load current and the inductor current, at the bottom the output voltage waveforms during at the end of function transient are shown. The actual state is not yet detected.

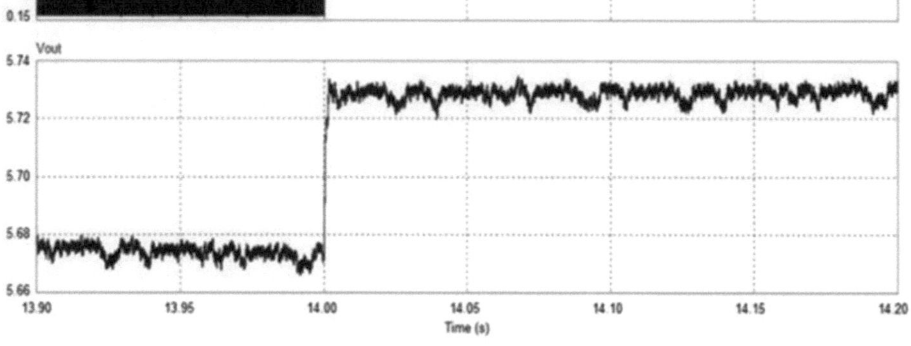

Fig. 36. Simulation results after turning on in photography mode. At the top the pulsed load current and the inductor current, at the bottom the output voltage waveforms are shown. The DSC state is detected and the current threshold is increased to allow the supercapacitor recharge.

Note that the instant at which the reference subsystem detects the actual DSC mode of operation is not related to the transient itself but above all on the history of the system since the start-up condition. Experimental results under turning-on in photography mode in the worst-case are shown in Fig.37. In this case, the actual mode of operation is detected after the end of transient. In Fig. 38, the actual mode of operation is detected before the end of transient. The discharge of the supercapacitor is thus limited to the beginning of the function transient.

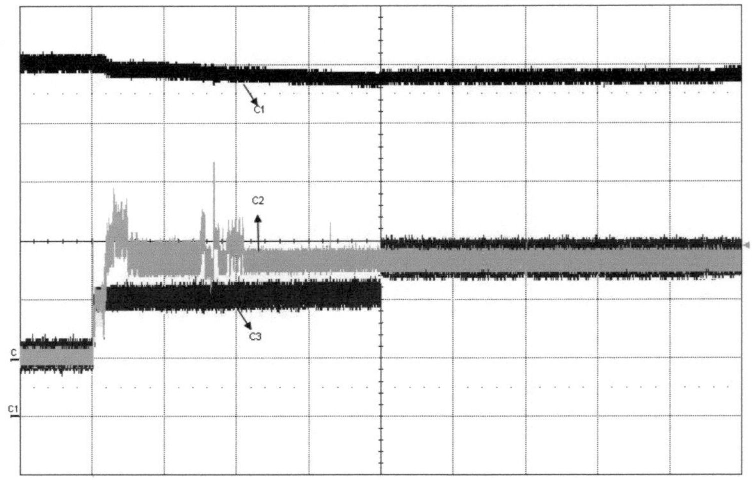

Fig. 37. Experimental results under turning on in photography mode. The DSC state is detected at the end of function transient. On C1 the output voltage (1V/div), on C2 the load current (200mA/div), on C3 the inductor current (200mA/div) are shown. Time base is set at 2s/div.

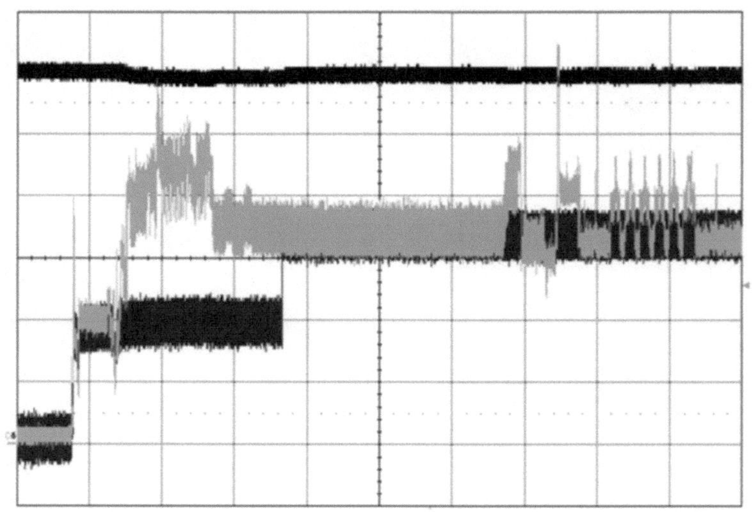

Fig. 38. Experimental results under turning on in photography mode. In this case the actual mode is detected before the end of transient. On C1 the output voltage (1V/div), on C2 the load current (200mA/div), on C3 the inductor current (200mA/div) are shown. Time base is set at 2s/div.

In Fig.39 simulation results under bracketing function are shown. At the top, the pulsed load current and the buck inductor current are shown. At the bottom, the output voltage is shown. The inductor current which is a scaled version of the fuel cell current is limited at the photography stand-by current limit over the entire transient time. The fuel cell supplies the standby current of the actual DSC mode of operation while the supercapacitor bank supplies the instantaneous peak power. The output voltage is affected by the supercapacitor discharge. Yet, any accidental turning-off is avoided thanks to the accurate design of the power stage. Further, if no-function is selected by user the supercapacitor bank will be recharged driving back the system to the nominal working conditions.

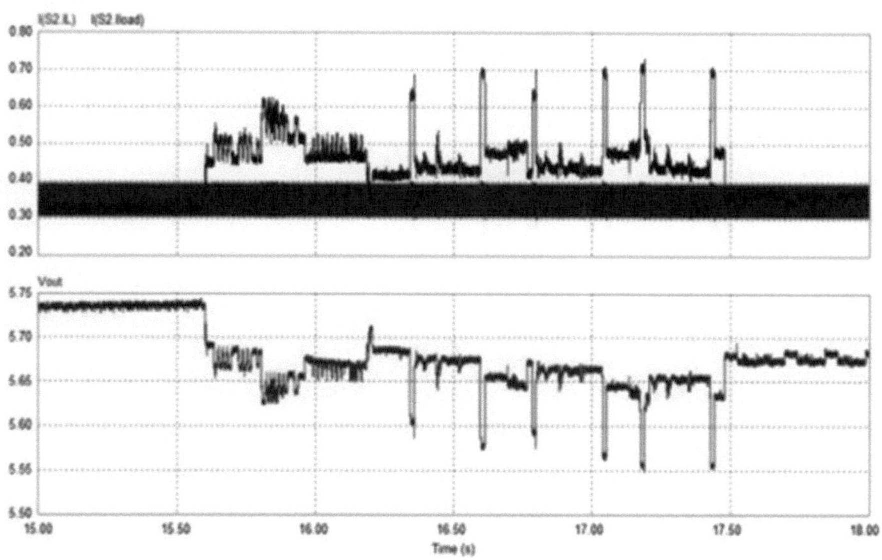

Fig. 39. Simulation results under bracketing function. At the top the pulsed load current and the inductor current, at the bottom the output voltage waveforms are shown.

Fig.40 shows simulation results under bracketing function. In this case, the system has not yet detected the actual mode of operation of the DSC. At the top the pulsed load current and the inductor current, at the bottom the output voltage waveforms are shown. The system is still in playback mode and the inductor current is limited to 240mA, lower and lower than the actual standby current. This is the worst-case for bracketing function. The fuel cell supplies the playback mode current while the supercapacitor is heavily discharged supplying both the pulsed current and the difference between the photography and playback standby currents. Yet, the discharge is not yet critical for the DSC working. Note that this condition is closely related to the history of the system.
Experimental results under bracketing function are shown in Fig.41. The output voltage (C1, 1V/div), the load current (C2, 200mA/div) and the inductor current (C4, 200mA/div) are shown. The time base is fixed at 500ms/div. Note the high accuracy of simulation results. The DSC current profile is accurately reproduced allowing the designer to test the control algorithms as closely as possible to the effective system behaviour. Since specific hybrid source features as life-cycle and transient response are directly controlled, high accuracy

modelling is a key step to achieve high-efficiency power management control algorithms. As expected by the performed behavioural simulations, experimental results confirm the high efficiency of the implemented algorithms.

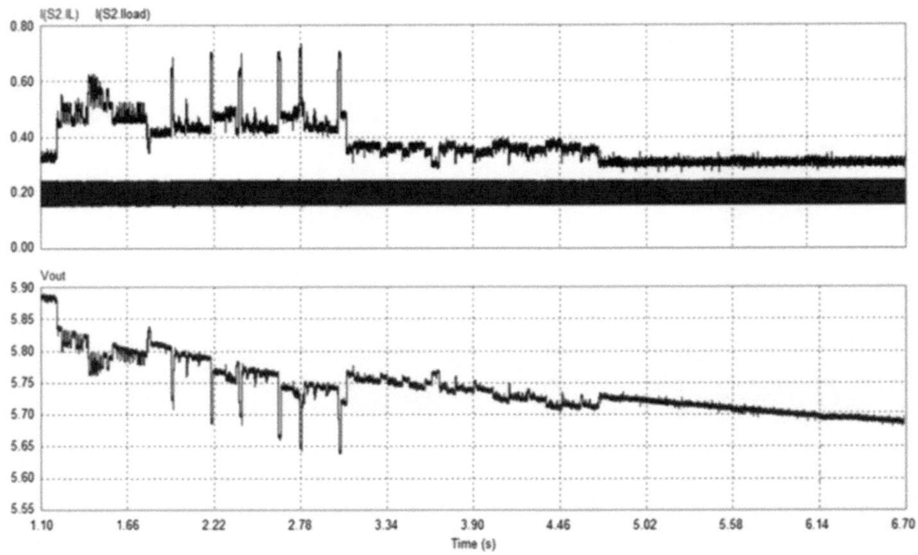

Fig. 40. Simulation results under bracketing function. The actual mode is not yet detected and the playback mode current limit is active. At the top the pulsed load current and the inductor current, at the bottom the output voltage waveforms are shown.

Simulation results under zoom function in playback mode are shown in Fig.42. At the top, the pulsed load current and the buck inductor current are shown. At the bottom, the output voltage is shown. The zoom function is not a critical function for the hybrid power supply. The inductor current is limited at the playback mode threshold. At the end of the transient time, the output voltage reaches again the nominal value. The net discharge of the supercapacitor bank could be neglected under the selected function running. The fuel cell supplies the standby current of the actual DSC mode of operation while the supercapacitor bank supplies the instantaneous peak power.

Fig.43 shows simulation results under multiple execution of zoom function in playback mode. At the top, the pulsed load current and the inductor current, at the bottom the output voltage waveforms are shown. In this case, the system has previously detected an excessive discharge of the supercapacitor bank. The current limit has been previously increased up to the movie mode threshold to allow a fast recharge. Yet, zoom function is actually selected by user and repeated several times. Note that in this case, the recharge is supplied by the fuel cell itself. The net recharge current is equal to the difference between the limited inductor current and the load current.

Experimental results under zoom function are shown in Fig.44. The output voltage (C1, 1V/div), the load current (C2, 200mA/div) and the inductor current (C3, 100mA/div) are shown. Time base is set to 20ms/div. As expected by simulation results, the output voltage is not affected by the zoom running.

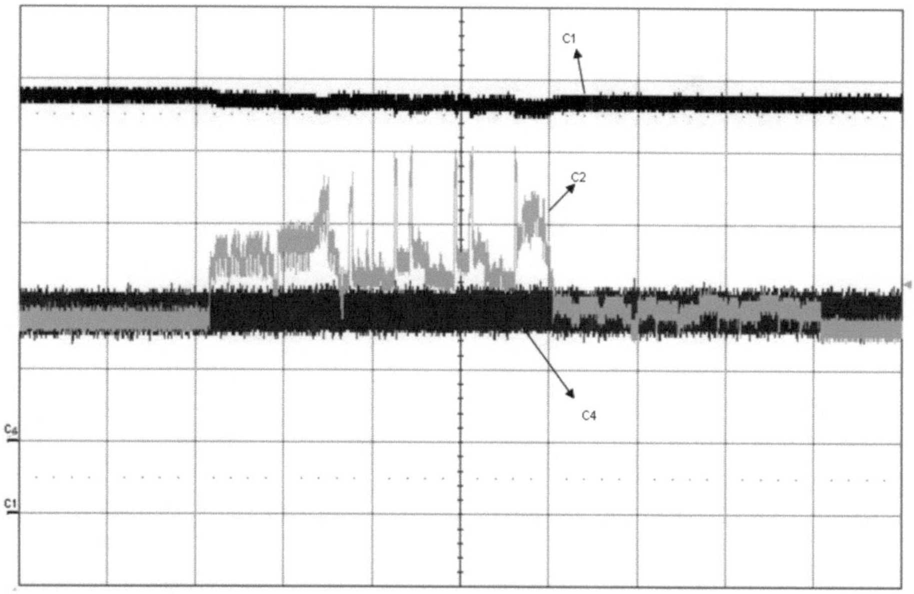

Fig. 41. Experimental results under bracketing function. The output voltage (C1, 1V/div), the load current (C2, 200mA/div), the buck inductor current (C4, 200mA/div) are shown. Time base is set to 500ms/div.

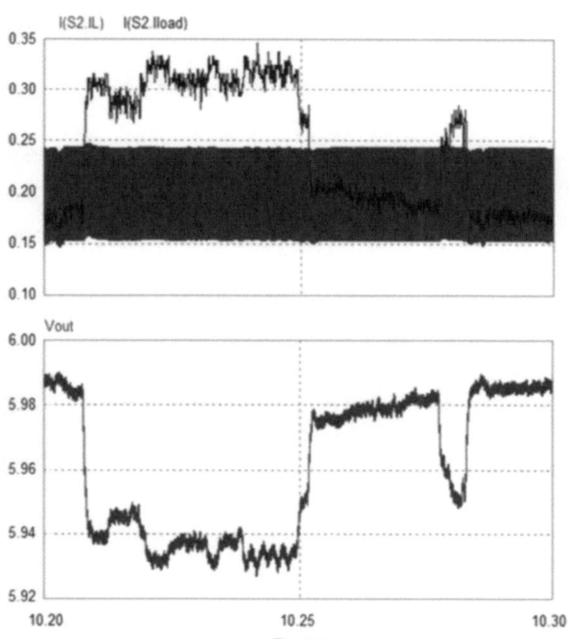

Fig. 42. Simulation results under zoom function in playback mode. At the top, the pulsed load current and the inductor current, at the bottom the output voltage waveforms are shown.

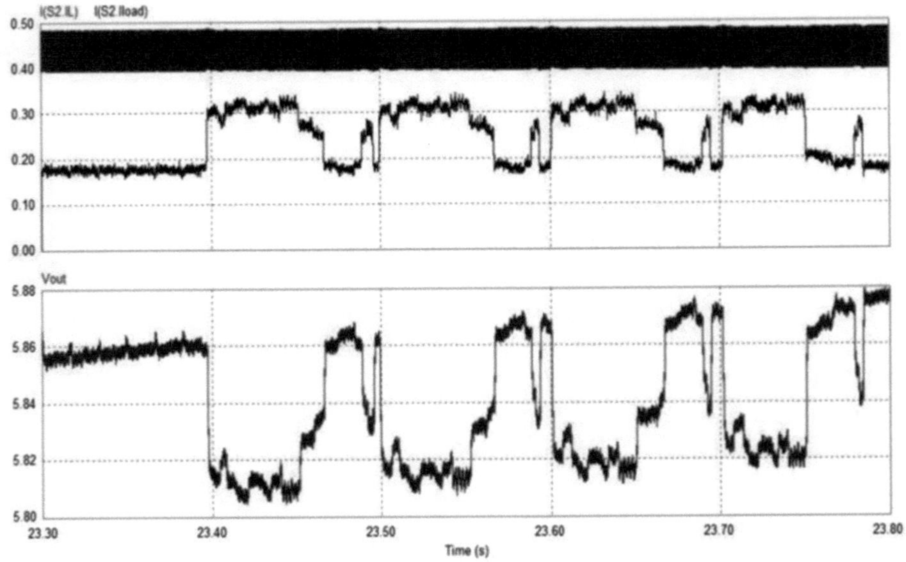

Fig. 43. Simulation results under zoom function in playback mode. The current limit is higher than the playback mode threshold to allow a fast recharge of the supercapacitor bank. At the top, the pulsed load current and the inductor current, at the bottom the output voltage waveforms are shown.

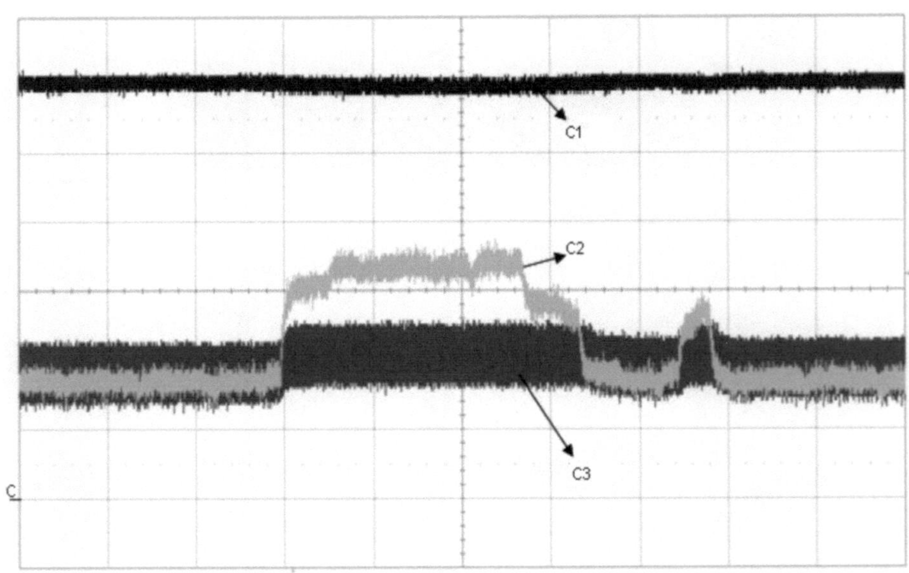

Fig. 44. Experimental results under zoom function in playback mode. The output voltage (C1, 1V/div), the load current (C2, 200mA/div), the buck inductor current (C3, 100mA/div) are shown. Time base is set to 20ms/div.

6. Conclusion

In this chapter, a high accuracy simulation set-up for hybrid power supplies is proposed. As an example, a fuel cell-supercapacitor hybrid power supply for a digital still camera is designed and tested. The system is modelled and tested in Simulink environment with the aid of *SimCoupler Module* for PSIM/Matlab co-simulation. The power management controller is implemented in PSIM environment while the fuel cell and the power load are accurately modelled by the means of Simulink library elements. A laboratory prototype has been realized and tested. Simulation results accurately match experimental results, highlighting the high efficiency of the proposed technique. The proposed modelling approach is suitable for each power supply system thanks to the powerful tools available in Matlab suite. Thanks to the powerful modelling approach, the need of a warm-up phase is highlighted since the simulation step. The fuel cell temperature has to be increased up to 40°C before the system start-up. Authors are working on an innovative power management system which overcomes this drawback by controlling the fuel cell temperature under start-up conditions.
The modelling approach is still a key design tool.

7. Acknowledgement

Authors would like to thank ST Microelectronics for supporting the research activity.

8. References

Alotto, P., Guarnieri, M. & Moro, F. (2008). Modelling and control of fuel cell-battery hybrid power systems for portable electronics. *Proceedings of IEEE Universities Power Engineering Conference,* ISBN: 978-1-4244-3294-3, Padova, Italy, December 2008.

Boscaino, V., Capponi G., Livreri, P. & Marino, F. (2008). Measurement-based load modelling for power supply system design, *Proceedings of IEEE International Conference on Control and modelling for Power Electronics,* ISBN: 978-1-4244-2550-1, Zürich, Switzerland, August 2008.

Boscaino, V., Capponi G. & Marino, F.(2009a). Experimental test on a fuel cell-supercapacitor hybrid power supply for a digital still camera, *Proceedings of IEEE Universities Power Engineering Conference,* ISBN: 978-1-4244-6823-2, Glasgow, Scotland, Sept. 2009.

Boscaino, V., Capponi, G. & Marino, F. (2009b). A steady-state and dynamic fuel cell model including temperature effects. *Proceedings of IEEE International Conference on Industrial Electronics,* ISBN: 978-1-4244-4648-3, Porto, Portugal, November 2009.

Gao L., & Dougal, R.A. (2003). Active Power Sharing in Hybrid Battery/Capacitor Power Sources. *Proceedings of Applied Power Electronics Conference and Exposition,* ISBN: 0-7803-7768-0, Miami, Florida, February *2003.*

Lin, C.J., Chen, A.Y.T., Chiou, C.Y., Huang, C.H., Chiang, H.D. , Wang, J.C. & Fekih-Ahmed, L.(1993). Dynamic load models in power systems using the measurement approach. *IEEE Transactions on Power Systems*, vol. 8, no. 1, (February 2003), pp. 309-315, ISSN: 0885-8950.

9

Calculating Radiation from Power Lines for Power Line Communications

Cornelis Jan Kikkert
James Cook University
Queensland
Australia

1. Introduction

The cost of electricity charged to consumers in Australia is predominantly set by state governments and does not vary depending on the actual cost that the electricity retailer has to pay the generators. This does not encourage users to reduce power at times of peak demand and the ratio between the peak demand and the average demand is growing. In the long term, user pays principle must apply and the cost of electricity charged will need to vary depending on the actual cost of production. This requires a communication system to be produced firstly to determine the date and time electricity is used, so that the usage and actual cost can be matched, and secondly to inform the consumer of the actual cost of electricity, so that appropriate actions can be taken, like turning off air conditioners when the cost per kW becomes high.

There are two ways that such a communication system can be developed. Firstly it can use the PLC for carrying the communication signals. Secondly the communication systems can be carried by third party suppliers. The WiMAX radio system currently being rolled out in Australia in Victoria and mobile phone based systems are examples of such systems. Using PLC has the advantage that the communication system is fully under the control of the electricity company and no fees need to be paid to third party operators.

In addition it is possible for the electricity supplier to use their power lines to provide BPL, giving internet access to customers, by putting communication signals up to 80 MHz onto the power lines. The frequency range used and bandwidth required for BPL is very different than that for PLC and the radiation losses are very different for BPL and PLC.

When a power line is used for transmitting communication signals, signal power is lost through electromagnetic radiation. This may cause interference to other users. There is a concern about the amount of radiation from power lines (ACMA 2005, 2007), with amateur radio operators claiming BPL creates excessive levels of radiation. Unfortunately much of the amateur radio literature does not distinguish between BPL and PLC. The second loss factor is resistive losses, which due to the skin depth causes an increasing attenuation with frequency.

The Matlab® program described in this paper and the results obtained from this program provide a rigorous basis for determining both the resistive losses and the radiation obtained from power lines. Electricity distribution companies and other communication providers can use this data to determine the feasibility of power line communications in their region.

SWER power lines are used in remote areas and are single phase lines where the ground is relied upon for the return path. As these power lines can be up to 300 km long, there is a significant economic incentive to read the power meter for those customers remotely since a 600 km trip on dirt roads is likely to cost more than the customer's electricity bill. To achieve this JCU has been carrying out a research project for the Queensland electricity retailer ERGON for developing a PLC communication system for SWER lines.

2. Fundamental principles

2.1 Line radiation theory

The existing travelling wave model of a long wire antenna (Balanis, 1997, Walter, 1970 and Ulaby, 1994) assumes that the antenna is less than 10 λ long and the current along the line is constant, implying that no power is lost in radiation. Neither of these assumptions apply for power lines, so that a radiation model based on fundamental equations had to be developed.

The power radiated for an infinitesimal current element, also called an elementary doublet is described in most antenna books. The model presented in this paper cascades many of these infinitesimal current element models to make up the whole transmission line. The power radiated by a small length of conductor of length l in the far field, is dependent on the current in the conductor, I_0, and is shown in (Balanis, 1997) to be:

$$P_{rad} = \eta \frac{\pi}{3}\left(\frac{l I_0}{\lambda}\right)^2 \tag{1}$$

where η_0 = 120 π, is the λ wavelength. Antenna radiation patterns for long wire antenna Because the line is long, I_0 will not be constant. Three factors affect I_0:

1. I_0 is reduced by dissipation due to series resistance. This series resistance varies with frequency due to the skin depth varying with frequency.
2. I_0 is altered in phase, along the line, due to wave propagation.
3. I_0 is progressively reduced because power is radiated.

Using the conventional spherical coordinates r, θ and φ, the far-field electric field E_θ and the far-field magnetic field H_φ for this elementary doublet is given by (Balanis 1997) as:

$$E_\theta = \frac{j\eta_0 k I_0 l e^{-jkr}\sin(\theta)}{4\pi r} = \frac{j\eta_0 I_0 l e^{-jkr}\sin(\theta)}{2\lambda r} = \frac{j60\pi I_0 l e^{-jkr}\sin(\theta)}{\lambda r} \tag{2}$$

$$H_\varphi = \frac{jk I_0 l e^{-jkr}\sin(\theta)}{4\pi r} = \frac{j I_0 l e^{-jkr}\sin(\theta)}{2\lambda r} \tag{3}$$

where the wave number, k = 2π/λ. Note that since the current I_0 has a magnitude and phase, both E_θ and H_φ are complex quantities.

$$P_{rad} = \frac{1}{2}\mathrm{Re}\left(\oint\!\!\oint_s E_\theta \times H_\varphi ds\right) \tag{4}$$

The far-field power radiated is obtained by integrating the Poynting vector over a closed surface, chosen to be a sphere of radius r, where r is much larger than the wavelength and the length of the power line dimensions as shown in equation (4). For an elementary doublet in free space, the inner integrand is independent of φ, resulting in a constant of 2π for that integration, so that:

$$\mathrm{P}_{rad} = \frac{\pi}{2\eta_0}\int_0^{2\pi}|E(\theta)|r^2\sin(\theta)d\theta = \frac{1}{240}\int_0^{2\pi}|E(\theta)|r^2\sin(\theta)d\theta \quad (5)$$

For a very long wire antenna, such as a power line, the magnitude and phase of the current I_0 and E_θ at a position along the line is iteratively determined by considering the radiation and resistive line losses up to that point. This is then be used to determine E_θ caused by the elementary doublet at that point. At a point along the line, the E_θ vector from the elementary doublet is added to the cumulative E_θ vector, to produce the new cumulative E_θ vector. For a line in free space, the cumulative fields are independent of φ, so that (5) can be used to evaluate the radiated power.

If the conductor is not in free space, but is a single power line, a distance h above an ideal groundplane, then equal and opposite image current will be induced below the groundplane. That changes the radiation pattern, so that the radiation is no longer independent of φ. A Medium Voltage (11 kV to 33 kV) single power line is typically 7 m above the ground. If this is used for power line communication signals up to 1 MHz, then the power line is far less than a quarter wavelength above the ground. The far-field electric field for an elementary doublet a distance h above a perfectly conducting ground plane will be:

$$E(\theta,\varphi) = E_\theta(2jSin(\frac{\pi 2h}{\lambda}Cos(\varphi)) = -\frac{120\pi I_0 le^{-jkr}\sin(\theta)}{\lambda r}Sin(\frac{\pi 2h}{\lambda}Cos(\varphi)) \quad (6)$$

The radiation pattern from the elementary doublet will then have a null along the conductor (θ=0), as it had for the free space conductor and in addition it will have a null along the groundplane (φ=90°) and a maximum perpendicular to the groundplane ($\theta = \varphi = 90°$). The field in this direction depends on 2h, the separation between the line and the return path. For SWER lines, the ground plane is not a perfectly conducting plane and the distance of the ground return path below the ground level is given by Carson's equation (Carson, 1926, Wang & Liu, 2001, Deri & Tevan, 1981):

$$D = 2(h + \sqrt{\left(\frac{\rho_s}{2\pi F\mu_0}\right)} \quad (7)$$

where h is the height of the SWER line above ground, ρ_s is the soil resistivity. To use this for a SWER line we replace the line separation 2h in equation (6) by D in equation (7).

At 50 Hz the return path is typically 1km below ground and at 100 kHz it is about 36 m below ground. In both cases the return path distance is still much less than a quarter wavelength, so no additional nulls appear in the field from the elementary doublet. Since the effective line spacing varies, the line capacitance and characteristic impedance also change with frequency.

Equation (6) can also be used to determine the radiation from overhead power lines where the PLC signals are applied in a differential form on two conductors with a line separation of *2h*.

From knowing the skin depth, the diameter of the conductor and its conductivity, the resistance of conductor for the elementary doublet length can be calculated. Knowing the current flowing through the elementary doublet, the resistive losses can then be calculated.

Knowing the current flowing into the present elementary doublet and keeping the characteristic impedance of the line fixed at the value for the operating frequency, the current I_0 flowing into the next elementary doublet can determined by subtracting the cumulated power lost in radiation and the cumulated resistive losses from the input power to the present elementary doublet as shown in (8).

$$I_0 = \sqrt{\frac{I_{in}^2 Z_0 - P_{rad} - P_{res}}{Z_0}} \tag{8}$$

This process of adding an elementary doublet, calculating the resulting cumulative E_θ, cumulative radiated power, resistive losses and evaluating the current I_0 flowing into the next elementary doublet, is repeated to determine the E_θ and the power radiated and the resistive losses for the whole line. The accuracy of this model has been verified by the authors (Reid & Kikkert, 2008) by comparing its results for short line lengths with those from standard equations.

2.2 Transmission line parameters

To calculate the resistive losses and radiation losses, accurate transmission line parameters need to be used. The fundamental equations for transmission line parameters are shown in (Johnson, 1950). Those equations have been used by the author (Kikkert & Reid, 2009) to derive the line parameters for power lines.

In a conductor, most of the current flows in the outer layer of the conductor, with a thickness of the skin depth (δ). The equation for the resistance of the line is given by equation (9) (Johnson 1950):

$$R = \frac{\rho}{\sqrt{2}\pi a \delta} \frac{ber(q)\frac{d}{dq}bei(q) - bei(q)\frac{d}{dq}ber(q)}{\left\{\frac{d}{dq}bei(q)\right\}^2 + \left\{\frac{d}{dq}ber(q)\right\}^2} \quad \Omega / m \tag{9}$$

where *ber* and *bei* are Kelvin-Bessel functions (Johnson 1950), a is the conductor radius, ρ is the resistivity of the conductor in ohm-meters, q is an intermediate constant and δ is the skin depth, F is the frequency in Hz and μ is the magnetic permeability ($4\pi \times 10^{-7}$ in free space), as given by equations (10) and (11).

$$q = \sqrt{2}\frac{a}{\delta} \qquad \delta = \sqrt{\frac{\rho}{\pi \mu F}} \tag{10}$$

$$R_{dc} = \frac{\rho}{\pi a^2} \quad \Omega / m \tag{11}$$

At high frequencies Fig 3.10 of (Johnson, 1950) shows equation (9) becomes approximately:

$$R = R_{dc}\frac{a}{2\delta} \tag{12}$$

To avoid calculation Kelvin-Bessel functions and considering that the conductor is made up of several strands with a steel core and aluminium cladding, equation (9) can be approximated to:

$$R = \sqrt{\frac{{R_{Cdc}}^2 {a_S}^2}{4\delta} + {R_{Wdc}}^2} \tag{13}$$

where R_{cdc} is the DC resistance of the whole conductor, if it were made from aluminium only, R_{Wdc} is the actual DC resistance of the whole conductor and a_s is the radius of each strand. At high frequencies the resistance is determined by the skin depth in the aluminium cladding and the low frequency asymptote is the actual DC resistance of the whole steel core bundled conductor. If a conductor is made up of solid steel or solid aluminium, then $R_{Cdc} = R_{Wdc}$. The difference between (9) and (13) for Steel Cored Galvanized Zinc (SCGZ) conductors is less than 3.4% for frequencies above 3 kHz. For Aluminium conductors, the error is less than 3.4% for frequencies above 30 kHz. Equation (9) cannot be applied to SCAC conductors, so that equation (13) is an acceptable equation for all conductors at PLC frequencies.
The line inductance for a line, can similarly be approximated to:

$$L_i = \frac{\mu_r \mu_0}{\sqrt{\frac{a^2}{4\delta^2} + 1}} \tag{14}$$

$$L = \frac{4}{10K} Log_e\left(\frac{D}{a} + L_i\right) \quad mH / km \tag{15}$$

where L is the inductance of the line, L_i is the internal inductance, D is the distance between the conductor and the one carrying the return path. For SWER lines, this is given by equation (7). K is a constant, where $K = 2$ if the transmission line consists of a conductor above a ground plane and $K = 1$ if the transmission line consists of a balanced line.

$$C = \frac{2K\varepsilon_r}{36 Log_e(\frac{D}{a})} \quad \mu F / km \tag{16}$$

$$Z = \sqrt{\frac{L}{C}} \tag{17}$$

3. Matlab® implementation

3.1 Transmission line parameters

For SWER lines, three types of conductors are commonly used. The oldest lines use Steel Core Galvanised Zinc (SCGZ) cables. These are basically fencing wire and typically have 3 strands, each of 2.75 mm diameter (Olex, 2006). The DC resistance at 20 °C is 11 Ω. The zinc coating is very thin and it's thickness is not adequately specified and varies with age. As a result these lines are modelled as steel lines.

Most SWER lines have a high current backbone, which then feeds many lower current spurs. The newer spurs use Steel Core Aluminium Clad (SCAC) cables. Typically these cables have 3 strands, each of 2.75 mm diameter (Olex, 2006), with an aluminium area of 5.91 mm^2 and a total area of 17.28 mm^2. The DC resistance at 20 °C is 4.8 Ω. The high power backbone typically uses Sultana (Olex, 2006) cables, which consist of 4 strands of Aluminium wires of 3 mm diameter around a galvanised steel core of 3 wires of 3 mm diameter. The DC resistance at 20 °C is 0.897 Ω. Since the conductivity of the steel is much less than the aluminium, these lines are modelled as pure aluminium conductors. Other power line conductor configurations are used in practice. They can be incorporated by simply specifying the correct wire diameter, the diameter of the whole conductor, the number of strands and for composite conductors, the area of Aluminium and the area of steel. In addition the conductivity and the permeability of the cable is also required. Those variables are listed at the start of the Matlab® program, the relevant ones for a SCAC conductor are as follows:

```
RhoC= 2.82e-8;     %resistivity of conductor 2.82e-8 for Al, 1.74e-7 for steel
RhoS= 30.0 ;     %resistivity of soil typical 30
DiaC= 2.75e-3;     %diameter of conductor strand in m for default 2.75mm
ALArea=5.91;     %Area of Aluminium in conductor SCAC
LineArea=17.82;     %Conductor Area SCAC
NSC=3;     %number of conductor strands default 3
DiaL=5.9e-3;  %Nominal Line Diameter m, 5.9 mm for SCGZ, SCAC
Er=4.5;     %Dielectric constant for the spacing between conductors. 4.5 for SWER from
measurements
RadC = DiaC/2.0;  %conductor radius for skin depth and resistance
RadL = DiaL/2.0; %Line radius for capacitance and inductance
Mu0=4.0*pi*1.0e-7;  %mu0 for free space
MuR=1.0;  % Mur=70 for steel (SCGZ), 1 for Aluminium (SCAC and Sultana)
MuC = Mu0*MuR;
Rdc = RhoC*1000.0/(NSC*pi*RadC*RadC);
RdcW = Rdc*LineArea/ALArea ;  %DC resistance of Aluminium part of the line.
```

For SCGZ conductors, the above values are changed to the SCGZ values. For SCGZ and pure aluminium conductors, the last line above is simply changed to:

```
RdcW = Rdc;  %DC resistance of Aluminium part of the line or Steel for a SCGZ line.
```

The Matlab® program uses these line parameters to calculates the skin depth using equation (10) and uses that together with equations (11) and (13) to determine the actual line resistance. The line inductance and characteristic impedance of the line is calculated using equations from (Johnson, 1950) and Carson's Depth equation (7) as needed. The transmission line impedance, is then used to determine the resistive losses of the transmission line and using equation (8) is used to determine the current flowing into the next elementary doublet. The relevant equations are:

```
SkinDepth = sqrt(2.0*RhoC/(twopi*Freq*MuC)); %Johnson 1950, pp 74
Rs = (sqrt(Rdc*Rdc*RadC*RadC/(4.0*SkinDepth*SkinDepth)+RdcW*RdcW));
  %Line resistance per km asymptote at actual DC resistance of line (RdcW).
Lr = 1.0/(sqrt(RadL*RadL/(4.0*SkinDepth*SkinDepth)+1));  % internal inductance
if FreeSpace == 'y';  %if 'y' Line in Free Space if 'n' line with groundplane or balanced
transmission line.
```

```
    RealZo = Mu0*c;   %Single line characteristic impedance in free space 376 ohm
else
if SWER == 'y';  %if 'y' SWER Line, use Carson for line separation, if 'n' have balanced line
      K1=2.0;  %for SWER K1=2 Line with Groundplane, like SWER line
      LineSep= 2.0*(h+sqrt(RhoS/(twopi*Freq*Mu0))); %Carson's depth
      Cl = Er*K1/(36.0*log(LineSep/RadL)); %Line Capacitance nF/m SWER line
   else
      K1=1.0;  %for SWER K1=2 Balanced line.
      LineSep = 2.0*h; %Line separation for differential line configuration
      Cl = Er/(36.0*log(LineSep/RadC)); %Line capacitance nF/m = uF/km Line in free
space
   end;
   Lkm = (4*log(LineSep/RadL)+MuR*Lr)/(K1*10);  %inductance (mH)/km
   Ckm = Cl*1000.0;  %line capacitance per km
   RealZo = sqrt(1.0e6*Lkm/Ckm); % Real part of Z for resistive losses.
end;
```

3.2 Radiated power

The evaluation of equation (6) is the core of the Matlab® program that is used to calculate the resulting E_θ fields for these cascaded line segments, using (2) to (3) and the intermediate equations shown in Reed & Kikkert, 2008. For a single line in space, the field is constant with respect to φ and equations (2) to (5) can be used to determine the radiation pattern and the radiated power. For a line above ground, equation (6) needs to be used and integration over both φ and θ need to be done. A 10 km line at 100 kHz is 3.33 wavelengths long and as shown in figure 1, has 14 main lobes.

Doubling the signal frequency, doubles the electrical length of the line and thus the number of lobes in the radiation pattern, and requires a halving of the angular interval for the determination of the radiated power for integrating equation (6) for E over θ and φ. In addition, the line has twice the number of elementary doublets, thus requiring 8 times number of calculations to be done. It is thus critical to get the optimum electrical line length for the elementary doublet and the optimum angular increment to obtain good accuracy, while minimising the number of calculations required. The initial work for this topic was done using a elementary doublet length of 0.01 λ or 0.1 km, whichever is the smallest, to ensure a high level of accuracy, so that for a 10 km line at 100 kHz, 299 line segments are used and at 100 MHz, 299980 line segments are used. For the results presented here the length for the elementary doublet is chosen to be 1/64 wavelength or 0.1 km, whichever is the smallest, since simulations showed that reducing the length below the 1/64 wavelength starts to affect the accuracy and 0.1 km is required since the printing of results are done at 0.1 km intervals. This then results in 200 elementary doublets for the line of figure 1.

The initial work for this topic was done at the 3600 angular intervals regardless of the signal frequency, to ensure that accurate fields were obtained for a 100 km long line at 100 kHz. It was found that one quarter of the number of elementary doublets used results in an accurate measure of radiated power, resulting in 50 angular intervals. The integration of the fields in the θ direction is done over the whole 0 to 360 degree region, and those in the φ direction only need to be done if from 0 to 90 degrees, due to symmetry. If the angular increment in the θ and φ directions are to be the same, then the number of angles is to be divisible by 4.

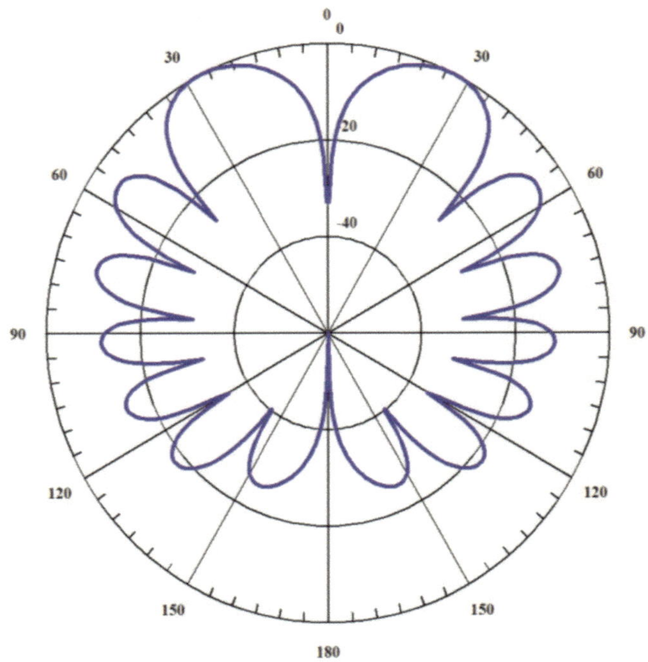

Fig. 1. Radiation pattern for 10 km long conductor in free space at 100 kHz.

As a result 52 angular intervals are required. This gives the same accuracy to 5 decimal places compared with 3600 angular intervals. To produce nice looking plots, as shown in figure 1, a minimum of 256 angles are used. The relevant code is shown below:

```
% N is the number of elementary douplets making up the
NumTh=4*round(N/16);  %number of angles per circle same as N by 4 as default.
if (NumTh > 3600) NumTh = 3600; end; %Limit to 0.1 degree.
if (NumTh < 256 ) NumTh = 256; end; %Limit to 256 for good looking plots
dtheta=twopi/NumTh;  %delta theta for a vector of angles and for integration 360 deg
```

For long power lines, the radiation pattern has many narrow lobes, as a result many angular intervals are required for the Matlab® evaluation of the radiation patterns. To avoid having to calculate sine and cosine for the same angles over and over again, these sine and cosine values are stored in an array, thus speeding up the calculations. This is done as follows:

```
% COMPUTE ANGLES, SINE OF ANGLES AND COSINE OF ANGLES
for angle=1:NumTh
   angles(angle)=dtheta*(angle-1) + 0.5*dtheta; %array of angles
   sinarr(angle)=sin(angles(angle));  %array of Sine used for both Theta and Phi
   cosarr(angle)=cos(angles(angle));  %array of Cos used for both Theta and Phi
end;
```

For a line in free space, this array is then used to calculate the cumulative $E(\theta)$ due to the elementary doublet length (dipL) having been added to $E(\theta)$ as shown below. This Esum(Theta) is the cumulative $E(\theta)$ and can then be used to calculate the cumulative radiated power as follows:

```
for segment=1:1:N  %N is number of segments
    if I>0
      for Theta=1:1:NumTh   %Loop to consider all angles Theta 0-360
          Eed_M(Theta) = 60*pi*edL*I*sinarr(Theta)*sin(EedPhi);
      %Field of elementary doublet of length edL, eqn (6), complex variable.
      end;
      edL_Ph=twopi_edL*(segment-1);   %Phase of I in current edL segment.
      for Theta=1:1:NumTh   %Loop to consider all angles Theta
        E_RE(Theta)= cos(edL_Ph*(cosarr(Theta)-1))*Eed_M(Theta);  % real E_ field
        E_IM(Theta)=-sin(edL_Ph*(cosarr(Theta)-1))*Eed_M(Theta); % imag E_ field
        Etp(Theta)=complex(E_RE(Theta),E_IM(Theta));  %Total E field
        Esum(Theta)=Esumd(Theta)+Etp(Theta); %Progressive sum
        Esumd(Theta)= Esum(Theta);  %store current value for next iteration
      end;
      % Calculate the radiated & dissipated power and attenuation
      PowerRadiated=0;
      for Theta=1:1:NumTh
        E_squared(Theta)= (real(Esum(Theta))*real(Esum(Theta)) +
          imag(Esum(Theta))*imag(Esum(Theta)))';
         PowerRadiated = (PowerRadiated +E_squared(Theta)*abs(sinarr(Theta))
            *dtheta)/240);  %Integration 360 deg, 240 = 4x60
      end;
      Pdiss = Pdiss + I*I*ResistperSegment;
      PdissN = Pdiss/Pin; %Resistive Loss, normalise wrt input.
        PRadN = PowerRadiated/Pin; %Radiated power, normalise wrt input.
      %calculate current at output of dipole.
      I2 = (Pin - PowerRadiated - Pdiss)/RealZo; %Current into next segment
      if I2>0
        I = sqrt(I2);
      else
        I = 0;  %No more current left all dissipated.
      end;
      AttenuationResulting = 20*log10(I/Io); %cumulative total attenuation of the line
      Pout = I*I*RealZo/Pin;
    end; %Exit if no current left.
  % more code writing to file, plotting etc.
end;
```

For a line above a ground plane, a 3 dimensional integration, with θ and φ must be made. Here the axis origin is at the groundplane and the maximum radiated field of the elementary doublet is perpendicular to the groundplane. The 3 dimensional field is calculated by adding another loop with a variable Phi, around the code for evaluation E(θ) as shown as follows:

```
if I>0
  for Phi=1:1:NumPhi   %Loop to consider all angles Phi (0-90)
    for Theta=1:1:NumTh   %Loop to consider all angles Theta 0-360
    Eed_M(Theta,Phi) = 60*pi*edL*I*sinarr(Theta)*sin(EedPhi(Phi)); % eqn (6)
```

```
      end;
    end;
    edL_Ph=twopi_edL*(segment-1);   %Phase of I in current edL segment.
    for Phi=1:1:NumPhi    %Loop to consider all angles Phi (0-90)
    for Theta=1:1:NumTh    %Loop to consider all angles Theta
        E_RE(Theta,Phi)= cos(edL_Ph*(cosarr(Theta)-1))*Eed_M(Theta,Phi);  % real E
        E_IM(Theta,Phi)=-sin(edL_Ph*(cosarr(Theta)-1))*Eed_M(Theta,Phi); % imag E
       Etp(Theta)=complex(E_RE(Theta),E_IM(Theta));  %Total E field
        Esum(Theta,Phi)=Esumd(Theta,Phi)+Etp(Theta,Phi); %Progressive sum
        Esumd(Theta,Phi)= Esum(Theta,Phi);   %store current value for next iteration
      end;
    end;
    % Calculate the radiated & dissipated power and attenuation
    PowerRadiated=0;
    for Phi=1:1:NumPhi    %Loop to consider all angles Phi (0-90)
      for Theta=1:1:NumTh
        E_squared(Theta,Phi)= (real(Esum(Theta,Phi))*real(Esum(Theta,Phi)) +
          imag(Esum(Theta,Phi))*imag(Esum(Theta,Phi)))';
        PowerRadiated = (PowerRadiated + E_squared(Theta,Phi)*abs(sinarr(Theta))
          *dtheta)/240);        %Integration 360 deg 240 = 6x60
      end;
     if Phi == 1
          PowerRad2D=PowerRadiated; % same as for 2D plot.
      end;
    end;
     PowerRadiated=2*PowerRadiated*dtheta/pi; %note dtheta=dphi 3D radiated power
    RadN2D = PowerRad2D*(0.5+0.65*power(LineSepe,1.8))/Pin;
      % derived from 2D plot, same value
      % as 3D plot. allows 2D calculations to be used for lines with groundplane.
     Pdiss = Pdiss + I*I*ResistperSegment;
      PdissN = Pdiss/Pin; %Resistive Loss, normalise wrt input.
      PRadN = PowerRadiated/Pin; %Radiated power, normalise wrt input.
      %calculate current at output of dipole.
      I2 = (Pin - PowerRadiated - Pdiss)/RealZo; %Current into next segment
      if I2>0
          I = sqrt(I2);
      else
          I = 0;  %No more current left all dissipated.
      end;
      AttenuationResulting = 20*log10(I/Io); %cumulative total attenuation of the line
      Pout = I*I*RealZo/Pin;
  end; %Exit if no current left.
  % more code writing to file, plotting etc.
```

The 3D calculation for a 10 km SWER line with a 100 kHz PLC signal takes a few minutes on a fast PC. The same calculations for a 300 kHz PLC signal take several hours and the calculations for a 1 MHz PLC signal are expected to take several weeks, since less than 1% of the calculations were done overnight. It is thus nearly impossible to evaluate the fields from long lines at high frequency. Since the separation between the line and the return path is far less than a quarter wavelength for signals below 1 MHz, and as a result the dependence of the E fields has little dependence on φ. The radiated power derived from the field along the line and perpendicular to the ground plane can be used as an accurate measure of the radiated power of the power line. The accurate 3 D radiated power was calculated for many different frequencies, line lengths and line heights above ground. As a result, the radiated power for all these variations can accurately be determined as follows:

PowerRadiated = PowerRad2D*(0.5+0.65*power(LineSepe,1.8));

PowerRad2D is the power obtained from the 2D field, LineSepe is the line separation in wavelengths. When the line separation is less than half a wavelength, the error due to the above approximation is better than 0.01%. A 2D calculation for the radiated power can thus be used reducing the calculation time by several orders of magnitude without loss of accuracy. The 3D radiated power is thus:

$$P_{rad}(\theta,\varphi)_{rms} = P_{rad}(\theta)_{rms} \times (0.5 + 0.65 * \left(\frac{2h}{\lambda}\right)^{1.8}) \qquad (18)$$

As a result of (18) the above Matlab® code can also be used for long lines above ground, or to find the radiation of overhead power lines with the PLC signals driven on two conductors in a balanced fashion.
The main Matlab® program is over 500 lines long, but only the core parts of the code have been described in this section.

4. Wobble

Figure 2 shows the field pattern from a 100 km long straight line, with the left figure being in free space and the right figure obtained from a SWER line 7 m above ground. The maximum gain for the free space line is 52.9 dB, while the maximum gain for the SWER line

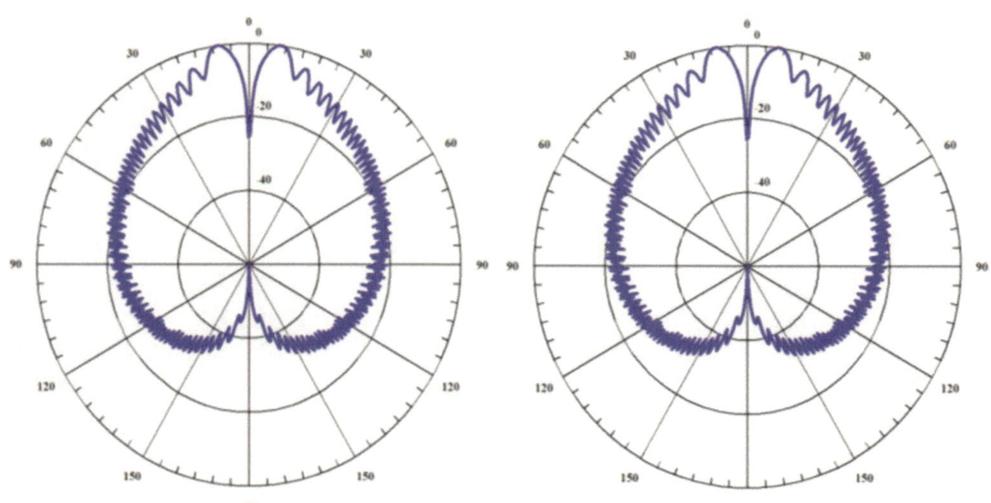

Fig. 2. Radiation Straight line, 100 kHz, 100 km long. Left free space, max gain 52.9 dB and Right SWER line max gain 21.6 dB.

is 21.6 dB. The radiation patterns look the same, so that the SWER line has 31.4 dB less peak radiated power than the free space line. The total radiated power from the SWER line is 32.4 dB less for the SWER line than the free space line.

Practical power-lines are not absolutely straight. Any small bends, as the line direction changes to follow the terrain, has a major impact on the radiation pattern. Figure 3 shows the effect of the radiation loss as the change in line direction, called *wobble* in this paper, is varied every 0.1 km by a random angle with the standard deviation indicated. Figure 3 is for a 1 km long SWER line with a 1 MHz carrier frequency. If the wobble is comparable to the spacing between the side lobes, large changes in attenuation can result.

For the radiation results presented in the rest of this chapter, a 50 mrad wobble is used as that reasonably represents the power line geometry, has sufficient randomness and results in a sufficient increase in radiation, while avoiding the rapid changes in attenuation associated with a larger wobble. Including the wobble, results in a significantly increase in radiated power. The average results for figure 3 are obtained from 10 simulations at each value of wobble.

Fig. 3. Radiation loss of a SWER line with bends.

Figure 4 shows the radiated power for a line in free space and a SWER line when wobble is applied. The right graph of figure 2, shows the radiation patterns of a 100 km long straight SCAC SWER line with a 100 kHz carrier frequency, the right graph of figure 4 shows the corresponding radiation pattern of a SWER line with a 50 mrad wobble. The line with wobble has a 0.0415% radiation loss and the straight line has a 0.0118% radiation loss. The wobble will thus increase the radiated power by close to 4 times. The free space straight line has a radiation loss of 20.7%, while the line with wobble has lost all its input power after 90.5 km with a radiation loss of 60% and a resistive loss of 40%. Figure 5a shows these radiation losses versus distance for these four lines. It is interesting to note that for very long straight lines, the radiated power decreases as the line becomes longer. This is due to some of the fields cancelling as new elementary doublets are added. Figure 5 shows that the wobble increases the radiated power significantly and on average, the radiated power keeps increasing as the distance increases. For short lines, less than 3 km, the lobes of radiation are broad and the wobble is small compared to the beamwidth, so that the straight line and the line with wobble result in virtually the same radiation. For long lines the wobble is comparable to or larger than the beamwidth of the radiation pattern lobes and the difference between the radiation from the straight line and the line with wobble becomes larger.

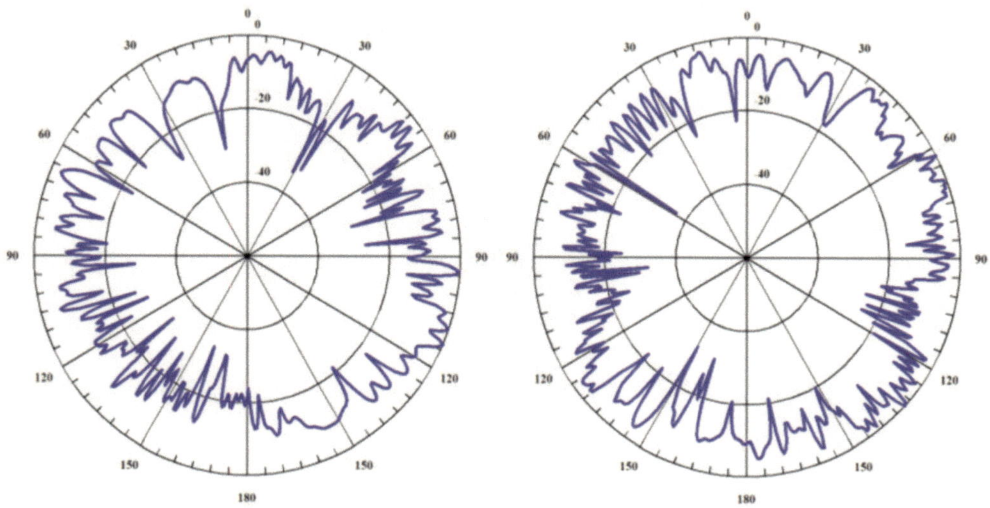

Fig. 4. Radiation line with 50 mrad wobble, 100 kHz, 100 km long. Left free space, max gain 49.8 dB and right SWER line max gain 18.4 dB.

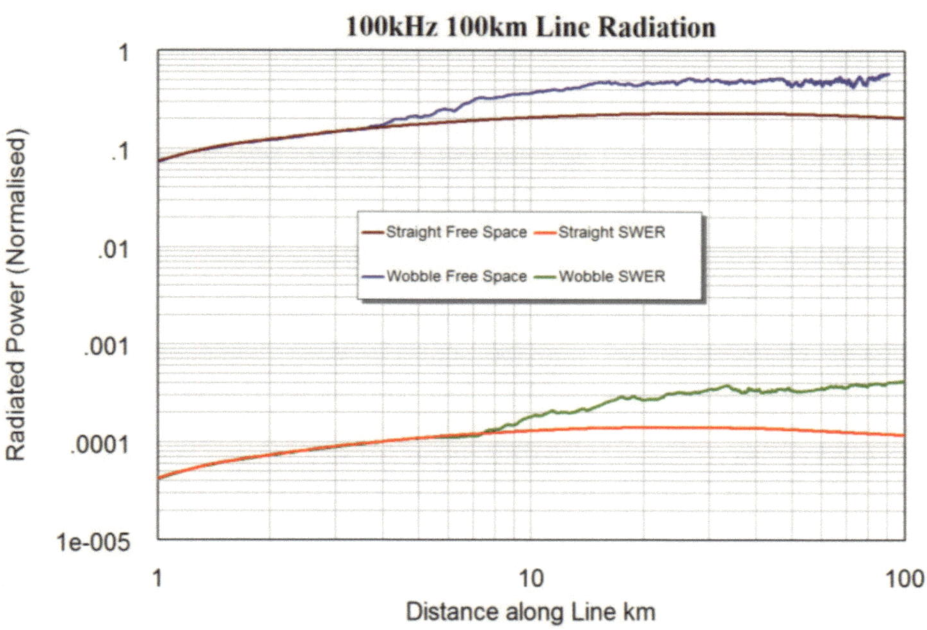

Fig. 5. a. Radiation loss for a 100 kHz signal on a 100 km long line.

Figure 5b shows the resistive loss corresponding to the radiation loss of figure 5a. Having a high radiation loss, results in a smaller current flowing along the line and thus less resistive (I^2R) losses. The radiation losses from SWER line are so small that the resistive loss with and without wobble is nearly the same.

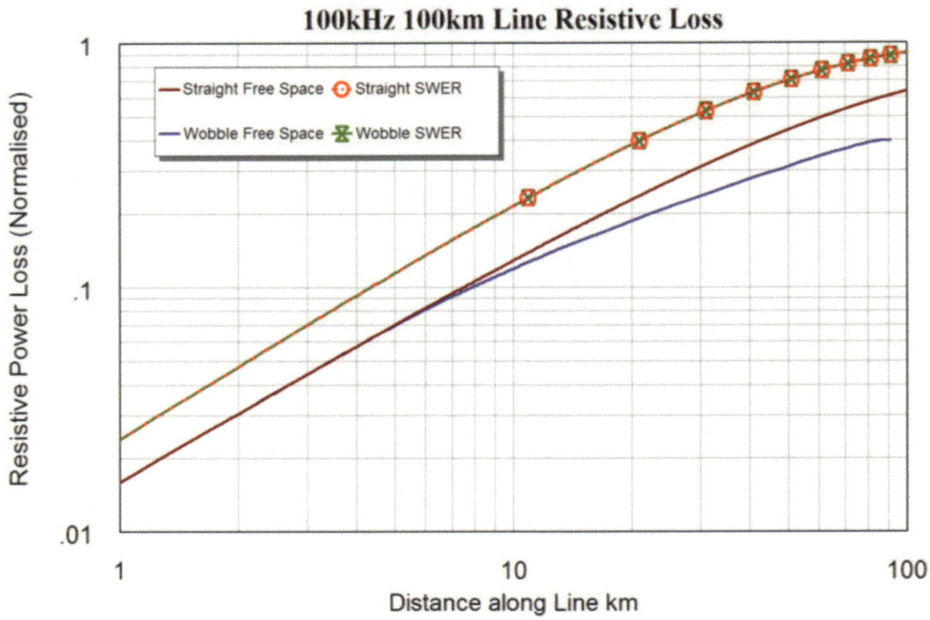

Fig. 5. b. Resistive loss for a 100 kHz signal on a 100km long line.

5. Results

5.1 SWER Lines

The first line type for which results are presented is a 3/2.75 SWER line consisting of either an aluminium clad steel (SCAC) or a galvanised steel (SCGZ) cable with three 2.75 mm diameter strands. The SWER line is typically 7 m above ground with the earth return distance varying according to equation (7). The author has made measurements on an 18 km long SCGZ SWER line SWER line (Kikkert & Reid 2009) at Mt Stewart station, 100 km west of Charters Towers in North Queensland, Australia. A comparison between the SWER line measurements and the results from the model presented here, using equations (7) to (17) and including the ground pad and earth return path resistance is shown in figure 6. It can be seen that there is a remarkable agreement, thus verifying the schematic model of the line using equations (7) to (17) and the corresponding Matlab® code in section 3.1.

The parameters for a 3/2.75 SCGZ SWER line obtained from the Matlab® program are shown in figure 7. The line resistance increases significantly with frequency. The earth return path depth (7) varies from close to 2 km at 10 Hz to 16 m at 10 MHz. Due to the current being carried in the steel conductor for SCGZ lines, the inductance varies with frequency. For aluminium or copper conductors, the internal inductance of equation (14) is negligible, so that the inductance is mainly governed by the external inductance. For steel conductors, with μ_r typically being 70, the internal inductance is larger, so that the inductance changes significantly with frequency. As a result of both of these effects, the characteristic impedance of the SWER line varies from 565 Ω at 50 Hz to 270 Ω at 100 kHz.

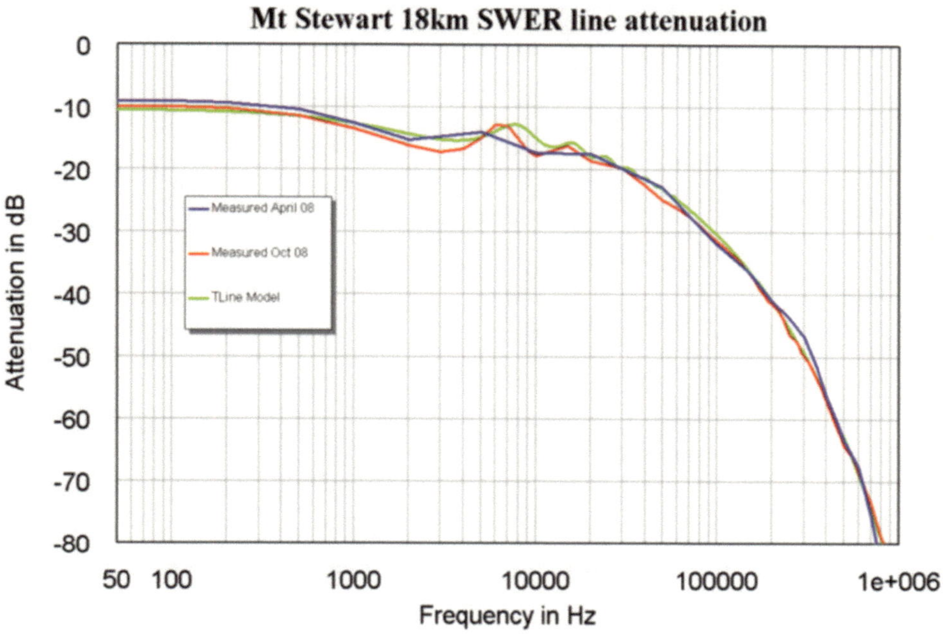

Fig. 6. Measurements and model comparison.

Figure 7 also shows the radiated power, expressed as a resistance. Below 300 kHz, the radiation is negligible, but at 5 MHz the same power is lost in radiation as in resistive losses. The radiation losses increase proportionally to the frequency$^{2.77}$. Figure 8 shows the same plots for a SCAC conductor. Comparing figures 7 and 8 shows that the corner frequency where the line resistance starts to increase is much lower for the SCGZ conductors.
The parameters for a 3/2.75 SCAC SWER line obtained from the Matlab® program are shown in figure 8. The line resistance increases significantly with frequency. Despite the earth return path depth (7) varying from close to 2 km at 10 Hz to 16 m at 10 MHz, the characteristic impedance of the SWER line only varies from 344 Ω at 50 Hz to 258 Ω at 100 kHz. Figure 8 also shows the difference between the resistance of the line of it were a pure Aluminium line and the resistance of the SCAC line. Above 1 MHz all the current is carried in the Aluminium cladding. Figure 8 also shows the radiated power, expressed as a resistance. Below 300 kHz, the radiation is negligible, but at 1.5 MHz the same power is lost in radiation as in resistive losses. Equation (18) shows that the radiation losses increase proportionally to the frequency raised to the power 2.77. Comparing figures 7 and 8 show that the resistive losses of the SCGZ line are much higher than the SCAC line.
Figure 9 shows the line losses for a 3/2.75 SCGZ SWER line. For frequencies below 1 MHz, the radiation losses are very small in comparison to the resistive losses. For a to 10 km line and 100 kHz, the radiated power is 0.008% and for lower frequencies it is smaller. As a result radiation is negligible for all CENELEC-A (9 kHz to 95 kHz) frequencies. The resistive losses for SCGZ lines are such that for a 70 km SWER line a 33 dB attenuation results. This is still well below the typical dynamic range of PLC modems.

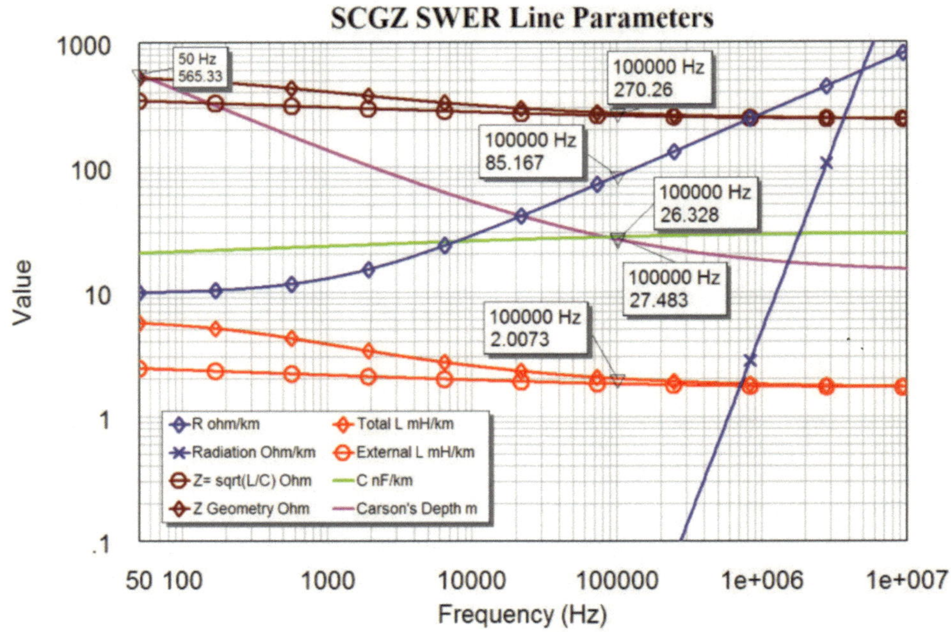

Fig. 7. Steel Core Galvanized Zinc (SCGZ) conductor per km transmission line parameters.

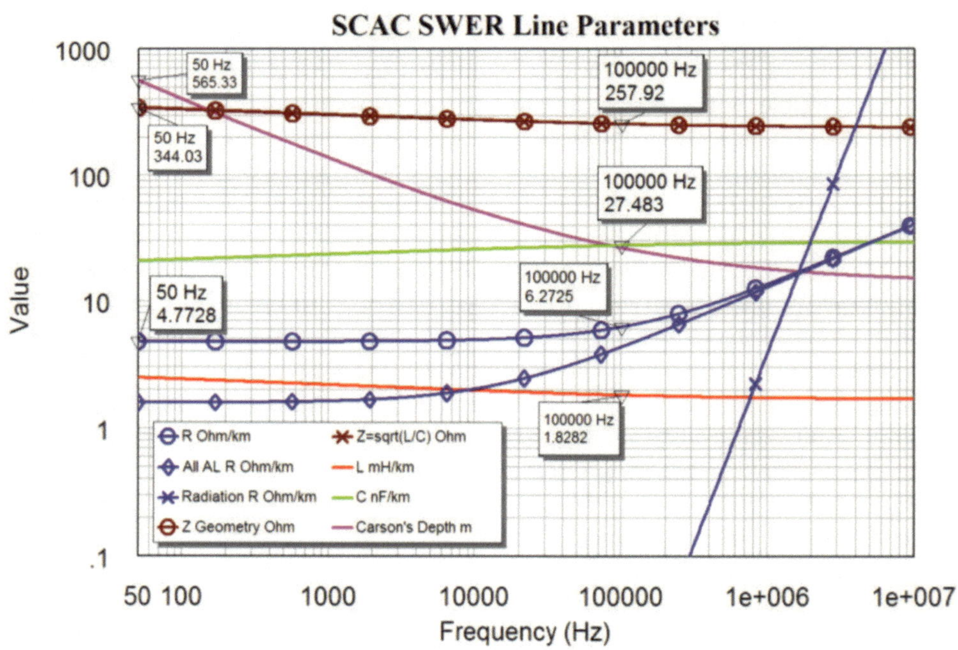

Fig. 8. Steel Core Aluminium Clad (SCAC) conductor per km transmission line parameters.

Figure 10 shows the corresponding line losses for a 3/2.75 SCAC SWER line. Comparing figures 9 and 10, show that for a 3/2.75 SCAC line the resistive losses are much lower. The radiation losses are the same, but the resistive losses are significantly smaller. A 300 km SCAC SWER line at 100 kHz has a 37 dB attenuation, similar to that of a 70 km SCGZ line.

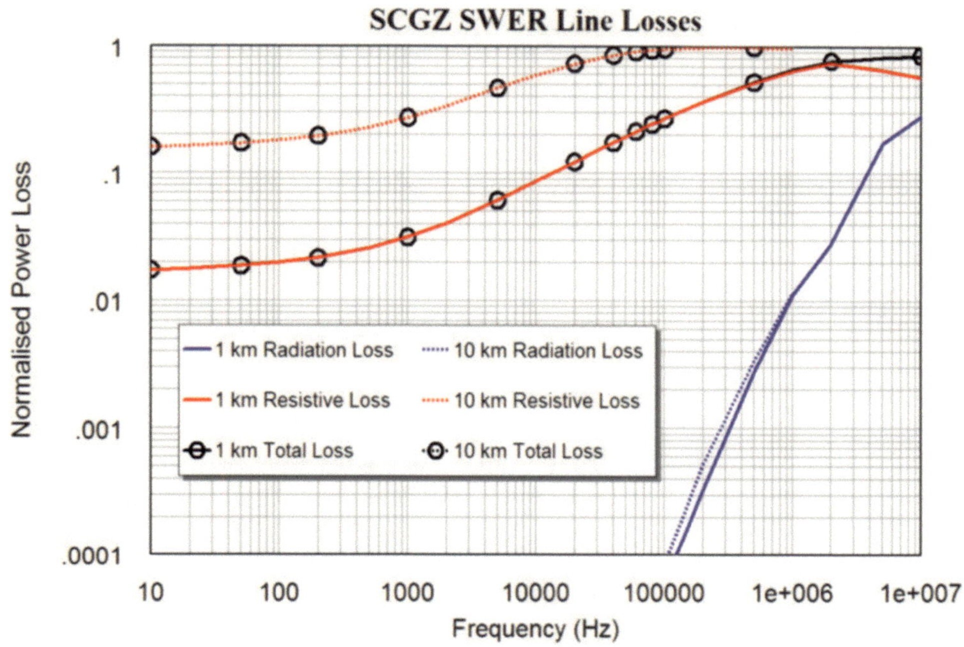

Fig. 9. SCGZ SWER line losses versus frequency.

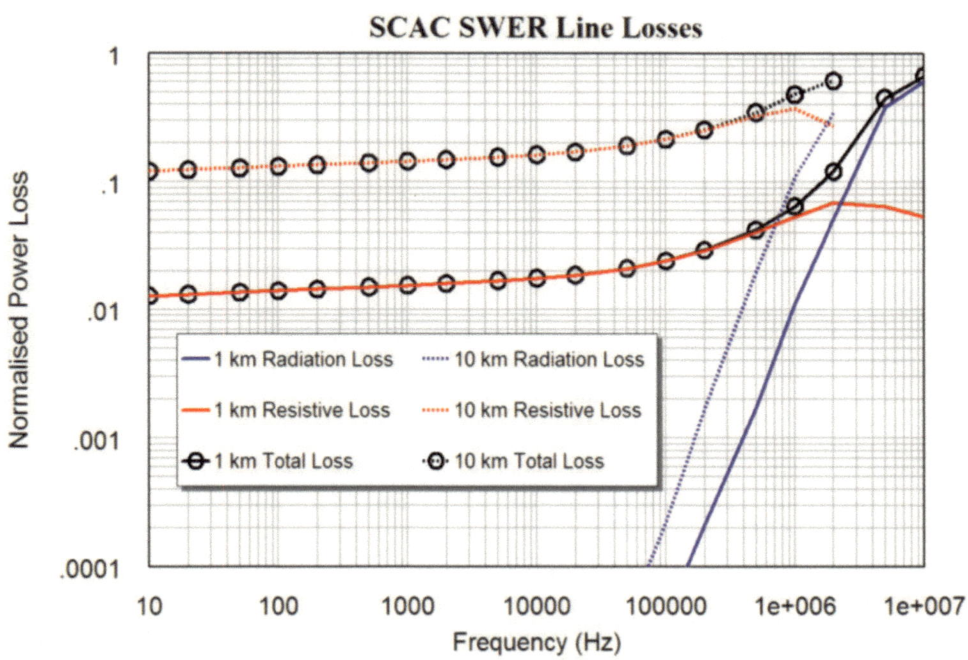

Fig. 10. SCAC SWER line losses versus frequency.

5.1.1 SWER line radiation resistance

The Matlab® program described in this chapter, prints the calculated normalised cumulative radiation and resistive losses every 100 m along the SWER line. Taking the difference between these cumulative results and averaging these for a line length of 30 km or when the total losses are less than half the input power, whichever is the shorter distance, allows a per km radiation resistance to be determined as a function of frequency. To ensure that the SWER line configuration is identical as the frequency is varied using different Matlab® program runs, the seed for the random wobble is initialised to the same value at the start of each run. Figure 11 shows the resulting radiation resistance for SCGZ and SCAC conductors for a SWER line 7 m above ground and a 50 mrad wobble every 100 m. Despite the resistive losses being very different, the per km radiation losses are nearly the same. Figure 11 also shows a least square error fit as follows:

$$R_{rad} = 1.35 \times 10^{-16} \times Frequency^{2.77} \quad \Omega / km \tag{19}$$

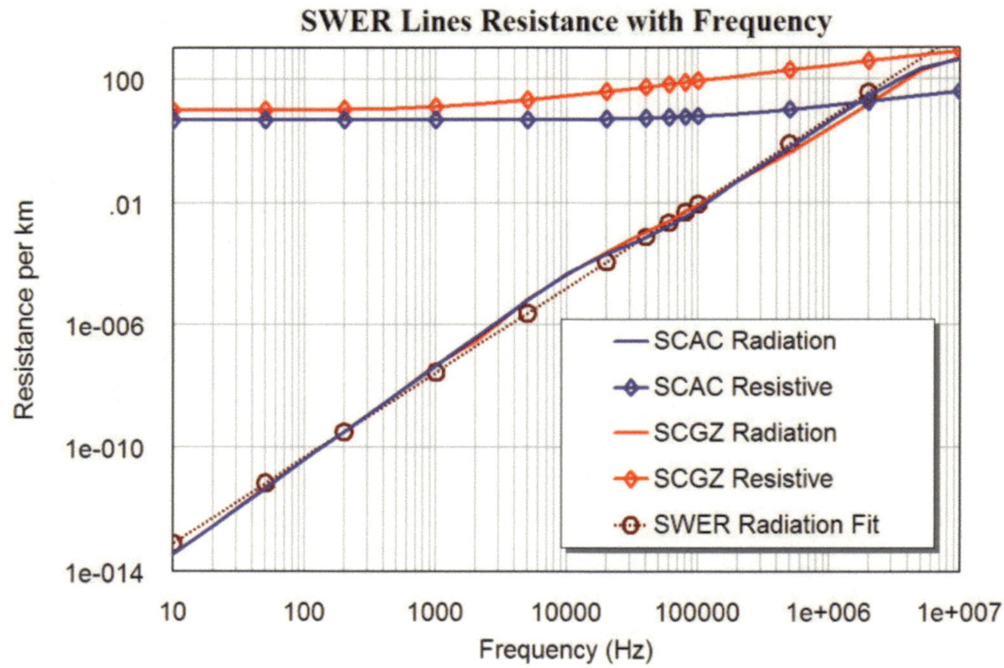

Fig. 11. SCAC SWER line resistances versus frequency.

Figure 11 shows that despite the coefficients of equation 21 being non-integer values, equation (19) gives a good approximation of the results obtained by the Matlab® program. At high frequencies, the radiation losses become quite high and within a short distance, all the input power is lost in resistive and radiation losses.

Figures 10 and 11 shows that for SCAC SWER line at 2 MHz, the radiation losses are equal to the resistive losses. For larger frequencies the radiation losses increase rapidly, causing a very high line attenuation. Since PLC transmissions by Electricity Utilities use frequencies below 150 kHz, figures 7 to 11, show that such PLC transmissions will not cause any interference as the radiated power is very small. However figures 7 to 11 show that SCAC SWER lines, SCGZ SWER lines and MV or LV three phase overhead power lines, where one phase is used for PLC and the earth path is used for the return path, are unsuitable for communication signals above 500 kHz, as the radiation losses will be significant, so that interference to other services in the MF band such as AM broadcast transmissions, may occur.

5.2 Overhead lines mounted on a crossarm

The second type of transmission line considered in this paper is the typical traditional open wire low voltage overhead (LVOH) line consisting of four All-Aluminium Conductor (AAC) cables each with 7 strands of 4.75 mm diameter mounted on a crossarm. The line consists of two sets of wires with a 550 mm spacing and a larger spacing between these sets of wires to accommodate the power pole. The results presented here are for a set of wires with a 550 mm spacing, which is typical in Australia for the outer sets of 240 V LVOH conductors on a crossarm.

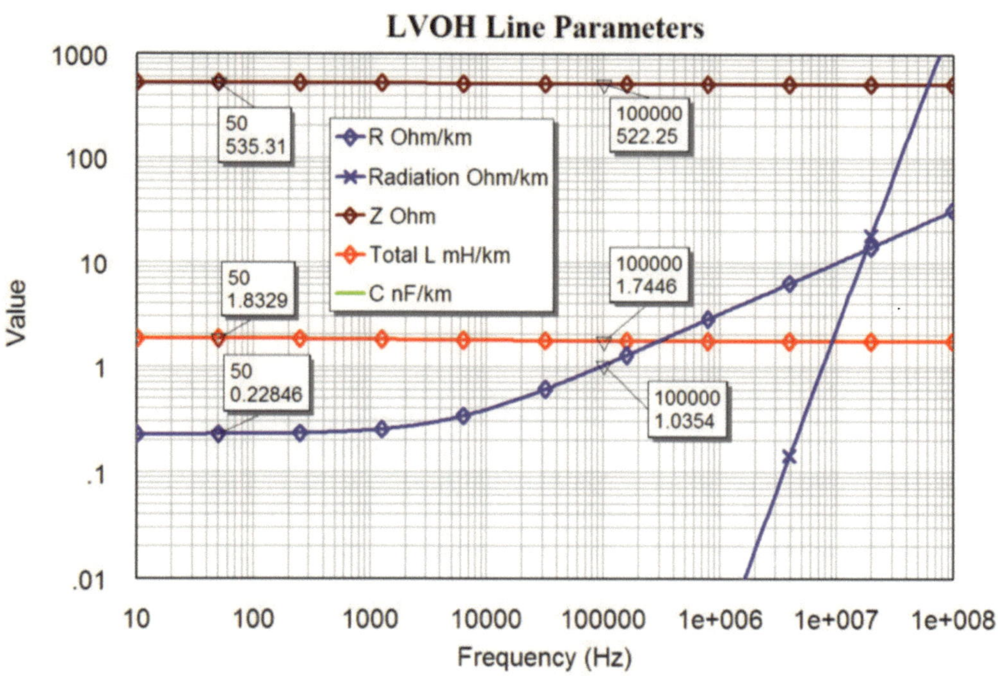

Fig. 12. LV overhead line on crossarm parameters versus frequency.

The parameters for the overhead line are shown in figure 12. The characteristic impedance of the line is 522 Ω and is virtually independent of frequency. There are only small variations of line inductance and capacitance with frequency. The plot for radiation in figure 12 corresponds to equation (20) and the OHL radiation curve fit in figure 14. For PLC applications, the signal is coupled onto these lines in a differential manner, and no ground return is used. Figure 13 shows that, the radiation losses of this line are much less than that of the SWER line.

Figure 14 shows the radiation and line resistance versus frequency for OHL and ABC lines as obtained from the Matlab® program described in this chapter. The least square error fit for frequencies above 1 kHz for OHL on crossarm conductors is:

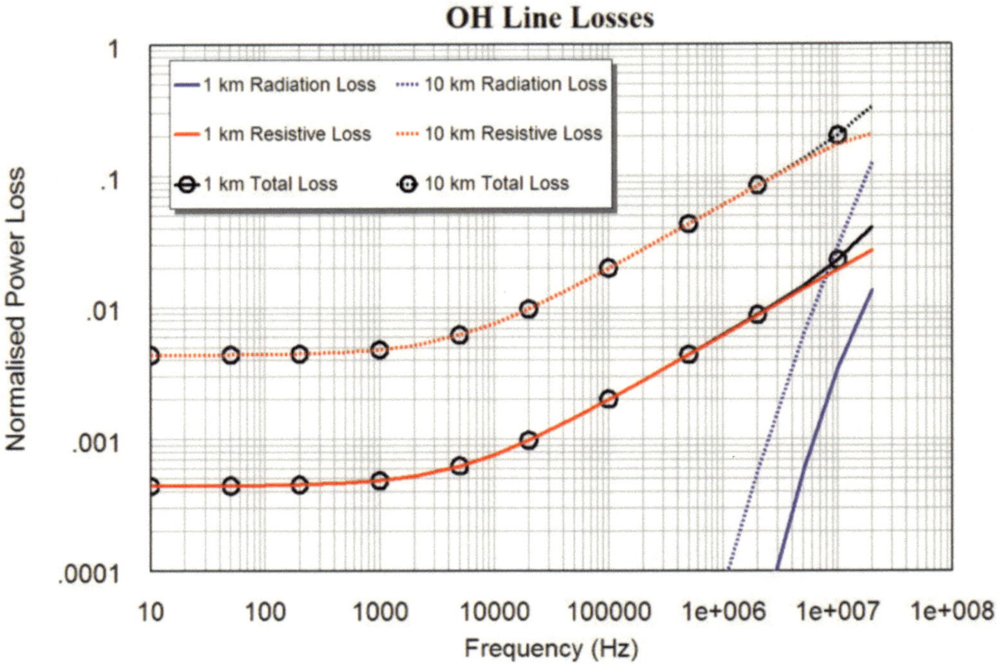

Fig. 13. LV overhead line line on crossarm losses versus frequency.

$$R_{rad} = 2.38^{-21} \times Frequency^3 \quad \Omega / km \tag{20}$$

The radiation resistance and the line resistance are the same at just above 20 MHz, so that these lines can be used at more than 10 times the frequency of SWER lines. If the PLC signal is coupled onto the all three phase lines in a common mode, i.e. the PLC signals is coupled onto all the lines in-phase, the neutral line is not connected to the PLC signal and the ground is used for a return path, then similar radiation losses to SWER lines are obtained. For a 10 km line, at 2 MHz, less than 0.05% of the input power is radiated and the line can thus be used for transmitting communication signals at those frequencies.

Broadband over Power Lines (BPL) uses signals in the frequency Range 525 kHz to 80 MHz. Field trials (ACMA 2007, ACMA 2009) have been carried out in Australia. The tests at Queanbean (ACMA2009) used frequencies in the range of 2.5 MHz to 22.8 MHz. Figure 13 shows that at 20 MHz and a 1 km line length, 15% of the power is lost in radiation while 25% is lost in resistive losses. BPL is thus not a suitable system to be used on LVOH lines. PLC signals using the CENELEC A band of 35 to 95 kHz for smart metering can be applied on these lines without any significant interference to existing radio services.

5.3 Aerial bundled conductors

The final type of transmission line considered is an Aerial Bundled Conductor (ABC), consisting of four insulated, compacted aluminium cables grouped together with common insulation. Each conductor is made up of 19 strands, 2.52 mm in diameter. Each compacted

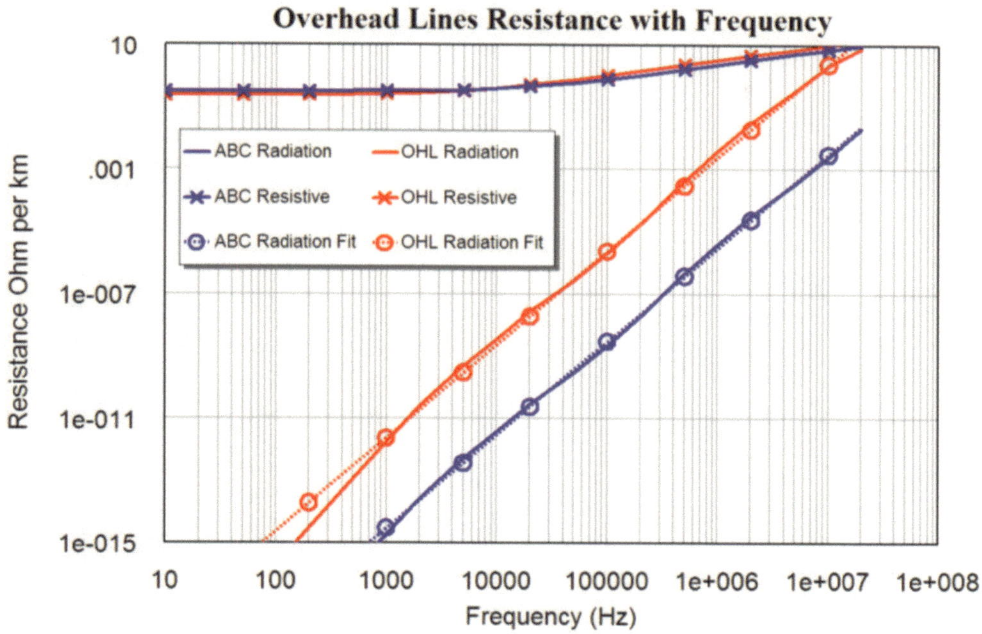

Fig. 14. LV overhead line resistances versus frequency.

conductor is 11.4 mm in diameter and the spacing between the centres of the conductors is 14.9 mm. The cable type is XDAB22AA004 from (Olex, 2008). The parameters of this line is shown in figure 15. The radiation resistance shown in figure 15 corresponds to equation (21) and the least curve fit for ABC in figure 14. For ABC lines, this corresponds to:

$$R_{rad} = 3.0^{-24} \times Frequency^3 \quad \Omega / km \tag{21}$$

Comparing equations (19), (20) and (21), shows that for OHL on crossarm and ABC liones, the radiation resistance increases with the third power of frequency, while for SWER lines the radiation resistance increases with the frequency raised to the power 2.77. The difference is due to the earth return path and thus the effective line separation for SWER lines changing with frequency as shown by Carson's equation (7). Because the effective line separation is much larger for SWER lines, the radiation from SWER lines is much larger than those for the OHL and ABC lines.

Figure 16 shows the losses for ABC conductors for 1 km and 10 km ABC lines. The corresponding figures for the SWER and OHL on crossarm conductors are figures 9, 10 and 13. Comparing these figures show that ABC conductors have very little radiation.

Comparing the resistive, conductor, losses for OHL on crossarm and ABC conductors in figure 14, shows that at low frequency ABC conductors have a higher resistance than OHL on crossarm conductors but at high frequencies ABC conductors have a lower resistance. This is because the ABC conductors have 19 strands in the conductor, while the Moon conductor (Olex, 2008) used for the OHL on crossarm conductor has 7 strands. As a result the skin effect is less severe for ABC conductors. The calculations presented here have not considered that the 19 strands of the ABC conductors are compressed and that this will reduce the conductor surface available at high frequencies and thus increase the line resistance above the value calculated. Unfortunately the extent of this increase is not presented in any cable manufacturer's catalogue, since the main application for these lines is at 50 or 60 Hz.

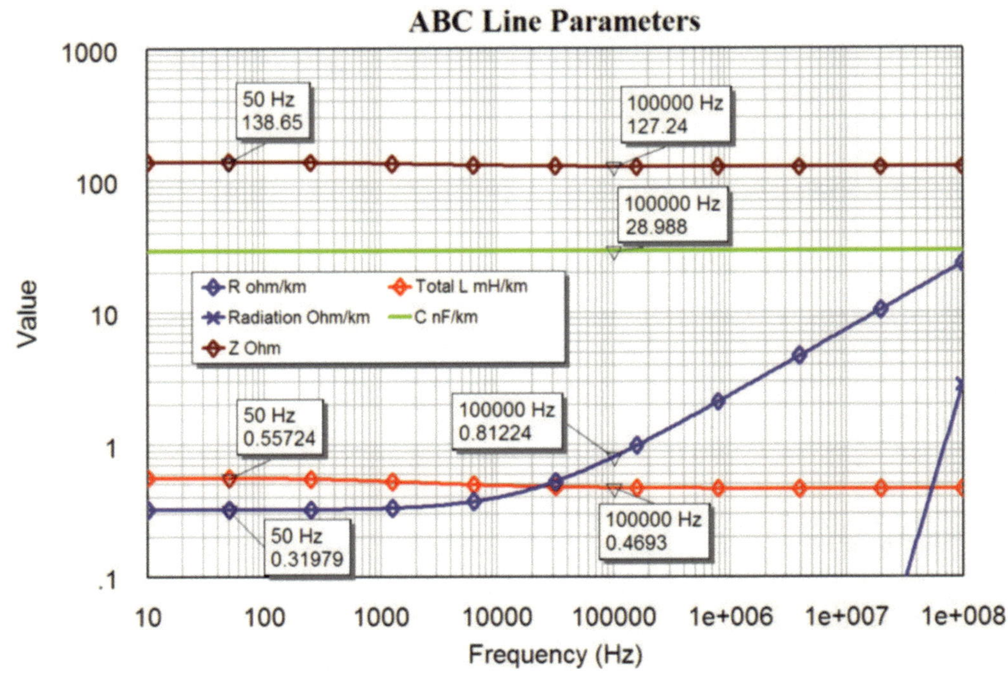

Fig. 15. Aerial Bundled Conductor line parameters versus frequency.

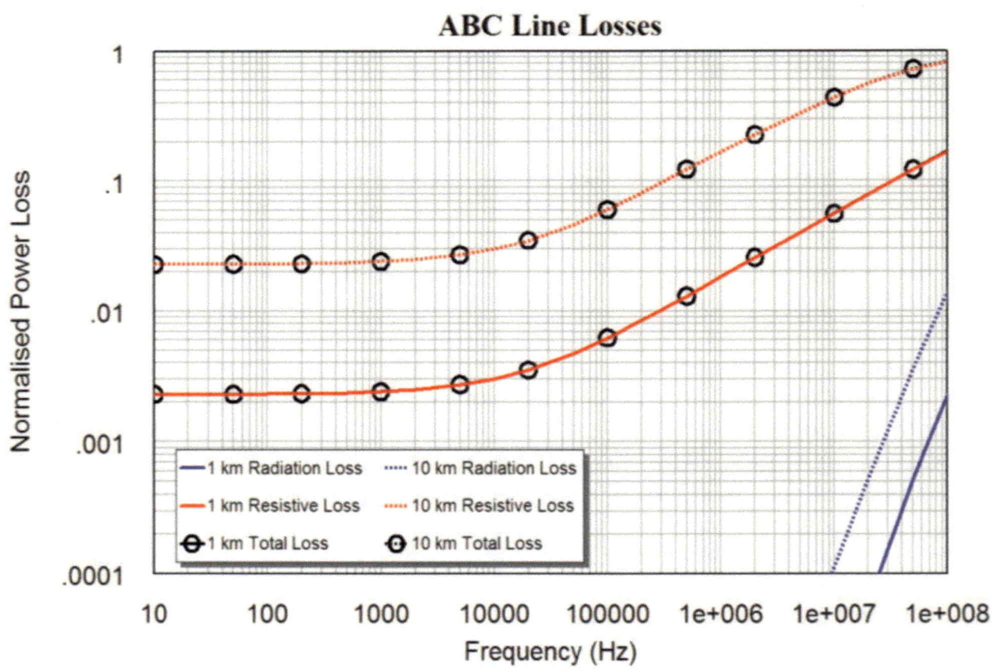

Fig. 16. Aerial Bundled Conductor line losses versus frequency.

Figure 16 shows that for frequencies below 100 MHz, the radiation losses are less than 2% of the input power. However the resistive losses are such that for frequencies above 20 MHz, all the input power is lost before the end of a 30 km line. The low level of radiation losses will ensure that no significant interference to other services will occur. ABC lines can thus be used for transmitting BPL signals at frequencies up to 100 MHz, however the resistive losses prevent great distances being reached.

Similar results will apply for underground cables, where all the active conductors are bundled together in one cable. BPL can thus safely be used on ABC lines and underground cables. The success of BPL on those lines will primarily depend on economic rather that technical matters.

PLC signals using the CENELEC A band for smart metering can be applied on these lines without any significant interference to existing services.

6. Conclusion

The radiation from power lines cannot be determined from expressions from long wire antennae, since those expressions assume that the signal current in the power line is constant, the power line is straight and its length is less than 5 wavelengths. None of these assumptions are true for powerlines and as a result the radiation patterns and the radiated power must be determined from first principles using a Matlab® program. This program can be used to determine the radiated power from both SWER lines and overhead power lines where the PLC signals are coupled to 2 lines in a differential mode.

The results presented here show that SWER line result in little radiation for frequencies below 100 kHz, typical overhead lines mounted on a crossarm have little radiation for frequencies up to 2 MHz and bundled conductors have little radiation at frequencies up to 100 MHz.

All lines can thus be used for the 9-95 kHz CENELEC A frequency band to permit PLC communication for smart-metering and network control. Conventional overhead lines mounted on crossarms will cause significant interference levels for signal frequencies above 2 MHz and should not be used for BPL. Bundled conductors, ABC and underground, can be used for BPL applications, with little radiation, but with significant resistive losses at high frequencies.

7. Acknowledgment

The author would like to thank ERGON ENERGY for their support in providing the funding for this research. The author would also like to thank the technical and academic staff at James Cook University, for their assistance and encouragement in this work. The author would like to acknowledge Mr. Geoffrey Reid for his contribution to writing the Matlab code for calculating the radiated fields.

8. References

ACMA "ACA Field Report Country Energy BPL Trial Queanbeyan NSW - February 2005" ACA URL: http://www.acma.gov.au/webwr /lib284/queanbeyan %20trial %20feb202005%20final%20public%20 report.pdf., 23 October 2009

Balanis, A., Antenna theory: analysis and design. 2nd edition ed. 1997: John Wiley & Sons, Inc.

Walter, C.H., Travelling Wave Antennas. 1970 ed. 1965: Dover Publications. 429.

Ulaby, F.T., Fundamentals of Applied Electromagnetics. Fifth Edition. 1994: Pearson Prentice Hall. 456.

Johnson, W.C., Transmission Lines and Networks. International Student Edition, 1950, McGraw-Hill.

Reid, G. D. and C. J. Kikkert, "Radiation from a single wire earth return power line", EEEvolution Symposium, Cairns 28-30 July 2008

Kikkert, C, J, and G. Reid, Radiation and Attenuation of Communication Signals on Power Lines. 7th International Conference on Information, Communications and Signal Processing, ICICS 2009, 7-10 December 2009, Macau.

Carson, J.R., Wave propagation in overhead wires with ground return. Bell Systems Technical Journal, 1926. 5.

Wang,Y., Liu, S. "A Review of Methods for Calculation of Frequency-dependent Impedance of Overhead Power Transmission Lines." 2001 Proc. Natl. Sci. Counc. ROC(A) Vol 25, No. 6, 2001. pp. 329-338

Deri, A.,Tevan, G., "The Complex Ground Return Plane: A Simplified Model for Homogeneous and Multi-layer Earth Return." IEEE Transactions on Power Apparatus and Systems, Vol. PAS-100, No. 8. August 1981.

Olex, Areal cable catalogue, March 2008 http://storage.baselocation.com/ olex.com.au/ Media/Docs/Aerial-Catalogue-b8c9b2b7-c2b0-42a2-a5a6-6c4d000f3df5.pdf

10

Automatic Modelling Approach for Power Electronics Converters: Code Generation (C S Function, Modelica, VHDL-AMS) and MATLAB/Simulink Simulation

Asma Merdassi, Laurent Gerbaud and Seddik Bacha
Grenoble INP/ Grenoble Electrical Engineering Laboratory (G2Elab) ENSE3
Domaine Universitaire
France

1. Introduction

Modelling and simulation are useful for the analysis and design process of power electronics systems. Power electronics models of static converters are used for component sizing, for control adjustment or behaviour simulation.

In this context, average models are a good compromise between complexity, computation time and acceptable accuracy for system simulation. So, the development of averaging methods has been a topic of interest for the power electronic community for over three decades (Chetty, 1982; Middlebrook & Cuk, 1976; Sun & Grostollen, 1992).

The modelling of simple DC/DC structures is easy on the continuous conduction mode (Bass & Sun, 1998; Maksimovic et al., 2001; Maranesi & Riva, 2003; Rajagopalan, 1987; Webster & Ngo, 1992). However, the modelling complexity increases with the number of switches and the nature of the operating mode (the state sequences separated by the switch commutations). In this context, average operating analysis is becoming more and more complicated and the modelling requires skilful handling of complicated mathematical expressions which is generally time consuming.

In the literature, several automatic averaged modelling techniques have been developed however they have many limitations. As (Sun & Grostollen, 1997) that proposes a package for the modelling of PWM structures, in hard or soft switching, but the modelling is only for power electronics structures alone. The automatic modelling of a three-phase electrical machine with static converter is not possible. So, the environment of the static converter is limited, e.g. the load can not be a three-phase synchronous machine.

In the Electrical Engineering Laboratory (G2Elab), (Verdiere et al., 2003) proposes a new software architecture for the average modelling of power electronics structures, but this software is limited to the treatment of DC/DC converters in the continuous conduction mode, the classic average model is only obtained automatically.

The same problem as (Sun & Grostollen, 1997), the automatic coupling of converter with electrical machine is not considered. Finally, the computing technologies used to the topological analyze of electrical circuit (e.g. Macsyma) are not up to date.

The originality of this chapter consists to improve, on one hand, the work of (Sun & Grostollen, 1997) and (Verdiere et al., 2003), by proposing a new automatic methodology deals with several models (average and exact models) for DC/DC, DC/AC and AC/AC converters, and on other hand, by modelling converters with or without their environment (e.g. electrical machines). The particularities of this approach are the generation of models in different forms: C S-Function, VHDL-AMS, Modelica and the automatic treatment of the static converters in the continuous and discontinuous conduction mode. In this chapter, only results for the continuous conduction mode are presented.
In the first part of this chapter, the modelling approach is explained and the main steps of this modelling are detailed. A causal approach for the modelling of static converters of a power electronics applications independently of their environment (i.e its sources and loads) is also presented.
In the second part, the implementation in the software tool (AMG for Average Model Generator) dedicated to this automatic building is described. The code generation in C S-function, VHDL-AMS and Modelica is illustrated for a boost converter.
In the last part, several applications results are presented and implemented in several software (e.g Matlab/Simulink), among them a resonant converter, a three phase inverter coupled with a three-phase machine and a multi-level converter.

2. Modelling approach

The modelling approach in the software tool AMG is defined by using an a priori on the static converter behaviour and considering some hypothesis (ideal switches OFF "open circuit" and ON "short circuit", linear and invariant passive components and perfect sources).
Every model is entirely made in an automatic way from a topological description of the static converter. This description is carried out from a Netlist file extracted by using simulation software (i.e PSpice) and a dedicated simplified component library is used.
The user must define the commutation mode (i.e the cyclic sequence of switched configurations in an operating period) and the switch control sequence of the static converter to be modelled, mainly the control links of switches. The switch control and the operating mode are deduced from the analysis of the studied static converter, e.g., by using simulation software (i.e Portunus, Psim, PSpice, Simplorer, Saber, etc.). These data information given by the user are introduced into the software tool AMG.
The approach of the automatic building includes three important steps:

1. the analysis of the circuit,
2. the extraction of the state matrixes for each configuration of the static converter,
3. the building of the global state model.

Steps of modelling are presented in Fig. 1.

2.1 Topological analysis

An electrical circuit can be represented by a directed graph. The edges of this graph then connect the nodes of the circuit pairs. It is therefore possible to extract a tree of this graph corresponding to a subset of edges covering all nodes in the graph, but not forming mesh. The topological analysis is to automatically determine a tree from a simple description of the topology of the circuit. This method has been tested and used in different works (Delaye et al., 2004).

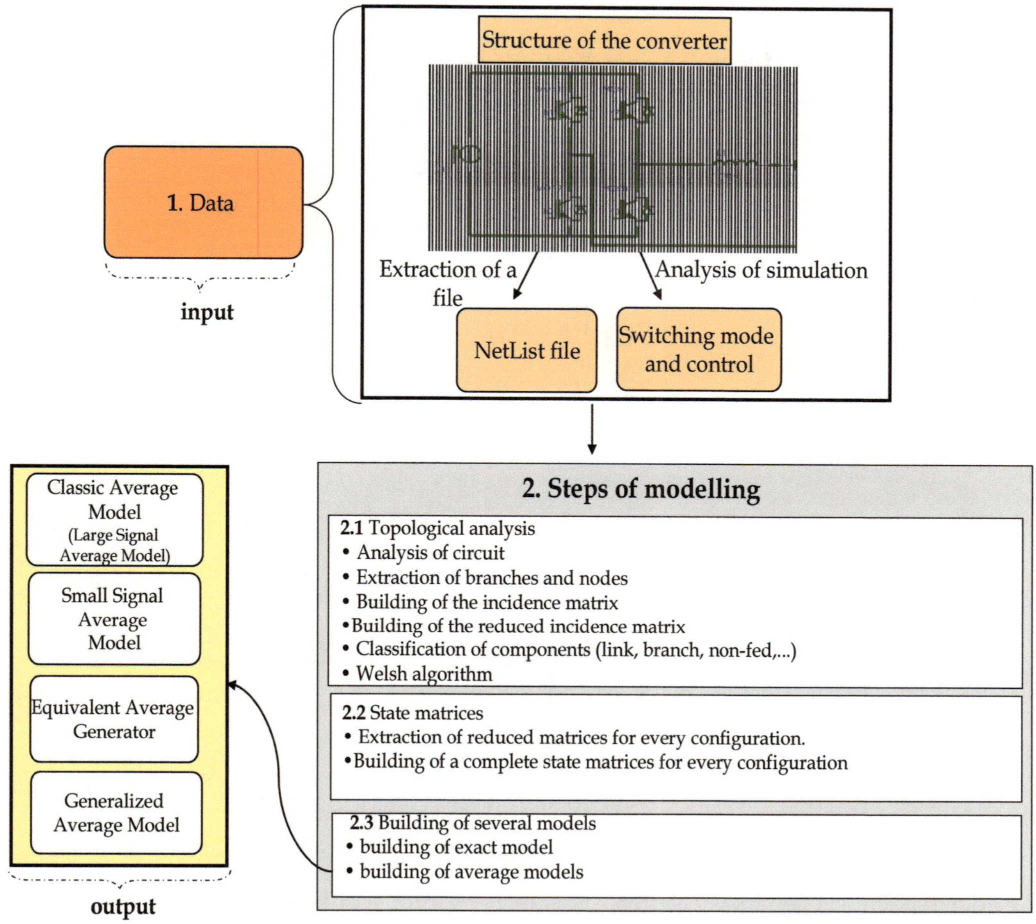

Fig. 1. Steps of modelling

Thus knowing the topology of any electrical circuit, it is possible to express the incidence matrix nodes/branches and then calculate the reduced incidence matrix.
In the incidence matrix, the rows correspond to nodes and the columns to the branches (see Fig. 2).

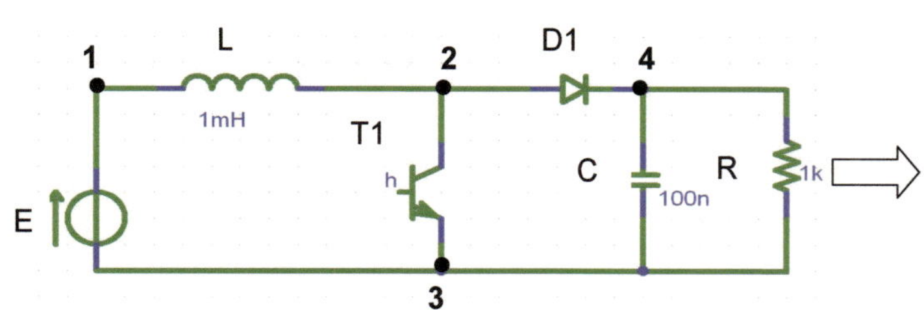

Incidence matrix

Nodes \ Components	D1	T1	E	C	R	L
1	0	0	-1	0	0	1
2	1	-1	0	0	0	-1
3	0	1	1	-1	1	0
4	-1	0	0	1	-1	0

Fig. 2. Incidence matrix of a boost converter

After, this matrix is reduced for each state, according to the conduction state of switches. A switch at state ON is considered as "short-circuit": the lines corresponding to its nodes are added or subtracted (to keep a resulting line with only 0, 1 and -1). A switch at state OFF is considered as an "open circuit": the switch column is suppressed.

Incidence matrix of a boost converter

D1	T1	E	C	R	L
0.0	0.0	-1.0	0.0	0.0	1.0
1.0	-1.0	0.0	0.0	0.0	-1.0
0.0	1.0	1.0	-1.0	1.0	0.0
-1.0	0.0	0.0	1.0	-1.0	0.0

Boost converter
Case1 : D1 ON & T1 OFF

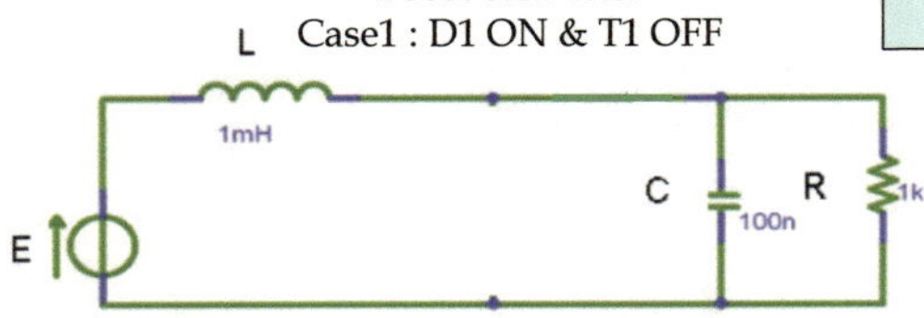

Reduced incidence matrix for case1

E	C	R	L
-1.0	0.0	0.0	1.0
0.0	1.0	-1.0	-1.0
1.0	-1.0	1.0	0.0

Boost converter
Case2: D1 OFF & T1 ON

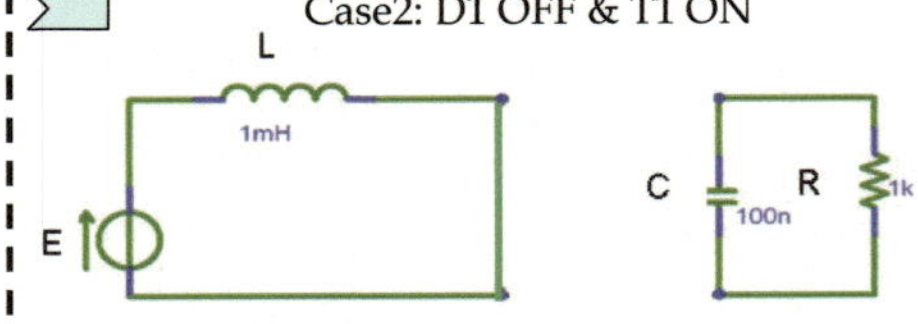

Reduced incidence matrix for case2

E	C	R	L
-1.0	0.0	0.0	1.0
1.0	-1.0	1.0	-1.0
0.0	1.0	-1.0	0.0

Fig. 3. The reduced incidence matrix for a boost converter (for case 1 and case 2)

Welsh algorithm is used to extract the relations between the voltages *U* and currents *I* of the circuit (Rajagopalan, 1987). It separates links components and branches variables:

- *Vmc, Vmr, Vml, Vmj* are respectively the vectors of links voltages for the capacitors, the resistors, the inductors and the sources.
- *Vbc, Vbr, Vbl, Ve* are respectively the vectors of branches voltages for the capacitors, the resistors, the inductors and the sources.
- *Ibe, Ibc, Ibr, Ibl* are respectively the vectors of branches currents for the sources, the capacitors, the resistors and the inductors.
- *Imc, Imr, Iml, Ij* are respectively the vectors of links currents for the capacitors, the resistors, the inductors and the sources.

So, Kirchhoff laws and relations between, on the one hand, the branches voltage and current and on the other hand, between links voltage and current are easily deduced.

We propose also a new extension of the Welsh algorithm that offers the possibility to deduce:

- non fed components
- short-circuited components

Finally, the topological analysis offers a first set of circuit equations in the form of relations between on the one hand, the branch current (*Ib*) and the link current (*Im*) and on the other hand, the branch voltage (*Vb*) and the link voltages (*Vm*).

2.2 State matrices

The state matrices of the static converter are extracted for each configuration from their simplified nodes equations. By combining the equations of voltage-current relations, a reduced state system is obtained (Kuo-Peng et al., 1997).

$$\frac{d}{dt}\begin{bmatrix} V_{bc} \\ I_{ml} \end{bmatrix} = A \cdot \begin{bmatrix} V_{bc} \\ I_{ml} \end{bmatrix} + B \cdot \begin{bmatrix} V_e \\ I_j \end{bmatrix} \tag{1}$$

$$\begin{bmatrix} I_e \\ V_{mj} \end{bmatrix} = C \cdot \begin{bmatrix} V_{bc} \\ I_{ml} \end{bmatrix} + D \cdot \begin{bmatrix} V_e \\ I_j \end{bmatrix} \tag{2}$$

The equations (1) and (2) are written as (3) and (4):

$$\frac{dx}{dt} = A \cdot x + B \cdot u \tag{3}$$

$$Y = C \cdot x + D \cdot u \tag{4}$$

Where:

x :the state vector (size[n])

$$x = \begin{bmatrix} V_{bc} \\ I_{ml} \end{bmatrix} \tag{5}$$

u : the input vector (the external sources) (size[p]).

$$u = \begin{bmatrix} V_e \\ I_j \end{bmatrix} \tag{6}$$

$Y(t)$: the output vector (size[q])

$$Y = \begin{bmatrix} I_e \\ V_{mj} \end{bmatrix} \tag{7}$$

A : the state matrix (size [n,n]).
B : the input matrix (size[n,p]).
C : the output matrix (size[q,n]).
D : the feedforward matrix (size[q,p]).

2.3 Building of the several models

The global global state model of the converter is made from the state equations for each configuration of the static converter. It consists in extracting the state system for each possible topology of circuit in order to create the converter model. The approach focuses on exact and average models (classic average model, equivalent average model, generalized average model and small signal average model). The models are generated according to the

nature of the power conversion (DC/DC, AC/DC) and the operating mode (continuous conduction or discontinuous conduction).
A Comparison between several models generated by AMG is presented in table 1 (Merdassi et al., 2010).

Models	Domain of validity	Results	Limitations
Exact model (Etxeberria-Otadui et al., 2002)	- DC and AC	- Most faithful model	- Not adapted for continuous control - Analyze of modes
Classic average model (Middlebrook & Cuk, 1976)	- DC-DC -Continuous conduction	- Sliding average - Not linear models	-Discontinuous conduction - Alternatives variables
Small signal average model (Bacha et al., 1994; Kanaan et al., 2005)	- DC and AC	- Linear models - Extraction of average values	-Validity around the balance operating point
Equivalent average generator (Sun & Grostollen, 1997)	-Discontinuous conduction - AC and DC	- Model of reduced dimension	- Precision missed in continuous conduction
Generalized average model (Sanders et al., 1990 ; Petitclair et al.,1996)	- Alternatives variables - DC and AC converters - Continuous conduction	- Transient mode (magnitude and phase)	- Complicated computation for higher harmonic range

Table 1. Comparison between the models generated by AMG

2.3.1 The exact model

The exact model represents the starting point to any average modelling operation (Bacha et al., 1994). Regarding the state of the various switches, the converter can be considered as a variable structure system with N possible configurations during a given commutation period T.
The state equation of each configuration of index i ($i = 1,..,N$) is defined by equation (8) in a corresponding time interval $t \in [t_{i-1}, t_i]$.

$$\frac{dx}{dt} = A_i' \cdot x + B_i' \cdot e \tag{8}$$

Where:

$$\sum_{i=1}^{N} t_i - t_{i-1} = T \tag{9}$$

T : the switching period.
N: the number of topologies (configurations) that happen during the switching period T.
x : the state vector (size [n]).
t_i : the commutation instant between configuration i and configuration $i+1$
A_i' : the state matrix for the ith configuration (size [n,n]).
B_i' : the input matrix (size [n,p]).
e : the external sources (size [p]).
By assembling these N equations, considering the continuous character of the state variable (vector x) and by assigning a discrete switching function $u_i(t) \in \{0,1\}$ or $\{-1,1\}$, representing both the operating mode and the control, the global behaviour of the static converter is formulated as the bilinear equation (10) (Sun & Grostollen, 1992).
Note that p switching functions can describe 2^p configurations.

$$\frac{dx}{dt} = A \cdot x + \sum_{i=1}^{p} u_i \cdot (B_i \cdot x + b_i) + d \tag{10}$$

Where:
x : the state vector (size [n]).
A: the global state matrix (size [n,n]).
B_i : input matrix (size [n,n])
u_i : the vector control (size [n,1]).
b_i, d: other input matrixes (size [n,1]).

2.3.2 The average model

The average value of the kth harmonic is defined by equation (11).

$$\langle x(t) \rangle_k = \frac{1}{T} \int_{t}^{t+T} x(\tau) \cdot e^{-jk\omega\tau} d\tau \tag{11}$$

Where:

$$\begin{cases} \omega = \dfrac{2\pi}{T} \\ x(\tau) = 0 \ \ pour \quad \tau < 0 \end{cases}$$

$\langle x(t) \rangle_k$ represents the harmonic coefficient of range k in the decomposition of the complex Fourier series. It's average is made on a sliding window and not on the static interval.
AMG deals with the following types of static converters: DC/DC, DC/AC and AC/AC.
It allows the automatic average modelling. In the literature, the following average models (classic average model, equivalent average generator, generalized average model and small-signal average model) are well known and presented in the papers (Chen & Sun, 2005; Etxeberria-Otadui et al., 2002; Verdiere et al., 2003 & Sanders et al., 1990).

3. Causality of the static converter

For the models of loads or sources that can not be simply described by a circuit representation, a Netlist or graphical approach is limited. So, it is useful to carry out models

of static converters without the description of their environment, by using only knowledge on the connection points of the converter with its environment. Then, the obtained models of the static converters are introduced into the global application.
Two possibilities are proposed: the static converter model is either oriented or non oriented, i.e. causal or non causal (Allain et al., 2009).

3.1 Oriented model

The global model of the static converter is described in a block (e.g. a C S-Function of Matlab/Simulink). Then, it is connected with the other blocks of the system. In this approach, the static converter is considered as a causal model, i.e. the solving sequence of its equations is imposed. So, the model has inputs and outputs.
The figure 4 illustrates this causality in the meaning of block representation and Bond Graph representation for a single-phase voltage inverter.

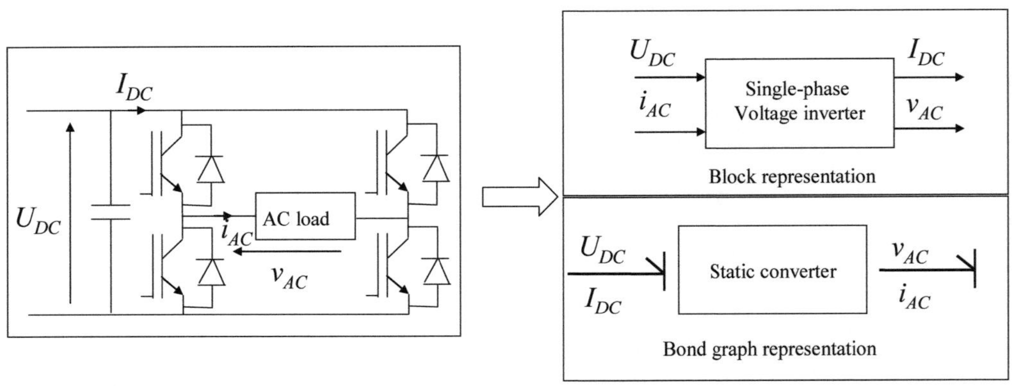

Fig. 4. Example of causality aspect for a single-phase voltage inverter

3.2 Non oriented model

The causality of the static converter can be determined by respecting the definition given in Bond Graph representation (Karnopp et al., 1990), but applied in the electrical domain. The model can be described in a non causal modelling language, e.g. VHDL-AMS, Verilog or Modelica (for the analog part). This means that the model equations are not oriented. Then the model of the static converter is connected to the models of the components thanks to the modelling language. Finally, the compilers of such languages manage automatically the causality (so the solving sequence of the model equations) at the start of the simulation running.
Practically, the static converter environment is defined with equivalent sources. Thus, a voltage source or a current source is imposed at every connection point (Mohan et al., 1989). However, in power electronics, according to their value, inductors may be compared to current sources whereas capacitors are compared to voltages sources.
In the viewpoint of ordinary differential equation solving, the integral causality requires a numerical integration to get the state variables, i.e. the currents across the inductor and the voltages through the capacitors. So, for the external connection of the static converter, current sources (respectively voltage sources) can be used to represent inductors or inductive phenomena (respectively capacitors or capacitive phenomena).

By considering the integral causality, defined as the preferential causality in Bond Graph, the causality of capacitors and inductors are defined (see Fig.5).

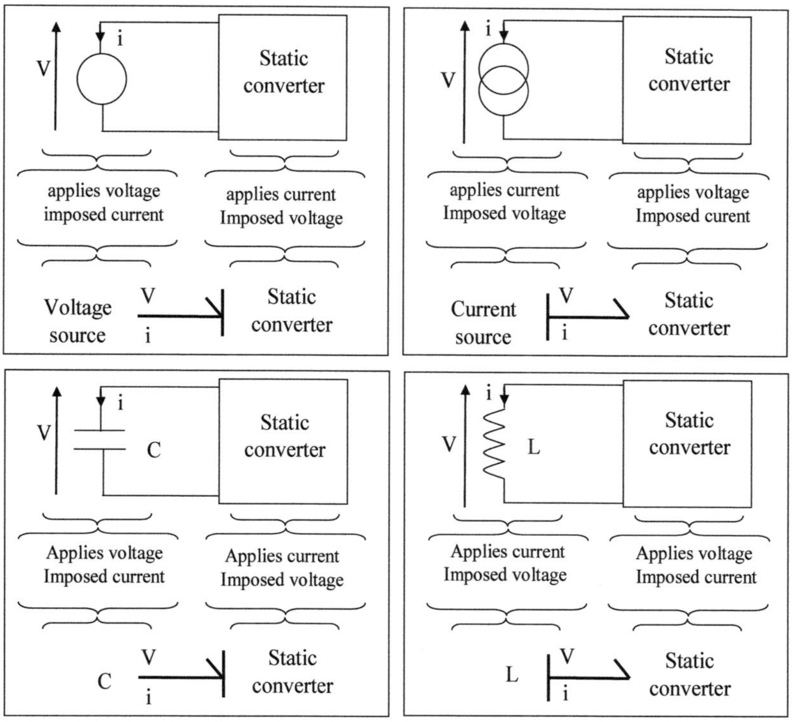

Fig. 5. Causality of a static converter

This approach proposes to generate automatically its models (exact and/or average) according to the nature of the state variables. However, to associate the generated model with other models, thanks to the static converter environment characterisation, the generated model has to give an expression for every complementary energetic variable of the equivalent sources that are connected to the converter. In this way, the current across voltage sources and the voltage through current sources have to be formulated.

The following outputs are formulated:

I_e : the sub-vector of the current in the voltage sources at the interface of the static converter.

V_{mj} : the sub-vector of the voltage on the current sources at the interface of the static converter.

Finally, models are obtained by using equation (2). This representation form of state equation is especially interesting for coupling models.

4. Implementation

AMG is implemented by using Java and Maple programming. Only symbolic treatments are in Maple. The building of the state matrixes A_i, B_i, C_i and D_i for every configuration (indexed i) is developed in Java by equations (1) and (2). The building of the exact and the average models (equations (10) and (11)) by a symbolic approach is made in Maple (Merdassi et al., 2008).

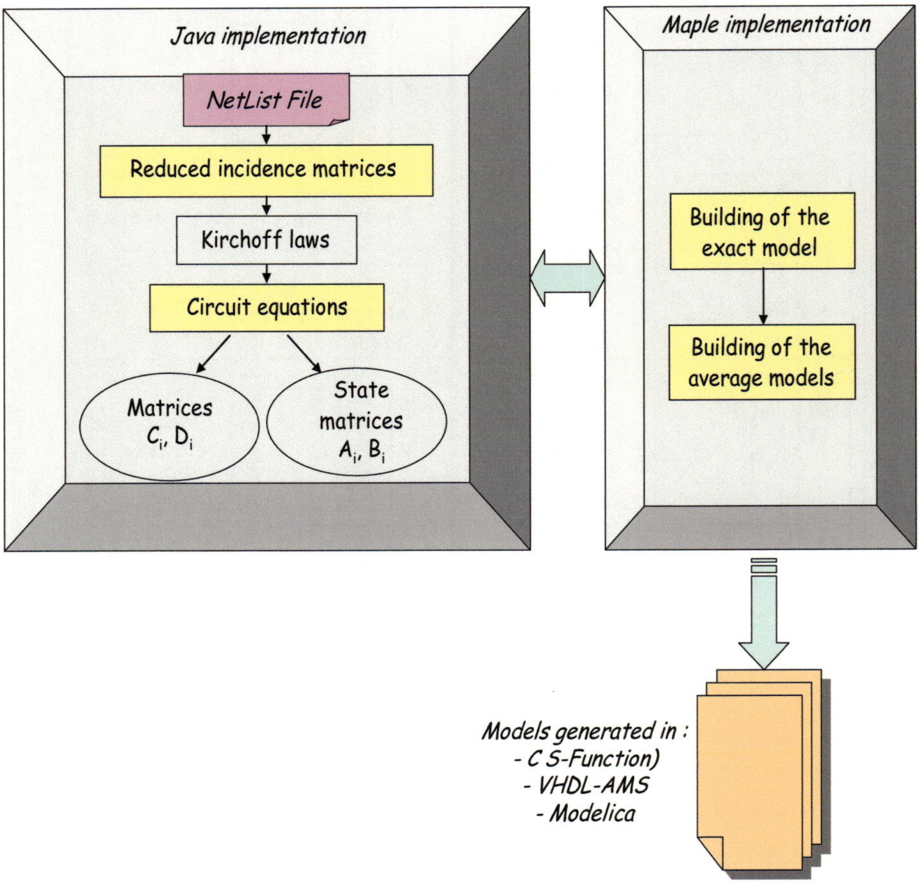

Fig. 6. Implementation in Java and Maple

In this section, an example of the generated C-S function, Modelica and VHDL-AMS code are presented for a boost converter.

```
// pour chaque entree
    InputRealPtrsType uPtrs0 = ssGetInputPortRealSignalPtrs(S,0);
    real_T            h1moy  = *uPtrs0[0];
    real_T            U1   = *uPtrs0[1];


    VC1moy=x[0];
    IL1moy=x[1];


dVC1moy_dt= -(VC1moy - IL1moy * R1 + IL1moy * R1 * h1moy) / C1 / R1;
dIL1moy_dt= (-VC1moy + VC1moy * h1moy + U1) / L1;
 dx[0] = dVC1moy_dt;
 dx[1] = dIL1moy_dt;
```

Fig. 7. The average model for a boost converter in C S-Function

```
---------- VHDLAMS MODEL hacpar_Exact ----------
LIBRARY ieee;
USE           ieee.ALL;
use ieee.math_real.all;
---------- ENTITY DECLARATION  hacpar_Exact ----------
  ENTITY  hacpar_Exact  IS
GENERIC(
  R1:real;
  L1:real;
  C1:real
);
PORT  (
  Quantity  h1:in real;
  Quantity  U1:in real;
  Quantity  VC1:out real;
  Quantity  iL1:out real
);
  END ENTITY  hacpar_Exact ;
---------- ARCHITECTURE DECLARATION  arch_hacpar_Exact -------
---
ARCHITECTURE  arch_hacpar_Exact  OF  hacpar_Exact  IS
BEGIN
VC1'dot== -(VC1 - iL1 * R1 + iL1 * R1 * h1) / C1 / R1;
iL1'dot== (-VC1 + VC1 * h1 + U1) / L1;
END ARCHITECTURE arch_hacpar_Exact ;
```

Fig. 8. The exact model for a boost converter in VHDL-AMS

```
model  hacpar_Exact
external connector InputReal = input Real;
parameter Real R1(fixed=false)=0.5 ;
parameter Real L1(fixed=false)=0.5 ;
parameter Real C1(fixed=false)=0.5 ;
  InputReal h1;
  InputReal U1;
  Real VC1;
  Real iL1;

equation
der(VC1)= -(VC1 - iL1 * R1 + iL1 * R1 * h1) / C1 / R1;
der(iL1)= (-VC1 + VC1 * h1 + U1) / L1;

end hacpar_Exact ;
```

Fig. 9. The exact model for a boost converter in Modelica

5. Applications in Matlab/Simulink

Many examples of converters are implemented in Matlab/Simulink. The results are presented for several applications on the continuous conduction mode among them a resonant converter, a three phase inverter coupled with a three-phase machine (modelled by a three-phase resistor-inductor load). Finally, a multi-level converter is also taken as an example to show the interest of using AMG for big power electronic structure.

5.1 Application 1: A resonant converter

The static converter has been modelled by AMG. The studied structure has an alternative level so the generalized average model is generated for the alternative and the continuous state variables. The equivalent average generator is also tested for this application.

5.1.1 Definition of the control

The mode and the control are deducted from a classic simulation of the structure to be studied in simulation software (e.g Portunus). In the example, these signals will be known as *h1* that controls (MOS1, MOS8) and *h2* that controls (MOS3, MOS6). Their complementary $\overline{h}_1$ and $\overline{h}_2$ respectively control (MOS7, MOS2) and (MOS5, MOS4).

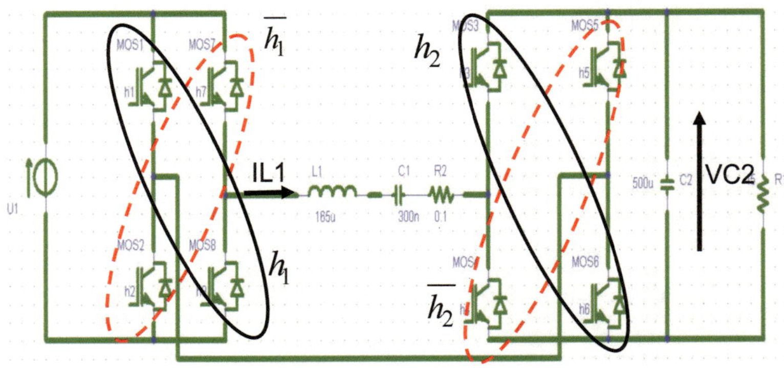

Fig. 10. Control associated to the switching cells

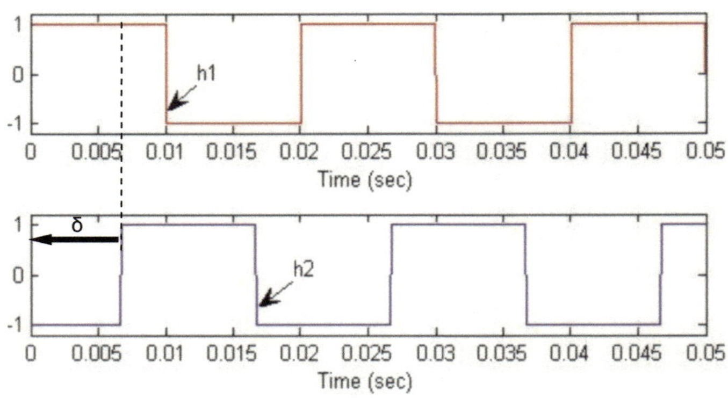

Fig. 11. Full wave control: *h1* et *h2* between [-1,1]

Square control signals are used for the switch control *h1* and *h2*. These signals are periodical and characterized by a 0.5 duty cycle and the phase shifting (δ) between the control *h1* and *h2*.

5.1.2 Simulation in Matlab/Simulink

The generalized average model allows to get the amplitude and the phase of alternative state variables. They are deduced from the real and imaginary expression of IL1.

In Fig. 13 and Fig. 14, the amplitude of the current inductor IL1 is shown for several values of delta (δ).

Finally, we remark that the envelope of the current inductor IL1 illustrates the good concordance between the model generated automatically and the real model.

For the continuous state variable (the voltage VC2), the classical average model, the exact model and the equivalent average generator are generated as shown on Fig. 15.

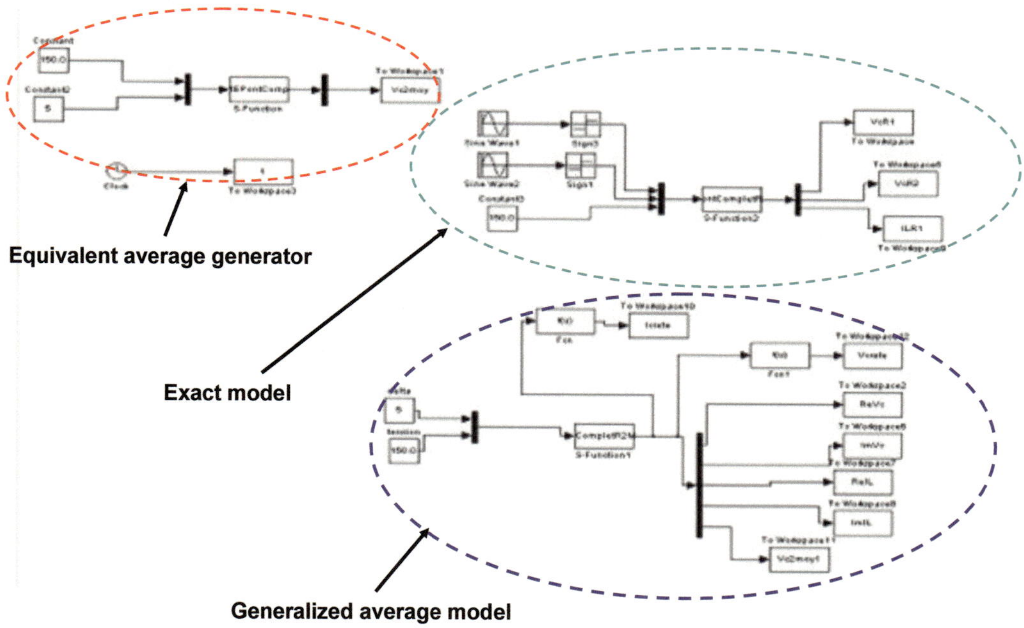

Fig. 12. Implementation of the models for a resonant converter in Matlab/Simulink

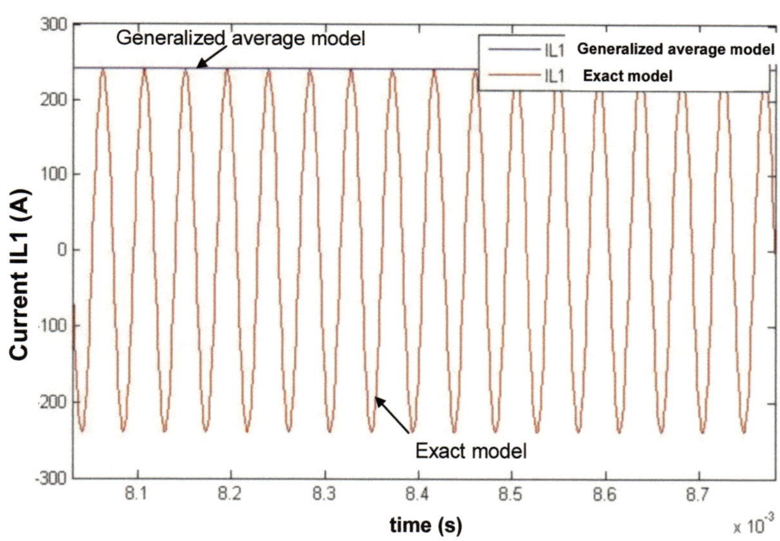

Fig. 13. Extraction of the current amplitude of IL1 from the generalized average model (for $\delta = 5$)

We can notice that, on the one hand, the average equivalent generator is not accurate for this example because it is not adapted to the converter operating in the continuous conduction mode. In fact, the equivalent average generator eliminates some dynamics of the system especially in the discontinuous conduction mode (cf. table 1). On the other hand, the classic average model is better suited for the converter.

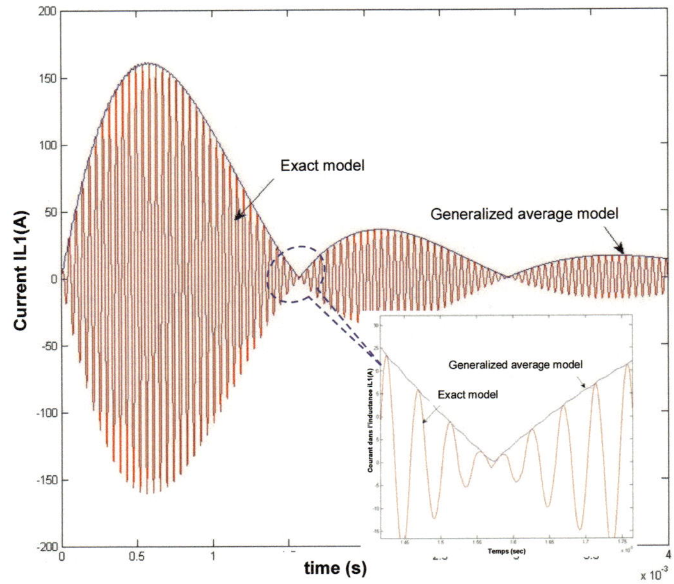

Fig. 14. Extraction of the current amplitude of IL1 from the generalized average model (for $\delta = 0$)

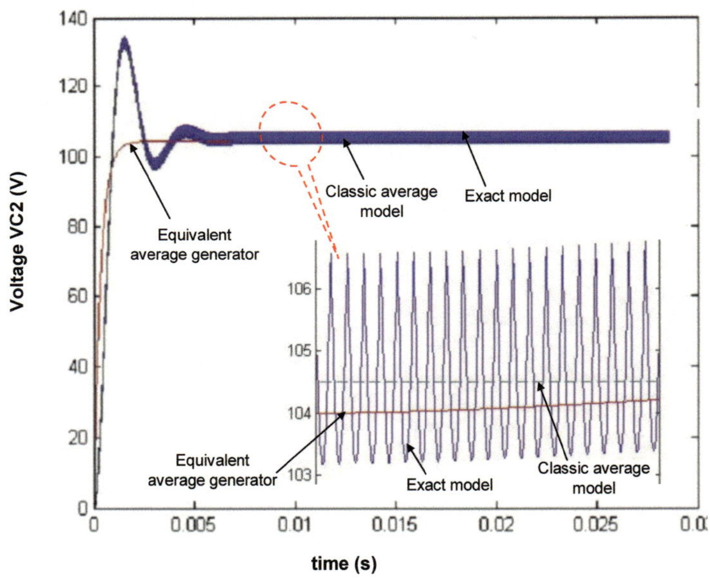

Fig. 15. Exact model, equivalent average generator and classic average model of the voltage VC2

5.2 Application 2: A three-phase voltage inverter

In this section, a voltage inverter feeding an electrical machine is studied. The proposed structure operates in continuous conduction mode, i.e., every switch commutation is controlled.

As explained above, AMG needs basic assumptions on the external equivalent electrical sources to define its environment to connect to it.

5.2.1 Definition of the control

In this static converter, each commutation cell is an inverter legs. For, one leg when a switch is controlled to be ON the other one is OFF. As a consequence, the inverter needs only three control signals corresponding to the upper switch of the switching cell (MOS1, MOS3 and MOS5). These signals will be known as *h1, h2* and *h3*, respectively controls MOS1, MOS3 and MOS5. So, their complementary $\overline{h}_1, \overline{h}_2$ and $\overline{h}_3$ respectively controls MOS2, MOS4 and MOS6.

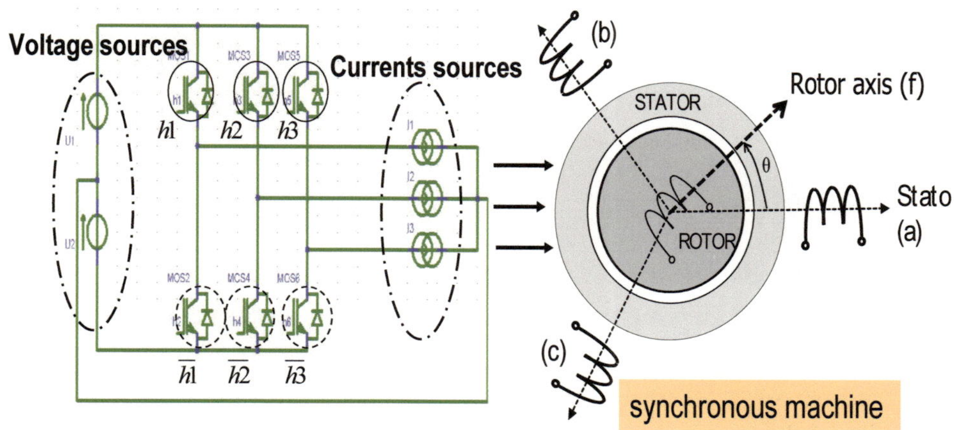

Fig. 16. Three phase voltage inverter coupled with synchronous machine

Here, for the average model, each control signal is a full wave control one. For this application, full wave control and Pulse Width Modulation (PWM) are applied.
For the full wave control, signals are periodical and characterized by a 0.5 duty cycle and $\delta = \frac{2\pi}{3}$ the phase shifting angle between the controls *h1, h2* and *h3*.

A C S-function is obtained. It contains equations of currents in the voltage sources and the voltage on the current sources according to the equation (4).
Analyzing the code (C S-Function), we can see the expression of the DC bus current (i.e. IU1 and IU2) as a function of:

- the control signals: h1, h2, h3
- the expressions of the currents in every phase: I1, I2 and I3

In the same way, the voltage drop applied in the phase is a function of:

- the DC bus voltages: U1, U2
- the control signals: h1, h2, h3.

5.2.2 Simulation in Matlab/Simulink

The model has been mixed with the equations of a three phase RL circuit (see Fig. 18) and three-phase synchronous machine which model is a Park Model. Park's transforms and inverse Park's transforms have been added in the machine model.

```
equation
IU1 = DC_H.i;
IU2 = DC_L.i;
U2 = DC_L.v;
U1 = DC_H.v;

VI1 = A.v;
VI2 = B.v;
VI3 = C.v;
I1 = A.i;
I2 = B.i;
I3 = C.i;

IU1= -0.3e1 / 0.8e1 * I1 * h1 + I1 * h1 * h3 / 0.8e1 - 0.3e1 /
0.8e1 * I1 + I1 * h3 / 0.8e1 + I1 * h1 * h2 * h3 / 0.8e1 + I1 * h1
* h2 / 0.8e1 + I1 * h2 * h3 / 0.8e1 + I1 * h2 / 0.8e1 + I2 * h1 *
h2 * h3 / 0.8e1 + I2 * h1 * h3 / 0.8e1 - 0.3e1 / 0.8e1 * I2 * h2 -
0.3e1 / 0.8e1 * I2 + I2 * h2 * h3 / 0.8e1 + I2 * h3 / 0.8e1 + I2 *
h1 * h2 / 0.8e1 + I2 * h1 / 0.8e1 - 0.3e1 / 0.8e1 * I3 * h3 - 0.3e1
/ 0.8e1 * I3 + I3 * h2 * h3 / 0.8e1 + I3 * h2 / 0.8e1 + I3 * h1 *
h2 * h3 / 0.8e1 + I3 * h1 * h2 / 0.8e1 + I3 * h1 * h3 / 0.8e1 + I3
* h1 / 0.8e1;
IU2= I1 * h3 / 0.8e1 + 0.3e1 / 0.8e1 * I1 - I1 * h1 * h3 / 0.8e1 -
0.3e1 / 0.8e1 * I1 * h1 + I1 * h2 / 0.8e1 - I1 * h2 * h3 / 0.8e1 -
I1 * h1 * h2 / 0.8e1 + I1 * h1 * h2 * h3 / 0.8e1 + I2 * h1 / 0.8e1
- I2 * h1 * h2 / 0.8e1 + 0.3e1 / 0.8e1 * I2 - 0.3e1 / 0.8e1 * I2 *
h2 + I2 * h3 / 0.8e1 - I2 * h2 * h3 / 0.8e1 - I2 * h1 * h3 / 0.8e1
+ I2 * h1 * h2 * h3 / 0.8e1 + I3 * h1 / 0.8e1 - I3 * h1 * h3 /
0.8e1 + 0.3e1 / 0.8e1 * I3 - 0.3e1 / 0.8e1 * I3 * h3 + I3 * h2 /
0.8e1 - I3 * h2 * h3 / 0.8e1 - I3 * h1 * h2 / 0.8e1 + I3 * h1 * h2
* h3 / 0.8e1;

VI1= -0.3e1 / 0.8e1 * U1 * h1 + U1 * h1 * h3 / 0.8e1 - 0.3e1 /
```

Fig. 17. Exact model for a three phase voltage inverter (in Matlab/Simulink C S-Function)

The interest of the AMG tool becomes obvious by looking at the equation generated for this very basic power converter structure. One can easily imagine the difficulty to build such a model without modelling tool, for more complex structures, such a multi-level converter.

5.3 Application 3: A multi-level converter

A multi-level converter is taken as an example to show the interest of using AMG for big power electronic structure.

5.3.1 Definition of the control

For this application, the static converter legs are supposed perfectly balanced. In this example, only the model of one leg is generated by AMG.

The switch commutations are controlled by the signals: *h1, h2, h3* and *h4* and their complementary values.

Each control signal is a pulse wave modulation. Each switching cell is control by the same sinusoidal modulation but with a $\pi/2$ phase displacement of its triangular waveform compared to the one of the switching cell where it is imbricated.

5.3.2 Simulation in Matlab/Simulink

The exact model of the current IL1 generated in C S-function (e.g Matlab/Simulink) is compared to the classical simulation from electrical software (e.g Portunus).

By using the exact model generated by AMG, simulation results represent the perfect behaviour of the multi-level converter. The same results are given with a comparison between the current IL1 obtained automatically (from the exact model by AMG) and the one obtained from the classical simulation (e.g Portunus). Finally, the automatic modelling approach is also approved for a complicated structure.

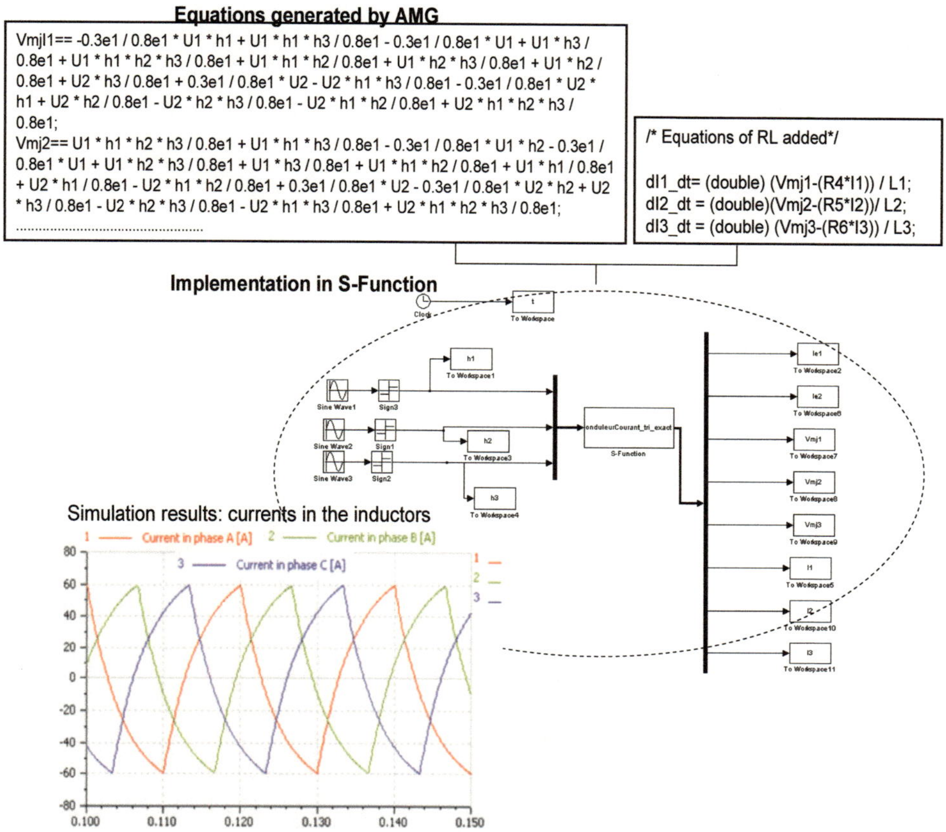

Fig. 18. Implementation in Matlab/Simulink: 3-phase RL load

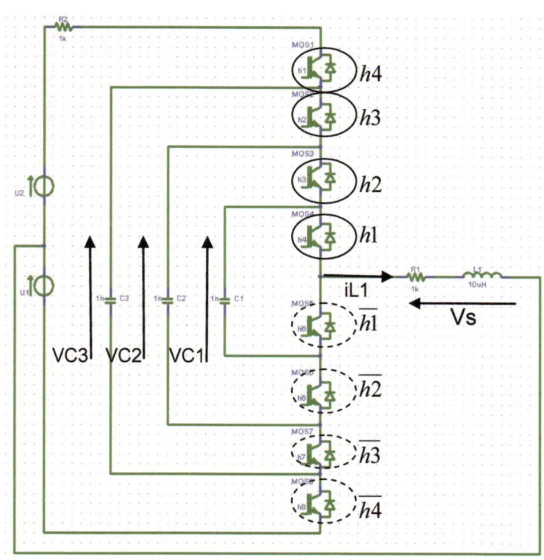

Fig. 19. One leg of the three phase multi-level circuit converter

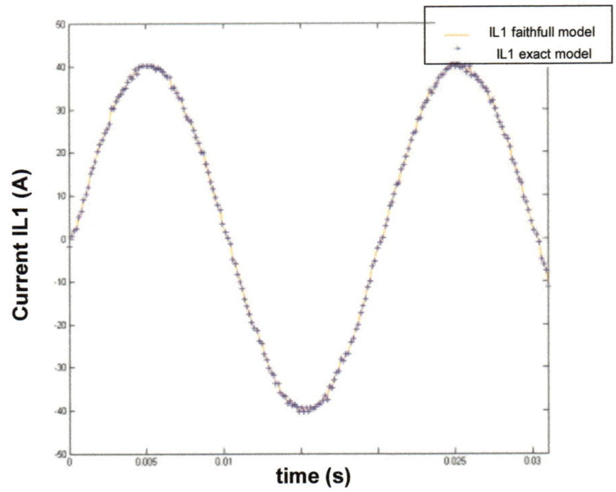

Fig. 20. Comparison between the current IL1 from the exact model (from i.e Matlab/Simulink) and the classical reference model (from i.e Portunus)

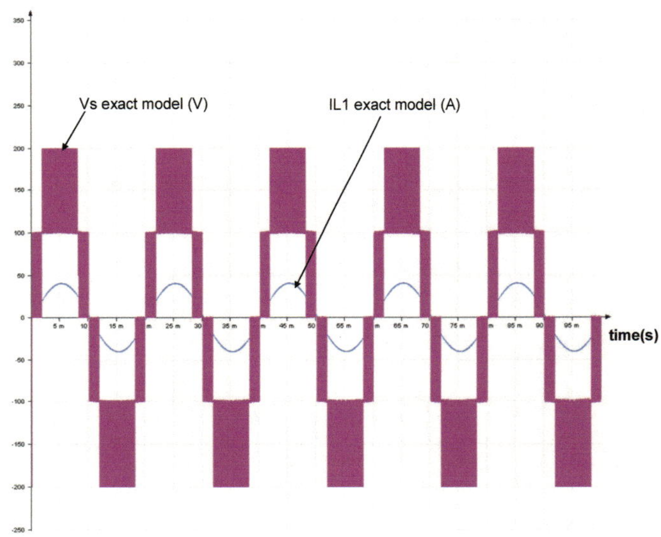

Fig. 21. Results of simulation of the exact model generated by AMG

6. Conclusion

This chapter proposes an automatic modelling process that allows to obtain different models of static converter according to the nature of the power conversion and the state variables. Every model is entirely made in an automatic way by the AMG software, from a description of the structure (here a Netlist file generated by PSpice), the commutation mode (cyclic sequence of switched configurations) and the switch control sequence of the static converter to model. This descriptive information is given by the AMG user.

The automatic generation is useful, especially for complex static converter structures. The generated models are also automatically translated into C-S Function, Modelica and VHDL-

AMS language. Indeed, models in such a language are easy to use in the power electronics simulation software like Matlab/Simulink, Portunus, Simplorer, Amesim, Dymola. This also allows to connect the generated model with others by managing automatically the model causality. This aspect is especially very interesting for coupling models.
Intrinsically, for the average modelling, AMG supposes an a priori on the behaviour of the studied static converters. In this way, the user must understand and analyze the behaviour of the static converter to study. It should also be interesting to extract automatically the control and the mode, by analyzing classical simulation.
A specific methodology for the treatment of the discontinuous conduction mode is also proposed with AMG but not presented in this chapter. However, this automatic treatment requires some knowledge about the converter operating in discontinuous conduction mode. Nowadays, it is only automatically applied for DC/DC converters so it will be interesting in the future to extend it to AC/DC and DC/AC converters.

7. Acknowledgment

This work has been supported by the French association ANR, in the context of the project C6E2-SIMPA2 on the simulation and modelling of mechatronic systems.

8. References

Allain, L.; Merdassi, A.; Gerbaud, L. & Bacha, S. (2009). Automatic modelling of Power Electronic Converter, Average model construction and Modelica model generation, *In Proceddings of the Modelica Conference*, Como Italy, September 2009.

Bacha, S.; Brunello, M. & Hassan, A. (1994). A general large signal model for DC-DC symmetric switching converters, *Electric Machines and Power Systems*, Vol 22, N° 4, July 1994 , pp 493-510.

Bass, R.M. & Sun, J. (1998). Using symbolic computation for power electronics, *Computers in Power Electronics*, 6th Workshop, 19-22 July 1998, pp I IV.

Chen, M. & Sun, J. (2005). A General Approach to Averaged Modelling and Analysis of Active-Clamped Converters, Applied Power Electronics Conference and Exposition, *in Proceedings of the Twentieth Annual IEEE* ,Volume 2, 6-10 March 2005, pp 1359 - 1365.

Chetty, P. R. K. (1982). Current injected equivalent circuit approach to modelling and analysis of current programmed switching DC-to-DC converters (discontinuous inductor conduction mode), *IEEE Transactions. on Industry Applications*, Vol. IA-18, N°3, pp 295-299.

Delaye, A.; Albert, L.; Gerbaud, L. & Wurtz, F. (2004). Automatic generation of sizing models for the optimization of electromagnetic devices using reluctances networks, *IEEE Transactions on Magnetics*, Volume 40, Issue2, Part 2, March 2004, pp.830-833.

Etxeberria-Otadui, I.; Manzo, V.; Bacha, S. & Baltes, F. (2002). Generalized average modelling of FACTS for real time simulation in ARENE, *in Proceedings of IEEE-IECON'02*, 5-8 Nov. 2002, Vol.2, pp 864 - 869.

Kanaan, H. Y.; Al-Haddad, K & Fnaiech, F. (2005). Modelling and control of three-phase/switch/level fixed-frequency PWM rectifier: state-space averaged model, *IEEE Proc. Electric Power Applications*, pp. 551-557, May 2005.

Karnopp, D.C.; Margolis, D.L. & Rosenberg, R.C. (1990). System dynamics: a unified approach, *John Wiley and Sons,* 2nd edition.

Kuo-Peng P.; Sdowski, N.; Bastos, J.P.A.; Carlson, R. & Batistela, N.J. (1997). A General Method for Coupling Static Converters with Electromagnetic Structures, *IEEE Transactions on. Magnetics.,* Vol.33, N°2, March1997.

Maksimovic, D.; Stankovic, A.M.; Thottuvelil, V.J. & Verghese, G.C. (2001). Modeling and simulation of power electronic converters, *Proceedings of the IEEE,* Vol. 89, Issue 6, pp 898 - 912.

Maranesi, P.G. & Riva, M. (2003). Automatic modelling of PWM DC-DC converters, *IEEE Power Electron.* Letters, Vol.1, N°4.

Merdassi, A.; Gerbaud, L. & Bacha, S. (2008). A New Automatic Average Modelling Tool for Power Electronics Systems, *IEEE Power Electron. Specialists Conference,* Greece Rhodes, 15-19 June 2008 pp:3425- 3431.

Merdassi, A.; Gerbaud, L. & Bacha, S. (2010). Automatic generation of average models for power electronics systems in VHDL-AMS and Modelica modelling languages, *Journal of Modelling and Simulation of Systems (JMSS),* Vol.1, Iss.3, pp. 176-186.

Middlebrook, R.D. & Cuk, S. (1976). A general unified approach to modelling switching converter power tages, *IEEE Power Specialists Conference,* pp 18-34, 1976.

Mohan, N.; Underland, T.M. & Robbins, W.P. (1989). Power Electronics: Converters, Applications and Design, 1ere Ed : ISBN: 0 471 61342 82eme :ISBN 0 471 505374, 1989.

Petitclair, P.; Bacha, S. & Rognon, J.p. (1996). Averaged modelling and nonlinear control of an ASVC (advanced static VAr compensator), *Power Electronics Specialists Conference, 27th Annual IEEE,* pp: 753 - 758 vol.1.

Rajagopalan, V. (1987). Computer-aided analysis of power electronic systems, New York, Marcel Dekker Inc.

Sun, J. & Grostollen, H. (1992). Averaged Modeling of switching power converters: Reformulation and theoretical basis, *Power Electronics Specialists Conference PESC Record.,* 23rd Annual IEEE, pp.1165-1172.

Sun, J. & Grostollen, H. (1997). Symbolic Analysis Methods for Averaged Modelling of Switching Power Converters, *IEEE Transactions on Power Electronics,* Vol 12, n° 3, pp 537-546.

Verdiere, F.; Bacha, S. & Gerbaud, L. (2003). Automatic modelling of static converter averaged models, *EPE,* Toulouse, pp 1-9.

Webster, R. & Ngo, K.D.T. (1992). Computer-based symbolic circuit analysis and simulation, *in Conference Proceedings APEC,* pp. 772-779.

11

PV Curves for Steady-State Security Assessment with MATLAB

Ricardo Vargas, M.A Arjona and Manuel Carrillo
Instituto Tecnológico de la Laguna
División de Estudios de Posgrado e Investigación
México

1. Introduction

Most of the problem solutions oriented to the analysis of power systems require the implementation of sophisticated algorithms which need a considerable amount of calculations that must be carried out with a digital computer. Advances in software and hardware engineering have led to the development of specialized computing tools in the area of electrical power systems which allows its efficient analysis. Most of the computational programs, if not all of them, are developed under proprietary code, in other words, the users does not have access to the source code, which limits its usage scope. These programs are considered as black boxes that users only need to feed the required input data to obtain the results without knowing anything about the details of the inner program structure. In the academic or research areas this kind of programs does not fulfill all needs that are required hence it is common the usage of programming tools oriented to the scientific computing. These tools facilitate the development of solution algorithms for any engineering problem, by taking into account the mathematical formulations which define the solution of the proposed problem. Besides, it is also common that most of these programs are known as script or interpreted languages, such as MATLAB, Python and Perl. They all have the common feature of being high level programming languages that usually make use of available efficient libraries in a straightforward way. MATLAB is considered as a programming language that has become a good option for many researchers in different science and engineering areas because of it can allow the creation, manipulation and operation of sparse or full matrices; it also allows to the user the programming of any mathematical algorithm by means of an ordered sequence of commands (code) written into an ascii file known as script files. These files are portable, i.e. they can be executed in most of software versions in any processor under the operating systems Linux or windows.

The main objective of this chapter consists in presenting an efficient alternative of developing a script program in the MATLAB environment; the program can generate characteristic curves power vs. voltage (PV curves) of each node in a power system. The curves are used to analyze and evaluate the stability voltage limits in steady state, and they are calculated by employing an algorithm known as continuous load flows, which are a variation of the Newton-Raphson formulation for load flows but it avoids any possibility of singularity during the solution process under a scenario of continuous load variation. To illustrate the application of this analysis tool, the 14-node IEEE test system is used to

generate the PV curves. The code presented allows any modification throughout its script file and therefore it can be used for future power system studies and research.
The formulation of the load flow problem is firstly presented to obtain the PV curves, there are some issues that need to be taken into account in the algorithm oriented to the solution of load flows such as: mathematical formulation of the load flow, its adaptation to the Newton-Rhapson method and the implementation of the continuation theory to the analysis of load flows. It is also presented the necessary programming issues to the development of the script that plots the PV curves, the recommendations that are needed in the creation, manipulation and operation of sparse matrices, the use of vector operations, triangular decompositions techniques (that used in the solution of the set on linear equations) and finally the reading of ascii files and Graphical User Interface (GUI) development are also given.

1.1 Antecedents

Nowadays there are commercial programs which have been approved and used for the electric utilities in the analysis of electric power systems. Simulation programs as the Power World Simulator (PWS) (PowerWorld Corporation, 2010) and PSS (Siemens, 2005) are some of the most popular in the control and planning of a power system, and some of them are adopted by universities, e.g. PWS, because of its elegant interface and easy usage. Most of them have friendly user interfaces. On the other hand, a bachelor or graduate student, who want to reproduce or test new problem formulations to the solution of power system problems, need a simulation tool suitable for the generation of prototype programs. The code reutilization is important for integrating in a modular form, new functions required for the power system analysis (Milano, 2010). Commercial programs does not fulfill these requirements and therefore a search for alternatives is usually carry out, such as a new programming language or for the scientific language MATLAB. It is possible to find open source projects in several websites, which are usually named as "Toolbox" by their authors, and they cover a vast diversity of topics as: load flows, transient stability analysis, nodal analysis, and electromagnetic transients. Some of most relevant projects and its authors are: PSAT by Federico Milano (Milano, 2006), MatPower by Zimmerman, Carlos E. Murillo-Sánchez and Deqiang Gan (Zimmerman et al., 2011), PST by Graham Rogers, Joe H. Chow and Luigi Vanfretti (Graham et al., 2009) and MatEMTP by Mahseredjian, J. Alvarado and Fernando L. (Mahseredjian et al., 1997).
Similar projects have been developed at the Instituto Tecnológico de la Laguna (ITL) and they have been the basis for several MSc theses which have been integrated into the power system program PTL (figure 1). These projects have made possible the incorporation of new applications making a more flexible and robust program for the steady-state analysis of an electric power system.

2. Conceptual design of the PTL simulator

In spite of the foundation of the PTL program, i.e. being an integration of several graduate projects at the ITL, its design offers an interface which permits an intuitive user interaction and at the same time it has a dynamic performance which is able to solve load flow problems for any electric network regardless the node number. It offers the feature of showing the information graphically and numerically and besides it generates a report of the activities performed and exports files with data for making stability studies. The above PTL features make it a simulation program suitable for investigations because it allows

Fig. 1. GUI of the PTL program.

integrating solution algorithms for economic dispatch, calculation and plotting of PV curves, testing of methods with distributed slacks, static var compensator (SVC) models, transmission lines, generators, etc. It is also an important tool in power system research, making the PTL more complete for the analysis or studies oriented to the operation and control of electric power systems.

2.1 Data input details

As any other simulation program (commercial or free), the PTL requires of information data as input, it is needed for the analysis process. The information can be given as a data file that contains basic information to generate the base study case: the base power of the system, nodal information (number of nodes, voltages, load powers and generation power), machine limits, system branches, SVC information (if applies). The simulation program PTL can handle two file extensions: cdf (standardized IEEE format) and ptl (proposed PTL format).

2.2 Simulator description

The input information for carrying out the search of the solution process, as the related data to the problem results of the load flow problem (for generating the base case) are stored in defined data structures (e.g. Dat_Vn, Dat_Gen, Dat_Lin, Dat_Xtr). These structures allow easily the data extraction, by naming each field in such a way that the programming becomes intuitive and each variable can be easily identified with the corresponding physical variable of the problem. An example with two structures used in the PTL program is shown in Table 1.
The MATLAB structures are composed of non-primitive variable types that allow storing different data types in a hierarchical way with the same entity (García et al., 2005). They are formed by data containers called fields, which can be declared by defining the structure name and the desired field considering its value, e.g. Dat_Vn.Amp=1.02.

Structure	Field	Description
Dat_Vn	Amp	Voltage magnitude
	Ang	Phase angle of voltages
Dat_Gen	NumNG	Generation and load nodes
	Nslack	Slack node
	V_Rem_bus	Voltage information
	Pgen	Generated active power
	Qgen	Generated reactive power
	Pmin	Minimum limit of generator active power
	Pmax	Maximum limit of generator active power
	Qmin	Minimum limit of generator reactive power
	Qmax	Maximum limit of generator reactive power

Table 1. Example of the information handled in the PTL.

2.3 Output information

The PTL program displays the results obtained from the load flow execution in a boxlist (uicontrol MATLAB) with a defined format: nodal information, power flows in branches and generators. It gives the option of printing a report in Word format with the same information. In addition, it has the option of generating a file with the extension f2s which is oriented for stability studies and it contains all necessary information for the initialization of the state machine variables by using the results of the current power flow solution.

The definition of the conceptual simulation program PTL is presented as a recommendation by taking into account the three basic points that a simulation program must include: to be completely functional, to be general for any study case and to facilitate its maintenance; in other words it must allow the incorporation of new functions for the solution of new studies, such that it allows its free modification as easy as possible.

3. Load flows

In a practical problem, the knowledge of the operating conditions of an electric power system is always needed; that is, the knowledge of the nodal voltage levels in steady-state under loaded and generating conditions and the availability of its transmission elements are required to evaluate the system reliability. Many studies focused to the electric power systems start from the load flow solution which is known as "base case", and in some cases, these studies are used to initialize the state variables of dynamic elements of a network (generators, motors, SVC, etc) to carry out dynamic and transient stability studies. Another study of interest, that it also requires starting from a base case, is the analysis of the power system security that will be discussed in next sections.

The mathematical equations used to solve this problem are known as power flow equations, or network equations. In its more basic form, these equations are derived considering the transmission network with lumped parameters under lineal and balanced conditions, similarly as the known operating conditions in all nodes of the system (Arrillaga, 2001).

3.1 Power flow equations

An electric power system is formed with elements that can be represented for its equivalent circuit RLC, and with components as load and generating units which cannot be represented as basic elements of an electrical network, they are represented as nonlinear elements. However, the analysis of an electrical power system starts with the formulation of a referenced nodal system and it describes the relationship between the electrical variables (voltages and currents) as it is stated by the second Kirchhoff´s law or nodal law.

$$\mathbf{I}_{BUS} = \mathbf{Y}_{BUS} \cdot \mathbf{V}_{BUS} \tag{1}$$

where $\mathbf{I}_{BUS}$ is a $n\times1$ vector whose components are the electrical net current injections in the n network nodes, $\mathbf{V}_{BUS}$ is a $n\times1$ vector with the nodal voltages measured with respect to the referenced node and $\mathbf{Y}_{BUS}$ is the $n\times n$ nodal admittance matrix of the electrical network; it has the properties of being symmetric and squared, and it describes the network topology.

In a real power system, the injected currents to the network nodes are unknown; what it is commonly known is the net injected power S_k. Conceptually, S_k is the net complex power injected to the k-th node of the electrical network, and it is determined by the product of voltage (V_k) and the current conjugate (I_k^*), where V_k and I_k are the voltages and nodal currents at the node k, that is, the k-th elements of vectors $\mathbf{V}_{BUS}$ y $\mathbf{I}_{BUS}$ in (1). Once the I_k is calculated using (1), the net complex power S_k can be expressed as:

$$S_k = V_k \cdot I_k^* = \mathrm{V}_k \cdot \left(\sum_{m=1}^{n} \mathrm{Y}_{k,m} \mathrm{V}_m \right)^* \text{, for } k = 1,2,\ldots..n \tag{2}$$

where $\mathrm{Y}_{k,m}$ is the element (k,m) of $\mathbf{Y}_{BUS}$ matrix in (1). S_k can also be represented for its real and imaginary components such as it is shown in the following expression:

$$S_k = P_k + jQ_k \text{ , for } k = 1,2,\ldots..n \tag{3}$$

where P_k and Q_k are the net active and reactive power injected at node k of the system, respectively. They are defined as:

$$P_k = P_k^{Gen} - P_k^{Load} \tag{4}$$

$$Q_k = Q_k^{Gen} - Q_k^{Load} \tag{5}$$

where the variables P_k^{Gen} and Q_k^{Gen} represent the active and reactive powers respectively. They are injected at node k for a generator and the variables P_k^{Load} and Q_k^{Load} represent the active and reactive Powers, respectively of a load connected to the same node.

By representing the nodal voltages in polar form, we have:

$$V_k = V_k e^{j\theta_k} = V_k \left(\cos\theta_k + j\sin\theta_k \right) \tag{6}$$

and each element of the admittance matrix $\mathbf{Y}_{BUS}$ as,

$$Y_{km} = G_{km} + jB_{km} \tag{7}$$

Using the above expressions in (2), it results,

$$S_k = V_k e^{j\theta_k} \cdot \left(\sum_{m=1}^{n} (G_{km} + jB_{km}) V_m e^{j\theta_m} \right)^* = V_k \cdot \left(\sum_{m=1}^{n} V_m (G_{km} + jB_{km})(cos\theta_{km} + j\sin\theta_{km}) \right)^*$$
$$\text{for } k=1,2,\ldots..n \qquad (8)$$

where $\theta_{km} = \theta_k - \theta_m$. By separating the real and imaginary parts as it is suggested in (3), it is obtained the following,

$$P_k = V_k^2 G_{kk} + V_k \sum_{\substack{m=1 \\ m \neq n}}^{n} V_m (G_{km} Cos(\theta_k - \theta_m) + B_{km} Sin(\theta_k - \theta_m)) \text{ for } k=1,2,\ldots..n \qquad (9)$$

$$Q_k = -V_k^2 B_{km} + V_k \sum_{\substack{m=1 \\ m \neq n}}^{n} V_m (G_{km} Cos(\theta_k - \theta_m) - B_{km} Cos(\theta_k - \theta_m)), \text{ for } k=1,2,\ldots..n \qquad (10)$$

The equations (9) and (10) are commonly known as Power flow equations and they are needed for solving the load flow problem (Arrillaga, 2001). By analyzing these equations it can be clearly seen that each system node *k* is characterized for four variables: active power, reactive power, voltage magnitude and angle. Hence it is necessary to specify two of them and consider the remaining two as state variables to find with the solution of both equations.

3.2 Bus types in load flow studies

In an electrical power network, by considering its load flow equations, four variables are defined at each node, the active and reactive powers injected at node P_k and Q_k, and the magnitude and phase voltage at the node V_k y θ_k. The latter two variables determine the total electrical state of the network, then, the objective of the load flow problem consists in determining these variables at each node. The variables can be classified in controlled variables, that is, its values can be specified and state variables to be calculated with the solution of the load flow problem. The controlled or specified variables are determined by taking into account the node nature, i.e. in a generator node, the active power can be controlled by the turbine speed governor, and the voltage magnitude of the generator node can be controlled by the automatic voltage regulator (AVR). In a load node, the active and reactive power can be specified because its values can be obtained from load demand studies. Therefore, the system nodes can be classified as follows:

- *Generator node PV*: It is any node where a generator is connected; the magnitude voltage and generated active power can be controlled or specified, while the voltage phase angle and the reactive power are the unknown state variables (Arrillaga, 2001).
- *Load node PQ*: It is any node where a system load is connected; the active and reactive consumed powers are known or specified, while the voltage magnitude and its phase angle are the unknown state variables to be calculated (Arrillaga, 2001).
- *Slack node* (Compensator): In a power system at least one of the nodes has to be selected and labeled with this node type. It is a generating node where it cannot be specified the generated active power as in the PV node, because the transmission losses are not known beforehand and thus it cannot be established the balance of active power of the loads and

generators. Therefore this node compensates the unbalance between the active power between loads and generating units as specified in the PQ and PV nodes (Arrillaga, 2001).

3.3 Solution of the nonlinear equations by the Newton-Rhapson method

The nature of the load flow problem formulation requires the simultaneous solution of a set of nonlinear equations; therefore it is necessary to apply a numerical method that guarantees a unique solution. There are methods as the Gauss-Seidel and Newton-Rhapson, in the work presented here, the load flow problem is solved with the Newton-Raphson (NR) (Arrillga, 2001).

The NR method is robust and has a fast convergence to the solution. The method has been applied to the solution of nonlinear equations that can be defined as,

$$\mathbf{f}(\mathbf{x}) = \mathbf{0} \tag{11}$$

where $\mathbf{f}(\mathbf{x})$ is a $n\times1$ vector that contains the n equations to be solved $f_i(\mathbf{x}) = 0$, $i=1,n$,

$$\mathbf{f}(\mathbf{x}) = \left[f_1(\mathbf{x}), f_2(\mathbf{x}), \ldots, f_n(\mathbf{x})\right]^T \tag{12}$$

and $\mathbf{x}$ is a $n\times1$ vector that contains the state variables, x_i, $i=1,n$,

$$\mathbf{x} = \left[x_1, x_2, \ldots, x_n\right]^T \tag{13}$$

The numerical methods used to solve (11) are focused to determine a recursive formula $\mathbf{x}^{k+1} = \mathbf{x}^k + \Delta\mathbf{x}$. The solution algorithm is based in the iterative application of the above formula starting from an initial estimate $\mathbf{x}^0$, until a convergence criterion is achieved $\max(\Delta\mathbf{x}) < \varepsilon$, where ε is a small numerical value, and the vector $\mathbf{x}^k$ is an approximation to the solution $\mathbf{x}^*$ of (11).

The Newton-Raphson method can be easily explained when it is applied to an equation of a single state variable (Arrillaga, 2001). A geometrical illustration of this problem is shown in figure 2.

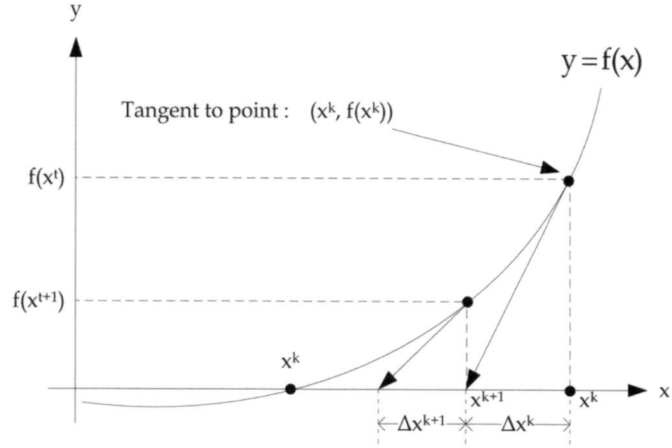

Fig. 2. Geometric interpretation of the NR algorithm.

From figure 2, it can be established that $\Delta x^k = x^{k+1} - x^k$

$$d\frac{f(x)}{dx}\bigg|_{x^k} = -\frac{f(x)}{\Delta x^k} \tag{14}$$

where,

$$\Delta x^k = -\left(f'(x_k)\right)^{-1} \cdot f(x_k) \tag{15}$$

As it can be seen in figure 2, the successive application of this correction $\Delta x^k, \Delta x^{k+1}, \Delta x^{k+2}$... leads to the solution $\mathbf{x}^*$ as nearer as desired.
To derive the recursive formula to be employed in the solution of the set of equations, and by expressing the equation (15) in matrix notation, it is obtained,

$$\Delta \mathbf{x}^k = -\left(\mathbf{f}'(\mathbf{x}_k)\right)^{-1} \cdot \mathbf{f}(\mathbf{x}_k) = -\left[\mathbf{J}(\mathbf{x}_k)\right]^{-1} \cdot \mathbf{f}(\mathbf{x}_k) \tag{16}$$

where

$$\mathbf{J}(\mathbf{x}_k) = \frac{\partial \mathbf{f}(\mathbf{x}_k)}{\partial \mathbf{x}} = \begin{bmatrix} \frac{\partial f_1(\mathbf{x})}{\partial x_1} & \frac{\partial f_1(\mathbf{x})}{\partial x_2} & \cdots & \frac{\partial f_1(\mathbf{x})}{\partial x_n} \\ \frac{\partial f_2(\mathbf{x})}{\partial x_1} & \frac{\partial f_2(\mathbf{x})}{\partial x_2} & \cdots & \frac{\partial f_2(\mathbf{x})}{\partial x_n} \\ \vdots & \vdots & \cdots & \vdots \\ \frac{\partial f_n(\mathbf{x})}{\partial x_1} & \frac{\partial f_n(\mathbf{x})}{\partial x_2} & \cdots & \frac{\partial f_n(\mathbf{x})}{\partial x_n} \end{bmatrix} \tag{17}$$

and the recursive formula is given by,

$$\mathbf{x}^{k+1} = \mathbf{x}^k + \Delta \mathbf{x} \tag{18}$$

3.4 Application of the NR to the power flow problem

The equations to be solved in the load flow problem, as it was explained in section 3.1, are here rewritten,

$$P_k^{esp} - \left[V_k^2 G_{kk} + V_k \sum_{\substack{m=1 \\ m \neq n}}^{n} V_m \left(G_{km} Cos(\theta_k - \theta_m) + B_{km} Sin(\theta_k - \theta_m) \right) \right] = 0 \tag{4}$$

$$Q_k^{esp} - \left[-V_k^2 B_{km} + V_k \sum_{\substack{m=1 \\ m \neq n}}^{n} V_m \left(G_{km} Cos(\theta_k - \theta_m) - B_{km} Cos(\theta_k - \theta_m) \right) \right] = 0 \tag{5}$$

for k= 1,2,.....n

The $2n$ equations to be solved are represented by (4) and (5). However, for all generator nodes, equation (5) can be omitted and for the slack node the equations (4) and (5) (Arrillaga, 2001). The resulting set of equations is consistent because for the neglected equations, its corresponding state variables P^{esp}, Q^{esp} are also omitted from them. All this operation gives as a result a set of equations to solve, where its state variables $\mathbf{x}$ only contain magnitudes of nodal voltages and its corresponding phase angles which are denoted by $\mathbf{V}$ y $\boldsymbol{\theta}$, which simplifies considerably a guaranteed convergence of the numerical method. Therefore, the set of equation can be represented in vector form as,

$$\mathbf{f}(\mathbf{x}) = \begin{bmatrix} \Delta\mathbf{P}(\mathbf{x}) \\ \Delta\mathbf{Q}(\mathbf{x}) \end{bmatrix} = \mathbf{0} \tag{19}$$

where $\Delta\mathbf{P}(\mathbf{x})$ represents the equation (4) for PV and PQ nodes, $\Delta\mathbf{Q}(\mathbf{x})$ represents the equation (5) for PQ nodes and $\mathbf{x}$ denotes the state variables $\mathbf{V}$ and $\boldsymbol{\theta}$, which are represented in vector notation as:

$$\mathbf{x} = \begin{bmatrix} \boldsymbol{\theta} \\ \mathbf{V} \end{bmatrix} \tag{20}$$

where:
$\mathbf{V}$ = ncx1 vector.
$\boldsymbol{\theta}$ = nc+n-1 vector.
nc = Number of PQ nodes.
n = Total number of nodes.
Considering equation (16), its matrix equation is obtained and it defines the solution of the load flow problem:

$$\underbrace{\begin{bmatrix} \Delta\boldsymbol{\theta} \\ \Delta\mathbf{V} \end{bmatrix}}_{\mathbf{x}^k} = -\underbrace{\begin{bmatrix} \dfrac{\partial \Delta\mathbf{P}}{\partial \boldsymbol{\theta}} & \dfrac{\partial \Delta\mathbf{P}}{\partial \mathbf{V}} \\ \dfrac{\partial \Delta\mathbf{Q}}{\partial \boldsymbol{\theta}} & \dfrac{\partial \Delta\mathbf{Q}}{\partial \mathbf{V}} \end{bmatrix}^{-1}}_{\mathbf{J}(\mathbf{x}^k)} \underbrace{\begin{bmatrix} \Delta\mathbf{P} \\ \Delta\mathbf{Q} \end{bmatrix}}_{\mathbf{f}(\mathbf{x}^k)} \tag{21}$$

By applying the recursive equation (18), the state variables ($\mathbf{V}$ y $\boldsymbol{\theta}$) are updated every iteration until the convergence criterion is achieved $\max(|\Delta\mathbf{P}(\mathbf{x})|) \le \varepsilon$ or $\max(|\Delta\mathbf{Q}(\mathbf{x})|) \le \varepsilon$ for a small ε or until the iteration number exceeds the maximum number previously defined which in this indicates convergence problems.
The Jacobian elements in (21) are,

$$\frac{\partial \Delta\mathbf{P}}{\partial \boldsymbol{\theta}} \tag{22}$$

They are calculated using (19), however, by taking into account that the specified powers P_k^{esp} are constants, we obtain,

$$\frac{\partial \Delta\mathbf{P}}{\partial \boldsymbol{\theta}} = -\frac{\partial \mathbf{P}}{\partial \boldsymbol{\theta}} \tag{23}$$

Therefore, equation (21) can be expressed as,

$$\begin{bmatrix} \Delta \mathbf{P} \\ \Delta \mathbf{Q} \end{bmatrix} = \begin{bmatrix} \frac{\partial \mathbf{P}}{\partial \boldsymbol{\theta}} & \frac{\partial \mathbf{P}}{\partial \mathbf{V}} \\ \frac{\partial \mathbf{Q}}{\partial \boldsymbol{\theta}} & \frac{\partial \mathbf{Q}}{\partial \mathbf{V}} \end{bmatrix} \cdot \begin{matrix} \Delta \boldsymbol{\theta} \\ \Delta \mathbf{V} \end{matrix} \tag{24}$$

where the Jacobian elements are calculated using equations (9) and (10), provided equation (21) is normalized.

To simplify the calculation of the Jacobian elements of (24), it can be reformulated as:

$$\begin{bmatrix} \Delta \mathbf{P} \\ \Delta \mathbf{Q} \end{bmatrix} = \begin{bmatrix} \mathbf{H} & \mathbf{N} \\ \mathbf{J} & \mathbf{L} \end{bmatrix} \begin{bmatrix} \Delta \boldsymbol{\theta} \\ \frac{\Delta \mathbf{V}}{\mathbf{V}} \end{bmatrix} \tag{25}$$

where the quotient of each element with its corresponding element V allows that some elements of the Jacobian matrix can be expressed similarly (Arrillaga, 2001). The Jacobian can be formed by defining four submatrixes denoted as **H**, **N**, **J** and **L** which are defined as,

If $k \neq m$ (off diagonal elements):

$$H_{km} = \frac{\partial P_k}{\partial \theta_m} = V_k V_m \left(G_{km} \sin\theta_{km} - B_{km} \cos\theta_{km} \right) \tag{26}$$

$$N_{km} = V_k \frac{\partial P_k}{\partial V_m} = V_k V_m \left(G_{km} \cos\theta_{km} + B_{km} \sin\theta_{km} \right) \tag{27}$$

$$J_{km} = \frac{\partial Q_k}{\partial \theta_m} = -V_k V_m \left(G_{km} \cos\theta_{km} + B_{km} \sin\theta_{km} \right) \tag{28}$$

$$L_{km} = V_k \frac{\partial P_k}{\partial V_m} = V_k V_m \left(G_{km} \sin\theta_{km} - B_{km} \cos\theta_{km} \right) \tag{29}$$

If $k=m$ (main diagonal elements):

$$H_{kk} = \frac{\partial P_k}{\partial \theta_k} = -Q_k - B_{kk} V_k^2 \tag{30}$$

$$N_{kk} = V_k \frac{\partial P_k}{\partial V_k} = P_k + G_{kk} V_k^2 \tag{31}$$

$$J_{kk} = \frac{\partial Q_k}{\partial \theta_m} = P_k - G_{kk} V_k^2 \tag{32}$$

$$L_{kk} = V_k \frac{\partial P_k}{\partial V_m} = Q_k - B_{kk} V_k^2 \tag{33}$$

It is important to consider that subscripts k and m are different, $L_{km} = H_{km}$ and $J_{km} = -N_{km}$, on the contrary, to the principal diagonal elements. Nevertheless, there is a relationship when the following equation is solved:

$$\begin{bmatrix} V_1 & 0 & \cdots & 0 \\ 0 & V_1 & \cdots & 0 \\ \vdots & \vdots & \ddots & \vdots \\ 0 & 0 & \cdots & V_n \end{bmatrix} \left(\begin{bmatrix} Y_{11} & Y_{12} & \cdots & Y_{1n} \\ Y_{21} & Y_{22} & \cdots & Y_{2n} \\ \vdots & \vdots & \cdots & \vdots \\ Y_{n1} & Y_{n1} & \cdots & Y_{nn} \end{bmatrix} \begin{bmatrix} V_1 & 0 & \cdots & 0 \\ 0 & V_1 & \cdots & 0 \\ \vdots & \vdots & \ddots & \vdots \\ 0 & 0 & \cdots & V_n \end{bmatrix} \right)^* \tag{34}$$

By simple inspection of (34), we can see that the operation for $-N_{km}$ and J_{km} results to be the real part of (34), while H_{km} and L_{km} are the imaginary component of it. The variant consists that all elements of the principal diagonal are calculated after (34) has been solved by subtracting or adding the corresponding P_k or Q_k as it can be seen in (30)-(33).
The Jacobian matrix has the characteristic of being sparse and squared with an order of the length of vector **X**, where its sub-matrixes have the following dimensions:
H: n-1 x n-1 matrix.
N: n-1 x nc matrix.
J: nc x n-1 matrix.
L: nc x nc matrix.

4. Voltage stability and collapse

The terms of voltage stability and collapse are closely related to each other in topics of operation and control of power systems.

4.1 Voltage stability

According to the IEEE, the voltage stability is defined as the capacity of a power system to maintain in all nodes acceptable voltage levels under normal conditions after a system disturbance for a given initial condition (Kundur, 1994). This definition gives us an idea of the robustness of a power system which is measured by its capability of keep the equilibrium between the demanded load and the generated power. The system can be in an unstable condition under a disturbance, increase of demanded load and changes in the topology of the network, causing an incontrollable voltage decrement (Kundur, 1994). The unstable condition can be originated for the operating limits of the power system components (Venkataramana, 2007), such as:
Generators: They represent the supply of reactive power enough to keep the power system in stable conditions by keeping the standardized voltage levels of normal operation. However, the generation of machines is limited by its capability curve that gives the constraints of the reactive power output due to the field winding current limitation.
Transmission lines: They are another important constraint to the voltage stability, and they also limit the maximum power that be transported and it is defined the thermal limits.
Loads: They represent the third elements that have influence on the stability voltage; they are classified in two categories: static and dynamic loads and they have an effect on the voltage profiles under excessive reactive power generation.

4.2 Voltage collapse

The voltage collapse is a phenomenon that might be present in a highly loaded electric power system. This can be present in the form of event sequence together with the voltage instability that may lead to a blackout or to voltage levels below the operating limits for a significant part of the power system (Kundur, 1994). Due to the nonlinear nature of the electrical network, as the phenomenon related to the power system, it is necessary to employ nonlinear techniques for the analysis of the voltage collapse (Venkataramana, 2007) and find out a solution to avoid it.

There many disturbances which contribute to the voltage collapse:

- Load increment.
- To reach the reactive power limits in generators, synchronous condensers or SVC.
- The operation of TAP changers in transformers.
- The tripping of transmission lines, transformers and generators.

Most of these changes have a significant effect in the production, consumption and transmission of reactive power. Because of this, it is suggested control actions by using compensator elements as capacitor banks, blocking of tap changers, new generation dispatch, secondary voltage regulation and load sectioning (Kundur, 1994).

4.3 Analysis methods for the voltage stability

Some of the tools used for the analysis of stability voltage are the methods based on dynamic analysis and those based in static analysis.

Dynamic Analysis. They consist in the numerical solution (simulation) of the set of differential and algebraic equations that model the power system (Kundur, 1994), this is similar as transients; however, this kind of simulations need considerable amount of computing resources and hence the solution time is large and they do not give information about the sensibility and stability degree.

Static analysis. They consist in the solution of the set of algebraic equations that represent the system in steady state (Kundur, 1994), with the aim of evaluating the feasibility of the equilibrium point represented by the operating conditions of the system and to find the critical voltage value. The advantage with respect to the dynamic analysis techniques is that it gives valuable information about the nature of the problem and helps to identify the key factors for the instability problem. The plotting of the PV curve helps to the analysis of the voltage stability limits of a power system under a scenario with load increments and with the presence of a disturbance such as the loss of generation or the loss of a transmission line.

4.4 PV curves

The PV curves represent the voltage variation with respect to the variation of load reactive power. This curve is produced by a series of load flow solutions for different load levels uniformly distributed, by keeping constant the power factor. The generated active power is proportionally incremented to the generator rating or to the participating factors which are defined by the user. The P and Q components of each load can or cannot be dependant of the bus voltage accordingly to the load model selected. The determination of the critical point for a given load increment is very important because it can lead to the voltage collapse of the system. These characteristics are illustrated in figure 3.

Some authors (Yamura et al, 1998 & Ogrady et al, 1999) have proposed voltage stability indexes which are based in some kind of analysis of load flows with the aim to evaluate the stability voltage limits. However, the Jacobian used in the load flows, when the Newton-Raphson is employed, becomes singular at the critical point, besides the load flow solutions at the points near to the critical region tend to diverge (Kundur, 1994). These disadvantages are avoided by using the method of continuation load flows (Venkataramana et al, 1992).

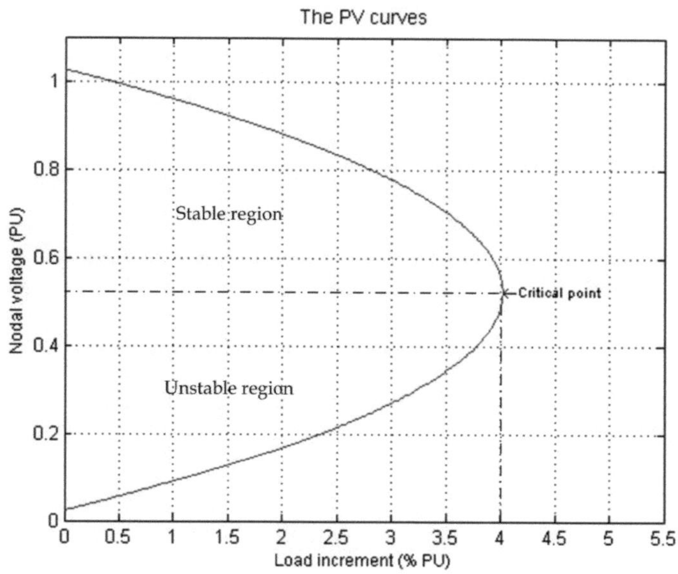

Fig. 3. PV curve

4.5 Application of the continuation method to the power flow problem

The continuous load flow procedure is based in a reformulation of the equations of the load flow problem and the application of the continuation technique with a local parameterization which has shown to be efficient in the trajectory plotting of PV curves.
The purpose of continuous load flows is to find a set of load flow solutions in a scenario where the load is continuously changing, starting from a base case until the critical point. Thereafter, the continuous load flows had been applied to understand and evaluate the problem of voltage stability and those areas that are likely to the voltage collapse. Besides, they have also been applied in other related problems like the evaluation of power transfer limits between regions.
The general principle of continuous load flows employs a predictor-corrector scheme to find a trajectory of solutions for the set of load flow equations (4) and (5) which are reformulated to include the load parameter λ.

$$\Delta P_i = \lambda\left(P_{Gi} - P_{Li}\right) - P_i = \lambda P_i^{esp} - P_i = 0 \tag{35}$$

$$\Delta Q_i = \lambda\left(Q_{Gi} - Q_{Li}\right) - Q_i = \lambda Q_i^{esp} - Q_i = 0 \tag{36}$$

$$1 \le \lambda \le \lambda_{critic} \tag{37}$$

The process is started from a known solution and a predictor vector which is tangent to the corrected solutions is used to estimate the future solutions with different values of the load parameter. The estimation is corrected using the same technique of the Newton-Rhapson employed in the conventional load flow with a new added parameter:

$$\mathbf{f}(\boldsymbol{\theta},\mathbf{V},\lambda)=\mathbf{0} \tag{38}$$

The parameterization plays an important role in the elimination of the Jacobian non-singularity.

4.5.1 Prediction of the new solution

Once the base solution has been found for λ=0, it is required to predict the next solution taking into consideration the appropriate step size and the direction of the tangent to the trajectory solution. The first task in this process consists in calculating the tangent vector, which is determined taking the first derivative of the reformulated flow equations (38).

$$d\mathbf{f}(\boldsymbol{\theta},\mathbf{V},\lambda)=\mathbf{f}_{\theta}d\boldsymbol{\theta}+\mathbf{f}_{V}d\mathbf{V}+\mathbf{f}_{\lambda}d\lambda=0 \tag{39}$$

where **F** is the vector [**ΔP**, **ΔQ**, 0] that is augmented in one row; in a factorized form, the equation is expressed as,

$$\begin{bmatrix}\mathbf{f}_{\theta} & \mathbf{f}_{F} & \mathbf{f}_{\lambda}\end{bmatrix}\begin{bmatrix} d\boldsymbol{\theta} \\ d\mathbf{V} \\ d\lambda \end{bmatrix}=0 \tag{40}$$

The left hand side of the equation is a matrix of partial derivatives that multiplies the tangent vector form with differential elements. The matrix of partial derivatives is known as the Jacobian of the conventional load flow problem that is augmented by the column $\mathbf{F}_{\lambda}$, which can be obtained by taking the partial derivatives with respect to λ (35) and (36), which gives:

$$\begin{bmatrix}\Delta P \\ \Delta Q\end{bmatrix}=\begin{bmatrix}\mathbf{H} & \mathbf{N} & -\mathbf{P}^{esp} \\ \mathbf{J} & \mathbf{L} & -\mathbf{Q}^{esp}\end{bmatrix}\begin{bmatrix} d\boldsymbol{\theta} \\ \dfrac{d\mathbf{V}}{\mathbf{V}} \\ d\lambda \end{bmatrix} \tag{41}$$

Due to the nature of (41) which is a set of $nc+n$-1 equations with $nc+n$ unknowns and by adding λ to the load flow equations, it is not possible to find a unique and nontrivial solution of the tangent vector; consequently an additional equation is needed.

This problem is solved by selecting a magnitude different from zero for one of the components of the tangent vector. In other words, if the tangent vector is denoted by:

$$\mathbf{t}=\begin{bmatrix} d\boldsymbol{\theta} \\ d\mathbf{V} \\ d\lambda \end{bmatrix}=0,\quad t_k=\pm 1 \tag{42}$$

which leads to:

$$\begin{bmatrix} \mathbf{H} & \mathbf{N} & -\mathbf{P}^{esp} \\ \mathbf{J} & \mathbf{L} & -\mathbf{Q}^{esp} \\ & \mathbf{e}_k & \end{bmatrix} \cdot \mathbf{t} = \begin{bmatrix} \mathbf{0} \\ \pm 1 \end{bmatrix} \tag{43}$$

where $\mathbf{e}_k$ is a vector of dimension m+1 with all elements equal to zero but the *k*-th one, which is equal to 1. If the index *k* is correctly selected, $t_k = \pm 1$ impose a none zero norm to the tangent vector and it guarantees that the augmented Jacobian will be nonsingular at the critical point (Eheinboldt et al, 1986). The usage of +1 or -1 depends on how the *k*-th state variable is changing during the trajectory solution which is being plotted. In a next section of this chapter, a method to select *k* will be presented. Once the tangent vector has found the solution of (43), the prediction is carried out as follows:

$$\begin{bmatrix} \boldsymbol{\theta}^* \\ \mathbf{V}^* \\ \lambda^* \end{bmatrix} = \begin{bmatrix} \boldsymbol{\theta} \\ \mathbf{V} \\ \lambda \end{bmatrix} + \sigma \begin{bmatrix} d\boldsymbol{\theta} \\ d\mathbf{V} \\ d\lambda \end{bmatrix} \tag{44}$$

where "*" denotes the prediction for a future value of λ (the load parameter) and σ is a scalar that defines the step size. One inconvenient in the control of the step size consists in its dependence of the normalized tangent vector (Alves et al, 2000),

$$\sigma = \frac{\sigma_0}{\|\mathbf{t}\|} \tag{45}$$

where $|t_k|$ is the Euclidian norm of the tangent vector and σ_0 is a predefined scalar. The process efficiency depends on making a good selection of σ_0, which its value is system dependant.

4.5.2 Parameterization and corrector

After the prediction has been made, it is necessary to correct the approximate solution. Every continuation technique has a particular parameterization that gives a way to identify the solution along the plotting trajectory. The scheme here presented is referred as a local parameterization. In this scheme, the original set of equations is augmented with one extra equation, which has a meaning of specifying the value of a single state variable. In the case of the reformulated equations, this has a meaning of giving a unity magnitude to each nodal voltage, the phase angle of the nodal voltage or the load parameter λ. The new set of equations involves the new definition of state variables as:

$$\mathbf{x} = \begin{bmatrix} \boldsymbol{\theta} \\ \mathbf{V} \\ \lambda \end{bmatrix} \tag{46}$$

where,

$$x_k = \eta \tag{47}$$

where $x_k \varepsilon \mathbf{x}$ and η represent the appropriate k-th element of **x**. Therefore, the new set of equations that substitute (38) is given by,

$$\begin{bmatrix} \mathbf{F(x)} \\ x_k - \eta \end{bmatrix} = 0 \tag{48}$$

After an appropriate index k has been selected and its corresponding value of η, the load flow is solved with the slightly modified Newton Raphson method (48). In other words, the k index used in the corrector is the same as that used in the predictor and η is equal to the obtained x_k from the corrector (44), thus the variable x_k is the continuation parameter.
The application of the Newton-Raphson to (38) results in,

$$\begin{bmatrix} H & N & -\mathbf{P}^{esp} \\ M & L & -\mathbf{Q}^{esp} \\ & \mathbf{e}_k & \end{bmatrix} \begin{bmatrix} \Delta\boldsymbol{\theta} \\ \Delta\mathbf{V} \\ \Delta\lambda \end{bmatrix} = \begin{bmatrix} \Delta\mathbf{P} \\ \Delta\mathbf{Q} \\ 0 \end{bmatrix} \tag{49}$$

where $\mathbf{e}_k$ is the same vector used in (43), and the elements $\Delta\mathbf{P}$ and $\Delta\mathbf{Q}$ are calculated from (35) and (36). Once the x_k is specified in (48), the values of the other variables are dependant on it and they are solved by the iterative application of (49).

4.5.3 Selection of the continuation parameter

The most appropriate selection corresponds to that state variable with the component of the tangent vector with the largest rate of change relative to the given solution. Typically, the load parameter is the best starting selection, i.e. λ=1. This is true if the starting base case is characterized for a light or normal load; in such conditions, the magnitudes of the nodal voltages and angles keep almost constants with load changes. On the other hand, when the load parameter has been increased for a given number of continuation steps, the solution trajectory is approximated to the critical point, and the voltage magnitudes and angles probably will have more significant changes. At this point, λ has had a poor selection as compared with other state variables. Then, once the first step selection has been made, the following verification must be made:

$$x_k \leftarrow \max\left\{ \frac{t_1}{x_1} \quad \frac{t_2}{x_2} \quad \cdots \quad \frac{t_{m-1}}{xm-1} \quad \frac{t_m}{x_m} \right\} \tag{50}$$

where m is equal to the state variables; including the load parameter and k corresponding to the maximum t/x component. When the continuation parameter is selected, the sign of the corresponding component of the tangent vector must be taken into account to assign +1 or -1 to t_k in (42) for the subsequent calculation of the tangent vector.

5. MATLAB resources for electrical networks

The reason why MATLAB is frequently chosen for the development of academic or research tools is because its huge amount of mathematical operations as those related to vectors and matrixes. In addition, it also has several specialized libraries (toolboxes) for more specific areas as control, optimization, symbolic mathematics, etc. In the area of power systems, it is possible to point it out several advantages considered as key points for the development of a script program, which are discussed below.

5.1 Sparse matrix manipulation

The electrical networks are studied using nodal analysis, as it was presented in section 3.1. In this frame of reference, the network matrixes as Ybus or Jacobian (1) and (21) have a sparse structure, considering that a node in an electrical network is connected to about 2.4 nodes in average. To illustrate this issue, if we consider the creation of a squared matrix with order 20, i.e. the matrix has 200 elements which 256 are zeros and the remaining are different from zero that are denoted as nz, as it is shown in figure 4. The sparsity pattern is displayed by using the MATLAB function *spy*.

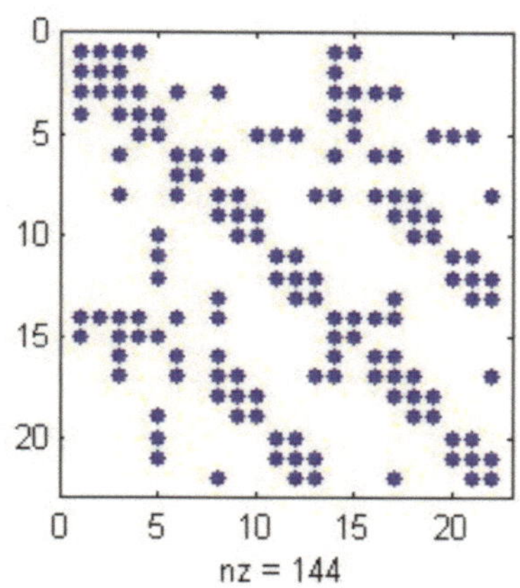

Fig. 4. An example of a sparse matrix.

The operation on this type of matrices with conventional computational methods leads to obtain prohibited calculation times (Gracia et al, 2005). Due to this reason, there have been adopted special techniques for deal with this type of matrixes to avoid the unnecessary usage of memory and to execute the calculation processes on the nonzero elements. It is important to point it out that this kind of matrixes is more related to a computation technique than to a mathematic concept.

MATLAB offers mechanisms and methods to create, manipulate and operate on this kind of matrixes. The sparse matrixes are created with the sparse function, which requires the specification of 5 arguments in the following order: 3 arrays to specify the position *i*, the position *j* - row and column- and the element values x that correspond to each position (i,j), and the two integer variables to determine the dimensions *mxn* of the matrix, for example:

```
>> A = sparse(i, j, x, m, n)
```

In MATLAB language, the indexing of full matrixes is equal to the sparse matrixes. This mechanism consists in pointing to a set of matrix elements through the use of two arrays that makes reference to each row and column of the matrix, e.g. **B** = **A[I, J]** or by simply pointing to each element o elements of the matrix to be modified, e.g. A[**I**, **J**] = **X.**

where **A** is a *mxn* spare matrix, I and J are the arrays that point to the rows and columns and **X** is the array that contains each element corresponding to each ordered pair (I_k, J_k). All mentioned arrays are composed for a number of *k* elements, such as $k < n$ and $k < m$.

MATLAB has a function called spdiags that is intended for the direct operation on any diagonal of the matrix, e.g. to make uniform changes on the elements of the diagonal "d" of matrix A:

>> A = spdiags(B, d, A)

A mechanism frequently used to form matrixes from other defined ones is called the *concatenation*. Even more, to form sparse matrixes by using other arrays of the same type but with specified dimensions in such a way that there is a consistency to gather into a single one, i.e. the concatenating is horizontal, the matrix rows must be equal to those of B matrix, e.g. C = [A B]. On the other hand, if the concatenating is vertical, then the columns of both matrices must be equal, e.g. C = [A; B].

5.2 The LU factorization for solving a set of equations

In electrical network applications, to find a solution of the algebraic system $\mathbf{Ax} = \mathbf{b}$ in an efficient way, one option is to use the triangular decomposition as the LU factorization technique.

The triangular factorization LU consists in decomposing a matrix (A) such that it can be represented as the product of two matrixes, one of them is a lower triangular (L) while the other is an upper triangular (U), $\mathbf{A} = \mathbf{L} \cdot \mathbf{U}$. This representation is commonly named explicit factorization LU; even though it is very related to the Gaussian elimination, the elements of L and U are directly calculated from the **A** elements, the principal advantage with respect to the Gaussian elimination (Gill et al., 1991) consists in obtaining the solution of an algebraic system for any **b** vector, if and only if the "**A**" matrix is not modified.

5.3 Sparse matrix ordering using AMD

The Approximate minimum degree permutation (AMD) is a set of subroutines for row and column permutation of a sparse matrix before executing the Cholesky factorization or for the LU factorization with a diagonal pivoting (Tim, 2004). The employment of this subroutine is made by using the function "amd" to the matrix to be permuted, e.g. P = amd(**A**).

5.4 Sparse matrix operations

Care must be taken with a several rules in MATLAB when operations are carried out that include full and sparse matrixes, for example, the operation eye(22) + speye(22) gives a full matrix.

5.5 Vector operations

An approach to develop the script programs in MATLAB to be executed faster consists in coding the algorithms with the use of vectors within the programs and avoiding the use of loops such as *for, while and do-while.* The vector operations are made by writing the symbol "." before the operation to be made, e.g. .+, .-, .*, ./. This discussion is illustrated by comparing two MATLAB script programs to solve the following operation:

$$\begin{bmatrix} C_1 \\ C_2 \\ \vdots \\ C_n \end{bmatrix} = \begin{bmatrix} A_1 \cdot B_1 \\ A_1 \cdot B_2 \\ \vdots \\ A_n \cdot B_n \end{bmatrix}$$

Script program with the loop command	Script program with vector operations.
for k = 1:1000 C(k,1) = k*k; end	A = 1:1000; B = 1:1000; C = A.*B;
Execution time: 0.002086 s	*Execution time*: 0.000045 s

It is evident that the use of the *for-loop* command to carry out the described operation gives a larger computation time than by using the vector operation **A.*B**.

6. MATLAB application for plotting the PV curves

The program for plotting the PV curves is integrated with four specific tasks:

- Reading of input data
- Generation of the flow base case
- Calculation of points for the PV curves at each node.
- Graphical interface for editing the display of PV curves.

Afterwards, the complete application code is listed. In case the code is copied and pasted into a new m-file, this will have the complete application, i.e. there is no necessity to add new code lines.

```
function main()
%% **************   READING OF INPUT DATA   **************

% -> The filename and its path are obtained:
  [file, trayectoria] = uigetfile( ...
    { '*.cdf;','Type file (*.cdf)'; '*.cf', ...
    'IEEE Common Format (*.cf)'}, 'Select any load flow file');

  if file == 0 & trayectoria == 0
    return;
  end
  archivo = [trayectoria file];

% -> the code lines are stored in the following variable:
  DATA = textread(archivo,'%s','delimiter','\n','whitespace','');

% -> Reading of nodal data:
  X_b = DATA{1};
  Sbase = str2double(X_b(32:37)); % Base power (MVA): Sbase

  X_b = DATA{2};
  N_Bus = findstr(X_b,'ITEMS');
  N_Bus = str2double(fliplr(strtok(fliplr(X_b(1:N_Bus-1)))));
  Nnod  = N_Bus; % Total number of buses
  N_Bus = 2+N_Bus;
  DN    = strvcat(DATA{3:N_Bus});
```

```
  No_B = str2num(DN(:,1:4));      % Number of buses: No_B
  Tipo = str2num(DN(:,25:26));    % Bus type: Tipo

  Nslack = find(Tipo == 3);   % Slack bus
  NumNG  = find(Tipo >= 2);   % Index of PV nodes
  NumNC  = find(Tipo == 0);   % Index of PQ nodes
  NumCG  = find(Tipo <= 2);   % Index of all nodes except slack

  Vabs = str2num(DN(:,28:33));    % Magnitude of nodal voltages.
  Tetan = str2num(DN(:,34:40));   % Phase angle of nodal voltages (degrees)
  Tetan = Tetan*pi/180;           % Degrees to radians conversion

  Pload = str2num(DN(:,41:49));   % Demanded active power (MW)
  Qload = str2num(DN(:,50:59));   % Demanded reactive power (MVAr)

  Pgen = str2num(DN(:,60:67));    % Generated active power (MW)
  Qgen = str2num(DN(:,68:75));    % Generated reactive power (MVAr)
  Pgen = Pgen(NumNG);     % PV nodes are selected
  Qgen = Qgen(NumNG);     %PV nodes are selected
  Gc   = str2num(DN(:,107:114)); % Compensator conductance
  Bc   = str2num(DN(:,115:122)); % Compensator susceptance
  NumND = find(Bc~=0);    % Indexes of all compensating nodes.
  Bcomp = Bc(NumND);      % Susceptance of all compensating nodes  NumND

% -> Branch data is read:
  X_b = DATA{N_Bus+2};
  N_Bra = findstr(X_b,'ITEMS');
  N_Bra = str2double(fliplr(strtok(fliplr(X_b(1:N_Bra-1)))));
  N_Bra1 = N_Bus+3;
  N_Bra2 = N_Bus+N_Bra+2;
  XLN = strvcat(DATA{N_Bra1:N_Bra2});

  X_b    = str2num(XLN(:,19));
  NramL  = find(X_b == 0);   % Indexes of transmission lines (LT)
  NramT  = find(X_b >= 1);   % Indexes of transformers (Trafos)
  PLi    = str2num(XLN(NramL,1:4));  % Initial bus for the transmission lines
  QLi    = str2num(XLN(NramL,6:9));  % Final bus for the transmission lines
  PTr    = str2num(XLN(NramT,1:4));  % Initial bus for the transformers
  QTr    = str2num(XLN(NramT,6:9));  % Final bus for the transformers

  RbrL =  str2num(XLN(NramL,20:29)); % Resistance of transmission lines (pu)
  XbrL =  str2num(XLN(NramL,30:40)); % Reactance of transmission lines (pu)
  Blin = str2num(XLN(NramL,41:50))/2; % Susceptance of transmission lines (pu)

  RbrX =  str2num(XLN(NramT,20:29)); % Resistance of transmission lines (pu)
  XbrX =  str2num(XLN(NramT,30:40)); % Reactance of transmission lines (pu)
```

```
  TAP  = str2num(XLN(NramT,77:82));  % TAP changers of transformers

% -> Admittance matrix:

  Ylin =1./(RbrL+1j*XbrL);       % Series admítanse of transmission lines
  Yxtr =(1./(RbrX+1j*XbrX))./TAP; % Series admítanse of transformers
%  Mutual admittances:
  Ynodo = sparse([ PLi;  PTr;  QLi;  QTr ],...
            [ QLi;  QTr;  PLi;  PTr ],...
            [-Ylin; -Yxtr; -Ylin; -Yxtr ], Nnod, Nnod);

 % Self admittances:
  Ynodo = Ynodo + ...
  sparse([      PLi;       QLi;      PTr;      QTr;   NumND],...
      [      PLi;       QLi;      PTr;      QTr;   NumND],...
      [Ylin+1j*Blin; Ylin+1j*Blin; Yxtr./TAP; Yxtr.*TAP; 1j*Bcomp],...
       Nnod, Nnod);

%% ******************   CASE BASE GENERATION    ********************

  Tol_NR  = 1e-3;   % Tolerance error
  Max_Iter = 60;    % Maximum number of possible iterations.

% -> Initialization:
  Vabs(NumNC) = 1.0;  % Voltage magnitude of PQ nodes
  Tetan      = zeros(Nnod,1);   % Phase angles in all nodes

 % -> Calculation of specified powers:
 % Active power:
  PLg = Pload(NumNG);
  QLg = Qload(NumNG);
  Pesp(NumNG,1)  = (Pgen-PLg)/Sbase;     % for PV nodes
  Pesp(NumNC,1)  = (-Pload(NumNC))/Sbase; % for PQ nodes
% Reactive power:
  Qesp  = -Qload/Sbase;  % for PQ nodes

  Ndim = Nnod + length(NumNC) - 1;   % Jacobian dimension.
  iter = 0;  % Initialization of iteration counter.
  tic

  while iter <= Max_Iter  % Limit of the number of iterations
%  -> Calculation of net active and reactive powers injected to each node:
    [Pnodo Qnodo] = scmplx();

%  -> Calculation of  misadjustment of reactive and active powers:
```

```
    DelP  = Pesp(NumCG) - Pnodo(NumCG);
    DelQ  = Qesp(NumNC) - Qnodo(NumNC);
    Pmismatch = [DelP; DelQ];

%  -> Check the convergence method.
    if max(abs(Pmismatch)) < Tol_NR
       tsol = toc;
       fprintf( 'The case has converged: %d iterations \n', iter);
       fprintf( 'in: %f seg. \n', tsol);
       break;
    end

%  -> Jacobian calculation:
    JB = Jacob();

%  -> Solution of the set of equations:
    DeltaX = linear_solver(JB, Pmismatch);

%  -> Update of magnitudes and angles of nodal voltages:
    Vabs(NumNC)  = Vabs(NumNC).*(1 + DeltaX(Nnod:Ndim));
    Tetan(NumCG) = Tetan(NumCG) + DeltaX(1:Nnod-1);

    iter = iter + 1;
  end

%% ******  CALCULATION OF POINTS OF PV CURVES AT EACH NODE    ******

  Ndim = Nnod + length(NumNC); % Augmented Jacobian dimension.

  sigma0   = 0.3966;    % Predictor step.
  Vpredict  = [Vabs];    % Predicted voltage values.
  Vexact   = [Vabs];    % Corrected voltage values.
  Carga    = [0];       % Load increment.
  lambda   = 0;         % Initial value of lambda.
  b(Ndim,1) = 1;         % Column vector of equation (43).
  Ix = Ndim;            % Index that indicates the continuation parameter.

 % Flag to indicate state before the critical point:
  Superior  = true;

 % Counter used to calculate exactly the number of points alter the critical point:
  Inferior  = 0;

  while(Superior == true) || (Inferior > 0)
%  -> After the critical point has been reached, only more 14 points are obtained.
    if (Superior == false) Inferior = Inferior - 1; end
```

```
% -> Calculation of the augmented Jacobian as in equation (43):
    JB = Jacob();
    JB(Ndim,Ix) = 1;
    JB(1:Ndim-1,Ndim) = [-Pesp(NumCG); -Qesp(NumNC)];

% -> Calculation of the tangent vector as in equation (43)
    t = linear_solver(JB, b);

% -> The critical point has been reached:
    if b(end) < 0
      if Superior == true;
        sigma0  = 0.25;  % Decrement of the predictor step
        Inferior = 14;   % Calculation of additional 14 points.
        Superior = false;

        Carga(end-1:end)      = [];
        Vpredict(:, end-1:end) = [];
        Vexact(:, end)        = [];
      end
    end

% -> Selection of the continuation parameter:
    x = [Tetan(NumCG); Vabs(NumNC); lambda];
    [xk Ix] = max(abs(t)./x);  % As in equation (50)

% -> Calculation of the predictor step as in equation (45):
    sigma = sigma0/norm(t);

% -> Calculation of predictor:
    Vabs(NumNC)  = Vabs(NumNC).*(1 + t(Nnod:Ndim-1)*sigma);
    Tetan(NumCG) = Tetan(NumCG) + t(1:Nnod-1)*sigma;
    lambda = lambda + sigma*t(end);

    Vpredict = [Vpredict Vabs]; % Calculated values with the predictor
    Carga  = [Carga lambda];   % Load increment

% -> Calculation with the corrector:
    iter = 0;
    while iter <= Max_Iter

      [Pnodo Qnodo] = scmplx();  % Computation of the complex power
%     -> Calculation of misadjustment  in active and reactive powers as in:
      DelP = Pesp(NumCG)*(1 + lambda) - Pnodo(NumCG); % Equation (35)
      DelQ = Qesp(NumNC)*(1 + lambda) - Qnodo(NumNC); % Equation (36)
      Pmismatch = [DelP; DelQ; 0];
```

```
        if max(abs(Pmismatch)) < Tol_NR    % Convergence criterion
           break;
        end
%      -> Calculation of the augmented Jacobian.
        JB = Jacob();
        JB(1:Ndim-1,Ndim) = [-Pesp(NumCG); -Qesp(NumNC)];
        JB(Ndim,Ix) = 1;

%      -> Calculation of the set of equations as in (49).
        DeltaX = linear_solver(JB, Pmismatch);

%      -> Checking if the critical point has been found.
        if DeltaX(end) < 0 && Superior == true
           b(Ndim,1) = -1;
           break;
        end

%      -> Update state variables in the corrector:
        Vabs(NumNC)  = Vabs(NumNC).*(1 + DeltaX(Nnod:Ndim-1));
        Tetan(NumCG) = Tetan(NumCG) + DeltaX(1:Nnod-1);
        lambda       = lambda + DeltaX(end);

        iter = iter + 1;
     end

     Vexact   = [Vexact Vabs];
     Vpredict = [Vpredict Vabs];
     Carga    = [Carga lambda];

  end

%% **   GRAPHICAL INTERFACE FOR DISPLAYING THE PV CURVES   **
  PV_PRINT( Carga, Vpredict, Vexact );

%% ***********************   Nested functions   ***********************
  function [P Q] = scmplx()

     Vfasor = Vabs.*exp(1j*Tetan);       % Complex form of nodal voltage using Euler.
     Scal =  Vfasor.*conj(Ynodo*Vfasor);   % Calculation of complex power as in (8).
     P = real(Scal); % Net active power injected to each node as in (9).
     Q = imag(Scal); % Net reactive power injected to each node as in (10).

end

  function Jac = Jacob()
```

```
    Jac = sparse(Ndim, Ndim);

    Vdiag = sparse(1:Nnod, 1:Nnod, Vabs.*exp(1j*Tetan));
    J2  = Vdiag*conj(Ynodo*Vdiag);   % Computation of equation (34)
    P = sparse(1:Nnod, 1:Nnod, Pnodo);
    Q = sparse(1:Nnod, 1:Nnod, Qnodo);

    H = ( imag(J2(NumCG, NumCG)) - Q(NumCG, NumCG));   % Equations  (26) and (30)
    N = ( real(J2(NumCG, NumNC)) + P(NumCG, NumNC));   % Equations (27) and (31)
    J = (-real(J2(NumNC, NumCG)) + P(NumNC, NumCG));   % Equations (28) and (32)
    L = ( imag(J2(NumNC, NumNC)) + Q(NumNC, NumNC));   % Equations (29) and (33)

    Jac = horzcat( vertcat(H, J), vertcat(N, L) );  % Submatrix concatenation as indicated in
(25)

  end

  function x = linear_solver(A, b)

    P = amd(A);            % Ordering of matrix A (Jacobian).
    [L, U]  = lu(A(P, P));  % Application of LU factorization.
  % The set of equations (b=A*x) are solved using the LU factorization:
    y     = L\b(P);
    x(P, 1) = U\y;

  end

end
```

As it was shown above, the four specific tasks of this application are integrated around the principal function: main(), which function is the sequential integration of these tasks. Even though the first three tasks are described in a set of continuous code lines, each task represents one independent process from each other; hence it is possible to separate them as external functions, such as the function PV_PRINT, which executes the four tasks. Additionally, it can be seen that the calculation tasks, flow case base and the points of PV curves use nested functions within the main function that are common to both tasks. The following nested functions are:

Scmplx: This function computes the net complex power injected to each node of the system and it returns its real and imaginary components.

Jacob: This function computes the Jacobian of the conventional load flow problem.

Linear_solver: This function solves the set of linear equations $\mathbf{A} \cdot \mathbf{x} = \mathbf{b}$ by using the LU factorization with previous reordering of **A** matrix.

6.1 Reading of input data

A program based on the solution of load flows requires of some input data that describes the network to be analyzed. The information can be included in a text file with a standardized format with the extension cdf (Common Data Format) (University of Washington electrical engineering, 1999). The reading of the complete information is achieved by using the MATLAB function textread. The reading includes the use of a standard uicontrol of MATLAB to locate the file path. This information is stored in a data matrix of string type, and it can be interpreted by using functions that operate on the variables of string type. There is basic information that is used in the developed program; the variables can be divided into two categories:

Nodal information:

Sbase : Base power of the system.

Nnod : Number of system nodes.

No_B : *n*x1 vector with the numbering of each system bus.

Name_B : *n*x1 vector with the name of each bus system.

Tipo : *n*x1 vector with the node type of the system.

Nslack : The number of the slack node.

Vn : *n*x1 vector with voltage magnitudes at each system node.

Vbase : *n*x1 vector with base values of voltages at each system bus.

Tetan : *n*x1 vector with phase angles at each nodal voltage.

PLoad and **QLoad** : *n*x1 vector with the active and reactive load powers, respectively.

Pgen and **Qgen** : *(n-nc)*x1 vector with the active and reactive power of generators, respectively.

Gc and **Bc** : *n*x1 vector with conductance and susceptance of each compensating element, respectively.

Branch information (transmission lines and transformers), where *l* denotes the total number of transmission lines and *t* is the number of transformers in the electrical network:

PLi and **PTr** : Vectors with dimensions *l*x1 y *t*x1, that indicate one side of transmission lines and transformers connected to the P node, respectively.

QLr and **QTr** : They are similar as PL and PT with the difference that indicates the opposite side of the connected branch to the Q node.

RbrL and **RbrX** : They are similar as the above two variables with the difference that indicate the resistance of each transmission line and transformer.

XbrL and **XbrX** : They are similar as the above with the difference that indicate the reactance of each transmission line and transformer.

Blin : *l*x1 vector with the half susceptance of a transmission line.

TAP : *t*x1 vector with the current position of the TAP changer of the transformer.

After reading the input data, the admittance matrix **Ynode**, and a series of useful pointers are created to extract particular data from the nodal and branch data:

- **NumNG**: An array that points to the PV nodes.
- **NumNC**: An array that points to the PQ nodes.
- **NumCG**: An array that points to all nodes but the slack node.

Tol_NR – the maximum deviations in power are lower to this value in case of convergence - and Max_Iter –is the maximum number of iterations – these variables are used to control the convergence and a value is assigned to them by default after reading of input data.

The program does not consider the checking of limits of reactive power in generator nodes neither the effect of the automatic tap changer in transformers, nor the inter-area power transfer, etc. Therefore the input data related to these controllers is not used in the program.

6.2 Graphical interface for editing the display of PV curves

In the last part of the program, a graphical user interface (GUI) is generated for the plotting of PV curves from the points previously calculated in the continuous load flows program. Even though the main objective of this interface is oriented to the plotting of PV curves, its design allows the illustration continuation method process, i.e. it has the option of displaying the calculated points with the predictor, corrector or both of them, for example, it can be seen in figure 5 the set of points obtained with the predictor-corrector for the nodes 10,12,13, and 14 of the 14-node IEEE test power system. This is possible by integrating the MATLAB controls called uicontrol's into the GUI design, the resultant GUI makes more intuitive and flexible its use.

The numbers 1-12, that are indicated in red color in figure 5, make reference to each uicontrol or graphical object that integrates the GUI. The graphical objects with its uicontrol number, its handle and its description are given in table 1.

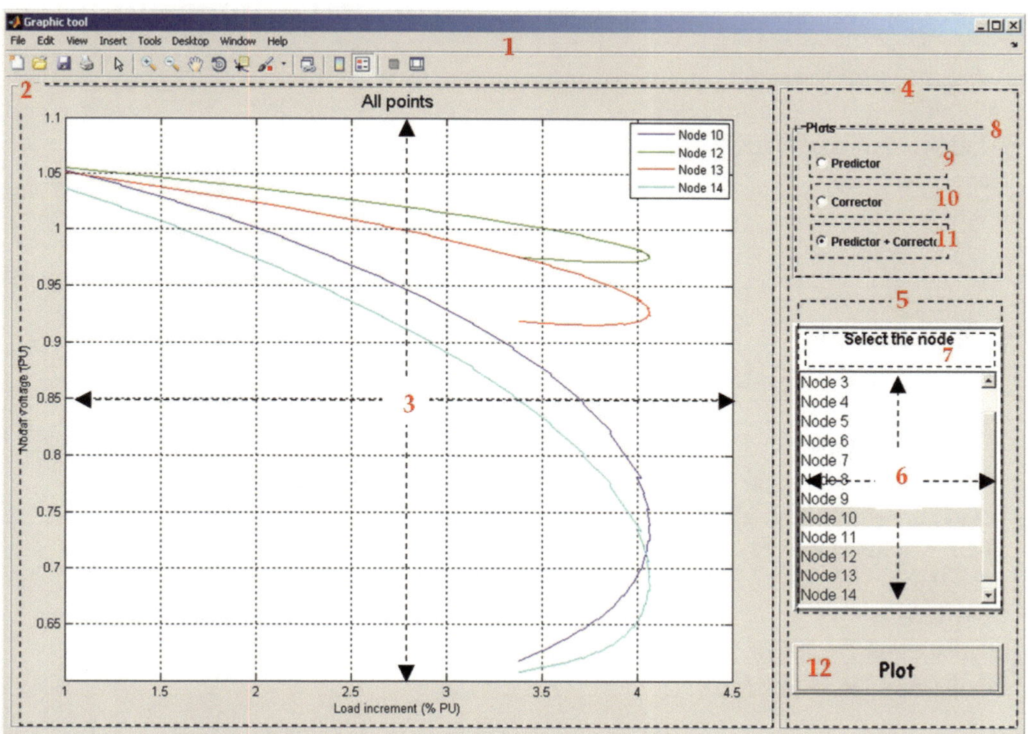

Fig. 5. GUI for plotting the PV curves for any node.

Uicontrol number	handle	Description
1	hPV	Graphical object known as figure
2	hPanel_print	Panel located to the left of hPV
3	hAxes_Curve	Object for 2D graphs known as axes
4	hPanel_control	Panel located to the right of hPV
5	hPanel	Panel located in the upper part of hPanel_control
6	hlb_log	Graphical object known as listbox
7	hlb_txt	Graphical object known as textbox
8	hChoice_PV	Set of objects known as radio buttons
9	opt0	Graphical objects known as radiobutton
10	opt1	Graphical objects known as radiobutton
11	opt2	Graphical objects known as radiobutton
12	- without handle-	Graphical objects known as pushbutton

Table 1. Description of each graphical object used in the GUI shown in figure 5.

The complete code of the function that generates the GUI is presented below, where the code lines for creating each graphical object mentioned in table 1 are fully described.

```
function PV_PRINT(lambda, predictor, corrector )

   [Nodos columnas] = size(predictor);
   clear columnas;
   etiqueta = {};

% Variable for registering the elements of listbox that relates the system nodes, which can
have plotted its PV curve
   for ii = 1:Nodos
      etiqueta{ii, 1} = ['Node ' num2str(ii)];
   end

 % Variables for configuring the graphical object, color and screen size.
   BckgrClr = get(0, 'defaultUicontrolbackgroundColor');
   Sc_Sz = get(0, 'ScreenSize');
   wF = 0.85;
   hF = 0.85;
   wF_Pix = wF*Sc_Sz(3);
   hF_Pix = hF*Sc_Sz(4);

 % Creation of the object type figure: main window.
   hPV = figure(...
        'Name', 'Graphic tool', ...
        'units', 'normalized', 'Color', BckgrClr,...
```

```
        'MenuBar', 'figure', 'numbertitle', 'off',...
        'visible', 'on', 'Position', [0.05 0.05 wF hF]);
    delete(gca);

% Generation of the left panel included in hPV.
    hPanel_print = uipanel('Parent', hPV, ...
        'Units', 'normalized', 'BackgroundColor', BckgrClr, ...
        'BorderType', 'etchedout', 'BorderWidth', 1,...
        'visible', 'on', 'Position', [0.005 0.01 0.75 0.98]);

% Declaration of axes object where the curves are to be plotted and it is located in hPanel_Print.
    hAxes_Curve = axes('Parent', hPanel_print, ...
        'units', 'normalized', 'Position',[0.07 0.07 0.88 0.88], ...
        'Box', 'on', 'Tag', 'hAxes_Curve', 'Visible', 'off');

% Generation of the right panel in hPV.
    hPanel_control = uipanel('Parent',hPV, ...
        'Units', 'normalized', 'BackgroundColor', BckgrClr, ...
        'BorderType', 'etchedout', 'BorderWidth', 1,...
        'visible', 'on', 'Position', [0.76 0.01 0.235 0.98]);

% Declaration of a panel inside the hPanel_control  and it contains the listbox and textbox.
    hPanel = uipanel('Parent', hPanel_control, ...
        'Units', 'normalized', 'BackgroundColor', BckgrClr, ...
        'BorderType', 'etchedout', 'BorderWidth', 3,...
        'visible', 'on', 'Position', [0.05 0.18 0.9 0.45]);

% Listbox located in hPanel and it is used for selecting the node or desired nodes for
displaying its curves.
    hlb_log = uicontrol('Parent', hPanel, ...
        'Units', 'normalized', 'BackgroundColor', [1 1 1], ...
        'FontName', 'Lucida Console', 'HorizontalAlignment', 'left',...
        'Tag', 'hlb_log', 'Position', [0 0 1 0.85], 'fontsize', 12,...
        'Enable', 'on', 'Style', 'listbox', 'String', etiqueta, ...
        'Max', Nodos, 'Min', 0, 'Clipping', 'off', 'Visible', 'on');

% Textbox located in hPanel and it is used for displaying any string.
    hlb_txt = uicontrol('Parent', hPanel,...
        'Units', 'normalized', 'HorizontalAlignment', 'center',...
        'style', 'text', 'fontname', 'Comic Sans MS',...
        'BackgroundColor', 'w', 'string', 'Select the node',...
        'fontsize', 12, 'fontweight', 'bold', 'visible', 'on',...
        'Position', [0.0 0.85 1 0.15]);

% Uicontrol of type optionbutton, and it is located in hPanel_control.
   hChoice_PV = uibuttongroup('Parent', hPanel_control, ...
```

```
        'Units', 'normalized', 'Position', [0.05 0.7 0.9 0.25], ...
        'BackgroundColor', BckgrClr, 'FontName', 'Lucida Console', ...
        'FontSize', 10, 'FontWeight', 'bold', 'Tag','hChoice_PV',...
        'Title', 'Plots', 'visible', 'off');

 % Optionbutton located in hChoice_PV which is used for ploting the points obtained with
the corrector.
    opt0 = uicontrol('Parent', hChoice_PV, ...
        'Units', 'normalized', 'pos', [0.1 0.68 0.8 0.25], ...
        'BackgroundColor', BckgrClr, 'FontName', 'Lucida Console', ...
        'FontSize', 9, 'FontWeight', 'bold', 'Style', 'Radio',...
        'String', 'Predictor', 'HandleVisibility', 'off');

 % Optionbutton located in hChoice_PV and it is used for plotting the points calculated with
the corrector.
    opt1 = uicontrol('Parent', hChoice_PV, ...
        'Units', 'normalized', 'pos', [0.1 0.4 0.8 0.25], ...
        'BackgroundColor', BckgrClr, 'FontName', 'Lucida Console', ...
        'FontSize', 9, 'FontWeight', 'bold', 'Style', 'Radio',...
        'String', 'Corrector', 'HandleVisibility', 'off');
 % Optionbutton located in hChoice_PV  and it is used for plotting the points obtained with
the predictor + corrector.
    opt2 = uicontrol('Parent', hChoice_PV, ...
        'Units', 'normalized', 'pos', [0.1 0.125 0.8 0.25], ...
        'BackgroundColor', BckgrClr, 'FontName', 'Lucida Console', ...
        'FontSize', 9, 'FontWeight', 'bold', 'Style', 'Radio',...
        'String', 'Predictor + Corrector', 'HandleVisibility', 'off');

 % Configuration of the graphical object hChoice_PV.
    set(hChoice_PV, 'SelectionChangeFcn', @selcbk);
    set(hChoice_PV, 'SelectedObject', opt0);
    set(hChoice_PV, 'UserData', 0);
    set(hChoice_PV, 'Visible', 'on');

% Generation of the command button which calls the function that generates the selected
graphs for the set of optionbutton located in hChoice_PV.
    uicontrol('Parent', hPanel_control, ...
        'Units', 'normalized', 'style', 'pushbutton',...
        'FontName', 'Comic Sans MS', 'visible', 'on',...
        'fontsize', 9, ...
        'callback', {@RefreshAxes, hChoice_PV, hAxes_Curve, hlb_log, lambda, predictor,
corrector},...
        'FontWeight', 'bold', 'string', 'Plot', ...
        'Position',[0.05 0.05 0.9 0.08]);

end
```

```
function selcbk(source, eventdata)

   switch get(eventdata.NewValue, 'String')
      case 'Predictor'
         set(source, 'UserData', 0);
      case 'Corrector'
         set(source, 'UserData', 1);
      otherwise
         set(source, 'UserData', 2);

   end

end

function RefreshAxes(source, eventdata, hChoice_PV, hAxes_Curve, hlb_log, lambda,
predictor, corrector)

  Nodos = get(hlb_log, 'Value');      % It is obtained the node(s) whose PV curves will be
plotted
   switch get(hChoice_PV, 'UserData') % Option selection for the object uibuttongroup

      case 0  % The points obtained with the predictor are plotted for the selected nodes.
         plot(hAxes_Curve, 1 + [lambda(1), lambda(2:2:end)], [predictor(Nodos, 1),
predictor(Nodos, 2:2:end)]);
         title(hAxes_Curve, 'Plot the points of predictor', 'FontSize', 14);

      case 1  % The points obtained with the corrector are plotted for the selected nodes.
         plot(hAxes_Curve, 1 + lambda(1:2:end), corrector(Nodos,:));
         title(hAxes_Curve, 'Plot the points of corrector ', 'FontSize', 14);
      otherwise
     % The points stored in the variable predictor are plotted for the selected nodes.
         plot(hAxes_Curve, 1 + lambda, predictor(Nodos, :));
         title(hAxes_Curve, ' All points ', 'FontSize', 14);

   end

    if length(Nodos) > 1
    % If there are more than one node, they are labeled for marking the shown curves
      etiqN = get(hlb_log, 'String');
      legend(hAxes_Curve, etiqN{Nodos});
   end

% The grid are shown in the plot.
   grid(hAxes_Curve, 'on');

% Automatic numbering of axes (selection of maximum and minimum limits for x-y axes)
```

```
  axis(hAxes_Curve, 'auto');

% Labeling of X and Y axes.
  xlabel(hAxes_Curve, 'Load increment (% PU)', 'FontSize', 10);
  ylabel(hAxes_Curve, 'Nodal voltage (PU)', 'FontSize', 10);

% The object becomes visible with the handle hAxes_Curve.
  set(hAxes_Curve, 'Visible', 'on');

end
```

Since the function PV_PRINT is external to the function main, the created variables within main cannot be read directly for the function PV_PRINT, hence it is required to declare arguments as inputs for making reference to any variable in main. The main advantage of using external functions consists in the ability to call them in any application just by giving the required arguments for its correct performance. In order to reproduce this application, it is necessary to copy the code in an m-file which is different from the main.

7. Conclusion

An electrical engineering problem involves the solution of a series of formulations and mathematical algorithm definitions that describe the problem physics. The problems related to the control, operation and diagnostic of power systems as the steady-state security evaluation for the example the PV curves, are formulated in matrix form, which involves manipulation techniques and matrix operations; however the necessity of operating on matrixes with large dimensions takes us to look for computational tools for handling efficiently these large matrixes. The use of script programming which is oriented to scientific computing is currently widely used in the academic and research areas. By taking advantage of its mathematical features which are normally found in many science or engineering problems allows us solving any numerical problem. It can be adapted for the development of simulation programs and for illustrating the whole process in finding a solution to a defined problem, and thus makes easier to grasp the solution method, such as the conventional load flow problem solved with the Newton-Raphson method.
MATLAB has demonstrated to be a good tool for the numerical experimentation and for the study of engineering problems; it provides a set of functions that make simple and straightforward the programming. It also offers mechanisms that allow dealing with mathematic abstractions such as matrixes in such a way that is possible to develop prototype programs which are oriented to the solution methods by matrix computations. The development of scripts or tools can be considered to be a priority in the academic area such that they allow achieving a valid solution. It is also advisable to take advantage of the MATLAB resources such as: vector operations, functions and mechanisms for operating on each matrix element without using any flow control for the program, i.e. for loop; this offers the advantage of decreasing the number of code lines of the script program. These recommendations reduce the computation time and allow its easy usage and modification by any user. Finally, MATLAB offers powerful graphical tools which are extremely useful for displaying the output information and to aid interpreting the simulation results. In this chapter, the plotting of the corrector points (PV curve) has been presented for a given load

that can be considered as critical point or voltage collapse of the power system. The technique for continuous load flow has been applied to determine the PV curves of the 14-node IEEE test system, and it has been shown that a 4.062% load increment can lead to the instability of the system, and it also has been determined that the node 14 is the weaker node of the system.

8. References

Arrillaga, J. & Walsion,N. (2001). *Computer Modeling of electrical Power Systems (2th)*, Whyley, ISBN 0-471-87249-0.

D. A. Alves, L. C. P. Da Silva, C. A. Castro, V. F. da Costa, "Continuation Load Flor Method Parametrized by Transmissión Line Powers", Paper 0-7801-6338-8/00 IEEE 2000

Garcia, J., Rodriguez, J.& Vidal, J. (2005). Aprenda Matlab 7.0 como si estuviera en primero, Universidad Politécnica de Madrid, Retrieved from http://mat21.etsii.upm.es/ayudainf/aprendainf/Matlab70/ matlab70primero.pdf

Gill, P., Murray, W. & Wrigth M., (1991). *Nuemric linear Algebra and optimization vol 1* (ed), Addison-wesley, ISBN 0-201-12647-4, Redwood City, US

Graham, R., Chow, J., &, Vanfretti, L. (2009). Power System Toolbox, In: Power System Toolbox Webpage, 15.03.20011, Available from: http://www.ecse.rpi.edu/pst/

Kundur, P. (1994). Voltage Stability, *Power System stability and control*, pp. 959-1024, Mc Graw Hill, ISBN 0-07-035959-X, Palo Alto, California

Mahseredjian, J., & Alvarado, F. (1997). MatEMTP, In: Creating an electromagnetic transients program in MATLAB, Available: 15.013.2011, http://minds.wisconsin.edu/handle/1793/9012

M. G. Ogrady, M. A. Pai, "Analysis of Voltage Collapse in Power Systems", Proceedings of 21st Annual North American Power Symposium, Rolla, Missouiri, October 1999ric Manufacturers Association, Washington, D.C.

Milano, F. (2010). *Power system modelling and scripting (1th)*, Springer, ISBN 9-783-642-13669-6, London, ___

Milano, F. (2006). PSAT, In: Dr. Federico Milano Website, 15.03.2011, http://www.power.uwaterloo.ca/~fmilano/psat.htm

PowerWorld Corporation (2010). http://www.powerworld.com

Siemens, PTI. (2005). http://www.energy.siemens.com/us/en/services/powertransmission-distribution/power-technologies-international/softwaresolutions/pss-e.htm

Tim, D. (2004), Research and software development in sparse matrix algorithms, In: AMD, 12.03.2011, Available from http://www.cise.ufl.edu/research/sparse/amd/

Venkataramana, A. (2007). *Power Computational Techniques for Voltage Stability Assessment and Control (1th)*, Springer, ISBN 978-0-387-26080-8.

Venkataramana Ajjarapu, Colin Christy, "The Continuation Power flor: A Tool for Steady State Voltaje Stability Analysis", Transactions on Power Systems, Vol. 7, No. 1, Fabruary 1992

W. C. Eheinboldt, J. B. Burkhardt, "A Locally Parametrized Continuation Process", ACM Transactions on Mathematical Software, Vol. 9 No. 2, June 1986, pp. 215-235.

University of Washington electrical engineering. (1999). 14 Bus, In: Power Systems Test Case Archive, 25.01.2011, Available from http://www.ee.washington.edu/research/pstca/.

Y. Yamura, K. Sakamoto, Y. Tayama, "Voltaje Instability Proximity Index baesd on Multiple Load Flor Solutions in Ill-Conditioned Power Systems". Proceedings of the 27th IEEE Conference on Decision and Control, Austin, Texas, December 1988

Zimmerman, R., Murillo, C., & Gan, D. (2011). MATPOWER, In: A MATLAB Power System Simulation Package, 15.03.2011, Available from: http://www.pserc.cornell.edu/matpower/

12

Application of Modern Optimal Control in Power System: Damping Detrimental Sub-Synchronous Oscillations

Iman Mohammad Hoseiny Naveh and Javad Sadeh
Islamic Azad University, Gonabad Branch
Islamic Republic of Iran

1. Introduction

The occurrence of several incidents in different countries during the seventies and the eighties promoted investigations into the cause of turbine-generator torsional excitation and the effect of the stimulated oscillations on the machine shaft. The best known incidents are the two shaft failures that occurred in the Mohave station in Nevada in 1970 and 1971, which were caused by sub-synchronous resonance (SSR) (Walker et al., 1975; Hall et al., 1976). A major concern associated with fixed series capacitor is the SSR phenomenon which arises as a result of the interaction between the compensated transmission line and turbine-generator shaft. This results in excessively high oscillatory torque on machine shaft causing their fatigue and damage. These failures were caused by sub-synchronous oscillations due to the SSR between the turbine-generator (T-G) shaft system and the series compensated transmission network. These incidents and others captured the attention of the industry at large and stimulated greater interest in the interaction between power plants and electric systems (IEEE committee report, 1992; IEEE Torsional Issues Working Group, 1997; Anderson et al., 1990; Begamudre, 1997).

Torsional interaction involves energy interchange between the turbine-generator and the electric network. Therefore, the analysis of SSR requires the representation of both the electromechanical dynamics of the generating unit and the electromagnetic dynamics of the transmission network. As a result, the dynamic system model used for SSR studies is of a higher order and greater stiffness than the models used for stability studies. Eigenvalue analysis is used in this research. Eigenvalue analysis is performed with the network and the generator modelled by a system of linear simultaneous differential equations. The differential and algebraic equations which describe the dynamic performance of the synchronous machine and the transmission network are, in general, nonlinear. For the purpose of stability analysis, these equations may be linearized by assuming that a disturbance is considered to be small. Small-signal analysis using linear techniques provides valuable information about the inherent dynamic characteristics of the power system and assists in its design (Cross et al., 1982; Parniani & Iravani, 1995).

In this research, two innovative methods are proposed to improve the performance of linear optimal control for mitigation of sub-synchronous resonance in power systems. At first, a technique is introduced based on shifting eigenvalues of the state matrix of system to the left

hand-side of s plane. It is found that this proposed controller is an extended state of linear optimal controller with determined degree of stability. So this method is called extended optimal control. A proposed design, which is presented in this paper, has been developed in order to control of severe sub-synchronous oscillations in a nearby turbine-generator. The proposed strategy is tested on second benchmark model and compared with the optimal full-state feedback method by means of simulation. It is shown that this method creates more suitable damping for these oscillations.
In some of genuine applications, measurement of all state variables is impossible and uneconomic. Therefore in this chapter, another novel strategy is proposed by using optimal state feedback, based on the reduced - order observer structure. It was shown also that the Linear Observer Method can mitigate Sub-synchronous Oscillations (SSO) in power systems. The proposed methods are applied to the IEEE Second Benchmark system for SSR studies and the results are verified based on comparison with those obtained from digital computer simulation by MATLAB.

2. System model

The system under study is shown in Fig. 1. This is the IEEE Second benchmark model, with a fixed series capacitor connected to it. This system is adopted to explain and demonstrate applications of the proposed method for investigation of the single-machine torsional oscillations. The system includes a T-G unit which is connected through a radial series compensated line to an infinite bus. The rotating mechanical system of the T-G set is composed of two turbine sections, the generator rotor and a rotating exciter (Harb & Widyan, 2003).

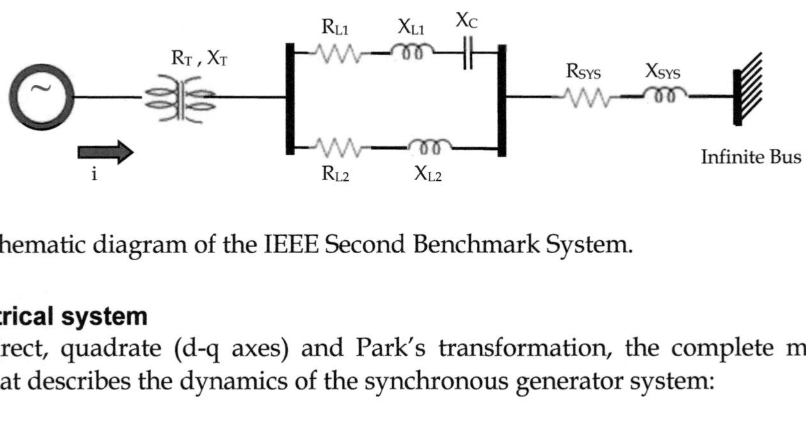

Fig. 1. Schematic diagram of the IEEE Second Benchmark System.

2.1 Electrical system

Using direct, quadrate (d-q axes) and Park's transformation, the complete mathematical model that describes the dynamics of the synchronous generator system:

$$\Delta\dot{X}_{Gen} = A_G \Delta X_{Gen} + B_{G1}\Delta U_1 + B_{G2}\Delta U_2 + B_{G3}\Delta U_3 + B_{G4}\Delta U_4 \quad (1)$$

$$\Delta y_{Gen} = C_G \Delta X_{Gen} \quad (2)$$

Where, C_G is an identity matrix. The following state variables and input parameters are used in (1):

$$\Delta X_{Gen}^T = [\Delta i_{fd} \;\; \Delta i_d \;\; \Delta i_{kd} \;\; \Delta i_q \;\; \Delta i_{kq}] \quad (3)$$

$$\Delta U_{Gen}{}^{T} = [\Delta V_O \quad \Delta\delta_g \quad \Delta\omega_g \quad \Delta E] \tag{4}$$

Where, ΔV_O is variation of infinitive bus voltage. In addition to the synchronous generator, the system also contains the compensated transmission line. The linearized model of transmission line is given by:

$$\Delta\dot{X}_{Line} = A_{Line}\Delta X_{Line} + B_{Line}\Delta U_{Line} \tag{5}$$

$$\Delta X_{Line}{}^{T} = [\Delta V_{Cd} \quad \Delta V_{Cq}] \tag{6}$$

$$\Delta U_{Line}{}^{T} = [\Delta i_d \quad \Delta i_q] \tag{7}$$

To obtain the electrical system, we can combine (1-7). Finally we can illustrate electrical system by below equations:

$$\Delta\dot{X}_{El} = A_{El}\Delta X_{El} + B_{El}\Delta U_{El} \tag{8}$$

$$\Delta X_{El}{}^{T} = [\Delta X_{Gen}{}^{T} \quad \Delta X_{Line}{}^{T}] \tag{9}$$

$$\Delta U_{El}{}^{T} = [\Delta U_{Gen}{}^{T}] \tag{10}$$

2.2 Mechanical system

The shaft system of the T-G set is represented by four rigid masses. The linearized model of the shaft system, based on a mass-spring-damping model is:

$$\Delta\dot{X}_{Mech} = A_M\Delta X_{Mech} + B_{M1}\Delta U_{M1} + B_{M2}\Delta U_{M2} \tag{11}$$

$$\Delta X_{Mech}^{T} = [\Delta\delta_1 \quad \Delta\omega_1 \quad \Delta\delta_g \quad \Delta\omega_g \quad \Delta\delta_2 \quad \Delta\omega_2 \quad \Delta\delta_3 \quad \Delta\omega_3] \tag{12}$$

$$\Delta U_{Mech}^{T} = [\Delta T_m \quad \Delta T_e] \tag{13}$$

The variation of electrical torque is denoted by ΔT_e and is given by:

$$\Delta T_e = P_1.\Delta i_{fd} + P_2.\Delta i_d + P_3.\Delta i_q + P_4.\Delta i_{kd} + P_5.\Delta i_{kq} \tag{14}$$

Parameters P_1 - P_5 can simplicity be founded by combination of electrical and mechanical system (Fig 2). Fig.3 illustrates the shaft system of the turbine-generator (T-G) in IEEE second benchmark model.

2.3 Combined power system model

The combined power system model is obtained by combining the linearized equations of the electrical system and mechanical system.
Let us define a state vector as $\Delta X_{Sys}{}^{T} = [\Delta X_{El}{}^{T} \ \Delta X_{Mech}{}^{T}]$. So we can write:

$$\Delta \dot{X}_{Sys} = A_{Sys} \Delta X_{Sys} + B_{Sys} \Delta U_{Sys} \tag{15}$$

$$\Delta U_{Sys}{}^{T} = [\Delta T_m \quad \Delta E] \tag{16}$$

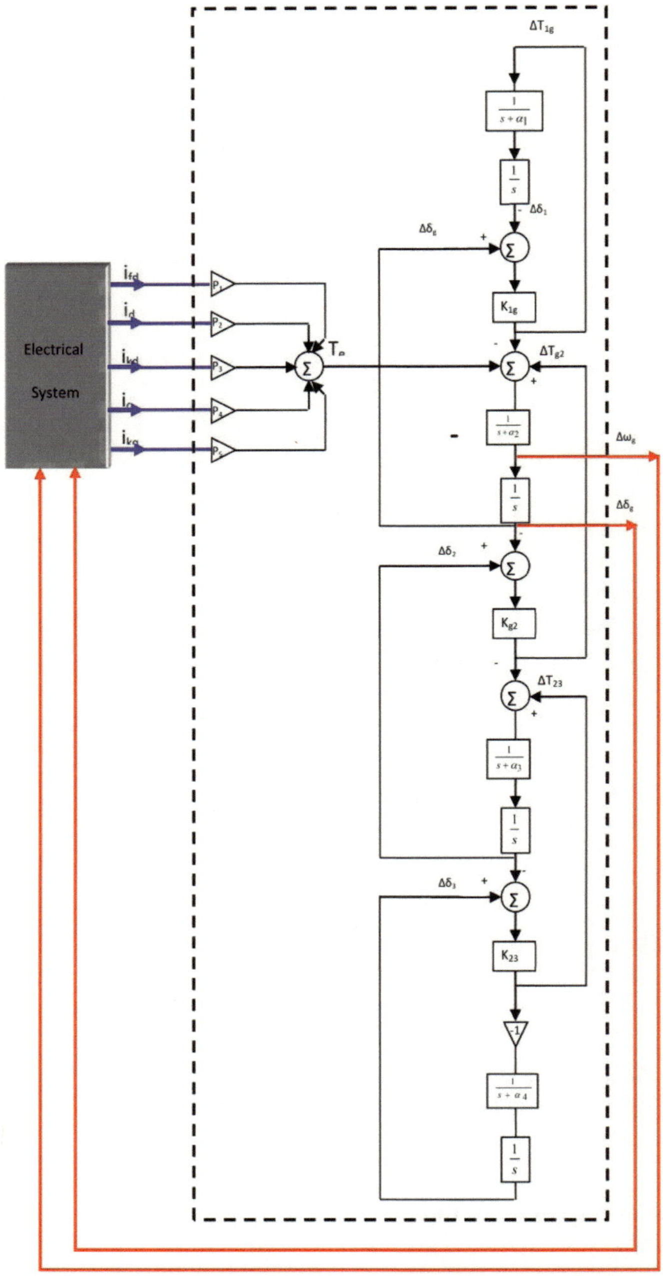

Fig. 2. Schematic diagram of calculation of T_e

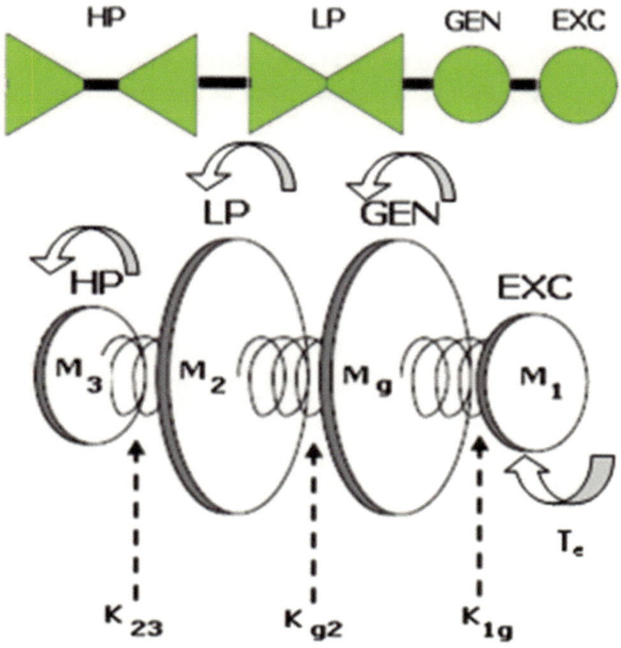

Fig. 3. Schematic diagram of the shaft system of the turbine-generator IEEE second benchmark model.

3. Modern optimal control

Optimal control must be employed in order to damp out the sub-synchronous oscillations resulting from the negatively damped mode. For the linear system, the control signal U which minimizes the performance index (Zhu et al., 1996; Patel & Munro, 1982; Khaki Sedigh, 2003; Ogata, 1990; Friedland, 1989; Kwakernaak, 1972):

$$J = \int [\Delta x_{Sys}{}^{T}(t) Q \Delta x_{Sys}(t) + \Delta u_{Sys}{}^{T} R_{\mu} \Delta u_{Sys}(t)] dt \tag{17}$$

It is given by the feedback control law in terms of system states:

$$U(t) = -K \cdot \Delta x_{Sys}(t) \tag{18}$$

$$K = R_{\mu}{}^{-1}.B_{Sys}{}^{T}.P \tag{19}$$

Where P is the solution of Riccati equation:

$$A_{Sys}{}^{T}.P + P.A_{Sys} - P.B_{Sys} R_{\mu}{}^{-1} B_{Sys}{}^{T}.P + Q = 0 \tag{20}$$

3.1 Extended optimal control

In this chapter, a strategy is proposed, based on shifting eigenvalues of the state matrix of system to the left hand-side of s plane, for damping all sub-synchronous torsional oscillations. In order to have a complete research, optimal full state feedback control is designed and the results are compared with extended optimal control as proposed method. It is found that we can design linear optimal controller to obtain special degree of stability in optimal closed loop system by using this method. In the other hand, we can design a new controller that it transfers all of poles of optimal closed loop system to the left hand-side of –α (a real value) in S plane. For a linear system by (15), we can rewrite the performance index using proposed method:

$$J = \int e^{2\alpha t}.[\Delta x_{Sys}{}^{T}(t) Q \Delta x_{Sys}(t) + \Delta u_{Sys}{}^{T} R_{\mu} \Delta u_{Sys}(t)]dt \tag{21}$$

For the linear system the control signal U which minimizes the performance index is given by the feedback control law in terms of system states:

$$U_{\alpha}(t) = -K_{\alpha} \cdot \Delta x_{Sys}(t) \tag{22}$$

$$K_{\alpha} = R_{\mu}^{-1}.B_{Sys}{}^{T}.P_{\alpha} \tag{23}$$

Where Pα is the solution of Riccati equation in this case:

$$(A_{Sys} + \alpha I_n)^T.P_{\alpha} + P_{\alpha}.(A_{Sys} + \alpha I_n) - P_{\alpha}.B_{Sys} R_{\mu}^{-1} B_{Sys}{}^{T}.P_{\alpha} + Q = 0 \tag{24}$$

Where I_n is an n×n identity matrix. So the state matrix of optimal closed loop system (A_{α}) is obtained by below:

$$(A_{Sys} + \alpha I_n)^T.P_{\alpha} + P_{\alpha}.(A_{Sys} + \alpha I_n) - P_{\alpha}.B_{Sys} R_{\mu}^{-1} B_{Sys}{}^{T}.P_{\alpha} + Q = 0 \tag{25}$$

In order to be asymptotically stable for Aα, we can write:

$$\lambda_i(A_{\alpha}) = \lambda_i(A_{Sys} + \alpha I_n - B_{Sys}.K_{\alpha}) = \lambda_i(A_{Sys} - B_{Sys}.K_{\alpha}) + \alpha \tag{26}$$

Where $\lambda_i(A_{\alpha})$ is eigenvalues of Aα for i=1,2,…,n. Because of $\mathrm{Re}[\lambda_i(A_{\alpha})] < 0$, we can write :

$$\mathrm{Re}[\lambda_i(A_{\alpha})] = \mathrm{Re}[\lambda_i(A_{Sys} - B_{Sys}.K_{\alpha}) + \alpha] = \mathrm{Re}[\lambda_i(A_{Sys} - B_{Sys}.K_{\alpha})] + \alpha < 0 \tag{27}$$

So we can write:

$$\mathrm{Re}[\lambda_i(A_{Sys} - B_{Sys}.K_{\alpha})] < -\alpha \tag{28}$$

In the other hand, all of eigenvalues of (A_{Sys}-B_{Sys}.K_{α}) are located on the left hand-side of –α in S plane. So the control signal U, which minimizes the performance index in (21), can create a closed lope system with determined degree of stability.

3.1.1 Numeral sample

This subsection gives a dimensional example in which the controllable system is to be designed in according to the proposed method. Suppose the nominal plant used for design of the controller is:

$$\frac{d}{dt}X = \begin{bmatrix} 0 & 1 \\ 0 & 0 \end{bmatrix}.X + \begin{bmatrix} 1 & 0 \\ 0 & 1 \end{bmatrix}.U \tag{29}$$

Where $X=[x_1(t)\ x_2(t)]^T$ and $U=[\mu_1(t)\ \mu_2(t)]^T$. We want to design an optimal controller in which the closed-loop system achieves to a favourite prescribed degree of stability. In this case, we chose $\alpha=2$. Suppose that

$$Q=\begin{bmatrix}1 & 1\\ 1 & 1\end{bmatrix} \quad , \quad R=\begin{bmatrix}1 & 0\\ 0 & 1\end{bmatrix} \tag{30}$$

The solution of Riccati equation in this case is equal to:

$$P_\alpha=\begin{bmatrix}3.9316 & 1.1265\\ 1.1265 & 4.4462\end{bmatrix} \tag{31}$$

To obtain the feedback control law in terms of system states, we can combine (23) with (29 - 31). Finally the optimal controller is given by:

$$U_\alpha(t)=-R^{-1}.B^T.P_\alpha.x(t)=\begin{bmatrix}-3.9316 & -1.1265\\ -1.1265 & -4.4462\end{bmatrix}.x(t) \tag{32}$$

And then the state matrix of optimal closed loop system (A_α) is obtained by:

$$A_\alpha=A+2I_n-B.K_\alpha=\begin{bmatrix}-3.9316 & -0.1265\\ -1.1265 & -4.4462\end{bmatrix} \tag{33}$$

So the poles of optimal closed loop system are located in -3.7321and -4.6458. It can be seen that both of them shift to the left hand-side of $-\alpha$ ($\alpha=2$) in S plane.

3.2 Reduced order observer

The Luenberger reduced-order observer is used as a linear observer in this paper. The block diagram of this reduced-order observer is shown in Fig. 3. For the controllable and observable system that is defined by (15), there is an observer structure with size of (n-1). The size of state vector is n and output vector is l. The dynamic system of Luenberger reduced-order observer with state vector of z(t), is given by:

$$\Delta z(t)=L.\Delta x_{Total}(t) \tag{34}$$

$$\dot{z}(t)=D.z(t)+T.y_{Total}(t)+R.u_{Total}(t) \tag{35}$$

To determine L, T and R is basic goal in reduced-order observer. In this method, the estimated state vector $\Delta\hat{X}_{Total}(t)$ includes two parts. First one will obtain by measuring $\Delta y_{Total}(t)$ and the other one will obtain by estimating $\Delta z(t)$ from (34). We can take:

$$\begin{bmatrix}\Delta y_{Total}(t)\\ \Delta z(t)\end{bmatrix}=\begin{bmatrix}C_{Total}\\ L\end{bmatrix}.\Delta\hat{X}_{Total}(t) \tag{36}$$

By assumption full rank $[C_{Total}^T \quad L^T]^T$, we can get:

$$\Delta\hat{X}_{Total}(t) = \begin{bmatrix} C_{Total} \\ L \end{bmatrix}^{-1} \cdot \begin{bmatrix} \Delta y_{Total}(t) \\ \Delta z(t) \end{bmatrix} \tag{37}$$

By definition:

$$\begin{bmatrix} C_{Total} \\ L \end{bmatrix}^{-1} = \begin{bmatrix} F_1 & F_2 \end{bmatrix} \tag{38}$$

We get:

$$\Delta\hat{X}_{Total}(t) = F_1.\Delta y_{Total}(t) + F_2.\Delta z(t) \tag{39}$$

Where:

$$F_1.C_{Total} + F_2.L = I_n \tag{40}$$

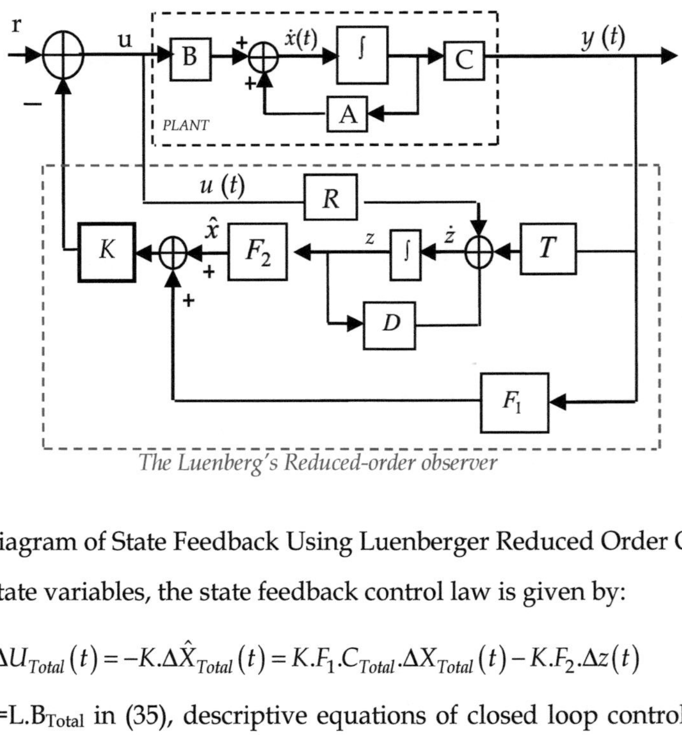

Fig. 4. Shematic Diagram of State Feedback Using Luenberger Reduced Order Observer

Using estimated state variables, the state feedback control law is given by:

$$\Delta U_{Total}(t) = -K.\Delta\hat{X}_{Total}(t) = K.F_1.C_{Total}.\Delta X_{Total}(t) - K.F_2.\Delta z(t) \tag{41}$$

By assumption R=L.B_{Total} in (35), descriptive equations of closed loop control system with reduced-order observer are:

$$\begin{bmatrix} \Delta\dot{X}_{Total}(t) \\ \Delta\dot{z}(t) \end{bmatrix} = \begin{bmatrix} A_{Total} - B_{Total}.F_1.C_{Total} & -B_{Total}.K.F_2 \\ T.C_{Total} - L.B_{Total}.K.F_1.C_{Total} & D - L.B_{Total}.K.F_2 \end{bmatrix} \cdot \begin{bmatrix} \Delta X_{Total}(t) \\ \Delta z(t) \end{bmatrix} \tag{42}$$

Dynamic error between linear combination of states of $L.\Delta X_{Total}(t)$ system and observer $\Delta z(t)$ is defined as:

$$\dot{e}(t) = \Delta\dot{z}(t) - L.\Delta\dot{X}_{Total}(t) \tag{43}$$

Combine (35) and (36), we get:

$$\begin{bmatrix} \Delta\dot{X}_{Total}(t) \\ \dot{e} \end{bmatrix} = \begin{bmatrix} A_{Total} - B_{Total}.K & -B_{Total}.K.F_2 \\ 0 & D \end{bmatrix} . \begin{bmatrix} \Delta X_{Total}(t) \\ e \end{bmatrix} \tag{44}$$

For stability of the observer dynamic system, the eigenvalues of D must lie in the left hand-side of s plane. By choosing D, we can calculate L, T and R (Luenberger, 1971).

3.2.1 Numeral sample

The longitudinal equations of an aircraft are presented in steady state format (Rynaski, 1982):

$$\frac{d}{dt}\begin{bmatrix} \Delta v(t) \\ \alpha(t) \\ \theta(t) \\ q(t) \end{bmatrix} = \begin{bmatrix} \alpha_{11} & a_{12} & 0 & -g \\ a_{21} & a_{22} & 1 & 0 \\ a_{31} & a_{32} & a_{33} & 0 \\ 0 & 0 & 1 & 0 \end{bmatrix} x(t) - \begin{bmatrix} b_1 \\ b_2 \\ b_3 \\ 0 \end{bmatrix} \delta_e(t) \tag{45}$$

Where Δv is variation of velocity, α is angle of attack, θ is pitch angle, δ_e is elevator angle and q is pitch rate. This equation in special state is presented by:

$$\frac{d}{dt}X(t) = \begin{bmatrix} -0.0507 & -3.861 & 0 & -9.8 \\ -0.00117 & -0.5164 & 1 & 0 \\ -0.000129 & 1.4168 & -0.4932 & 0 \\ 0 & 0 & 1 & 0 \end{bmatrix} X(t) - \begin{bmatrix} 0 \\ -0.0717 \\ -1.645 \\ 0 \end{bmatrix} \delta_e(t) \tag{46}$$

$$y = \begin{bmatrix} 1 & 0 & 0 & 0 \\ 0 & 1 & 0 & 0 \end{bmatrix} X(t) \tag{47}$$

So Δv and α are measurable state variables. Therefor we can get final result by MATLAB simulations.

4. Simulation results

Eigenvalue analysis is a fast and well-suited technique for defining behavioral trends in a system that can provide an immediate stability test. The real parts of the eigenvalue represent the damping mode of vibration, a positive value indicating instability, while the imaginary parts denote the damped natural frequency of oscillation.

As mentioned earlier, the system considered here is the IEEE second benchmark model. It is assumed that the fixed capacitive reactance (X_C) is 81.62% of the reactance of the transmission line (X_{L1}=0.48 P.u).

The simulation studies of IEEE-SBM carried out on MATLAB platform is discussed here. The following cases are considered for the analysis.

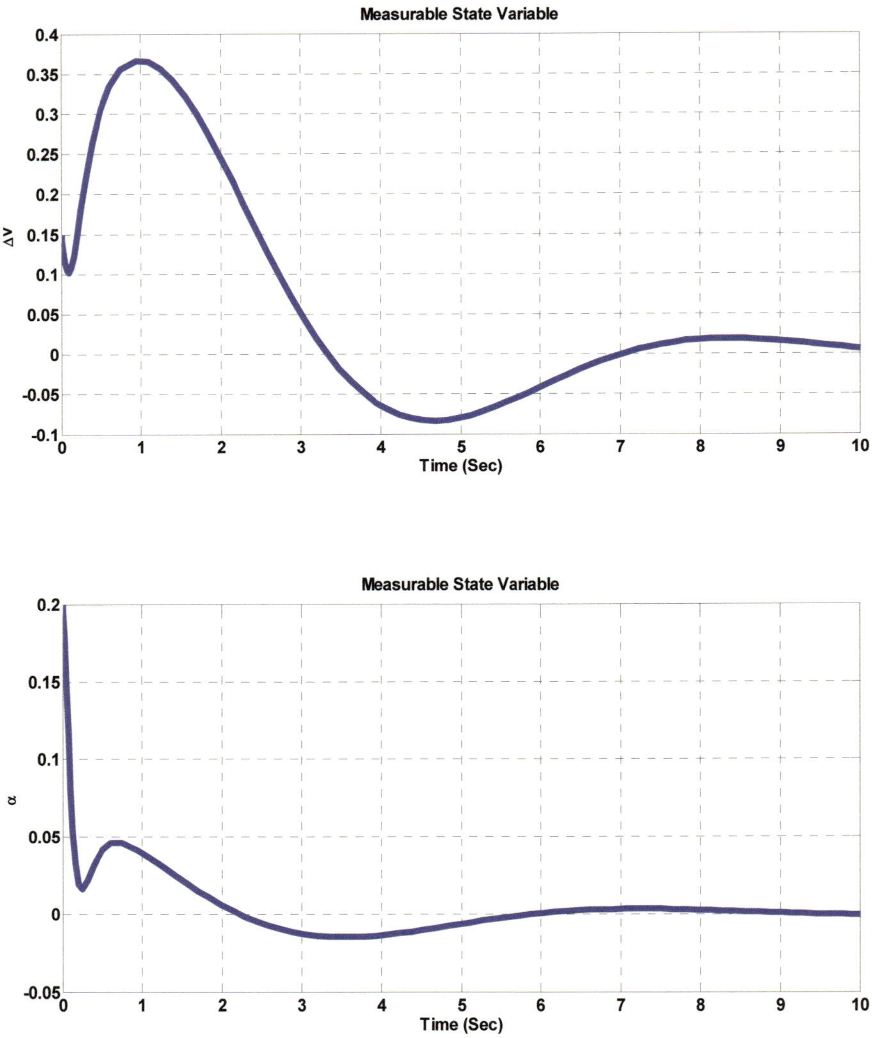

Fig. 5. Variation of Measurable State Variables

4.1 Without controller

In the first Case, second benchmark model is simulated without any controller in initial conditions. Fig. 7 shows the variation of torque of the rotating mechanical system of the T-G set. It can be seen that variations of torque of the mechanical system are severe unstable and then power system tends to approach to the SSR conditions.

The study is carried out with heavily loaded synchronous generator of P_G=0.9 p.u, Q_G=0.43 p.u and V_t=1.138 p.u. Figure. 8 shows the variation of real and imaginary parts of the eigenvalues of A_{Sys} with the compensation factor $\mu_C=X_C/X_{L1}$. It can be observed that the first torsional mode is the most unstable modes at μ_C=81.62%. The unstable range of variation of torsional modes has been illustrated in Fig. 8.

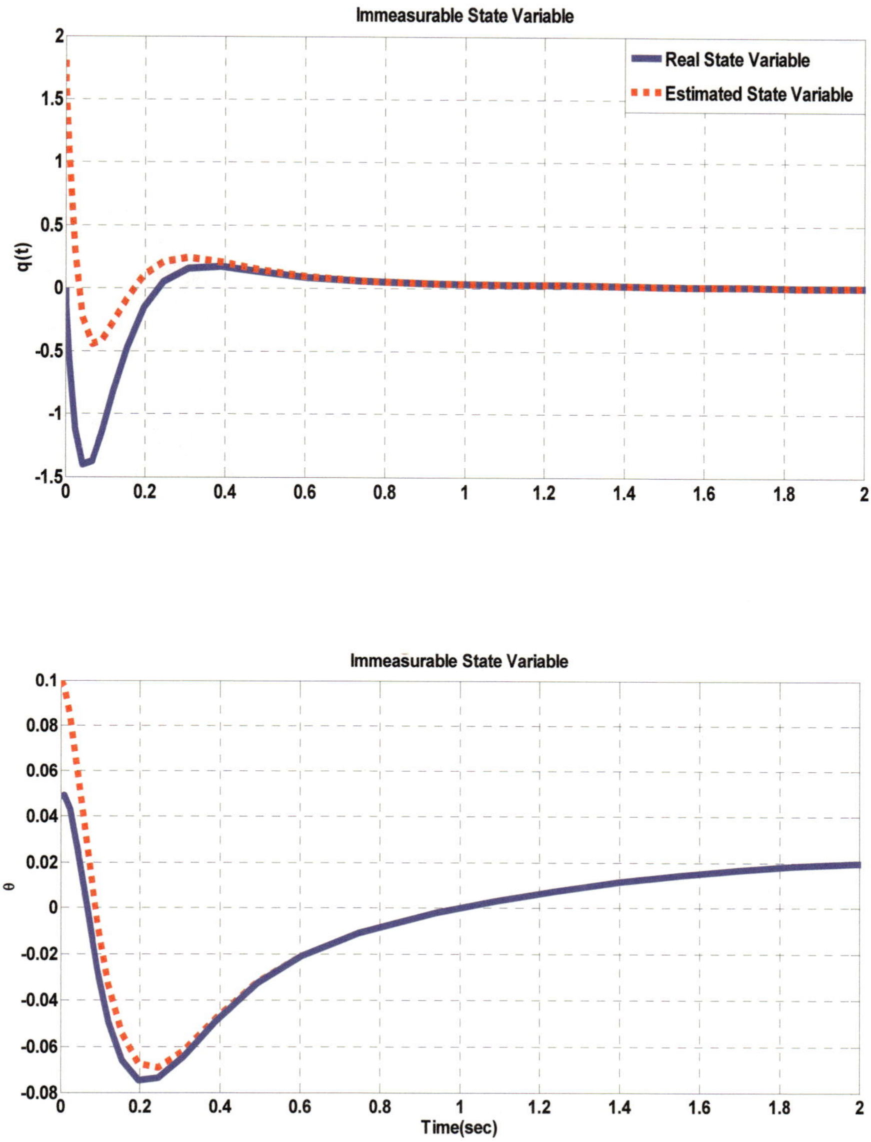

Fig. 6. Variation of Immeasurable State Variables

4.2 With proposed controller: Extended optimal control

For presentation of the first proposed controller, power system is simulated by extended optimal control with using (20-24). Proposed method is carried out on second benchmark simultaneously. The obtained results have been compared with prevalent optimal control in (17-20) by Fig. 9-(a). It is observed that the proposed method has created more suitable damping for first torsional mode of second benchmark model than prevalent method. As

similar way, this proposed method has suitable results on second torsional mode. Fig. 9-(b) clearly illustrates this point.
Fig. 10 illustrates variation of torque of the mechanical system in T-G set. It can be observed that the proposed method has more effect on the output of power system than prevalent method.

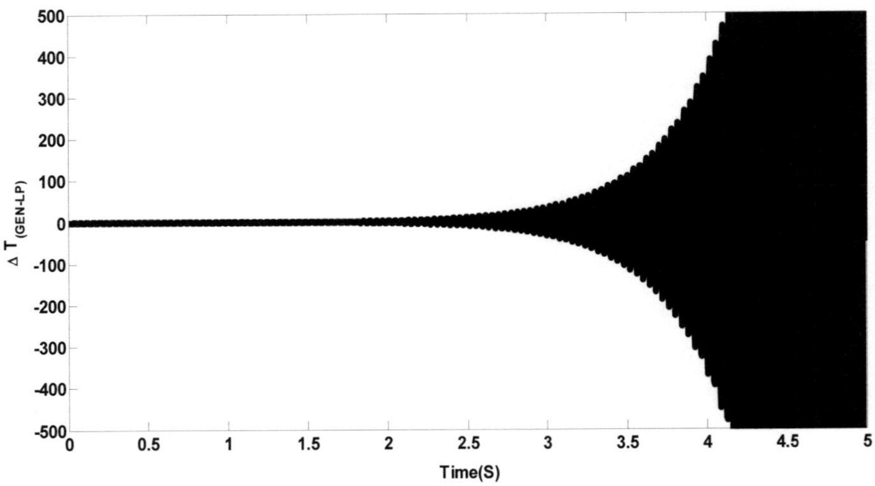

Fig. 7. Variation of torque of generator – low pressure turbine in the T-G set for μ_C=81.62% without any controller.

4.3 With proposed controller: Reduced order observer

In order to have a complete research, optimal full state feedback control is designed and the results are compared with reduced-order method. Some parameters, such as Δi_{kd} and Δi_{kq}, are not physical variables. ΔV_{Cd} and ΔV_{Cq} are transmission line parameters that they are not accessible. So let us define:

$$\Delta \hat{X}_{Sys}{}^{T} = [\Delta i_{kd} \quad \Delta i_{kq} \quad \Delta V_{Cd} \quad \Delta V_{Cq}] \tag{48}$$

$$\Delta y_{Sys}{}^{T} = [\Delta T_{EXC-GEN} \quad \Delta T_{GEN-LP} \quad \Delta T_{LP-HP}] \tag{49}$$

Where $\Delta y_{Sys}{}^{T}$ is used to obtain variation of torque of the rotating mechanical system of the T-G set . Full order observer estimates all the states in a system, regardless whether they are measurable or immeasurable. When some of the state variables are measurable using a reduced-order observer is so better.
In this scenario, proposed method is carried out on second benchmark model simultaneously. The obtained results have been illustrates in Fig. 11. It is observed that the reduced-order method has created a suitable estimation from immeasurable variables that are introduced in (48).
Fig. 12 shows variation of torque of the mechanical system in T-G set. It can be observed that the proposed method has small effect on the output of power system

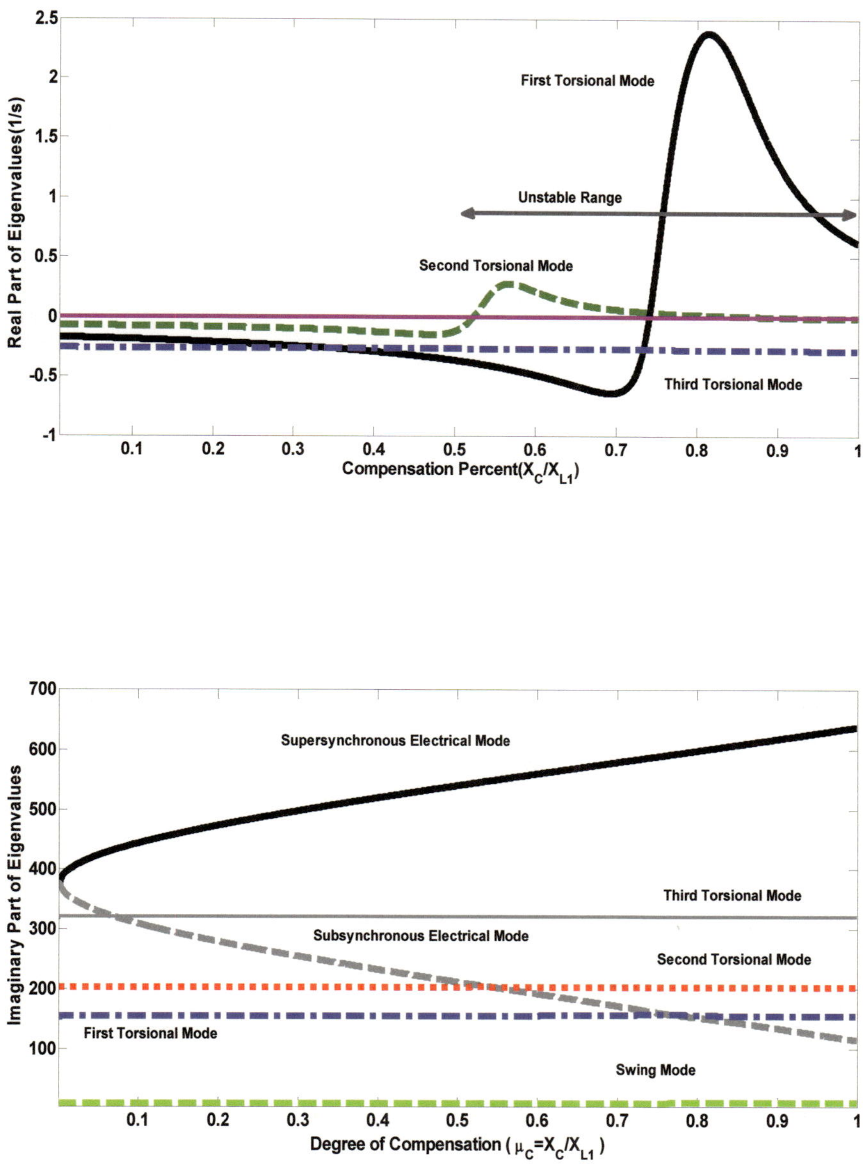

Fig. 8. Variation of real and imaginary parts of eigenvalues as a function of μ_C

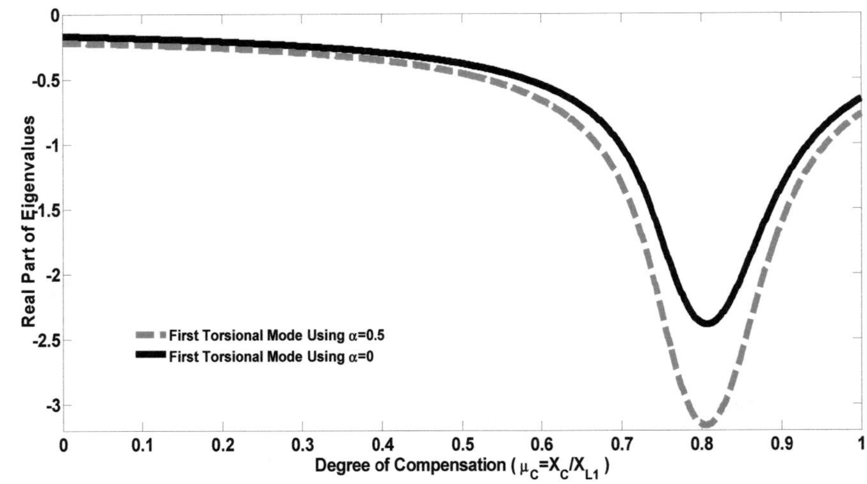

(a)

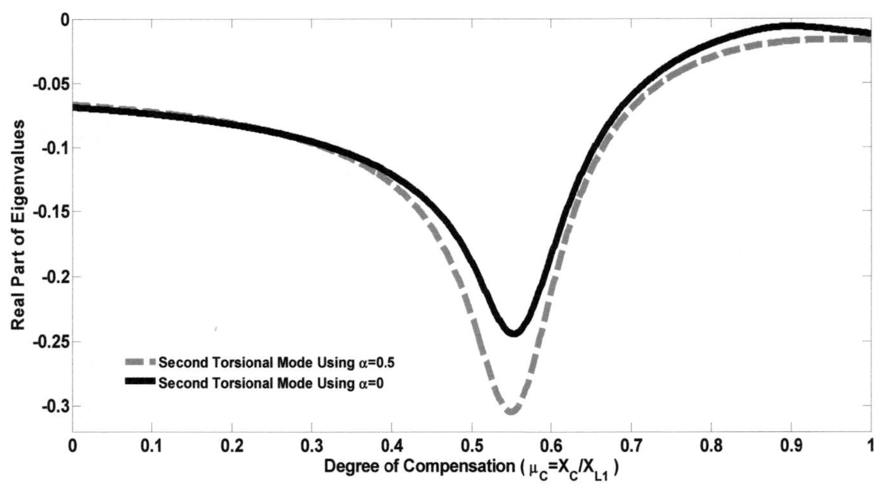

(b)

Fig. 9. Variation of first torsional mode (a) and second mode (b) in IEEE second benchmark to degree of compensation: Dotted (proposed controller), Solid (prevalent controller).

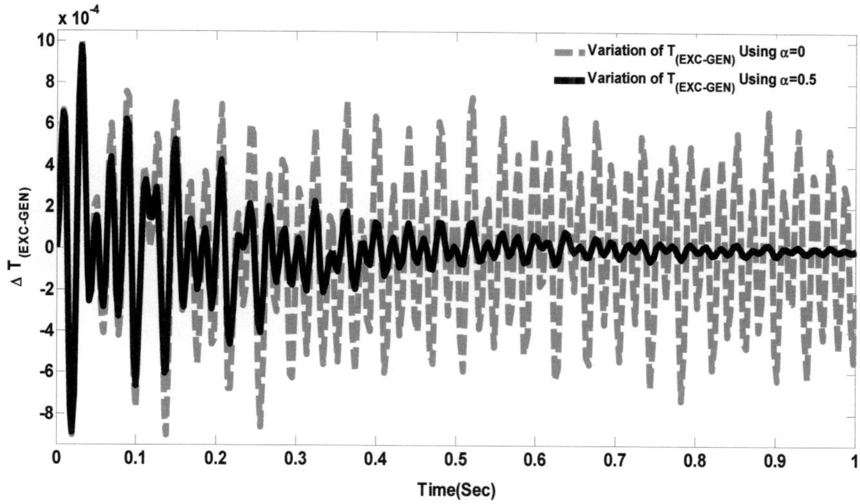

(a)

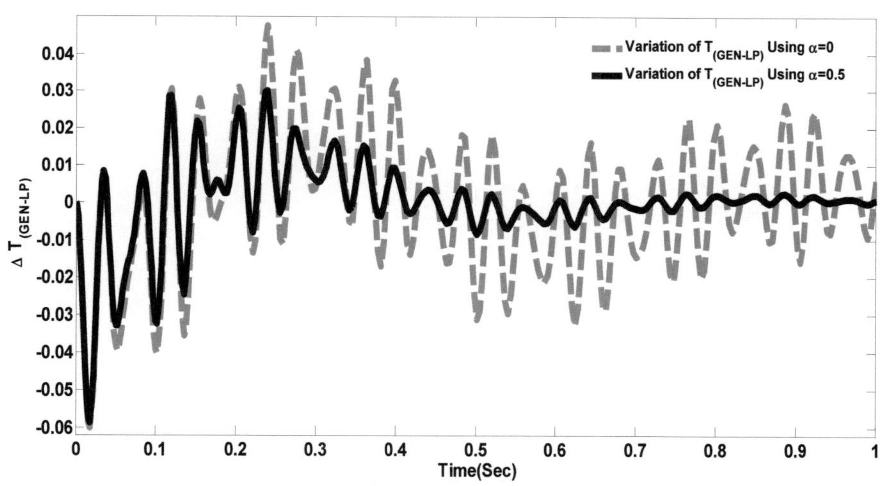

(b)

Fig. 10. Variation of torque of exciter-generator (a) and generator-low pressure (b): (proposed controller), Dotted (prevalent controller).

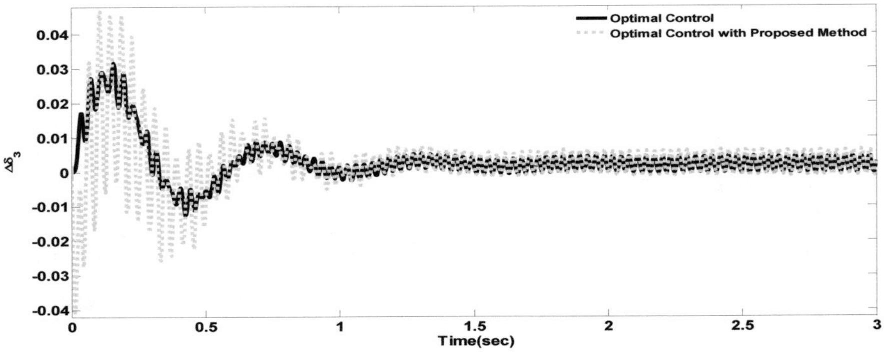
Optimal Control
Optimal Control with Proposed Method
0.04
0.03
0.02
0.01
0
-0.01
-0.02
-0.03
-0.04
$\Delta\delta_3$
0
0.5
1
1.5
2
2.5
3
Time(sec)

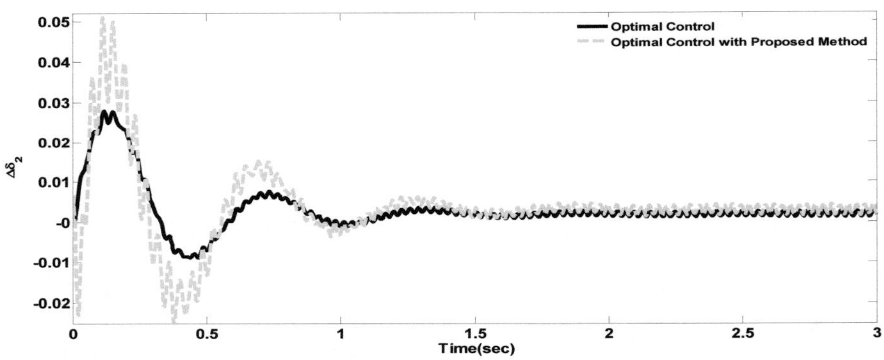
Optimal Control
Optimal Control with Proposed Method
0.05
0.04
0.03
0.02
0.01
-0
-0.01
-0.02
$\Delta\delta_2$
0
0.5
1
1.5
2
2.5
3
Time(sec)

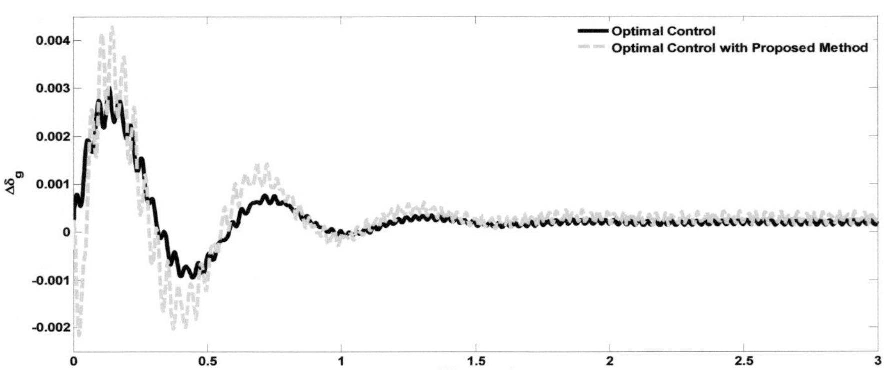
Optimal Control
Optimal Control with Proposed Method
0.004
0.003
0.002
0.001
0
-0.001
-0.002
$\Delta\delta_g$
0
0.5
1
1.5
2
2.5
3
Time(sec)

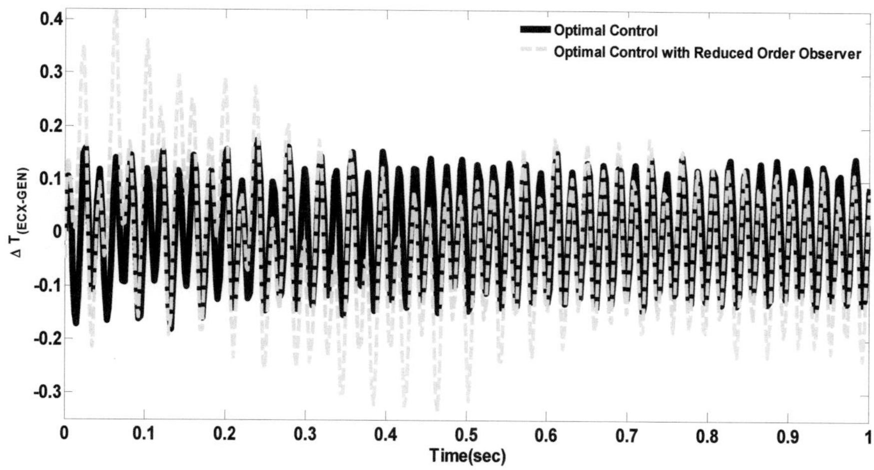

Fig. 11. Variation of δg, δ2and δ3: Solid (optimal full state feedback), Dotted (reduced-order observer control).

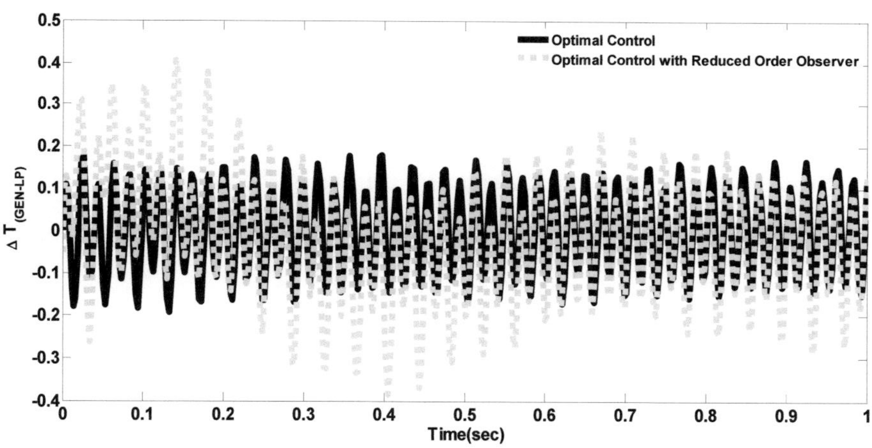

Fig. 12. Variation of torque of exciter - generator and generator - low pressure turbine in the T-G set: (reduced-order observer control), Solid (optimal full state feedback).

5. Conclusion

Fixed capacitors have long been used to increase the steady state power transfer capabilities of transmission lines. A major concern associated with fixed series capacitor is the sub-synchronous resonance (SSR) phenomenon which arises as a result of the interaction between the compensated transmission line and turbine-generator shaft. This results in excessively high oscillatory torque on machine shaft causing their fatigue and damage.

This chapter presents two analytical methods useful in the study of small-signal analysis of SSR, establishes a linearized model for the power system, and performs the analysis of the SSR using the eigenvalue technique. It is believed that by studying the small-signal stability of the power system, the engineer will be able to find countermeasures to damp all sub-synchronous torsional oscillations.

The first strategy is proposed, based on shifting eigenvalues of the state matrix of system to the left hand-side of s plane, for damping all sub-synchronous torsional oscillations. The proposed method is applied to The IEEE Second Benchmark system for SSR studies and the results are verified based on comparison with those obtained from digital computer simulation by MATLAB. Analysis reveals that the proposed technique gives more appropriate results than prevalent optimal controller. In the practical environment (real world), access to all of the state variables of system is limited and measuring all of them is also impossible. So when we have fewer sensors available than the number of states or it may be undesirable, expensive, or impossible to directly measure all of the states, using a reduced-order observer is proposed. Therefore in this chapter, another novel approach is introduced by using optimal state feedback, based on the Reduced - order observer structure. Analysis reveals that the proposed technique gives good results. It can be concluded that the application of reduced-order observer controller to mitigate SSR in power system will be provided a practical viewpoint. Also this method can be used in a large power system as a local estimator.

6. Acknowledgement

The authors would like to express their sincere gratitude and appreciations to the Islamic Azad University, Gonabad Branch, as collegiate assistances in all stages of this research.

7. Appendix (Nomenclature)

ΔX_{Gen}	State Vector for Generator System Model
A_G	State Matrix for Generator System Model
B_{Gi}	i^{th} Input Matrix for Generator System Model
Δy_{Gen}	Output Vector for Generator System Model
ΔU_{Gen}	Input Vector for Generator System Model
Δi_{fd}	Variation of Field Winding Current
$\Delta i_d, \Delta i_q$	Variation of Stator Currents in the d-q Reference Frame
$\Delta i_{kd}, \Delta i_{kq}$	Variation of Damping Winding Current in the d-q Reference Frame
$\Delta \delta_g$	Variation of Generator Angle
$\Delta \omega_g$	Variation of Angular Velocity of Generator
ΔX_{Mech}	State Vector for Mechanical System Model
A_M	State Matrix for Mechanical System Model
B_{Mi}	i^{th} Input Matrix for Mechanical System Model
Δy_{Mech}	Output Vector for Mechanical System Model
ΔU_{Mech}	Input Vector for Mechanical System Model
ΔT_m	Variation of Mechanical Torque
ΔT_e	Variation of Electrical Torque
ΔX_{Line}	State Vector for Transmission Line System
A_{Line}	State Matrix for Transmission Line System
B_{Line}	Input Matrix for Transmission Line System
ΔU_{Line}	Input Vector for Transmission Line System
ΔX_{Sys}	State Vector for Combined Power System Model

$\mathbf{A_{Sys}}$	State Matrix for Combined Power System Model
$\mathbf{B_{Sys}}$	Input Matrix for Combined Power System Model
$\mathbf{\Delta U_{Sys}}$	Input Vector for Combined Power System Model
$\mathbf{\Delta E}$	Variation of Field Voltage
J	Performance Index
K	Gain Feedback Vector in Linear Optimal Control
K_α	Gain Feedback Vector in Linear Optimal Control with Determined Degree of Stability
P	Solution of Riccati Equation in Linear Optimal Control
$\mathbf{P_\alpha}$	Solution of Riccati Equation in Linear Optimal Control with Determined Degree of Stability

8. References

Walker D.N.; Bowler C.L., Jackson R.L. & Hodges D.A. (1975). Results of sub-synchronous resonance test at Mohave, *IEEE on Power Apparatus and Systems,* pp. 1878–1889

Hall M.C. & Hodges D.A. (1976). Experience with 500 kV Subsynchronous Resonance and Resulting Turbine-Generator Shaft Damage at Mohave Generating Station, *IEEE Publication,* No.CH1066-0-PWR, pp.22-29

IEEE Committee report. (1992). Reader's guide to Subsynchronous Resonance. *IEEE on Power Apparatus and Systems,* pp. 150-157

IEEE Torsional Issues Working Group. (1997). Fourth supplement to a bibliography for study of sub-synchronous resonance between rotating machines and power systems, *IEEE on Power Apparatus and Systems,* pp. 1276–1282

Anderson P.M. ; Agrawal B. L. & Van Ness J.E. (1990). *Sub-synchronous Resonance in Power System,* IEEE Press, New York

Begamudre R.D. (1997). *Extra High Voltage A.C Transmission Engineering,* New Age International (P) Limited, New Delhi

Gross G,; Imparato C. F., & Look P. M. (1982). A tool for comprehensive analysis of power system dynamic stability, *IEEE on Power Apparatus and Systems,* pp. 226–234, Jan

Parniani M. & Iravani M. R. (1995). Computer analysis of small-signal stability of power systems including network dynamics, *Proc. Inst. Elect. Eng. Gener. Transmiss. Distrib.,* pp. 613–617, Nov

Harb A.M. & Widyan M.S. (2004). Chaos and bifurcation control of SSR in the IEEE second benchmark model, *Chaos, Solitons and Fractals,* pp. 537-552. Dec

Zhu W.; Mohler R.R., Spce R., Mittelstadt W.A. & Mrartukulam D. (1996). Hopf Bifurcation in a SMIB Power System with SSR, *IEEE Transaction on Power System,* pp. 1579-1584

Patel R.V. & Munro N. (1976). *Multivariable System Theory and Design,* Pergamon Press

Khaki Sedigh A. (2003). *Modern control systems,* university of Tehran, Press 2235

Ogata K. (1990). *Modern Control Engineering,* Prentice–Hall

Friedland B. (1989). *Control System Design : An Introduction to State – Space Methods,* Mc Graw–Hill

Kwakernaak H. & Sivan R. (1972). *Linear Optimal Control Systems,* Wiley- Intersciences

Luenberger D.G. (1971). An Introduction to Observers, *IEEE Trans On Automatic Control,* pp 596-602 , Dec

Rynaski E.J. (1982). Flight control synthesis using robust output observers, *Guidance and Control Conference*, pp. 825-831, San Diego

13

A New Approach of Control System Design for LLC Resonant Converter

Peter Drgoňa, Michal Frivaldský and Anna Simonová
University of Žilina, Faculty of Electrical Engineering, Žilina Slovakia

1. Introduction

Main task of power semiconductor converter is transfer of electrical energy from its input to the output and to the load. This energy flow is provided by control of the switching process of one or more semiconductor devices. Based on converter application it is necessary to choose correct control algorithm for selected switching frequency of converter. Algorithm itself has to be utilized with suitable hardware platform, whereby through the set of instructions the turn - on and turn - of control pulses are generated. Control system also has to secure other important functions for secondary processes. Nowadays a huge number of converter topologies exists, whereby each type should be suited for different conditions of use. For example uninterruptible power supply must generate constant output voltage with constant frequency and constant amplitude for wide range of output power. Converters for electric drive applications have to control their speed through generation of three phase voltage system with configurable amplitude and speed. From mentioned above it is clear to say that for each topology of power converter, the different type of control modulation (PWM - Pulse Width Modulation, PSM - Phase Shift Modulation, FM - Frequency Modulation) and different structure of regulator has to be used. Therefore selection of suitable control system depends on number of various factors, which are output power of converter, type of switching devices, type of load, possibility of hardware implementation and ways of switching.
In the field of DC/DC converters for switching power supplies, the main focus is on implementation of digital control, which means use of microcontrollers or DSP with implemented control algorithms and functions for communication with user as well. Analog control systems are well known and its design procedure is mastered, so it is easy to convert analog (continuous) controller into discrete and consequently implementing in microcontroller and DSP. But this approach ignore sample and hold effect of A/D converter and computing time of microprocessor. For proper discrete controller design, the method named direct digital design can be used. This method uses transfer function of converter in discrete form, including effect of sampling and computation delay.
For controller design purposes, transfer function of converter is necessary. This transfer function is based on model of power stage of controller. For PWM converters such as buck, boost, etc. the averaging method is widely used, but for new resonant topologies such as LLC converter, with this averaging method, the control to output transfer function cannot be used. In this chapter, new simulation based method for obtaining the transfer function of converter is discussed. This method uses MATLAB and OrCad PSPICE environments for

revealing the transfer function. Advantage of this method is, that it can be used for every type of power converter. Next in the chapter, the direct digital design of controller based on transfer function is discussed. This method uses MATLAB environment for designing the discrete controller.

2. The ways of regulation of electric quantities in power converters

From the various types of regulation of electric quantities (voltage, current) the most well - known are PWM, PSM, and FM. In pulse width modulation (PWM) technique, the mean value of output voltage or current is controlled through the change of on-time (t_{on}) or off-time (t_{off}) of power transistor. Generation of PWM signals is based on comparison between repeating sequence (sawtooth signal or triangular signal with constant frequency) and between reference value of voltage (u_{reg}) which is generated from regulator. This principle is for analog and digital system almost the same. The only difference in the case of analog system is that repeating sequence is generated from op-amplifier and consequently compared with reference value in analog comparator. For generation of repeating sequence the digital system instead of op-amplifier utilizes digital timer. Comparator is replaced by compare register. The proportional on-time in the case of direct quantities is called duty cycle - D, and is defined as follows:

$$D = t_{on}/T \tag{1}$$

where t_{on} is on-time of semiconductor devices, and T_s is switching period of converter.
In the case of phase shift modulation (PSM) the mean value of output voltage is controlled by phase shift of on-times of two or more semiconductor devices, such two transistors in upper or lower leg of fullbridge converter are switched simultaneously, whereby switching frequency and duty cycle are constant. The application of PSM is well suited in ZVS (Zero Voltage Switching) and ZCS (Zero Current Switching) resonant converters.
Frequency modulation is basically similar to PWM. Difference is that duty cycle in this case is always constant (D = const.), but frequency of switching signal is varying (f_{sw} = var.). Based on the change of control voltage u_{reg}, the switching frequency of PWM signal is being changed. In the case of analog circuits the frequency modulation is realized through utilization of voltage control oscillator (VCO). On the other hand, in the case of digital implementation the VCO is not required, because frequency of timer is able to be changed directly.
These previously mentioned ways of regulation of electric quantities in power converters are basic types, whereby also their combination is being utilized in practical applications.

3. LLC converter - properties and principle of operation

LLC resonant converter is multi-resonant converter and is characterized by its unique DC - gain characteristic, which has two resonant frequencies (f_{r1} and f_{r2}). This converter has several advantages compared to standard serial LC resonant topology. One of them is possibility of stable regulation of output voltage in a wide range of input voltages together with the change of output power from 1% to 100%. The next advantage is achievement of ZVS switching mode during various operational modes. LLC resonant converter is composed of three functional parts (Fig. 1a). It deals about pulse generator, resonant circuit with high-frequency transformer and rectifier with capacitive filter. Operation of LLC converter in different operational modes is described by DC gain characteristic (Fig. 1b), which should be divided into ZVS and/or ZCS region. ZVS region in dependency on the switching frequency can be further divided into:

- region with switching frequency equal to resonant ($f_{sw} = f_{r1}$)
- region1 with switching frequency higher than resonant ($f_{sw} > f_{r1}$)
- region2 with switching frequency lower than resonant ($f_{sw} < f_{r1}$)
- region3 with switching frequency lower than resonant and with voltage gain < 1

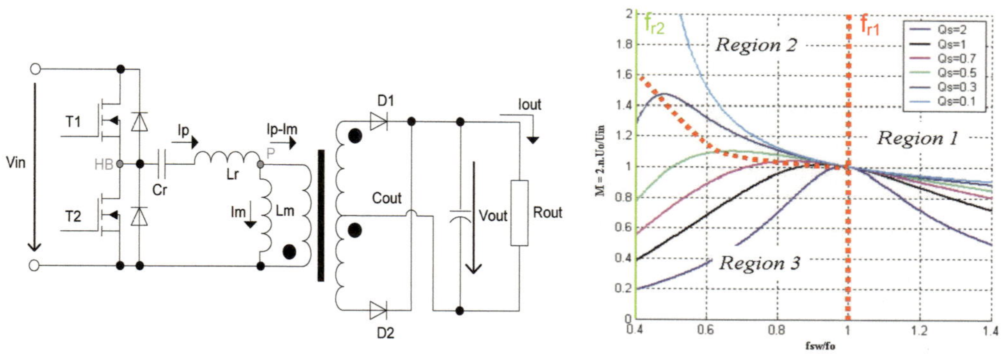

a) b)

Fig. 1. a) Principle schematics of LLC converter, b) DC-gain characteristic of LLC converter

According to the operational modes of resonant converters the operation of LLC resonant converter is rather difficult. The principal waveforms of transformer and output diode during each operating mode are shown in Fig. 2. The impedance of series resonant circuit at the resonant frequency is equal to zero. Therefore the reflected output voltage is equal to the input voltage, what is described by the unity of voltage gain thus the circuit then operates optimally. LLC resonant converter can achieve greater gain, lower or equal to 1. If the switching frequency is less than the resonant frequency, magnetization inductance is involved into the resonance of the circuit so the converter can deliver higher gain.

For analysis of operation of LLC converter it is necessary to exactly examine voltage gain characteristic. Voltage gain characteristic is possible to be made from equivalent circuit of converter. Output part together with rectifier and load is replaced by equivalent output resistance which is marked as R_{AC}.

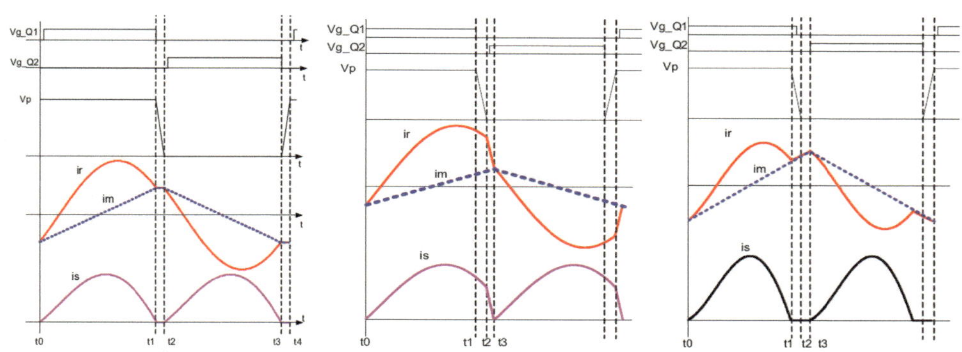

a) b) c)

Fig. 2. Waveforms of currents and voltages of LLC converter at different operating conditions a) $f_{sw} = f_{r1}$, b) $f_{sw} > f_{r1}$, c) $f_{sw} < f_{r1}$

Considering, that converter is working with almost resonant frequency, only first harmonic is transferred through resonant circuit, and therefore it is possible to utilize simple approximation, where rectangular pulses are substituted by sinusoidal waveforms.

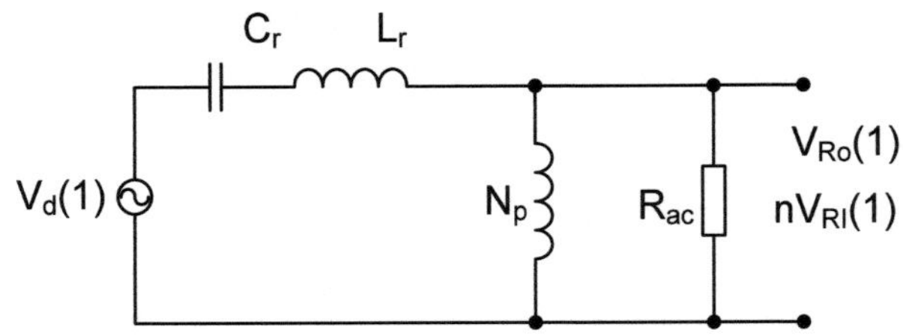

Fig. 3. Equivalent circuit of LLC converter

For voltage expressions of this equivalent circuit next formulas are valid:

$$V_{RI(1)} = \frac{4 \cdot V_o}{\pi} \cdot \sin(\omega t) \tag{2}$$

$$V_{d(1)} = \frac{4}{\pi} \cdot \frac{V_{in}}{2} \cdot \sin(\omega t) \tag{3}$$

where V_{RI} is voltage at the output of resonant circuit, and V_d is first harmonic part of supply voltage.
The equivalent circuit of converter is then similar to that which is shown on Fig.3. Equation of voltage gain characteristic is then equal to:

$$M = \frac{2nV_o}{V_{in}} = \left| \frac{\left(\frac{\omega^2}{\omega_{r1}^2}\right).\sqrt{m.(m-1)}}{\left(\frac{\omega^2}{\omega_{r2}^2} - 1\right) + j.\left(\frac{\omega}{\omega_{r1}}\right).\left(\frac{\omega^2}{\omega_{r1}^2} - 1\right).(m-1).Q} \right| \tag{4}$$

where:

$$f_{r1} = \frac{1}{2\pi.\sqrt{L_R.C_R}} \tag{5}$$

$$f_{r2} = \frac{1}{2\pi\sqrt{(L_M + L_R).C_R}} \tag{6}$$

$$Q = \frac{\sqrt{\frac{L_R}{C_R}}}{R_{AC}} \tag{7}$$

$$R_{AC} = \frac{8.n^2}{\pi^2}.R_O \tag{8}$$

Voltage gain characteristic of proposed converter is shown on Fig. 4. X-axis is defined as switching frequency, or better said frequency of input sinusoidal voltage. Ratio between output voltage and input voltage is marked on y-axis. Each wave is related to different loads of converter (quality factors Q). Main parameters of converter are: $\mathbf{V_{in} = 400\ V}$, $\mathbf{V_{out} = 60\ V}$, $\mathbf{L_r = 6.6\ \mu H}$, $\mathbf{C_r = 900\ nF}$, $\mathbf{L_m = 36\ \mu H}$, $\mathbf{L_{r2} = 3\ \mu H}$, $\mathbf{R_{omin} = 2.4\ \Omega}$, $\mathbf{I_{max} = 25\ A}$

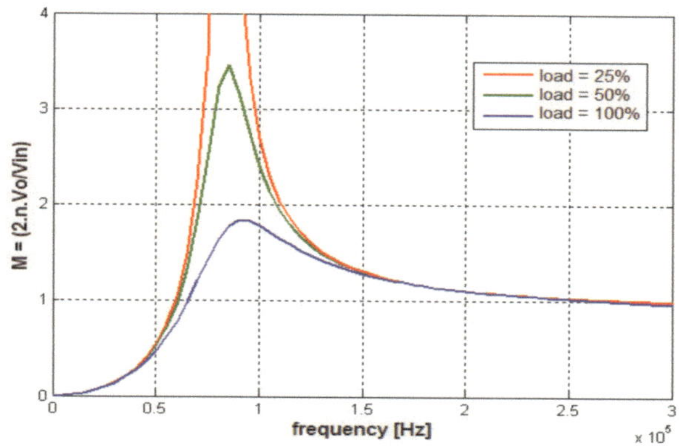

Fig. 4. Voltage gain characteristic of proposed converter.

3.1 Regulation of LLC converter

The regulation algorithm for the LLC converter maintains the requested value of output voltage, during the change of input voltage or output load. The LLC converter is controlled by variations of switching frequency, so the active part of the regulator is a voltage controlled oscillator (VCO) in analog or digital (software) form. The change of the output frequency is based on the input voltage of the VCO. As mentioned above, the switching frequencies of the LLC converter are between f_{r1} and f_{r2} during normal operation. The regulation algorithm works as follows: The normal operating point (Fig. 5a point 1) is characterized by V_{IN}=400 V, U_{OUT}=60 V. If the input voltage drops below 400 V, the regulation algorithm reacts in form of switching frequency reduction, so the operating point of the converter moves from the point 1 to the point 2. In this point, the converter works with the increased gain to maintain the output voltage at the constant value (60 V). The minimal input voltage is defined as 325V, so it is not possible to maintain the output voltage on 60V below this value.
If the input voltage rises back to 400V, the control system increases the switching frequency - voltage gain decreases and the operating point of the converter moves back to the point 1. The next operating condition for the LLC converter is variation of the output load. Fig. 5b shows the point 1, where the converter works with full load, the operating point is on the curve with Q=100%. When the output load drops, the operating point moves from the curve with Q=100% to the curve with Q=10%, which means that for the constant switching frequency, the output voltage rises to 60% above the nominal value, so the regulation algorithm rises the switching frequency which leads to lower voltage gain and output voltage decrease to nominal value.
Specific case of operation is the start of the converter, when the switching frequency is higher than the resonant frequency f_{r1} to avoid current inrush during the initial charge of the output capacitor C_{OUT}. Generally, for the soft start, the switching frequency is two or three times higher than the resonant frequency. Voltage gain on this frequency is lower (Fig. 4), so the charging current of the output capacitor stays on an acceptable level.

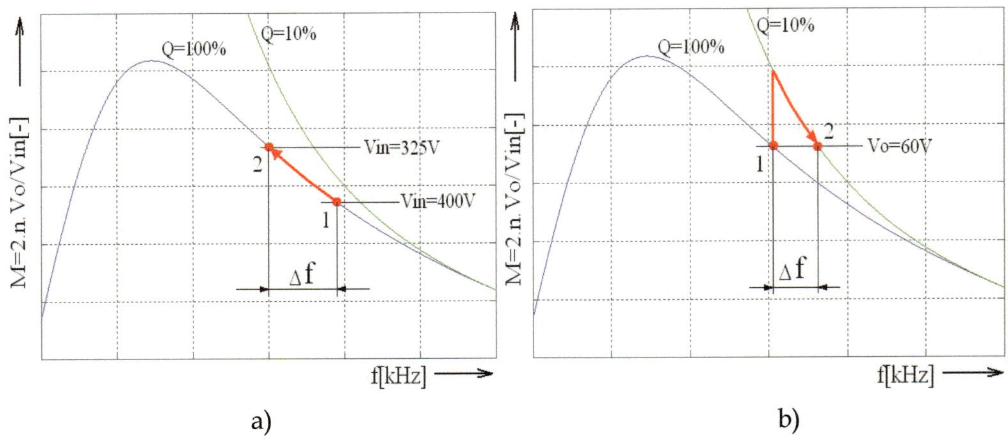

Fig. 5. Regulation of output voltage a) during input supply voltage decrease, b) during load variations

3.2 Simulation of LLC converter in OrCad PSPICE

For verification and mathematical model design, first, the simulation in Orcad PSPICE has been made. Data acquired from simulations in PSPICE are used in MATLAB for design of mathematical model. For best performance and accuracy of switching waveforms, all parasitic components were included into simulation.

For power transistors the IPW60R165CP model was used, and MUR10015CT was used for output diodes. For transformer, the leakage inductance with all parasitic components was also simulated.

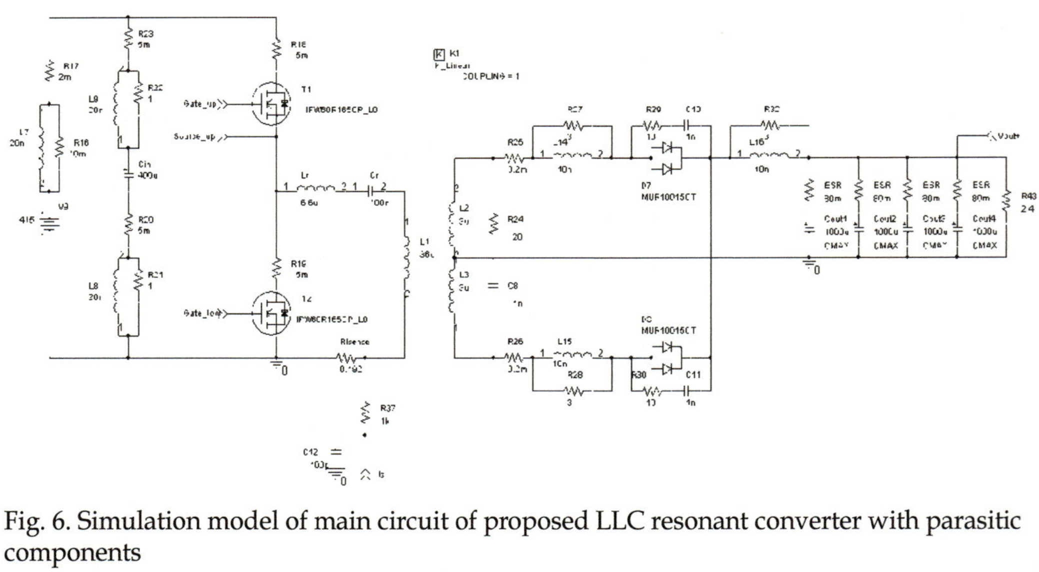

Fig. 6. Simulation model of main circuit of proposed LLC resonant converter with parasitic components

In Fig.7 the basic waveforms of LLC converter are shown. This simulation experiment was performed with full input voltage 425V and with output power 1kW. Fig. 8 shows another waveforms, with lower input voltage at 325V and output power of 1kW. All operation conditions including soft start and overload were also verified in simulation experiments.

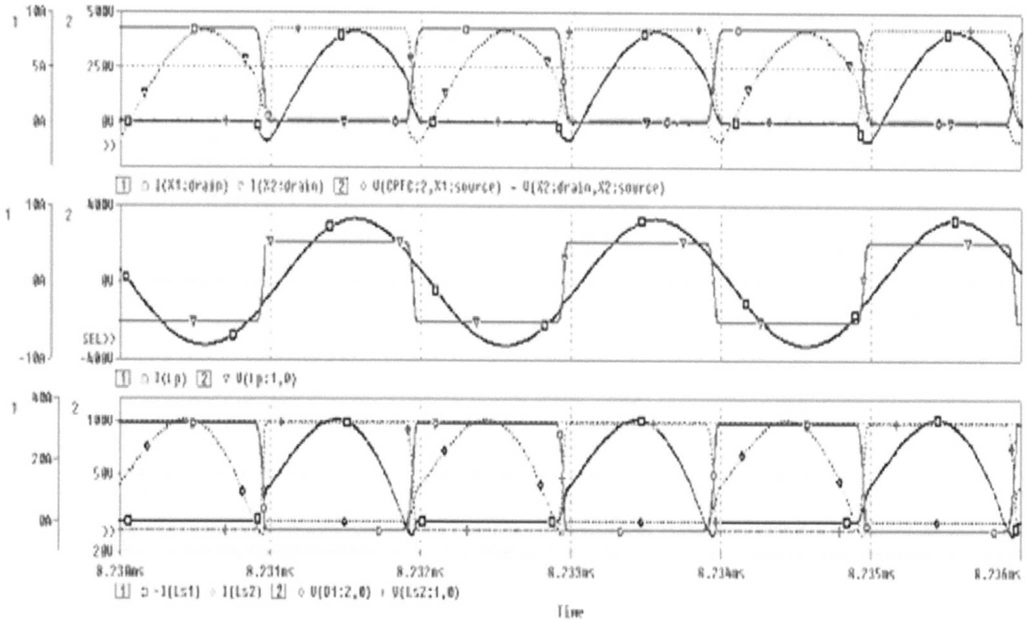

Fig. 7. Time waveforms of voltages and currents during the simulation experiment: Uin = 425V, Pout = 1008W (from top: transistor T1and T2, transformer primary side, output diode D1 and D2)

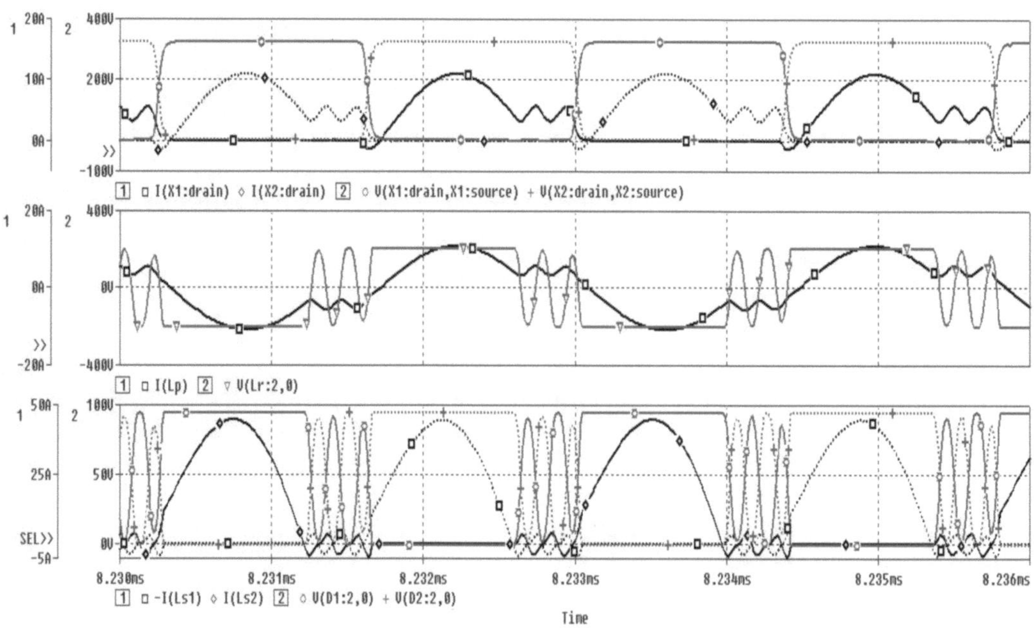

Fig. 8. Time waveforms of voltages and currents during the simulation experiment: Uin = 325V, Pout = 1008W (from top - transistor X1a X2, transformer primary side, output diode D1 and D2)

From simulations above, it's clear to say, that design procedure was very accurate and results are showing acceptable performance.

4. Transfer function for controller

In previous sections, a operating principle of LLC converter was briefly mentioned, together with simulation of main circuit. Accurate simulation is critical for design and optimization of the control system for the LLC converter. For the design of control structure and the actual control system, a transfer function is necessary, which will describe response of output voltage and current to the change of the control variable.

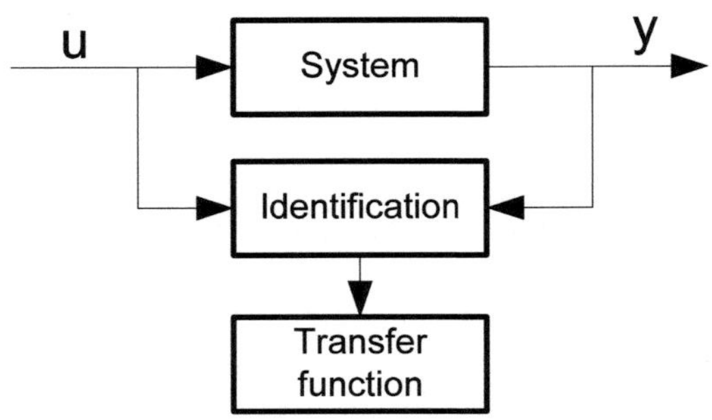

Fig. 9. Process of transfer function acquiring

Mathematical model of LLC converter requires control-to-output transfer function. Based on this transfer function, digital controller can be obtained. For PWM converters, standard "averaged" methods can be used for revealing the transfer function of converter. One of method with good results is "direct circuit averaging". This method can be easily implemented for standard PWM converters such as boost, buck, flyback etc. Transfer function obtained with this method has duty cycle as an input value and output voltage as an output value.

Unlike the PWM converters, the control transfer function of frequency controlled resonant converters cannot be obtained by state space averaging method, due to different ways of energy processing. While state space averaging methods eliminates the information about switching frequency, they cannot predict dynamic properties of resonant converters, so the proper control-to-output transfer function cannot be evaluated.

There is a several methods for solving this problems, but some of them are too simplified and idealized, others are too complex and difficult to use. In this paper, new simulation based method for revealing the control transfer function is proposed. This method is based on PSPICE simulation, which was discussed in previous chapter, and use of System Identification Toolbox in MATLAB environment. First, the simulation of main circuit in PSPICE must be created. Using of PSPICE simulation, the dependency of output (voltage, current) on input (switching frequency, duty cycle) can be simulated.

Another option for creation of the mathematical model is use of block called SLPS in MATLAB. This block creates interface between circuit model in PSPICE and mathematical models in MATLAB environment. Data acquired from simulation in PSPICE are used in MATLAB for creation of transfer function of LLC multiresonant converter. For obtaining of the transfer function in s-domain, the MATLAB System Identification Toolbox was used.

Whole process is shown on Fig. 10. First, the simulation of dynamic step response of LLC converter on control value (switching frequency) was created in OrCad PSPICE environment. Result from this simulation was dynamic output voltage response (output value) on step of switching frequency (input value). This simulated results from OrCad PSPICE, were used in MATLAB as input values for identification of this dynamic system.

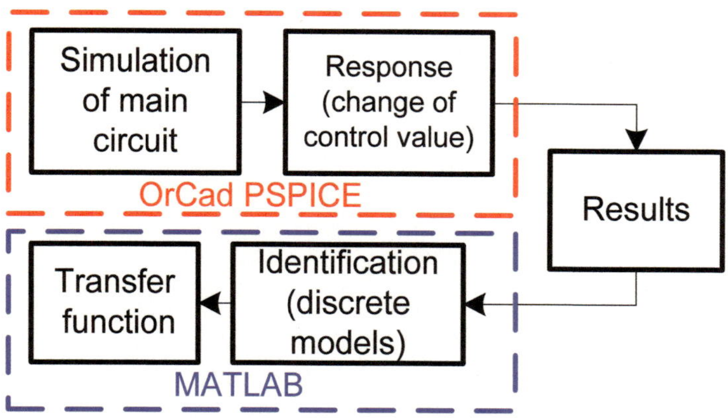

Fig. 10. Simulation based method for identification of transfer function

Use of System Identification Toolbox offers several models for identification of dynamic system. With use of different models from System Identification Toolbox (SIT), identification of all converters is possible.

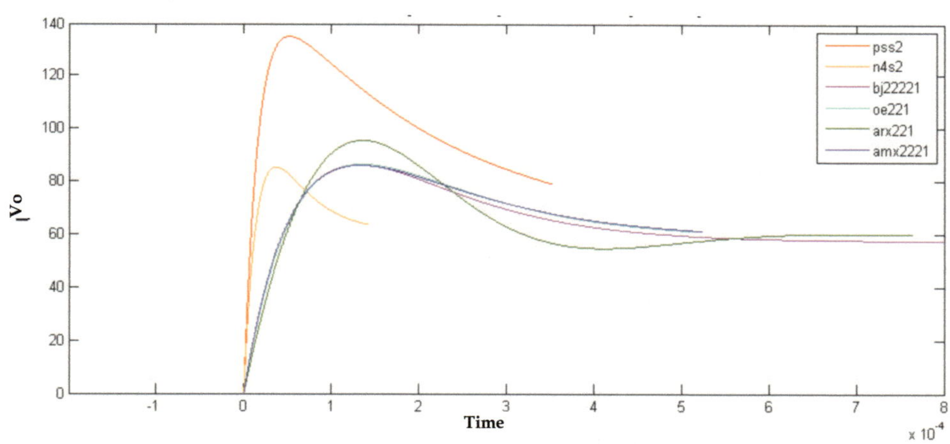

Fig. 11. Accuracy of some model types from SIT with different degree (step response)

System Identification Toolbox includes number of models in continuous or discrete form, which can be used for identification of systems: ARX (Auto Regresive Exogeneous Input Model), ARMAX (Auto Regresive Moving Average Exogeneous Input Model) OE (Output Error Model), BJ (Box-Jenkins Model), SS (State-Space Model). Accuracy of the models depends on degree of polynomials used in transfer function. Fig. 11 shows accuracy of identified transfer functions for different model types from simulated results of LLC converter. All models are in discrete form (z-domain), so the exact specification of sampling interval is necessary, which means, that the integration step which was used in OrCad PSPICE, must be also used for MATLAB. From Fig. 11 can be seen, that the best accuracy has ARX and ARMAX model.

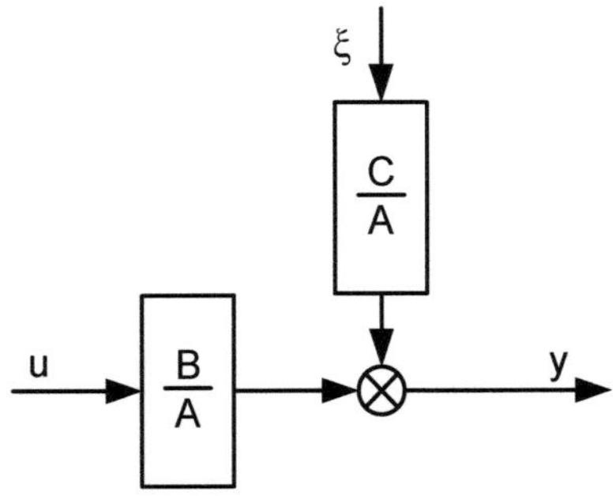

Fig. 12. Structure of ARMAX model

The ARMAX model, whose structure is on Fig. 12, is similar to ARX model, but with better accuracy. It extends the ARX model with polynomial C(z) - equation of average value of perturbation function. The ARMAX model is suitable for those systems, where perturbation function affects input variable u(n). Searched transfer function has the same form as in ARX model, but the computing algorithm is different. The equation for ARMAX model is as follows:

$$A(z)y(n) = \left(B(z)u(n-k) + C(z)\xi(n)\right) \tag{9}$$

Structure of the model is shown on Fig. 12. After adjusting, the form of Eq. (10) is:

$$y(n) = \frac{1}{A(z)}\left(B(z)u(n-nk) + C(z)\xi(n)\right) \tag{10}$$

Due to best accuracy of ARMAX model, only this model was used for revealing the transfer function. Another parameter necessary for the transfer function revealing, is degree of its polynomials. Fig. 13 shows accuracy of ARMAX model with different degree. Best accuracy offers model of 2nd degree, which means, that polynomials A(z), and C(z) are just 2nd degree. We can say, that the control to output transfer function of LLC converter has same degree as ARMAX model.

4.1 Transfer function

As mentioned above, the sampling interval used for models in SIT must be equivalent with integration step used for simulation in OrCad PSPICE. If sampling interval used in SIT differs from integration step in PSPICE, the dynamic results (from step response) will have different time representation in MATLAB, so the searched transfer function will have incorrect form.

Requested discrete transfer function is in form:

$$G(z) = \frac{B(z)}{A(z)} = \frac{b_0 + b_1 z^{-1} + b_2 z^{-2} + \ldots + b_{nb} z^{-nb}}{a_0 + a_1 z^{-1} + a_2 z^{-2} + \ldots + a_{na} z^{-na}} \tag{11}$$

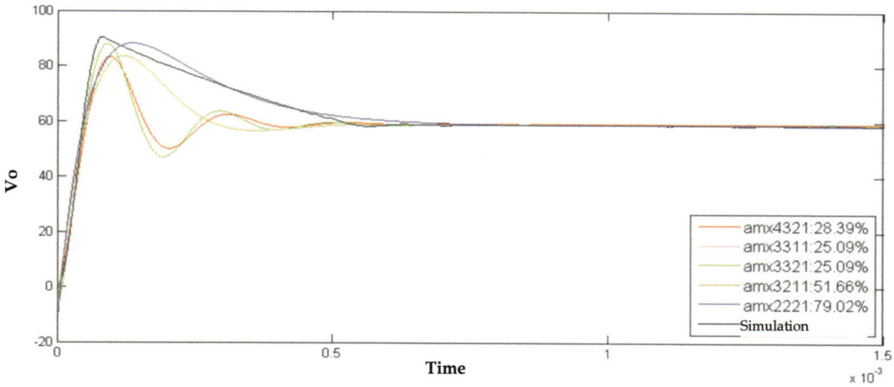

Fig. 13. Accuracy of ARMAX models with different degree (up to down 4,3,2)

For better view, Fig.14 shows comparison of ARMAX 2221 model, used for transfer function, with simulated dynamic step response from OrCad PSPICE.

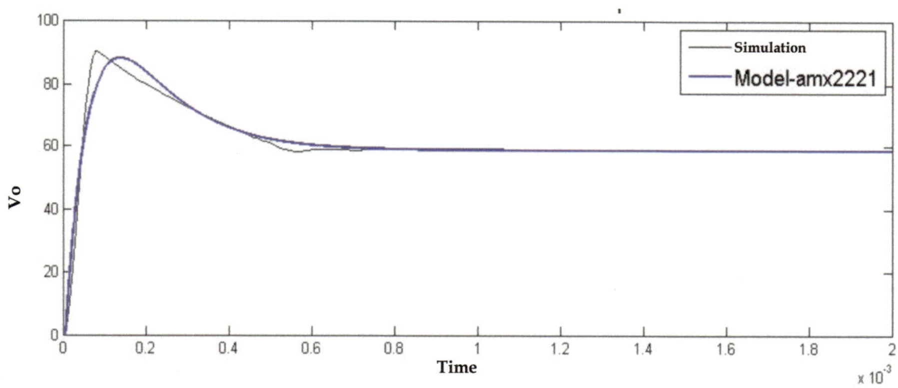

Fig. 14. Comparison of simulated results (PSPICE) with ARMAX model of 2nd degree (MATLAB)

For LLC converter, whose waveforms are in Fig. 7 and Fig. 8, resulting transfer function is in Eq. (12).

$$G(s) = \frac{2.054 \cdot 10^6 s + 6.895 \cdot 10^9}{s^2 + 2.29 \cdot 10^4 s + 1.176 \cdot 10^8} \tag{12}$$

After acquiring of transfer function, we can obtain basic mathematical model of LLC converter. This mathematical model can be used for design of discrete model, with all effects from discrete control system. The following figures show the bode characteristics of the systems marked G_{dlyz3} and G_{dlyz4} with discrete controllers. The design of controllers was made in Matlab using the SISOTOOL. This tool allows to design not only regulators, but also analyze the characteristics and quality of the proposed control circuit.

5. Design of discrete controller

Due to implementation in microprocessor, the controller must be in discrete form. There are two ways to design a discrete controller - design by emulation and direct digital design.

In the design by emulation approach, also known as digital redesign method, first an analog controller is designed in the continuous domain, by ignoring the effects of sampling and hold of A/D converter and computing delay of microprocessor. In next step, the controller can be converted into discrete-time domain by one of discretization method. This approach is good for systems of lower degree, but in discrete systems of higher degree, the transient responses does not reflect the required values because of ignoring sample and hold and computation delay effects.
On the other side, direct digital design approach offers design of controller directly in z-domain, without conversion, including effects of A/D converter and microprocessor. Block diagram of this approach is on Fig. 15.

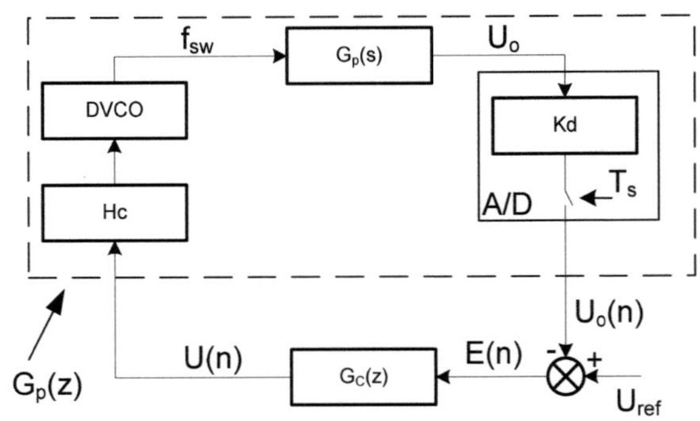

Fig. 15. Direct digital design control loop

Sampling of measured value with A/D converter can be represented by ideal Zero-Order-Hold block with sample time Ts. Gain of A/D converter is represented by block K_{adc}. Computing delay of microprocessor, also with delay from PWM module are represented by block T_{comp}. A/D converter with PWM module together form a sampling-and-hold device. Sample and hold block brings additional time delay of Ts/2 and phase lag of ωTs/2, which means, that reconstructed signal has time or phase lag. Block T_{comp} represents delay between conversion of A/D converter and PWM duty cycle or modulo update. Time between this two events is necessary for computing the values for PWM block. Discrete transfer function of whole converter including Zero-Order block, Sample-and-Hold effect and gain of A/D converter is:

$$G(z) = Z\left\{\frac{1}{s}\left(1 - e^{sT_s}\right)\cdot H_C(s)\cdot G_P(s)\cdot K_d\right\}$$

Fig. 16 shows effect of sampling interval with computing delay on stability of closed control loop. Tab. 1 shows transfer functions with different sampling intervals and different computational delays. Sampling times were used from A/D converter included in DSC 56F8013, the computing times were used from same processor. Application was for digital control system for 200kHz LLC multiresonant converter. In this system discrete regulator of third order was used.
For design of controller in z-domain, all above mentioned delays must be taken into account. With use of MATLAB Siso Design Tool, the proper discrete controller can be designed. Advantage of this tool is possibility of direct placing of zeroes and poles of controller on bode diagram of closed or open loop. After placing the poles or zeros

of controller, the different responses of closed control loop can be displayed for verification.

Sampling time T_s	Computing delay T_{comp}	Mark
5μs	0	Gz1
10μs	0	Gz2
5μs	3μs	Gdlyz1
10μs	3μs	Gdlyz2
5μs	6μs	Gdlyz3
10μs	6μs	Gdlyz4

Table 1. Sampling times and computational delays for transfer functions in Fig. 16

From Fig. 16 is clear, that computing delay has significant effect on stability of the control loop. With rising computing and sampling time stability of system drops.

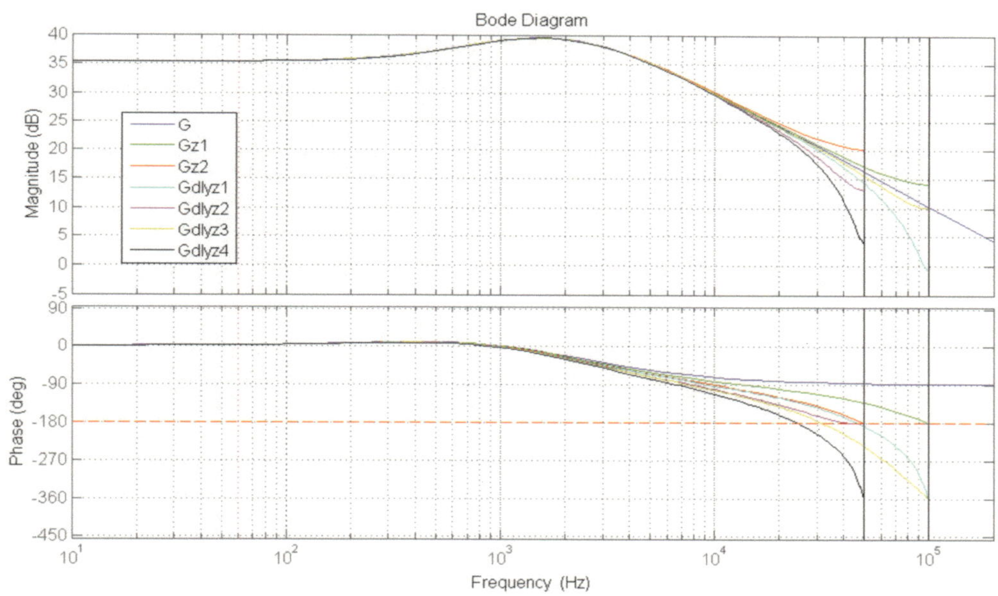

Fig. 16. Effect of sample and hold and computation delay on stability of control loop

Fig. 17 shows the system G_{dlyz3} with poles and zeros of the regulated system (blue) and regulator (red). Fig. 18 shows the closed-loop response of the system to a unitary jump. Time of control settling is about 70 microseconds, overshoot as high as 17%.
Transfer function of designed controller is in form:

$$G_c(z) = 0.041204 \cdot \frac{z-0.886}{z-0.995} \tag{13}$$

Fig.19 shows the bode characteristics of system marked G_{dlyz4}, with the proposed controller. Poles and zeros of the transfer function of the regulated system are shown blue, poles and zeros of the controller are shown red. As in the previous case, in Fig. 20 a closed control loop response to unitary jump is shown. Time of control settling is 100 microseconds, overshoot is 20%, which is caused by a longer interval sampling interval of system Gdlyz4.

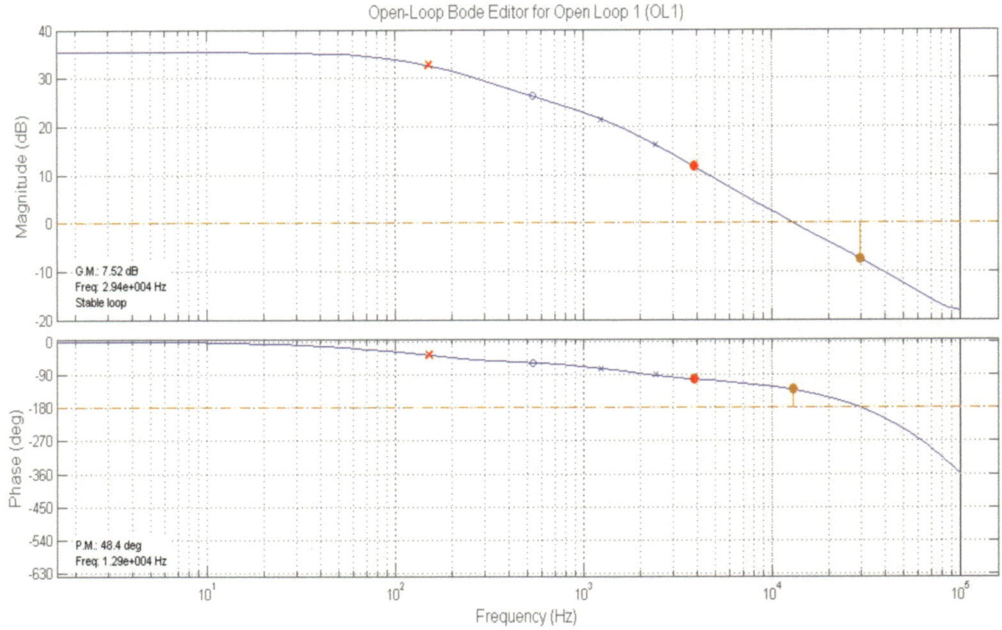

Fig. 17. Design of controller using transfer function of open loop for system G_{dlyz3}

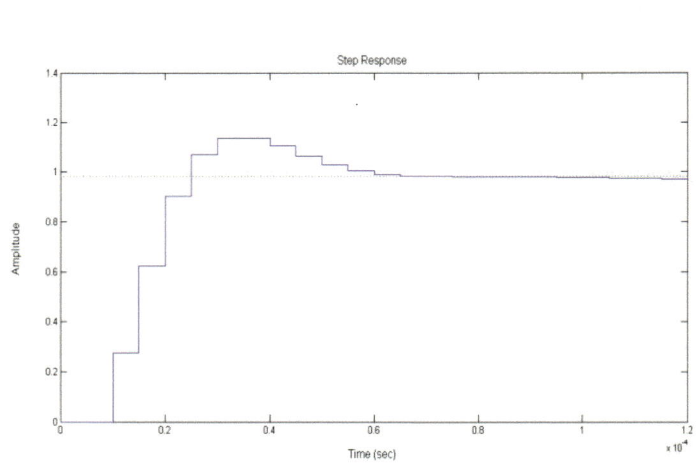

Fig. 18. Closed-loop response with designed controller for unitary jump

Both designed controllers controls at 97% of requested value, due to the reduction of regulators gain, because of limitation of overshoot below 20% of the requested value. The elimination of this problem was realized by increasing the requested value of the output voltage by 3%

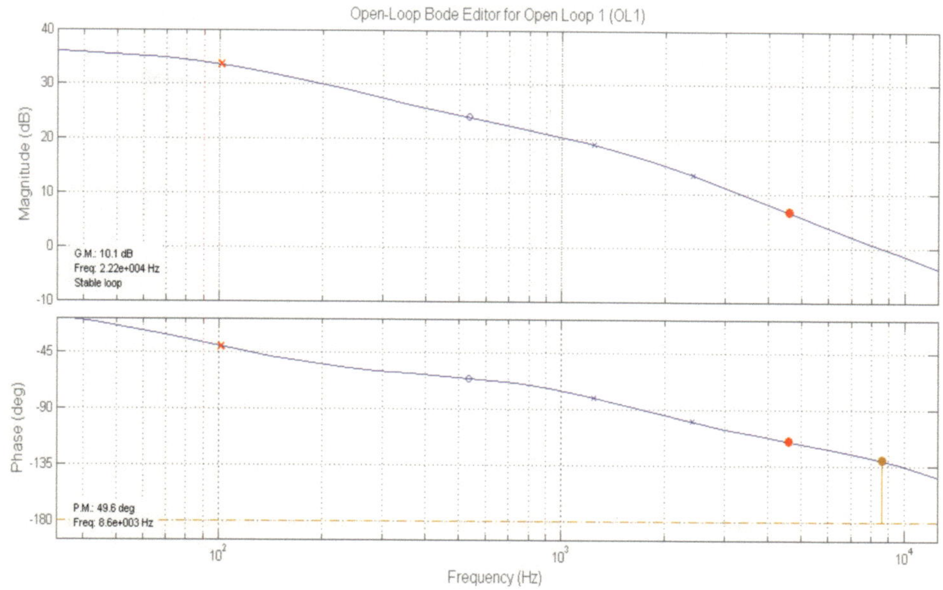

Fig. 19. Design of controller using transfer function of open loop

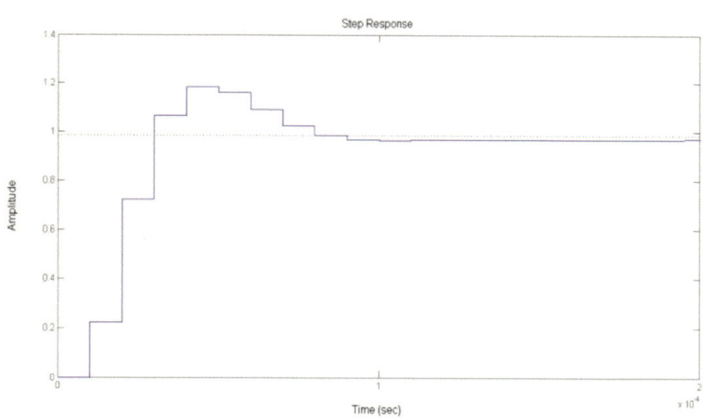

Fig. 20. Closed-loop response with designed controller for unitary jump

Transfer function of designed controller is in form:

$$G_C = 0.028539 \cdot \frac{z - 0.748}{z - 0.994} \tag{14}$$

SISOTOOL enables also the analysis of the quality and stability of the regulatory circuit. The advantage is, that information on the quality and stability control is available directly during the design procedure of the controller. As seen from figures 4.7 and 4.9 the systems with closed loop are stable , with safety margin about 50°.

5.1 Implementation in DSC

Discrete controller proposed in previous chapter was implemented into 16b digital signal controller (DSC) Freescale 56F8013, which is primary designed for motor and converter control. Advantage of this microprocessor are high performance peripherals which can operate with 96Mhz clock frequency. On the other side, disadvantage of this processor is low core frequency - 32 MHz, and fixed point arithmetic. For better performance, fraction arithmetic with intrinsic functions were used in this DSC.
Block scheme of digital control system with DSC 56F8013 on 200 kHz LLC converter is on Fig. 21. For better performance and lower amount of additional hardware, the concept with microprocessor on secondary side of converter was used. Also, new available fast digital isolators were used instead of standard optocouplers.

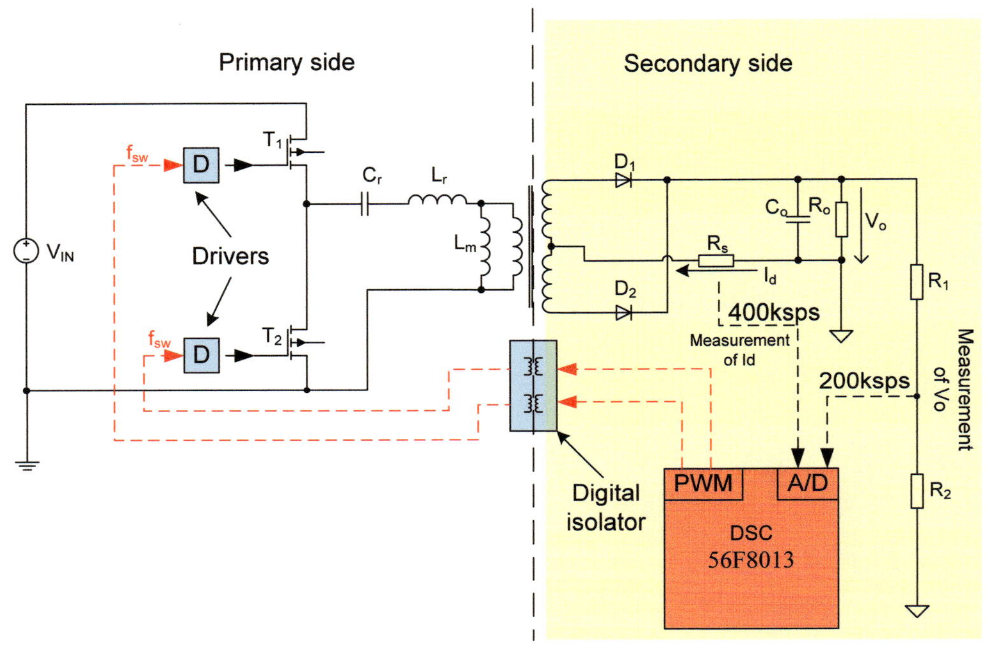

Fig. 21. Block scheme of full digital control system with DSC 56F8013

Processor	**Bits**	*Core frequency*	*A/D sampling time*	*Computing of control loop*	*Computing of current value*
56F8013	16b	32Mhz	1.126μs	2.98μs	3.01μs
ColdFireV1	32b	50,3Mhz	2.252μs	1.8μs	1.12μs

Table 2. Sampling times and computational delays for two processors

Another option for implementation is use of 32b microprocessor ColdFire V1 which offers better computing performance, but sampling time of A/D converter is twice as in DSC

56F8013. For measurement of output voltage, this time is sufficient, but for current sensing, the A/D converter on ColdFire is too slow. This problem was eliminated by use of special algorithm for computing of diode current from value of output voltage, value of load and ripple of output voltage. This algorithm is based on computing of output current from output voltage drop, during load connection. Detailed method is described in. Times required for computing on both processors are in Tab. 2.

6. Conclusion

The method for creation of mathematical model discussed in this chapter is based on circuit model of LLC converter in OrCAD PSPICE and use of MATLAB System Identification Toolbox. This approach eliminates the problems of transfer function obtaining, whose results from use of standard "averaging" methods. Instead of that, this approach uses simulation in OrCad PSPICE, based on circuit model of converter, for acquiring the results and subsequent use of MATLAB for creation of accurate control to output transfer function (in s- or z- domain). Advantage of this method is in use of all parasitic components (resistors, capacitances, inductors) in OrCad PSPICE simulation, so the transfer function is very accurate. Also, the approach for identification of the system, proposed in this paper, uses new, discrete model based method. This method allows rapid acquiring of mathematical model of converter with use of computing power of modern PC. Another advantage of this method is possibility of use for any type of converter without limitation in structure of converter.

7. Acknowledgement

Results of this work were made with support of national grant agency APVV project No. 0535-07 and to R&D operational program Centre of excellence of power electronics systems and materials for their components No. OPVaV-2008/01-SORO, ITMS 2622012003 funded by European regional development fund (ERDF).

8. References

Maksimovic, D. Zane, R. Erickson, R. (2004). Impact of Digital Control in Power Electronic, *Proceedings of 2004 International Symposium on Power Semiconductor Devices*, ISBN 4-88686-060-5, Kitakyushu, May 2004

Moudgalya, K. N. (2007). In: *Digital Control*, John Wiley and Sons, pp.157-237, John Wiley and Sons, ISBN 978-0-470-03144-5, Chichester

Hangseok, Ch. (2007). Analysis and design of LLC resonant converter with integrated transformer, *Proceedings of Applied Power Electronics Conference*, ISBN 1-4244-0714-1/07, Anaheim USA, March 2007

Hargas, L. Hrianka, M. Lakatos, J. Koniar, D. (2010). Heat fields modelling and verification of electronic parts of mechatronics systems, *Metalurgija (Metallurgy)*, vol. 49, (February 2010), ISSN 1334-2576

Frivaldský, M. Drgona, P. Prikopova, A. (2009). Design and modeling of 200kHz 1,5kW LLC power semiconductor resonant converter, *Proceedings of Applied Electronics*, ISBN 978-80-7043-781-0, September 2009

Frivaldský, M. Drgoňa, P. Špánik, P. (2009). Optimization of transistor´s hard switched commutation mode in high - power, high frequency application, *Proceedings of 15th International Conference on ELECTRICAL DRIVES and POWER ELECTRONICS*, ISBN 953-6037-55-1, Dubrovnik Croatia, October 2009

Part 4

Motor Applications

14

Wavelet Fault Diagnosis of Induction Motor

Khalaf Salloum Gaeid and Hew Wooi Ping
University of Malaya
Malaysia

1. Introduction

The early 1980s saw the emergence of wavelets, an analysis tool that drew a lot of attention from scientists of various disciplines, mathematicians in particular, due to its promising applications.
The roots of wavelet techniques go back to 1807, when Joseph Fourier presented his theories of frequency analysis. By the 1930s, investigations were being carried out on scale-varying basis functions that would conserve energy in the computation of functional energy. Between 1960 and 1980, Guido Weiss and Ronald R. Coifman studied the reconstruction of functional elements using 'atoms'. Later, Grossman and Morlet would provide a quantum physics definition of wavelets. Stephane Mallat made an important contribution to the development of wavelets through his work in digital signal processing in 1985. The first non-trivial, continuously differentiable wavelets were created by Y.Meyer. Not long after, Ingrid Daubechies constructed a set of orthonormal basis functions that form the foundation of modern day wavelet applications (Nirmesh Yadav et al, 2004).
The present demand in the industry is for high performance electric drives that are capable of achieving speed commands accurately. Control methods have had to reach higher levels of sophistication accordingly. Induction motors, with their advantages in terms of size, cost and efficiency, are best suited to meet these growing needs (Khalaf Salloum Gaeid&Hew Wooi Ping, 2010).
In costly systems, maintenance and protection are especially essential in the prevention of system breakdowns and catastrophes. Thanks to advances in signal processing technology, it is now possible to utilize wavelet principles to efficiently diagnose and protect industrial induction motors.
Motor Current Signature Analysis (MCSA) of the stator current with wavelet to detect the fault in a broken rotor bar in the transient region was done by (Douglas et al, 2003).The analysis of the sensorless control system of induction motor with a broken rotor for diagnostics using wavelet techniques has been presented by (Bogalecka et al, 2009). (Zhang et al, 2007), used the empirical model decomposition(EMD) which deals with nonlinear systems to detect the broken rotor bar using wavelet discrete transform (WDT).(Cao Zhitong et al, 2001), used the multi resolution wavelet analysis (MRA) method to detect broken rotor bars according to the analysis of stator current. The signal was filtered, differentiated and then supplied to the Daubechies wavelet with 5 levels. (Faiz, Ebrahimi et al, 2007) presented a novel criterion to detect the broken rotor bar using time stepping finite element (TSFE) to model the broken bar faults in induction motor. (Yang et al, 2007), presented a novel method to detect the rotor broken bar using Ridge wavelet. In this paper, only one phase of the

stator currents was shown to be enough to extract the characteristics of the frequency component of broken bar.(Pons-Llinares et al, 2009), presented a new method to detect a broken bar in the transient region using time motor current signature analysis (TMCSA) via frequency B-Splines. (Pineda-Sanchez et al, 2010), used fractional Fourier transform as a spectral analysis tool with the TMCSA to detect the rotor broken bar. The single mean square of discrete wavelet function computation measures whether the status of the broken rotor bar of the induction motor is healthy or faulty, using Field Programmable Gate Array(FPGA). A novelty to the weighting function was introduced by (Ordaz Moreno et al, 2008). (Abbas zadeh et al, 2001) presented a novel approach to detect the broken bar fault in squirrel cage induction motors. Two 3 HP induction motors with cast aluminum rotor bars were employed for this experiment. (Cabal-Yepez et al, 2009), used FPGA to detect a number of faults in the squirrel cage such as unbalance, faulty bearing and broken bars using parallel combination of fused fast Fourier transform(FFT) and wavelet. (J.Antonino-Daviu et al, 2009) ,presented new techniques for the detection of broken bars using high order discrete wavelet (db40) and compared it with classical methods such as the Fourier transform. To remedy the shortcomings of the FFT, (Cusido, Rosero et al, 2006) introduced spectral density on the wavelet to detect many faults in the induction motor for different load conditions (7% and 10%).A few issues were seen to feature in the use of the MCSA method for fault detection, especially when the load torque was varied. (Cusido et al, 2007& Cusido et al, 2010) presented an online system for fault detection using many wavelets like the Mexican Hat, Morlet and the Agnsis mother wavelet to detect broken bar faults.

The drawbacks of using FFT, like corrupted frequency components,the noises or other phenomena such as load torque fluctuations or supply voltage oscillations (J. Pons-Llinares et al , 2010), have been investigated by many authors for detection of broken rotor bars. The Daubechies (db) is commonly employed as the mother function to avoid low level overlapping with adjacent bands.

A 0.1 Hz resolution to detect faults in an induction motor using a combination of wavelets and power spectral density was obtained by (Hamidi et al, 2004).

The fault detection in the transient region for a broken rotor bar using the instantaneous power FFT as a medium for fault detection was presented by (Douglas, H& Pillay, P, 2005). A wavelet was used to decompose the residual stator current after filtering the noise using a Notch filter.

The wavelet indicator for detecting the broken rotor bars by calculating the absolute values of the summed coefficients in the third pattern which were normalized against the summation of the wavelet coefficient, the number of scales, and the number of samples used was presented by (Supangat et al, 2006& Supangat et al,2007).

The V/F control to detect a broken rotor bar in the induction motor was made according to the probability distribution of different operation statuses of healthy and faulty motors used by (Samsi et al, 2006). In this paper, the difference in entropy was used as a measurement indication of fault.

DWT to detect the broken rotor bar in the transient region using the slip dependant fault component according to the energy ratio of the current signal to the wavelet signal was done by Riera-Guasp et al, 2008).

The detection of the broken rotor bar fault using optimized DWT and FFT in the steady state was proposed by (J. Antonino et al, 2006). (Kia et al,2009) presented a discrete wavelet transform (DWT) for broken bar detection and diagnosis faults in induction machines in which an energy test of bandwidth with time domain analysis is performed first, after which it is applied to the stator current space vector to obtain the different broken bar fault severities and load levels.

Eigen vector as a fault indicator of stator inter turn short circuit using the Eigen vector and an energy Eigen value which contain the necessary information of the electromagnetic torque signal was presented by (Liu & Huang, 2005).

The finite element (FE) modelling of the internal faults of an induction motor. They solved the equation by the time stepping approach of a broken bar and stator shorted turns using db10 wavelet for both sinusoidal and non-sinusoidal cases has been used by (Mohammed et al, 2006& Mohammed et al, 2007).

Software diagnosis of short inter turn circuit and open circuit of the stator winding as an incipient fault was performed by (Ponci et al, 2007) to avoid any hardware cost and difficulty using wavelet decomposition for different values of stator resistance.

The MCSA technique and a wavelet to detect faults but performed the stator teeth harmonic variation using dq0 components instead of stator currents (I_{abc})was done by (Cusido et al, 2006). (Gang Niu et al, 2008) employed Bayesian belief fusion and multi agent fusion as a classifier tool to detect different faulty collected data using the signal processing techniques for smoothing and then used DWT to decompose the signals into different ranges of frequency.

Detection and diagnosis for rotor asymmetries in the induction motor based on the analysis of the stator start-up current has been done by (M. Riera-Guaspa et al, 2009). The authors extracted the harmonic component introduced by this fault. The left sideband component from the stator startup current, digital low-pass filtering (DLPF) and (DWT) are used in this technique. (C. Combastel et al, 2002) presented a comparison between model-based and signal-based approaches in the fault detection of the induction motor. The electrical variables are described according to the Park transformation model. Broken rotor and stator winding failures were investigated and the parameter variations due to heating were taken into account. (S. Radhika et al, 2010), in her MCSA-based fault diagnosis, classified WT extracted features using a Support Vector Machine (SVM). (Chen & Loparo, 1998) proposed the computation of a fault index for the stator winding faults. (Khan& Rahman, 2006) used two DWT to detect and classify the faults.

The continuous wavelet is a part of the wavelet used to detect faults especially when the overlapping between the frequency supply signal and the adjacent signal cannot be recognized. The work presented by (Ayaz et al, 2006) involved the use of six accelerometers that measured the vibration data of 5 kW and were put in independent places around the motor to detect the bearing damage.

A new technique for detecting and diagnosing faults in both stator and rotor windings using wound rotor induction motor was presented by (Saleh et al, 2005). This technique is based on a wavelet transform multi resolution analysis (WTMRA). (Cusido et al, 2007) presented both continuous and discrete wavelet to detect many mechanical and electrical induction motor faults using MCSA. (Sayed-Ahmed et al, 2007) studied the inter-turn short circuit in one phase of a stator winding of an induction motor energized from a vector controlled drive.

The induction motor requires a variable frequency three phase source for variable speed operation. One can realize this source by using a power converter system consisting of a rectifier connected to an inverter through a DC link.

In some control schemes where a three phase, variable frequency current source is required, current control loops are added to force the motor currents to follow an input reference.

Vector control techniques have been widely used for the high performance drive of induction motors. Like DC motors, torque control of induction motor is achieved by controlling the torque and flux components independently (Mohamed Boussak and Kamel Jarray, 2006). The similarities between DC and vector control are why the latter is referred to as decoupling, orthogonal or trans-vector control (Archana S. Nanoty, and A. R. Chudasama, 2008).
In this chapter, we investigate the use of the wavelet in the fault detection of vector-controlled induction motors, detection of the broken rotor bar and stator short winding faults as well as the verification of wavelet fault detection models using MATLAB.
Finally, two approaches for the protection of induction motor are examined. The first uses the Automatic Gain Control (AGC) to compensate the voltage of the induction motor to maintain satisfactory operation. The second halts operation when the fault severity becomes high. Without delving into excessively detailed results, we analyse the output relevant to wavelet detection and diagnosis.

2. Model of induction motor

The d-q dynamic model of the squirrel cage induction motor with the reference frame fixed to the stator is given by (Anjaneyulu, N .Kalaiarasi and K.S.R 2007):

$$V_s = R_s i_s + \frac{d\lambda_s}{dt} + j\omega_s M\lambda_s \tag{1}$$

$$V_r = R_r i_r + \frac{d\lambda_r}{dt} + (\omega_s - \omega_r) M\lambda_r \tag{2}$$

The electromagnetic torque is found as:

$$T_e = \frac{2pL_m}{3L_r}(i_{qs}i_{dr} - i_{ds}i_{qr}) \tag{3}$$

$$T_e = \frac{2pL_m}{3L_r}(i_{qs}\varphi_{dr} - i_{ds}\varphi_{qr}) \tag{4}$$

$$\varphi_{ds} = L_r i_{dr} + L_m i_{ds} \tag{5}$$

The field orientation is based on the following assumption:

$$\varphi_{qr} = 0 \tag{6}$$

$$\varphi_{dr} = constant \tag{7}$$

The (vector) field orientation control performs the following calculations

$$\begin{bmatrix} i_{qs} \\ i_{ds} \end{bmatrix} = \begin{bmatrix} \cos\varphi_s & \sin\varphi_s \\ -\sin\varphi_s & \cos\varphi_s \end{bmatrix} \tag{8}$$

d-q to abc transformation is:

$$\begin{bmatrix} i_{as} \\ i_{bs} \\ i_{cs} \end{bmatrix} = \begin{bmatrix} 1 & 0 \\ -0.5 & -\sqrt{3}/2 \\ -0.5 & -\sqrt{3}/2 \end{bmatrix} \begin{bmatrix} i_{qs} \\ i_{ds} \end{bmatrix} \tag{9}$$

Accordingly, the rotor flux and the torque can be controlled individually through the stator current in the dq-axis so that the induction motor is transformed to a linear current and torque relationship.

3. Vector control of the induction motor

Vector control was invented by Hasse in 1969 and by Blaschke in 1972 when they demonstrated that an induction motor can be controlled like a separately excited dc motor. This brought a renaissance in the high performance control of AC drives.
Vector control of the squirrel cage induction motor is considered a fast response and high performance method to achieve variable speeds using a variable frequency source as shown in Fig.1

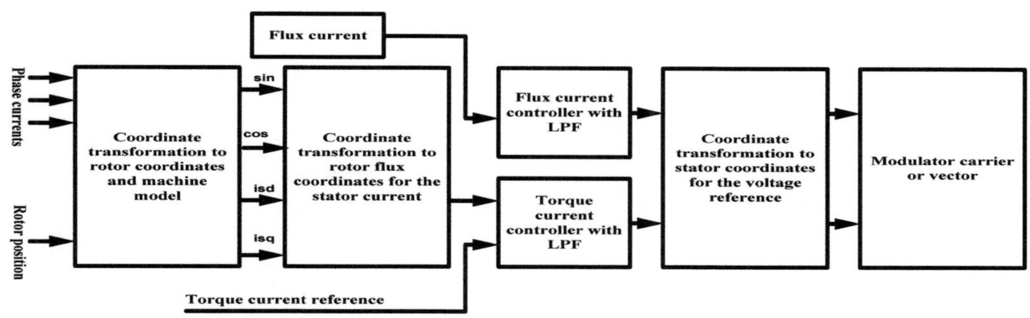

Fig. 1. Vector control principle

In the vector control method, the induction motor can be operated like a separately excited DC motor for high performance applications.
To achieve better performance, numerous speed closed loop systems have been improved. However, desired drive specifications still cannot be perfectly satisfied and/or their algorithms are too complex (J.L. Silva Neto&Hoang Le-Huy, 1996) as shown in Fig.2.

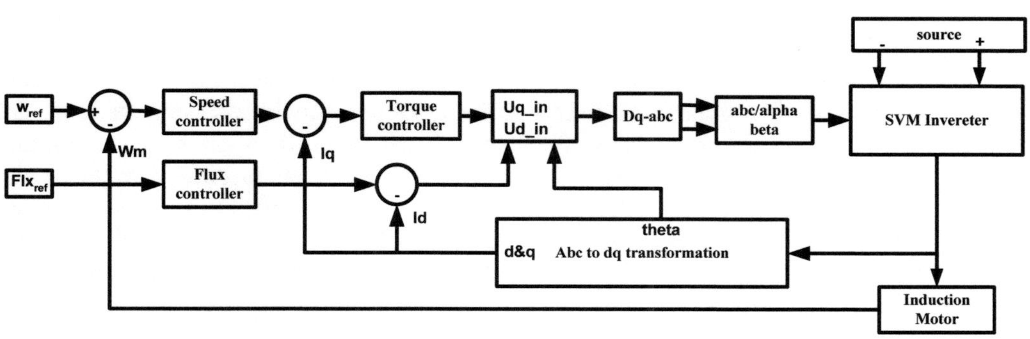

Fig. 2. Vector control implementation

Vector controlled machines need two constants as input references; the torque component (aligned with the q-axis coordinate) and the flux component (aligned with d-axis coordinate) which is simply based on projections as the control structure handles instantaneous electrical quantities. This behavior yields accurate control in both the steady state and transients and is independent of the bandwidth mathematical model of the induction motor.

Vector control is an especially advantageous solution to the problem of motor control because the torque and flux components of stator flux are easily accessible. Besides, it is free from a number of complexities that beset direct torque control (BPRA073, 1998).

There are two different strategies in vector control to obtain the rotor flux:

- Indirect control, in which the rotor flux vector is either measured by a flux sensor mounted in the air-gap or measured using the voltage equations starting from the electrical machine parameters.
- Direct control, in which the rotor flux parameter can be calculated by direct rotor speed measurement.

The condition to apply vector control to induction motors is the formulation of dynamic model equations to calculate and control the variables (AN2388, 2006) as can be seen in Fig.3, which shows the Simulink implementation of vector control using the current regulation technique. Note that both the magnitude and phase alignment of vector variables is controlled.

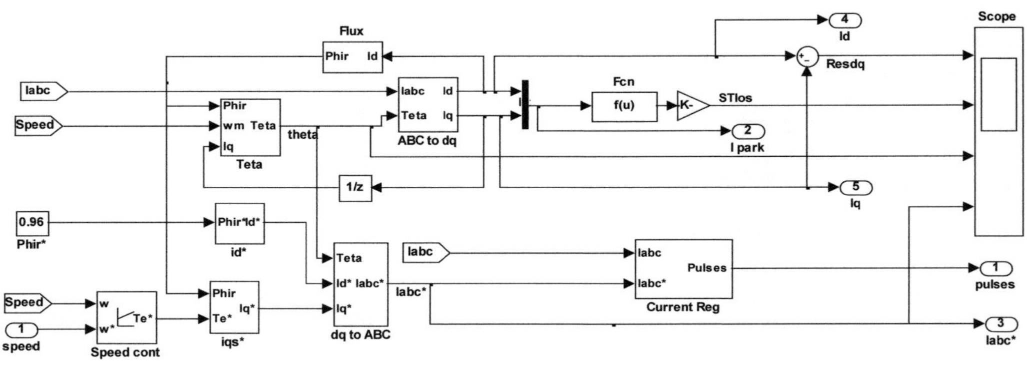

Fig. 3. Vector control implemented using Simulink.

4. Discrete wavelet transform fault detection

Wavelet techniques are new in the field of fault diagnosis. They are useful due to their ability to extract all the information in both time and frequency domain. They provide a sensitive means to diagnose the faults in comparison to other signal processing methods like the Fourier Transform, the drawbacks of which include the need to use a single window function in all frequency components and the acquisition of linear resolution in the whole frequency domain. This is an important reason for the interest in wavelets in time-frequency analysis as can be seen in (M. Riera-Guaspa et al, 2009). (Andrew K.S. et al, 2006) presented a review of the diagnosis of machines using the condition-based maintenance approach. There are two levels of fault diagnosis:

1. Traditional control
2. Knowledge based fault diagnosis

Fault diagnosis techniques contain the feature extraction module (wavelet), feature cluster module and the fault decision module (1). Indicators of faults include the negative sequence current, impedance and the Park's vector.
Motor Current Signature Analysis (MCSA) is used to diagnose the stator short circuit fault.
Multi resolution analysis and good time localization are particularly useful characteristics of wavelets in the context of fault diagnosis.
Signal processing techniques like the FFT are based on the assumptions of constant stator fundamental frequency, load, motor speed and the assumption that the load is sufficient.
Wavelet transformation is of many kinds but in this chapter the authors will introduce the most important among them:

1. Discrete wavelet transformation
2. Continuous wavelet transformation
3. Wavelet packet decomposition transformation

The wavelet is divided into two main groups. One is the discrete wavelet transform represented in the following Eq.:

$$DWT(m,k) = \frac{1}{\sqrt{a_0^m}} \Sigma x(n) g\left(\frac{k - nb_0 a_0^m}{a_0^m}\right) \tag{10}$$

Where $g(n)$ is the mother wavelet $x(n)$ is the input signal and the scaling and translation parameters " a "and " b " are functions of the integer parameter m (M. Sushama et al, 2009).
The second wavelet type is the continuous wavelet transform (CWT) which can be represented as follows:

$$\omega(m,n) = \int_{-\infty}^{\infty} f(t) \psi^{*}_{m,n}(t) dt \tag{11}$$

* denotes the complex conjugate, where f (t) is the waveform signal and ψ (t) is a wavelet.

$$\psi_{m,n}(t) = 2^{-1/2} \psi(2^{-m} t - n) \tag{12}$$

Where m and n are the wavelet dilation and translation used to transform the original signal to a new one with smaller scales according to the high frequency components. This relation is valid for the orthogonal basis of wavelet transform (a =2 and b =1). In the following continuous wavelet transform, a is the scale parameter, b is the time parameter.

$$\omega_{a,b}(t) = \left| a \right|^{-1/2} \psi\left(\frac{t-b}{a}\right) \tag{13}$$

CWT is divided into the Real wavelet as can be seen in table 1 and the Complex wavelet as in table 2.
In digital computers, the discrete wavelet transform is a good choice. The mother wavelet is scaled to the power of 2 (R. Salehi Arashloo&A. Jalilian, 2010).
The continuous wavelet transform (CWT) was developed as an alternative approach to overcome the resolution problem as is shown in Table 1 (Lorand SZABO et al, 2005).

Beta Wavelet	$\psi_{beta}(t/\alpha,\beta)=(-1)dp(t/\alpha,\beta)/dt$
Hermitian Wavelet	$\psi_n(t)=(2n)^{-n/2}C_n H_n(t/\sqrt{2})e^{(-1/2n)t^2}$
Mex.hat wavelet	$\psi(t)=(2/\sqrt{3}\sigma\pi^{1/4})(1-t^2/\sigma^2)e^{(-t^2/2\sigma^2)}$
Shannon wavelet	$\psi(t)=2\sin c(2t)-\sin c(t)$

Table 1. Continuous real wavelet transform

Mexican hat wavelet	$\psi(t)=\frac{2}{\sqrt{3}}\pi^{-0.25}\left(\sqrt{\pi}(-t^2)e^{-0.5t^2}-\right.$ $\left.-\sqrt{2}\,it\sqrt{\pi}erf\left(\frac{i}{\sqrt{2}}t\right)(1-t^2)\,e^{-0.5t^2}\right)$
Morlet wavelet	$\psi(t)=(C\pi^{-(1/4)})e^{-1/2t^2}(e^{it}-k)$
Shannon wavelet	$\psi(t)=\sin c(t)e^{-j\pi t}$
Modified Morlet wavelet	$\psi(t)=C_\psi\cos(\omega_o t)\sec h(t)$

Table 2. Continuous complex wavelet transform

Two properties of the wavelet are noteworthy:

1. When a wavelet satisfies an admissibility condition, a signal with finite energy can be reconstructed without needing all values of its decomposition. The admissibility condition is represented by the following equation:

$$\int\frac{|\psi(\omega)|^2}{|\omega|}d\omega<+\infty \tag{14}$$

Where ψ (ω) is the Fourier transform of the wavelet function ψ (t) used to investigate the signals and then to reconstruct them without losing any information. According to the admissibility condition, the Fourier transform goes to zero as is shown in the following equation:

$$|\psi(\omega)|^2=0 \tag{15}$$

Another important property of the wavelet is:

$$\int\psi(\omega)=0 \tag{16}$$

2. To remedy the squared relationship between the time bandwidth product of the wavelet transform and the input signal, certain regularity conditions are imposed so as to ensure the smoothness and concentration of the wavelet function in both time and frequency domains.

The decomposition can be implemented using filtering and down-sampling, and can be iterated, with successive approximation as in (Turkmenoglu, 2010).

The total decomposition levels (L) can be calculated according to the following relationship:

$$L \geq \frac{\log(fs/f)}{\log(2)} + 1 \tag{17}$$

These bands can't be changed unless a new acquisition with different sampling frequency is made, which complicate any fault detection based on DWT, particularly in time-varying conditions (Yasser Gritli et al, 2011).

When (18) is applied at a sampling frequency of 1 kHz, a six level decomposition occurs. Table 3 depicts the frequency bands for each wavelet signal.

$$L = \frac{\log(1000/50)}{\log(2)} + 1 = 6 \text{ levels} \tag{18}$$

Approximations «aj»	Frequency bands (Hz)	Details «dj»	Frequency bands (Hz)
a_6	[0-16.125]	d_6	[16.125-32.25]
a_5	[0-32.25]	d_5	[32.250-64.5]
a_4	[0 - 64.50]	d_4	[64.50-125.0]
a_3	[0 – 125.0]	d_3	[125.0-250.0]
a_2	[0- 250.0]	d_2	[250.0-500.0]
a_1	[0-500.0]	d_1	[500.0-1000.0]

Table 3. Frequency bands for the six levels of wavelet signals

The data required to analyze the signal depends on both the sampling frequency ( ) and the resolution (R) as in (19):

$$D_{required} = f_s / R \tag{19}$$

The interpretation of the above table is shown in Fig 4:

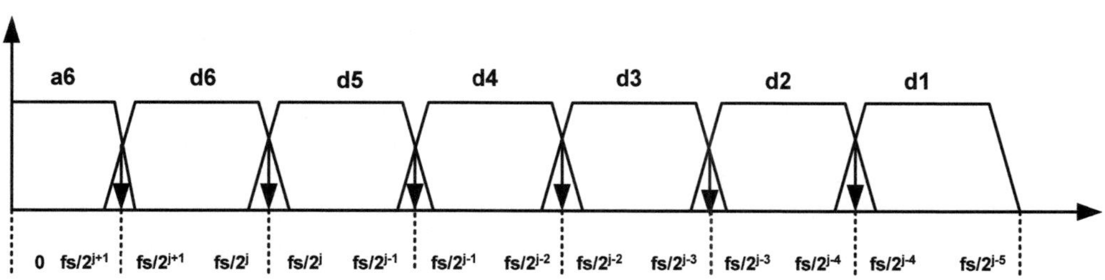

Fig. 4. Frequency range covers for details and final approximation

The MATLAB signal processing toolbox software provides the Filter Design and Analysis tool (FDATool) that enables the design of a low pass filter and high pass filter and then export the filters coefficients to a matching filter implemented as can be seen in the Fig.5.

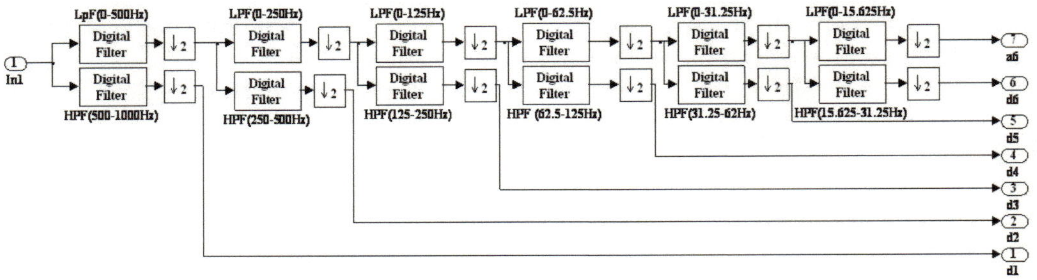

Fig. 5. Wavelet decomposition levels using FDA matlab tool box

An alternative way to performing the same task is through the DWT dyadic filter from MATLAB/Simulink. Although for this method, the wavelet coefficients may need to be calculated using the following MATLAB instruction:

$$[Lo\_D, Hi\_D, Lo\_R, Hi\_R] = \text{wfilters}(\text{'db10'}) \tag{20}$$

Where Lo_D,Hi_D,Lo_R,Hi_R represent low pass filter decomposition,high pass filter decomposition ,low pass filter reconstruction and high pass filter reconstruction respectively. This is shown in Fig.6.

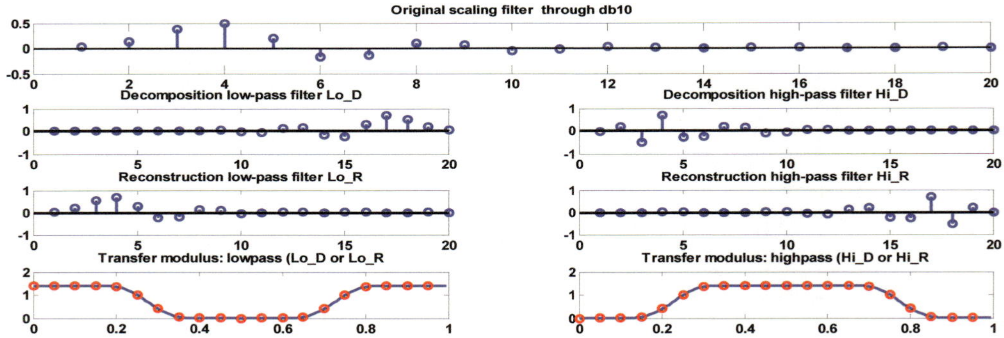

Fig. 6. Wavelet decomposition and reconsstruction f filters

The decomposition of the wavelets was impemented using the above relation as can be seen in Fig.7.

The above two circuits are exactly the same. A wavelet-transform-based method was developed for diagnosis and protection the induction motor against broken rotor bar and short stator windings. Detailed information is obtained from the high pass filters and the approximation information is obtained from low pass filter. Daubechies wavelet (db10) is used to analayze stator current as in Fig8.

The construction of DWT is followed by implementing the criterion of fault detection of induction motor faults. The criteria used to detect the induction motor faults depend on the relationship between maximum detail energy (d6) and the original stator current (*Ia*) as is shown in Fig.9.

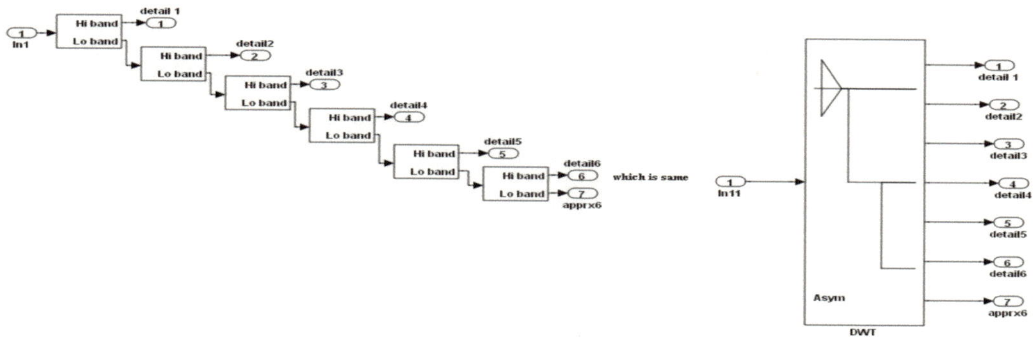

Fig. 7. DWT filters and levels using simulink

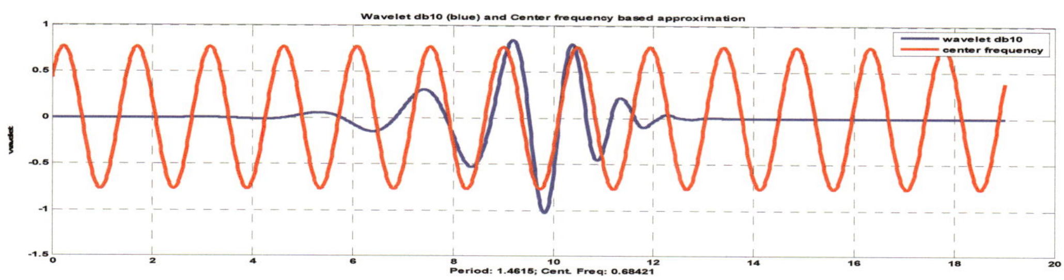

Fig. 8. Daubechies wavelet (db10) and central frequency

Offline calculations of maximum energy were done using MATLAB instructions as in the following wavelet program:

```
load Ia
[C, L] = wavedec (Ia, 6,'db10');
[Ea, Ed] = wenergy(C, L)
```

Ea is the percentage of energy corresponding to the approximation, Ed is the vector containing the percentages of energy corresponding to the details, C is the wavelet decomposition vector and L is the bookkeeping vector.

Ea = 99.5370(a6)

Ed =0.0000(d1) 0.0000(d2) 0.0000(d3) 0.0001(d4) 0.0010(d5) 0.4619(d6)

The Wavelet coefficients, the energy of the details of any signal at level j can be expressed as (M. Sabarimalai Manikandan, and S. Dandapat, 2007):

$$E_j = \sum d_{j,k}^{\ 2} \tag{21}$$

$$d_{j,k} = \langle x(t), \psi_{j,k} \rangle = \frac{1}{\sqrt{2^j}} \int x(t)\psi(2^j t - k)dt \tag{22}$$

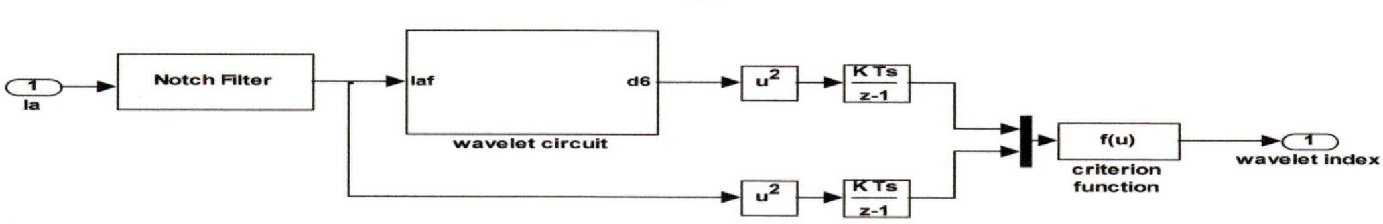

Fig. 9. Wavelet index unit with conditioning signal

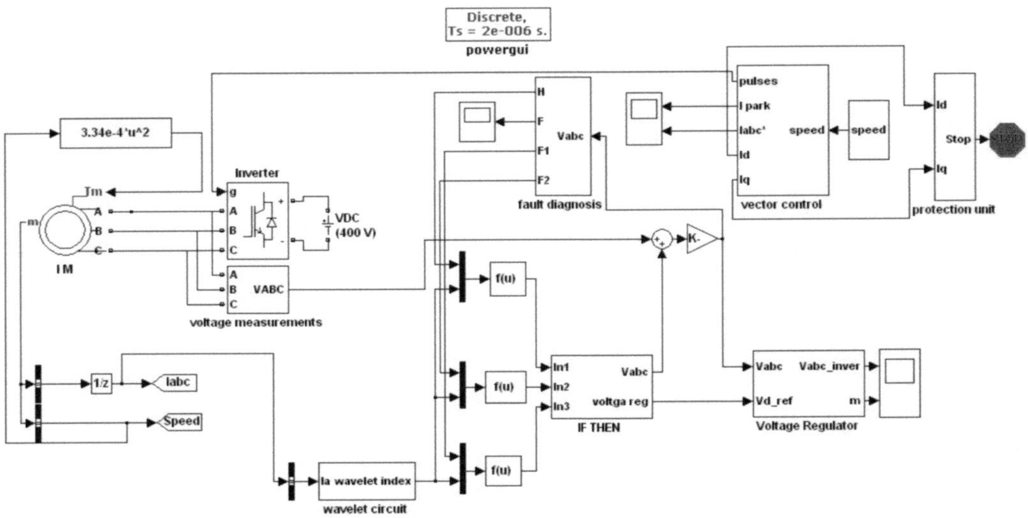

Fig. 10. Proposed circuit of induction motor fault diagnosis with wavelet

M. specifications	Unit	Value
power	w	370
Current	ampere	1.7
Voltage (delta)	volt	230
Rated speed	RPM	2800
No. of pole		2
Moment of inertia	Kgm^2	3.5e-4
Stator resist.	ohm	24.6
Rotor resist.	ohm	16.1
Stator induct.	henry	40e-3
Rotor induct.	henry	40e-3

Table 4. Induction motor specifications

5. Fault detection

Electric drives are used in safety-critical applications or industrial processes where the immense costs of unplanned stops are unacceptable. Fault detection depends on the availability of information from the system. In this work, the fault detection is done using wavelet for analysis of stator current as can be shown in Fig.11 for the healthy case, Fig.12 for broken rotor bar case and Fig.13 for the stator short winding case respectively.
The wavelet criterion of fault detection is:

$$W_{indx} = abs(energy(d6)) / average(energy(Ia)) \tag{23}$$

In MATLAB/Simulink, an assessment of operating features of the proposed scheme is performed. Two faults are investigated: stator short winding and broken rotor bar.

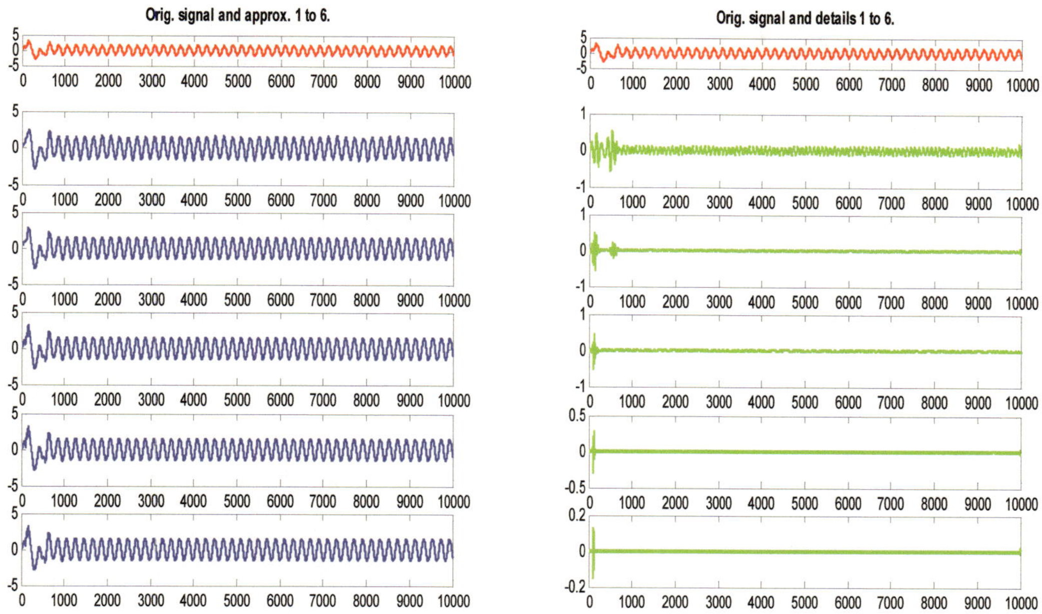

Fig. 11. Approximation and details signal in healthy motor

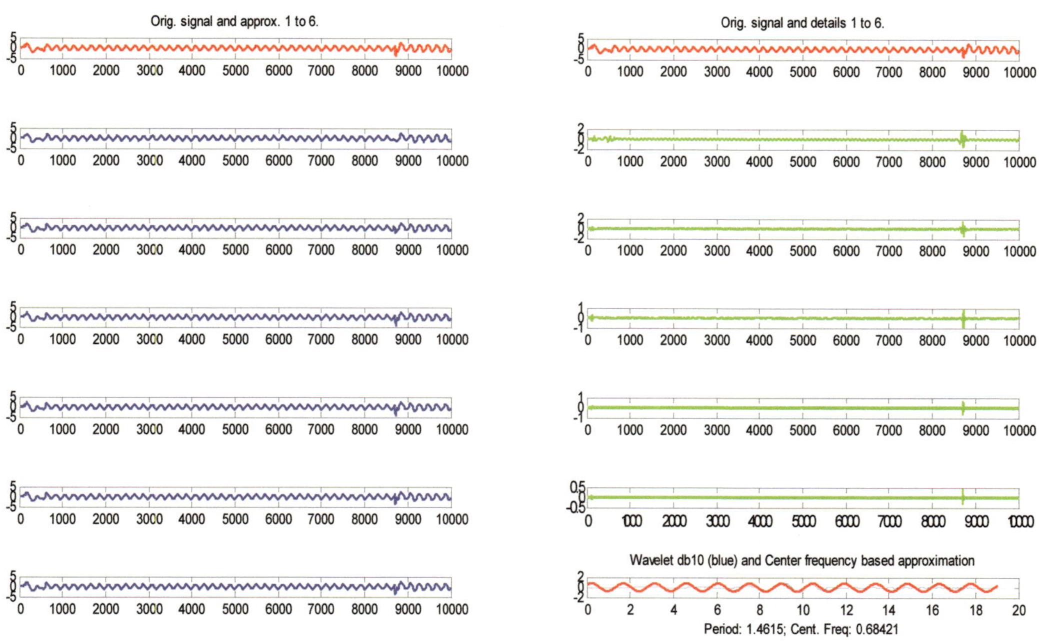

Fig. 12. Approximation and details signal in one broken rotor bar fault

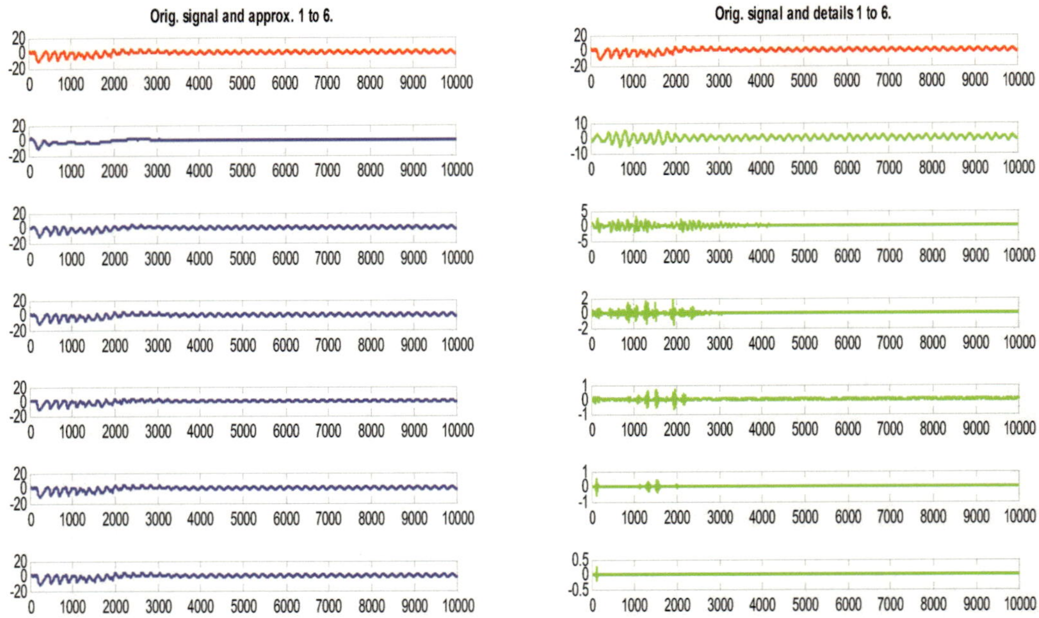

Fig. 13. Approximation and details signal in short stator winding fault

This wavelet is also used as fault indicator or wave index as is shown in Fig14.

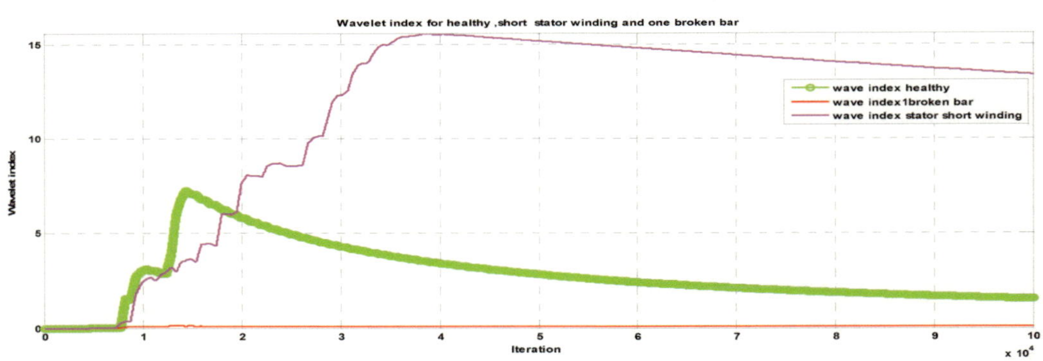

Fig. 14. Wavelet index for fault detection

5.1 Broken rotor bar

Key reasons for a broken rotor bar are (Ahmed Y. Ben Sasi et al, 2006):

1. Direct on line starting which leads to excessive heating and mechanical problems.
2. Variable mechanical load.
3. Unsatisfactory rotor cage manufacturing.

Broken rotor bar faults can be simulated by connecting three resistances with the rotor resistance so that by increasing one of the rotor phase resistances, the broken rotor bar equivalent resistance can be computed as in (24).

$$R_{brk} \cong (0.33/4) R_r z_{nb} / N^2_s \tag{24}$$

The external added resistances are changed in 0.0833 Ω steps, which represents the difference between the reference rotor resistance and the original rotor resistance for one broken rotor bar .Reference rotor resistance depends on the number of broken bars and the total number of rotor bars (Hakan Calıs& Abdulkadir Cakır, 2007). The resistance of induction motor rotor bar is assumed to be high.
(Levent Eren, & Michael J. Devaney, 2004), presented the bearing fault defects of the induction motor WPT decomposition of 1 Hp induction motor stator current through the test of RMS for both healthy and faulty bearings.

5.2 Stator shorting the winding

More than 30% of all motor faults are caused by failure of the motor winding due to insulation problems. For the stator short circuit winding fault, the stator resistance of the induction motor is connected to the parallel variable resistance which is reduced according to the following formula:

$$R_{sh} = 0.1R_{org} \tag{25}$$

The majority of induction motor winding failures proceed gradually from lower short circuit current to a higher level and finally break as can be seen in (Dimas et al, 2010).
To check the validity of the wavelet fault detection of both stator winding and broken rotor bar units as well as when the motor is in a healthy condition,MATLAB/Simulink's Predicted Model Block (PED) is used to verifiy the wavelet detection units as is shown in subsequent figures.
In the healthy induction motor, transfer finction of the wavelet unit (interval test) is:

$$G_{healthy} = \frac{-1.3e-166z^3 + 8.2e-167z^2}{z^4 - 0.5z^3 - 0.5z^2 + 7.7067e-8z - 1.1592e-8} \tag{26}$$

And the noise model of unit is:

$$G_{Noise} = \frac{z^4 + 0.0027766z^3 + 0.00025661z^2}{z^4 - 2.3152z^3 + 1.2203z^2 + 0.5013z - 0.40632} \tag{27}$$

The predicted and noise model of the wavelet detection unit in the healthy case is shown in Fig15.

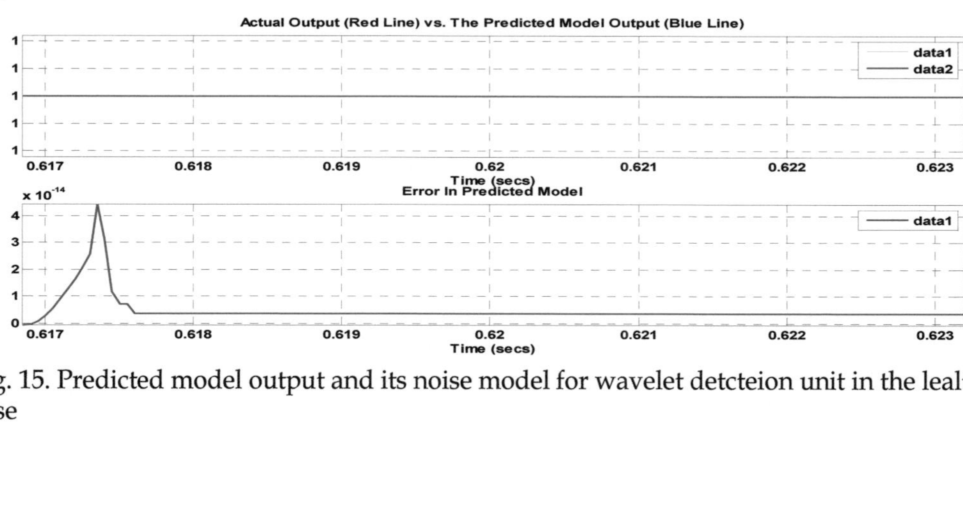

Fig. 15. Predicted model output and its noise model for wavelet detcteion unit in the lealthy case

In the stator short winding fault, transfer function of the wavelet unit (interval test) is:

$$G_{statorshort} = \frac{1.1665e-158z^3 - 2.2477e-158z^2}{z^4 - 0.5z^3 - 0.5z^2 + 2.9406e-10z - 3.5998e-11} \quad (28)$$

The noise model of the unit is:

$$G_{noise\,model} = \frac{z^4 + 0.0020325z^3 - 0.00119535z^2}{z^4 - 2.4623z^3 + 1.4434z^2 + 0.5z - 0.48113} \quad (29)$$

The predicted and noise model of the wavelet detection unit in this case is shown in Fig16.

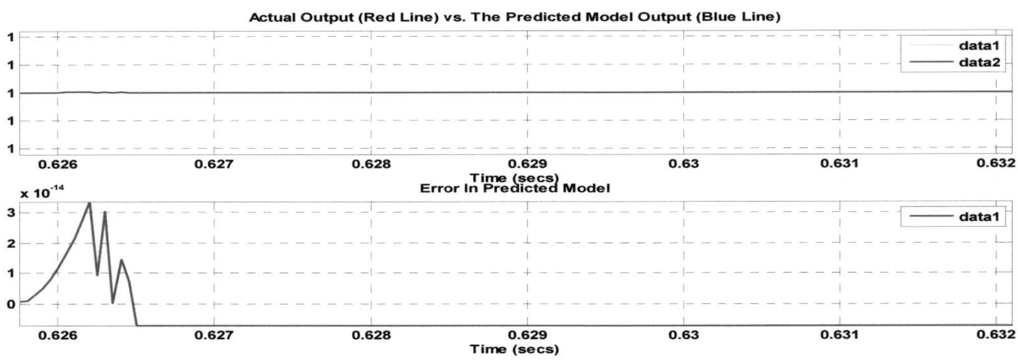

Fig. 16. predicted model output and its noise model for wavelet detcteion unit in the stator short winding case

In the broken rotor bar fault, transfer function of the wavelet unit (interval test) is:

$$G_{brokenbar} = \frac{1.17382e-159z^3 - 2.0472e-159z^2}{z^4 - 0.5z^3 - 0.5z^2 - 3.4564e-11z - 4.1663e-11} \quad (30)$$

The noise model of the unit is:

$$G_{noise\,model} = \frac{z^4 + 0.0035537z^3 - 0.0011322z^2}{z^4 - 2.1078z^3 + 0.90396z^2 + 0.503z - 0.30002} \quad (31)$$

The predicted and noise model of the wavelet detection unit in this case is shown in Fig17.

6. Protection circuit

In the protection stage of the induction motor, there are many steps to perform exact or optimal protection of the circuit like: condition monitoring which is the process of monitoring a parameter of condition in machinery, such that a significant change is indicative of a developing failure. Many condition-monitoring methods, which monitor the motor's condition using only the currents and voltages of the motor, are preferred due to their low cost and non-intrusiveness (Zhang et al, 2011). For reliable operation of ajustable

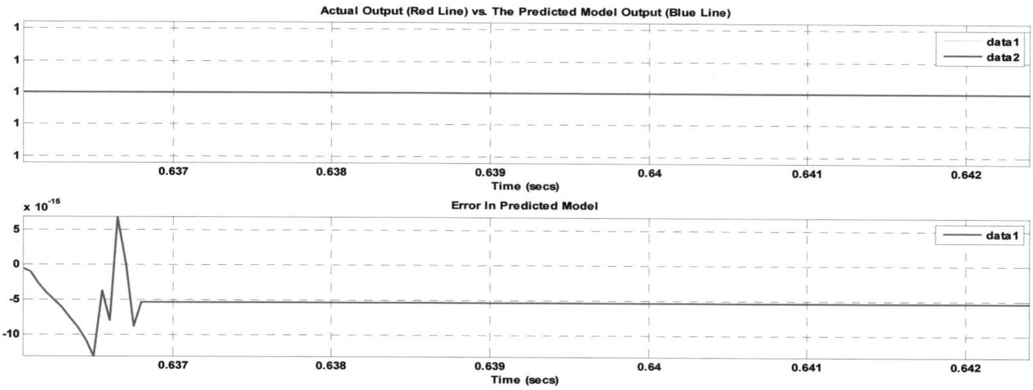

Fig. 17. Predicted model output and its noise model for wavelet detcteion unit in the broken rotor.

speed drive systems, the vulnerable components of the power converter, cable, and motor must be monitored, since failure of a single component can result in a forced outage of the entire system (Lee, et al, 2011).

In this chapter, two approaches are used to treat the faults mentioned above. First, voltage regulation with automatic gain control (AGC) is used to control the voltage after the occurrence of fault and hence the speed to maintain the operation of the induction motor as in (32):

$$AGC = reciprocal(mean(real(f_{vd})^2 + real(f_{vq})^2) \quad (32)$$

This is shown in Fig18:

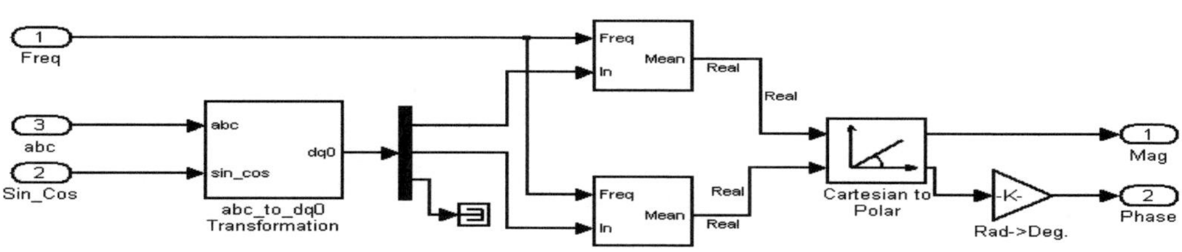

Fig. 18. Automatic gain controller circuit

The fault diagnosis condition depends also upon an optimization technique of induction motor flux as in (33).

$$\varphi_{optimal} = |T_e * \sqrt{R_r / (3/2 * p)}| \quad (33)$$

The proposed circuit of the wavelet fault diagnosis is shown in Fig10. The last stage of the protection is to stop the motor operation when the fault severity becomes high and cannot be controlled according to the following criteria.

$$\textit{if}\ \max(Iq) > 180\ \ \&\textit{bad flux due to bad torque}\ \ \textit{then stop the operation} \tag{34}$$

The protection circuit as in the Fig.19

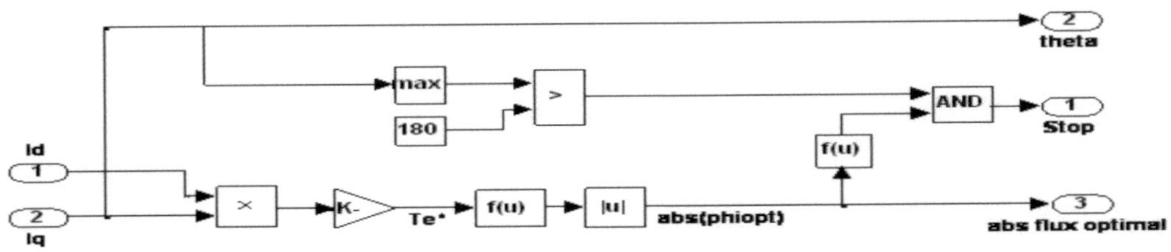

Fig. 19. Protection and checking of the optimal flux unit

Since this work focuses on the wavelet, the results of this stage are not included here. They are expected to be presented by the authors in a paper dealing with the protection of induction motors.

7. Simulation results

Computer simulations using Matlab/Simulink have been performed for assessment of operating features of the proposed scheme. The simulation involved a startup of an induction motor 0.5Hp, 230V, 50 Hz as is shown in Table 4. All pertinent mathematical models have been developed individually, using Simulink blocks for the power, electronic converters and the motor. The developed torque increases rapidly due to the slip speed, which is maximum at starting and decreases as the speed of the motor is increased. The classic vector control scheme consists of the torque and flux control loops. For the vector control of induction motors, the rotor field orientation has the advantage of easy decoupling of the torque and flux components of the controlled variable. The speed loop utilizes a PI controller to produce the quadrature axis currents which serves as the torque command (K_p =18 and K_i=5). Better PI tuning results in a better wavelet waveform. One phase of stator current is used as the input to the wavelet circuit. It is clear from Fig.11, Fig.12 and Fig.13 that detailed information is extracted from the high pass filter and approximation data from the low pass filter to show the exact location and time of the fault even for the transient response of the healthy case. A higher order of wavelet introduces better signal accuracy. Fig.14 shows the wavelet index with the threshold of the healthy case between 2.5 and 7. In this work, the stator short winding was high index (16.6), the range of this fault being 7-17 due to the severity of fault; the broken rotor bar was very light (0.12) and the range of this fault was between 0 and 0.2.The figure did not start from zero because there is a 1 sec delay for protection. Careful tuning of AGC is needed for the PID controller to get best results, in this work (K_i=100, K_p = 1 and K_d=0).

Fig.15, Fig.16 and Fig.17 show the outputs of the PEM (Predictive Error Method) estimator block which estimates linear input-output polynomial models in Simulink for the healthy case, stator short winding and broken rotor bar respectively. The monitoring of the optimal flux is another fault diagnosis indicator in this work which depends on both torque and rotor resistance as well as on the poles of the induction motor.

The last stage of the operation is the protection. Fig.19 shows the optimal flux and protection mechanism which depends on both torque, flux and on the phase of I_q. If this phase is more than 180, this will lead to bad torque and flux and will indicate the need to stop the operation of induction motor.

8. Conclusion

The scalar control of induction motor drives have many drawbacks including slow response, unsuitable performance, torque ripple and impossibility of operation at all points of speed torque curve, vector control is implemented on an induction motor drive to solve these imperfections.
Three phase sinusoidal voltage is converted to dc voltage with the help of universal diode bridge rectifier. Current source inverters which dominate modern adjustable speed AC drives are not free from certain disadvantages.
In particular the high switching rate needed for good quality of the current fed to the motor cause's losses, electromagnetic interference etc.Accords to the results, the algorithm used is very effective and have been succeeded in maintain both speed and torque.
There are many conclusions can be included due to this work:

- The wavelet is considered as powerful tools in the fault detection and diagnosis of induction motors.
- Many wavelet classes can be generated by different kinds of mother wavelets and can be constructed by filters banks.
- The improvement of fault detection and diagnosis can be exploiting the wavelet properties to get high detection and diagnostics effectiveness.
- Theories of wavelet need to be pushed forward to insure best choosing of mother wavelet.
- The wavelet index can distinguish correctly between the faults and healthy induction motor.
- Matlab/Simulink axcellent package for both simulations and practicle experiments in the diagnostic of induction machines with wavelet.

9. References

Abbas zadeh, K., Milimonfared, J., Haji, M., & Toliyat, H. (2001). Broken bar detection in induction motor via wavelet transformation. *The 27th Annual Conference of the IEEE Industrial Electronics Society*, Vol.1, pp. 95 -99.

Ahmed Y. Ben Sasi, Fengshou Gu, Yuhua Li and Andrew D. Ball (2006). A validated model for the prediction of rotor bar failure in squirrel-cage motors using instantaneous angular speed. *Mechanical Systems and Signal Processing*, Vol.20, No 7, pp. 1572-1589.

Hakan Calıs& Abdulkadir Cakır (2007). Rotor bar fault diagnosis in three phase induction motors by monitoring fluctuations of motor current zero crossing instants. *Electric Power Systems Research*, Vol.77, pp. 385–392.

Andrew K.S. Jardine, Daming Lin, Dragan Banjevic (2006). A review on machinery diagnostics and prognostics implementing condition-based maintenance. *Mechanical Systems and Signal Processing,* Vol.20, pp.1483–1510.

Anjaneyulu, N .Kalaiarasi and K.S.R (2007). Adaptive Vector Control of Induction Motor Drives. *International Journal of Electrical and Engineering*, Vol.1 .No.2, 239-245.

Archana S. Nanoty, and A. R. Chudasama (2008). Vector Control of Multimotor Drive. *Proceedings of World Academy of Science, Engineering and Technology*, Vol.35, pp. 2070-3740.

Ayaz, E., Ozturk, A., & Seker, S. (2006). Continuous Wavelet Transform for Bearing Damage Detection in Electric Motors. *IEEE Electrotechnical Conference, MELECON.* Mediterranean, pp. 1130 -1133.

Bogalecka, Piotr Kołodziejek and Elz bieta (2009). Broken rotor bar impact on sensorless control of induction machine. *The International Journal for Computation and Mathematics in Electrical and Electronic Engineering*, Vol.28, No.3, pp.540-555.

BPRA073. (1998). Field Orientated Control of 3-Phase AC-Motors. *Texas Instruments Europe.*

C. Combastel, S. Lesecq, S. Petropol, S. Gentil (2002). Model-based and wavelet approaches to induction motor on-line fault detection. *Control Engineering Practice*, Vol.10, No.5, pp.493–509.

Cabal-Yepez, E., Osornio-Rios, R., Romero-Troncoso, R., Razo-Hernandez, J., & Lopez-Garcia, R. (2009). FPGA-Based Online Induction Motor Multiple-Fault Detection with Fused FFT andWavelet Analysis. *International Conference on Reconfigurable Computing and FPGAs*, pp. 101 -106.

Cao Zhitong, Chen Hongping, He Guoguang, Ritchie, E (2001). Rotor fault diagnosis of induction motor based on wavelet reconstruction"*Proceedings of the Fifth International Conference on Electrical Machines and Systems*, ICEMS, Vol.1, pp. 374 - 377.

Chen, C.-M., & Loparo, K. (1998). Electric fault detection for vector-controlled induction motors using the discrete wavelet transform. *Proceedings of the American Control Conference*, Vol.6, pp. 3297 -3301.

Cusido, J., Rosero, J., Cusido, M., Garcia, A., Ortega, J. L., & Author, Q. (2007). On-Line System for Fault Detection in Induction Machines based on Wavelet Convolution. *IEEE Conf.On Power Electronics Specialists, PESC*, pp. 927-932.

Cusido, J., Rosero, J., Cusido, M., Garcia, A., Ortega, J., & Romeral, L. (2007). On-Line System for Fault Detection in Induction Machines Based on Wavelet Convolution. *IEEE Instrumentation and Measurement Technology Conference Proceedings, IMTC*, pp. 1 - 5.

Cusido, J., Rosero, J., Ortega, J., Garcia, A., & Romeral, L. (2006). Induction Motor Fault Detection by using Wavelet decomposition on dq0 components. *IEEE International Symposium on Industrial Electronics*, Vol.3, pp. 2406 -2411.

Cusido, J., Rosero, J., Romeral, L., Ortega, J., & Garcia, A. (2006). Fault Detection in Induction Machines by Using Power Spectral Density on the Wavelet Decompositions. *37th IEEE Conference on Power Electronics Specialists PESC*,pp. 1-6.

Dimas Anton A, Syafaruddin, Dicky N Wardana, M.H.Purnomo, Takashi Hiyama (2010). Characterization of Temporary Short Circuit in Induction Motor Winding using Wavelet Analysis. *Proceedings of the International Conference on Modelling, Identification and Control*, pp. 477 -482.

Douglas, H., & Pillay, P. (2005). The impact of wavelet selection on transient motor current signature analysis. *IEEE International Conference on Electric Machines and Drives*, pp. 80 - 85.

Douglas, H., Pillay, P., & Ziarani, A. (2003). Detection of broken rotor bars in induction motors using wavelet analysis. *International IEEE Conf. On Electric Machines and Drive, IEMDC*, Vol.2, pp. 923 -928.

Levent Eren and Michael J. Devaney (2004). Bearing Damage Detection via Wavelet Packet Decomposition of the Stator Current. *IEEE Transactions on Instrumentation and Measurement*, Vol.53, No.2, pp. 431-436.

Faiz, J., Ebrahimi, B., Asaie, B., Rajabioun, R., & Toliyat, H. (2007). A criterion function for broken bar fault diagnosis in induction motor under load variation using wavelet transform. *International Conference on Electrical Machines and Systems, ICEMS*, pp. 1249 -1254.

Gang Niu, Achmad Widodo, Jong-Duk Son, Bo-Suk Yang, Don-Ha Hwang , Dong, Sik Kang (2008). Decision level fusion based on wavelet decomposition for induction motor fault diagnosis using transient current signal. *Expert Systems with Applications*, Vol.35, pp.918–928.

Hamidi, H., Nasiri, A., & Nasiri, F. (2004). Detection and isolation of mixed eccentricity in three phase induction motor via wavelet packet decomposition. *5th Asian Control Conference*, Vol.2, pp. 1371 -1376.

J. Antonino-Daviu, M. Riera-Guasp, J. Roger-Folch, F.Martinez-Gimenez, A. Peris (2006). Application and optimization ofthe discrete wavelet transform for the detection of broken rotor bars in induction machines. *Applied and Computational Harmonic Analysis*, Vol.21, No.2, pp.268–279.

J. Cusido,L. Romerala, J.A. Ortega, A. Garcia and J.R. Riba. (2010). Wavelet and PDD as fault detection techniques. *Electric Power Systems Resaerch*, Vol.80, No.8, pp 915-924.

J.Antonino-Daviu, P.Jover Rodriguez, M.Riera-Guasp M. Pineda-Sanchez, A.Arkkio (2009). Detection combined faults in induction machines with stator parallel branches through the DWT of the startup current. *Mechanical Systems and Signal Processing*, Vo.23, pp.2336–2351.

J.L. Silva Neto, Hoang Le-Huy (1996). Fuzzy Logic Based Controller for Induction Motor Drives. *IEEE, IECON*, pp. 631-634.

Mohamed Boussak and Kamel Jarray (2006). A High Performance Sensorless Indirect Stator Flux Orientation Control of Induction Motor Drive. *IEEE trans. Industrial Electronics*, Vol. 53, pp. 41-49.

Nirmesh Yadav, Sharad Sharma, Vikram M. Gadre, &ldquo (2004). Wavelet Analysis and Applications. *New Age International Publishers*, ISBN 81-224-1515-6.

Khalaf Salloum Gaeid, Hew Wooi ping(2010). Diagnosis and Fault Tolerant Control of the Induction Motors Techniques: A review. *Australian Journal of Basic and Applied Sciences*, Vol.4 No.2, pp. 227-246.

Khan, M., & Rahman, M. (2006). Discrete Wavelet Transform Based Detection of Disturbances in Induction Motors. *Electrical and Computer Engineering, ICECE*, pp. 462 -465.

Kia, S., Henao, H., & Capolino, G.-A. (2009). Diagnosis of Broken-Bar Fault in Induction Machines Using Discrete Wavelet Transform without Slip Estimation. *IEEE Transactions on Industry Applications*, Vol.45, No.4, pp1395 -1404.

Lee, S. B.; Yang, J.; Hong, J.; Yoo, J.-Y.; Kim, B.; Lee, K.; Yun, J.; Kim, M.; Lee, K.-W.; Wiedenbrug, E. J.; Nandi, S. (2011). A New Strategy for Condition Monitoring of Adjustable Speed Induction Machine Drive Systems. *IEEE Transactions on Power Electronics*, Vol.26, No.2, pp.389 - 398.

Liu, T., & Huang, J. (2005). A novel method for induction motors stator interturn short circuit fault diagnosis by Systems, Proceedings *of the Eighth International Conference on Electrical Machines and Systems, ICEMS*, Vol. 3, pp. 2254 - 2258.

Lorand SZABO, JenoBarna DOBAI, Karoly Agoston BIRO (2005). Discrete Wavelet Transform Based Rotor Faults Detection Method for Induction Machines. *Intelligent Systems at the Service of Mankind*, Vol. 2, pp. 63-74.

M. Riera-Guaspa, J. Antonino-Daviua,J. Rusekb, J. Roger Folch (2009). Diagnosis of rotor asymmetries in induction motors based on the transient extraction of fault components using filtering techniques. *Electric Power Systems Research*, Vol.79, No.8, pp.1181–1191.

M. Sabarimalai Manikandan, and S. Dandapat (2007). Wavelet energy based diagnostic distortion measure for ECG. *Biomedical Signal Processing and Control*, Vol.2, No.2, pp. 80-96.

M. Sushama, G. Tulasi Ram Das and A. Jaya Laxmi (2009). Detection of High-Impedance Faults in Transmission. ARPN *Journal of Engineering and Applied Sciences*, Vol.4, No. 3, pp.6-12.

Mohammed, O., Abed, N., & Ganu, S. (2006). Modelling and Characterization of Induction Motor Internal Faults Using Finite-Element and Discrete Wavelet Transforms. *IEEE Transactions on Magnetics*, Vol.42, No.10, pp.3434 -3436.

Mohammed, O., Abed, N., & Garni, S. (2007). Modeling and characterization of induction motor internal faults using finite element and discrete wavelet transforms. *IEEE Symposium on Electric Ship Technologies, ESTS*, pp. 250 – 253.

AN2388 Application Note, (2006). Sensor Field Oriented Control (IFOC) of Three-Phase AC Induction Motors Using ST10F276.

Ordaz Moreno, A. de Jesus Romero-Troncoso, R. Vite-Frias (2008). Automatic Online Diagnosis Algorithm for Broken-Bar Detection on Induction Motors Based on Discrete WaveletTransform for FPGA Implementation. *IEEE Transactions on Industrial Electronics*, Nol.55, No.5, pp2193 -2202.

Pineda-Sanchez, M., Riera-Guasp, M., Antonino-Daviu, J. A., Roger-Folch, J., Perez-Cruz, J., & Puche-Panadero, R. (2010). Diagnosis of Induction Motor Faults in the Fractional Fourier Domain. *IEEE Transactions on Instrumentation and Measurement*, Vol.59, No 8, pp.2065 - 2075.

Ponci, F., Monti, A., Cristaldi, L., & Lazzaroni, M. (2007). Diagnostic of a Faulty Induction Motor Drive via Wavelet Decomposition. *IEEE Transactions on Instrumentation and Measurement*, Vol. 56 No.6, pp. 2606 -2615.

Pons-Llinares, J., Antonino-Daviu, J., Riera-Guasp, M.-S. M., & Climente-Alarcon, V. (2009). Induction motor fault diagnosis based on analytic wavelet transform via Frequency B-Splines. *IEEE International Symposium on Diagnostics for Electric Machines, Power Electronics and Drives, SDEMPED*, pp. 1-7.

R. Salehi Arashloo, A. Jalilian (2010). Design, Implementation and Comparison of Two Wavelet Based Methods for the Detectionof Broken Rotor Bars in Three Phase Induction Motors. *1st Power Electronic & Drive Systems & Technologies Conference, PEDSTC*, pp. 345 -350.

Riera-Guasp, M., Antonino-Daviu, J., Pineda-Sanchez, M., Puche-Panadero, R., & Perez-Cruz, J. (2008). A General Approach for the Transient Detection of Slip-Dependent Fault Components Based on the Discrete Wavelet Transform. *IEEE Transactions on Industrial Electronics*, Vol.55, No.12, pp.4167 -4180.

S. Radhika, G.R. Sabareesh, G. Jagadanand, V. Sugumaran (2010). Precise wavelet for current signature in 3φIM. *Expert Systems with applications*, Vol.37, No.1, pp.450-455.

Saleh, S., Khan, M., & Rahman, M. (2005). Application of a wavelet-based MRA for diagnosing disturbances in a three phase induction motor. *5th IEEE Conf. on Diagnostics for Electric Machines, Power Electronics and Drives, SDEMPED*, pp. 1-6.

Samsi, R., Rajagopalan, V., & Ray, A. (2006). Wavelet-based symbolic analysis for detection of broken rotor bars in inverter-fed induction motors. *American Control Conference*, pp. 3032-3038.

Sayed-Ahmed, A., Sizov, G., & Demerdash, N. (2007). Diagnosis of Inter-Turn Short Circuit for a Polyphase Induction Motor in Closed-Loop Vector-Controlled Drives. *IEEE ,42nd IAS Annual Meeting*, pp. 2262 - 2268.

Supangat, R., Ertugrul, N. W., & Grieger, J. (2006). Detection of broken rotor bars in induction motor using starting-current analysis and effects of loading. *IEEE Proceedings on Electric Power Applications*, Vol.153:6, pp. 848 -855.

Supangat, R., Grieger, J., Ertugrul, N., Soong, W., Gray, D., & Hansen, C. (2007). Detection of Broken Rotor Bar Faults and Effects of Loading in Induction Motors during Rundown. *IEEE International Conference on Electric Machines & Drives, IEMDC*, Vol.1, pp. 196 - 201.

Turkmenoglu, M. A. (2010). Wavelet-based switching faults detection in. *IET Science, Measurement and Technology*, Vol.4, No.6, pp.303–310.

Yang, C., Cui, G., Wei, Y., & Wang, Y. (2007). Fault Diagnosis for Induction Motors Using the Wavelet Ridge. *Second International Conference on Bio-Inspired Computing: Theories and Applications, BIC-TA*, pp. 231 - 235.

Yasser Gritli, Andrea Stefani,Claudio Rossi, Fiorenzo Filippetti and Abderrazak Chatt (2011). Experimental validation of doubly fed induction machine electrical faults diagnosis under time-varying conditions. *Electric Power Systems Research*, Vol.81, No.3, pp.751-766.

Zhang Jian wen, Zhu Ning-hui, Yang Li, Yao Qi, Lu Qing (2007). A Fault Diagnosis Approach for Broken Rotor Bars Based on EMD and Envelope Analysis. *Journal of China University Mining & Technology*, Vol.17, No. 2, pp.205-209.

Zhang, Pinjia; Du, Yi; Habetler, T.G.; Lu, Bin (2011). A Survey of Condition Monitoring and Protection Methods for Medium-Voltage Induction Motors. *IEEE Transactions on Industry Applications*, Vol.47, No.1, pp.34 - 46.

Pons-Llinares, J.; Antonino-Daviu, J.; Roger-Folch, J.; Morinigo-Sotelo, D.; Duque-Perez, O.; (2010). Eccentricity Diagnosis in Inverter Fed Induction Motors via the Analytic Wavelet Transform of Transient Currents. *XIX International Conference on Electrical Machines (ICEM)*, pp.1 -6.

15

Implementation of Induction Motor Drive Control Schemes in MATLAB/Simulink/dSPACE Environment for Educational Purpose

Christophe Versèle, Olivier Deblecker and Jacques Lobry
Electrical Engineering Department, University of Mons
Belgium

1. Introduction

Squirrel-cage induction motors (IM) are the workhorse of industries for variable speed applications in a wide power range that covers from fractional watt to megawatts. However, the torque and speed control of these motors is difficult because of their nonlinear and complex structure. In the past five decades, a lot of advanced control schemes for IM drive appeared. First, in the 1960's, the principle of speed control was based on an IM model considered just for steady state. Therefore, the so-called "scalar control methods" cannot achieve best performance during transients, which is their major drawback. Afterwards, in the 1970's, different control schemes were developed based on a dynamic model of the IM. Among these control strategies, the vector control which is included in the so-called field oriented control (FOC) methods can be mentioned. The principle of vector control is to control independently the two Park components of the motor current, responsible for producing the torque and flux respectively. In that way, the IM drive operates like a separately excited dc motor drive (where the torque and the flux are controlled by two independent orthogonal variables: the armature and field currents, respectively). Since the 1980's, many researchers have worked on improvements of the FOC and vector control which have become the industry's standard for IM drives. Moreover, these researches led to new control strategies such as direct self control (DSC) or direct torque control (DTC). The principle of DTC is to control directly the stator flux and torque of the IM by applying the appropriate stator voltage space vector.

With vector control, FOC, DSC and DTC, the major drawback of the scalar control is overcome because these control schemes are based on a model of the IM which is considered valid for transient conditions (Santisteban & Stephan, 2001). Both DTC and DSC possess high torque dynamics compared to vector control and FOC (Böcker & Mathapati, 2007). However, these two first control techniques have the drawbacks of variable switching frequency and higher torque ripple. The use of space vector pulse-width-modulation (SV-PWM) in conjunction with DTC (called, in this chapter, DTC-space vector modulation or DTC-SVM) has been proposed as a solution to overcome these drawbacks (Rodriguez et al., 2004), but sticking to the fundamental concept of DTC.

The objective of this chapter is neither to do an overview of all IM control methods, as is done, e.g., in (Böcker & Mathapati, 2007; Santisteban & Stephan, 2001), nor to try to

ameliorate them. Its aim is to present a powerful tool to help students to understand some IM control schemes, namely the scalar control method, the vector control and the DTC-SVM, of a voltage-fed inverter IM drive using a dSPACE platform and Matlab/Simulink environment. First, they determine the IM parameters using a procedure based on the implemented vector control scheme. The accuracy of these measurements is very important because the considered control methods need precise information about the motor parameters (Böcker & Mathapati, 2007). Then, after concluding off-line simulations, they perform some experiments in speed regulation and speed tracking.
The remainder of this chapter is organized as follows. First, the experimental system is presented. Then the IM models used therein are described and the determination of the IM parameters as well as the implementation of the control methods are exposed. Finally, typical results are presented and the educational experience is discussed.

2. Experimental system

The experimental system consists of three essentials parts: (1) the power driver, (2) the control system and (3) the transducers. Fig. 1 shows a synoptic scheme of the experimental platform.
The power driver consists of a voltage-fed inverter and two machines: one squirrel-type IM of rated power 5.5 kW and a dc-machine with a separately excited field winding of rated power 14.6 kW. These machines are mechanically coupled and the dc-machine is used as the load of the IM.

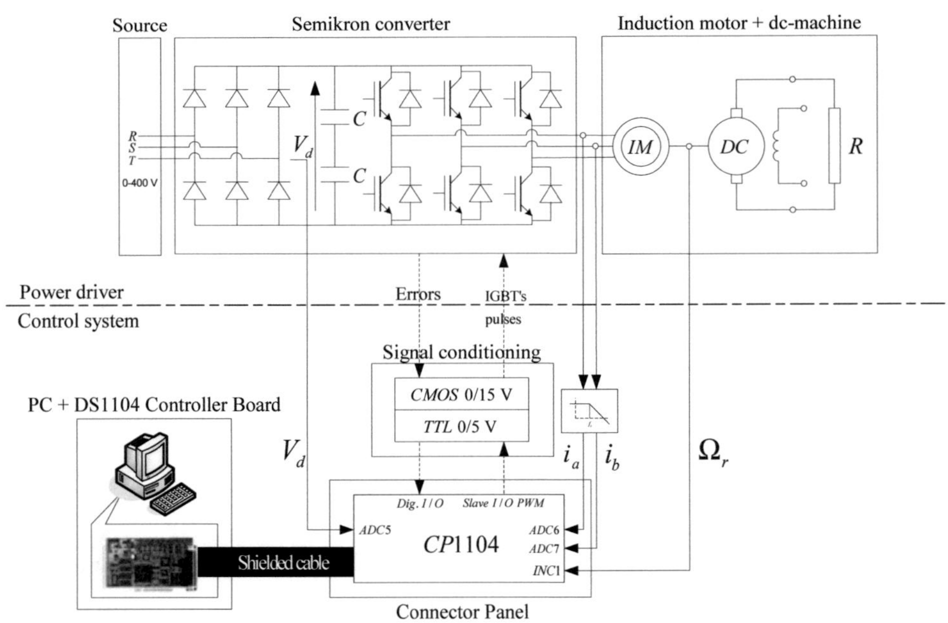

Fig. 1. Synoptic scheme of the experimental platform

The control system is based on the DS1104 Controller Board by dSPACE plugged in a computer. Its development software operates under Matlab/Simulink environment (Bojoi et al., 2002) and is divided into two main components: Real Time Interface (RTI) which is the implementation software and ControlDesk which is the experimentation software. RTI is a Simulink toolbox which provides blocks to configure models (Bojoi et al., 2002). These blocks allow the users to access to the dSPACE hardware. ControlDesk allows, as for it, the users to control and monitor the real-time operation by using a lot of virtual instruments and building a control window.

When using dSPACE, the several steps required to implement a control system on the DS1104 Controller Board are described below. The first step consists in modeling the control system with Simulink and configuring the I/O connections of the Connector Panel thanks to the RTI toolbox. After that, the Real-Time Workshop (RTW) toolbox, using RTI, automatically generates the C-code for the board. Once the execution code has been generated, the dSPACE hardware can perform a real-time experiment which can be controlled from a PC with ControlDesk. ControlDesk can be used to monitor the simulation progress, adjust parameters online, capture data (in a format compatible with Matlab) and communicate easily with the upper computer real-time (Luo et al., 2008). Fig. 2 presents the connections between Matlab and dSPACE.

The experimental system contains several current and voltage LEM transducers as well as a speed sensor. Moreover, the measured currents must be filtered in order to avoid aliasing when they will be converted into digital signals. Therefore, an anti-aliasing filter is added to each current transducer. The cut-off frequency of this filter is estimated at 500 Hz (an order of magnitude above the rated frequency of 50 Hz).

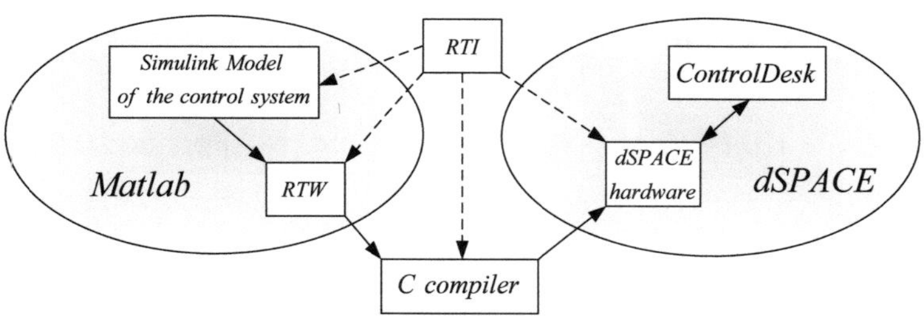

Fig. 2. Connections between Matlab and dSPACE (Mäki et al., 2005)

3. IM modeling

A simple per phase equivalent circuit model of an IM is interesting for the analysis and the performance prediction at steady-state condition. Such a model is therefore used in this chapter for scalar control. In the two other considered control schemes, namely vector control and DTC-SVM, the transient behaviour of the IM has to be taken into account. So, the dynamic d-q model of the IM based on the Park's transformation is considered. These two well-known types of IM models are available in literature (see, e.g., (Bose, 2002; Mohan, 2001)) and are briefly recalled in this section.

3.1 Steady-state model of IM

The considered steady-state IM model, based on complex phasors, is shown in Fig. 3(a). This model is an equivalent circuit with respect to the stator and can easily be established from the short-circuited transformer-equivalent circuit (Bose, 2002).

The synchronously rotating air gap flux wave generates an electromotive force E_s which differs from the stator terminal voltage V_s by the drop voltage in stator resistance R_s and stator leakage inductance l_s. The stator current I_s consists of the magnetizing current I_m and the rotor current I_r (referred to the stator in Fig. 3(a)) which is given by (Bose, 2002):

$$I_r = \frac{E_s}{\frac{R_r}{s} + j \cdot 2 \cdot \pi \cdot f \cdot l_r}. \tag{1}$$

where R_r is the rotor resistance (referred to the stator), l_r is the rotor leakage inductance (referred to the stator), s is the slip and f is the stator supply frequency. Finally, in Fig. 3(a), L_m is the magnetizing inductance and R_m is the equivalent resistance for the core loss.
The equivalent circuit of Fig. 3(a) can be further simplified as shown in Fig. 3(b) where the resistance R_m has been dropped and the inductance l_s has been shifted to the other side of the inductance L_m.

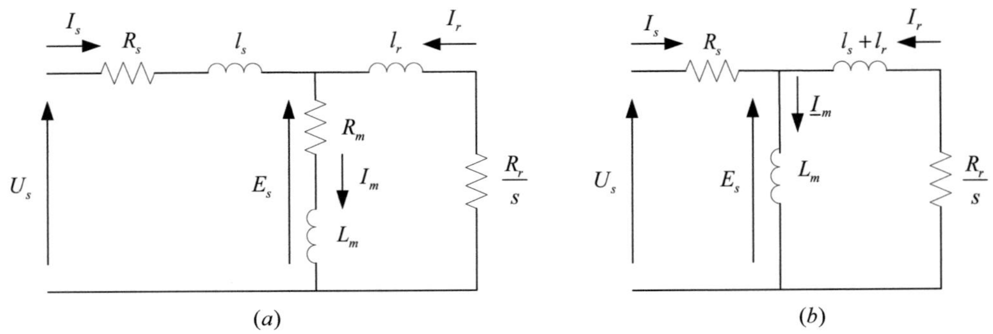

Fig. 3. (a) Equivalent circuit with respect to the stator and (b) Approximate per phase equivalent circuit

This approximation is easily justified as the value of the magnetizing inductance is, at least, one order of magnitude greater than the value of the stator leakage inductance. Moreover, the performance prediction by the approximate equivalent circuit typically varies within 5% from that of the actual machine (Bose, 2002).
Based on the equivalent circuit of Fig. 3(b), it can be demonstrated (see, e.g., (Bose, 2002)) the following expression of the electromagnetic torque:

$$T_e = 3 \cdot P \cdot R_r \cdot \frac{(s \cdot \omega) \cdot \psi^2}{R_r^2 + (s \cdot \omega)^2 \cdot (l_s + l_r)^2} \tag{2}$$

where P is the number of poles pairs and ψ is the stator flux. It should also be emphasized that for small slip values, (2) can be rewritten as:

$$T_e = \frac{3 \cdot P \cdot \psi^2}{R_r} \cdot (s \cdot \omega) = K_T \cdot (s \cdot \omega) \tag{3}$$

where K_T is a constant if the flux is kept constant.
Finally, for steady-state operation of IM, the rotational speed Ω_r can be calculated by:

$$\Omega_r = (1 - s) \cdot \frac{2 \cdot \pi \cdot f}{P}. \tag{4}$$

3.2 Dynamic model of IM

Applying the usual space vector transformation to a three-phase system, it is possible to obtain the following set of equations, based on space vectors, that describes the IM dynamic behavior in a stator fixed coordinate system (Rodrigez et al., 2004):

$$\mathbf{v_s} = R_s \cdot \mathbf{i_s} + \frac{d\boldsymbol{\psi}_\mathbf{s}}{dt} + j \cdot \omega_1 \cdot \boldsymbol{\psi}_\mathbf{s} \tag{5}$$

$$\mathbf{v_r} = 0 = R_r \cdot \mathbf{i_r} + \frac{d\boldsymbol{\psi}_\mathbf{r}}{dt} + j \cdot (\omega_1 - P \cdot \Omega_r) \cdot \boldsymbol{\psi}_\mathbf{r} \tag{6}$$

$$\boldsymbol{\psi}_\mathbf{s} = l_s \cdot \mathbf{i_s} + L_m \cdot (\mathbf{i_s} + \mathbf{i_r}) \tag{7}$$

$$\boldsymbol{\psi}_\mathbf{r} = l_r \cdot \mathbf{i_r} + L_m \cdot (\mathbf{i_s} + \mathbf{i_r}) \tag{8}$$

where ω_1 is the rotational speed of the d-q reference frame, $\mathbf{v_s}$ and $\mathbf{v_r}$ are respectively the stator and rotor voltages, $\mathbf{i_s}$ and $\mathbf{i_r}$ are respectively the stator and rotor currents and $\boldsymbol{\psi}_\mathbf{s}$ and $\boldsymbol{\psi}_\mathbf{r}$ are respectively the stator and rotor fluxes.

The electromagnetic torque developed by the IM can be expressed in terms of flux and current space vector by several analog expressions. In this chapter, two of them are useful:

$$T_e = \frac{3}{2} \cdot P \cdot \frac{L_m}{L_r} \cdot [\boldsymbol{\psi}_\mathbf{r} \times \mathbf{i_s}] \tag{9}$$

and

$$T_e = \frac{3}{2} \cdot P \cdot \frac{L_m}{\sigma \cdot L_s \cdot L_r} \cdot [\boldsymbol{\psi}_\mathbf{s} \times \boldsymbol{\psi}_\mathbf{r}] \tag{10}$$

where L_s ($L_s = L_m + l_s$) and L_r ($L_r = L_m + l_r$) are respectively the stator and rotor inductances and σ is the leakage factor of the IM defined as:

$$\sigma = 1 - \frac{L_m^2}{L_s \cdot L_r} \cdot \tag{11}$$

The speed Ω_r cannot normally be treated as a constant (Bose, 2002). It can be related to torque using the IM drive mechanical equation which is:

$$T_e = J \cdot \frac{d\Omega_r}{dt} + B \cdot \Omega_r \tag{12}$$

where J and B denote respectively the total inertia and total damping of the IM coupled to the dc-machine.

Finally, the dynamic model of the IM is shown in Fig. 4 in its complex form for compact representation.

4. Control schemes

4.1 Scalar control

Scalar control is due to magnitude variation of the control variables only and disregards the coupling effect in the machine (Bose, 2002). Although having inferior performances than the

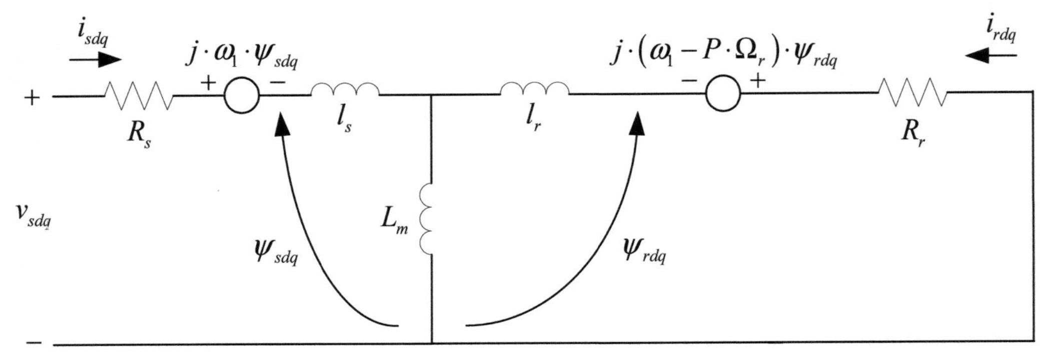

Fig. 4. Dynamic model of IM

two other considered control schemes, it is considered in this chapter because it has been widely used in industry and it is easy to implement. So, this is a good basis for the study of IM drive. Among the several scalar control techniques, the open loop Volts/Hz control of IM, which is the most popular method of speed control of a voltage-fed inverter IM, is used. For adjustable speed applications, frequency control appears to be natural considering (4). However, the stator voltage is required to be proportional to frequency so that the flux:

$$\psi = \frac{U_s}{2 \cdot \pi \cdot f} \tag{13}$$

remains constant (normally equal to its rated value), neglecting the stator resistance voltage drop. Indeed, if an attempt is made to reduce the frequency at the rated stator voltage, the flux will tend to saturate, causing excessive stator current and distortion of the flux waveforms (Bose, 2002). Therefore, in the region below the base frequency f_b (which can be different from the rated frequency), a reduction of the frequency should be accompanied by the proportional reduction of the stator voltage in order to maintain the flux to its rated value. Fig. 5 shows the torque-speed curves. It can be shown in this figure that in the region below the base frequency, the torque-speed curves are identical to each other and that the maximum torque T_{em} (which can be deduced from (2)) is preserved regardless of the frequency, except in the low-frequency region where the stator resistance voltage drop must be compensated by an additional boost voltage U_{boost} in order to restore the T_{em} value (as shown in Fig. 5).

Once the frequency increases beyond the base frequency, the stator voltage is kept constant and, therefore, the flux decreases. As shown in Fig. 5, in this flux-weakening region, the torque-speed curves differ from the previous ones and the developed torque decreases. An advantage of the flux-weakening mode of operation is that it permits to increase the speed range of the IM.

Fig. 6 shows the block diagram of the Volts/Hz speed control method. The frequency f^*, which is approximately equal to the speed neglecting the slip, is the primary control variable. The secondary control variable is the stator voltage U_s^* which is directly generated from the frequency command using the gain factor G so that the flux remains constant or a flux-weakening mode of operation is achieved. Moreover, at low-frequencies, corresponding to a low rotational speed of the IM, the boost voltage is added in order to have the maximum torque available at zero speed. Note that the effect of this boost voltage becomes negligible when the frequency grows. Finally, the f^* command signal is integrated to generate the angle signal θ^* which in combination with U_s^* produce the sinusoidal voltages.

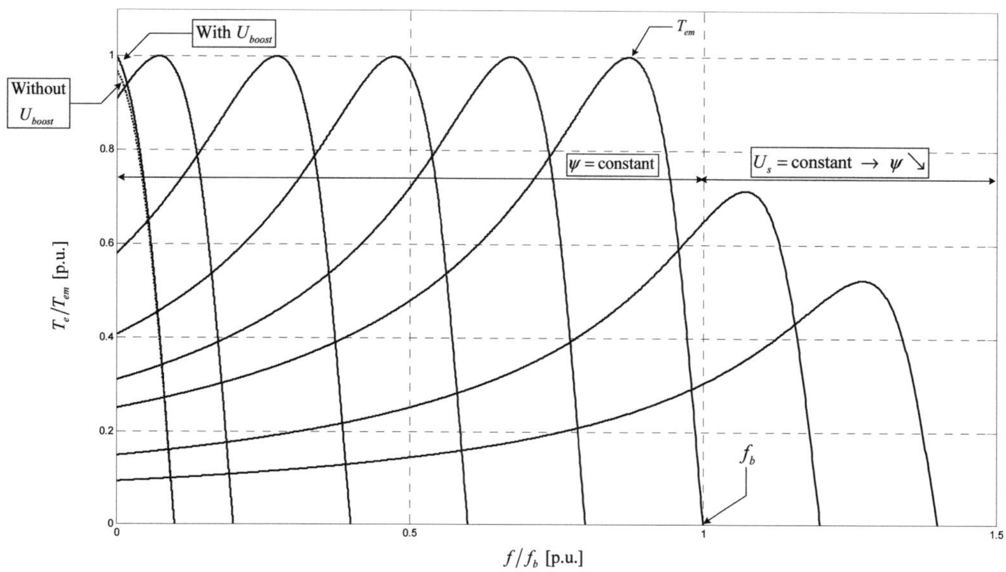

Fig. 5. Torque-speed curves at constant Volts/Hz region and in flux-weakening region

Note that an improvement of the open-loop Volts/Hz control is the close-loop speed control by slip regulation (see, e.g., (Bose, 2002)).

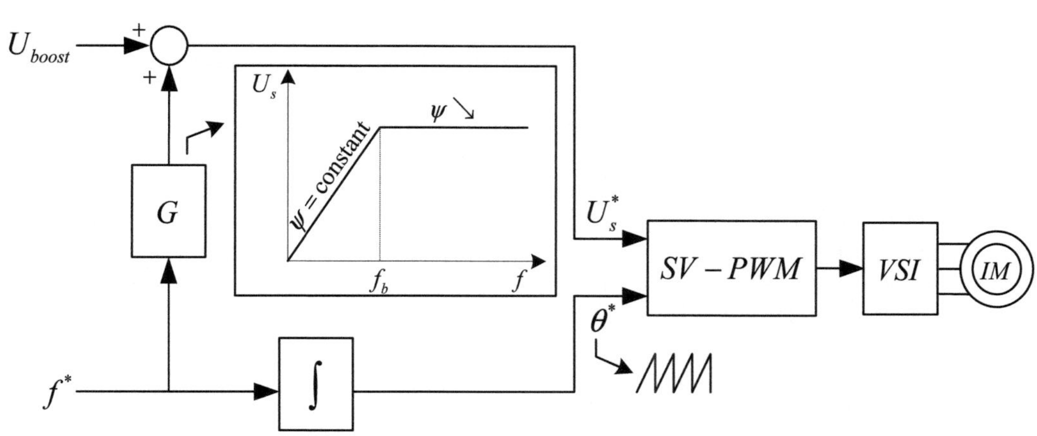

Fig. 6. Open-loop Volts/Hz control of IM

4.2 Vector control

The objective of vector control of IM is to allow an IM to be controlled just like a separately excited dc motor drive (where the torque and the flux are controlled by two independent orthogonal variables: the armature and field currents, respectively). This is achieved by a

proper choice of the so-called Park's rotating frame (*d-q* axes) in which the space vector equations (5)-(8) are separated into *d-q* ones.
In the *d-q* frame, (9) can be rewritten:

$$T_e = \frac{3}{2} \cdot P \cdot \frac{L_m}{L_r} \cdot \left(\psi_{rd} \cdot i_{sq} - \psi_{rq} \cdot i_{sd}\right) \tag{14}$$

where ψ_{rd} and ψ_{rq} are the rotor fluxes and i_{sd} and i_{sq} are the stator current in the dq-axes.
In this chapter, a direct vector control strategy in which the *d-q* frame rotates along with the rotor flux (which is maintained at its rated value) is considered. The *d*-axis is aligned with the direction of the rotor flux. Therefore, the *q*-axis component of the rotor flux is null and the expression of the electromagnetic torque simplifies as follows:

$$T_e = \frac{3}{2} \cdot P \cdot \frac{L_m^2}{L_r} \cdot i_{mr} \cdot i_{sq} \tag{15}$$

where i_{mr} is the rotor magnetizing current defined by:

$$\psi_{rd} = L_m \cdot i_{mr} \cdot \tag{16}$$

Using (6) and (7) projected in the *d-q* frame as well as (16), the rotor magnetizing current can be expressed in terms of the *d*-axis stator current as follows:

$$i_{mr} + T_r \cdot \frac{di_{mr}}{dt} = i_{sd} \tag{17}$$

where T_r ($T_r = L_r/R_r$) is the rotor time constant.
From (15) and (17), one can conclude that the *d*-axis stator current (i_{sd}) is controlled to maintain the flux at its rated value whereas the *q*-axis stator current (i_{sq}) is varied to achieve the desired electromagnetic torque. Therefore, the IM can be controlled just like a separately excited dc motor drive because the *d-* and *q*-axes are orthogonal.
Note that, at each sample time, direct vector control of the IM requires to know the module and phase of the rotor flux. Therefore, a flux observer is used. Its task is to provide an estimate of the rotor flux (or rotor magnetizing current) in module and phase using the measured stator currents (converted in *d-q* components) and speed.
Once a flux estimate is available, the torque can easily be computed using (15). The flux observer implemented in the Simulink/dSPACE environment is shown in Fig. 7. As can be seen in this figure, the phase μ of the rotor magnetizing current is obtained by integrating the angular speed ω_1 of the *d-q* axes in the fixed stator reference frame.
In vector control, the IM is fed by a Voltage Supply Inverter (VSI) and a SV-PWM is used to produce the instantaneous generation of the commanded stator voltages. The required *d*-axis and *q*-axis stator voltages (v_{sd} and v_{sq}) that the VSI must supply to the IM, in order to make the stator currents (i_{sd} and i_{sq}) equal to their reference values are expressed as follows:

$$v_{sd} = R_s \cdot \left[i_{sd} + T_s \cdot \left(\sigma \cdot \frac{di_{sd}}{dt} + (1-\sigma) \cdot \frac{di_{mr}}{dt} - \sigma \cdot \omega_1 \cdot i_{sq} \right) \right] \tag{18}$$

$$v_{sq} = R_s \cdot \left[i_{sq} + T_s \cdot \left(\sigma \cdot \frac{di_{sq}}{dt} + (1-\sigma) \cdot \omega_1 \cdot i_{mr} - \sigma \cdot \omega_1 \cdot i_{sd} \right) \right] \tag{19}$$

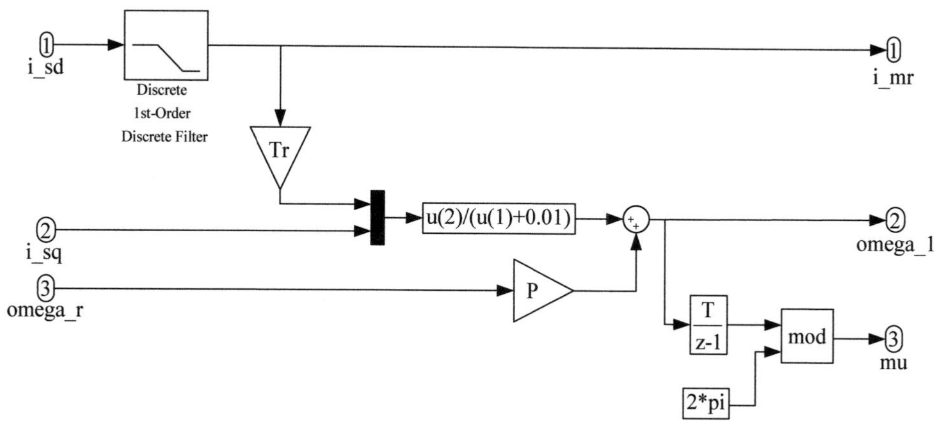

Fig. 7. Flux observer implemented in Matlab/Simulink/dSPACE environment

where T_s ($T_s = L_s/R_s$) is the stator time constant.
In the *d*-axis (respectively *q*-axis) voltage equation, only the first two terms of the right-hand side are due to the *d*-component (respectively *q*-component) of the stator current, i_{sd} (respectively i_{sq}). The other terms, due to i_{mr} and i_{sq} (respectively i_{mr} and i_{sd}) can be considered as disturbances (Mohan, 2001). So, (18) and (19) can simply be rewritten as:

$$v'_{sd} = R_s \cdot \left[i_{sd} + \sigma \cdot T_s \cdot \frac{di_{sd}}{dt} \right] \tag{20}$$

$$v'_{sq} = R_s \cdot \left[i_{sq} + \sigma \cdot T_s \cdot \frac{di_{sq}}{dt} \right]. \tag{21}$$

Note that, in order to account for the terms considered as disturbances, a "decoupling compensator" block is incorporated in the vector control scheme.
The vector control scheme is shown in Fig. 8 with the reference values indicated by '*'. This control scheme matches to a direct vector control strategy in which the rotor flux is assigned to a reference value (its rated value as mentioned above).
The *d*-axis reference current, i^*_{sd}, controls the rotor flux (through the rotor magnetizing current) whereas the *q*-axis current, i^*_{sq}, controls the electromagnetic torque developed by the IM. The reference currents in the *d*- and *q*-axes are generated by a flux control loop and a speed control loop, respectively. The *d*-axis and *q*-axis voltages, v'_{sd} and v'_{sq}, are calculated from the given reference currents and using (20) and (21). To obtain these command signals, two PI controllers (in two inner current loops) are employed and it is assumed that the compensation is perfect. The terms considered as disturbances are then added to the voltages v'_{sd} and v'_{sq} in the "decoupling compensator" block. Hence, the *d*-axis and *q*-axis reference voltages, v_{sd} and v_{sq}, are obtained. Finally, these reference voltages are converted into the reference three-phase voltages v_a, v_b and v_c and supplied (in an approximate fashion over the switching period) by the VSI using the SV-PWM technique. Note that the four controllers are tuned by the pole-zero compensation technique.

4.3 DTC-SVM

Direct torque control of IM consists in closed-loop control of the stator flux and torque using estimators of these two quantities (Trzynadlowski et al., 1999).

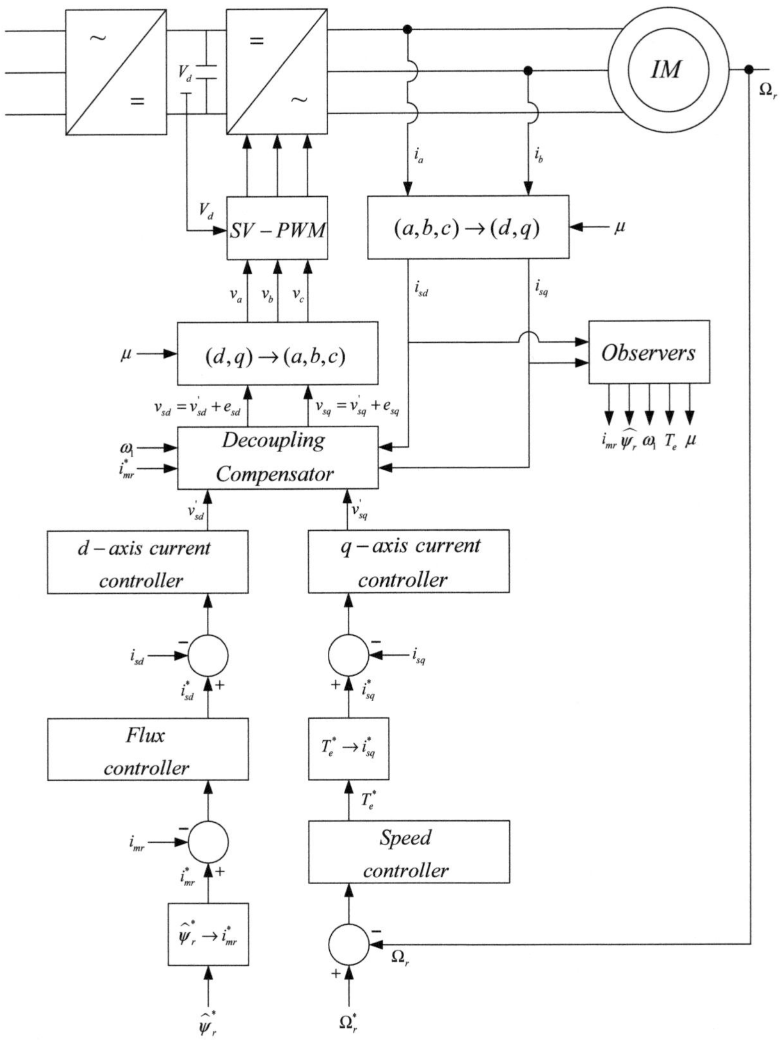

Fig. 8. Vector control scheme

From the IM dynamic model (5)-(8), the following equation can be obtained:

$$\frac{d\boldsymbol{\psi}_r}{dt} + \left(\frac{1}{\sigma \cdot T_r} - j \cdot P \cdot \Omega_r \right) \cdot \boldsymbol{\psi}_r = \frac{L_m}{\sigma \cdot T_r \cdot L_s} \cdot \boldsymbol{\psi}_s \tag{22}$$

which shows that the relationship between the stator and rotor fluxes is of low-pass filter type with time constant $\sigma \cdot T_r$ (Casadei et al., 2005). Otherwise stated, the rotor flux will follow a change in the stator flux with some delay (typically of the order of a few tenths of ms).

Equation (10) can also be rewritten as follows:

$$T_e = \frac{3}{2} \cdot P \cdot \frac{L_m}{\sigma \cdot L_s \cdot L_r} \cdot \psi_s \cdot \psi_r \cdot \sin\delta \tag{23}$$

where δ is the angle between the stator and rotor fluxes.
Based on the previous expression, it is clear that it is possible to achieve machine torque control directly by actuating over the angle δ (Rodriguez et al., 2004). DTC is founded on this consideration.
Due to slow rotor flux dynamic, the easiest way to change δ is to force a variation in the stator flux. Neglecting the effect of the voltage drop across the stator resistance, the stator flux vector in (5) is the time integral of the stator voltage vector. Hence, for sampling time Δt sufficiently small, (5) can be approximated as (Rodriguez et al., 2004):

$$\Delta \boldsymbol{\psi}_s \approx \Delta t \cdot \mathbf{v}_s \tag{24}$$

which means that the stator flux can be changed in accordance with the stator voltage vector supplied to the IM.
In the conventional DTC drive, the flux and torque magnitude errors are applied to hysteresis comparators. The outputs of these comparators are used to select the appropriate stator voltage vector to apply to the IM by means of a pre-designed look-up table. This scheme is simple and robust but it has certain drawbacks such as variable switching frequency and large current and torque ripples. Note that these ripples are imposed by the hysteresis-band width chosen for the hysteresis comparators.
In this chapter, the conventional DTC scheme is not considered but the so-called DTC-SVM scheme, which is discussed in details in (Rodriguez et al., 2004) and briefly presented below, is used. The objective of this alternative DTC scheme is to select the exact stator voltage vector that changes the stator flux vector according to the δ angle reference (calculated from the torque reference), while keeping the stator flux magnitude constant. SV-PWM technique is used to apply the required stator voltage vector to the IM.
The DTC-SVM scheme is shown in Fig. 9 with the reference values once again indicated by '*'. In this scheme, the torque reference is obtained from the speed reference thanks to the same speed controller as the one used in vector control. The error between the estimated torque and its reference value is processed through a PI controller to calculate the δ angle. From this angle, as well as the module of the stator flux (imposed at its rated value) and the estimated phase of the rotor flux, the block "Flux calculator" gives the stator flux reference according to:

$$\boldsymbol{\psi}_s^* = |\boldsymbol{\psi}_s|^* \cdot \cos(\delta + \angle\boldsymbol{\psi}_r) + j \cdot |\boldsymbol{\psi}_s|^* \cdot \sin(\delta + \angle\boldsymbol{\psi}_r) \tag{25}$$

The error between this reference quantity and the estimated stator flux is then divided by Δt, according to (24), in order to obtain the reference stator voltage vector. An approximation of that vector (over the switching period) is then supplied to the IM by the VSI using SV-PWM.
As explained above, the stator and rotor fluxes as well as the torque must be estimated. This is realized by the block "Torque and flux estimators". The rotor flux estimator is based on the IM model and implemented as follows:

$$\boldsymbol{\psi}_r = \frac{1}{T_r}\int \left(L_m \cdot \mathbf{i}_s - \left(1 - j \cdot T_r \cdot P \cdot \Omega_r\right) \cdot \boldsymbol{\psi}_r\right) \cdot dt\,. \tag{26}$$

The stator flux is, as for it, derived from:

$$\boldsymbol{\psi}_s = \sigma \cdot L_s \cdot i_s + \frac{L_r}{L_m} \cdot \boldsymbol{\psi}_r\,. \tag{27}$$

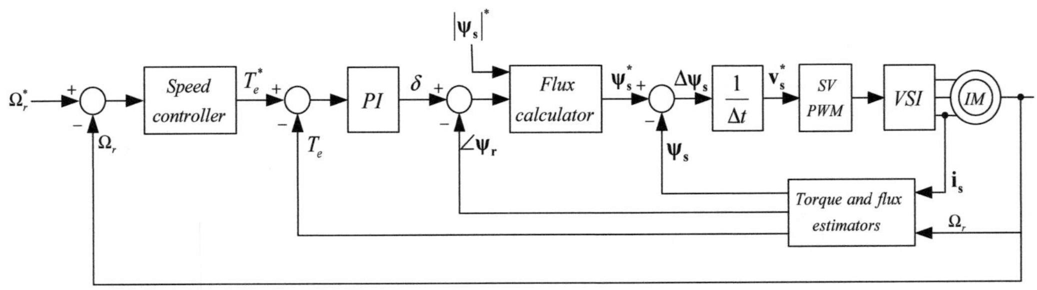

Fig. 9. DTC-SVM scheme

Once the stator and rotor fluxes estimates have been made available, the torque can be easily computed using (23). The observers of the stator and rotor fluxes implemented in the Matlab/Simulink/dSPACE environment are shown in Fig. 10.
The speed controller is tuned by the pole-zero compensation technique whereas the PI, that generates the δ angle reference, is tuned through a method based on the relay feedback test (Padhy & Majhi, 2006).

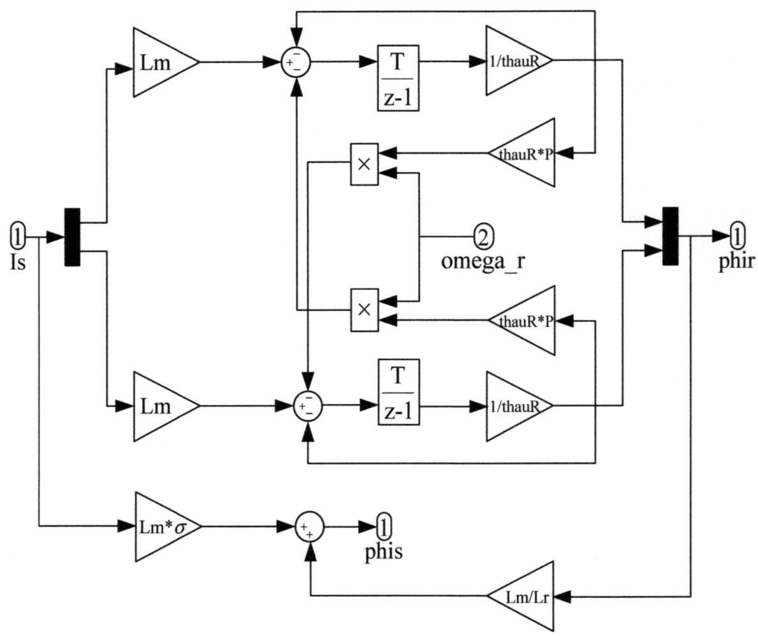

Fig. 10. Fluxes observers implemented in Matlab/Simulink/dSPACE environment

5. Determination of IM parameters

As it is well known, the control methods of IM require an accurate determination of machine parameters. Typically, five parameters need to be determined:

- R_s, R_r - the stator and rotor resistances;
- l_s, l_r - the stator and rotor leakage inductances;
- L_m - the magnetizing inductance.

In this chapter, the above parameters are determined both by a procedure founded on the vector control scheme (discussed in details in (Bose, 2002; Khambadkon et al., 1991)) and by a conventional method (no-load and blocked rotor tests).

The method based on the vector control scheme is divided into eight steps. Initially, the name plate machine parameters are stored into the computer's memory. Precisely, the method needs to know the rated stator voltage and current, the rated frequency and the number of poles pairs of the IM.

In a second step, the stator resistance is determined by a test at dc level. Next, the stator transient time constant is measured. Thanks to the stator resistance and transient time constant, the two inner current loops of the vector control scheme can be tuned. In the fifth step, the rotor time constant is determined. Next, the magnetizing inductance is measured. Note that, in this sixth step, the value of the rotor time constant is adjusted online in order to achieve $i_{sd} = i_{mr}$. Therefore, its value is verified because it is the most important parameter to obtain accurate rotor flux estimation. Thanks to the value of the rotor time constant, the flux controller of the vector control scheme can be tuned in the seventh step. Finally, the mechanical parameters of the IM coupled with the dc-machine (see below) are determined and the speed controller can be tuned.

The method based on the vector control structure has the major advantage that it can be automated. Therefore, this procedure can evaluate the motor parameters at each start-up of the experimental platform. All the results are reported in Table 1. As can be seen, very small differences are obtained between the two approaches, whatever the parameters. Therefore, one can conclude that all the IM parameters are properly determined.

Moreover, the procedure based on the vector control structure permits to determine the mechanical parameters of the IM coupled with the dc-machine. Three parameters need to be determined:

- J - the total inertia;
- T_m - the mechanical time constant;
- B - the total damping factor.

All the results are reported in Table 2.

Parameters	**Conventional method**	**Method based on the vector control scheme**
R_s	0.81 Ω	1.26 Ω
R_r	0.57 Ω	0.42 Ω
l_s	4 mH	3.9 mH
l_r	4 mH	3.9 mH
L_m	160 mH	164 mH

Table 1. IM parameters

Parameters	**Values**
J	0.0731 kg·m^2
T_m	2.1 s
B	0.00348 kg·m$^{2/s}$

Table 2. Mechanical parameters

6. Experimental results

After concluding off-line simulations using the blocks of the SimPowerSystem toolbox in Simulink software, the three control schemes are tested and compared by means of speed reference tracking, torque dynamic and flux regulation. To do so, the validated control strategies are transferred to the digital control board. Fig. 11 and 12, respectively, show the vector control algorithm implemented with Simulink and the corresponding window of the ControlDesk software which controls the dSPACE hardware. Note that more details about this work can be found in (Versèle et al., 2008; Versèle et al. 2010).

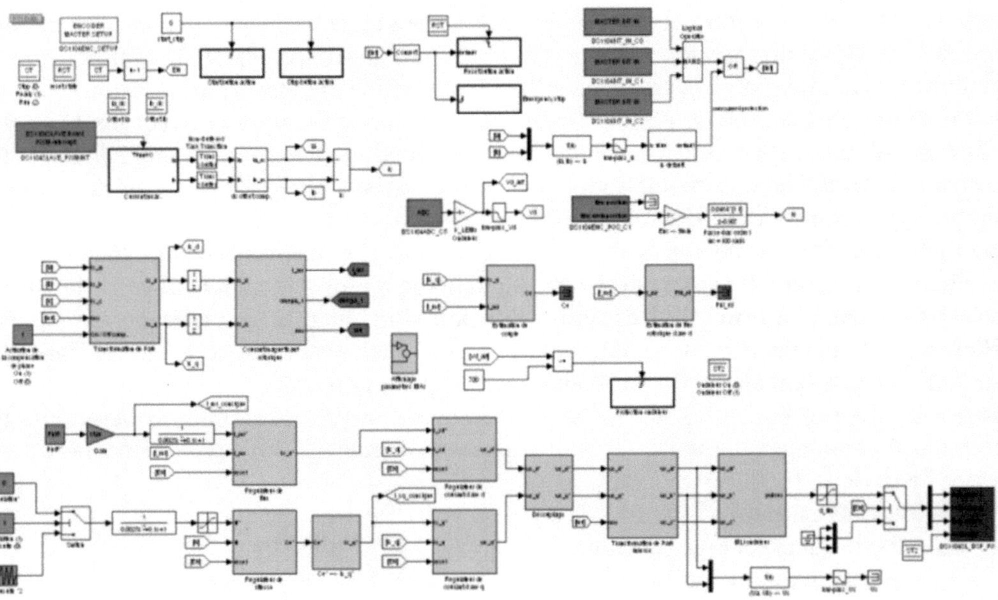

Fig. 11. Vector control algorithm implemented with Simulink

After the algorithms implementation, several tests can be carried out in order to plot the torque-speed curves in scalar control as well as to evaluate the vector control and DTC-SVM behavior in speed regulation and speed tracking. For all these tests, the switching frequency of the VSI is set at 9 kHz. The sample frequency is chosen equal to the switching frequency.

6.1 Scalar control

Fig. 13 shows the predetermined torque-speed curves (solid line) for several supplied frequencies in scalar control (in the constant flux region and in the flux-weakening region) as well as the measured torque-speed curves (circles). Note that the base frequency has been arbitrarily chosen equal to 40 Hz. It should also be noticed that, for the smaller frequencies (viz. 30 Hz, 35 Hz and 40 Hz), the measures have been stopped when instability, which can appear at low-speed and light-load operation (Kishimoto et al., 1986), is observed. One can easily conclude a very good agreement between the predetermined torque-speed curves and the measures. This confirms that the parameters are properly determined.

Fig. 14 shows the torque-speed curves in scalar control and constant rotor frequency ($s{\cdot}f$) operation. Note that this rotor frequency is maintained equal to 1 Hz by adjusting the slip by

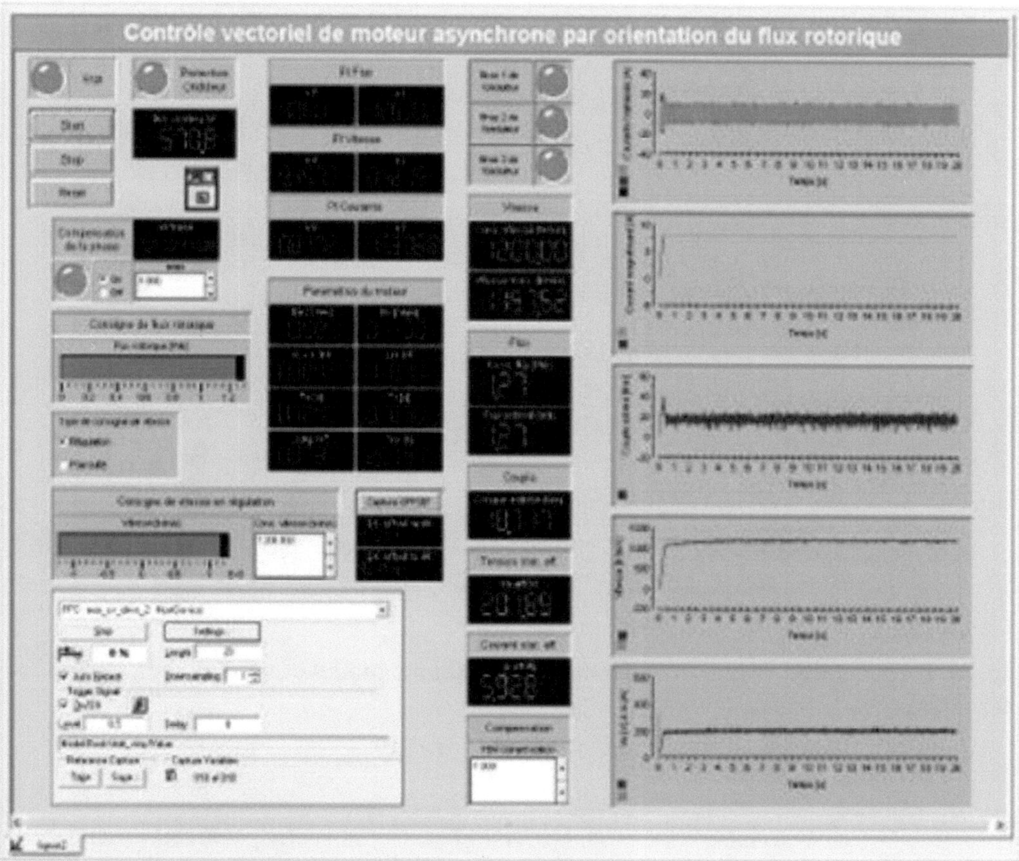

Fig. 12. ControlDesk virtual control panel

acting on the excitation of the dc-machine. Once again, one can conclude a good agreement between the predetermined curve (in solid line) and the measures performed from 30 Hz to 60 Hz (circles). Moreover, considering (3), the results can easily be explained. Indeed, in the constant flux region (below the base speed Ω_{base}), the torque is constant as the rotor frequency and the flux are constant (see (3)). Then, in the flux-weakening region, the rotor frequency remains constant but the flux decreases in inverse proportion to the frequency (and, so, to the speed). Therefore, according to (3), the torque decreases in inverse proportion to the square of the speed.

Finally, some measures have been performed in close-loop speed control with Volts/Hz control and slip regulation. Due to the slip regulation, the IM is able to rotate at the synchronous speed (900 rpm at 30 Hz and 1500 rpm at 50 Hz as P = 2) and, therefore, the torque-speed curves become vertical lines as shown in Fig. 15. As a final point, Fig. 16 shows a linear evolution of the torque as a function of the rotor frequency which can be explained on the basis of (3). Moreover, the slope of the regression lines, viz. 29.29 Nm/Hz at 30 Hz and 16.34 Nm/Hz at 50 Hz, are very close to the theoretical values of K_T (see (3)), viz. 28.92 Nm/Hz at 30 Hz and 16.27 Nm/Hz at 50 Hz. One can also conclude that the statistics of the regression, i.e. the R^2 and R^2_{Adj}, are very good (close to 1 and close to each other).

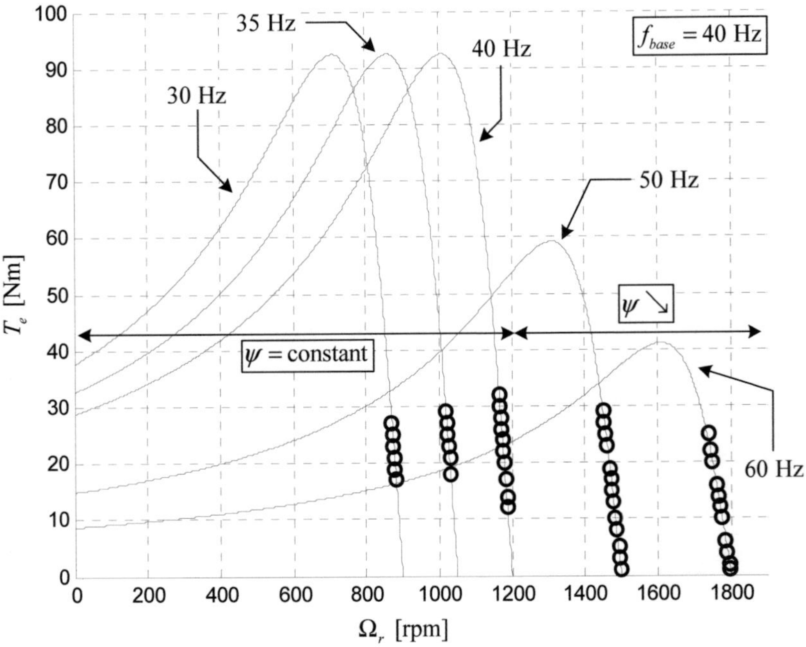

Fig. 13. Torque-speed curves in scalar control (solid line: predetermined curves; circles: measures)

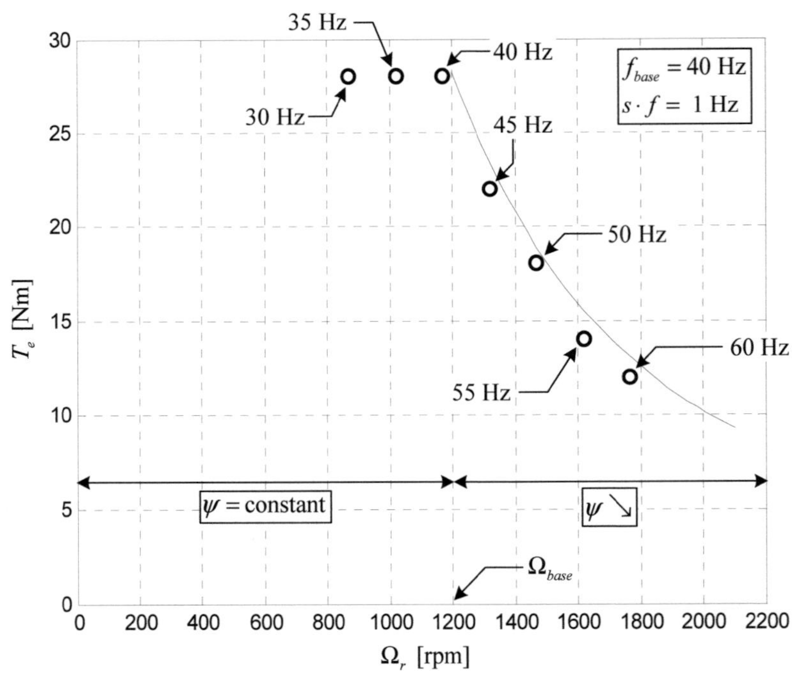

Fig. 14. Torque-speed curves in scalar control and constant rotor frequency (solid line: predetermined curves; circles: measures)

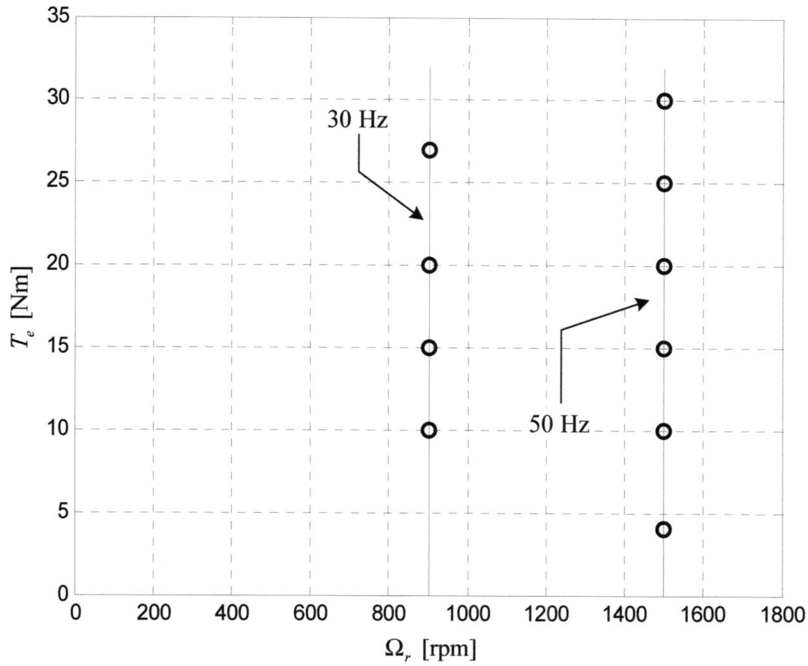

Fig. 15. Torque-speed curves in close-loop speed control with Volts/Hz control and slip regulation

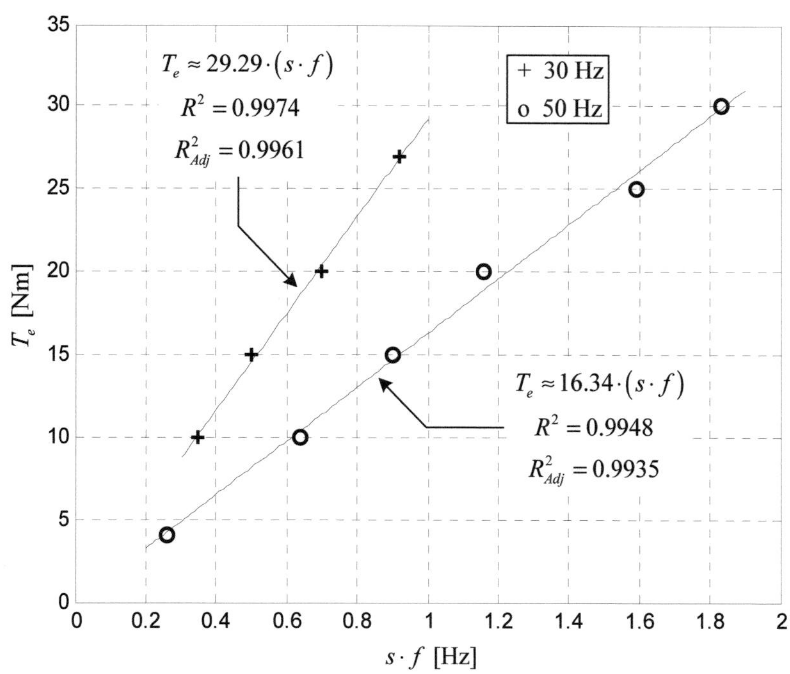

Fig. 16. Evolution of the torque as a function of the rotor frequency in close-loop speed control with Volts/Hz control and slip regulation

6.2 Vector control and DTC-SVM

In this sub-section, the results in vector control and DTC-SVM are presented and discussed. First, a speed regulation test is carried out at no-load (the load generator remains coupled to the shaft) by supplying a speed reference of 1000 rpm. In Fig. 17, the response using vector control is shown. Similarly, Fig. 18 shows the response with DTC-SVM. The speed, flux magnitude and torque are represented (from the top to the bottom). One can conclude that vector control and DTC-SVM schemes have similar dynamic responses and good speed reference tracking. One can also observe that, in vector control scheme, the rotor flux is correctly regulated and that, in DTC-SVM, the stator flux is properly regulated as well.

Then, a speed tracking test is performed at no-load. To do so, the speed reference varies from 1000 rpm to -1000 rpm as can be seen in Fig. 19 and 20. In these figures, one can observe a good response to the speed profile in vector control (Fig. 19) as well as in DTC-SVM (Fig. 20). Note that, as in the previous tests, the fluxes are correctly regulated.

In this sub-section, the two considered control schemes for IM are compared in similar operating conditions. According to the experimental results presented, one can conclude that vector control and DTC-SVM of IM drive produce comparable results in speed regulation and tracking. However, the DTC-SVM is simplest and easiest to implement than vector control. Indeed, no coordinate rotation and less PI controllers are needed. Moreover, less torque ripple is observed with DTC-SVM compare to vector control.

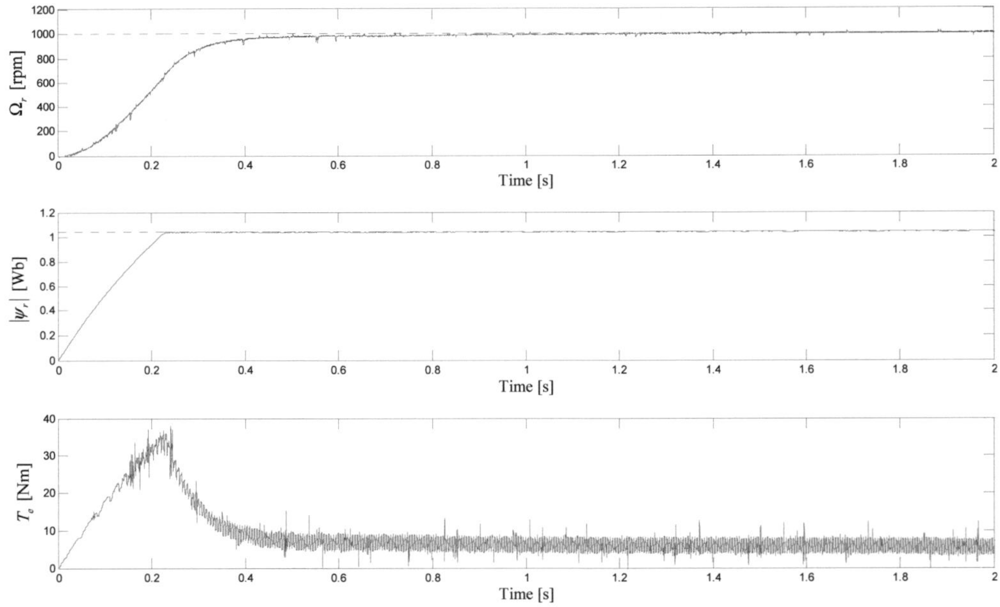

Fig. 17. Speed regulation in vector control (dotted line: speed reference; solid line: speed measured)

Finally, the effects of a load variation in vector control are shown in Fig. 21. One can conclude that such load variation does not affect the flux regulation and that, after a transient phase, the speed remains regulated at the considered speed reference (viz. 1200 rpm).

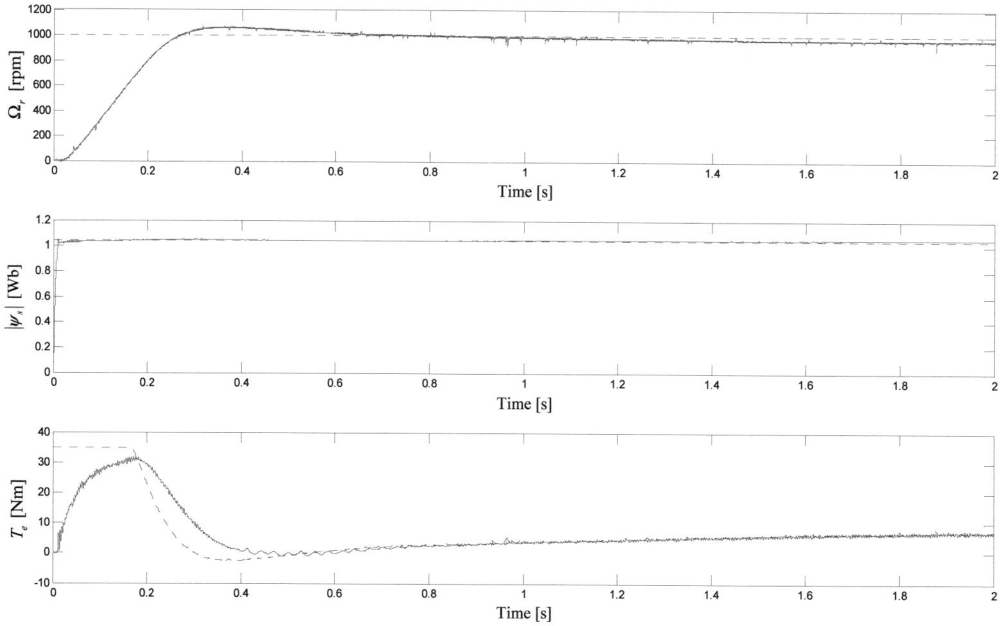

Fig. 18. Speed regulation in DTC-SVM (dotted line: speed reference; solid line: speed measured)

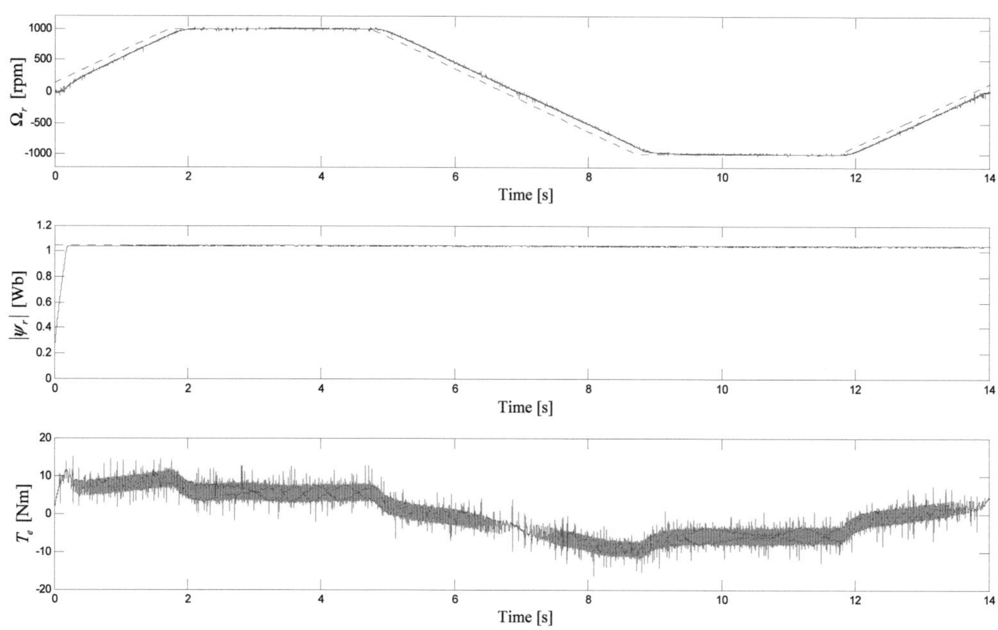

Fig. 19. Speed tracking in vector control (dotted line: speed reference; solid line: speed measured)

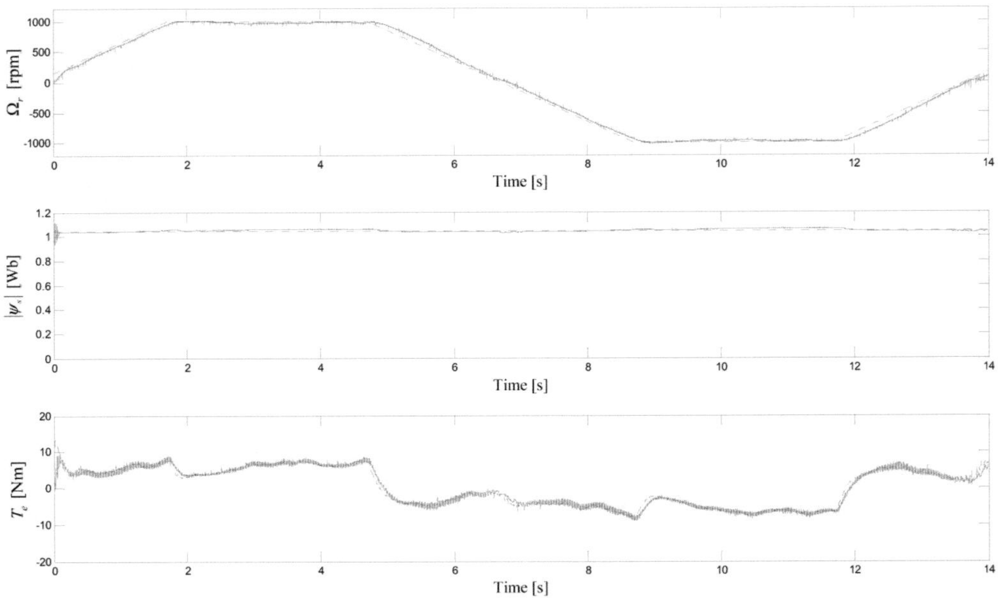

Fig. 20. Speed tracking in DCT-SVM (dotted line: speed reference; solid line: speed measured)

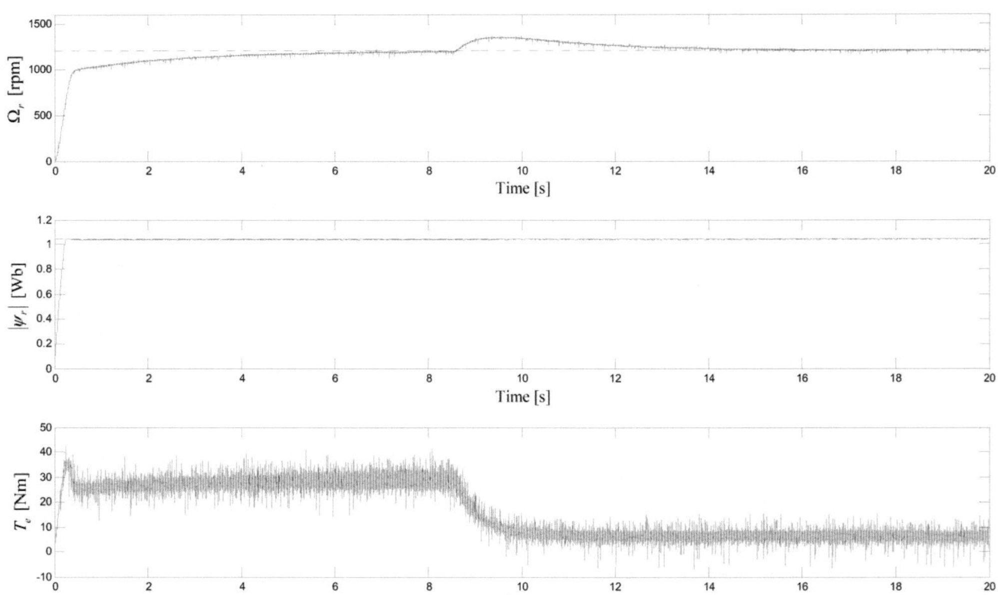

Fig. 21. Load variation in vector control (dotted line: speed reference; solid line: speed measured)

7. Educational experience

During the lectures, students become familiar with the steady-state and dynamic models of IM and the three control schemes. Then, through the experimental setup, they are made sensitive to many aspects concerning:

- modeling and simulation using the Matlab/Simulink/dSPACE environment;
- IM parameters determination;
- IM motor drives;
- some practical aspects concerning inverters and SV-PWM.

From the students' point of view, the experimental setup presented in this chapter helps them in understanding IM parameters determination, IM steady-state as well as dynamic models and IM drives. They also found that the dSPACE platform and Matlab/Simulink environment could be used for practical teaching in other courses.
From the authors' point of view, dSPACE material offers multiple advantages from the point of education and gives a powerful tool for the teaching of IM parameters identification and drives. Moreover, thanks to this experimental setup, the students can easily put into practice a lot of theoretical knowledge.

8. Conclusion

This chapter has dealt with the implementation of three control schemes of a voltage-fed inverter IM drive, namely scalar control, vector control and DTC, using a dSPACE platform and Matlab/Simulink environment. This has been successfully integrated into "Electric Drives" course which is, usually, attended by students during their fourth year of five-year electrical engineering degree at the Faculty of Engineering (FPMs) of the University of Mons (UMons) in Belgium. It helps greatly the students in understanding the theoretical concepts taught during the lectures.
Furthermore, the dSPACE platform and Matlab/Simulink environment give a powerful tool for teaching IM parameters identification and drives. The authors are planning to use more and more this experimental system in others teaching projects.

9. References

Böcker, J. & Mathapati, S. (2007). State of the art of induction motor control, *Proceedings of 2007 International Conference on Electric Machines & Drives*, ISBN 1-4244-0743-5, Antalya, Turkey, May 2007.

Bojoi, R.; Profume, F.; Griva, G.; Teodorescu, R. & Blaabjerg, F. (2002). Advanced research and education in electrical drives by using digital real-time hardware-in-the-loop simulation, *Proceedings of the 10th International Power Electronics and Motion Control Conference*, ISBN 0-7803-7089-9, Cavtat & Dubrovnik, Croatia, September 2002.

Bose, B. K. (2002). Modern Power Electronics and AC Drives, Prentice Hall PTR, ISBN 0-13-016743-6, New Jersey, USA.

Casadei, D.; Serra, G.; Tani, A. & Zarri, L. (2005). A review on the direct torque control of induction motors, *Proceedings of the 11th International Conference on Power Electronics and Applications*, ISBN 90-75815-07-7, Dresden, Germany, September 2005.

Khambadkon, A. M. & Holtz, J. (1991). Vector-controlled induction motor drive with a self-commissioning scheme, *IEEE Transactions on Industrial Electronics*, vol. 38, no. 5, (March 1991), pp. 322-327, ISSN 0278-0046.

Kishimoto, T.; Matsumoto, K.; Kamakure, T. & Daijo, M. (1986). Stability analysis of a voltage source PWM inverter-fed induction motor drive system, *Electrical Engineering in Japan*, vol. 106, no. 6, (June 1986), pp. 32-41, ISSN 0424-7760.

Luo, G.; Liu, W.; Song, K. & Zeng, Z. (2008). dSPACE based permanent magnet motor HIL simulation and test bench, *Proceedings of the 2008 IEEE International Conference on Industrial Technology*, ISBN 978-1-4244-1706-3, Chengdu, China, April 2008.

Mäki, K.; Partanen, A.; Rauhala, T.; Repo, S. & Järventausta, P. (2005). Real-time simulation environment for power system studies using RTDS and dSPACE simulators, *Proceedings of the 11th International Conference on Power Electronics and Applications*, ISBN 90-75815-07-7, Dresden, Germany, September 2005.

Mohan, N. (2001). Advanced Electric Drives: Analysis, Control and Modeling using Simulink ®, Edition MPERE, ISBN 0-9715292-0-5, Minneapolis, USA.

Padhy, P. K. & Majhi, S. (2006). Relay based PI-PD design for stable and unstable FOPDT processes, *Computer and Chemical Engineering*, vol. 30, no. 5, (April 2006), pp. 790-796, ISSN 0098-1354.

Rodriguez, J. ; Pontt, J. ; Silva, C. ; Kouro, S. & Miranda, H. (2004). A novel direct torque scheme for induction machines with space vector modulation, *Proceedings of 35th Annual IEEE Power Electronics Specialists Conference*, ISBN 0-7803-8399-0, Aachen Germany, June 2004.

Santisteban, J. A. & Stephan, R. M. (2001). Vector control methods for induction machines: an overview, *IEEE Transactions on Education*, vol. 44, no. 2, (May 2001), pp. 170-175, ISSN 0018-9359.

Trzynadlowski, A. M.; Kazmierkowski, M. P.; Graboswski, P. Z. & Bech M. M. (1999). Three examples of DSP applications in advanced induction motor drives, *Proceedings of the 1999 American Control Conference*, ISBN 0-7803-4990-3, San Diego, USA, June 1999.

Versèle, C.; Deblecker, O. & Lobry, J. (2008). Implementation of a vector control scheme using dSPACE material for teaching induction motor drives and parameters identification, *Proceedings of the 2008 International Conference on Electrical Machines*, ISBN 978-1-4244-1736-0, Vilamoura, Portugal, September 2008.

Versèle, C.; Deblecker, O. & Lobry, J. (2010). Implementation of advanced control schemes using dSPACE material for teaching induction motor drive, *International Journal of Electrical Engineering Education*, vol. 47, no. 2, (April 2010), pp. 151-167, ISSN 0020-7209.

16

Linearization of Permanent Magnet Synchronous Motor Using MATLAB and Simulink

A. K. Parvathy and R. Devanathan
Hindustan Institute of Technology and Science, Chennai
India

1. Introduction

Permanent magnet machines, particularly at low power range, are widely used in the industry because of their high efficiency. They have gained popularity in variable frequency drive applications. The merits of the machine are elimination of field copper loss, higher power density, lower rotor inertia and a robust construction of the rotor (Bose 2002).
In order to find effective ways of designing a controller for PM synchronous motor (PMSM), the dynamic model of the machine is normally used. The dynamic model of PM motor can be derived from the voltage equations referred to direct (d) and quadrature (q) axes (Bose 2002).The model derived essentially has quadratic nonlinearity. Linear control techniques generally fail to produce the desired performance. Feedback linearization is a technique that has been used to control nonlinear systems effectively.
By applying exact linearization technique (Cardoso & Schnitman 2011) it is possible to linearize a system and apply linear control methods. But this requires that certain system distributions have involutive property. An approximate feedback linearization technique was formulated by Krener (Krener 1984) based on Taylor series expansion of distributions for non-involutive systems.
Chiasson and Bodson (Chiasson & Bodson 1998) have designed a controller for electric motors using differential geometric method of nonlinear control based on exact feedback linearization. But from a practical point of view, this technique suffers from singularity issues. If the system goes into a state, during the course of the system operation, where the singularity condition is satisfied, then the designed controller will fail.
Starting with the quadratic model of PMSM, we apply quadratic linearization technique based on coordinate and state feedback. The linearization technique used is the control input analog of Poincare's work (Arnold 1983) as proposed by Kang and Krener (Kang & Krener 1992) and further developed by Devanathan (Devanathan 2001,2004) .The quadratic linearization technique proposed is on the lines of approximate linearization of Krener (Krener 1984) and does not introduce any singularities in the system compared to the exact linearization methods reported in (Chiasson & Bodson 1998).
MATLAB simulation is used to verify the effectiveness of the linearization technique proposed. In this chapter, MATLAB/SIMULINK modeling is used to verify the effectiveness of the quadratic linearization technique proposed. In particular, the application of MATLAB and SIMULINK as tools for simulating the following is described:

i. Dynamic model of a sinusoidal Permanent Magnet Synchronous machine(PMSM)
ii. Application of nonlinear coordinate and state feedback transformations to linearize the PMSM model and
iii. Tuning the transformations against a linear system model put in Brunovsky form employing error back propogation.

As these applications were somewhat sophisticated , customization and improvisation of the MATLAB/SIMULINK tools were essential. These applications are described in detail in this chapter.

In section 2, linearization of dynamic model of PMSM is discussed and simulation results using MATLAB are given. In section 3, linearization of PMSM machine model is given. Construction of PMSM model using SIMULINK and verification of linearization of PMSM SIMULINK model is given in Section 4. Tuning of the linearizing transformations to account for unmodelled dynamics is discussed in Section 5. In section 6, the chapter is concluded.

2. Linearization of dynamic model of PMSM

2.1 Dynamic model of PMSM

The dynamic model of a sinusoidal PM machine, considering the flux-linkage λ_f to be constant and ignoring the core-loss, can be written as (Bose 2002).

$$\dot{i}_d = \frac{v_d}{L_d} - \frac{R}{L_d} i_d + \frac{L_q}{L_d} p\omega_r i_q \tag{1}$$

$$\dot{i}_q = \frac{v_q}{L_q} - \frac{R}{L_q} i_q - \frac{L_d}{L_q} p\omega_r i_d - \frac{\lambda_f p\omega_r}{L_q} \tag{2}$$

$$\dot{\omega}_r = \frac{1.5p}{J}[\lambda_f i_q + (L_d - L_q) i_d i_q] \tag{3}$$

where all quantities in the rotor reference frame are referred to the stator.
L_q, L_d are q and d axis inductances respectively; R is the resistance of the stator windings; i_q, i_d are q and d axis currents respectively; v_q, v_d are q and d axis voltages respectively; ω_r is the angular velocity of the rotor; λ_f is the amplitude of the flux induced by the permanent magnets of the rotor in the stator phases and p is the number of pole pairs.
Using linear coordinate and state feedback transformations (Kuo 2001) the dynamic model can be written with the linear part put in Brunovsky form (Parvathy et. al. 2005,2006) as

$$\dot{x} = Ax + Bu + f^{(2)}(x) \tag{4}$$

where u=$[\, u_1 \quad u_2 \,]^T = [\, v_q \quad v_d \,]^T ; x = [i_q \quad i_d \quad \omega_e]^T$

$$A=\begin{bmatrix} 0 & 1 & 0 \\ 0 & 0 & 1 \\ 0 & 0 & 0 \end{bmatrix} \quad B=\begin{bmatrix} 0 & 0 \\ 0 & 1 \\ 1 & 0 \end{bmatrix}; \; f^{(2)}(x)=\begin{bmatrix} b_1x_2x_3 \\ b_2x_1x_3 \\ b_3x_1x_2 \end{bmatrix}$$

where b_1, b_2, b_3 are constants derived from the motor parameters.

2.2 Linearization of the dynamic model

Coordinate and state feedback transformations in quadratic form (Kang & Krener 1992)

$$y = x + \phi^{(2)}(x) \tag{5}$$

$$u = (I_2 + \beta^{(1)}(x))v + \alpha^{(2)}(x) \tag{6}$$

Where

$$y = \begin{bmatrix} y_1 & y_2 & y_3 \end{bmatrix}^T ; v = \begin{bmatrix} v_1 & v_2 \end{bmatrix}^T$$

$\phi^{(2)}(x);\alpha^{(2)}(x)$ and $\beta^{(1)}(x)$ are derived by solving the Generalized Homological Equations (Kang & Krener 1992) .Applying the transformations (5) and (6), (4) is reduced to

$$\dot{y} = Ay + Bv + O^{(3)}(y,v)$$

where $O^{(3)}(y,v)$ represent third and higher order nonlinearities .

2.3 Verification of linearization using MATLAB function

The problem now is to apply MATLAB to verify the theoretical result on quadratic linearization of the dynamic model (4). Expanding (4), we can see that the expression of the derivative of each state variable has the other two state variables in it. This becomes difficult to solve using manual methods of differential equation solution. The tool selected for solving the dynamic equations is the MATLAB function called ODE45.

ODE45 is a MATLAB function that solves initial value problems for ordinary differential equations (ODEs). It uses the iterative Runge Kutta method of solving equations. Hence, this function does not return the solution as an expression, but the values of the solution function at discrete instants of time. ODE45 is based on an explicit Runge-Kutta formula, the Dormand-Prince pair. It is a *one-step* ode45 –in the sense that, in computing $y(t_n)$, it needs only the solution at the immediately preceding time point $y(t_{n-1})$ .In general, ode45 is the best function to apply as a "first try" for most problems.

[t,Y] = ode45(odefun,tspan,y0) with tspan = [t0 tf] integrates the system of differential equations from time t0 to tf with initial conditions y0. Function f = odefun(t,y) is defined, where t corresponds to the column vector of time points and y is the solution array. Each row in y corresponds to the solution at a time returned in the corresponding row of t. To obtain solutions at the specific times t0, t1,...,tf (all increasing or all decreasing), we use tspan = [t0,t1,...,tf].

[t, Y] = ode45(odefun,tspan,y0,options) solves as above with default integration parameters replaced by property values specified in 'options'. Commonly used properties include a scalar relative error tolerance RelTol (1e-3 by default) and a vector of absolute error tolerances AbsTol (all components are 1e-6 by default).

The PLOT function is used to create a computer-graphic plot of any two quantities or a group of quantities with respect to time.

A simulation of (4) was carried out for different values of inputs u_1 and u_2 in the open loop before applying the linearizing transformations where b_1 = -0.0165*(10^-3) ; b_2 -186.96; b_3 =5754386. Fig 1 shows a plot of x_3 (angular velocity) versus time for pulse inputs

u_1= 0.1{u(t)-u(t-1)} and u_2=0.1{u(t)-u(t-1)} where u(t) is a unit step function . The system is oscillatory as seen from Fig 1. Fig. 2 shows the result of simulation of equation (4) after the linearizing transformations (5) and (6) are applied to the system. It shows a plot of y_1,y_2,y_3 against time for pulse inputs v_1=0.2{u(t)-u(t-1)}, v_2=0.2{u(t)-u(t-1)}. From Fig 2 it is seen that the system shows a stable response for a pulse input in v_1 and v_2 even under open loop conditions..

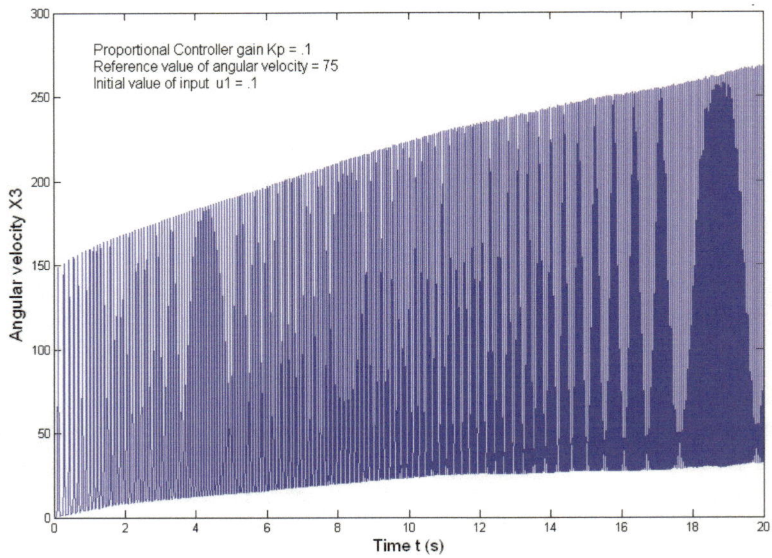

Fig. 1. Time response of angular velocity with v_1=0.1 and v_2=0.1

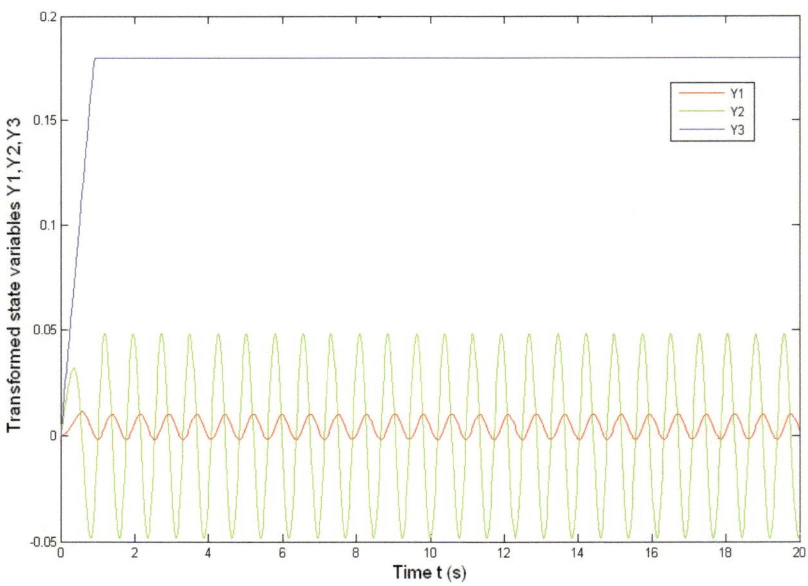

Fig. 2. Time response of Y_1 ,Y_2 ,Y_3 with v_1=0.2 and v_2=0.2

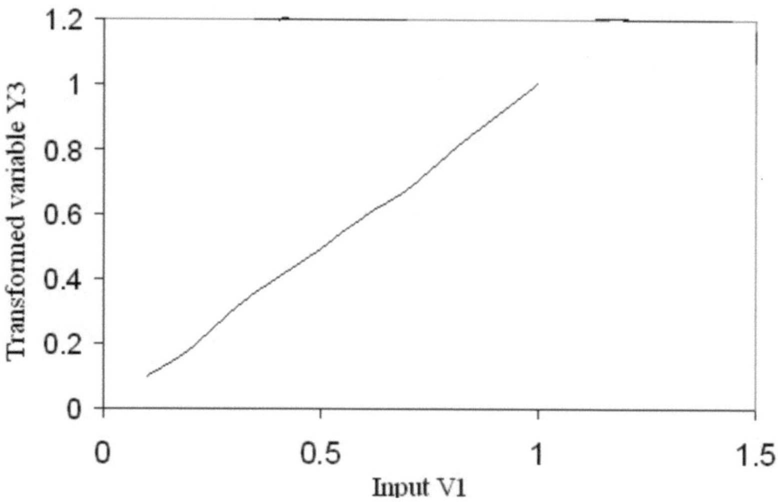

Fig. 3. Variation of transformed variable Y_3 with input v_1 (keeping v_2=0.1)

Fig. 3 shows the steady state gain of y_3 with respect to v_1 while v_2 is maintained constant. It is observed that the plot between y_3 and v_1 is almost linear, thus verifying that the linearizing system is almost linear. A similar test before linearization revealed that the steady gain of x_3 with respect to input u_1 varied over a large range thus revealing the nonlinearity.
Thus the linearization of the dynamic model of PMSM was verified through the use of MATLAB function ODE45 .

3. Linearization of PMSM machine model

3.1 PMSM model in normal form

The 4 - dimensional PM machine model can be derived as below (Bose 2002).

$$\begin{aligned} \dot{x} &= Ax + Bu + f^{(2)}(x) \\ x &= \begin{bmatrix} x_1 & x_2 & x_3 & x_4 \end{bmatrix}^T = \begin{bmatrix} \theta & \omega_e, & i_q, & i_d \end{bmatrix}^T; \\ u &= \begin{bmatrix} u_1 & u_2 \end{bmatrix}^T = \begin{bmatrix} v_q & v_d \end{bmatrix}^T \end{aligned} \tag{7}$$

where v_q, v_d, i_q, i_d represent the quadrature and direct axis voltages and currents respectively and θ, ω_e represent rotor position and angular velocity respectively.

$$A = \begin{bmatrix} 0 & 1 & 0 & 0 \\ 0 & 0 & \frac{1.5p\lambda}{J} & 0 \\ 0 & \frac{-\lambda p}{L_q} & \frac{-R}{L_q} & 0 \\ 0 & 0 & 0 & \frac{-R}{L_d} \end{bmatrix}; B = \begin{bmatrix} 0 & 0 \\ 0 & 0 \\ \frac{1}{L_q} & 0 \\ 0 & \frac{1}{L_d} \end{bmatrix}; f^{(2)}(x) = \begin{bmatrix} 0 \\ \frac{1.5p(L_d - L_q)i_d i_q}{J} \\ \frac{-L_d p \omega_e i_d}{L_q} \\ \frac{L_q p \omega_e i_q}{L_d} \end{bmatrix}$$

λ is the flux induced by the permanent magnet of the rotor in the stator phases. L_d, L_q are the direct and quadrature inductances respectively. R is the stator resistance. p is the number of pole pairs and J is the system moment of inertia.
The model (7) can be reduced to normal form for two inputs (Brunovsky 1970), in a standard way using the following transformations (Kuo 2001),

$$x = \begin{bmatrix} a_1c_1 & 0 & 0 & 0 \\ 0 & a_1c_1 & 0 & 0 \\ 0 & 0 & c_1 & 0 \\ 0 & 0 & 0 & a_4 \end{bmatrix} y$$
$$u = \begin{bmatrix} 1 & 0 \\ 0 & a_4/c_2 \end{bmatrix} u' + \begin{bmatrix} 0 & -a_1a_2 & -a_3 & 0 \\ 0 & 0 & 0 & -a_4^2/c_2 \end{bmatrix} y \tag{8}$$

where

$$a_1 = \frac{1.5p\lambda}{J};\; a_2 = \frac{-\lambda p}{L_q}, a_3 = \frac{-R}{L_q},\; a_4 = \frac{-R}{L_d};\; c_1 = \frac{1}{L_q}; c_2 = \frac{1}{L_d}$$

The Brunovsky form for two inputs is given below (where x, u, A and B are retained for simplicity of notation).

$$\dot{x} = Ax + Bu + f^{(2)}(x) \tag{9}$$

Where

$$A = \begin{bmatrix} 0 & 1 & 0 & 0 \\ 0 & 0 & 1 & 0 \\ 0 & 0 & 0 & 0 \\ 0 & 0 & 0 & 0 \end{bmatrix}; B = \begin{bmatrix} 0 & 0 \\ 0 & 0 \\ 1 & 0 \\ 0 & 1 \end{bmatrix}; f^{(2)}(x) = \begin{bmatrix} 0 \\ k_1x_3x_4 \\ k_2x_2x_4 \\ k_3x_2x_3 \end{bmatrix}$$

$$k_1 = \frac{1.5p(L_d - L_q)a_4}{Ja_1}, k_2 = \frac{-L_dpa_1a_4}{L_q}, k_3 = \frac{L_qC_1^{\,2}a_1}{L_da_4}$$

3.2 Linearization of PMSM normal form model

Given the 4 dimensional model of a PM synchronous motor (IPM model) of the form (9), the system can be linearized using the following transformations

$$y = x + \phi^{(2)}(x) \tag{10}$$

$$u = (I_2 + \beta^{(1)}(x))v + \alpha^{(2)}(x) \tag{11}$$

where $u=[u_1 \quad u_2]^T ; v=[v_1 \quad v_2]^T$

$$\phi^{(2)}(x)=\begin{bmatrix}0\\0\\k_1x_3x_4\\0\end{bmatrix},\alpha^{(2)}(x)=\begin{bmatrix}-k_2x_2x_4\\-k_3x_2x_3\end{bmatrix},\beta^{(1)}(x)=-\begin{bmatrix}k_1x_4 & k_1x_3\\0 & 0\end{bmatrix}$$

where I_2 is the identity matrix of order 2. The system then reduces to

$$\dot{y}=Ay+Bv+O^{(3)}(y,v)$$

where $O^{(3)}(y,v)$ represents third and higher order nonlinearities .

4. Linearization of PMSM model using SIMULINK

4.1 Construction of PMSM model

Customization of PMSM machine model using MATLAB/SIMULINK tools had to be carried out as the standard library available contained only special cases. The PM motor drive simulation was built in several steps through the construction of q-axis circuit, d-a xis circuit, torque block and speed block.

4.1.1 q-axis circuit

By using the following system equation the q-axis circuit is constructed.

$$v_q=R_qi_q+\omega_r(L_di_d+\lambda_f)+\rho L_qi_q$$

q-axis circuit in the SIMULINK is shown in Fig.4 .

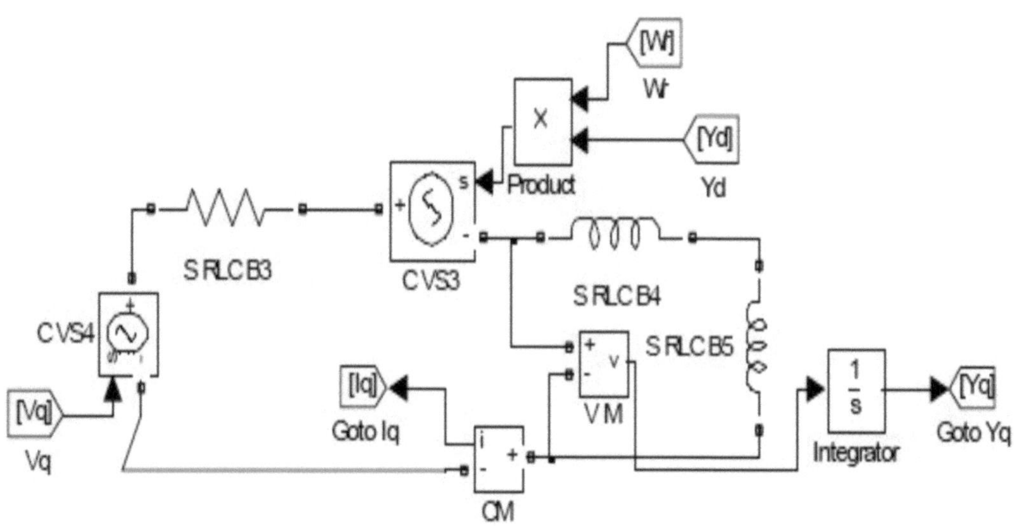

Fig. 4. q-axis circuit

4.1.2 d-axis circuit

By using the following system equation the d-axis circuit is constructed.

$$v_d = R_d i_d + \omega_r (L_q i_q) + \rho(\lambda_f + L_d i_d)$$

Simulation of the d-axis circuit is shown in Fig. 5.

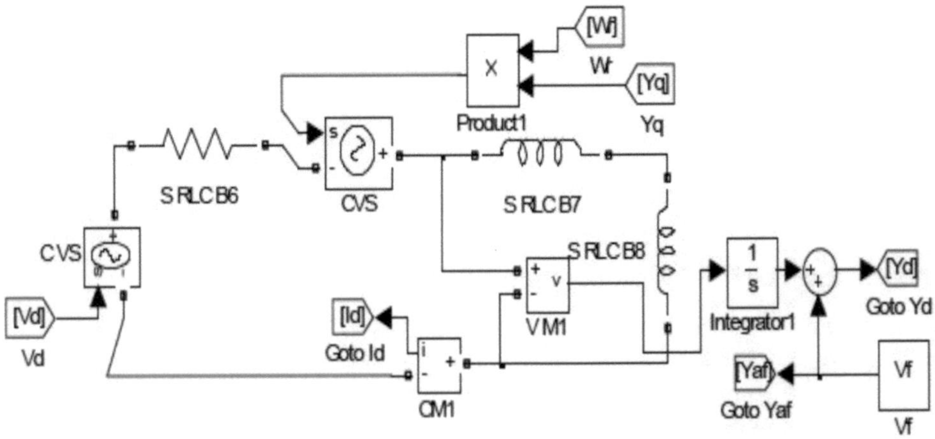

Fig. 5. d-axis circuit

4.1.3 Torque block

By using the following torque equation the torque block is constructed.

$$T_e = (3/2)(p/4)(\lambda_d i_q - \lambda_q i_d)$$

The simulation of torque T_e circuit is shown in the Fig 6.

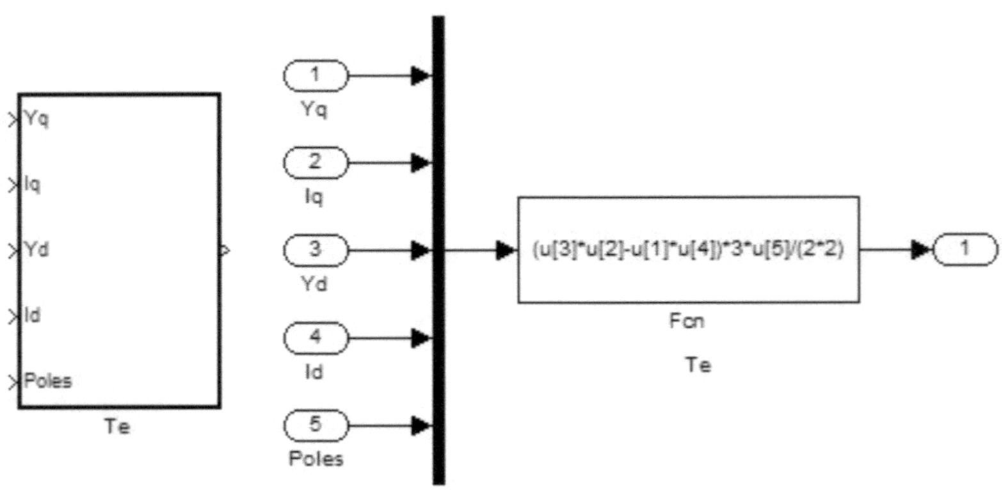

Fig. 6. T_e Block in Simulink

4.1.4 Speed block

By using the following equations the speed block is constructed.

$$\omega_m = \int (T_e - T_l - B\omega_m)/J dt$$

$$\omega_m = \omega_r (2/p)$$

The simulation of ω_m circuit is shown in the Fig.7.

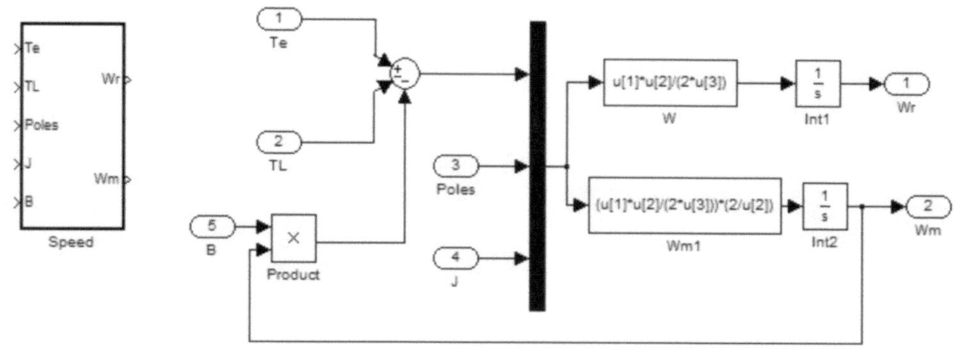

Fig. 7. Speed Block in Simulink

4.1.5 Designed PMSM with V_q and V_d as inputs

The PMSM is constructed by using q-axis, d-axis, torque and speed blocks (figures 4,5, 6, and 7) and is shown in figure 8.

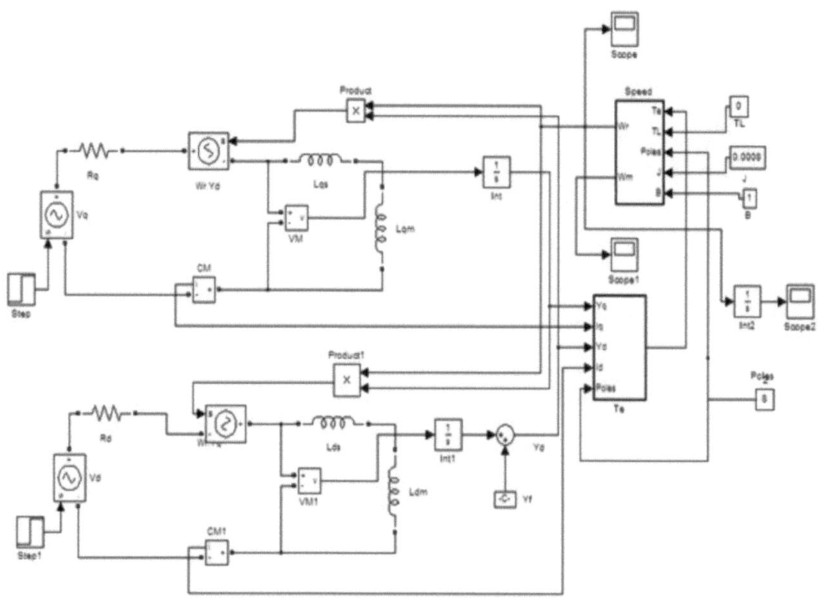

Fig. 8. Permanent Magnet Synchronous Motor with V_q and V_d as inputs

4.2 Linearization of PMSM SIMULINK model

The PMSM model is first converted to controller normal form of the linear part (9) using transformations as given in (8). Then linearization of the PMSM is carried out using quadratic coordinate and state feedback as given in (10) and (11). Fig.9 gives the PMSM model including linearization blocks. N_1 and N_2 include the linear transformations (8) while L_1 and L_2, denote the nonlinear transformations (11) and (10) respectively.
N_1, N_2, L_1 and L_2 are implemented using function blocks.

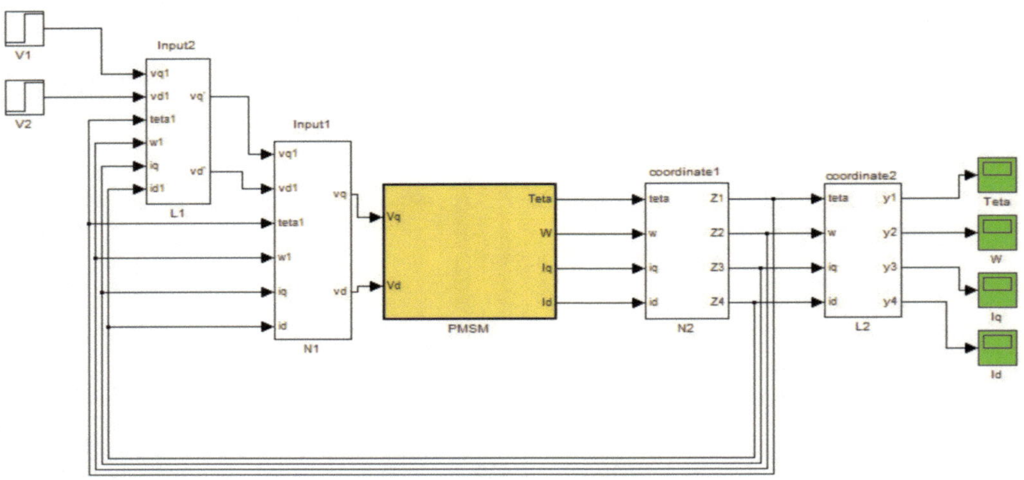

Fig. 9. Linearization of PMSM model

4.3 Verification of linearization of PMSM-simulation results

For the Interior PMSM, parameters are taken as follows:
Stator resistance R = 2.875Ω; q- axis Inductance L_q = 9mH; d-axis Inductance L_d = 7mH;
Flux induced in magnets λ_f = 0.175 wb; Moment of Inertia J = 0.0008 kg.m^2
Friction factor B = 1 N.m.s; No. of pole pairs p = 4

v_q	ω_e	K=d ω_e / d v_q
5	2.55	-
10	4.7709	0.44418
15	6.4706	0.33994
20	7.6082	0.22752
25	8.2567	0.1297
30	8.5326	0.05518

Table 1. Steady state gain of ω_e versus v_q for the system in open loop (Prior to linearization)

v_1	y_2 *10^(-6)	K=d y_2 /d v_1 *10^(-6)
5	2.176	-
10	4.366	0.438
15	6.585	0.4438
20	8.845	0.452
25	11.162	0.4634
30	13.55	0.4776

Table 2. Steady state gain of y_2 vs v_1 for the linearized system in open loop

Prior to linearization, the open loop steady state gain of ω_e versus v_q of the PMSM model is investigated and the results are given in Table 1. In Table 1, it is observed that the open loop steady state gain of ω_e versus v_q (keeping v_d constant) is not constant because of the system nonlinearity. To verify the linearity of the system after linearization, we investigated the variation of its gain of y_2 (a scaled version of ω_e as can be seen from (8) and (10)) with input v_1 (see Fig. 9) and the results are given in Table 2. The table reveals that the gain of the system is nearly constant thus verifying that by applying the homogeneous linearizing transformation, the PMSM model is made nearly linear for the given set of inputs.

Figures 10 and 11 show the time response of angular velocity ω_e by closing the loop around PMSM model (Fig. 8) before linearization when v_q = 5 units and 30 units respectively. It is observed that the dynamic response for v_q = 5 is more oscillatory compared to the case of v_q = 30 with a fixed controller of proportional gain = 50 and integral constant =2. This is to be expected since the loop gain is higher in the former case with a higher static gain in the plant or motor as can be seen from Table I.

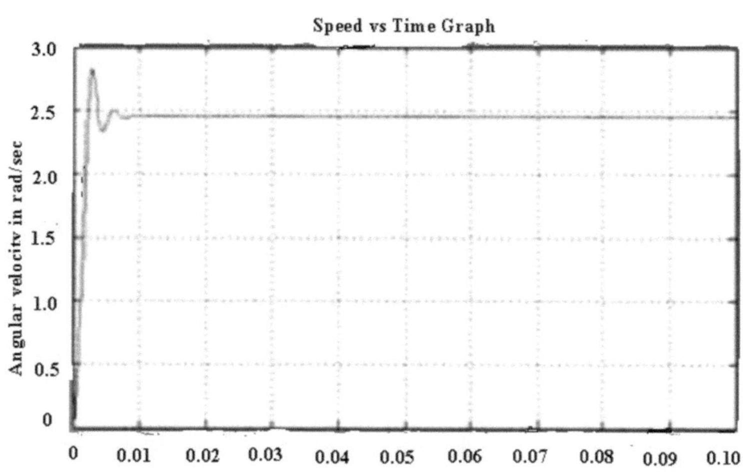

Fig. 10. Time response of angular velocity in closed loop when $v_q = 5$; $k_p = 50; k_i = 2$ (before linearization)

Figures 12 and 13 show the time response of y_2 of the transformed PMSM system (Fig. 9) in closed loop when v_1 = 5 units and 30 units respectively . It is observed that a uniform output response is obtained in the closed loop after linearization when the reference is varied. Since the static gain in Table II is nearly uniform, the loop gain is also nearly constant for the extreme points in the operating range, thus resulting in the uniform dynamic responses in Fig. 12 and 13.
Simulation results show that the nearly constant gain of the linearized model, results in a uniform response on a range of set point and load inputs with a fixed controller. This is in contrast to the case before linearization under the corresponding conditions.

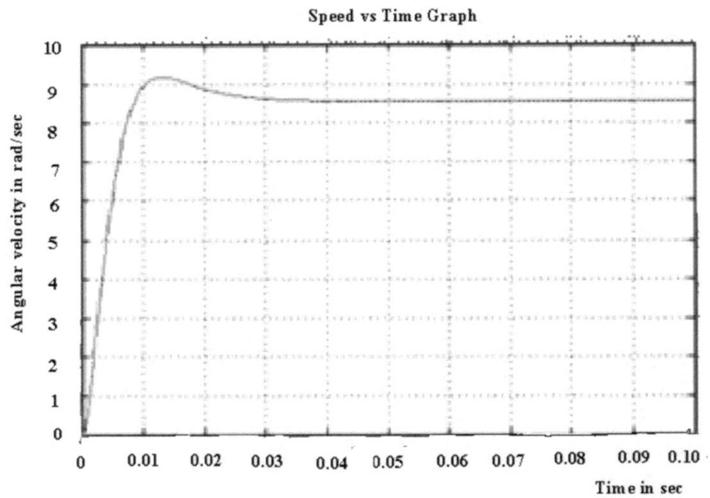

Fig. 11. Time response of angular velocity in closed loop when $v_q = 30$; $k_p = 50; k_i = 2$ (before linearization)

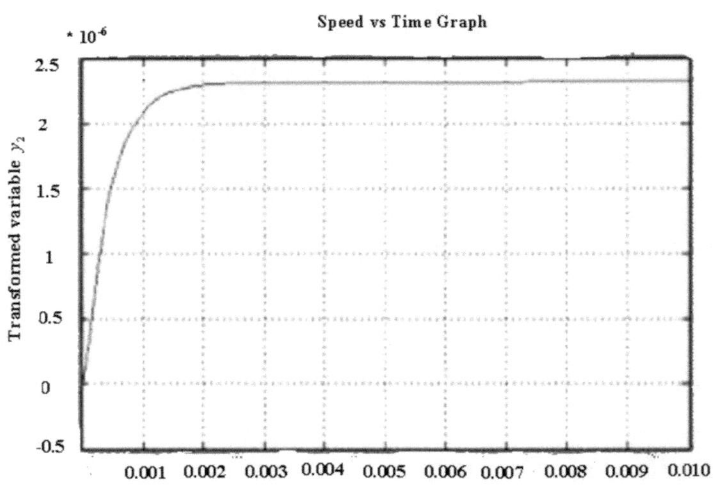

Fig. 12. Time Response of y_2 for the linearized system in closed loop when $v_1 = 5$; $k_p = 50; k_i = 2$

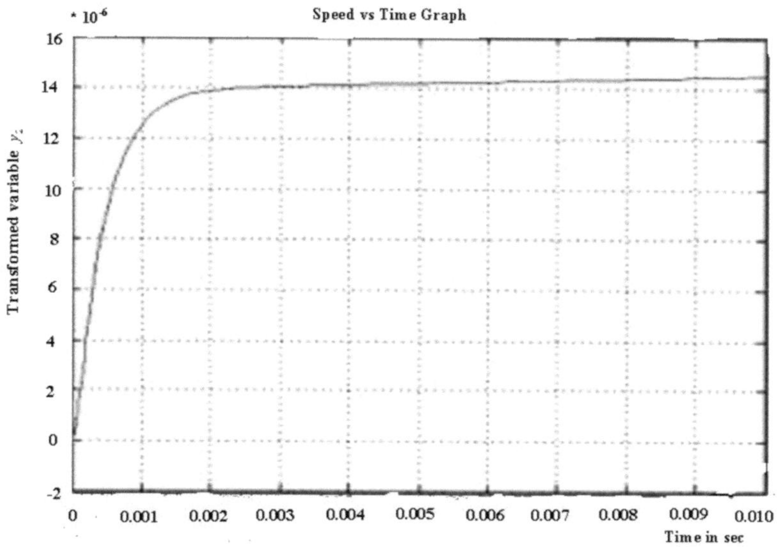

Fig. 13. Time Response of y_2 for the linearized system in closed loop when $v_1 = 30$; $k_p = 50; k_i = 2$

5. Tuning linearizing transformations

Unmodelled dynamics coupled with the third and higher order nonlinearities introduced due to quadratic linearization, are best accounted for by tuning the transformations (Levin & Narendra 1993).

To further improve the linearity of the system taking into account unmodelled dynamics and higher order nonlinearities, tuning of the transformation parameters against an actual PM machine is done on the lines similar to those proposed by Narendra (Levin & Narendra 1993). Fig 14 shows the block diagram for tuning.

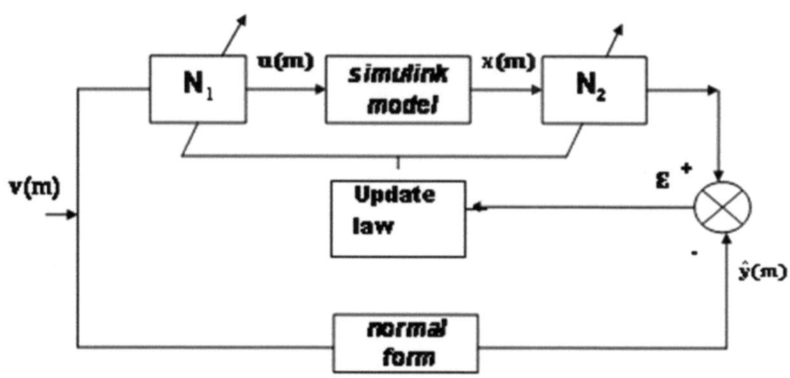

Fig. 14. Block diagram for tuning of transformation

Referring to Fig. 14, error (E) can be calculated as

$$E = (\varepsilon^T \varepsilon) = \left[(y-\hat{y})^T (y-\hat{y})\right]^{1/2} \tag{12}$$

where $\varepsilon = (\varepsilon_1 \quad \varepsilon_2 \quad \varepsilon_3 \quad \varepsilon_4)^T$; $\varepsilon_i = y_i - \hat{y}_i; i = 1,2,3,4$

The error can be written as

$$E = \left(\varepsilon_1^2 + \varepsilon_2^2 + \varepsilon_3^2 + \varepsilon_4^2\right)^{1/2}$$

Since $\phi^{(2)}(x)$ and $\beta^{(1)}(x)$ are both functions of k_1, we shall redefine

$$\phi^{(2)}(x) = \begin{bmatrix} 0 \\ 0 \\ k_1 x_3 x_4 \\ 0 \end{bmatrix}$$

and

$$\beta^{(1)}(x) = -\begin{bmatrix} k_1' x_4 & k_1' x_3 \\ 0 & 0 \end{bmatrix}$$

so that $\phi^{(2)}(x)$ and $\beta^{(1)}(x)$ can be independently tuned by tuning k_1 and k_1' respectively and $\alpha^{(2)}(x)$ is not varied.

5.1 Updation of N_2 transformation coefficients

Tuning of N_2 transformation implies the tuning of $\phi^{(2)}(x)$. As $\phi^{(2)}(x)$ is a function of only $k_1 x_3 x_4$, the coefficient k_1 has to be updated based on the error between the outputs of quadratic linearized system and normal form. The updation law is derived as follows.

$$\Delta k_1 = \frac{\partial E}{\partial k_1} = \frac{\partial E}{\partial y}\frac{\partial y}{\partial k_1}$$

From (12), it is seen that

$$\frac{\partial E}{\partial y_i} = \frac{\varepsilon_i}{E}; i = 1,2,3,4$$

Hence

$$\frac{\partial E}{\partial y} = \begin{bmatrix} \frac{\varepsilon_1}{E} & \frac{\varepsilon_2}{E} & \frac{\varepsilon_3}{E} & \frac{\varepsilon_4}{E} \end{bmatrix}.$$

$$\therefore \Delta k_1 = \begin{bmatrix} \frac{\varepsilon_1}{E} & \frac{\varepsilon_2}{E} & \frac{\varepsilon_3}{E} & \frac{\varepsilon_4}{E} \end{bmatrix} \begin{bmatrix} 0 \\ 0 \\ x_3 x_4 \\ 0 \end{bmatrix} = \frac{\varepsilon_3}{E} x_3 x_4 \qquad (13)$$

Updation of $\phi^{(2)}(x)$ is done by using the formula:

$$k_1(m) = k_1(m-1) - \rho\Delta k_1(m); 0 < \rho < 1 \qquad (14)$$

where m corresponds to the updating step and ρ correspond to the accelerating factor.

5.2 Updation of N_1 transformation coefficients

Tuning of N_1' transformation is achieved by tuning of $\beta^{(1)}(x)$. As $\beta^{(1)}(x)$ is a function of $k_1' x_3$ and $k_1' x_4$, the coefficient k_1' has to be updated based on the error between the outputs of quadratic linearized system and normal form . The updation law is derived as follows.

$$\Delta k_1' = \frac{\partial E}{\partial k_1'} = \frac{\partial E}{\partial y}\frac{\partial y}{\partial x}\frac{\partial x}{\partial u_1}\frac{\partial u_1}{\partial k_1'}$$

where ; $\frac{\partial E}{\partial y} = \begin{bmatrix} \frac{\varepsilon_1}{E} & \frac{\varepsilon_2}{E} & \frac{\varepsilon_3}{E} & \frac{\varepsilon_4}{E} \end{bmatrix}$

$$\frac{\partial y}{\partial x} = \begin{bmatrix} 1 & 0 & 0 & 0 \\ 0 & 1 & 0 & 0 \\ 0 & 0 & (1+k_1' x_4) & k_1' x_3 \\ 0 & 0 & 0 & 1 \end{bmatrix}; \frac{\partial x}{\partial u_1} = \begin{bmatrix} 0 \\ -1/k_2x_4 \\ 0 \\ -1/k_2x_2 \end{bmatrix}$$

Assuming that the steady state of the Simulink model is reached within the tuning period.

$$\frac{\partial u_1}{\partial k_1'} = -v_1x_4 - v_2x_3$$

Hence

$$\Delta k_1' = \frac{(v_1x_4 + v_2x_3)}{E}\left(\frac{\varepsilon_2}{k_2x_4} + \frac{\varepsilon_3 k_1' x_3 + \varepsilon_4}{k_2x_2}\right) \qquad (15)$$

Tuning of the quadratic linearizing transformations is done by updating the transformation coefficients of vector polynomials $\phi^{(2)}(x)$ and $\beta^{(1)}(x)$.

5.3 Construction of controller tuning blocks

Updation of $\phi^{(2)}(x)$ is done by using (14) and Δk_1 can be obtained from (13).
The tuning is done using Memory blocks and they are constructed in simulink as shown. Fig. 15 shows the construction of Del k_1 block. Similar construction can be done for Del k_1' where $\Delta k_1'$ can be obtained from (14).
Simulation of updation of $\phi^{(2)}(x)$ and $\beta^{(1)}(x)$ can be done using the simulation diagrams Fig. 15, 16 and 17.

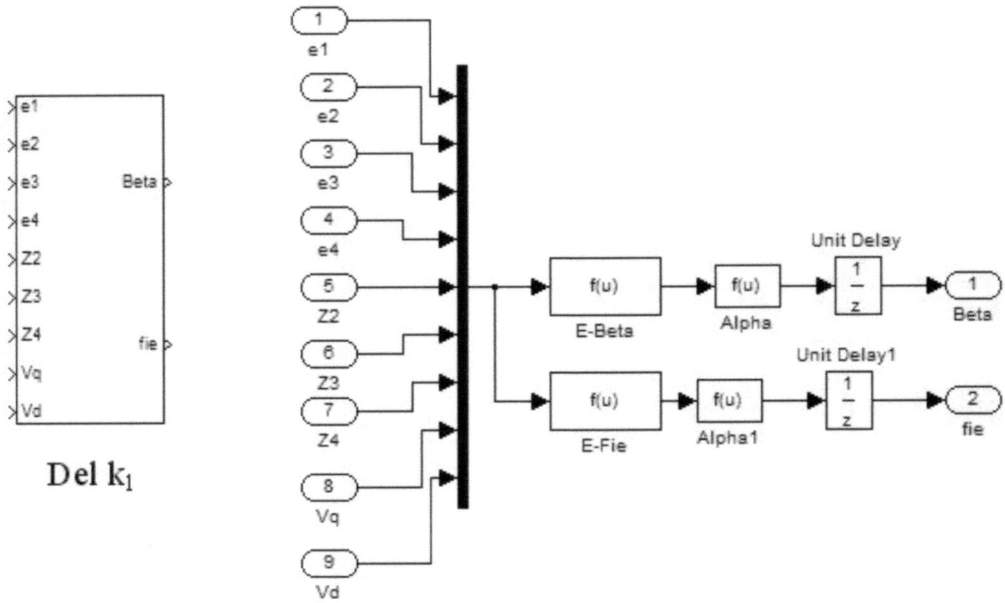

Fig. 15. Calculation of del K_1 for the updation of $\phi^{(2)}(x)$

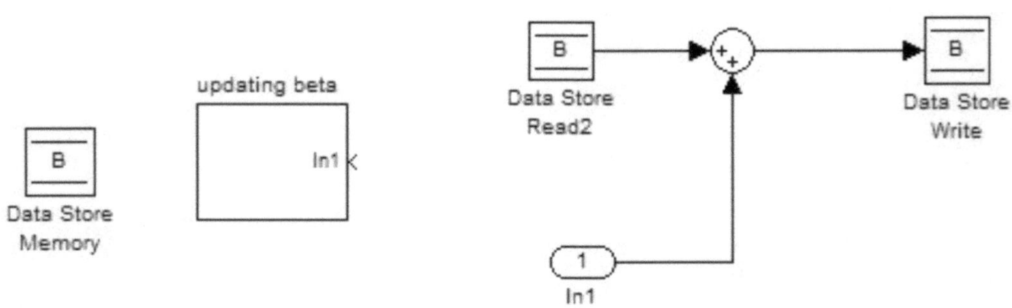

Fig. 16. Updation rule using Memory Read and memory Write Blocks

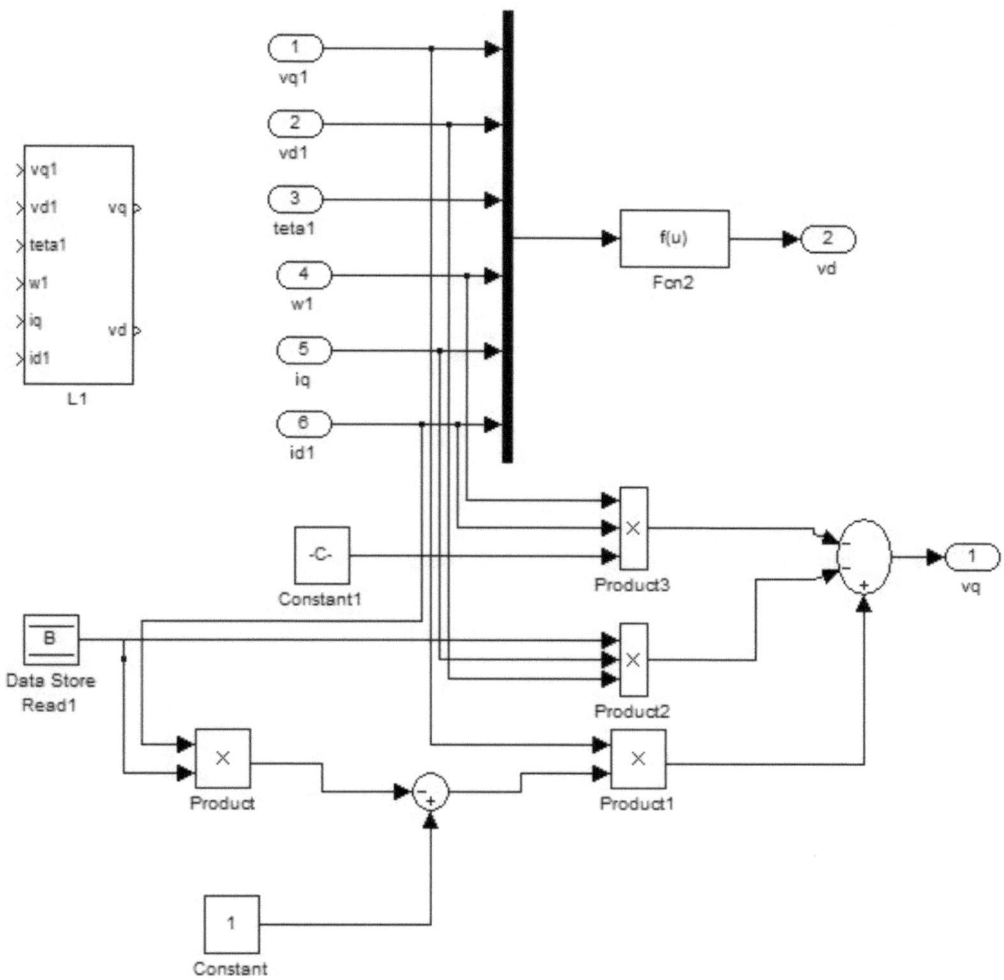

Fig. 17. Updation of input transformation

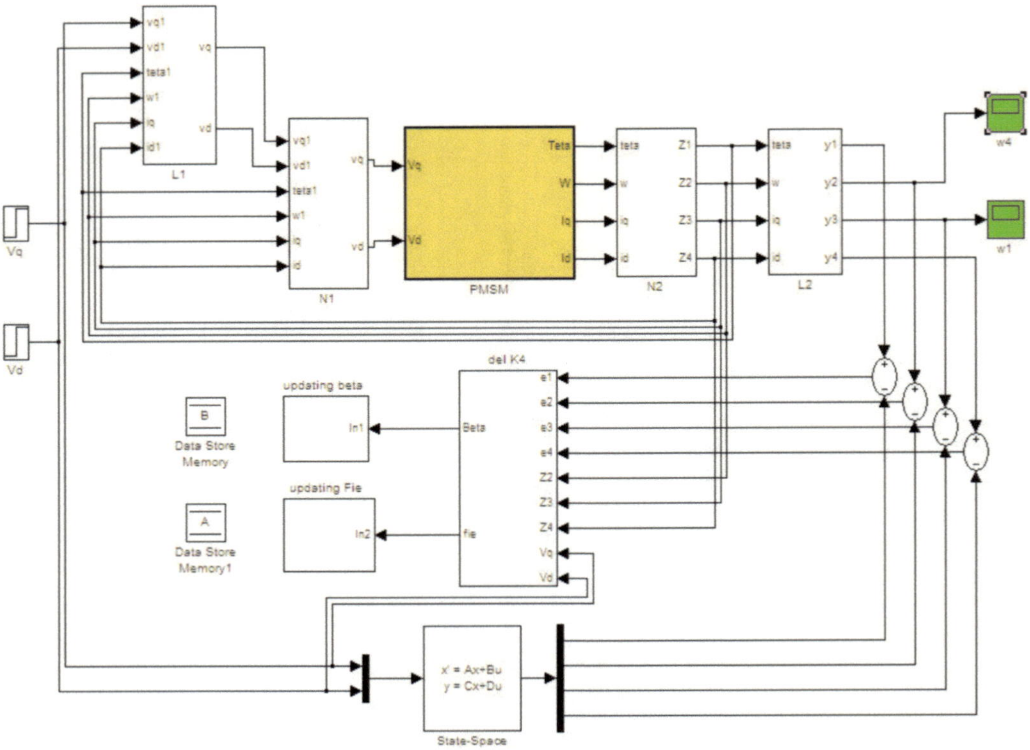

Fig. 18. Simulation diagram including controller tuning

v_1	y_2 *10^-6	K=d y_2 / d v_1 *10^(-6)
106	7.142	--
108	7.38	0.048
110	7.334	0.048
112	7.43	0.048
114	7.525	0.0475
116	7.62	0.0475
118	7.714	0.047

Table 3. Steady state gain of y_2 versus v_1 for the linearized system in open loop after tuning

Complete simulation diagram including conversion to Brunovsky form, linearization and tuning is given in Fig.18. It is seen that the error after tuning is reduced to 0.01.
In Table 3, improvements are obtained for the steady state gain of y_2 versus v_1 for the linearized system after incorporating tuning of the transformation parameters. Table 3 reveals that the gain of the system is even more constant compared to that shown in Table 2, thus verifying that by tuning the homogeneous linearizing transformation, the linearity of the system has been improved for the given set of inputs.

6. Conclusion

Application of MATLAB and SIMULINK tools for the verification of linearization of permanent magnet synchronous motor is considered in this chapter. Simulation is done using the dynamic model of PMSM, application of nonlinear coordinate and state feedback transformations to the SIMULINK model which is customized to PMSM and tuning the transformations against a linear system model employing error back propogation to account for unmodelled dynamics.
Initially, linearization of PMSM is verified using the dynamic model of PMSM. The dynamic model of a PM synchronous motor involving quadratic nonlinearity is linearized and simulated using MATLAB. Steps are given to perform dynamic simulation for the nonlinear system using the dynamic equations based on parameters of the machine, together with the state and input transformations using MATLAB function ODE45.
The SIMULINK model of Interior Permanent Magnet machine is specially developed by integrating various blocks as standard library functions do not cater to generic purposes . The PMSM machine model, together with the state and input transformations, are simulated using SIMULINK. The simulation results show that the linearizing transformations effectively linearize the system thus supporting the theory.
To account for the unmodelled dynamics and third and higher order nonlinearities, tuning of the transformation parameters is done by comparing the output of the linearized system with a normal form output. Tuning the transformation functions $\phi^{(2)}(x)$ and $\beta^{(1)}(x)$ is shown further to improve the linearity of the resulting system.
More details of the simulation results are given in (Parvathy et. al. 2011).

7. Acknowledgement

The authors acknowledge the financial support rendered by the management of Hindustan Institute of Technology and Science, Chennai in publishing this chapter.

8. References

Bimal .K. Bose(2002) *Modern Power Electronics and Ac Drives* , Pearson Education.
Gildeberto S. Cardoso & Leizer Schnitman (2011) Analysis of exact linearization and approximate feedback linearization techniques. *www.hindawi.com/journals/mpe/aip/205939.pdf*
Krener A.J. (1984) Approximate linearization by state feedback and coordinate change. *Systems and control Letters.* Vol. 5,pp. 181-185.

John Chiasson& Marc Bodson (1998) .Differential - Geometric methods for control of lectric motors. *International Journal of Robust and Nonlinear Control.* No.8, pp.923-954.

Arnold V.I.(1983) *Geometric methods in the theory of ordinary differential equations.* Springer-Verlag, NewYork, pp 177-188.

Kang .W & Krener.A.J. (1992) . Extended quadratic controller normal form and dynamic state feedback linearisation of nonlinear systems. *SIAM Journal of Control and optimization* . No.30,pp.1319-1337.

Devanathan R. (2001) ._Linearisation Condition through State Feedback_ *IEEE transactions on Automatic Control* .ol 46,no.8,pp.1257-1260

Devanathan R. (2004). Necessary and sufficient conditions for quadratic linearisation of a linearly controllable system. *INT.J. Control,* Vol.77, No.7,pp. 613-621

Benjamin.C.Kuo(2001) . *Automatic Control Systems.* Prentice-Hall India.

A.K.Parvathy, Aruna Rajan, R.Devanathan (2005) . Complete Quadratic Linearization of PM Synchronous Motor Model. , *proceedings of NEPC conference.* IIT Karagpur, pp 49-52.

A.K.Parvathy, R.Devanathan (2006) Linearisation of Permanent Magnet Synchronous Motor Model.*proc.of IEEE ICIT 2006*,pp. 483-486.

Pavol Brunovsky (1970) *A classification of linear controllable systems.* Kybernetika,Vol. 6. No.3, pp. 173-188

Asriel U Levin & Kumpati S Narendra (1993). Control of nonlinear dynamical systems using neural networks: controllability and stabilization. *IEEE Transactions on neural networks.*Vol-4, No.2,1993, pp.192-206.

A.K.Parvathy, V.Kamaraj & R.Devanathan (2011) A generalized quadratic linearization technique for PMSM. accepted for publication in , *European Journal of Scientific Research.*

Part 5

Vehicle Applications

17

Automatic Guided Vehicle Simulation in MATLAB by Using Genetic Algorithm

Anibal Azevedo
State University of São Paulo
Brazil

1. Introduction

The prodigious advances in robotics in recent times made the use of robots more present in modern society. One important advance that requires special attention is the development of an unmanned aerial vehicle (UAV), which allows an aircraft to fly without having a human crew on board, although the UAVs still need to be controlled by a pilot or a navigator.

Today's UAVs often combine remote control and computerized automation in a manner that built-in control and/or guidance systems perform deeds like speed control and flight-path stabilization. In this sense, existing UAVs are not truly autonomous, mostly because air-vehicle autonomy field is a recently emerging field, and this could be a bottleneck for future UAV development.

It could be said that the ultimate goal in the autonomy technology development is to replace human pilots by altering machines decisions in order to make decisions like humans do. For this purpose, several tools related with artificial intelligence could be employed such as expert systems, neural networks, machine learning and natural language processing (HAYKIN, 2009). Nowadays, the field of autonomy has mostly been following a bottom-up approach, such as hierarchical control systems (SHIM, 2000).

One interesting methodology from the hierarchical control systems approach is the subsumption architecture that decomposes complicated intelligent behavior into many "simple" behavior modules, which are organized into layers. Each layer implements a particular goal and higher layers are increasingly more abstract. The decisions are not taken by a superior layer, but by listening to the information that are triggered by sensory inputs (lowest layer). This methodology allows the use of **reinforcement learning** to acquire behavior with the information that comes with experience.

Inspired by old behaviorist psychology, **reinforcement learning** (RL) concerned with how an *agent* ought to take *actions* in an *environment,* so as to maximize some notion of cumulative *reward.* Reinforcement learning differs from standard supervised learning in that correct input/output pairs which are never presented (HAYKIN, 2009). Furthermore, there is a focus on an on-line performance, which involves finding a balance between exploration (of uncharted territory) and exploitation (of current knowledge). The reinforcement learning has been applied successfully to various problems, including robot control, elevator scheduling, telecommunications, backgammon and chess (SHIM, 2000).

Genetic algorithms (GAs) are developed in order to emulate the process of genetic evolution found in nature, and then perform artificial evolution. They were developed by John Holland [11] in the early 70s, and have been successfully applied to numerous large and complex search space problems ever since (MICHALEWICZ, 1996).
In nature, organisms have certain characteristics that affect their ability to survive and reproduce. These characteristics are contained in their genes. Natural selection ensures that genes from a strong individual are presented in greater numbers in the next generation, rather than those from a weak individual. Over a number of generations, the fittest individuals, in the environment in which they live, have the highest probability of survival and tend to increase in number; while the less fit individuals tend to die out. This is the Darwin's principle of the survival-of-the-fittest and constitutes the basic idea behind the GAs. In order to perform computational tests on how the reinforcement learning could cope with genetic algorithms to provide good rules for the navigation of an automatic vehicle (STAFYLOPATIS, 1998), a program that emulates a navigation environment was developed in a Matlab. This Chapter will describe how the ideas developed by (STAFYLOPATIS, 1998) could be employed to study the integration of the GAs and RL to produce rules for automatic guided vehicles searching for a better performance. The main contributions of this Chapter are: the vehicle, its sensors, and also the environment for training are different from the ones presented in (STAFYLOPATIS, 1998); a new equation for the reinforcement learning was proposed; the influence of the parameters that control the production of automatic generation of rules for vehicle control navigation are also tested. Sections 2 and 3 describe how the navigation decision rules could be encoded in a vector. Sections 4 and 5 show how the reinforcement learning and genetic algorithm uses the encoding of Section 2 to cope with the production of vehicle control navigation rules. In Section 6, some results are presented and finally, in Section 7, some conclusions and future works are given. All the proposed approach had been implemented in a Matlab.

2. Navigation problem representation

The navigation problem could be defined as how a vehicle could be guided through an ambient with many obstacles and barriers using the information available from the information given by the vehicle radar, as it can be seen in Figure 1.
Figure 1 also details how the vehicle radar works. The radar has 9 sectors in order to better acquire the information of how near is a vehicle to an object. The information of existence of an obstacle for each section is stored in vector **v** of nine positions using the following rule: if one object is in one section, then value 1 is attributed. If not, then value 0 is attributed. Figure 2 details a situation where there are obstacles in sector 1 and 2 and the correspondent representation by a vector. Once the objects had been detected by the radar, it is necessary to implement an appropriate action which could be one of the following three: turn 15° degrees to the left, keep the trajectory or turn 15° degrees to the right. For the sake of clarity, but without loss of generality, velocity v_c of the vehicle was assumed to be constant. With these three possible decisions, a new concept could be created, which is a rule. A **rule** is a vector that combines the one that describes the situation for the vehicle in terms of obstacles, like the one presented in Figure 2, and a new component that decides the vehicle action in turn to avoid a set of obstacles: 0 – turn left, 1 – keep the trajectory, 2 – turn right. An example of a rule for the situation showed in Figure 2 is described in Figure 3.

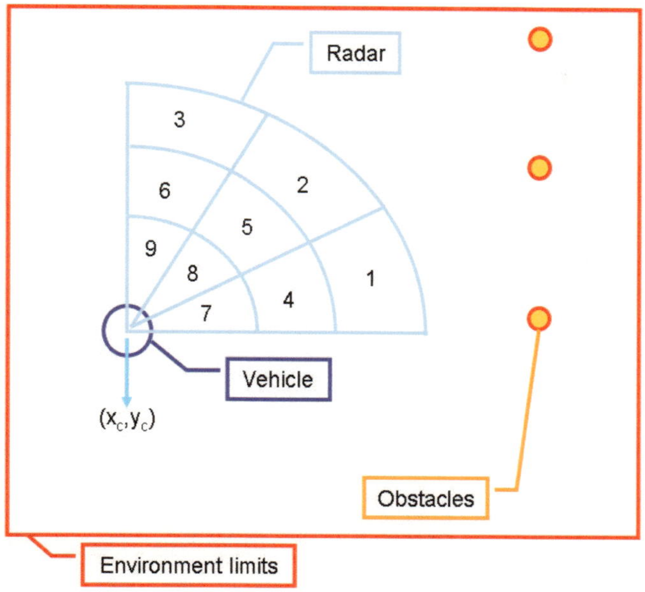

Fig. 1. Description of the elements of the developed environment in Matlab.

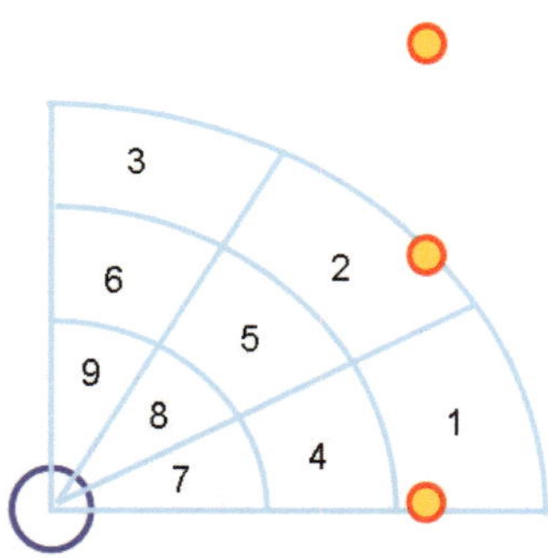

Situation	1	1	0	0	0	0	0	0	0
Vector Index	0	1	2	3	4	5	6	7	8
Sector	1	2	3	4	5	6	7	8	9

Fig. 2. The correspondence between the obstacles detected by a radar vehicle and a vector with binary information.

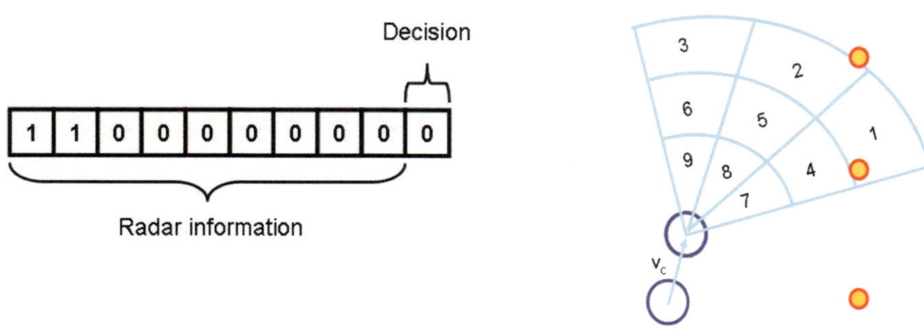

Fig. 3. The correspondence between a rule and decision taken by the vehicle.

3. Navigation control

The previous binary representation scheme has a main drawback since before every vehicle movement decision demanded to store $3 \times 2^9 = 1536$ vectors (rules) to precisely describe which action should be performed for each scenario detected by the radar information. This implies that before every step performed by the vehicle, a control action should compare, in the worst case, 1536 vectors in order to find the proper decision to be taken. This scheme is illustrated in Fig. 4.

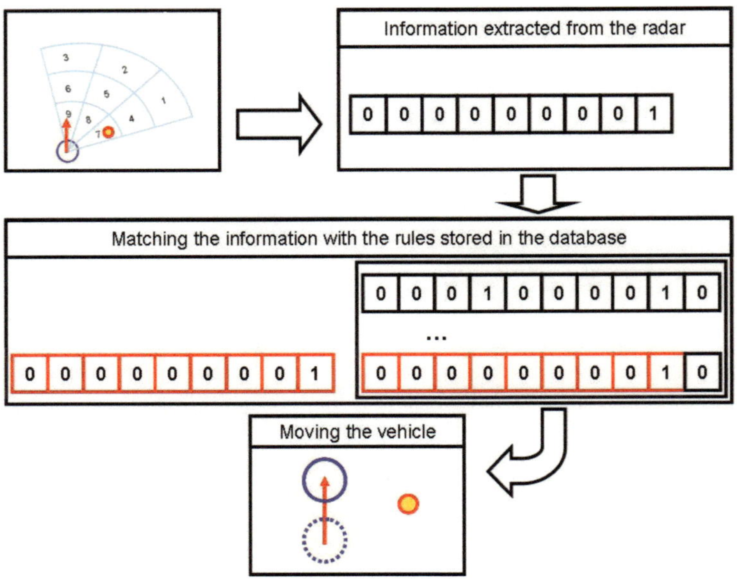

Fig. 4. Decision scheme followed by the automatic guided vehicle.

This computational work could be avoided by introducing a new symbol 2, for the radar information section, which means that "it could have or not an obstacle at this sector". The advantage of the definition of this new symbol is that it will help to reduce the number of necessary information to be kept by the vehicle control. The disadvantage of using this new symbol is that it could group different situations where the decisions should not be the same. Fig. 5 gives an example of this situation.

The example showed in Fig. 5 emphasizes the importance to construct the rules in a manner that the parts of the rule which do not affect the decision should be numbered as 2, and the other parts that have a great influence in the final behavior of the vehicle should be numbered as most specific as possible or, in other words, with the numbers 0 or 1. Fig. 6 illustrates the application of this concept.

Fig. 6 also gives a guideline procedure for another problem that could emerge, which is the appearance of more than one rule that matches the current radar information when symbol 2 is used. One criteria that will be adopted is to select the rules which match the environment situation, but with as much specific information as possible. For this purpose Eq. (1) will be adopted.

$$S_i = \frac{(n - k_i)}{n} \qquad i = 1, \cdots, R \tag{1}$$

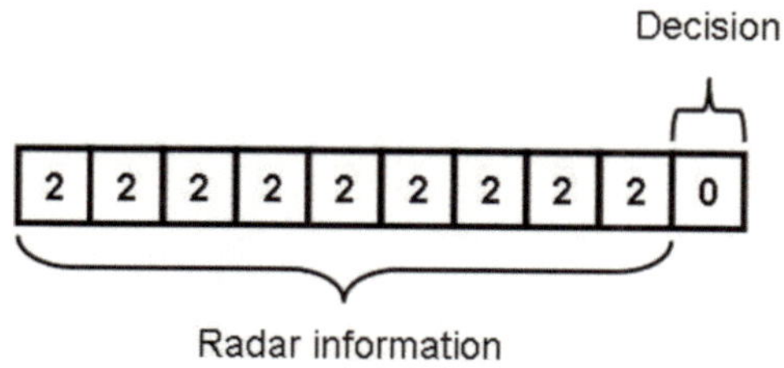

(A) The rule that match the acquired information obtained by the vehicle radar.

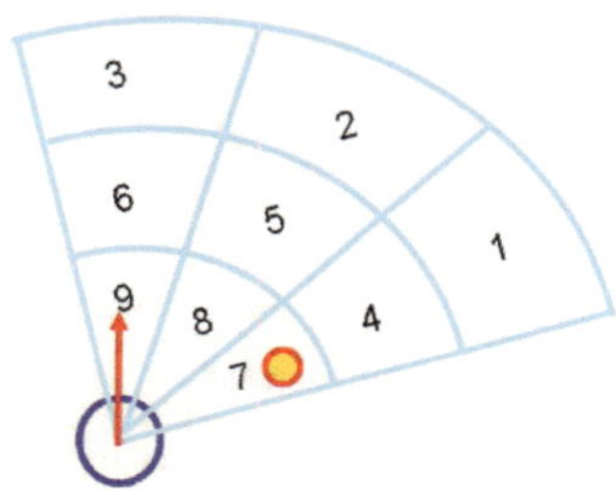

(B) Employing the rule - Step 1, Situation 1.

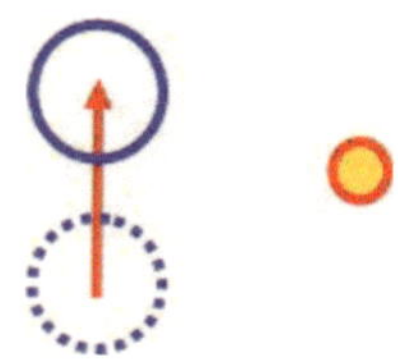

(C) Employing the rule - Step 2, Situation 1.

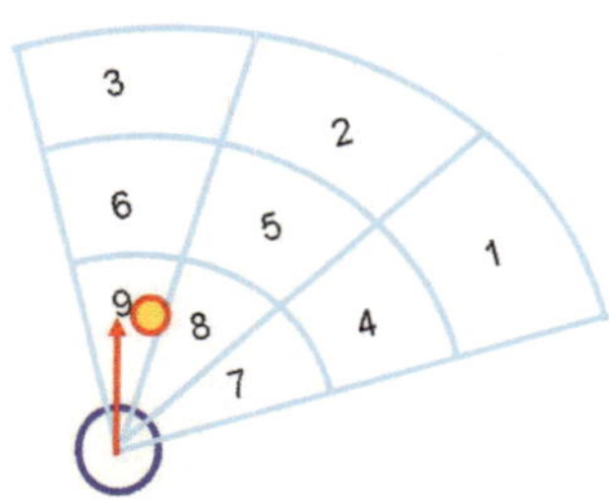

(D) Employing the rule - Step 1, Situation 2.

(E) Employing the rule - Step 2, Situation 2.

Fig. 5. Employing the same rule in different scenarios and the corresponding consequences.

Where: S_i is the measure of how specific is rule i, n is the number of sectors the vehicle radar has, k_i is the number of digits marked with value 2, and R is the number of rules. Thus $S_i \in [0,1]$ and note that variable S_i becomes 0 when every rule digit related with the sector state is marked with value 2 (lowest specificity) and S_i becomes 1, if value 2 does not appear in rule i (highest specificity).

This discussion also shows that the efficiently vehicle navigation control depends on more than one rule, and this leads to the objective of finding the set of rules that could properly control the vehicle. To achieve this objective the next sections will discuss concepts on how to automatically construct this set of rules by employing computational tools such as Reinforcement Learning and Genetic Algorithm.

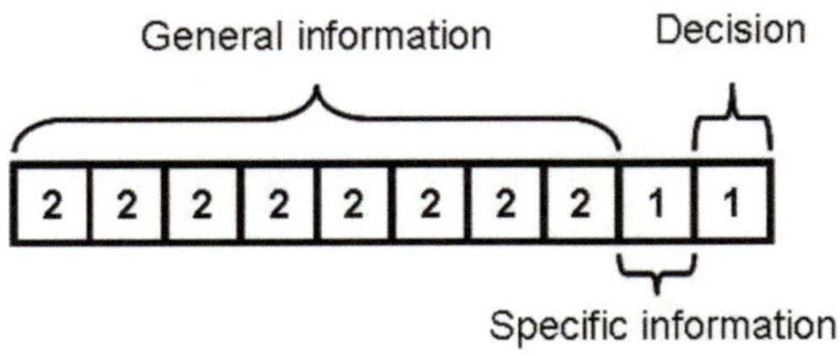

(A) The rule that matches the acquired information obtained by the vehicle radar.

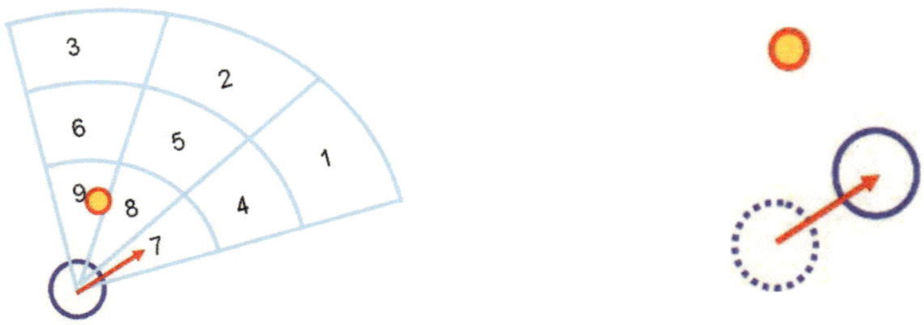

(B) Employing the rule - Step 1. (C) Employing the rule - Step 2.

Fig. 6. Employing a rule that combines general (number 2) with specific (number 0 or 1) knowledge.

4. Reinforcement learning

The developed program starts with rules totally generated at random and which quality, in terms of helping the vehicle navigation control, is unknown. Then, it was created a system that evaluates the quality of rules used through the vehicle navigation performed by a computational simulation. As it was seen before, during the navigation, more than one rule could be necessary and the system must punish or reward not only a rule, but also all rules employed that lead the vehicle to a collision or to avoid an obstacle, respectively. One difficulty related with this scheme is to know the correct contribution weight of each rule in a possible vehicle collision. It is also difficult to estimate the reward value for a set of rules that helps the vehicle to avoid an immediate collision, because this set could put the vehicle in a trajectory that leads to a future collision with another obstacle. Besides those problems, the initial credit received for each rule is modified by Eq. (2), if there are no collisions on the current vehicle step t.

$$C_{it+1} = C_{it} + kS_{it}C_{it} \tag{2}$$

Where: i is the rule that perfectly matches with the current vehicle situation; in order words, rule i is the one which S_{it} value is as greater as possible at the step t of the vehicle, C_{it} is the credit value assigned for each rule i at the step t, and k is a constant that indicates the learning rate.

When the vehicle crashes at some obstacle a punishment must be applied to the rules mostly related to the event. To avoid the storage of large amounts of historical record about what rules where used, and to punish just the rules mostly related to the collision, only the last three employed rules will have their credit updated by Eq. (3).

$$C_{it+1} = C_{it} / 2 \tag{3}$$

Eq. (3) was considered by (STAFYLOPATIS, 1998), but it represents that the rules that lead the vehicle to perform more than 200 steps without a collision will suffer the same punishment as the rules that conduct the vehicle to perform only 20 steps without a collision, for example. To avoid this problem, this book Chapter proposes, for the first time, a punishment formula which is a function on the number of steps as showed in Eq. (4) and (5).

$$C_{it+1} = k_p C_{it} \tag{4}$$

$$k_p = \frac{1}{1 + \exp^{-(ns+1)/np}} \tag{5}$$

The behavior of Eq. (5) for $np = 20$ is showed in Fig. 7.

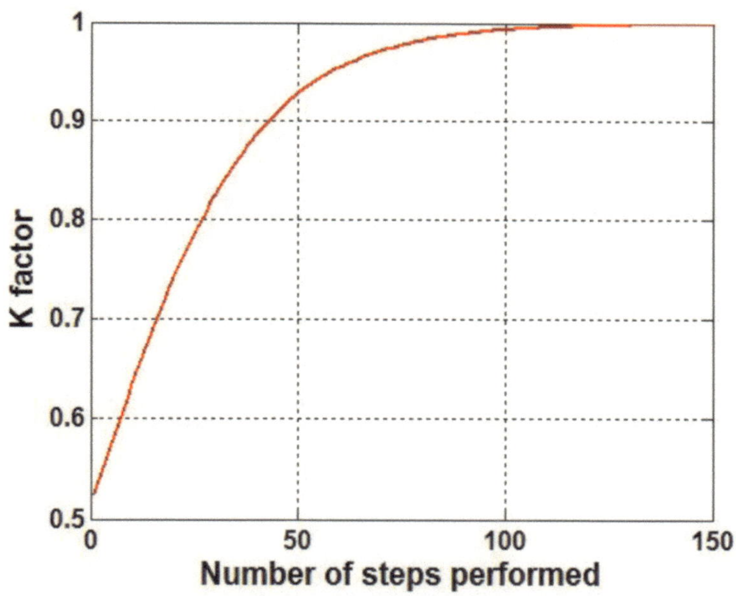

Fig. 7. Behavior of the parameter penalty factor k_p for $np = 20$.

The purpose of Eq. (4) and (5) is to punish the rules according with total number of steps (ns) performed by the vehicle before the collision, and it was reflected in a different credit actualization. For example, if the three last used rules lead to only 25 steps without a collision, then the new credit value will be 75% of the old credit value (see Fig. 7). The system proposed by Eq. (2) and (3) or (4) and (5) starts by assigning the same value, same credit, for every rule. Then, the rules performance is evaluated in an environment, created in Matlab, where the vehicle control is simulated, and during the simulation, after each step performed by the vehicle, it is verified whether there is a collision (then the Eq. (3) or Eq. (4) and (5) is used) or not (then the Eq. (2) is used) following the scheme described in Fig. 8.

```
function EvaluateRules (MR)
  % Initial learning rate for each step without a collision.
  k = 0.2;
  collision = 0;
 % Initial credit assignment for all rules.
 for i=1:R
   C(i) = 0.2;
 end
 % Starts the initial conditions of the environment and the objects that appear in the radar
 % vehicle.
 [vE, E]=Starts();
 ns = 0;            % Number of steps.
 Records = [ ];  % Stores the index of the rules used.
 % Loop that evaluates the rules inside MR while there is no collision.
 While (collision == 0)
   % Determining the rules that matches with the actual environment.
   [vm]=Match(MR, vE);
   % Verifying the measure of how specific each matching rule is (use Equation (1)).
   MRE = MR(vm,:);
   [sm]=Specific(MRE);
   [value, indexsmax] = max(sm);
   % Using the matching rule with maximum Sit value and verifying the consequences.
   VRM = MRE(indexsmax,:);
   % Update the vehicle in environment by using the selected rule. It also returns if
   % a collision happened (collision == 1).
   [collision, vE, E]= Simulate(VRM, E) ;
   % There is no collision with the rule application, then update the credit according
   % with the equation (2).
   If (collision == 0)
     % Update the credit of the rule applied.
     C(vm(indexsmax)) = (1 + k*sm(indexsmax))*C(vm(indexsmax))
     % Store the index of what rule was applied in a certain vehicle step.
     Records = [Records vm(indexsmax)];
     ns = ns + 1;
    % There is a collision after the rule application then update the credit of the last three
    % rules used according with equation (3) or (4) and (5).
   else
     indexp = Records(end-2:end);
     % Or use: kp = 1/(exp(-(ns+1)/20)+1); C(indexp)=C(indexp)*kp;
     C(indexp) = C(indexp)/2;
      ns = 0;
   end
 end
```

Fig. 8. The scheme to reward or to punish the rules during a simulation in the environment.

The functions and symbols used in Fig. 8 are defined as follows:

C	- Vector containing the credit associated to a set of rules.
E	- Matrix with all data about the current simulation environment state.
vE	- Vector with information extracted from the radar, as show in Figure 2.
MR	- Matrix with a set of rules. Each matrix line represents one rule.
Vm	- The vector with the index of the rules that matches the information extracted from vehicle radar (contained in vE).
MRE	- Matrix with only the rules that match the information extracted from vehicle radar.
Specific	- This function evaluates all the rules contained in matrix MRE according with the equation Eq. (1) in order to measure how specific is each rule.
sm	- Vector with all rules specific measure.
max	- This function determines which specific measure is the biggest (value) and the corresponding line of MRE (indexsmax).
VRM	- Vector with the rule selection to be used in current environment state.
Simulate	- This function simulates the vehicle through environment using VRM rules.
collision	- Variable that indicates whether a vehicle collides (equals to 1) or not (equals to 0).
indexsmax	- Index of the rule with maximum matching value.
Records	- Vector that stores the index of the rules used in a certain vehicle step through the environment.
indexp	- Vector with the index of the last three rules applied before the vehicle collision and which will be punished by a credit decreasing.
ns	- Number of steps without a collision.
kp	- Penalization factor applied in the credit of the last three rules when a collision occurs.

The system showed in Fig. 8 tries to establish a reward and a punishment scheme among the rules and their impact in the vehicle navigation through equations that monitor the performance, although the random generation of rules can also produce sets of rules which lead to a bad control navigation performance. After a pre-specified number of collisions, the set of rules could be changed by a new randomly generated set of rules formed with the insertion of new rules, the exclusion of rules with a bad performance (low credit value), and the maintenance of rules that help to avoid the obstacles (high credit value). To perform the formation of this new set of rules, a genetic algorithm was coupled to the credit evaluation scheme described in Fig. 8, as could be seen in Fig.9.

The complete description of the Genetic Algorithm developed is described in Section 5.

5. Genetic algorithm

The genetic algorithm keeps a population of individuals, represented by: $A(t) = \{A_1^t, ..., A_n^t\}$ for each generation (iteration) t, and each individual represents a rule to guide the vehicle through the environment and to avoid the obstacles. In the computational implementation adopted here, the population is stored in a matrix $A(t)$ and each column A_i^t represents a rule. Each rule A_i^t is evaluated according to the number of vehicle movements without a collision, and then, the *fitness*, a measure of how this individual is sucessful for the problem, is calculated. The *fitness* is calculated for the entire population and is based on this new population that combines the most capable individuals that will form generation t+1.

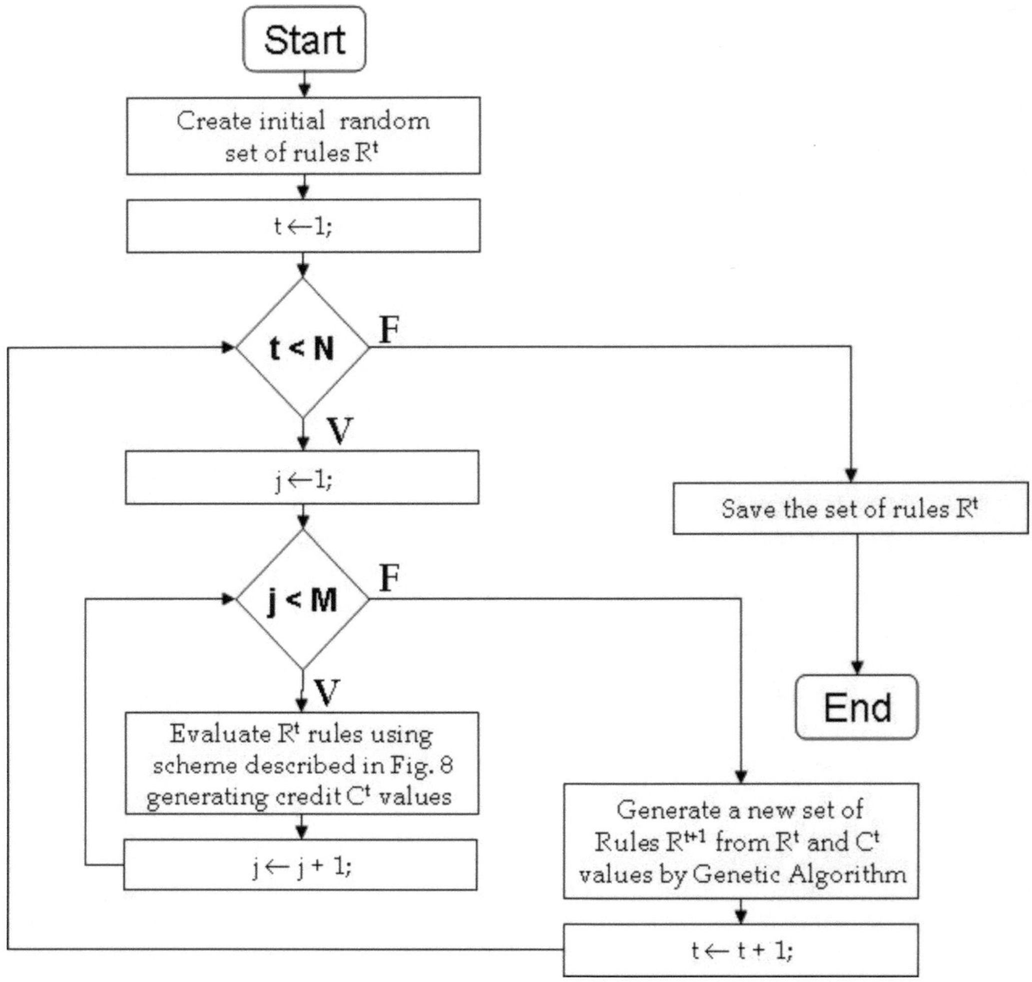

Fig. 9. Composition of the credit scheme and Genetic Algorithm.

During the formation of the new population, some individuals from generation *t* are submitted to a transformation process by genetic operators in order to form new rules. These transformations include unary operators m_i (mutation), that allow the creation of new rules by small changes in the individual attributes (m_i: $A_i \rightarrow A_i$), and superior order transformation c_j (crossover) that produces new individuals by combining one or more individuals (c_j: $A_j \times \ldots \times A_k \rightarrow A_j$). This process is carried out until a previous specified maximum number of generations is reached (MICHALEWICZ, 1996).

During the vehicle navigation along the environment different situations may occur, and each one of them could require a proper action implying the necessity of using more than just one rule. For this reason, the **reinforcement leaning** is acopled with a population produced by the genetic algorithm and, when a collision occurs, a proper number of rules used before the collision are penalized (STAFYLOPATIS, 1998). This system consists in firstly give the same value for each rule of the population, and then, evaluate each rule according to the number of times it was used until a collision happened.

The implementation details adopted for the Genetic Algorithm are as follows:

(A) Data structure codification for each individual:

Each genetic algorithm individual is associated to a rule by using a vector v with 10 elements and values inside the elements 1 to 9, corresponding to the presence (value 1) or not (value 0) or whatever (value 2) in the corresponding vehicle radar section, respectively (see Fig. 3). The value inside the position 10 indicates the decision that has to be made: 0 - turn 15º degrees to the left, 1 – keep the trajectory and 2 - turn 15º degrees to the right. The set of rules is stored in a matrix and each column represents a rule, as showed in Fig. 10. In the Example showed in Fig. 10, the first column contains a vector $\mathbf{v}_1$ with 10 positions which each position meaning explained in Fig. 2.

Sector	Rule 1	Rule 2
1	0	2
2	0	2
3	1	1
4	2	0
5	2	2
6	2	2
7	2	2
8	2	2
9	2	1
Decision	0	1
	v_1	v_2

Fig. 10. Relation between the genetic algorithm individual encoding and a rule. Matrix A has two rules.

Once the individual is defined, the population which consists in *numpop* individuals stored in a matrix A of dimension *10 × numpop* can also be defined. For the vehicle navigation, the value of *numpop* equals to 100 was adopted. Since each column of matrix *A* represents individuals/solutions, then every element $A(i,j) = k$ means what situation (i equals 1 to 9) or decision (i equals to 10) for the rule j should be made if the solution given from individual j is chosen. For example, $A(1,1) = 2$ means that the individual/solution 1 vehicle radar does not care (value 2) whether there is or not an object in sector 1 of the vehicle radar.

(B) Fitness evaluation and assignment:

The fitness evaluation or *fitness* is responsible to rank the individual among the population in a generation t. Then, the fitness is constructed in manner that the solutions with less credit measure have the higher fitness value. This explanation justifies why the fitness for each individual A_i is calculated with Eq. (6), given as follows:

$$Fit(A_i) = f(A_i) \tag{6}$$

Where: $f(A_i)$ is the fitness evaluation as defined by the credit value C_{it}, and it corresponds to the number of steps performed with rule *i* without a collision, according to the rule stored in vector A_i, through the environment.

(C) Individual Selection for the next generation:

The population formation process employed is the *"Roulette Wheel"*, in order words, a random raffle where the probability $Q(A_i)$ to choose the individual A_i for the next generation, in a population with *b* individuals, is used. The value $Q(A_i)$ can be obtained by using Eq. (7).

$$Q(A_i) = Fit(A_i) / \sum_{i=1}^{numpop} (Fit(A_i)) \tag{7}$$

The better individual of the actual generation is always kept to be on the next generation.

(D) Crossover OX:

The Crossover operators try to generate new individuals to form the next population by combining information from past generations that is present in the individuals. This work used two crossover operators which is described as follows.

Two individuals, A_1 and A_2, with *N* elements are randomly chosen from a population in generation t. Then, an integer number δ in the interval [1, *N-1*] is drawn and elements of A_1 that are in positions δ until *N* are exchanged with the elements of A_2 that are in positions δ until *N*. This exchange will produce two new individuals, nA_1 and nA_2, that can appear in the next generation.

(E) Mutation operator:

The mutation operator modifies *10*numpop*pm* elements of matrix A, where *pm* is the percentage of total bits to be muted (mutated). The selection of which element A_{ij} to be mutated consist in randomly select the line index and the column index, and then change it.

Fig. 11 shows how the genetic algorithm components described before are combined.

One important observation is that the best individual of generation A_t is always kept for the next generation A_{t+1}. Furthermore, the size of subpopulations $As_1{}^t$ and $As_2{}^t$ are the same and is equal to 5% of the total population (*numpop*).

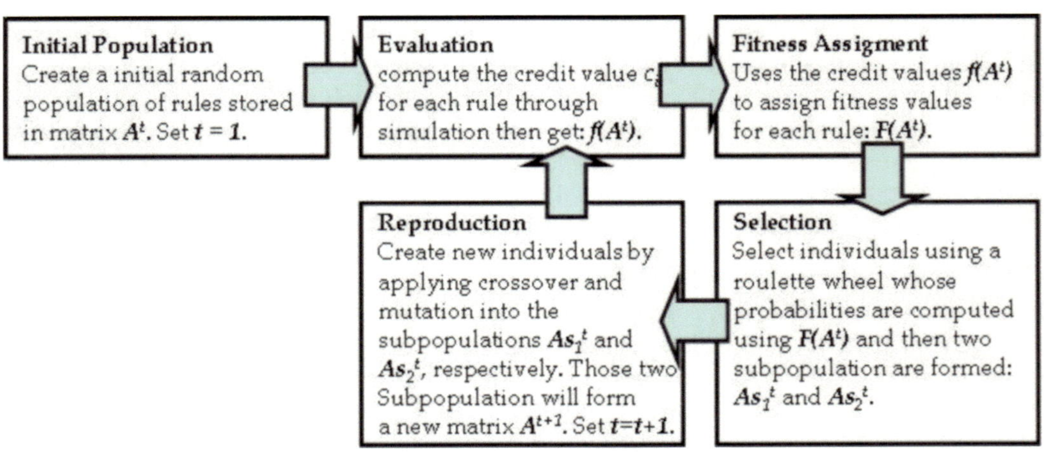

Fig. 11. How the genetic algorithm elements are combined into a unique algorithm.

6. Tests and results

Table 1 sumarizes the description of the parameters necessary to perform tests with the developed approach described in sections 4 and 5.

Parameter	Description
C_{i0}	Initial credit assigment for a set of rules.
k	reinformecent learning rate parameter.
pb0	percentance of digits equals to 0 for the initial population.
pb1	percentance of digits equals to 1 for the initial population.
pb2	percentance of digits equals to 2 for the initial population.
numpop	number of individuals in the genetic algorithm population.
pc	Crossover rate.
pm	Mutation rate.
pg	size of the subpopulation in terms of the A matrix (5%).
M	number of collisions before applying the genetic algorithm (10).
N	number of genetic algorithm aplication(14).

Table 1. Parameters used for the developed approach and their meanings.

It was also tested two environments whose obstacles initial position are shown in Fig. 12.
As shown in Fig. 12, the obstacles could be clustered in two groups: the obstacles that delimits the environment bounds have their position fixed and the obstacles that are in the interior of the environment, whose positions are actualized in a different manner for each environment:

- Environment 1: The moving obstacles actualize their x-positions according to Eq. (8).

$$x_i^t = x_i^t + \varepsilon \tag{8}$$

Where: x_i^t is the x-position for obstacle *i* in step *t* of the vehicle, ε is a random uniform variable in the interval [0, 1].

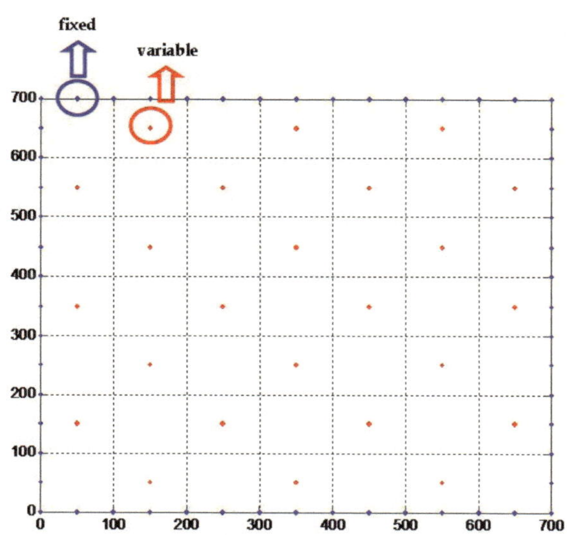

Fig. 12. Detailed description of the obstacles initial position in the environment.

- Environment 2: The user could also specify a positive value to a *radius* parameter and the moving obstacles actualize their x and y-positions according to Eq. (9).

$$\begin{aligned} x_i^t &= x_i^t + radius * \cos(x_i^t) \\ y_i^t &= y_i^t + radius * \sin(y_i^t) \end{aligned} \tag{9}$$

For all tests performed in environment 2, the radius value was fixed in 5. Five runs with the values listed in Table 2 had been performed in order to carry the best set of values for all the parametes listed in Table 1. Each row in Table 2 corresponds to a new configuration.

Set	C_{i0}	k	Pb0	Pb1	Pb2	numpop	pc	pm	pg	M	N	Environment
1	20	2	2.5%	2.5%	95%	100	30	1	5	10	14	1
2	20	2	2.5%	2.5%	95%	100	1	30	5	10	14	1
3	20	2	2.5%	2.5%	95%	100	30	1	5	20	5	1
4	20	2	2.5%	2.5%	95%	100	1	30	5	20	5	1
5	20	2	10%	10%	80%	100	30	1	5	20	5	1
6	20	2	10%	10%	80%	100	1	30	5	20	5	1
7	20	2	2.5%	2.5%	95%	100	1	30	5	20	5	2
8	20	2	10%	10%	80%	100	30	1	5	20	5	2

Table 2. List of values assigned for each parameter.

Each row of Table 3 corresponds to the number of the steps that could be taken with the final set of rules obtained after the application of the scheme described in Fig. 9 using the parameters described in Table 2 and the **reinforcement learning** that follows Eq. (3).

Set	Test 1	Test 2	Test 3	Test 4	Test 5	Best Number
1	16	7	7	7	7	16
2	7	110	7	7	80	110
3	28	57	78	16	7	78
4	177	32	48	21	18	177
5	151	18	15	32	116	151
6	34	32	19	32	106	106
7	32	163	20	106	84	163
8	38	15	31	108	31	108

Table 3. The number of maximum steps without a collision performed by the best set of rules produced by each set of parameters (described in Table 2) and Eq. (3).

In Table 3, the first column indicates the set of parameters and the corresponding obtained set of rules which lead to the number of maximum steps without a collision described in the second column until the sixth column. The results for the set of parameters 1 to 6 show that for environment 1 the best choices of parameters are sets 4 and 5. Those two sets were also tested in environment 2 in order to verify set parameters robustness in order to produce adequate rules for different environments. Configuration 7 had the best performance and three tests were sucessfull in producing rules which could make the vehicle able to take more than 80 steps without a collision.

The new proposed reinforcement learning formula proposed by Eq. (4) and (5) was also tested for $np = 20$ for the parameter values showed in Table 2.

Set	Test 1	Test 2	Test 3	Test 4	Test 5	Best Number
1	20	7	15	7	11	20
2	7	121	7	7	105	121
3	36	20	27	7	41	41
4	37	279	339	296	15	339
5	15	205	100	126	15	205
6	84	34	31	617	29	617
7	32	34	16	37	12	37
8	31	33	165	31	77	165

Table 4. The number of maximum steps without a collision performed by the best set of rules produced by each set of parameters (described in Table 2) and Eq. (4) and (5).

Fig. 13 shows the simulation of the vehicle control navigation with the best set of rules obtained from the fourth set of parameters.
The data in Table 4 also attest the better performance of the new reinforcement learning scheme proposed by Eq. (4) and (5) (see Table 4) since almost all set of parameters (expections are 3 and 7) created a set of rules with a number of steps without a collision which is bigger than the set of rules created by Eq. (3) (see Table 3).

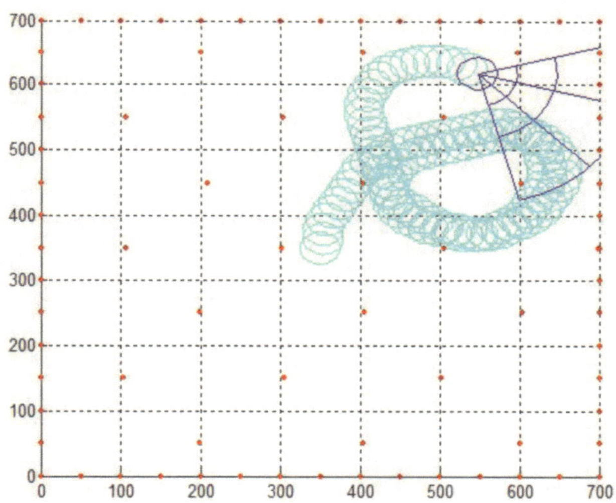

Fig. 13. The simulation of the vehicle navigation with best rules obtained with set 4.

7. Conclusions and future works

This Chapter discussed mathematical techniques that could help the ultimate unmanned aerial vehicle (UAVs) objective, which is the development of rules to replace human pilots by altering machines decisions in order to make decisions like humans do. For this purpose,

several tools related with artificial intelligence could be employed such as expert systems, neural networks, machine learning and natural language processing (HAYKIN, 2009).
Two methodologies, reinforcement learning and genetic algorithms, are described and combined. The methodologies had been implemented in a Matlab and were successfully applied in order to create rules that keep the vehicle away from the obstacles from random initial rules. This Chapter also described how the ideas developed by (STAFYLOPATIS, 1998) could be modified, particularly the setting of parameters and a new reinforcement learning methodology, to provide a better integration of the Genetic Algorithms (GAs) and Reinforcement Learning (RL) which produce rules for automatic guided vehicles with a better performance.
The main contributions of this Chapter were: the vehicle, its sensors, and also the environment for training which are different from the ones presented in (STAFYLOPATIS, 1998); a new equation for the reinforcement learning was proposed; the influence of the parameters that control the production of automatic generation of rules for vehicle control navigation are also tested. The results presented attested the better performance of the new reinforcement learning scheme proposed, implemented in Matlab. For future works, it could be applied a genetic algorithm for finding the better configuration of the parameters for the combined scheme of reinforcement learning and the genetic algorithm used to find the rules.
For future works more tests could be performed by using other equations for the reinforcement learning process and also other methods like Beam Search (SABUNCUOGLU and BAVIZ, 1999; DELLA CROCE and T'KINDT, 2002) could replace the Genetic Algorithm. A more detailed and complex decisions could also be incorporated such as the possibility of increasing or reducing the velocity of the vehicle.

8. References

Della Croce, F.; T'Kind, V., A Recovering Beam Search Algorithm for the One-Machine Dynamic Total Completation Time Scheduling Problem, Journal of the Operational Research Society, vol. 54, p. 1275-1280, 2002.

Haykin, , S. Neural Networks and Learning Machines, 3rd edition, Prentice Hall, 2009.

Sutton, R.S., Barto, A.G., *Reinforcement Learning: An Introduction*, MIT Press, 1998.

Stafylopatis, A., Blekas, K., Autonomous vehicle navigation using evolutionary reinforcement learning, European Journal of Operational Research, Vol. 108(2), p. 306-318, 1998.

Shim, D. H, Kim, H. J., Sastry, S., Hierarchical Control System Synthesis for Rotorcraft-based Unmanned Aerial Vehicles, AIAA Guidance, Navigation, and Control Conference and Exhibit, v. 1, p. 1-9, 2000.

Holland, J. H., Adaptation in natural and artificial systems. The University of Michigan Press, 1975.

Michalewicz, Z. Genetic Algorithms + Data Structures = Evolution Programs, 3rd edition, Springer-Verlag, 1996.

Sabuncuoglu, I., Baviz, M., Job Shop Scheduling with Beam Search, European Journal of Operational Research, vol. 118, pp. 390-412.

18

Robust Control of Active Vehicle Suspension Systems Using Sliding Modes and Differential Flatness with MATLAB

Esteban Chávez Conde[1], Francisco Beltrán Carbajal[2],
Antonio Valderrábano González[3] and Ramón Chávez Bracamontes[3]
[1]Universidad del Papaloapan, Campus Loma Bonita
[2]Universidad Autónoma Metropolitana, Unidad Azcapotzalco, Departamento de Energía
[3]Universidad Politécnica de la Zona Metropolitana de Guadalajara
[4]Instituto Tecnológico de Cd. Guzmán
México

1. Introduction

The main control objectives of active vehicle suspension systems are to improve the ride comfort and handling performance of the vehicle by adding degrees of freedom to the system and/or controlling actuator forces depending on feedback and feedforward information of the system obtained from sensors.

Passenger comfort is provided by isolating the passengers from undesirable vibrations induced from irregular road disturbances, and its performance is evaluated by the level of acceleration which vehicle passengers are exposed. Handling performance is achieved by maintaining a good contact between the tire and the road to provide guidance along the track.

The topic of active vehicle suspension control system, for linear and nonlinear models, in general, has been quite challenging over the years and we refer the reader to some of the fundamental work in the area which has been helpful in the preparation of this chapter. Control strategies like Linear Quadratic Regulator (LQR) in combination with nonlinear backstepping control techniques are proposed in (Liu et al., 2006). This strategy requires information about the state vector (vertical positions and speeds of the tire and car body). A reduced order controller is proposed in (Yousefi et al., 2006) to decrease the implementation costs without sacrificing the security and the comfort by using accelerometers for measurements of the vertical movement of the tire and car body. In (Tahboub, 2005) a controller of variable gain that considers the nonlinear dynamics of the suspension system is proposed. It requires measurements of the vertical positions of the car body and the tire, and the estimation of other states and of the road profile.

On the other hand, many dynamical systems exhibit a structural property called differential flatness. This property is equivalent to the existence of a set of independent outputs, called flat outputs and equal in number to the control inputs, which completely parameterizes every state variable and control input (Fliess et al., 1995). By means of differential flatness the analysis and design of controller is greatly simplified. In particular, the combination of differential flatness with sliding modes, which is extensively used when a robust control scheme is required, e.g., parameter uncertainty, exogenous disturbances and un-modeled dynamics (see Utkin, 1978), qualifies as an adequate robust control design approach to get high vibration attenuation level in active vehicle suspension systems. Sliding mode control of a differentially flat system of two degrees of freedom, with vibration attenuation, is presented in (Enríquez-Zárate et al., 2000).

This chapter presents a robust active vibration control scheme based on sliding modes and differential flatness for electromagnetic and hydraulic active vehicle suspension systems. Measurements of the vertical displacements of the car body and the tire are required for implementation of the proposed control scheme. On-line algebraic estimation of the states variables is used to avoid the use of sensors of acceleration and velocity. The road profile is considered as an unknown input disturbance that cannot be measured. Simulation results obtained from Matlab are included to show the dynamic performance and robustness of the active suspension systems with the proposed control scheme. This chapter applies the algebraic state estimation scheme proposed by Fliess and Sira-Ramírez (Fliess & Sira-Ramírez, 2004a, 2004b; Sira-Ramírez & Silva-Navarro, 2003) for control of nonlinear systems, which is based on the algebraic identification methodology of system parameters reported in (Fliess & Sira-Ramírez, 2003). The method is purely algebraic and involves the use of differential algebra. This method is applied to obtain an estimate of the time derivative from any signal, avoiding model reliance of the system at least in the estimation of states. Simulation and experimental results of the on-line algebraic estimation of states on a differentially flat system of two degrees of freedom are presented in (García-Rodríguez, 2005).

This chapter is organized as follows: Section 2 presents the linear mathematical models of vehicle suspension systems of a quarter car. The design of the controllers for the active suspension systems are introduced in Sections 3 and 4. Section 5 divulges the design of the algebraic estimator of states, while Section 6 shows the use of sensors for measuring the variables required by the controller. The simulation results are illustrated in Section 7. Finally, conclusions are brought out in Section 8.

2. Dynamic model of quarter-car suspension systems

2.1 Linear mathematical model of passive suspension system

A schematic diagram of a quarter-car suspension system is shown in Fig. 1(a). The mathematical model of the passive suspension system is given by

$$m_s\ddot{z}_s + c_s(\dot{z}_s - \dot{z}_u) + k_s(z_s - z_u) = 0 \tag{1}$$

$$m_u\ddot{z}_u - c_s(\dot{z}_s - \dot{z}_u) - k_s(z_s - z_u) + k_t(z_u - z_r) = 0 \tag{2}$$

where m_s represents the mass of a quarter car, m_u represents the mass of one wheel with the suspension and brake equipment, c_s is the damper coefficient of suspension, k_s and k_t are the spring coefficients of the suspension and the tire, z_s and z_u are the displacements of car body and the wheel and z_r is the terrain input disturbance. This simplified linear mathematical model of a passive suspension system has been widely used in many previous works, such as (Liu et al., 2006; Yousefi et al., 2006).

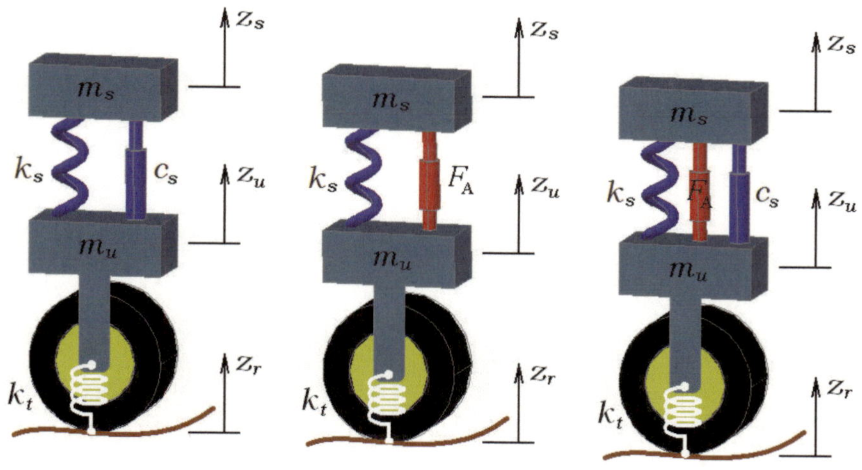

(a) (b) (c)

Fig. 1. Schematic diagram of a quarter-vehicle suspension system: (a) passive suspension system, (b) electromagnetic active suspension system and (c) hydraulic active suspension system.

2.2 Linear mathematical model of the electromagnetic active suspension system

A schematic diagram of a quarter-car active suspension system is illustrated in Fig.1 (b). The electromagnetic actuator replaces the damper, forming a suspension with the spring. The friction force of an electromagnetic actuator is neglected. The mathematical model of the electromagnetic suspension system, presented in (Martins et al., 2006), is given by:

$$m_s\ddot{z}_s + k_s(z_s - z_u) = F_A \tag{3}$$

$$m_u\ddot{z}_u - k_s(z_s - z_u) + k_t(z_u - z_r) = -F_A \tag{4}$$

where m_s, m_u, k_s, k_t, z_s, z_u and z_r represent the same parameters and variables shown in the passive suspension system. The electromagnetic actuator force is represented by F_A.

2.3 Linear mathematical model of hydraulic active suspension system

A schematic diagram of an active quarter-car suspension system is shown in Fig. 1(c). The mathematical model of the hydraulic suspension system is given by

$$m_s\ddot{z}_s + c_s(\dot{z}_s - \dot{z}_u) + k_s(z_s - z_u) = -F_f + F_A \tag{5}$$

$$m_u\ddot{z}_u - c_s(\dot{z}_s - \dot{z}_u) - k_s(z_s - z_u) + k_t(z_u - z_r) = F_f - F_A \tag{6}$$

where m_s, m_u, . k_s ., k_t, z_s, z_u and z_r represent the same parameters and variables shown in the passive suspension system. The hydraulic actuator force is represented by F_A, and F_f represents the friction force generated by the seals of the piston with the cylinder wall inside the actuator. This friction force has a significant magnitude ($> 200N$) and cannot be ignored (Martins et al., 2006; Yousefi et al., 2006). The net force given by the actuator is the difference between the hydraulic force F_A and the friction force F_f.

3. Control of electromagnetic suspension system

The mathematical model of the electromagnetic active suspension system illustrated in Fig. 1(b) is given by the equations (3) and (4). Defining the state variables $x_1 = z_s$, $x_2 = \dot{z}_s$, $x_3 = z_u$ and $x_4 = \dot{z}_u$ for the model of the equations mentioned, the representation in the state space form is,

$$\dot{x}(t) = Ax(t) + Bu(t) + Ez_r(t); \qquad x(t) \in \mathbb{R}^4, A \in \mathbb{R}^{4\times4}, B \in \mathbb{R}^{4\times1}, E \in \mathbb{R}^{4\times1},$$

$$\begin{bmatrix} \dot{x}_1 \\ \dot{x}_2 \\ \dot{x}_3 \\ \dot{x}_4 \end{bmatrix} = \begin{bmatrix} 0 & 1 & 0 & 0 \\ -\dfrac{k_s}{m_s} & 0 & \dfrac{k_s}{m_s} & 0 \\ 0 & 0 & 0 & 1 \\ \dfrac{k_s}{m_u} & 0 & -\dfrac{k_s + k_t}{m_u} & 0 \end{bmatrix} \begin{bmatrix} x_1 \\ x_2 \\ x_3 \\ x_4 \end{bmatrix} + \begin{bmatrix} 0 \\ \dfrac{1}{m_s} \\ 0 \\ -\dfrac{1}{m_u} \end{bmatrix} u + \begin{bmatrix} 0 \\ 0 \\ 0 \\ \dfrac{k_t}{m_u} \end{bmatrix} z_r \tag{7}$$

with $u = F_A$, the force provided by the electromagnetic actuator as control input.

3.1 Differential flatness

The system is controllable and hence, flat (Fliess et al., 1995; Sira-Ramírez & Agrawal, 2004), with the flat output being the positions of body car and wheel, $F = m_s x_1 + m_u x_3$, in (Chávez-Conde et al., 2009). For simplicity in the analysis of the differential flatness for the suspension system assume that $k_t z_r = 0$. In order to show the parameterization of all the state variables and control input, we firstly compute the time derivatives up to fourth order for F, resulting in

$$\begin{aligned} F &= m_s x_1 + m_u x_3 \\ \dot{F} &= m_s x_2 + m_u x_4 \\ \ddot{F} &= -k_t x_3 \\ F^{(3)} &= -k_t x_4 \\ F^{(4)} &= \frac{k_t}{m_u} u - \frac{k_s k_t}{m_u}(x_1 - x_3) + \frac{k_t^2}{m_u} x_3 \end{aligned}$$

Then, the state variables and control input are differentially parameterized in terms of the flat output as follows

$$\begin{aligned} x_1 &= \frac{1}{m_s}\left(F + \frac{m_u}{k_t}\ddot{F}\right) \\ x_2 &= \frac{1}{m_s}\left(\dot{F} + \frac{m_u}{k_t}F^{(3)}\right) \\ x_3 &= -\frac{1}{k_t}\ddot{F} \\ x_4 &= -\frac{1}{k_t}F^{(3)} \end{aligned}$$

$$u = \frac{m_u}{k_t}F^{(4)} + \left(\frac{k_s m_u}{k_t m_s} + \frac{k_s}{k_t} + 1\right)\ddot{F} + \frac{k_s}{m_s}F$$

3.2 Sliding mode and differential flatness control

The input u in terms of the flat output and its time derivatives is given by

$$u = \frac{m_u}{k_t}F^{(4)} + \left(\frac{k_s m_u}{k_t m_s} + \frac{k_s}{k_t} + 1\right)\ddot{F} + \frac{k_s}{m_s}F \tag{8}$$

where $F^{(4)} = v$ defines an auxiliary control input. This expression can be written in the following form:

$$u = d_1 F^{(4)} + d_2 \ddot{F} + d_3 F \tag{9}$$

where $d_1 = \frac{m_u}{k_t}$, $d_2 = \frac{k_s m_u}{k_t m_s} + \frac{k_s}{k_t} + 1$ and $d_3 = \frac{k_s}{m_s}$.

Now, consider a linear switching surface defined by

$$\sigma = F^{(3)} + \beta_2 \ddot{F} + \beta_1 \dot{F} + \beta_0 F \tag{10}$$

Then, the error dynamics restricted to $\sigma = 0$ is governed by the linear differential equation

$$F^{(3)} + \beta_2 \ddot{F} + \beta_1 \dot{F} + \beta_0 F = 0 \tag{11}$$

The design gains $\beta_2, \ldots, \beta_0$ are selected to verify that the associated characteristic polynomial $s^3 + \beta_2 s^2 + \beta_1 s + \beta_0$ be Hurwitz. As a consequence, the error dynamics on the switching surface $\sigma = 0$ is globally asymptotically stable. The sliding surface $\sigma = 0$ is made globally attractive with the continuous approximation to the discontinuous sliding mode controller as given in (Sira-Ramírez, 1993), i.e., by forcing to satisfy the dynamics,

$$\dot{\sigma} = -\mu[\sigma + \gamma sign(\sigma)] \tag{12}$$

where μ, γ denote positive real constants and "sign" is the standard signum function. The sliding surface is globally attractive, $\sigma\dot{\sigma} < 0$ for $\sigma \neq 0$, which is a very well known condition for the existence of sliding mode presented in (Utkin, 1978). One then obtains the following sliding-mode controller:

$$u = d_1 v + d_2 \ddot{F} + d_3 F \tag{13}$$

$$v = -\beta_2 F^{(3)} - \beta_1 \ddot{F} - \beta_0 \dot{F} - \mu[\sigma + \gamma sign(\sigma)]$$

This controller requires the measurement of all the state variables of the suspension system, z_s, $\dot{z}_s$, z_u and $\dot{z}_u$, corresponding to the vertical positions and velocity of the body of the car and the wheel. The variables $\dot{z}_s$ and $\dot{z}_u$ are calculated through an online algebraic estimator, shown in Section 5.

4. Control control of hydraulic suspension system

The mathematical model of the hydraulic active suspension system shown in Fig. 1(c) is given by the equations (5) and (6). Defining the state variables $x_1 = z_s$, $x_2 = \dot{z}_s$, $x_3 = z_u$ and $x_4 = \dot{z}_u$ for the model of the equations mentioned, the representation in the state space form is, $\dot{x}(t) = Ax(t) + Bu(t) + Ez_r(t);\ x(t) \in \mathbb{R}^4, A \in \mathbb{R}^{4\times4}, B \in \mathbb{R}^{4\times1}, E \in \mathbb{R}^{4\times1}$,

$$\begin{bmatrix} \dot{x}_1 \\ \dot{x}_2 \\ \dot{x}_3 \\ \dot{x}_4 \end{bmatrix} = \begin{bmatrix} 0 & 1 & 0 & 0 \\ -\frac{k_s}{m_s} & -\frac{c_s}{m_s} & \frac{k_s}{m_s} & \frac{c_s}{m_s} \\ 0 & 0 & 0 & 1 \\ \frac{k_s}{m_u} & \frac{c_s}{m_u} & -\frac{k_s + k_t}{m_u} & -\frac{c_s}{m_u} \end{bmatrix} \begin{bmatrix} x_1 \\ x_2 \\ x_3 \\ x_4 \end{bmatrix} + \begin{bmatrix} 0 \\ \frac{1}{m_s} \\ 0 \\ -\frac{1}{m_u} \end{bmatrix} u + \begin{bmatrix} 0 \\ 0 \\ 0 \\ \frac{k_t}{m_u} \end{bmatrix} z_r \qquad (14)$$

with $u = F_A - F_f$, the net force provided by the hydraulic actuator as control input (the net force provided by the actuator is the difference between the hydraulic force F_A and the frictional force F_f).

4.1 Differential flatness

The system is controllable and hence, flat (Fliess et al., 1995; Sira-Ramírez & Agrawal, 2004), with the flat output being the positions of body car and wheel, $F = m_s x_1 + m_u x_3$, in (Chávez-Conde et al., 2009). For simplicity in the analysis of the differential flatness for the suspension system assume that $k_t z_r = 0$. In order to show the parameterization of all the state variables and control input, we firstly compute the time derivatives up to fourth order for F, resulting in

$$\begin{aligned} F &= m_s x_1 + m_u x_3 \\ \dot{F} &= m_s x_2 + m_u x_4 \\ \ddot{F} &= -k_t x_3 \\ F^{(3)} &= -k_t x_4 \\ F^{(4)} &= \frac{k_t}{m_u} u - \frac{c_s k_t}{m_u}(x_2 - x_4) - \frac{k_s k_t}{m_u}(x_1 - x_3) + \frac{k_t^2}{m_u} x_3 \end{aligned}$$

Then, the state variables and control input are parameterized in terms of the flat output as follows

$$\begin{aligned} x_1 &= \frac{1}{m_s}\left(F + \frac{m_u}{k_t}\ddot{F}\right) \\ x_2 &= \frac{1}{m_s}\left(\dot{F} + \frac{m_u}{k_t}F^{(3)}\right) \\ x_3 &= -\frac{1}{k_t}\ddot{F} \\ x_4 &= -\frac{1}{k_t}F^{(3)} \end{aligned}$$

$$u = \frac{m_u}{k_t} F^{(4)} + \left(\frac{c_s m_u}{k_t m_s} + \frac{c_s}{k_t} \right) F^{(3)} + \left(\frac{k_s m_u}{k_t m_s} + \frac{k_s}{k_t} + 1 \right) \ddot{F} + \frac{c_s}{m_s} \dot{F} + \frac{k_s}{m_s} F$$

4.2 Sliding mode and differential flatness control

The input u in terms of the flat output and its time derivatives is given by

$$u = \frac{m_u}{k_t} v + \left(\frac{c_s m_u}{k_t m_s} + \frac{c_s}{k_t} \right) F^{(3)} + \left(\frac{k_s m_u}{k_t m_s} + \frac{k_s}{k_t} + 1 \right) \ddot{F} + \frac{c_s}{m_s} \dot{F} + \frac{k_s}{m_s} F \tag{15}$$

where $F^{(4)} = v$ defines the auxiliary control input. The expression can be written in the following form:

$$u = \eta_1 v + \eta_2 F^{(3)} + \eta_3 \ddot{F} + \eta_4 \dot{F} + \eta_5 F \tag{16}$$

where $\eta_1 = \frac{m_u}{k_t}$, $\eta_2 = \frac{c_s m_u}{k_t m_s} + \frac{c_s}{k_t}$, $\eta_3 = \frac{k_s m_u}{k_t m_s} + \frac{k_s}{k_t} + 1$, $\eta_4 = \frac{c_s}{m_s}$ and $\eta_5 = \frac{k_s}{m_s}$.

Now, consider a linear switching surface defined by

$$\sigma = F^{(3)} + \beta_2 \ddot{F} + \beta_1 \dot{F} + \beta_0 F \tag{17}$$

Then, the error dynamics restricted to $\sigma = 0$ is governed by the linear differential equation

$$F^{(3)} + \beta_2 \ddot{F} + \beta_1 \dot{F} + \beta_0 F = 0 \tag{18}$$

The design gains $\beta_2, \ldots, \beta_0$ are selected to verify that the associated characteristic polynomial $s^3 + \beta_2 s^2 + \beta_1 s + \beta_0$ be Hurwitz. As a consequence, the error dynamics on the switching surface $\sigma = 0$ is globally asymptotically stable. The sliding surface $\sigma = 0$ is made globally attractive with the continuous approximation to the discontinuous sliding mode controller as given in (Sira-Ramírez, 1993), i.e., by forcing to satisfy the dynamics

$$\dot{\sigma} = -\mu[\sigma + \gamma sign(\sigma)] \tag{19}$$

where μ, γ denote positive real constants and "sign" is the standard signum function. The sliding surface is globally attractive, $\sigma\dot{\sigma} < 0$ for $\sigma \neq 0$, which is a very well known condition for the existence of sliding mode presented in (Utkin, 1978). One then obtains the following sliding-mode controller:

$$u = \eta_1 v + \eta_2 F^{(3)} + \eta_3 \ddot{F} + \eta_4 \dot{F} + \eta_5 F \tag{20}$$

$$v = -\beta_2 F^{(3)} - \beta_1 \ddot{F} - \beta_0 \dot{F} - \mu[\sigma + \gamma sign(\sigma)]$$

This controller requires the measurement of all the variables of state of suspension system, z_s, $\dot{z}_s$, z_u and $\dot{z}_u$ corresponding to the vertical positions and velocity of the body of the car and the tire, respectively. The variables $\dot{z}_s$ and $\dot{z}_u$ are calculated through an online algebraic estimator, shown in Section 5.

5. On-line algebraic state estimation of active suspension system

5.1 First time derivative algebraic estimation

The algebraic methodology proposed in (Fliess & Sira-Ramírez, 2003) allows us to estimate the derivatives of a smooth signal considering a signal model of $n-th$ order, thus it is not necessary to design the time derivative estimator from a specific dynamic model of the plant. Through valid algebraic manipulations of this approximated model in the frequency domain, and using the algebraic derivation with respect to the complex variable s, we neglect the initial conditions of the signal. The resulting equation is multiplied by a negative power s^{n-1} and returned to the time domain. This last expression is manipulated algebraically in order to find a formula to estimate the first time derivative of $y(t)$.

Consider a fourth order approximation of a smooth signal $y(t)$,

$$\frac{d^4 y(t)}{dt^4} = 0 \tag{21}$$

This model indicates that $y(t)$ is a signal whose behavior can be approximated by a family of polynomials of third order, thus the fourth time derivative is assumed close to zero. The order of this approximation can be increased to enhance the estimation quality of the algebraic estimator. From (21) it is possible to design a time derivative algebraic estimator. First, we apply Laplace transform to (21),

$$s^4 Y(s) - s^3 Y(0) - s^2 \dot{Y}(0) - s\ddot{Y} - Y^{(3)} = 0 \tag{22}$$

Now, taking successive derivatives until a number of three with respect to the complex variable s, we obtain a expression which is free of initial conditions,

$$\frac{d^4\left(s^4 Y\right)}{ds^4} = 0 \tag{23}$$

Expanding this expression and multiplying by s^{-3},

$$24s^{-3}Y + 96s^{-2}\frac{dY}{ds} + 72s^{-1}\frac{d^2Y}{ds^2} + 16\frac{d^3Y}{ds^3} + s\frac{d^4Y}{ds^4} \tag{24}$$

Returning to the time domain,

$$\frac{d}{dt}(t^4 z(t)) - 16t^3 z(t) + 72\int_0^t \lambda_1^2 z(\lambda_1)d\lambda_1$$
$$-96\int_0^t\int_0^{\lambda_1} \lambda_2 z(\lambda_2)d\lambda_2 d\lambda_1 + 24\int_0^t\int_0^{\lambda_1}\int_0^{\lambda_2} z(\lambda_3)d\lambda_3 d\lambda_2 d\lambda_1 = 0$$

From the last equation is possible to obtain the following algebraic estimator,

$$\frac{dz}{dt} = \frac{12t^3 z + 96\int_0^t\int_0^{\lambda_1}\lambda_2 z(\lambda_2)d\lambda_2 d\lambda_1 - 24\int_0^t\int_0^{\lambda_1}\int_0^{\lambda_2} z(\lambda_3)d\lambda_3 d\lambda_2 d\lambda_1}{t^4} \tag{25}$$

This formula is valid for $t > 0$. Since (25) provides an approximated value of the first derivative, this is only valid during a period of time. So the state estimation should be calculated periodically as follows,

$$\left.\frac{dz}{dt}\right|_{t_i}^{t} = \frac{12(t-t_i)^3 z + 96\int_{t_i}^{t}\int_{t_i}^{\lambda_1}\lambda_2 z(\lambda_2)d\lambda_2 d\lambda_1 - 24\int_{t_i}^{t}\int_{t_i}^{\lambda_1}\int_{t_i}^{\lambda_2} z(\lambda_3)d\lambda_3 d\lambda_2 d\lambda_1}{(t-t_i)^4}, \quad \forall (t-t_i) > 0 \tag{26}$$

where (t_i, t) is the estimation period.
In order to obtain a better and smoother estimated value of the vertical velocity, we have implemented simultaneously two algebraic estimators for each velocity to estimate. Proceeding with an out-of-phase policy for one of these algebraic estimators, the outputs of both are combined properly to obtain a final estimated value.

6. Instrumentation of the active suspension system

The only variables required for the implementation of the proposed controllers are the vertical displacements of the body of the car z_s and the vertical displacement of the wheel z_u. These variables are needed to measure by some sensor. In (Chamseddine et al., 2006) the use of sensors in experimental vehicle platforms, as well as in commercial vehicles is presented. The most common sensors used for measuring the vertical displacement of the body of the car and the wheel are laser sensors. This type of sensors could be used to measure the variables z_s and z_s needed for controller implementation. An accelerometer or another type of sensor is not needed to measure the variables $\dot{z}_s$ and $\dot{z}_u$, these variables are estimated with the use of algebraic estimators from knowledge of the variables z_s and z_u. Fig. 2 shows a schematic diagram of the instrumentation for the active suspension system.

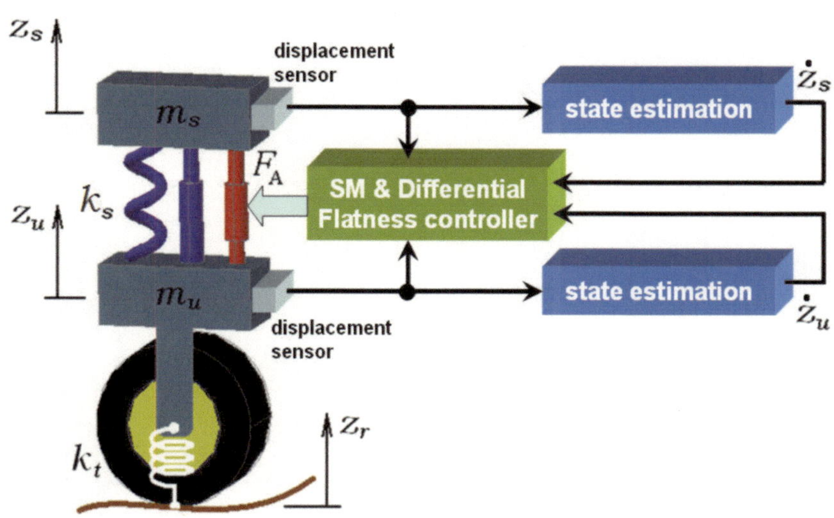

Fig. 2. Schematic diagram of the instrumentation of the active suspension system.

7. Simulation results

The simulation results were obtained by means of MATLAB/Simulink®, with the Runge-Kutta numerical method and a fixed integration step of $1ms$. The numerical values of the quarter-car model parameters (Sam & Hudha, 2006) are presented in Table 1.

Parameter	Value
Sprung mass (m_s)	282 $[kg]$
Unsprung mass (m_u)	45 $[kg]$
Spring stiffness (k_s)	17900 $\left[\frac{N}{m}\right]$
Damping constant (c_s)	1000 $\left[\frac{N \cdot s}{m}\right]$
Tire stiffness (k_t)	165790 $\left[\frac{N}{m}\right]$

Table 1. Quarter-car model parameters

In this simulation study, the road disturbance is shown in Fig. 3 and set in the form of (Sam & Hudha, 2006):

$$z_r = a\frac{1 - cos(8\pi t)}{2}$$

with $a = 0.11$ [m] for $0.5 \leq t \leq 0.75$, $a = 0.55$ [m] for $3.0 \leq t \leq 3.25$ and 0 otherwise.

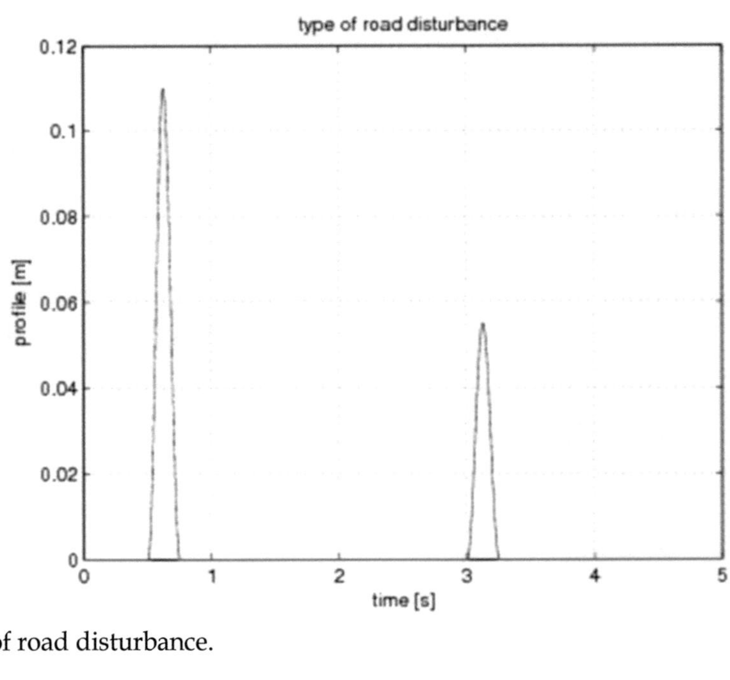

Fig. 3. Type of road disturbance.

It is desired to stabilize the suspension system at the positions $z_s = 0$ and $z_u = 0$. The gains of both electromagnetic and hydraulic suspension controllers were obtained by forcing their closed loop characteristic polynomials to be given by the following Hurwitz polynomial: $(s+p)(s^2+2\zeta\omega_n s+\omega_n^2)$ with $p=100$, $\zeta=0.5$, $\omega_n=90$, $\mu=95$ y $\gamma=95$.
The Simulink model of the sliding mode and differential flatness controller of the active suspension system is shown in Fig. 4. For the electromagnetic active suspension system, it is assumed that c_z = *0*. In Fig. 5 is shown the Simulink model of the sliding mode and differential flatness controller with algebraic state estimation.

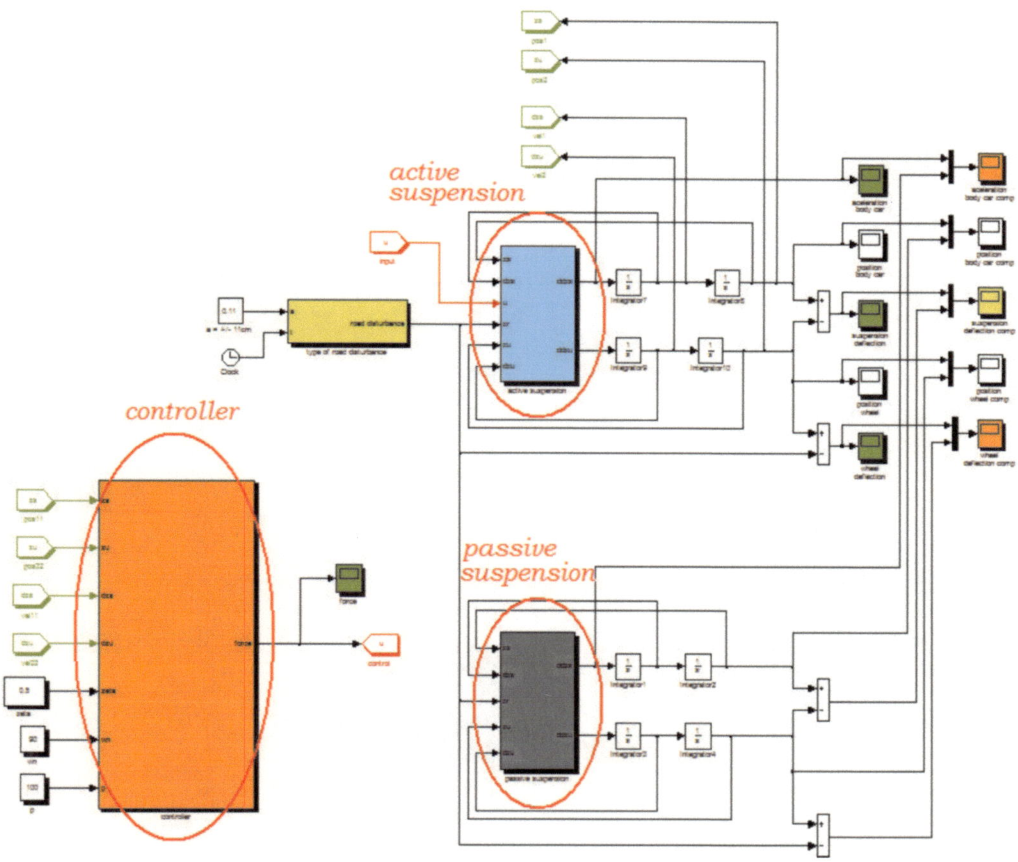

Fig. 4. Simulink model of the sliding mode and differential flatness controller.

In Fig. 6 is depicted the robust performance of the electromagnetic suspension controller. It can be seen the high vibration attenuation level of the active vehicle suspension system compared with the passive counterpart. Similar results on the implementation of the hydraulic suspension controller are depicted in Fig. 7.
In Fig. 8 is presented the algebraic estimation process of the velocities of the car body and the wheel. There we can observe a good and fast estimation. In Figs. 9 and 10 are shown the simulation results on the performance of the electromagnetic and hydraulic suspension controllers using the algebraic estimators of velocities. These results are quite similar to those gotten by the controllers using the real velocities.

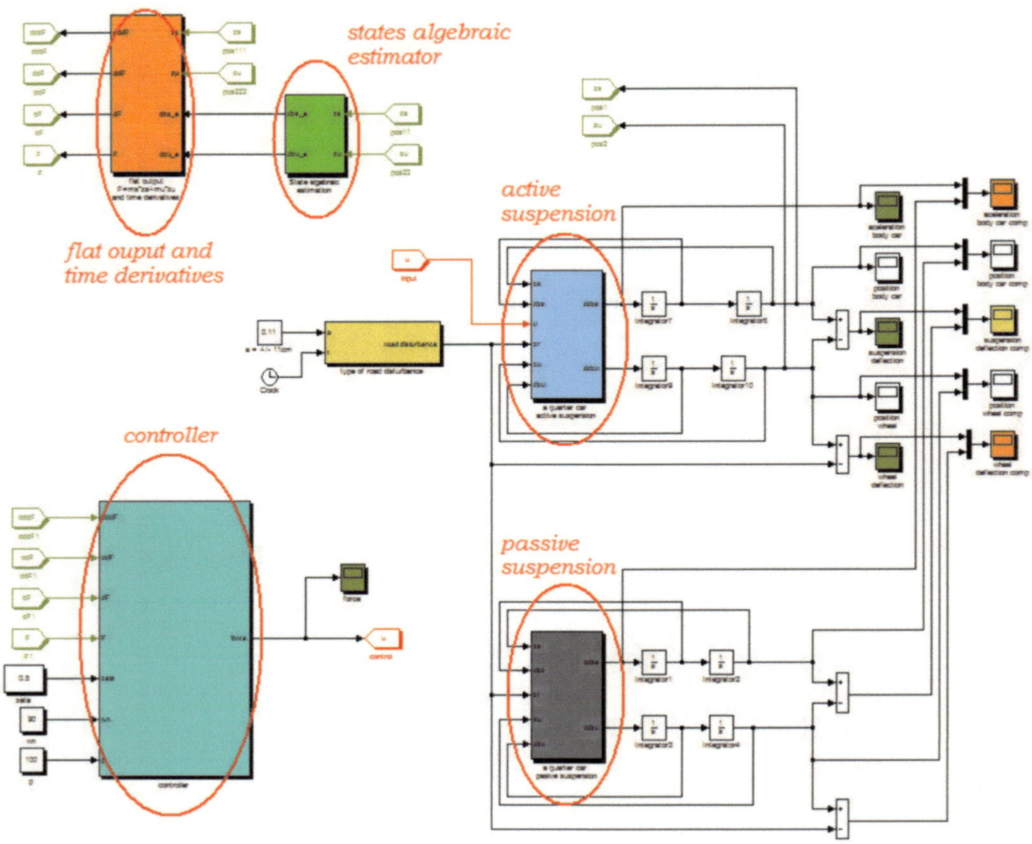

Fig. 5. Simulink model of the sliding mode and differential flatness controller with state estimation.

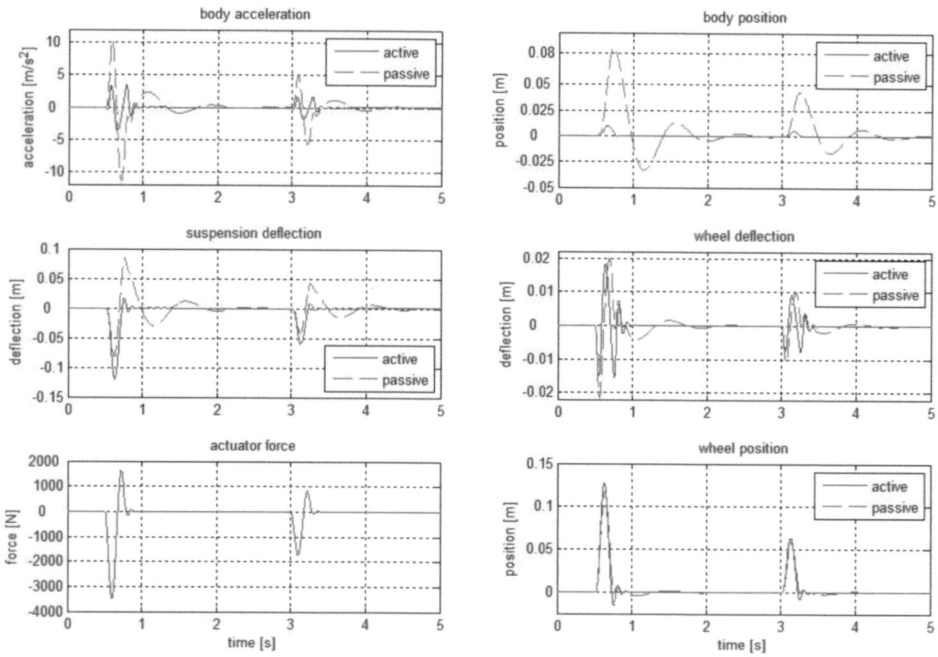

Fig. 6. Electromagnetic active vehicle suspension system responses with sliding mode and differential flatness based controller.

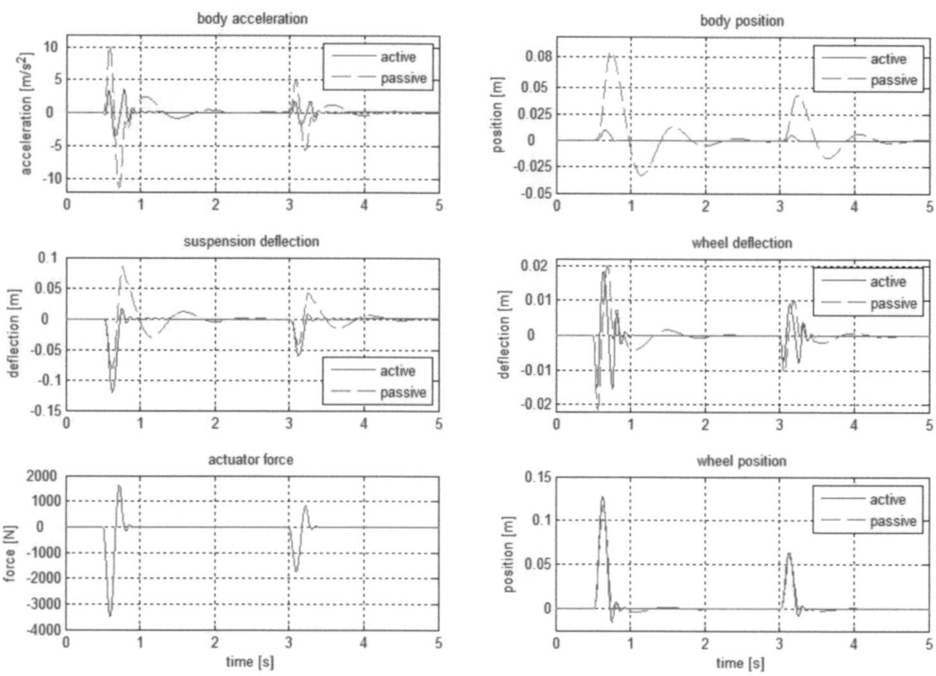

Fig. 7. Hydraulic active vehicle suspension system responses with sliding mode and differential flatness based controller.

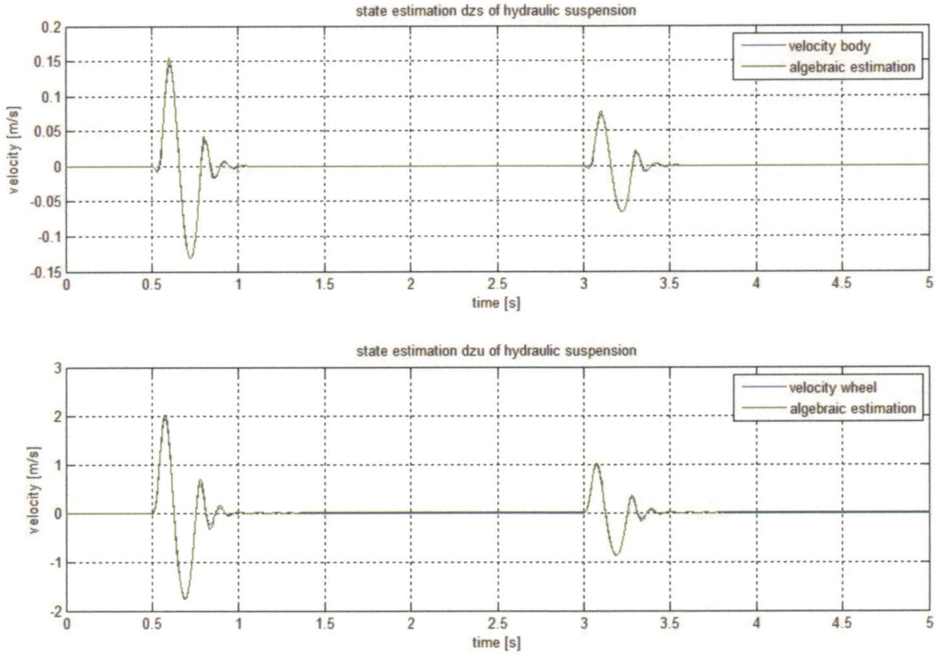

Fig. 8. On-line algebraic state estimates of the hydraulic active suspension system.

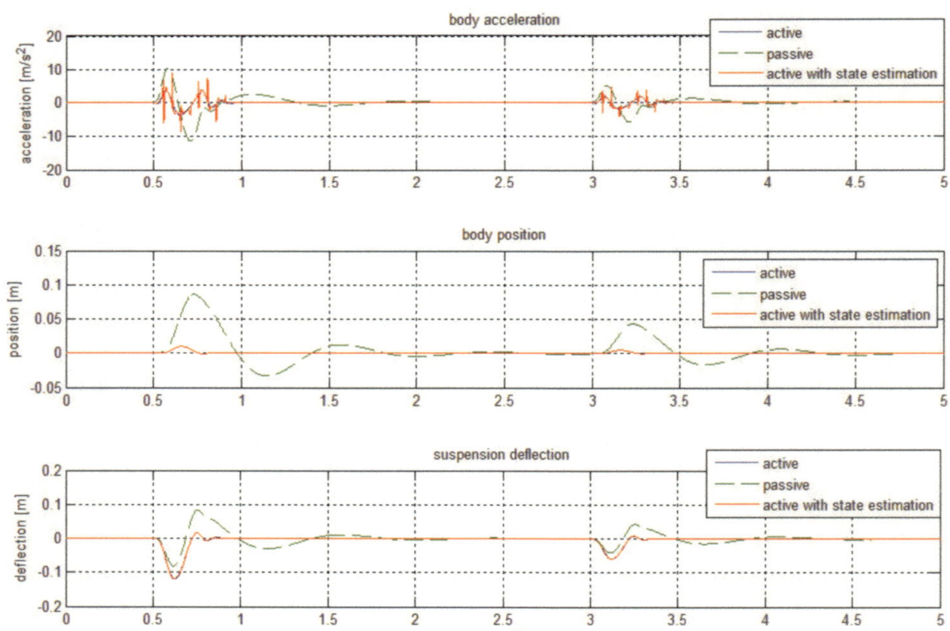

Fig. 9. a. Electromagnetic active vehicle suspension system responses with sliding mode and differential flatness based controller using algebraic state estimation.

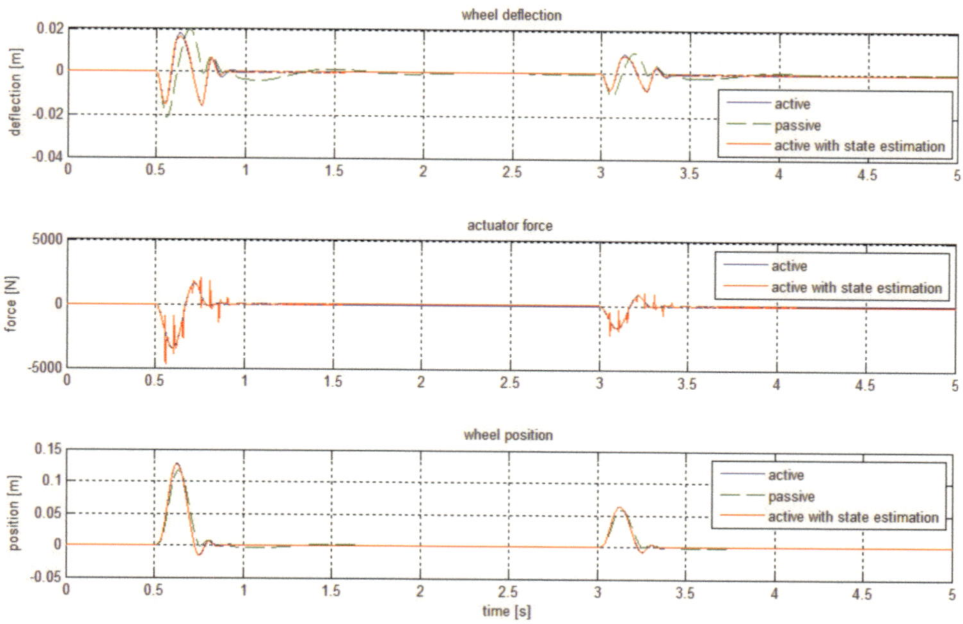

Fig. 9. b. Electromagnetic active vehicle suspension system responses with sliding mode and differential flatness based controller using algebraic state estimation.

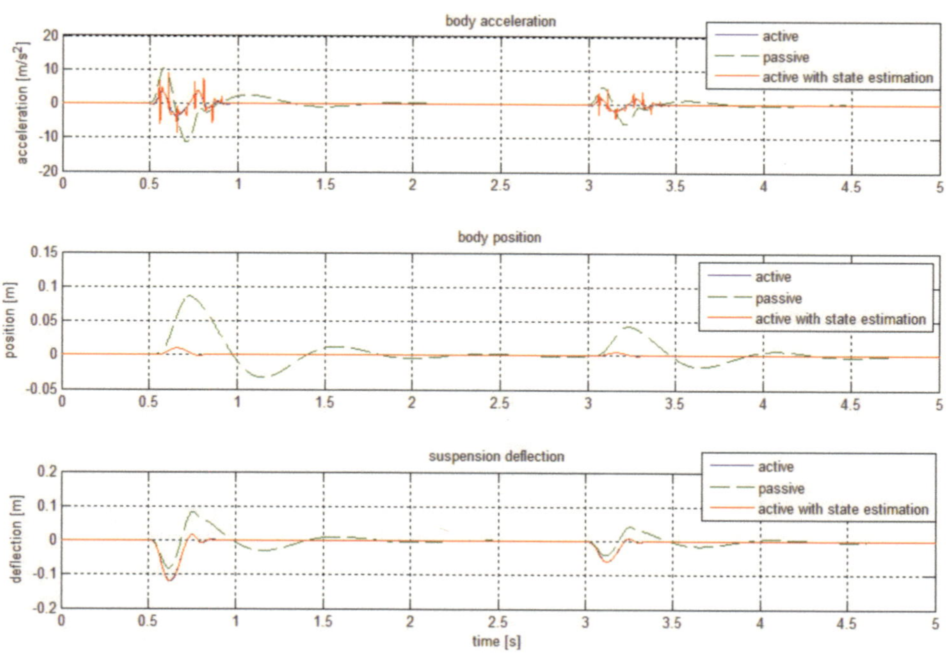

Fig. 10. a. Hydraulic active vehicle suspension system responses with sliding mode and differential flatness based controller using algebraic state estimation.

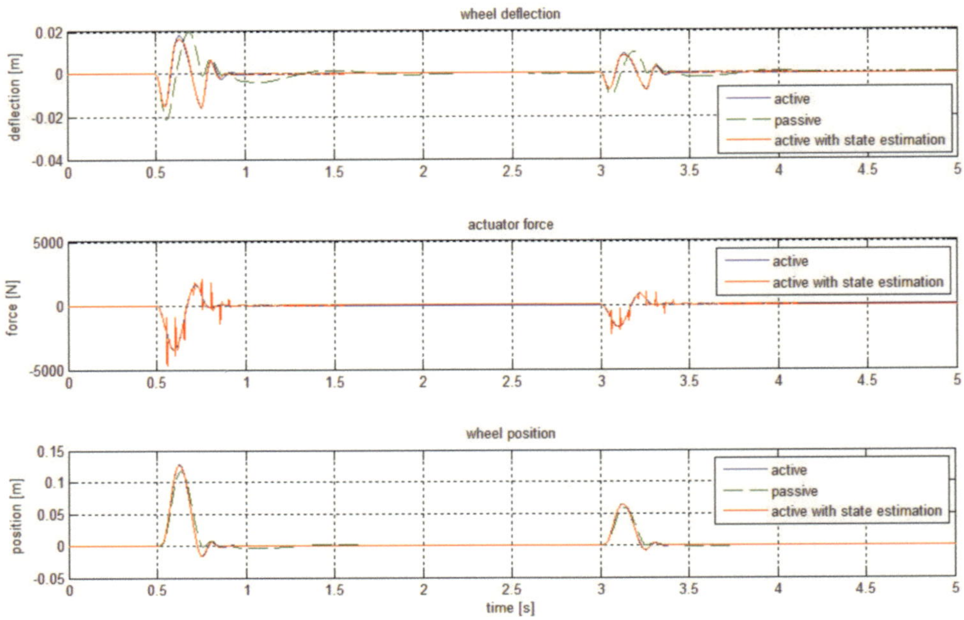

Fig. 10. b. Hydraulic active vehicle suspension system responses with sliding mode and differential flatness based controller using algebraic state estimation.

8. Conclusions

The stabilization of the vertical position of the quarter of car is obtained in a time much smaller to that of the passive suspension system. The sliding mode based differential flatness controller requires the knowledge of all the state variables. Nevertheless the fast stabilization with amplitude in acceleration and speed of the body of the car very remarkable is observed. On-line state estimation is obtained successfully, however when it is used into the controller one can observe a deterioration of the control signal. This can significantly improve with a suitable interpolation between the estimated values at each restart of the integrations. In addition, the simulations results show that the stabilization of the system is obtained before the response of the passive suspension system, with amplitude of acceleration and speed of the body of the car very remarkable. Finally, the robustness of the controllers is observed to take to stabilize to the system before the unknown disturbance.

9. References

Chamseddine, Abbas; Noura, Hassan; Raharijaona, Thibaut "Control of Linear Full Vehicle Active Suspension System Using Sliding Mode Techniques", 2006 IEEE International Conference on Control Applications. pp. 1306-1311, Munich, Germany, October 4-6, 2006.

Chávez-Conde, E.; Beltrán-Carbajal, F.; Blanco-Ortega, A.; Méndez-Azúa, H. "Sliding Mode and Generalized PI Control of Vehicle Active Suspensions", 2009 IEEE International Conference on Control Applications. Saint Petersburg, Russia, July 8-10, 2009.

Enríquez-Zárate, J.; Silva-Navarro, G.; Sira-Ramírez, H. "Sliding Mode Control of a Differentially Flat Vibrational Mechanical System: Experimental Results", 39th IEEE Conference on Decision and Control. pp. 1679-1684, Sydney, Australia, December 2000.

Flies, M.; Lévine, J.; Martin, Ph.; Rouchon, P. "Flatness and defect of nonlinear systems: introductory theory and examples", Int. Journal of Control. Vol. 61, pp. 1327-1361, 1995.

Fliess, M.; Sira-Ramírez, H. "Reconstructeurs d'états". C.R. Acad. Sci. Paris, I-338, pp. 91-96, 2004.

Fliess, M.; Sira-Ramírez, H. "Control via state estimations of some nonlinear systems", 4th IFAC Nolcos Conference. Germany, 2004.

Fliess, M.; Sira-Ramírez, H. "An Algebraic Framework For Linear Identification", ESAIM Control, Optimization and Calculus of Variations. Vol 9, pp. 151-168, January. 2003.

García-Rodríguez, C. "Estimación de estados por métodos algebraicos", Master of Thesis. CINVESTAV-IPN, México, D.F., México, 2005.

Liu, Zhen; Luo, Cheng; Hu, Dewen, "Active Suspension Control Design Using a Combination of LQR and Backstepping", 25th IEEE Chinese Control Conference, pp. 123-125, Harbin, Heilongjiang, August 7-11, 2006.

Martins, I.; Esteves, J.; Marques, D. G.; Da Silva, F. P. "Permanent-Magnets Linear Actuators Applicability in Automobile Active Suspensions", IEEE Trans. on Vehicular Technology. Vol. 55, No. 1, pp. 86-94, January 2006.

Sam, Y. M.; Hudha, K. "Modeling and Force Tracking Control of Hydraulic Actuator for an Active Suspension System", IEEE ICIEA, 2006.

Sira-Ramírez, H. "A dynamical variable structure control strategy in asymptotic output tracking problems", IEEE Trans. on Automatic Control. Vol. 38, No. 4, pp. 615-620, April 1993.

Sira-Ramírez, H.; Silva-Navarro, G. "Algebraic Methods in Flatness, Signal Processing and State Estimation", Innovación Editorial Lagares de México, November 2003.

Sira-Ramírez, H.; Agrawal, Sunil K. "Differentially Flat Systems", Marcel Dekker, N.Y., 2004.

Tahboub, Karim A. "Active Nonlinear Vehicle-Suspension Variable-Gain Control", 13th IEEE Mediterranean Conference on Control and Automation, pp. 569-574, Limassol, Cyprus, June 27-29, 2005.

Utkin,V. I. “Sliding Modes and Their Applications in Variable Structure Systems”. Moscow: MIR, 1978.

Yousefi, A.; Akbari, A and Lohmann, B., “Low Order Robust Controllers for Active Vehicle Suspensions”, IEEE International Conference on Control Applications, pp. 693-698, Munich, Germany, Octuber 4-6, 2006.

19

Thermal Behavior of IGBT Module for EV (Electric Vehicle)

Mohamed Amine Fakhfakh, Moez Ayadi,
Ibrahim Ben Salah and Rafik Neji
University of Sfax/Sfax
Tunisia

1. Introduction

EVs are divided into three categories: the pure EV, the hybrid EV, and the fuel cell EV. Although these three types of electric vehicle have different system configuration, one (or more) motor drive system is always needed to convert electrical power into mechanical ones. Among the drive systems used for EV, induction motor system and permanent magnet motor systems are mostly used for their high power density, high efficiency.

The motor drive system for electric vehicle (EV) is composed of a battery, three phase inverter, a permanent magnet motor, and a sensor system. The inverter is a key unit important among these electrical components which converts the direct current of the battery into the alternating current to rotate the motor. Therefore, for predicting the dynamic power loss and junction temperature, the electro-thermal coupling simulation techniques to estimate the power loss and to calculate the junction temperature become important.

This paper describes a compact thermal model suitable for the electro-thermal coupling simulation of EV inverter module for two current control methods. We can predict the dynamic temperature rise of Si devices by simulating the inverter operation in accordance with the real EV running.

2. Dynamic model of the EV

As shown in Figure 1 and table 1, there are six forces acting on the electric vehicle: the rolling resistance force, the aerodynamic force, the aerodynamic lift force, the gravity force, the normal force, and the motor force.

2.1 Rolling resistance force

Rolling resistance is due the tires deforming when contacting the surface of a road and varies depending on the surface being driven on. It can be model using the following equation:

$$F_1 = f\,M_v\,g \tag{1}$$

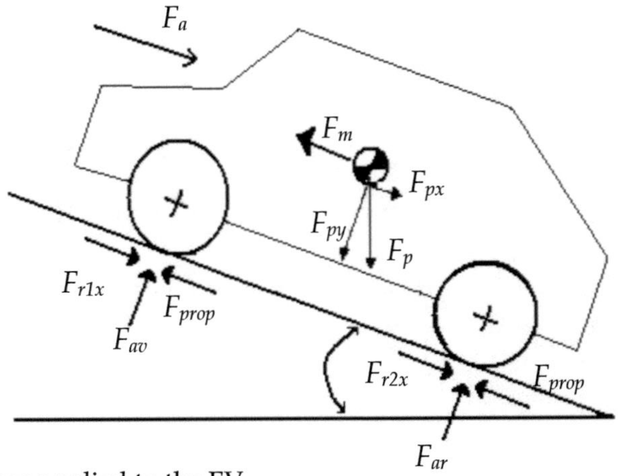

Fig. 1. Diagram of forces applied to the EV

F_{r1x}	Rolling resistance force
F_{r2x}	Rolling resistance force
F_{av}	Normal force
F_{ar}	Normal force
F_a	Aerodynamic force
F_{prop}	Thrust force
F_p	Gravity force
F_m	Motor force
θ	Slope angle with the horizontal

Table 1. Applied forces to EV

2.2 Aerodynamic force

Aerodynamic drag is caused by the momentum loss of air particles as they flow over the hood of the vehicle. The aerodynamic drag of a vehicle can be modeled using the following equation:

$$F_2 = \frac{1}{2} \rho S_f C_x V^2 \tag{2}$$

2.3 Gravity force

The gravity force can be calculated as follows:

$$F_3 = M_v g \sin\theta \tag{3}$$

2.4 Motor force

Using Newton's Second Law, we can deduce the motor force; it can be obtained by the following equation:

$$M_v \frac{dV}{dt} = \sum \vec{F}_{ext} = \vec{F}_m + \vec{F}_p + \vec{F}_a + \vec{F}_r \tag{4}$$

By projection on the (O, x) axis, we obtain:

$$F_m = M_v \frac{dV}{dt} + F_a + F_p + F_r \tag{5}$$

The power that the EV must develop at stabilized speed is expressed by the following equation:

$$P_{vehicle} = F_m V = (F_r + F_a + F_p + M_v \frac{dV}{dt})V \tag{6}$$

We deduce the expression of the total torque by multiplying equation (5) with the wheel radius R:

$$C_{vehicle} = C_r + C_a + C_p + M_v R \frac{dV}{dt} \tag{7}$$

Neglecting the mechanical losses in the gearbox, the t electromagnetic torque C_{em} developed by the motor is obtained by dividing the wheels torque $C_{vehicle}$ by the ratio reduction r_d.

$$C_{em} = \frac{1}{r_d}\left(C_r + C_a + C_p + M_v R \frac{dV}{dt}\right) \tag{8}$$

Figure 2 presents the dynamic model of the EV load, implemented under Matlab/simulink.

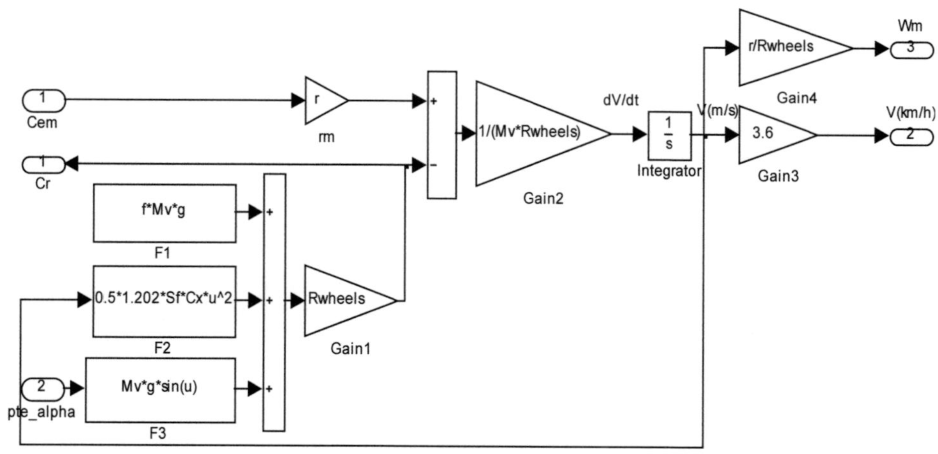

Fig. 2. SIMULINK dynamic model of electric vehicle

3. Electric motor control

Control of permanent magnet synchronous motor is performed using field oriented control. The stator windings of the motor are fed by an inverter that generates a variable frequency variable voltage. The frequency and phase of the output wave are controlled using a position sensor as shown in figure 3.

In our studie, we have used two types of current control, Hysteresis and PWM.

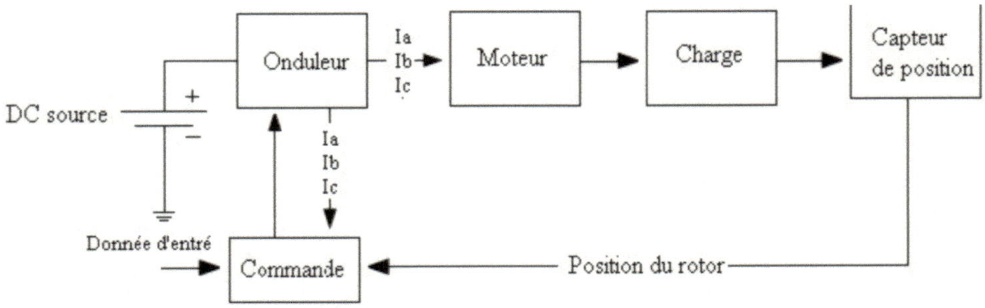

Fig. 3. Drive system schematic

3.1 PWM current controller

PWM current controllers are widely used. The switching frequency is usually kept constant. They are based in the principle of comparing a triangular carrier wave of desire switching frequency and is compared with error of the controlled signal [Bose, 1996].

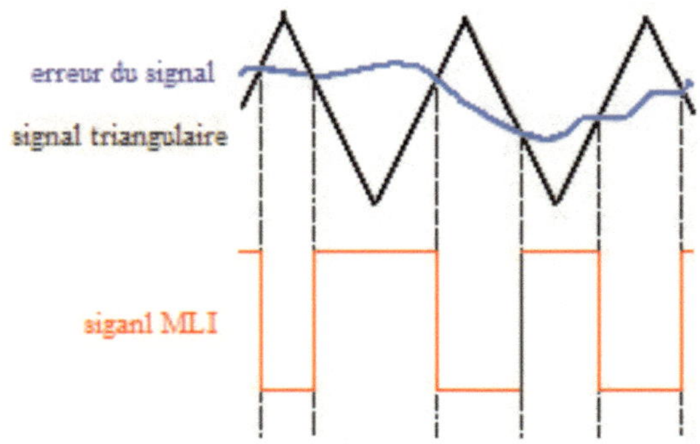

Fig. 4. PWM current controller

3.2 Hysteresis current controller

Hysteresis current controller can also be implemented to control the inverter currents. The controller will generate the reference currents with the inverter within a range which is fixed by the width of the band gap [Bose, 1996; Pillay et al., 1989].

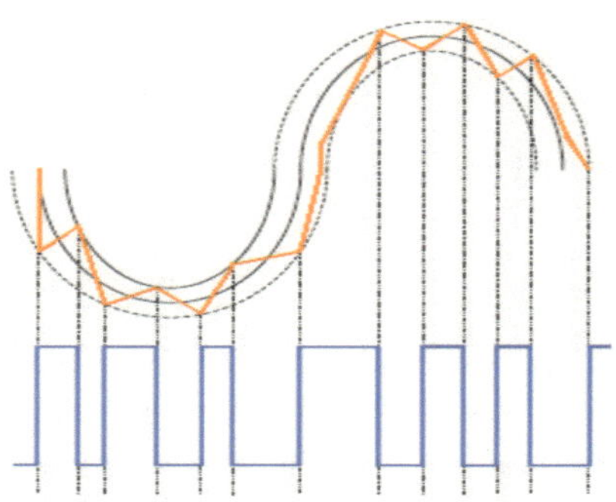

Fig. 5. Hysteresis current controller

4. Thermal model of IGBT module

The studied module is the Semikron module SKM 75GB 123D (75A/1200V) which contains two IGBTs and with two antiparallel diodes. The structure of the module contains primarily eight layers of different materials, each one of it is characterized by its thickness Li, its thermal conductivity Ki, density ρi and its heat capacity Cpi. Table 2 show the materials properties of the various layers of module as shown in figure 6. These values are given by the manufacturer and/or of the literatures [Dorkel et al., 1996; Uta et al., 2000; Thoams et al., 2000].

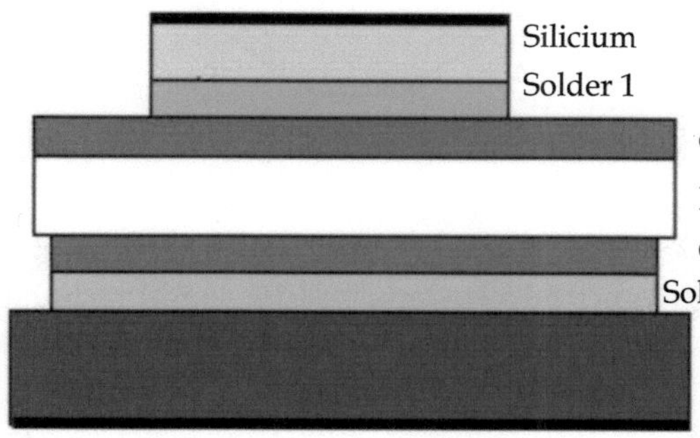

Fig. 6. Example of the module structure

Material	*L (mm)*	*K (W/mK)*	*ρCp (J/Kcm³)*
Silicium	0.4	140	1.7
Solder 1	0.053	35	1.3
Copper	0.35	360	3.5
Isolation	0.636	100	2.3
Copper	0.35	360	3.5
Solder 2	0.103	35	1.3
Base plate	3	280	3.6
Grease	0.1	1	2.1

Table 2. Thermal parameters of a power module

In the power module, the heating flow diffuses vertically and also laterally from the heating source. So, a thermal interaction happens inside the module between the adjacent devices when they operate together.

This thermal interaction depends from [Kojima et al., 2006; Ayadi et al., 2010; Fakhfakh et al., 2010]:

- The dissipated power value of the various components.
- The disposition of the chip components.
- The boundary condition at the heat spreader.

Figure 7 shows the thermal influence between the different components of the module. We notice that each component has a thermal interaction with the others and we supposed that each module have zero interaction with other modules.

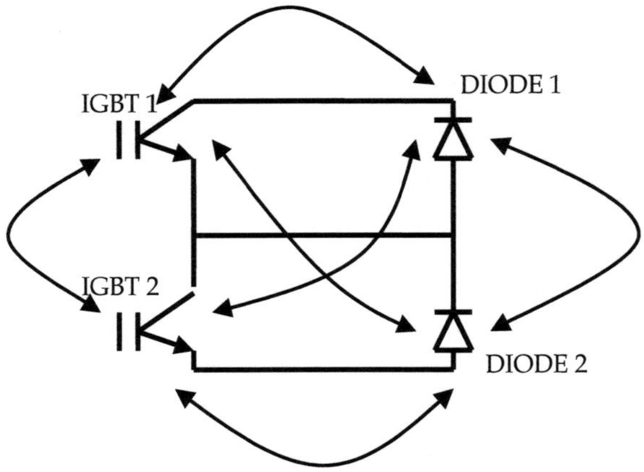

Fig. 7. Different thermal influences between the module components

Literature proposes some thermal circuit networks for electrothermal simulation for the semiconductor device. For example the finite difference method (FDM) and the finite element method (FEM). In our study we have used the FEM technique to model our inverter module. Figure 8 shows the thermal circuit example obtained by the FEM of IGBT1 without thermal interaction.

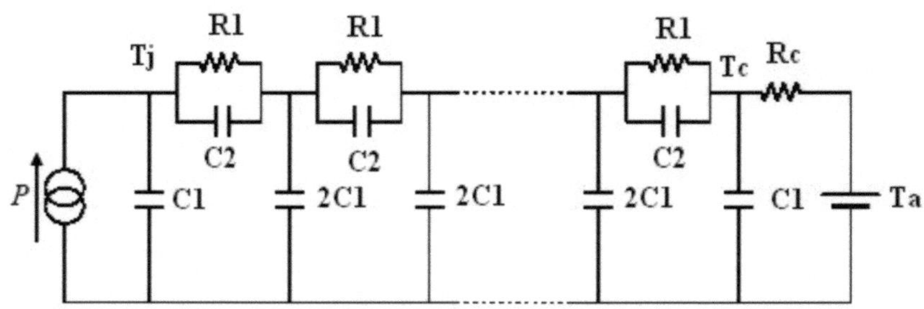

Fig. 8. Thermal circuit obtained by the FEM

Where:

- P is the input power dissipation device.
- Tj is the junction temperature.
- R1 is the thermal resistance.
- Rc is the convection resistance.
- C1 and C2 are thermal capacitance.
- Ta is the ambient temperature.

In order to introduce the thermal interaction between the different components of the module, we inserted three other current sources P1, P2 and P3. These sources are deduced from the structure of IGBT module [Drofenik et al., 2005; Hamada et al., 2006; Usui et al., 2006].

The source P1 is the power loss of DIODE1; it is introduced at the interface between the silicon and the copper materials because the IGBT1 and the DIODE1 ships are bounded on the same copper area. The source P2 and P3 are power loss of IGBT2 and DIODE2, they are introduced between solder 2 and base plate because all module components have the base plate as a common material. So the thermal circuit network of IGBT1 becomes as the figure 9.

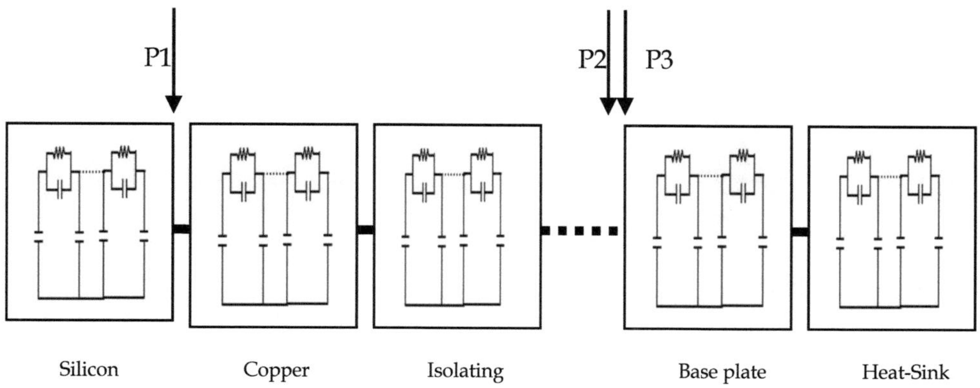

Fig. 9. Thermal model of IGBT module

5. Simulation and results

The PM motor drive simulation was built in several steps like abc phase transformation to dqo variables, calculation torque and speed, and control circuit [Ong, 1998; Roisse et al., 1998].
Parks transformation used for converting Iabc to Idq is shown in figure 10 and the reverse transformation for converting Idq to Iabc is shown in figure 11.

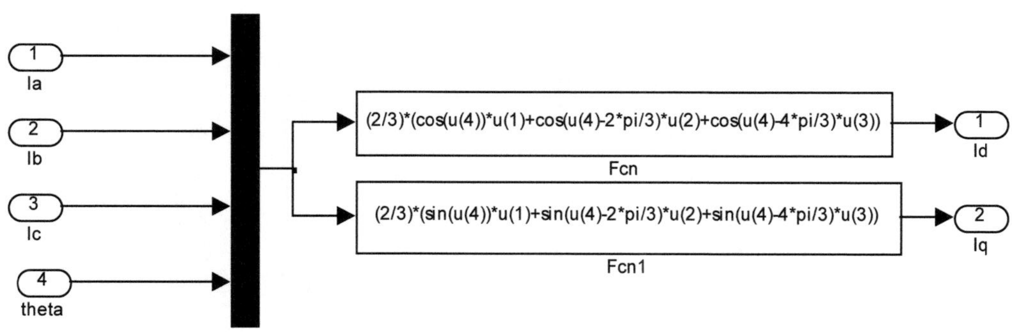

Fig. 10. Iabc to Idq bloc

The inverter is implemented in Simulink as shown in figure 12. The inverter consists of the "universal bridge" with the parameters of the IGBT module studied. All the voltages and the currents in the motor and the inverter can be deducted. The following figure shows the model of the inverter used.
For proper control of the inverter using the reference currents, current controllers are implemented generate the gate pulses for the IGBT's. Current controllers used are shown in figure 13 and 14.

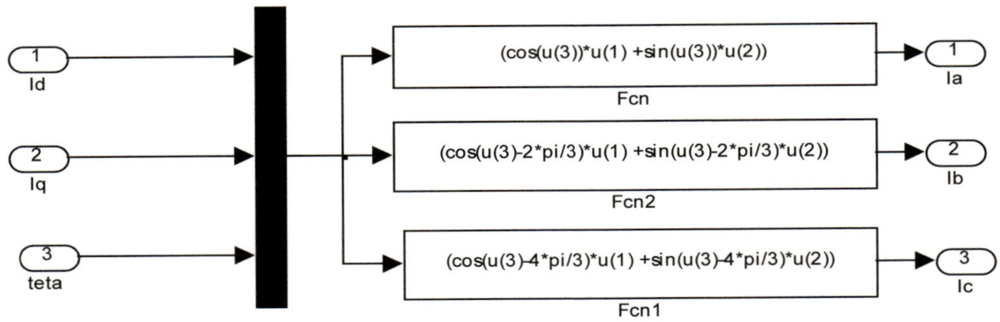

Fig. 11. Idq to Iabc bloc

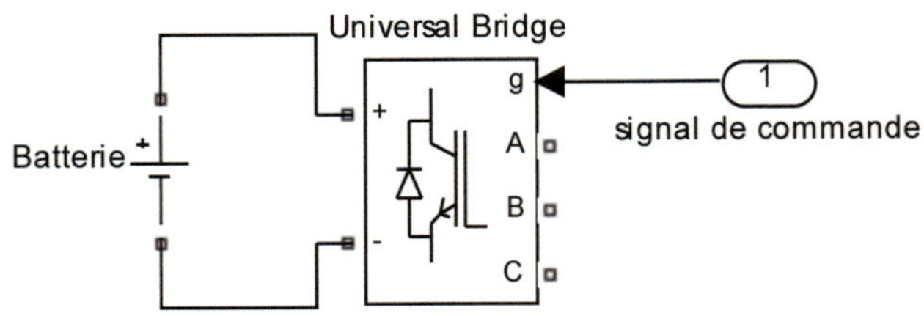

Fig. 12. Inverter model

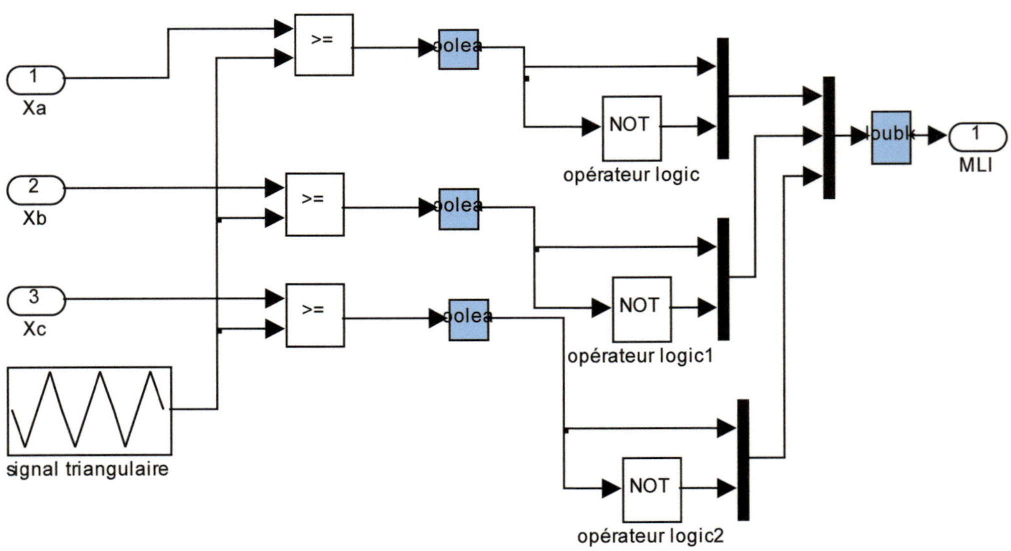

Fig. 13. PWM current controller

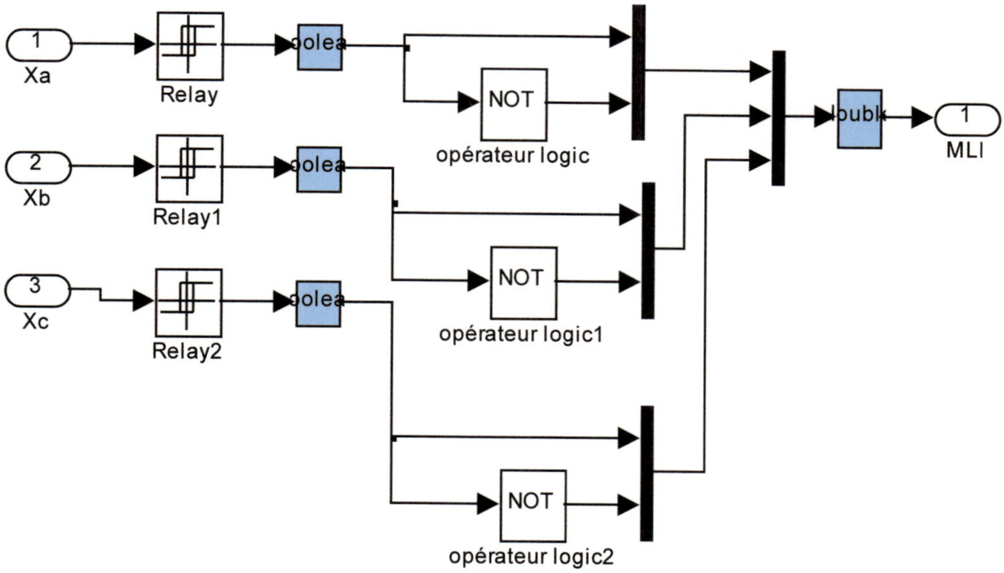

Fig. 14. Hysteresis controller

The complete system used for simulation and implemented in MATLAB / Simulink, is shown in Figure 15. This system was tested with two current controls, hysteresis and PWM control. The motor used is an axial flux Permanent Magnet Synchronous Motor (PMSM). For the simulation, we controlled the speed of EV at 30km / h.

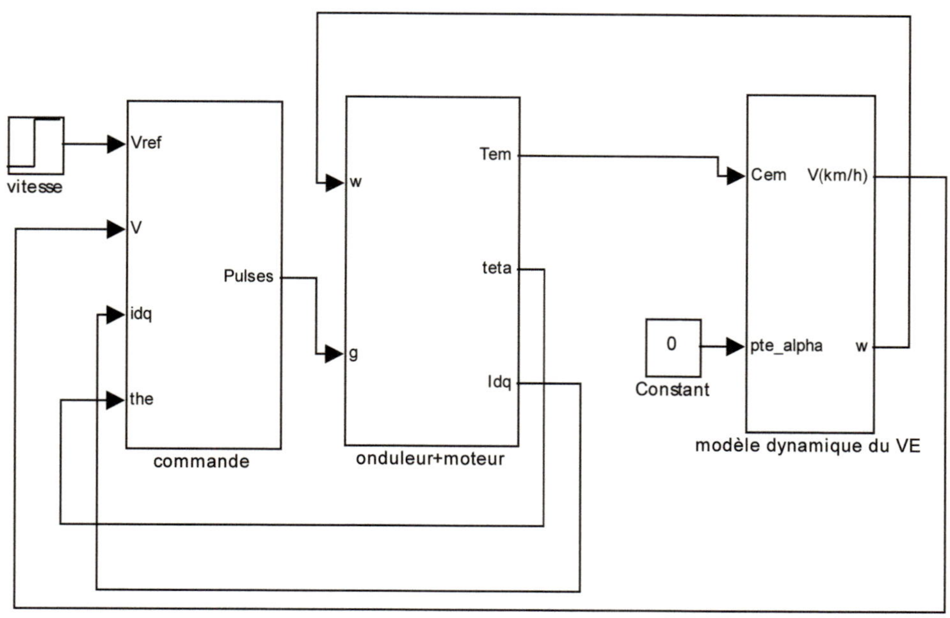

Fig. 15. PMSM in a traction chain

Figure 16 shows the EV speed regulated at 30km / h for the two types of control. We note that with the hysteresis control, we reach faster the steady state.

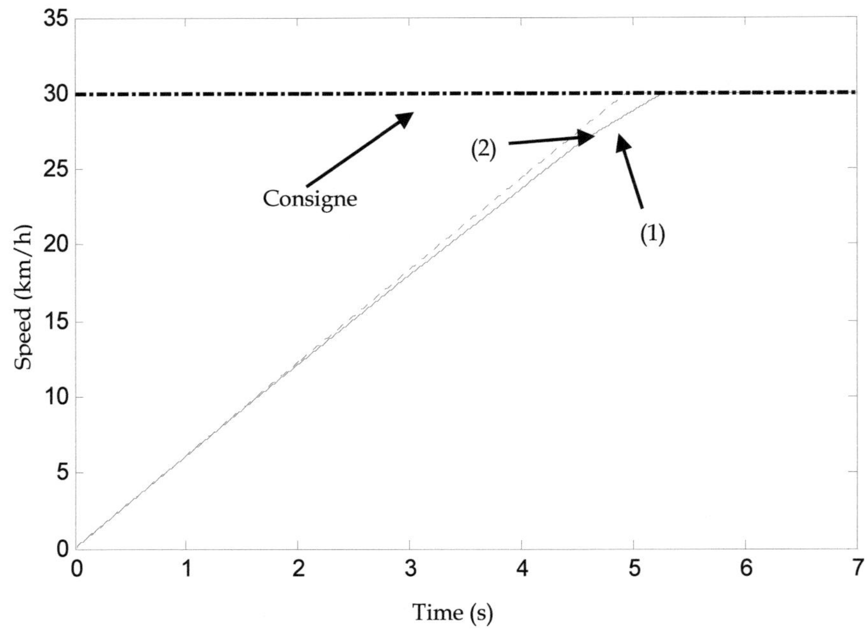

Fig. 16. EV speed; (1): with PWM controller; (2): with hysteresis controller

The stator phase currents corresponding to this regulation are represented by figure 17 and 18 Figure 19 and 20 show the IGBT1 and DIODE1 power losses for hysteresis and PWM current control respectively.

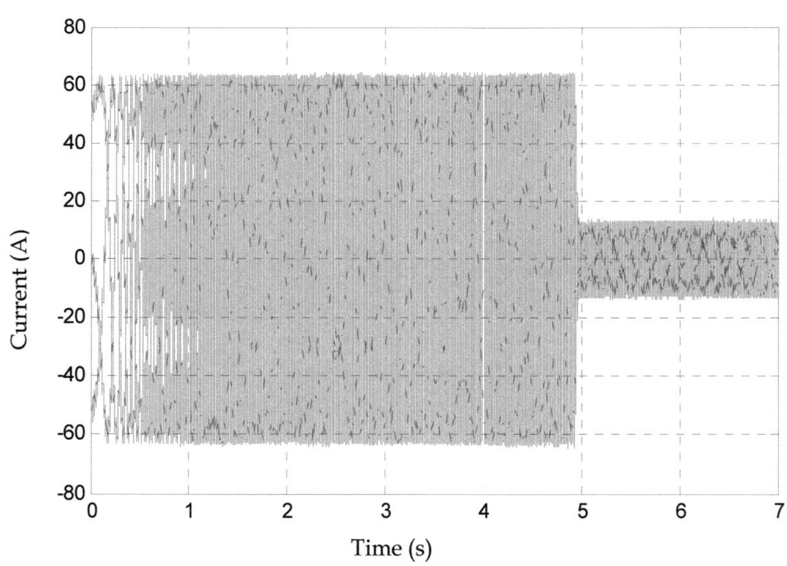

Fig. 17. Iabc currents with hysteresis control

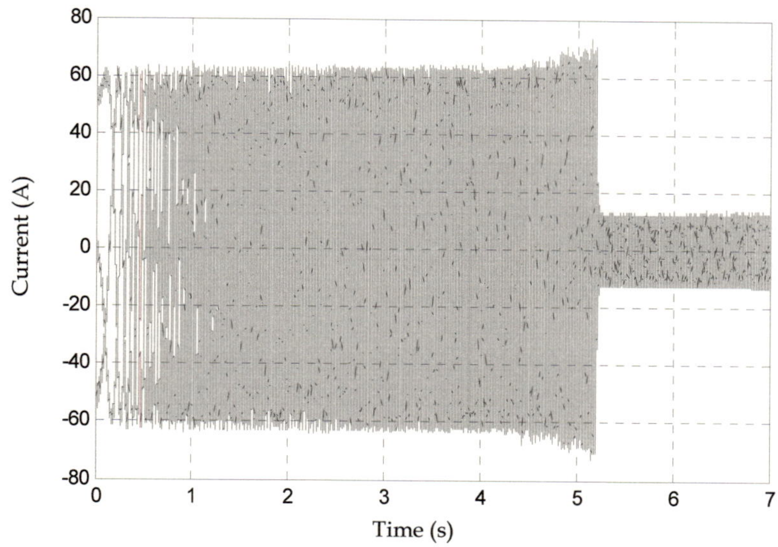

Fig. 18. Iabc currents with PWM control

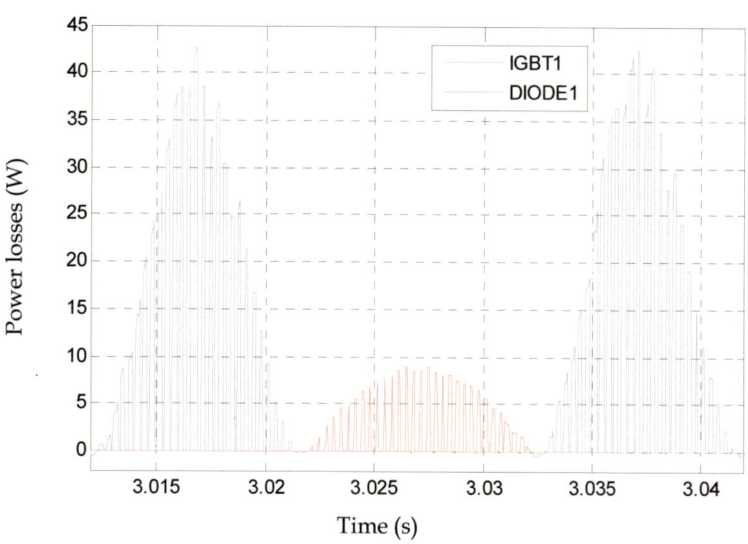

Fig. 19. IGBT1 and DIODE1 power losses with PWM control

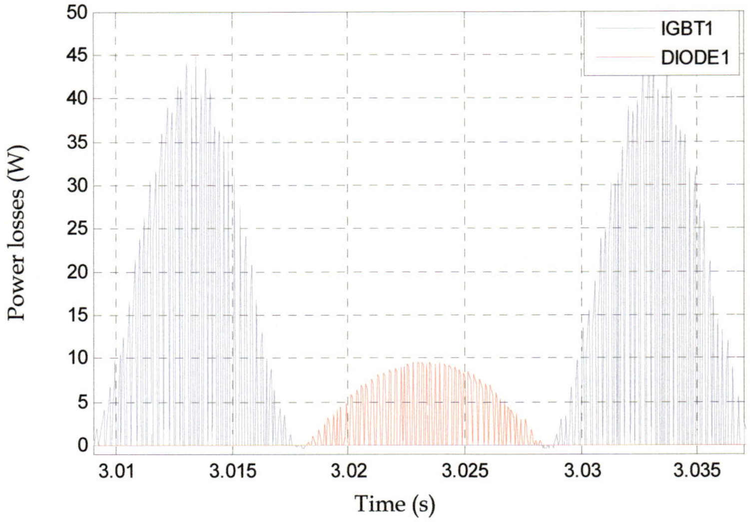

Fig. 20. IGBT1 and DIODE1 power losses with hysteresis control

Figure 21 and 22 show the IGBT1and DIODE1 junction temperature obtained by the two types of current control. It is very clear that the junction temperature of IGBT1 and DIODE1 is higher for the hysteresis control; this is due by the increase of power dissipation of the module components this type of control.

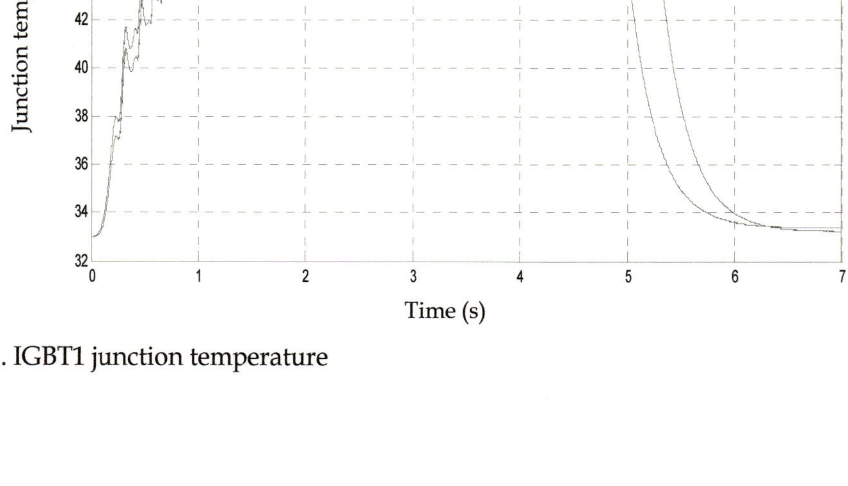

Fig. 21. IGBT1 junction temperature

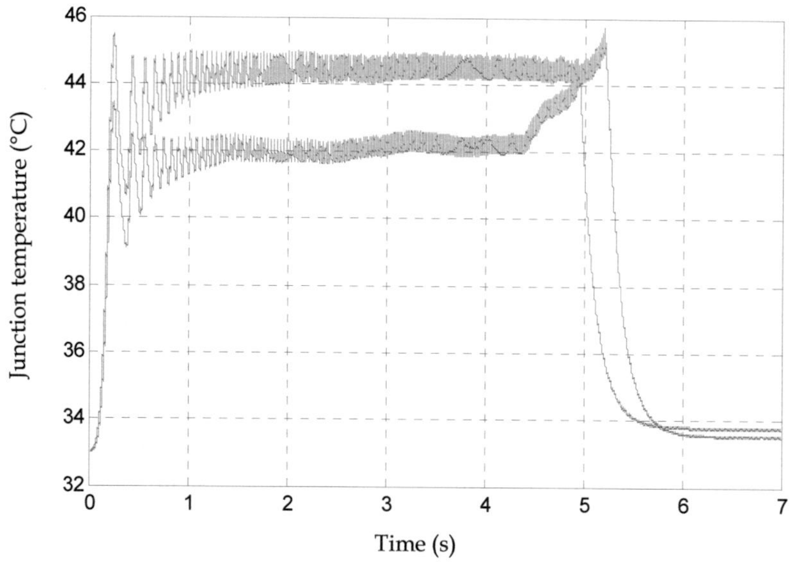

Fig. 22. DIODE1 junction temperature

6. Conclusion

A detailed dynamic model for EV was studied using two current control systems. MATLAB / Simulink were chosen from several simulation tools because of its flexibility in working with analog and digital devices, it is able to represent real-time results with the simulation time reduced. A comparative study was carried out in terms of switching frequency for power dissipated by the components of the inverter and junction temperature. The hysteresis current control has a variable switching frequency that depends on the hysteresis band, this type of control allows for fast simulations with a shorter time. The PWM current control has a fixed frequency switching and allows having junction temperatures lower than the hysteresis control.

7. References

B. K. Bose, Power Electronics and Variable Frequency Drives. (1996). 1 ed: Wiley, John & Sons

P. Pillay & R. Krishnan. (1989). Modeling, simulation, and analysis of permanent-magnet motor drives. I. The permanent-magnet synchronous motor drive. *Industry Applications, IEEE Transactions on*, vol. 25, pp. 265-273

Jean-Marie Dorkel, Patrick Tounsi, & Philippe Leturcq. (1996). Three-Dimensional thermal Modeling Based on the Two-Port Network Theory for Hybrid or Monolithic Integrated Power Circuits. IEEE Transaction on Electronics Devices, vol. 19, NO. 4, pp. 501-507

Uta Hecht & Uwe Scheuermann. (2000). Static and Transient Thermal Resistance of Advanced Power Modules. *Semikron Elektronik GmbH*, Sigmundstr. 200, 90431 Nürnberg (Germany).

Thomas Stockmeier. (2000). Power semiconductor packaging-a problem or a resource? From the state of the art to future trends. *Semikron Elektronik GmbH*, Sigmundstr. 2000, 90431 Nürnberg (Germany)

M. Ayadi, M.A. Fakhfakh, M. Ghariani, & R. Neji. (2010). Electrothermal modeling of hybrid power modules. *Emerald, Microelectronics International (MI)*, volume 27, issue 3, 2010, pp. 170-177

M.A. Fakhfakh, M. Ayadi, and R. Neji. Thermal behavior of a three phase inverter for EV (Electric Vehicle). *in Proc of 15th IEEE Mediterranean Electromechanical Conference (MELECON'10)*, Valletta, Malta, April 25-28, 2010, C4P-E24-3465, pp.1494-1498.

Kojima, et al. Novel Electro-thermal Coupling Simulation Technique for Dynamic Analysis of HV (Hybrid Vehicle) Inverter. *Proceedings of PESCO6*, pp. 2048-2052, 2006.

Hamada. Novel Electro-Thermal Coupling Simulation Technique for Dynamic Analysis of HV (Hybrid Vehicle) Inverter," Proc. of 7thIEEE Power Electronics Specialists Conference (PESC 2006), pp.2048-2052, 2006

U. Drofenik & J. Kolar. (2005). A Thermal Model of a Forced-Cooled Heat Sink for Transient Temperature Calculations Employing a Circuit Simulator. *Proceedings of IPECNiigata* 2005, pp. 1169-1177, 2005

M. Usui, M. Ishiko, "Simple Approach of Heat Dissipation Design for Inverter Module," Proc. of International Power Electronics Conference (IPEC 2005), pp. 1598-1603, 2005.

C. M. Ong. (1998). Dynamic simulation of electric machinery using MATLAB/Simulink.

H. Roisse, M. Hecquet, P. Brochet. (1998). Simulation of synchronous machines using a electric-magnetic coupled network model. IEEE Trans. on Magneticss, vol.34, pp.3656-3659, 1998.

Part 6

Robot Applications

20

Design and Simulation of Legged Walking Robots in MATLAB® Environment

Conghui Liang, Marco Ceccarelli and Giuseppe Carbone
LARM: Laboratory of Robotics and Mechatronics, University of Cassino
Italy

1. Introduction

It is well known that legged locomotion is more efficient, speedy, and versatile than the one by track and wheeled vehicles when it operates in a rough terrain or in unconstructed environment. The potential advantages of legged locomotion can be indicated such as better mobility, obstacles overcoming ability, active suspension, energy efficiency, and achievable speed (Song & Waldron, 1989). Legged walking robots have found wide application areas such as in military tasks, inspection of nuclear power plants, surveillance, planetary explorations, and in forestry and agricultural tasks (Carbone & Ceccarelli, 2005; González et al., 2006; Kajita & Espiau, 2008).

In the past decades, an extensive research has been focused on legged walking robots. A lot of prototypes such as biped robots, quadrupeds, hexapods, and multi-legged walking robots have been built in academic laboratories and companies (Kajita & Espiau, 2008). Significant examples can be indicated as ASIMO (Sakagami et al., 2002), Bigdog (Raibert, 2008), Rhex (Buehler, 2002), and ATHLETE (Wilcox et al., 2007). However, it is still far away to anticipate that legged walking robots can work in a complex environment and accomplish different tasks successfully. Mechanical design, dynamical walking control, walking pattern generation, and motion planning are still challenge problems for developing a reliable legged walking robot, which can operate in different terrains and environments with speedy, efficient, and versatility features.

Mechanism design, analysis, and optimization, as well as kinematic and dynamic simulation of legged walking robots are important issues for building an efficient, robust, and reliable legged walking robot. In particular, leg mechanism is a crucial part of a legged walking robot. A leg mechanism will not only determine the DOF (degree of freedom) of a robot, but also actuation system efficiency and its control strategy. Additionally, it is well understood that a torso plays an important role during animal and human movements. Thus, the aforementioned two aspects must be taken into account at the same time for developing legged walking robots.

Computer aided design and simulation can be considered useful for developing legged walking robots. Several commercial simulation software packages are available for performing modeling, kinematic, and dynamic simulation of legged walking robots. In particular, Matlab® is a widely used software package. It integrates computation, visualization, and programming in an easy-to-use environment where problems and solutions are expressed in familiar mathematical notation. By using a flexible programming environment, embedded functions, and several useful simulink® toolboxes, it is relative easy and fast to perform kinematic and dynamic analysis of a robotic mechanical system (Matlab manual, 2007). Additionally, motion control and task planning algorithms can be tested for a proposed mechanism design before implementing them on a prototype.

In this chapter, the applications of Matlab® tool for design and simulation of legged walking robots are illustrated through three cases, namely a single DOF biped walking robot with Chebyshev-Pantograph leg mechanisms (Liang et al., 2008); a novel biologically inspired tripod walking robot (Liang et al., 2009 & 2011); a new waist-trunk system for biped humanoid robots (Carbone et al., 2009; Liang et al., 2010; Liang & Ceccarelli, 2010). In details, the content of each section are organized as follows.

In the first section, operation analysis of a Chebyshev-Pantograph leg mechanism is presented for a single DOF biped robot. The proposed leg mechanism is composed of a Chebyshev four-bar linkage and a pantograph mechanism. Kinematic equations of the proposed leg mechanism are formulated and programmed in Matlab® environment for a computer oriented simulation. Simulation results show the operation performance of the proposed leg mechanism with suitable characteristics. A parametric study has been carried out to with the aims to evaluate the operation performance as function of design parameters and to achieve an optimal design solution.

In the second section, a novel tripod walking robot is presented as inspired by tripod gaits existing in nature. The mechanical design problem is investigated by considering the peculiar requirements of leg mechanism to have a proper tripod walking gait. The proposed tripod walking robot is composed of three leg mechanisms with linkage architecture. The proposed leg mechanism is modeled for kinematic analysis and equations are formulated for simulation. A program has been developed in Matlab® environment to study the operation performance of the leg mechanism and to evaluate the feasibility of the tripod walking gaits. Simulation results show operation characteristics of the leg mechanism and feasible walking ability of the proposed tripod walking robot.

In the third section, a new torso design solution named waist-trunk system has been proposed for biped humanoid robots. The proposed waist-trunk system is composed of a six DOFs parallel manipulator and a three DOFs orientation parallel manipulator, which are connected in a serial chain architecture. In contrast to the traditional torso design solutions, the proposed new waist-trunk system has a high number of DOFs, great motion versatility, high payload capability, good stiffness, and easy-operation design features. A 3D model has been built in Matlab® environment by using its Virtual Reality (VR) toolbox. Kinematic simulations have been carried out for two operation modes, namely walking mode and manipulation mode. Operation performances have been evaluated in terms of displacements, velocities, and accelerations. Simulation results show that the simulated waist-trunk system can be very convenient designed as the torso part for humanoid robots.

2. A single DOF biped robot

A suvery of existing biped robots shows that most of their leg mechanisms are built with an anthropomorphic architecture with three actuating motors at least at the hip, knee, and ankle joints. These kinds of leg mechanisms have an anthropomorphic design, and therefore they show anthropomorphic flexible motion However, mechanical design of these kinds of leg systems is very complex and difficult. Additionally, sophisticated control algorithms and electronics hardware are needed for the motion control. Therefore, it is very difficult and costy to build properly a biped robot with such kinds of leg mechanisms.

A different methodology can be considered such as constructing a biped robot with reduced number of DOFs and compact mechanical design. At LARM, Laboratory of Robotics and Mechatronics in the University of Cassino, a research line is dedicated to low-cost easy-operation leg mechanism design. Fig. 1 shows a prototype of a single DOF biped robot fixed on a supporting test bed. It consists of two leg mechanisms with a Chebyshev-Pantograph linkage architecture.The leg mechanisms are connected to the body with simple revolute joints and they are actuated by only one DC motor through a gear box. The actuated crank angles of the two leg mechanisms are 180 degrees synchronized. Therefore, when one leg mechanism is in non-propelling phase another leg mechanism is in propelling phase and vice versa. A big U shaped foot is connected at the end of each leg mechanism with a revolute joint equipped with a torsion spring. The torsion spring makes the foot contact with the ground properly so that it has adaptability to rough terrain and the walking stability of the biped robot is improved.

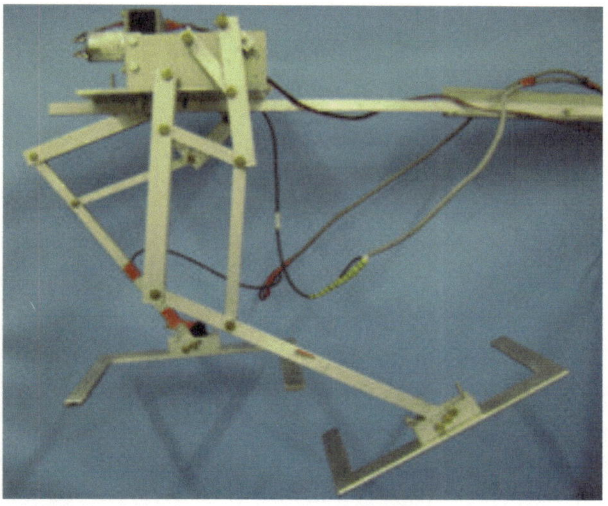

Fig. 1. A prototype of a single DOF biped robot with two Chebyshev-Pantograph leg mechanisms at LARM

2.1 Mechanism description

The built prototype in Fig. 1 consists of two single DOF leg mechanisms, which is composed of a Chebyshev four-bar linkage LEDCB and a pantograph mechanism PGBHIA, as shown in Fig. 2. The Chebyshev mechanism LEDCB can generate an ovoid curve for the point B, so that the leg mechanism can perform a rear-forth and up-down motion in sagittal plane with only one actuation motor. In Fig. 2, the crank is LE, the rocker is link CD, and the coupler triangle is EDB. Joints at L, C, and P are fixed on the body of the biped robot. The offsets a, p, and h between them will greatly influence the trajectory shape of point A. The pantograph mechanism PGBHIA is used to amplify the input trajectory of point B into output trajectory with the same shape at point A. In particularly, unlike the traditional design solution, the point P is fixed on the body of the robot instead of the point B in order to have a more compact robust design. However, drawbacks will exist and in this work the aim is to maintain them within certain limits. The amplify ratio of the pantograph mechanism depends on the length of link HI and link IA or the ratio of PA and PB.

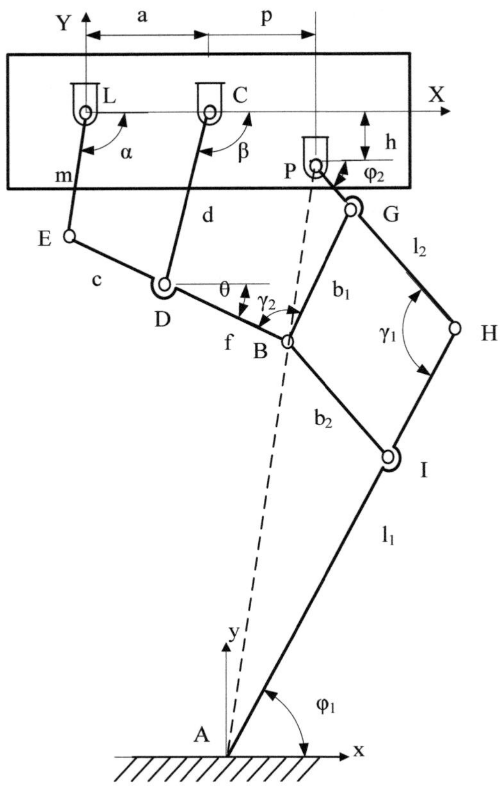

Fig. 2. A kinematic scheme of the single DOF Chebyshev-Pantograph leg mechanism

2.2 A kinematic analysis

A kinematic analysis has been carried out in order to evaluate the operation performance of the single DOF leg mechanism by using Matlab® programming. Actually, the pantograph mechanism amplifies the input motion that is produced by the Chebyshev linkage, as well as parameters p and h affect location and shape of the generated ovoid curve. A kinematic study can be carried out separately for the Chebyshev linkage and pantograph mechanism.

A scheme of the Chebyshev four-bar linkage LEDCB with design parameters is shown in Fig. 2. When the crank LE rotates around the point L an output ovoid curve can be traced by point B. Assuming a reference frame XY fixed at point L with X axis laying along in the direction of straight line LC, it is possible to formulate the coordinates of point B as a function of input crank angle α in the form, (Ottaviano et al., 2004),

$$x_B = m\cos\alpha + (c+f)\cos\theta$$

$$y_B = -m\sin\alpha - (c+f)\sin\theta \quad (1)$$

where

$$\theta = 2\tan^{-1}\left(\frac{\sin\alpha - (\sin^2\alpha + B^2 - D^2)^{1/2}}{B+D}\right) \quad (2)$$

and

$$B = \cos\alpha - \frac{a}{m} \tag{3}$$

$$C = \frac{a^2 + m^2 - c^2 + d^2}{2\,m\,d} - \frac{a}{d}\cos\alpha$$

$$D = \frac{a}{c}\cos\alpha - \frac{a^2 + m^2 - c^2 + d^2}{2\,m\,c}$$

The five design parameters a, m, c, d, and f characterize the Chebyshev four-bar linkage, which have a fixed ration with each other as reported in (Artobolevsky, 1979). A numerical simulation can be carried out by using Eqs. (1), (2), and (3) with proper value of the design parameters.

The pantograph mechanism PGBHIA with design parameters is shown in Fig. 2. The point P is fixed and point B is connected to the output motion that is obtained by the Chebyshev four-bar linkage. The transmission angles γ_1 and γ_2 are important parameters for mechanism efficiency. A good performance can be ensured when $|\gamma_i - 90^\circ| < 40^\circ$ (i=1, 2) according to practice rules for linkages as reported in (Hartenberg and Denavit, 1964).

Referring to the scheme in Fig. 2, kinematic equations of the pantograph mechanism can be formulated after some algebraic manipulation in the form, (Ottaviano et al., 2004),

$$\varphi_1 = 2\tan^{-1}\frac{1-\sqrt{1+k_1^2-k_2^2}}{k_1-k_2}$$

$$\varphi_2 = 2\tan^{-1}\frac{1-\sqrt{1+k_2^2-k_4^2}}{k_3-k_4} \tag{4}$$

with

$$k_1 = \frac{x_B - p}{y_B - h}$$

$$k_2 = \frac{b_1^2 + y_B^2 + x_B^2 - (l_2 - b_2)^2 + p^2 + h^2 - 2px_B - 2hy_B}{2b_1(y_B - h)}$$

$$k_3 = \frac{p - x_B}{y_B - h}$$

$$k_4 = \frac{-b_1^2 + y_B^2 + x_B^2 + (l_2 - b_2)^2 + p^2 + h^2 - 2px_B - 2hy_B}{2(l_2 - b_2)(y_B - h)} \tag{5}$$

Consequently, from Fig. 2 transmission angles γ_1 and γ_2 can be evaluated as $\gamma_1=\varphi_1+\varphi_2$ and $\gamma_2=\pi-\theta-\varphi_1$, respectively. The coordinates of point A can be given as

$$x_A = x_B + b_2\cos\varphi_2 - (l_1 - b_1)\cos\varphi_1$$

$$y_A = y_B - b_2\sin\varphi_2 - (l_1 - b_1)\sin\varphi_1 \qquad (6)$$

By using Eqs. (4), the transmission angles γ_1 and γ_2 can be computed to check the practical feasibility of the proposed mechanism. By derivating Eqs. (6), the motion velocities of point A can be easilty computed. Accelerations can be also computed through a futher derivative of the obbtained equations of velocities. Similarly, the velocities and accelerations at point B can be computed through the first and second derivatives of Eqs. (1), respectively.
By using velocity and acceleration analysis for the generated ovoid curve, kinematic performance of the proposed leg mechanism can be evaluated.

2.3 Simulation results

A simulation program has been developed in Matlab® environment to study kinematic performance of the proposed leg mechanism, as well as the feasible walking ability of the single DOF biped robot. The elaborated code in m files are included in the CD of this book. Design parameters of the simulated leg mechanism are listed in Table 1.

a	b	c	d	h	m
50	20	62.5	62.5	30	25
f	p	l_1	l_2	b_1	b_2
62.5	30	300	200	75	150

Table 1. Design parameters of a prototype leg mechanism at LARM with structure of Fig. 2 (sizes are in mm)

Examples of simulation results of one leg mechanism are shown in Fig. 3. When the input crank LE rotates around point L with a constant speed, the motion trajectories of point A and point B can be obtained in the form of ovoid curves. A scheme of the zoomed view of the ovoid curve in Fig. 3(a) is shown in Fig. 3(b) in which four characteristic angles of the input crank actuation are indicated. The dimension of the ovoid curve is characterized by the length L and height H. The generated ovoid curve is composed of an approximate straight-line and a curved segment with a symmetrical shape. The straight-line segment starts at the actuation angle α=90 degs and ends at α=270 degs. Actually, during this 180 degs interval the leg mechanism is in the non-propelling phase and it swings from rear to forth. During the next 180 degs interval the actuation angle goes from α=270 degs to α=90 degs corresponding to the coupler curve segment. In this period, the foot grasps the ground and the leg mechanism is in the propelling phase. The leg mechanism is in a almost stretched configuration when α=0 deg just as the leg scheme shows in Fig. 3(a).
Fig. 4 shows simulation results of the biped robot when it walks on the ground. In Fig. 4, the right leg is indicated with solid line when in contact with the ground and the crank actuation angle is at α=0 deg, the left leg is indicated with dashed line when the crank is at angle α=180 degs and it swings from rear to forth. The trajectories of points A and point B are also plotted as related to the non-propelling phase. It is noted that at the beginning and the end of the trajectory, the density of the points is higher than in the middle segment. Since the time periods are same between each plotted points, the velocity of the swinging leg mechanism in the middle is higher than that at the start and end of one step.

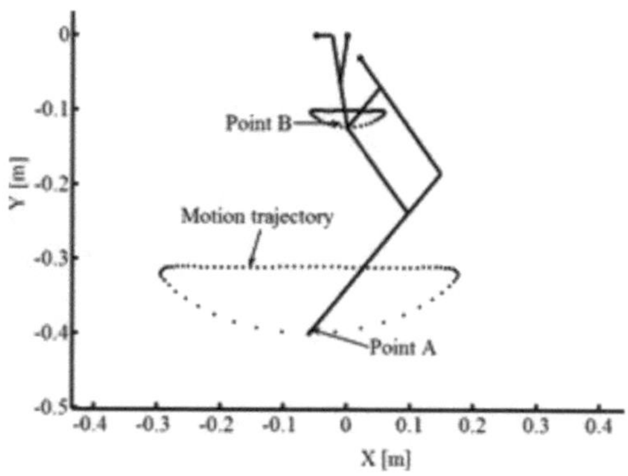

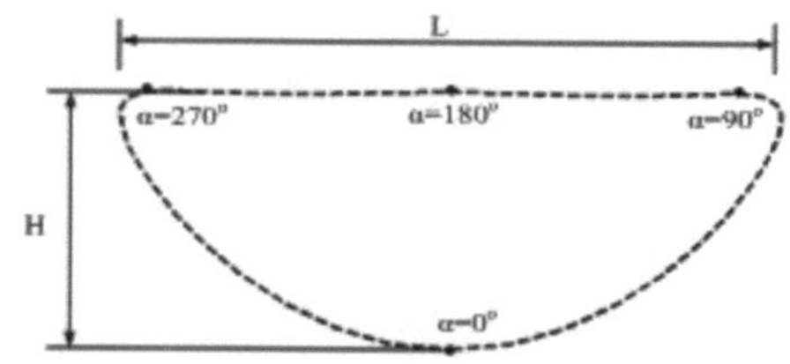

(a) (b)

Fig. 3. Simulation results of one leg mechanism: (a) computed trajectories of points A and B; (b) generated ovoid curve at point A

A scheme of the biped motion and trajectories of critical points are shown in Fig. 5(a). Referring to Fig. 5(a), when the leg mechanism is in a non-propelling phase, it swings from rear to forth and the supporting leg propels the body forward. The swinging leg mechanism has a relative swing motion with respect to the supporting leg mechanism. Therefore, the velocity of point B1 in a non-propelling phase with respect to the global inertial frame is larger than that during a supporting phase. This is the reason why the size of curve a-b-c is larger than that the size of curve c-d-e in Fig. 5(b) even if the Chebyshev mechanisms produce the motion with only 180 degs phase differences at the points B1 and B2.

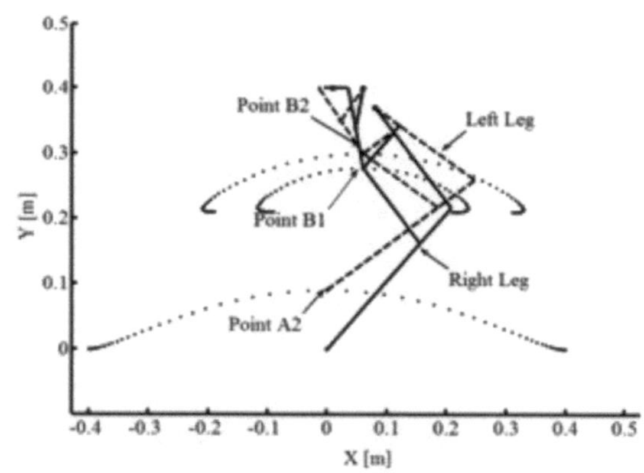

Fig. 4. Simulation results for motion trajectories of the leg mechanisms during biped walking

Fig. 5(b) shows the trajectories of points A1, A2, B1, and B2 in a biped walking gait. The trajectories are plotted with solid lines for the right leg mechanism and with dashed lines for the left leg mechanism, respectively. The motion sequences of points B1 and A1 are indicated with alphabet letters from a to e and a' to e', respectively. In Fig. 5(b), the trajectory segments a-b-c of point B1 and a'-b'-c' of point A1 are produced by the right leg mechanism while it swings from rear to forth. The trajectory segments c-d-e are produced while the right leg is in contact with the ground. Correspondingly, c', d', and e' are at the same point. The trajectories of points A2 and B2 for left leg mechanism are similar but have 180 degs differences with respect to the right leg mechanism. There are small circles in the trajectories of point B1 and point B2 during the transition of the two walking phases. This happens because there is a short period of time during which both legs are in contact with the ground and a sliding back motion occus for the body motion of the biped robot.

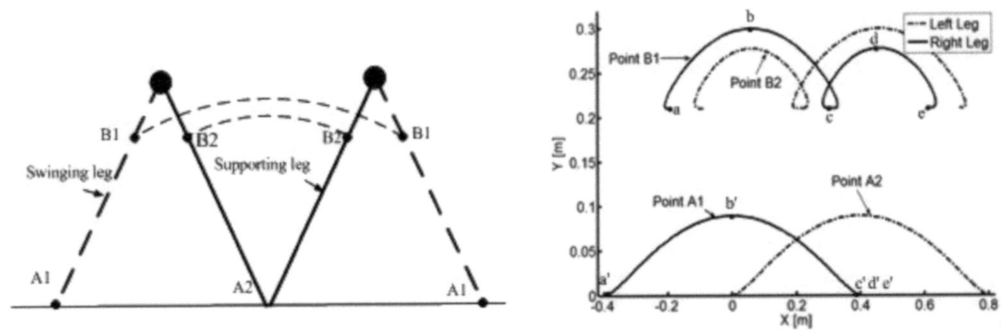

(a) (b)

Fig. 5. Simulation results of biped walking: (a) motion trajectories of the leg mechanisms; (b) a characterization of the computed trajectories of points A1, A2, B1, and B2

Fig. 6(a) shows plots of the computed transmission angles γ_1 and γ_2 of the right leg mechanisms as function of the input crank angles α_1. The value of the transmission angles are computed between 50 degs and 120 degs. The transmission angles for left leg mechanism have 180 degs time differences. Therefore, the proposed leg mechanism has an efficient motion transmission capability. Fig. 6(b) shows the computed plots for angles φ_1 and φ_2 of the right leg mechanism. The value of φ_1 is between 18 degs and 100 degs as a good contact with the ground. The value of φ_2 is between -5 degs and 100 degs and there is no confliction between the legs and body.

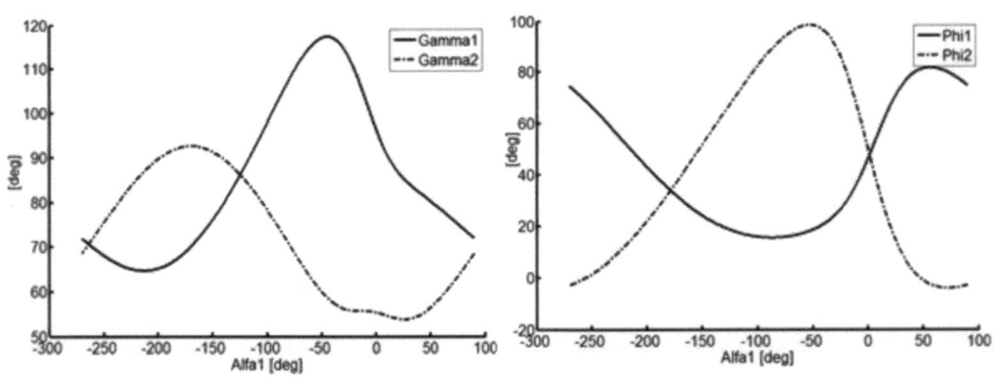

(a) (b)

Fig. 6. Characterization angles of the right leg mechanism as function of angle α_1: (a) angles γ_1 and γ_2; (b) angles φ_1 and φ_2

The acceleration of point A is computed by using kinematics equations, which are computed in Matlab® m files. Fig. 7(a) shows the computed acceleration values of point A along X axis and Y axis, respectively. Similarly, Fig. 7(b) shows the accelerations of point P on the body of the biped robot.

In Fig. 7(a), the acceleration of point A at the end of leg mechanism is computed between -1 ms^2 to 10 m/s^2 along X axis and between -10.5 m/s^2 to -3.5 m/s^2 along Y axis. The acceleration along X axis reaches the maximum value when the input crank angle is at t=0.5 s (α=20 degs) and the minimum value when it is at t=7.3 s (α=325 degs).

In Fig. 7(b), the acceleration at point P is computed between -2.3 m/s^2 to 9 m/s^2 along X axis and between -10.2 m/s^2 to -0.2 m/s^2 along Y axis. The acceleration in X axis reaches the maximum value when one leg mechanism is in the middle of supporting phase and acceleration in Y axis reaches the minimum value, correspondingly. The acceleration in X axis reaches the minimum value during the transition phase of leg mechanisms and the negative value shows that the biped robot in a double supporting phase and produces a back sliding motion.

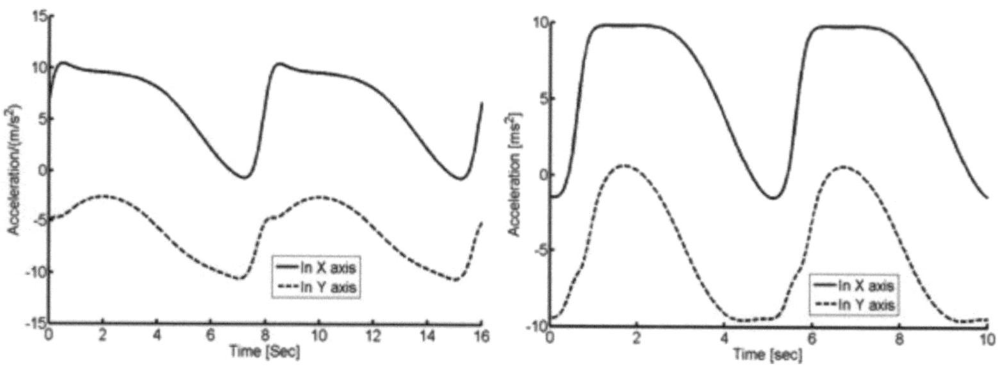

(a) (b)

Fig. 7. Computed accelerations during one biped walking gait: (a) accelerations of point A in X and Y axes; (b) accelerations of point P in X and Y axes

An optimal design of the leg mechanism can perform an efficient and practical feasible walking gait. By using the flexibility of Matlab® environment with the elaborated simulation codes. A parametric study has been proposed to characterize the operation performance of the proposed single DOF biped robot as function of its design parameters. Actually, the lengths of the linkages determine a proper shape and size of the generated ovoid curve that is produced by the Chebyshev linkage through an amplification ration of the pantograph mechanism as shown in Fig. 2. Therefore, only three parameters a, p, and h can be considered as significant design variables. In Fig. 8, results of the parametric study are plotted as function of parameter a as output of Matlab® m files.

By increasing the value of parameter a, size of the ovoid curve is decreased in X axis and is increased in Y axis as shown in Fig. 8(a). Particularly, the ovoid curve with an approximately straight line segment is obtained when a=0.05 m. Fig. 8(b) shows the corresponding trajectories of COG (center of gravity) and the feet of swinging leg when the other leg mechanism is in contact with the ground. The step length L decreases and step height H increases as function of the value of parameter a, as shown in Fig. 8(b).

In Fig. 9, results of parametric study are plotted as function of parameter p. In Fig. 9(a), by varying parameter p the ovoid curve generated at point A has only displacements along X

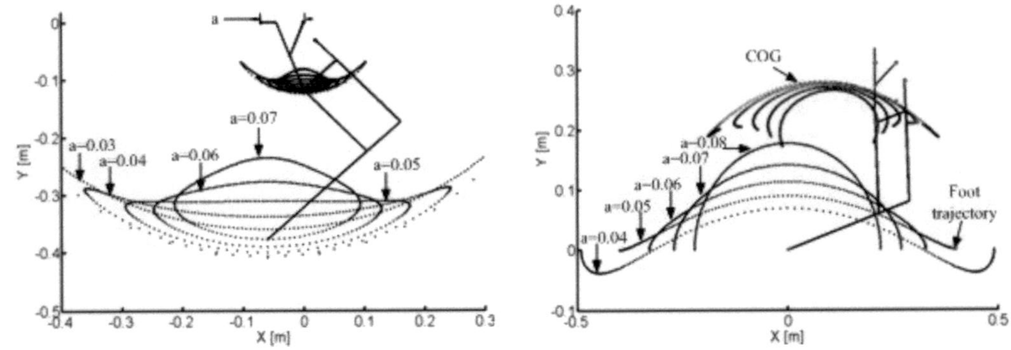

(a) (b)

Fig. 8. A parametric study of the leg mechanism as function of parameter a in Fig. 2: (a) generated ovoid curves at point A; (b) trajectories of COG and foot trajectories of the swinging leg

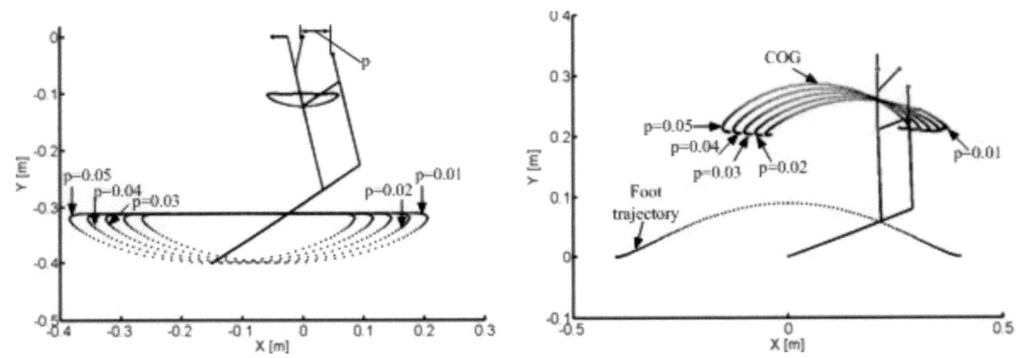

(a) (b)

Fig. 9. A parametric study of the biped robot as function of parameter p in Fig. 2: (a) generated ovoid curves at point A; (b) trajectories of COG and foot point of swinging leg

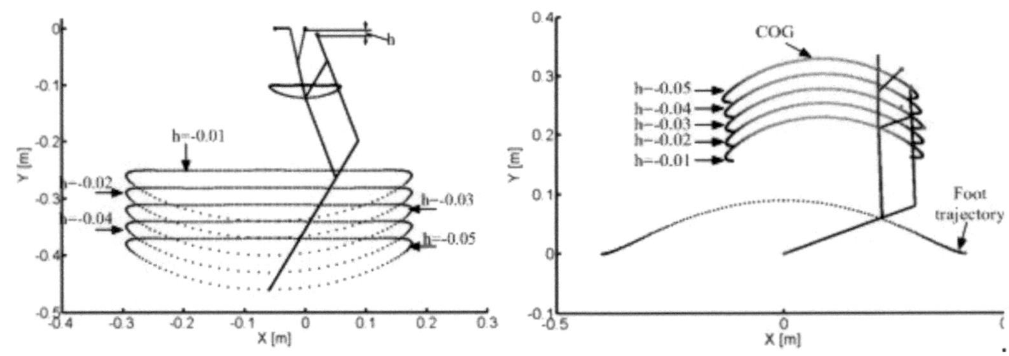

(a) (b)

Fig. 10. A parametric study of the biped robot as function of parameter h in Fig. 2: (a) generated ovoid curves at point A; (b) trajectories of COG and foot point of swinging leg

without change of the step length L and step height H. The COG of the biped robot has corresponding displacements along X axis. Similarly, by varying parameter h, the COG of the biped robot has displacements along Y axis as shown in Fig. 10.
Therefore, the position of point P determines the location of the ovoid curve without any shape change. Correspondingly, the location of COG of the biped robot can be as function of the position of point P since the mass center of the leg mechanism varies correspondingly.
The parametric study have analyzed the shape of the generated ovoid curve as function of three parameters a, p, and h. The parametric study whose main results are shown in Fig. 8, 9, and 10 has been aimed to check the motion possibility and design sensitivity of the proposed leg mechanism. Interesting outputs of the parametric study can be considered in the following aspects:

- The kinematic behaviour in terms of point trajectories is robust and well suited to walking tasks.
- Variations of main design parameters do not affect considerably main characteristics of the walking operation.
- The size of the walking step can be modified by changing the parameter a only.
- The size of height of swinging leg motion can be modified by changing the parameter h only.

Therefore, an optimized mechanical design for leg mechanism and an efficient walking gait for minimizing input crank torque can be determined by selecting proper design parameters.

3. A biologically inspired tripod walking robot

Legged locomotion in walking robots is mainly inspired by nature. For example, biped robots mimic the human walking; quadruped robots perform leg motion like dogs or horses and eight legged robots are inspired to spider-like motion (Song & Waldron, 1989; González et al., 2006). Most of animals have an even number of legs with symmetry character. With this important character animals can move easily, quickly and stably. However, among legged walking robots, biped walking robots are the human-like solutions but sophisticated control algorithms are needed to keep balance during operation (Vukobratovic, 1989). Multi legged robots have a good stable walking performance and can operate with several walking gaits. However, the number of motors increases together with legs. How to coordinate control the motors and gaits synthesis are still difficult problems.
Actually, there are some tripod walking experiences in nature, even around our daily life. A significant example of tripod walking can be recognized in old men walking with a cane. Two human legs and a walking cane as a third leg can produce a special tripod walking gait. With this kind of tripod walking gait, old people with aged or illness nervous system can walk more stably since they always keep two legs in contact with the ground at the same time. Additionally, a standing phase is more stable since there are three legs on the ground and forms a rigid triangle configuration. By talking into account of the advantages of a tripod walking gait, a novel tripod walking robot has been proposed as shown in Fig. 11.
In Fig. 11, the tripod walking robot consists of three single DOF Chebyshev-Pantograph leg mechanisms, a body frame, and a balancing mechanism, which is mounted on the top of body frame. Three leg mechanisms are installed on the body frame in a triangle arrangement with one leg mechanism ahead and two leg mechanisms rear in the same line. The main specifications of the designed model are listed in Table. 2.

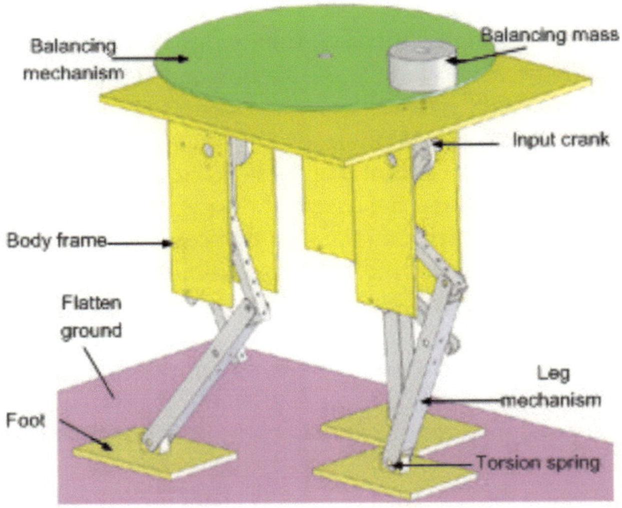

Fig. 11. A 3D model of the proposed tripod walking robot in SolidWorks® environment

Degrees of freedom	7 (3 for legs, 1 for balancing mechanism, 3 for passive ankle joints)
Weight	10 kg
Dimension	300×300×600 mm
Walking speed	0.36 km/h
Step size	300 mm/step
Walking cycle	1 sec/step

Table 2. Main specifications of the 3D model for the tripod walking robot in Fig. 11

The tripod walking robot is developed for payload transportation and manipulation purposes. The proposed design of the tripod walking robot will be capable of moving quickly with flexibility, and versatility within different environments. Therefore, in the mechanical design, particular attentions have been focused to make the tripod walking robot low-cost easy-operation, light weight, and compact. Particularly, commercial products have been extensively used in the designed model to make it easy to build. Aluminum alloy is selected as the material of the tripod walking robot since it has proper stiffness, mass density, and cheap price.

3.1 The proposed mechanical design

The mechanism design problem can be started by considering a concept of a tripod waking robot model as shown in Fig. 12(a). The scheme of the mechanism in Fig. 12(a) is a simplified structure with two DOFs that can perform a required back and forth, up and down movement in saggital plane. Actuation motors are fixed at the point C1, C2 and C3. Two feet grasp the ground at point A1 and point A2 while the third leg swings from back to forth. The two legs in contact with the ground together with the robot body form a parallel mechanism.

A scheme of the proposed leg mechanism for tripod walking robot is shown in Fig. 12(b). The tripod walking robot is mainly composed of three one-DOF leg mechanisms. The three leg mechanisms are the same design which is installed on the robot body to have a triangle configuration in horizontal plane. All the three legs are fixed on the body and actuated by DC motors. The leg mechanism is sketched with design parameters in Fig. 12(b).

The basic kinematics and operation characters of the proposed leg mechanism are investigated in the work (Liang et al., 2009). This one-DOF leg mechanism is composed of a Chebyshev four-bar linkage CLEDB and a pantograph mechanism BGMHIA. Points L, C and M are fixed on the body. The Chebyshev mechanism and pantograph mechanism are jointed together at point B through which the actuation force is transmitted from the Chebyshev linkage to the pantograph leg. Linkage LE is the crank and α is the input crank angle. The transmission angles γ_1 and γ_2 of the leg mechanism are shown in the Fig. 12(b).

When the crank LE rotates around point L, an ovoid curve with an approximate straight line segment and symmetry path as traced by foot point. Each straight line segment has a 180° phase in the crank rotation input. The straight line segment represents the supporting phase and the curve segment represents the swinging phase. When the leg mechanism operates in a supporting phase it generates a horizontal motion to points L, C and M which are fixed at the body. Therefore, the body of the robot is propelled forward without force conflict between two legs contacting the ground.

In a tripod walking gait each leg must has 2/3 period of time in supporting phase and another 1/3 time in swinging phase. In order to avoid the problem of force conflict between legs, a solution is that the two legs on the ground can produce a straight line motion in horizontal plane with the same speed and without waving in vertical direction. A careful analysis will help to define a propel operation of the leg mechanism.

A feasible solution requires that the actuation speed of the input crank is twice during swinging phase as compared with supporting phase. A_i (i=1, 2, 3) are the end points of three leg mechanisms. They trace the same ovoid curve but with 90°actuation phase differences in supporting phase. Therefore, there will be always two legs in contact with the ground and another leg swings in the air.

3.2 Simulation results

Simulations have been carried out in the Matlab® environment with suitable codes of the proposed formulation. The design parameters of the mechanisms for simulation are listed in Table.3. The rotation velocity of the input crank actuation angle is set at 270 degs/s. Each step lasts in 1/3 second for each leg, and numerical simulation has been computed for 2 seconds to evaluate a walking behavior in a stationary mode.

Chebyshev mechanism (mm)		Pantograph mechanism (mm)		Leg location (mm)
d=62.5	m=25	l_1=330	l_2=150	H_1=100
c=62.5	a=50	b_1=110	b_2=100	H_2=100
f=62.5	p=230	p=230	_	H_3=240

Table 3. Simulation parameters of the single DOF leg mechanism for the tripod walking robot

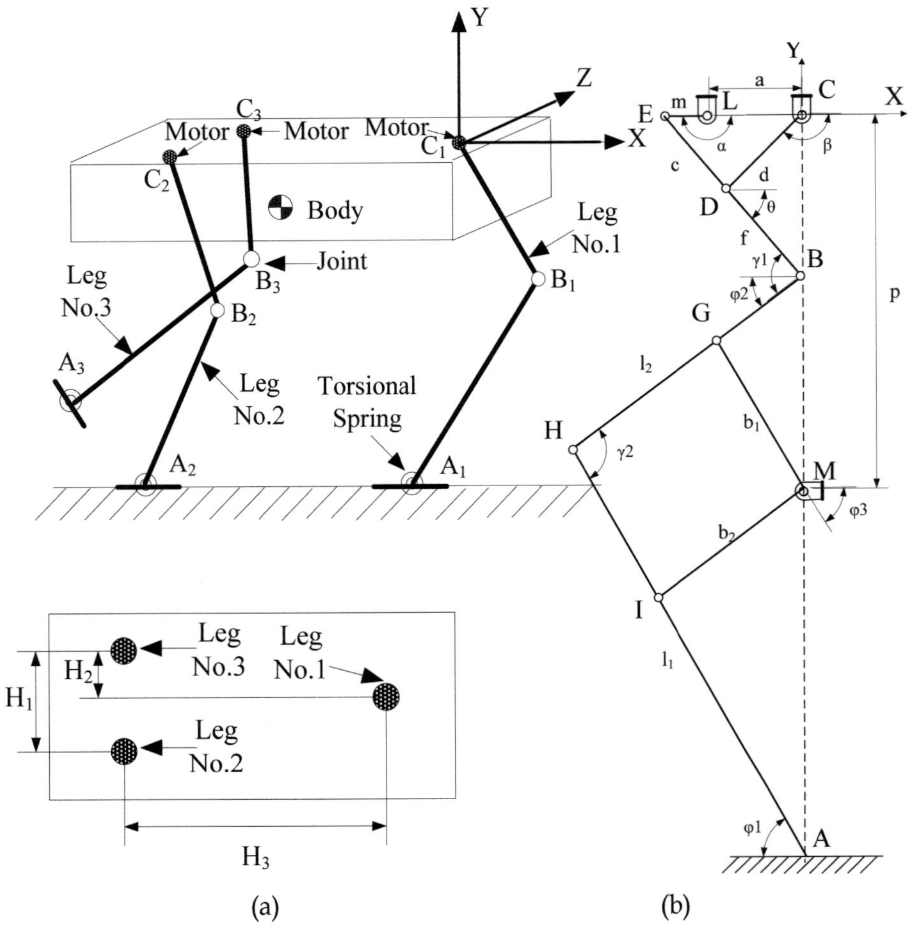

Fig. 12. The proposed tripod walking robot: (a) configurations of three leg mechanisms; (b) a scheme of one leg mechanism with design parameters

In Fig. 13, the tripod walking robot is given at initial configuration with the input crank angles α_1=180 degs, α_2=90 degs, and α_3=270 degs. At this initial time, the three legs are on the ground with two legs in supporting phase and the third leg is about to get into swinging phase.

In Fig. 14, a sequence of snapshots are shown for the tripod walking robot walks in three dimension space as computed in the numerical simulation. The trajectories of points A_i (i=1,2, 3) of the feet are depicted with small curves. In Fig. 15, the movements of the legs for tripod walking robot are shown in saggital plane. The positions of three feet are also shown in horizontal plane as referring to the computed snapshots.

As shown in Fig. 15, at each step, there are always two legs contacting the ground. Actually, a balancing mechanism can be installed on the body of the robot to adjust the gravity center between the two legs, which grasp the ground at each step. A simple rotation mechanism with a proper mass at end is likely to be installed on the body of robot as a balancing mechanism. Therefore, with a very simple control algorithm and specially sized balancing mechanism the tripod walking robot can walk with a static equilibrium even while it is walking.

A typical walking cycle for the proposed tripod walking robot can be described as following by referring to Fig. 13 and Fig. 15. The leg No.3 leaves the ground and swings from back to forth in the so-called swinging phase; at the same time the leg No.1 and the leg No.2 are in the supporting phase, since they are in contact with the ground and they propel the body forward. The speed of the input crank in leg No.3 is twice than in leg No.2 and Leg No.1. When the swinging leg No.3 touches the ground, it starts the propelling phase and the leg No.1 is ready to leave the ground. When Leg No.2 touches the ground, the tripod robot completes one cycle of walking.

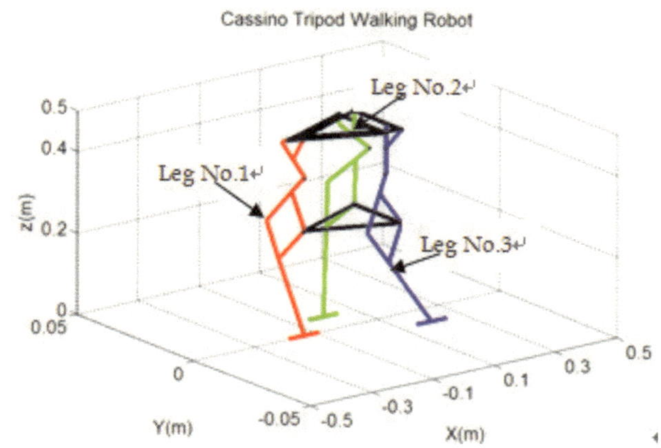

Fig. 13. The tripod walking robot at initial configuration with α_1=180 degs, α_2=90 degs, and α_3=270 degs

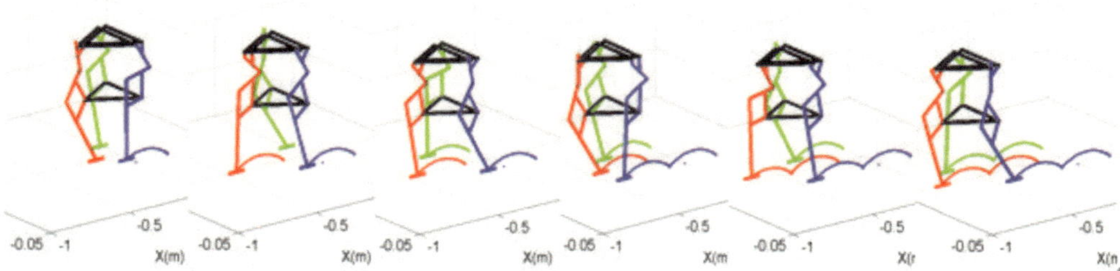

(a) (b) (c) (d) (e) (f)

Fig. 14. Walking snapshots of the tripod walking robot as function of the input for leg motion: (a) α_1=270 degs; (b) α_1=90 degs; (c) α_1=180 degs; (d) α_1=270 degs; (e) α_1=90 degs; (f) α_1=180 degs

In order to investigate the operation characteristics and feasibility of the proposed mechanism, the plots of transmission angles γ_1 , γ_2 and leg angles φ_1, φ_2 for three legs are shown as function of time in Fig. 16(a) and Fig. 16(b), respectively.
The plots are depicted for each leg. It can be found out that the transmission angle γ_1 varies between 60 degs and 170 degs and γ_2 varies between 70 degs and 120 degs. According to the kinematics rule of linkages, a feasible and effective transmission can be obtained for the proposed leg mechanism.

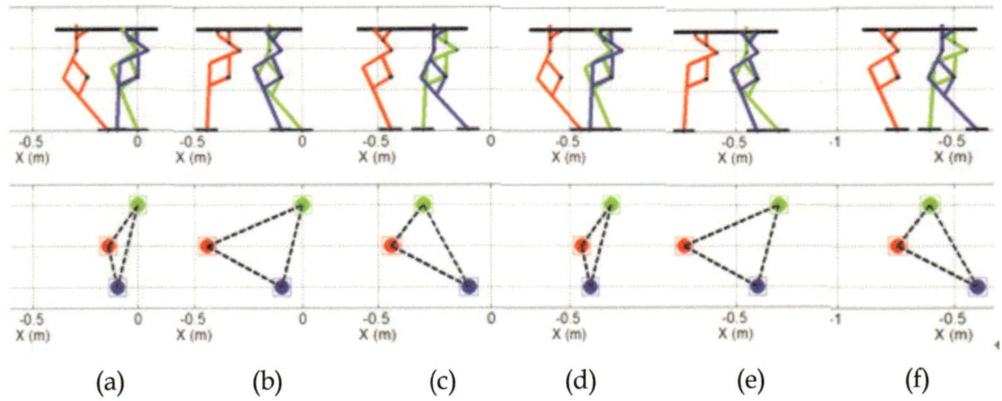

Fig. 15. Walking sequences and trajectories of the feet in saggital plane and position of the three feet in horizontal plane: (a) α_1=270 degs; (b) α_1=90 degs; (c) α_1=180 degs; (d) α_1=270 degs; (e) α_1=90 degs; (f) α_1=180 degs

The plots of leg angles $\varphi_{1,}$ φ_2 are shown in Fig. 17. Angle φ_1 varies in a feasible region between 45 degs and 95 degs. It reaches the maximum value at the transition point from swinging phase to supporting phase and the minimum value vice versa. Angle φ_2 varies between 5 degs and 72 degs. Therefore, no conflict exists between pantograph mechanism and Chebyshev linkage in the proposed leg mechanism.

Fig. 18(a) shows plots the motion trajectories in saggital plane for points A_i (i=1, 2, 3). Dimension of the length and height for each step are depicted as L and H, respectively. These two dimension parameters are useful to evaluate walking capability and obstacles avoidance ability for the tripod walking robot. They have been computed as L=300 mm and H=48 mm for each step.

A tripod walking gait is composed of three small steps. Fig. 18(b) shows the positions of points of C_i (i=1, 2, 3) in saggital plane. It can be noted that the trajectories are approximate straight lines with very small waving. Therefore, the body of the tripod walking robot has a very small movement of less 5 mm in vertical direction and can be seem as an energy efficiency walking gait. It is computed that the body of robot is propelled forward 100 mm for each leg step. Therefore, the body is propelled forward 300 mm in a cycle of tripod walking gait. The walking speed can be computed as 0.3 m/s. However, there is a period of time that points C_2 and C_3 do not maintain the rigid body condition, but they move very slightly with respect to each other. Actually, this happens because the propelling speeds of two supporting legs are different. Therefore, a small difference of the motions between points C_2 and C_3 have been computed in the simulation of the walking gait.

Fig. 19 shows those differences between the positions of points C_i (i=1, 2, 3) as corresponding to Fig. 12(a), during the tripod walking. Fig. 19(a) shows the differences in X axis and Fig. 19(b) in Y axis, respectively. The difference in X axis is less than ΔX_2=5 mm and difference in Y axis is less than ΔY_2=1.6 mm. The difference in Y axis can be used as compliance capability during the walking also to smooth the ground contacts. The difference in X axis can be compensated by installing a passive prismatic translation joint on the leg joints at the robot body.

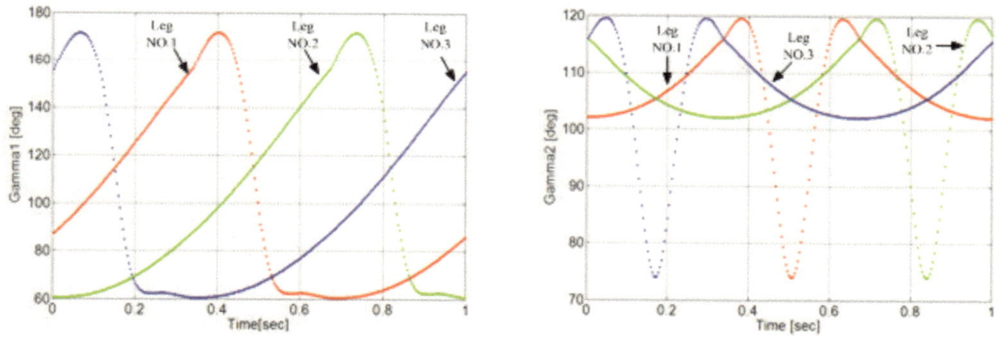

(a) (b)

Fig. 16. The transmission angles of the three leg mechanisms during a simulated walking as function of time; (a) transmission angle γ_1; (b) transmission angle γ_2

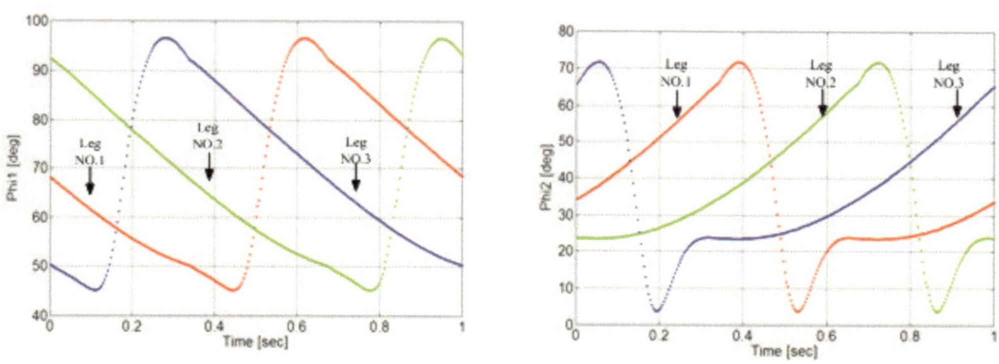

(a) (b)

Fig. 17. The transmission angles of three leg mechanisms as function of time; (a) transmission angle φ_1; (b) transmission angle φ_2

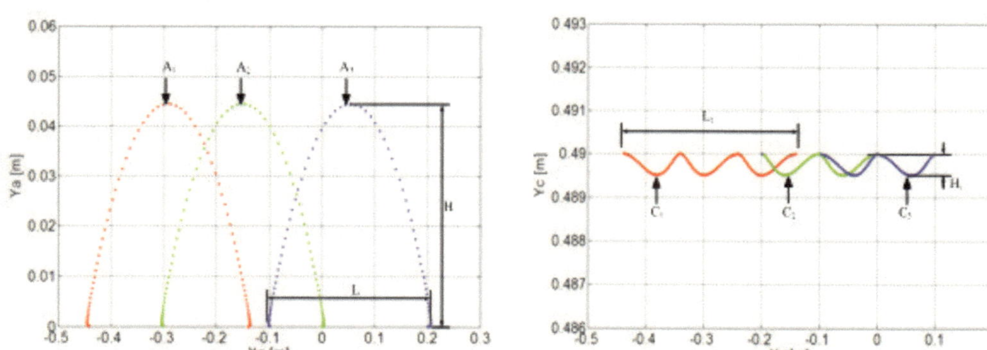

(a) (b)

Fig. 18. The position of point A and point C in Saggital XY plane for three legs; (a) positions of points A_i (i=1, 2, 3); (b) positions of points C_i (i=1, 2, 3)

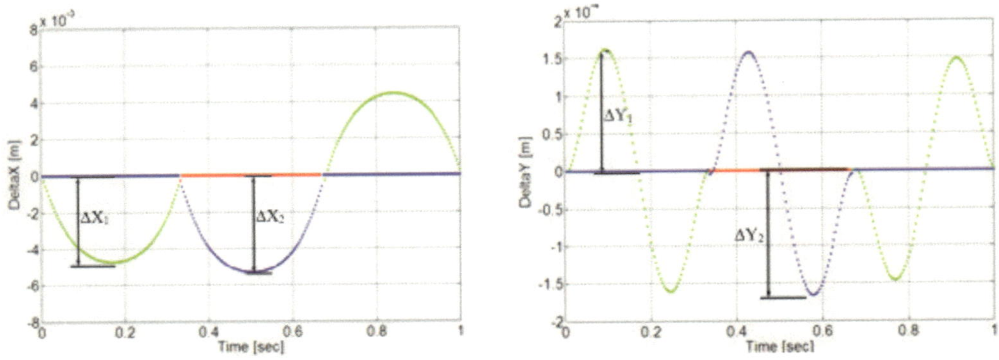

(a) (b)

Fig. 19. The errors between points C_i (i=1, 2, 3) as function of time: (a) errors in X axis; (b) errors in Y axis

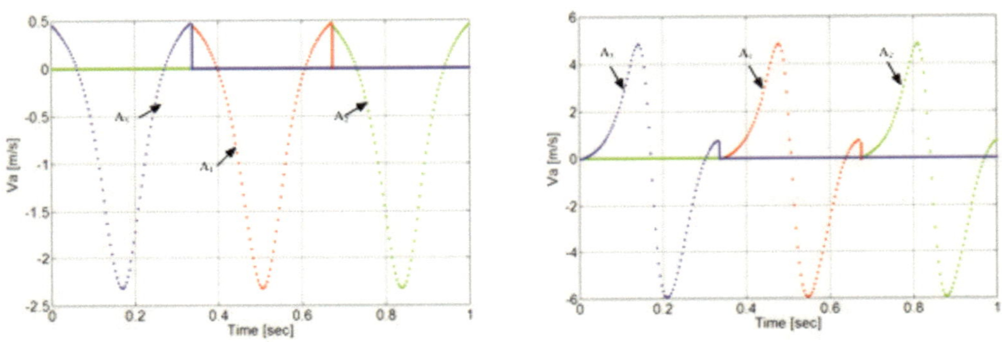

(a) (b)

Fig. 20. The velocity of points A_i (i=1, 2, 3). as function of time: (a) velocity in X axis ; (b) velocity in Y axis

The plots of velocity at points A_i (i=1, 2, 3) in X and Y axis are shown in Fig. 20(a) and .Fig. 20(b), respectively. It can be noted that the velocity reaches the maximum value when the legs move to the highest point in a swinging phase in X axis. At the same point the velocity in Y axis is zero and the sign of velocity is changed. In the supporting phase because points A_i (i=1, 2, 3) are on the ground, the velocity is zero. Since the input crank speed is twice time in swinging phase than that in supporting phase, the plots are discontinuous at the transition point. Actually, this can be modeled as an impact between feet and ground that can be smoothed by the above mentioned differences in the paths of C_i points.
Matlab® programming has been suitable and indeed efficient both for performance computation and operation simulation by using the formulated model for the design and operation of the proposed tripod walking robot.

4. A New waist-trunk system for humanoid robots

Humanoid robots are designed as directly inspired by human capabilities. These robots usually show kinematics similar to humans, as well as similar sensing and behaviour.

Therefore, they can be better accommodated in our daily life environment (home, office, and other public places) by providing services for human beings (Kemp et al., 2008). This research field has attracted large interests since two decades and a lot of prototypes have been built in the laboratories or companies. Significant examples of biped humanoid robots can be indicated for example in ASIMO developed by HONDA Corporation (Sakagami et al., 2002), HRP series developed at AIST (Kaneko et al., 2004), WABIAN series at the Takanishi laboratory in the Waseda University, Japan (Ogura et al., 2006), HUBO series built at KAIST in Korea (Ill-Woo et al., 2007), and BHR series built in the Beijing Institute of Technology, China (Qiang et al., 2005).

A survey on the current humanoid robots shows that their limbs (arms and legs) are anthropomorphically designed as articulated link mechanisms with 6 or 7 DOFs. However, torsos of humanoid robots are generally treated as rigid bodies, which are passively carried by the biped legs. The torsos of the existing humanoid robots like ASIMO, HRP, and HUBO have almost a box shaped body with a small number of DOFs. A motivation of this kind of designs is that the torso is used to store the computer, battery, sensors, and other necessary devices, so that the whole system can be designed as compact, robust, and stiff. In addition, due to mechanical design difficulties and complexity of controlling multi-body systems, torsos have been designed by using serial mechanism architectures. However, this kind of designs introduces several drawbacks, which give limitations on the motion capability and operation performances for humanoid robots (Carbone et al., 2009). Therefore, it is promising to design an advanced torso for humanoid robots by adopting parallel mechanisms with a relative high number of DOFs.

Actually, the human torso is a complex system with many DOFs, and plays an important role during human locomotion such as in walking, turning, and running. Humans unconsciously use their waists and trunks to perform successfully tasks like bending, pushing, carrying and transporting heavy objects. Therefore, an advanced torso system is needed for humanoid robots so that they can be better accommodated in our daily life environment with suitable motion capability, flexibility, better operation performances, and more anthropomorphic characteristics.

In the literature, there are few works on design and control issues of the torso system for humanoid robots. A humanoid robot named WABIAN-2R has been developed at Takanishi laboratory in the Waseda University with a 2 DOFs waist and 2 DOFs trunk, (Ogura et al., 2006). The waist and trunk of WABIAN-2R is a serial architecture and it is used for compensating the moment that is generated by the swinging legs when it walks, and to avoid the kinematics singularity in a stretched-knee, heel-contact and toe-off motion. A musculoskeletal flexible-spine humanoid robot named as Kotaro has been built at the JSK laboratory in the University of Tokyo. Kotaro has an anthropomorphic designed trunk system with several DOFs and a complicated sensor system, and it is actuated by using artificial muscle actuators. However, it is not able to walk, (Mizuuchi, 2005). A 3 DOFs parallel manipulator named as CaPaMan2 bis at LARM has been proposed as the trunk module for a low-cost easy-operation humanoid robot CALUMA with the aim to keep balance during walking and for manipulation movements, (Nava Rodriguez et al., 2005). However, these torso systems are fundamentally different from the proposed waist-trunk system.

4.1 A new waist-trunk system

Human torso is an important part of human body. It can be recognized as the portion of the human body to which the neck, upper and lower limbs are attached. Fig. 21(a) shows a scheme of the skeleton of human torso. It can be noted that the human torso consists of three main parts: thorax, waist, and pelvis (Virginia, 1999). The rib cages and spine column of the upper part contribute to thorax. In the thorax, the heart and lungs are protected by the rib cage. The human spine is composed of 33 individual vertebrae, which are separated by fibrocartilaginous intervertebral discs and are secured to each other by interlocking processes and binding ligaments. In particular, the lumbar spine, which is the waist segment, is the most important and largest part of human spine. The main function of the lumbar spine is to bear the weight of the human body. The spine is connected with the pelvis by sacrum and the pelvis is connected with two femurs in the lower part. Additionally, there are hundred pairs of muscles, flexible tendons, and ligaments, complex blood and nervous system with different functions to make a human torso an important part of the human body. Since the human torso is composed of three portions, namely the thorax, waist, and pelvis. In Fig. 21(a), three black rectangles have been indicated on the skeleton of the human torso as reference platforms for the thorax, waist, and pelvis, respectively. Fig. 21(b) shows the corresponding positions of these three parts on the human spine. Therefore, a simply model with three rigid bodies has been proposed as shown in Fig. 22(a), which is expected to imitate the function of human torso during difference human movements.

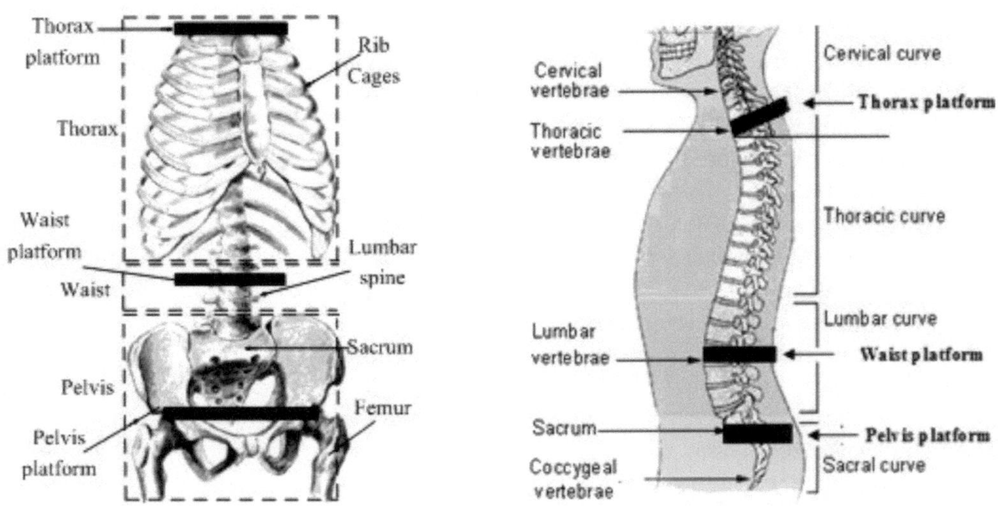

(a) (b)

Fig. 21. Schemes of human torso with reference platforms: (a) skeleton structure; (b) S curve of a human spine

The proposed model in Fig. 22(a) is composed of three rigid bodies namely thorax platform, waist platform, and pelvis platform, from the top to the bottom, respectively. The thorax platform can be connected together to the waist platform by using parallel mechanism with suitable DOFs, which has been named as the trunk module. The thorax platform is expected to imitate the movements of human thorax. Arms, neck, and head of humanoid robots are assumed to be installed a connected to the thorax platform. The pelvis platform is connected to the waist platform with suitable mechanism, which has been named as the waist module. Two legs are expected to be connected to pelvis platform.

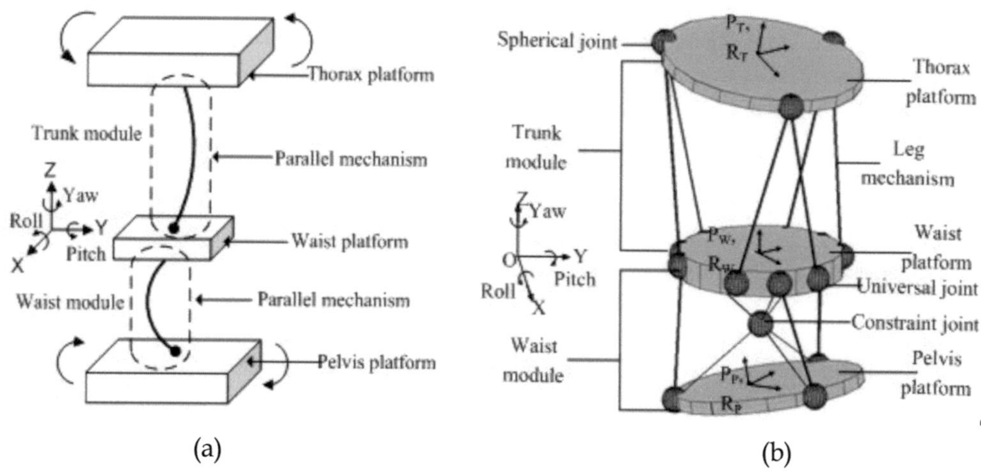

Fig. 22. A new waist-trunk system for humanoid robots: (a) a model for imitating the movements of human torso; (b) the proposed new waist-trunk system as modeled in Matlab® environment

The proposed waist-trunk system is illustrated in Fig. 22(b) as a kinematic model that has been elaborated in Matlab® environment. The design sizes of the proposed waist-trunk system are close to the human torso dimensions as reported in (Kawuchi and Mochimaru, 2005).

In Fig. 22(b), upper part of the proposed waist-trunk system is named as trunk module, which consists of a thorax platform, a waist platform, and six identical leg mechanisms to obtain a 6 DOFs parallel manipulator structure. Actually, the proposed trunk module has the same structure of a Stewart platform (Tsai, 1999; Ceccarelli, 2004).

In the trunk module, each leg mechanism is composed of a universal joint, a spherical joint, and an actuated prismatic joint. The trunk module has six DOFs with the aim to imitate the function of human lumbar spine and thorax to perform three rotations (flexion-extension, lateral-bending, and transverse-rotation movements) and three translation movements. In particular, head, neck, and dual-arm systems can be installed on the thorax platform in a humanoid robot design

The lower part in Fig. 22(b) is named as waist module, which consists of a pelvis platform, a waist platform, and three identical leg mechanisms to obtain a 3 DOFs orientation parallel manipulator structure. This 3 DOFs orientation parallel platform is a classical parallel mechanism, which has been designed as the hip, wrist, and shoulder joints for humanoid robots as reported in a rich literature (Sadjadian & Taghirad, 2006). The waist module shares waist platform with the trunk module but the leg mechanisms are installed on the counter side in a downward architecture.

The pelvis platform is connected to the waist platform with three leg mechanisms and a passive spherical joint. There are six bars connected with the passive spherical joint with the waist platform and pelvis platform with the aim to make it very stiff. The waist module is an orientation platform and has three rotation DOFs for yaw, pitch, and roll movements. The rotation center is a passive spherical joint, which plays a role like the symphysis pubis in the human pelvis to carrry the weight of the human body. The waist module is aimed to imitate the function of human pelvis during walking, running, and other movements. In particular, a biped leg system can be connected to the moving pelvis platform.

4.2 A kinematic simulation

Simulations have been carried out with the aim to evaluate the operation feasibility of the proposed waist-trunk system for a biped humanoid design solution. In Fig. 23(a) a biped humanoid robot with the proposed waist-trunk system has been modeled in Matlab® virtual reality toolbox environment by using VRML language (Vitual Reality Toolbox Users' Manual, 2007). VRML is a standard file format for representing 3D interactive vector graphics, which has been extensively used in robotic system simulation applications (Siciliano and Khatib, 2008). OpenHRP® is a simulation software package developed for performing dynamic simulation of the famous HRP series humanoid robots by using VRML language (Kanehiro et al., 2004). In a VRML file, the geometric sizes and dynamics parameters of the humanoid robot can be defined as a text-based format.

In Fig. 23(a), the modeled biped humanoid robot is composed of several balls, cuboids, and cylinders with the aim to avoid the complex mechanical design of a humanoid robot. Fig. 23(b) shows the modeling details of the waist-trunk system for a biped humanoid robot. In particular, universal joint and spherical joint are modeled by using balls. Motion constraints have been applied for each joint so that they have the proposed motion capability for a mechanical design solution. The geometry sizes and dynamics parameters of the modeled VRML model are close to the design specifications of most current humanoid robots.

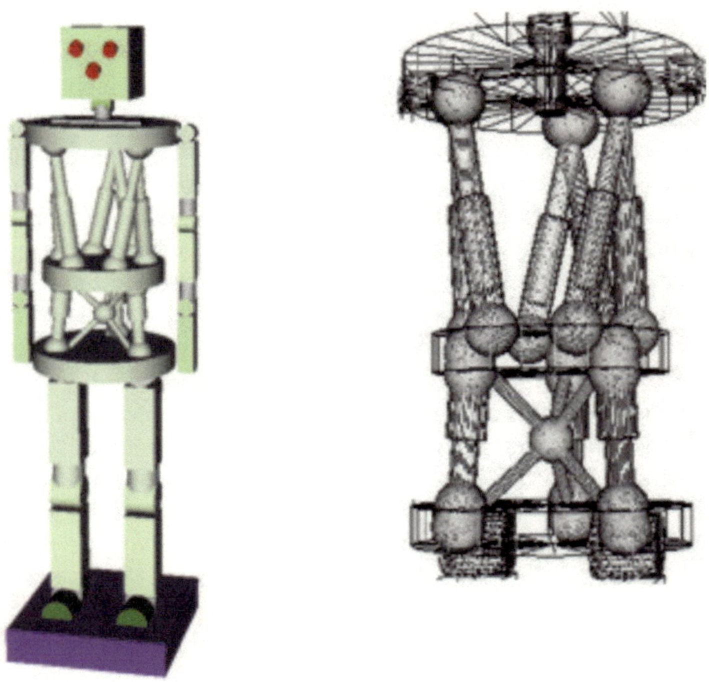

(a) (b)

Fig. 23. 3D models in VRML: (a) a biped humanoid robot; (a) modeling details of the waist-trunk system

In Fig. 24, a simulation procedure of the biped humanoid robot in Matlab® virtual reality toolbox is shown in several steps as described in the following:

Step 1. Movements of the moving platforms are computed according to assigned tasks. For a walking mode, motion trajectory of the waist platform is determined as based on the prescribed ZMP (zero momentum point) and COM (center of mass) trajectories. The movements of the pelvis platform are functions of the walking gait parameters. For a manipulation mode, the movements of waist platform and thorax platform depend on the locations of the manipulated objects.

Step 2. The prescribed movements are the inputs of a motion pattern generator, where walking pattern or manipulation pattern is generated for the simulated biped humanoid robot.

Step 3. The computed reference trajectories of the actuated joints are the inputs of a direct kinematics solver. By solving the direct kinematics of the biped humanoid robot, positions and orientations of each component can be computed.

Step 4. The position and orientation for each component of the VRML model are updated for each step of simulation. The computed movements of the simulated biped humanoid robot are shown in animations, which are stored as videos in AVI format.

Therefore, two different operation modes of the proposed waist-trunk system can be simultated and its operation performances can be conveniently characterized by using elaborated codes included in the CD of this book.

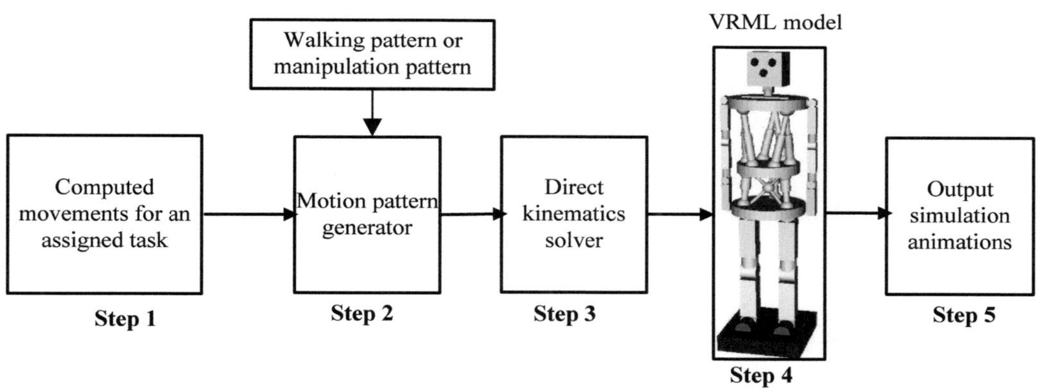

Fig. 24. A scheme for a simulation procedure of the biped humanoid robot in Matlab® virtual reality toolbox simulation environment

4.3 Simulation results

In this section, simulation results of the simulated VRML biped humanoid robot are illustrated for a walking task and a bending-manipulation task. The movements of the wais-trunk system are prescribed with suitable equations according to the assigned tasks. Operation performances of the simulated waist-trunk system have been characterized in terms of displacement, velocity, and acceleration. Simulation results show that the proposed waist-trunk system has satisfied operation characteristics as a mechanical system and has a capability of well imitating different movements of human torso.

4.3.1 Simulation of the walking mode

For a walking mode of the wais-trunk system, the waist platform is assumed to be the fixed base. Thus, positions and orientation angles of the thorax platform and the pelvis platform

can be conveniently prescribed. During a normal walking, the movements of the pelvis platform and thorax platform can be prescribed by using the equations listed in Table 4.
In Table 4, $A_\varphi(v, h)$ is the magnitude of the rotation angle around roll axis as function of the walking parameters that can be determined by the walking speed v and step height l. A_θ is the magnitude of the rotation angle around pitch axis as function of the slope angle α of the ground. In particular, for a flat ground it is $A_\theta(\alpha)=0$. $A_\psi(v, l)$ is the magnitude of the rotation angle around yaw axis as function of the walking parameters of the walking speed v and step length l. $\varphi_{W,0}$ and $\psi_{W,0}$ are the initial phase angles. $\omega=\pi/T_s$ is the walking frequency. T_s is the time period for one step of walking. The expressions in Table 4 can describe the periodical motion of the walking. A similar motion generation method is also presented in (Harada et al., 2009). The motion trajectories of the thorax platform can be prescribed similarly but in opposite motion direction in order to have a counter rotation with respect to the pelvis movements. This is aimed to preserve the angular monument generated by the lower limbs for walking stability. Particularly, only the orientation angles have been prescribed in the trunk module in the reported simulation. However, the position can be prescribed independently since the thorax platform has 6 DOFs.

	Positions (mm)	Orientation angles (degs)
Waist platform	$X_W = 0$	$\varphi_W = A_\varphi(v, h)\sin(\omega t+\varphi_{W,0})$
	$Y_W = 0$	$\theta_W = A_\theta(\alpha)$
	$Z_W = 0$	$\psi_W = A_\psi(v, l)\sin(\omega t+\psi_{W,0})$
Thorax platform	$X_T = 0$	$\varphi_T = - A_\varphi(v, h)\sin(\omega t+\varphi_{T,0})$
	$Y_T = 0$	$\theta_T = - A_\theta(\alpha)$
	$Z_T = 0$	$\psi_T = - A_\psi(v, l)\sin(\omega t+\psi_{T,0})$

Table 4. Prescribed movements for the moving platforms in a walking mode

Simulation time has been prescribed in 1.5s to simulate the function of waist-trunk system in a full cycle of humanoid robot normal walking (Ts=0.75 s/step). An operation has been simulated with 150 steps. In general, the range of motion of human pelvis is between 5 degrees and 20 degrees, and therefore, the orientation capability of the waist module has been designed within a range of 25 degrees. Thus, the waist module can imitate different movements of human pelvis through proper operations.
Fig. 25 shows the movements of the simulated biped humanoid robot, which have been simulated for two steps of walking in Matlab® environment by using the computed data in the previous analysis. The inverse kinematics analysis results have been imported to actuate the VRML model in Fig. 23. It is convenient to output the characterization values and annimations by using the flexible programming environment in Matlab®. The simulated humanoid robot shows a smooth motion which well imitates the movements of human thorax and pelvis during a walking task. In addition, it can be noted that the proposed waist-trunk system shows suitable motions to imitate the movements of the human torso during a normal walking.

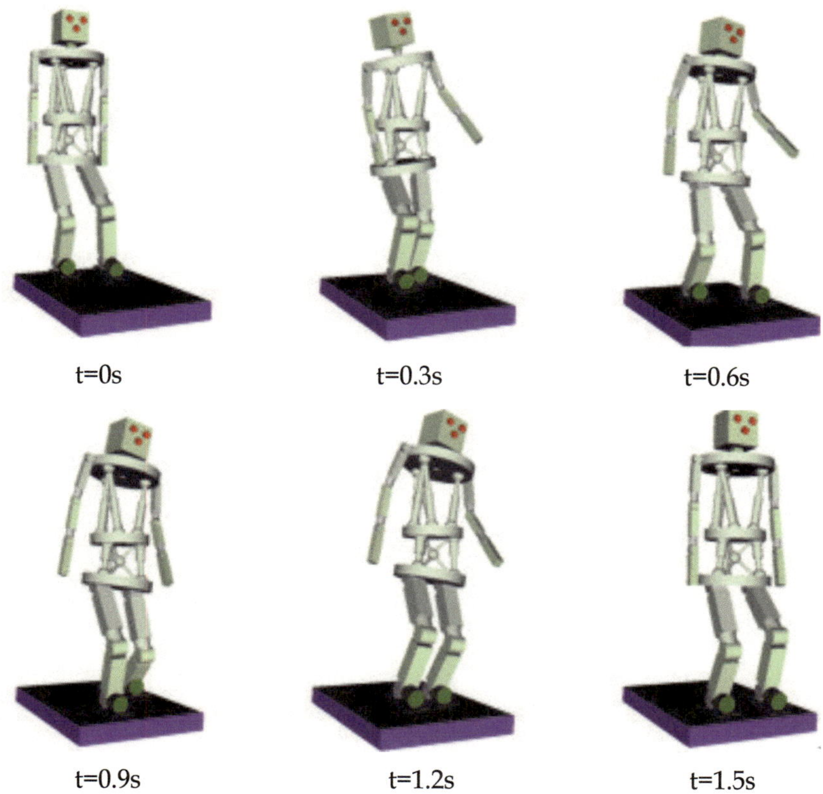

Fig. 25. Simulation snapshots of the movements of a biped humanoid robot in a walking procedure

The prescribed orientation angles of the trunk module and waist module are shown in Fig. 26(a) and Fig. 26(b). The solid and dashed lines represent rotation angle around the roll axis and yaw axes, respectively. The rotation magnitudes have been set as 20 degs and 10 degs, respectively. The dot-dashed line represents the rotation angle around the pitch axis, which has been set as a small value to avoid the computation singularity problem in the ZYZ orientation representation. The computed displacements of the prismatic joints L_i (i=1,...,6) of the trunk module are shown in Fig. 27. Fig. 28 shows the computed displacements for the prismatic joints S_k (k=1,2,3) of the waist module.

Fig. 29 and Fig. 30 show the computed velocities and accelerations for the waist and trunk modules, respectively.

It can be noted that the characterization plots are quite smooth. The proposed waist-trunk system shows a human-like behaviour for an assigned walking task because of the smooth time evaluation of the motion characteristics. The maximum velocity has been computed as 58 mm/s along Y axis for the trunk module and 120 mm/s along Y axis for the waist module. The maximum acceleration has been computed as 240 mm/s^2 along Y axis for the trunk module and 460 mm/s^2 along Y axis for the waist module. These values are feasible in proper regions for the operation of both the parallel manipulators and they properly simulate the operation of the human torso. Particularly, it can be noted that the velocity and acceleration curves of the trunk module and waist module have different signs, as an indication of the counter rotation of thorax platform and pelvis platform.

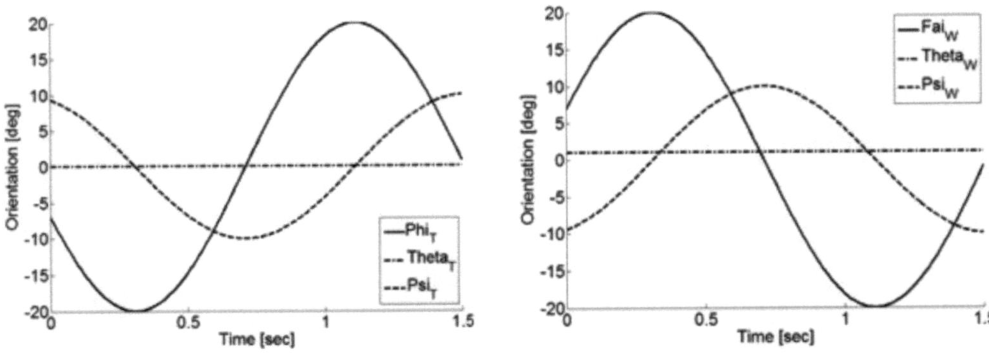

(a) (b)

Fig. 26. Prescribed orientation angles for an operation of walking mode: (a) thorax platform; (b) pelvis platform

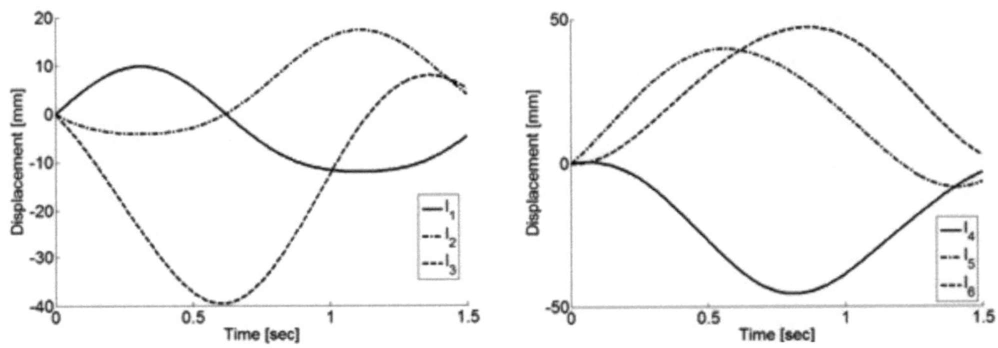

(a) (b)

Fig. 27. Computed leg displacement of the trunk module: (a) for legs 1, 2, and 3; (b) for legs 4, 5, and 6

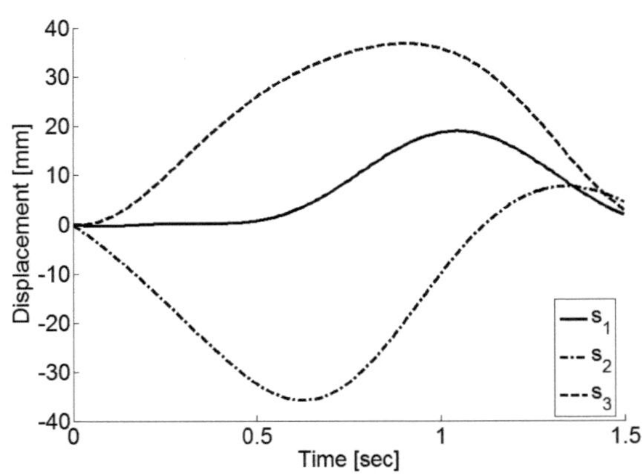

Fig. 28. Computed leg displacements of the waist module for the three legs

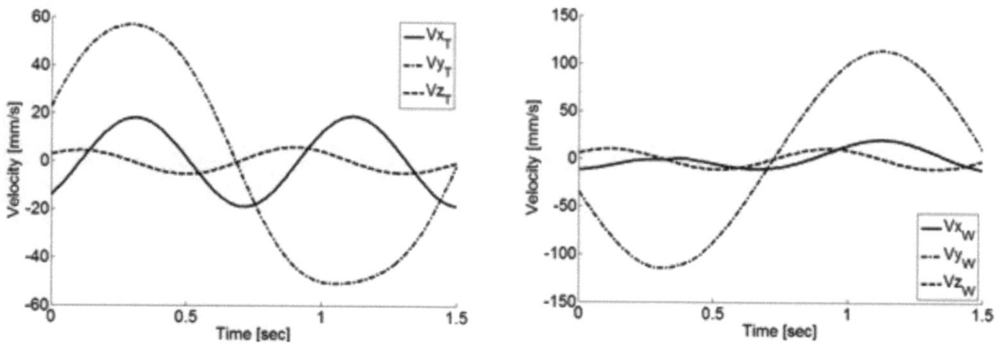

(a) (b)

Fig. 29. Computed velocities in Cartesian space: (a) thorax platform; (b) pelvis platform

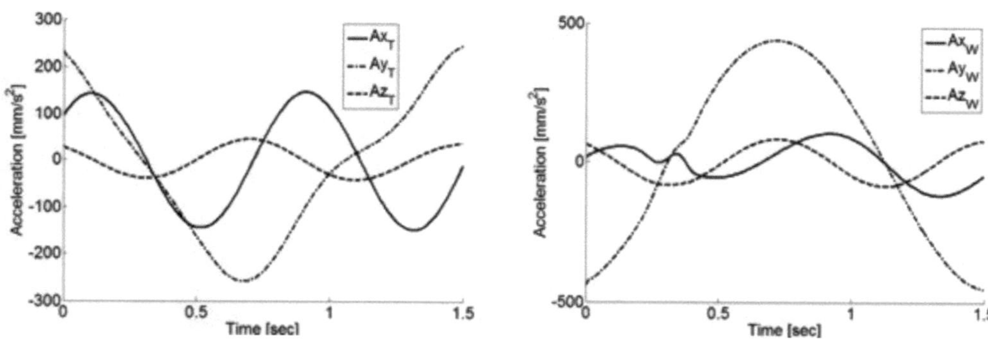

(a) (b)

Fig. 30. Computed accelerations in Cartesian space: (a) thorax platform; (b) pelvis platform

4.3.2 Simulation of the manipulation mode

The movements of the waist module and trunk module are combined together in a manipulation mode. The waist-trunk system is a redundant serial-parallel structure with totally 9 DOFs. The inverse kinematics and motion planning are challenge issues for this peculiar serial-parallel structure. The pelvis platform has been assumed to be the fixed base, and the motion trajectories of the center point of the thorax platform and waist platform have been prescribed independently. A simulation has been carried out for a bending-manipulation procedure in order to evaluate the operation performance for a simultaneous action of the two parallel manipulator structures. The movements of the moving platforms have been prescribed by using the equations in Table 5.

Fig. 31 shows a sequence of snapshots of the simulated biped humanoid robot performing a bending-manipulation movement. The biped humanoid robot bends his torso and tries to manipulate the object that is placed on the top of a column on the ground. The double-parallel architecture gives a great manipulation capability for the biped humanoid robot, which is a hard task for current humanoid robots to accomplish. From the motion sequences in Fig. 31, it can be noted that the proposed waist-trunk system shows a suitable motion which well imitates the movements of a human torso during a bending-manipulation procedure. It is remarkable the smooth behaviour of the overall operation that makes the waist-trunk system to show a human-like motion characteristic and it can be very convenient designed as the torso part for humanoid robots.

	Positions (mm)	Orientation angles (degs)
Thorax platform	$X_T = X_{t,0} + 120\sin(\omega t)$	$\varphi_T = 0$
	$Y_T = 0$	$\theta_T = 30\sin(\omega t + \theta_0)$
	$Z_T = Z_{T,0} - 80\sin(\omega t)$	$\psi_T = 0$
Waist platform	$X_W = X_W(\varphi_W, \theta_W, \psi_W)$	$\varphi_W = 0$
	$Y_W = 0$	$\theta_W = 30\sin(\omega t + \theta_0)$
	$Z_W = Z_W(\varphi_W, \theta_W, \psi_W)$	$\psi_W = 0$

Table 5. Prescribed movements of the moving platforms for a bending-manipulation motion

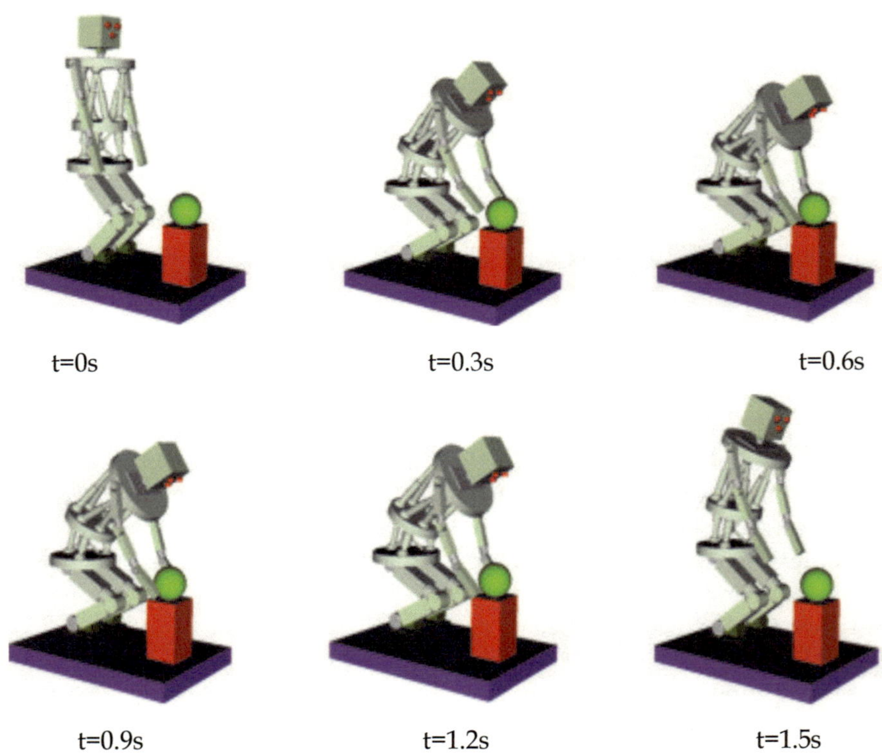

Fig. 31. Simulation snapshots of the movements of a biped humanoid robot in a bending-manipulation procedure

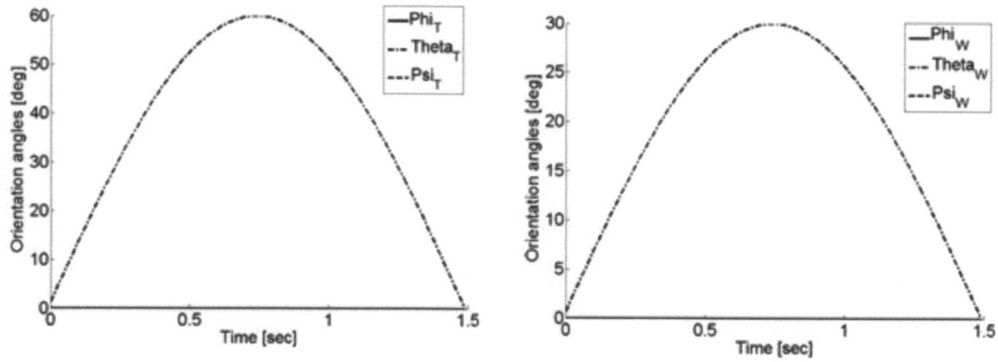

(a) (b)

Fig. 32. Prescribed orientation angles for a simulated operation of bending-manipulation movement: (a) thorax platform; (b) waist platform

The prescribed orientation angles of the thorax platform and waist platform are shown in Fig. 32(a) and Fig. 32(b), respectively. The thorax platform rotates 60 degs around its pitch axis and the waist platform rotates 30 degs around its pitch axis. The prescribed positions are plotted in Fig. 33(a) and Fig. 33(b). The center point of the thorax platform moves 120 mm along X axis and 80 mm along Z axis. The center point of the waist platform moves 66 mm along X axis and 17 mm along Y axis. Particularly, since the waist module is an orientation parallel manipulator, the positions of the waist platform are coupled with its orientation angles and they can be computed when the orientation angles are known. Fig. 34 shows the computed displacements of the prismatic joints S_k (k=1,2,3) of the waist module. The computed displacements of the prismatic joints L_i (i=1,…,6) of the trunk module are shown in Fig. 35.

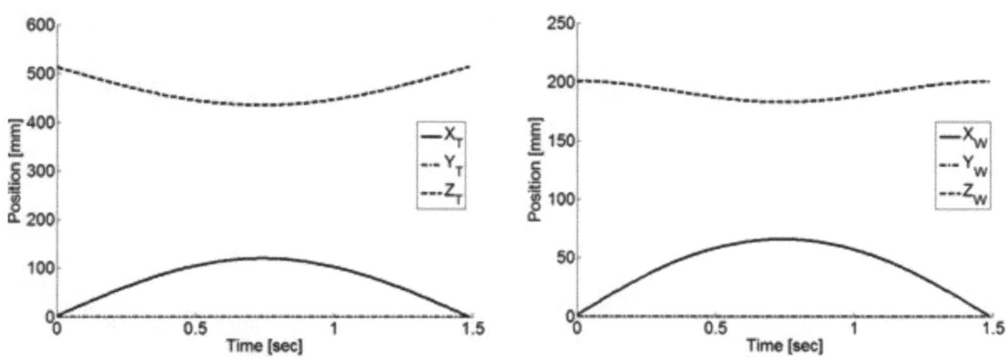

(a) (b)

Fig. 33. Prescribed positions in Cartesian space for a simulated operation of bending-manipulation movement: (a) thorax platform; (b) waist platform

Fig. 36 shows the computed velocities for the waist and trunk modules. The maximum velocity has been computed as 600 mm/s along X axis of the thorax platform and 80 mm/s along X axis of the waist platform. Fig. 37 shows the computed accelerations in the Cartesian space with the maximum acceleration as 1000 mm/s² along X axis of the thorax platform

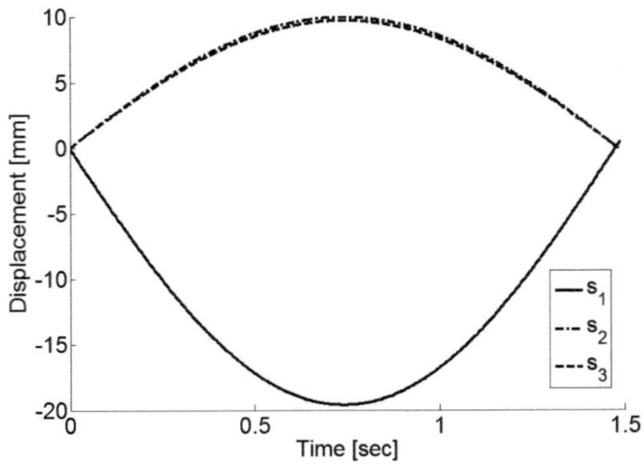

Fig. 34. Computed leg displacements of the waist module

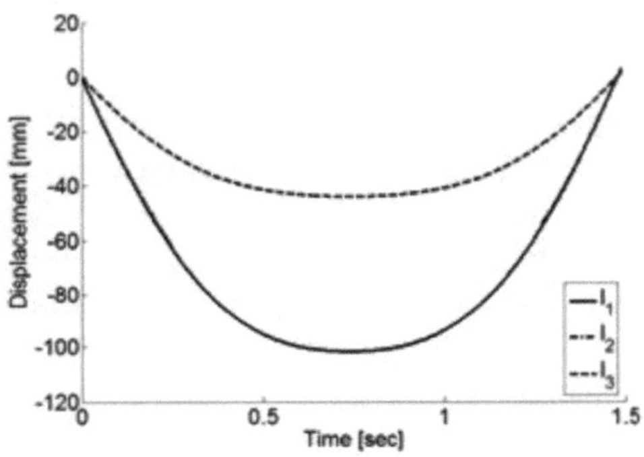

(a)

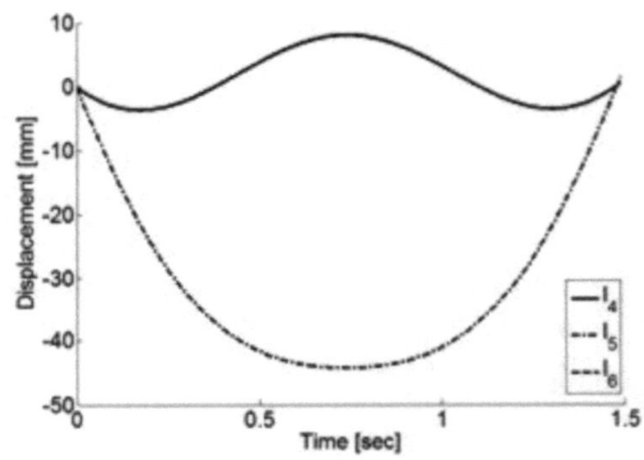

(b)

Fig. 35. Computed leg displacements of the trunk module: (a) for legs 1, 2, and 3; (b) for legs 4, 5, and 6

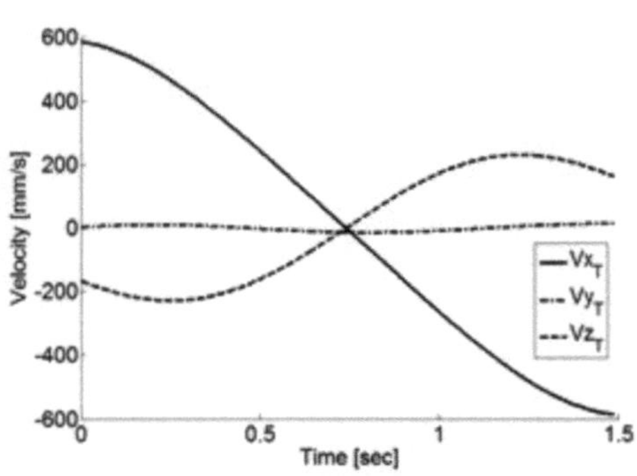

(a)

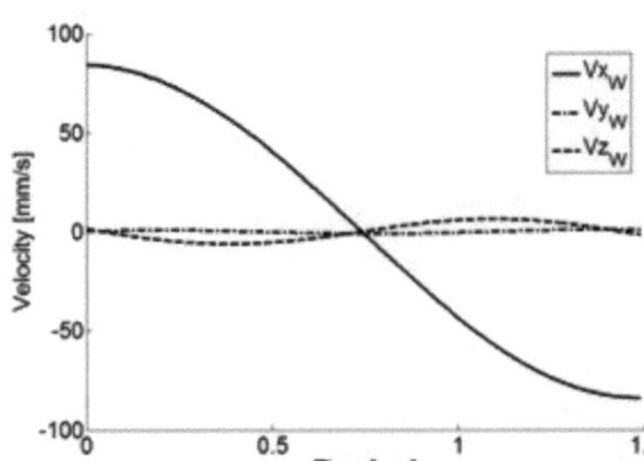

(b)

Fig. 36. Computed velocities in Cartesian space: (a) thorax platform; (b) waist platform

and 170 mm/s² along X axis of the waist platform. It can be noted that the characterization plots are quite smooth. The characterization values are feasible in proper regions for the operation of both the parallel manipulators and the proposed waist-trunk system has suitable and feasible operation performances for a robotic system as reported in the characterization plots from Fig. 32 to Fig. 37.

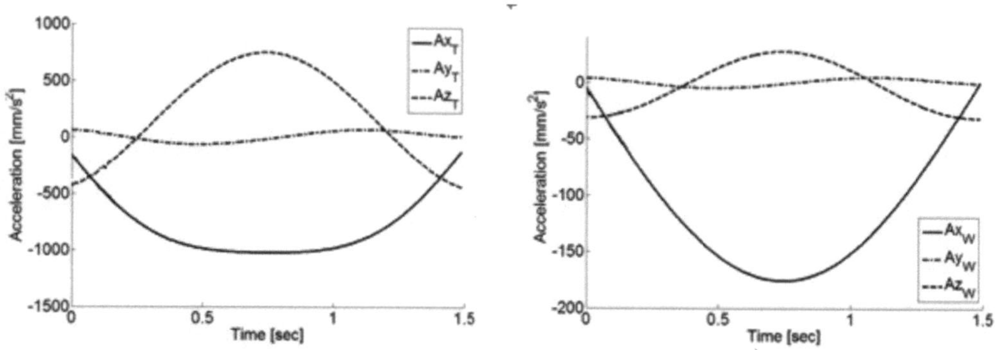

(a) (b)

Fig. 37. Computed accelerations in Cartesian space: (a) thorax platform; (b) waist platform

From the reported simulation results, it is worth to note that a complex mechanical system such as a humanoid robot can be conveniently modeled and evaluated in Matlab® environment due to its flexible programming environment and its powerful toolbox.

5. Conclusion

In this chapter, design and simulation issues of legged walking robots have been addressed by using modeling and simulation in Matlab® environment. In particular, Matlab® is a powerful computation and simulation software package, which is quite useful for the design and operation performances evaluation of legged robotic systems. Three examples are illustrated and they have been studied for motion feasibility analysis and operation performances characterizations by taking advantages of Matlab® features. Contributions of this chapter can be indicated as follows.

A kinematic study of a Chebyshev-Pantograph leg mechanism has been carried out, and equations are formulated in the Matlab® environment. From the reported simulation results, it shows that the practical feasible operation performance of the Chebyshev-Pantograph leg mechanism in a single DOF biped robot. Additionally, a parametric study has been developed by using the elaborated Matlab® analysis code to look for an optimized mechanical design and to determine an energy efficient walking gait.

A novel biologically inspired tripod walking robot is proposed by defining suitable design and operation solution for leg mechanism. Simulation results show the proposed design performs a tripod walking gait successfully. Operation performance of the leg mechanisms and the tripod walking robot are reported and discussed by using results from Matlab® simulations.

A new waist-trunk system for humanoid robots has been proposed by using suitable parallel architectures. The proposed system shows an anthropomorphic design and operation with several DOFs, flexibility, and high payload capacity. Simulation results show that the proposed waist-trunk system can well imitate movements of human torso for walking and manipulation tasks. Additionally, the proposed design has practical feasible operation performances from the reported simulation results.

6. Acknowledgment

The first author likes to acknowledge Chinese Scholarship Council (CSC) for supporting his Ph.D. study and research at LARM in the University of Cassino, Italy for the years 2008-2010.

7. References

Song, S.M. & Waldron K.J. (1989). *Machines That Walk-The Adaptive Suspension Vehicle*, The MIT press, Cambridge, USA.

Carbone, G. & Ceccarelli, M. (2005). *Legged Robotic Systems*, Cutting Edge Robotics ARS Scientific Book, pp. 553-576, Wien, Austria.

González-de-Santos, P.; Garcia, E. & Estremera, J. (2006). *Quadrupedal Locomotion: An Introduction to the Control of Four-legged Robots*, Springer-Verlag, New York, USA.

Kajita, S. & Espiau, Bernard. (2008). *Springer Handbook of robotics, Part G-16, Legged Robots*, Springer-Verlag, Berlin Heidelberg, Germany.

Sakagami, Y.; Watanabe, R.; Aoyama, C.; Matsunaga, S.; Higaki, N. & Fujimura, K. (2002). The Intelligent ASIMO: System Overview and Integration, *Proceedings of the 2002 IEEE/RSJ International Conference on Intelligent Robots and System*, Lausanne, September 30-October 4, pp. 2478-2483.

Raibert, M. (2008). *BigDog, the Rough-Terrain Robot*, Plenary talk of the 17th IFAC world congress.

Buehler, M. (2002). Dynamic Locomotion with One, Four and Six-Legged Robots, *Journal of the Robotics Society of Japan*, Vol. 20, No.3, pp. 15-20.

Wilcox, B.H.; Litwin, T.; Biesiadecki, J.; Matthews, J.; Heverly, M.; Morrison, J.; Townsend, J.; Ahmad, N.; Sirota, A. & Cooper, B. (2007). Athlete: A Cargo Handling and Manipulation Robot for The Moon, *Journal of Field Robotics*, Vol. 24, No.5, pp. 421-434.

Matlab manual, (2007). The MathWorks, Inc. Available from http://www.mathworks.com

Liang, C.; Ceccarelli, M.; & Takeda, Y. (2008). Operation Analysis of a One-DOF Pantograph Leg Mechanism, *Proceedings of the 17th International Workshop on Robotics in Alpe-Adria-Danube Region, RAAD'2008*, Ancona, Italy, September 15-17, Paper No. 50.

Liang, C.; Ceccarelli, M.; & Carbone, G. (2009). A Novel Biologically Inspired Tripod Walking Robot, *Proceedings of the 13th WSEAS International Conference on Computers, WSEAS'2009*, Rodos Island, Greece, July 23-25, n. 60-141, pp. 83-91.

Liang, C.; Gu, H.; Carbone, G.; & Cecarelli, M. (2010). Design and Operation of a Tripod Walking Robot via Dynamics Simulation, *Robotica*, doi: 10.1017/S02635747100000615.

Carbone, G.; Liang, C.; & Ceccarelli, M. (2009). *Using Parallel Architectures for Humanoid Robots*, Kolloquium Getriebetechnik 2009, Aachen, Germany, September 16-18, pp. 177-188.

Liang, C.; Cecarelli, M.; & Carbone, G. (2010). Design and Simulation of a Waist-Trunk System of a Humanoid Robot, *Theory and Practice of Robots and Manipulators 18th*

CISM-IFToMM Symposium on Robotics, ROMANSY'2010, Udine, Italy, July 5-8, pp. 217-224.

Liang, C.; Nava Rodriguez, N.E.. & Ceccarelli, M. (2010). Modelling and Functionality Simulation of A Waist-Trunk System with Mass Payloads, *Proceeding of the 28th Congreso Nacional de Ingeniería Mecánica, XVIII CNIM*, Ciudad Real, Spain, November 3-5, Paper no: 249.

Liang, C. & Ceccarelli, M. (2010). An Experimental Characterization of Operation of a Waist-Trunk System with Parallel Manipulator, *In Proceeding of the First IFToMM Asian Conference on Mechanism and Machine Science*, Taipei, Taiwan, October 21-25, paper no. 250042.

Artobolevsky I. (1979). *Mechanisms in Modern Engineering Design Volume V Part 1*, MIR Publishers, Moscow, Russia, pp. 405-406.

Hartenberg, R. & Denavit, J. (1964). Kinematics synthesis of linkages, McGraw-Hill Inc., New York, USA.

Ottaviano, E.; Ceccarelli M. & Tavolieri, C. (2004). Kinematic and Dynamic Analyses of A Pantograph-Leg for A Biped Walking Machine, *Proceeding of the 7th International Conference on Climbing and Walking Robots CLAWAR2004*, Madrid, Spain, September 22-24, Paper A019.

Vukobratovic, M.; Borova, B.; Surla, D.; & Storic, D. (1989). *Biped Locomotion: Dynamic Stability, Control and Application*, Springer-Verlag, New York, USA.

Kemp, C.; Fitzpatrick, P.; Hirukawa, H.; Yokoi, K.; Harada, K. & Matsumoto, Y. (2008), *Springer Handbook of Robotics, Part G. Humanoid Robots*, Springer-Verlag, Berlin Heidelberg, Germany.

Kaneko, K.; Kanehiro, F.; Kajita, S.; Hirukawa, H.; Kawasaki, T.; Hirata, M.; Akachi, K.; & Isozumi, T. (2004), Humanoid robot HRP-2, *Proceedings of 2004 IEEE International Conference on Robotics and Automation*, New Orleans, LA, USA, pp. 1083-1090.

Ogura, Y.; Shimomura, K.; Kondo, A.; Morishima, A.; Okubo, A.; Momoki, S.; Hun-ok, L. & Takanishi, A. (2006). Human-Like Walking with Knee Stretched Heel-Contact and Toe-Off Motion by A Humanoid Robot, *Proceedings of the 2006 IEEE/RSJ International Conference on Intelligence Robots and Systems*, Beijing, China, pp. 3976-3981.

Ill-Woo, P.; Jung-Yup, K.; Jungho, L. & Jun-Ho, O. (2007). Mechanical Design of the Humanoid Robot Platform, HUBO, *Advanced Robotics*, pp. 1305-1322.

Qiang, H.; Zhaoqin, P.; Weimin, Z.; Lige, Z. & Kejie, L. (2005). Design of Humanoid Complicated Dynamic Motion Based on Human Motion Capture, *Proceedings of 2005 IEEE/RSJ International Conference on Intelligent Robots and Systems*, Edmonton, pp. 3536-3541.

Mizuuchi, I. (2005). *A Musculoskeletal Flexible-Spine Humanoid Kotaro Aiming At the Future in 15 Years' Time, In Mobile Robots - Towards New Applications*, Verlag, Germany, pp. 45-56.

Nava Rodriguez, N.E.; Carbone, G. & Ceccarelli, M. (2005). CaPaMan 2bis as Trunk Module in CALUMA (CAssino Low-Cost hUMAnoid Robot), *In Proceeding of the 2nd IEEE International Conference on Robotics, Auto*mation and Mechatronics, RAM 2006, Bangkok, Thailand, pp. 347-352.

Virginia, C. (1999). *Bones and Muscles: An Illustrated Anatomy*, Wolf Fly Press, South Westerlo, New York, USA.

Kawauchi, M. & Mochimaru, M. (2010). AIST Human Body Properties Database, Digital Human Laboratory (AIST, Japan), Available on line: http://www.dh.aist.go.jp, 2010.

Tsai, L.-W. (1999). *Robot Analysis – The Mechanics of Serial and Parallel Manipulator,* John Wiley & Sons, New York, USA.

Ceccarelli, M. (2004). *Fundamental of Mechanics of Robotic Manipulator,* Kluwer Academic Publishers, Dordrecht, Germany.

Sadjadian, H.; & Taghirad, H.D. (2006). Kinematic, Singularity and Stiffness Analysis of the Hydraulic Shoulder: A 3-d.o.f. Redundant Parallel Manipulator, *Journal of Advanced Robotics,* Vol. 20, n. 7, pp. 763–781.

Visual Reality Toolbox User's Guide. (2007). The MathWorks, Inc. Available from http://www.mathworks.com/access/helpdesk/help/pdf_doc/vr/vr.pdf

Siciliano, B. & Khatib, O. (2008). *Springer Handbook of robotics,* Springer-Verlag, Berlin Heidelberg, Germany.

Harada, K.; Miura, K.; Morisawa, M.; Kaneko, K.; Nakaoka, S.; Kanehiro, F.; Tsuji, T. & Kajita, S. (2009). Toward Human-Like Walking Pattern Generator. *In Proceedings of the 2009 IEEE/RSJ international Conference on intelligent Robots and Systems,* St. Louis, MO, USA, pp. 1071-1077.

21

Modeling, Simulation and Control of a Power Assist Robot for Manipulating Objects Based on Operator's Weight Perception

S. M. Mizanoor Rahman[1], Ryojun Ikeura[2] and Haoyong Yu[1]
[1]National University of Singapore
[2]Mie University
[1]Singapore
[2]Japan

1. Introduction

1.1 Power assist robot and its current applications

Power assist robot is a human-robot cooperation that extends human's abilities and skills in performing works (Kazerooni, 1993). Breakthrough in power assist robots was conceived in early 1960s with "Man-amplifier" and "Hardiman" (Kazerooni, 1993), but the progress of research on this significant field is not satisfactory yet. It is found through literature that power assist systems are currently being developed mainly for sick, physically disabled and old people as healthcare and rehabilitation supports (Kong *et al.*, 2009; Seki, Ishihara and Tadakuma, 2009). Few power assist systems have also been developed for other applications such as for lifting baby carriage (Kawashima, 2009), physical support for workers performing agricultural jobs (Tanaka *et al.*, 2008), hydraulic assist for automobiles (Liu *et al.*, 2009), skill-assist for manufacturing (Lee, Hara and Yamada, 2008), assisted slide doors for automobiles (Osamura *et al.*, 2008), assist-control for bicycle (Kosuge, Yabushita and Hirata,2004), assist for sports training (Ding, Ueda and Ogasawara, 2008), etc.

1.2 Manipulating heavy objects in industries with power assist robots

We think that handling heavy objects, which is common and necessary in many industries, is another potential field of application of power assist robots. It is always necessary to move heavy objects in industries such as manufacturing and assembly, mining, construction, logistics and transport, disaster and rescue operations, forestry, agriculture etc. Manual manipulation of heavy objects is very cumbersome and it causes work-related disabilities and disorders such as back pain to humans. On the contrary, handling objects by autonomous systems may not provide required flexibility in many cases. Hence, it is thought that the uses of suitable human-robot cooperation systems such as power assist systems may be appropriate for handling heavy objects in industries. However, suitable power assist systems are not found in industries for this purpose because their design has not got much attention yet.

1.3 Weight illusion for power assist robots

A power assist robot reduces the perceived heaviness of an object manipulated with it (Kazerooni, 1993), as illustrated in Fig.1. Hence, load force (manipulative force tangential to grip surfaces) required to manipulate an object with a power assist robot should be lower than that required to manipulate the object manually. But, the limitations with the conventional power assist systems are that the operator cannot perceive the heaviness of the object correctly before manipulating it with the system and eventually applies excessive load force. The excessive load force results in sudden increase in acceleration, fearfulness of the operator, lack of maneuverability and stability, fatal accident etc. Fig.2 further explains the interaction processes and phenomena between a power assist robot and its operator for object manipulation. A few power assist systems are available for carrying objects (Doi *et al.*, 2007; Hara, 2007; Lee *et al.*, 2000; Miyoshi and Terashima, 2004). But, their safety, maneuverability, operability, naturalness, stability and other interactions with users are not so satisfactory because their controls do not consider human characteristics especially weight illusion and load force features.

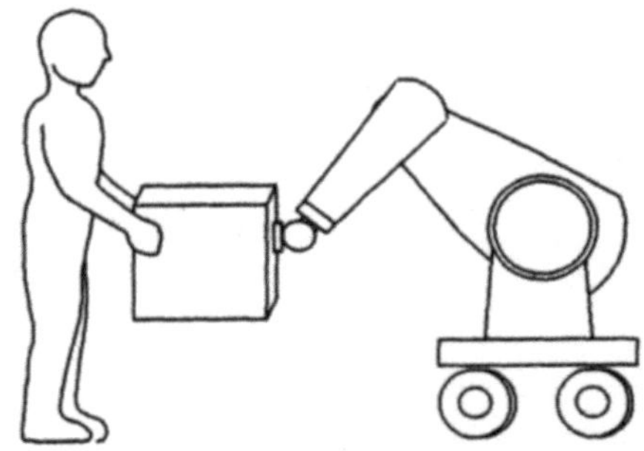

Fig. 1. A human manipulates (lifts) an object with a power assist robot and feels a scaled-down portion of the weight.

1.4 Distinctions between unimanual and bimanual manipulation

It is noticed in practices in industries that workers need to employ one or two hands to manipulate objects and they decide this on the basis of object's physical features such as shape, size, mass etc. as well as of task requirements (Bracewell *et al.*, 2003; Giachritsis and Wing, 2008; Lum, Reinkensmeyer and Lehman, 1993;Rahman *et al.*, 2009a). We assume that weight perception, load force and object motions for unimanual manipulation may be different from that for bimanual manipulation, and these differences may affect modeling the control. Hence, it seems to be necessary to study unimanual weight perception, load force and motion features and to compare these to that for bimanual manipulation, and to reflect the differences in modeling the power-assist control. We studied distinctions between unimanual and bimanual manipulation in our previous works though it is still necessary to deeply look into their differences to make the control more appropriate (Rahman *et al.*, 2009a , 2011a).

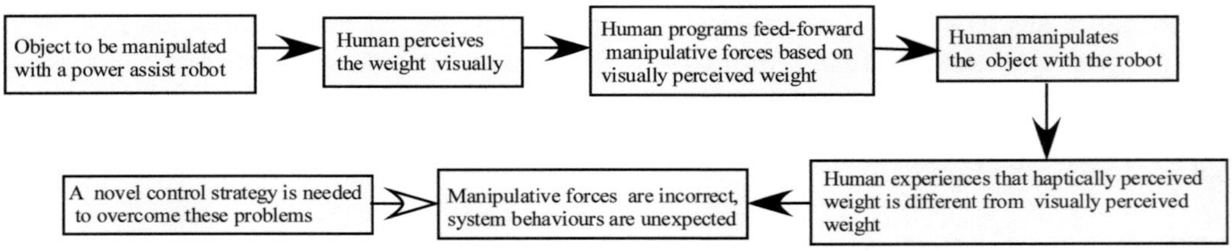

Fig. 2. Interaction processes and phenomena between robot and human when manipulating an object with a power assist robot.

1.5 Lifting, lowering and horizontal manipulation

In industries, workers need to transfer objects in different directions such as vertical lifting (lift objects from lower to higher position), vertical lowering (lower objects from higher to lower position), horizontal manipulation etc. in order to satisfy task requirements. We assume that maneuverability, heaviness perception, load force and motions for manipulating objects among these directions may be different from each other and these differences may affect the control and the system performances. Hence, it seems to be necessary to study object manipulation in all of these directions, compare them to each other, and to reflect the differences in the control (Rahman et al., 2010a, 2011a). However, such study has also not been carried out yet in detailed.We studied lifting objects in vertical direction in our previous works (Rahman *et al.*, 2009a, 2010c, 2011a), but manipulating objects in horizontal direction is still unaddressed though horizontal manipulation of objects is very common in practical fields. A few power-assist robotic systems consider manipulating objects in horizontal direction. But, they are not targetted to industrial applications and they have limitations in performances as they do not consider human characteristics in their control modeling (Hara, 2007).

1.6 The chapter summary

This chapter presents a power assist robot system developed for manipulating objects in horizontal direction in cooperation with human. Weight perception was included in robot dynamics and control. The robot was simulated for manipulating objects in horizontal direction. Optimum maneuverability conditions for horizontal manipulation of objects were determined and were compared to that for vertical lifting of objects. Psychophysical relationships between actual and perceived weights were determined, and load forces and motion features were analyzed for horizontal manipulation of objects. Then, a novel control scheme was implemented to reduce the excessive load forces and accelerations, and thus to improve the system performances. The novel control reduced the excessive load forces and accelerations for horizontal manipulation of objects, and thus improved the system performances in terms of maneuverability,safety, operability etc. We compared our results to that of related works. Finally, we proposed to use the findings to develop human-friendly power assist robots for manipulating heavy objects in various industries.

This chapter provides information to the readers about the power assist robot system- its innovative mechanical design, dynamics, modeling, control, simulation, application etc. Thus this chapter introduces a new area of applications of power assist robot systems and also introduces innovations in its dynamics, modeling, control etc. On the other hand, the readers will get a detailed explanation and practical example of how to use Matlab/Simulink to develop and simulate a dynamic system (e.g., a power assist robot system). The readers will also receive a practical example of how to measure and evaluate human factors subjectively for a technical domain (e.g., a power assist robot system). As a whole, this chapter will enrich the readers with novel concepts in robotics and control technology, Matlab/Simulink application, human factors/ergonomics, psychology and psychophysics, biomimetics, weight perception, human-robot/machine interaction, user interface design, haptics, cognitive science, biomechanics etc. The contents of this chapter were also compared to related works available in published literatures. Thus, the readers will get a collection of all possible works related and similar to the contents of this chapter.

2. The experimental robotic system: Configuration, dynamics and control

2.1 Configuration

We developed a 1-DOF (horizontal translational motion) power assist robot system using a ball screw assembly actuated by an AC servomotor (Type: SGML-01BF12, made by Yaskawa, Japan). The ball screw assembly and the servomotor were coaxially fixed on a metal board and the board was horizontally placed on a table. Three rectangular boxes were made by bending aluminum sheets (thickness: 0.5 mm).These boxes were horizontally manipulated with the power assist robot system and were called the power-assisted objects (PAOs). A PAO (box), at a time, could be tied to the ball nut (linear slider) of the ball screw assembly through a force sensor (foil strain gauge type, NEC Ltd.) and be manipulated by a human subject. The dimensions (length x width x height) of the boxes were 16 x 6 x 5cm, 12 x 6 x 5cm and 8.6 x 6 x 5cm for the large, medium and small size respectively. The bottom, left and right sides of each PAO were open. The complete experimental setup of the power assist robot system is depicted in Fig.3. The servodrive receives a command signal (voltage signal) from the controller through a D/A converter, amplifies the signal, and transmits electric current to the servomotor in order to produce motion proportional to the commanded signal. The position sensor (encoder with counter) reports (pulse signal) object's actual displacement back to the servodrive. The servodrive then compares the actual displacement to the desired displacement. It then alters the commanded signal to the motor so as to correct for any error in the displacement. Human force is sensed by the force sensor attached between the ball nut and the object. The force is sensed as voltage signal, amplified by the amplifier and then sent to the control system via an A/D converter. Human force gives only motion (acceleration) to the object.

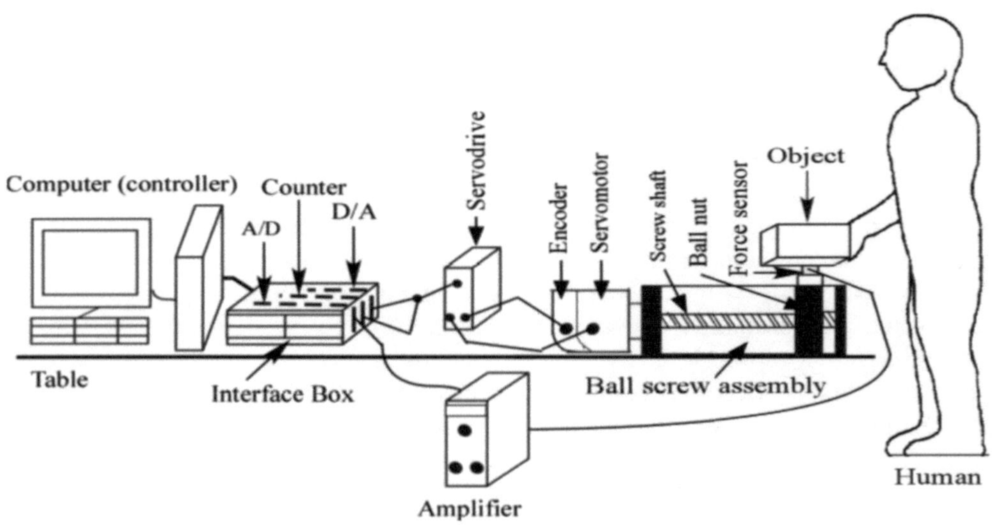

Fig. 3. Experimental setup of the 1-DOF power assist robot system.

2.2 Dynamics

According to Fig.4, the dynamics of the PAO when it is manipulated horizontally by a subject with the power assist robot system is described by Eq.(1), where F_o=mg. If we include our hypothesis in the dynamics, then Eq.(1) changes to Eq.(2). Both m_1 and m_2 stand for mass, but m_1 forms inertial force and m_2 forms gravitational force, $m_1 \neq m_2 \neq m, m_1 \ll m$, $m_2 \ll m$, $|m_1\ddot{x}_d| \neq |m_2 g|$. A difference between m_1 and m_2 arises due to the difference between human's perception and reality regarding the heaviness of the object manipulated with the power assist system (Kazerooni, 1993).

$$m\ddot{x}_d = f_h + F_0 \tag{1}$$

$$m_1\ddot{x}_d = f_h + m_2 g. \tag{2}$$

Where,
$m = Actual\ mass\ of\ the\ object$
$x_d = Desired\ displacement\ of\ the\ object$ $f_h = Load\ force\ applied\ by\ the\ subject$
$g = Acceleration\ of\ gravity$

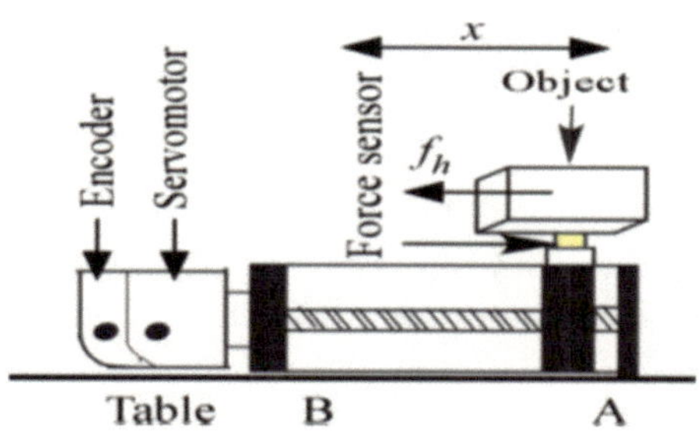

Fig. 4. Dynamics of 1-DOF power assist system for horizontal manipulation of objects. The PAO tied to the force sensor is moved by the subject from 'A' to 'B' position.

2.3 Control

We derived Eqs. (3)- (5) from Eq. (2). We then diagrammed the power-assist control based on Eqs.(3)-(5), which is shown in Fig.5. Eq. (3) gives the desired acceleration. Then, Eq. (3) is integrated and the integration gives the desired velocity ($\dot{x}_d$). Then, the velocity is integrated and the integration gives the desired displacement (x_d).

$$\ddot{x}_d = \frac{1}{m_1}(f_h + m_2 g) \tag{3}$$

$$\dot{x}_d = \int \ddot{x}_d \, dt \tag{4}$$

$$x_d = \int \dot{x}_d \, dt \tag{5}$$

$$\dot{x}_c = \dot{x}_d + G(x_d - x) \tag{6}$$

If the system is simulated using Matlab/Simulink in the velocity control mode of the servomotor, the commanded velocity ($\dot{x}_c$) to the servomotor is calculated by Eq. (6). The commanded velocity is provided to the servomotor through the D/A converter. During simulation, the servodrive determines the error displacement signal by comparing the actual displacement to the desired displacement and generates the control.

The following three types of control methods are usually used in power assist systems:-

1. Position based impedance control
2. Torque/force based impedance control
3. Force control

Position based impedance control and torque/force based impedance control produce good results. Results may be different for force control for reducing excessive force. Our control as introduced above is limited to position based impedance control. We used position based impedance control for the following reasons (advantages):

1. Position based impedance control automatically compensates the effects of friction, inertia, viscosity etc. In contrast, these effects are needed to consider for force control, however, it is very difficult to model and calculate the friction force for the force control. Dynamic effects, nonlinear forces etc. affect system performances for force control for multi-degree of freedom system.
2. Ball-screw gear ratio is high and actuator force is less for position control. However, the opposite is true for the force control.
3. It is easy to realize the real system for the position control for high gear ratio. However, the opposite is true for the force control.

However, there are some disadvantages of position control as the following:

1. Instability is high in position control. If we see Fig.5 we find that a feedback loop is created between x and f_h when human touches/grasps the object for manipulation. This feedback effect causes instability. In contrast, force control has less or no stability problem.
2. Motor system delay affects the stability more intensively for position control.
3. Value of G and velocity control also can compensate the effects of friction, inertia, viscosity etc., but the effects are not compensated completely, which may affect human's weight perception.

If the difference between m and m_1 is very large i.e., if $(m\text{-}m_1)$ is very big, the position control imposes very high load to the servomotor that results in instability, which is not so intensive for force control. Force control is better in some areas, but position control is better in some other areas. However, position control is to be effective for this chapter. Force control may be considered in near future.

The control shown in Fig.5 is not so complicated. However, there is novelty in this control that human's perception is included in this control. Again, another novel control strategy is also derived from this control that includes human features. This control can be recognized as an exemplary and novel control for human interactive robot control.

3. Experiment 1: Analyzing maneuverability,heaviness perception, force and motion features

3.1 Subjects

Ten mechanical engineering male students aged between 23 and 30 years were nominated to voluntarily participate in the experiment. The subjects were believed to be physically and mentally healthy. The subjects did not have any prior knowledge of the hypothesis being tested. Instructions regarding the experiment were given to them, but no formal training was arranged.

3.2 Evaluation criteria for power assist robot systems

Power assist can be defined as augmenting the ability or adjusting to the situation when human operates and works. In particular, in case of supporting for elderly and disabled people, the purpose of power assist is improvement of QOL (Quality of Life), that is, support for daily life. It has two meanings. One is support for self-help and the other is support for caring. The former is to support self-sustained daily life, and the latter is to decrease burden of caregiver.

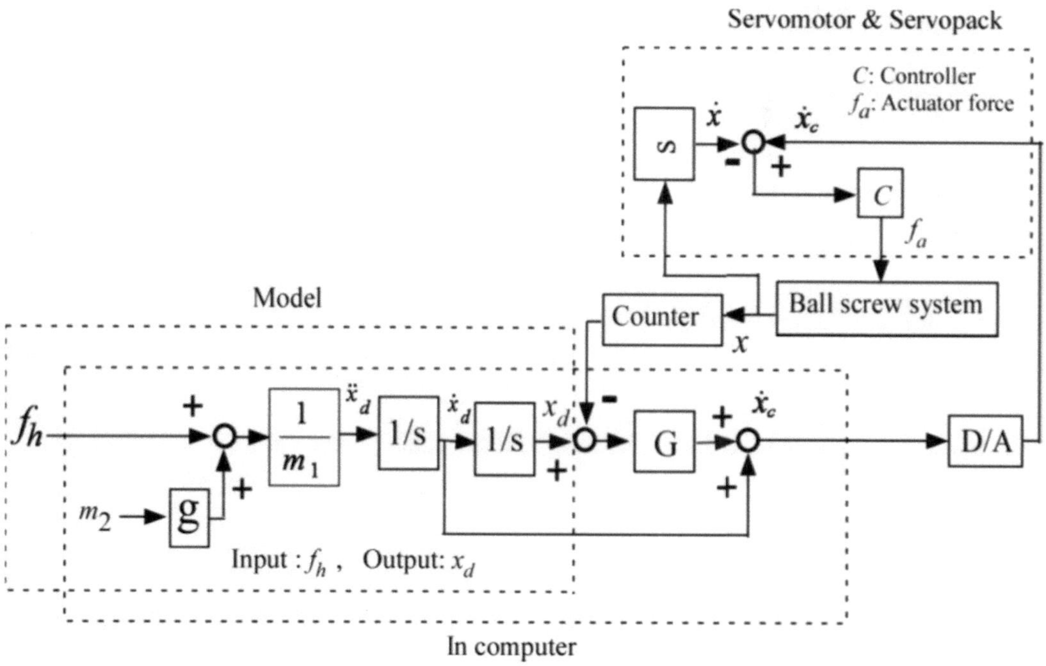

Fig. 5. Block diagram of the power-assist control, where G denotes feedback gain, D/A indicates D/A converter and x denotes actual displacement. Feedback position control is used with the servomotor in velocity control mode.

There are two requirements for power assist systems. The first requirement is amplification of human force, assistance of human motion etc. This is the realization of power assist itself, and there may have problems such as its realization method and stability of human-robot system. The second is safety, sense of security, operability, ease of use etc. This requirement does not appear as specific issue comparing to the first requirement, and it is difficult to be taken into account. However, in order to make power assist systems useful, the second requirement is more important than the first requirement. In case of lifting objects, we think that the main requirements for the power assist systems are maneuverability, safety and stability. Again, these requirements are interrelated where maneuverability plays the pivotal role.

Some basic requirements of a power assist system regarding its maneuverability have been mentioned by Seki, Iso and Hori (2002).However, we thought that only the light (less force required), natural and safe system can provide consistent feelings of ease of use and comfort though too light system may be unsafe, uneasy and uncomfortable. Hence, we considered operator's ease of use and comfort as the evaluation criteria for maneuverability of the power assist robot system.

3.3 Objectives

Objectives of experiment 1 were to (i) determine conditions for optimum maneuverability, (ii) determine psychophysical relationships between actual and perceived weights, (iii) analyze load force and determine excess in load force, (iv) analyze object's motions-displacement, velocity and acceleration etc. for manipulating objects with the power assist robot system in horizontal direction.

3.4 Design of the experiment

Independent variables were m_1 and m_2 values, and visual object sizes. Dependent variables were maneuverability, perceived weight, load force, and object's motions (displacement, velocity and acceleration).

3.5 Experiment procedures

The system shown in Fig.5 was simulated using Matlab/Simulink (solver: ode4, Runge-Kutta; type: fixed-step; fundamental sample time: 0.001s) for twelve m_1 and m_2 sets (Table 1) separately. The ranges of values of m_1 and m_2 were nominated based on our experience. The program for simulation is shown in Fig.6. We set the parameters of three custom-derived blocks such as counter, D/A converter and A/D converter before the simulation started. Fig. 7 shows what the parameters were and how they were set.

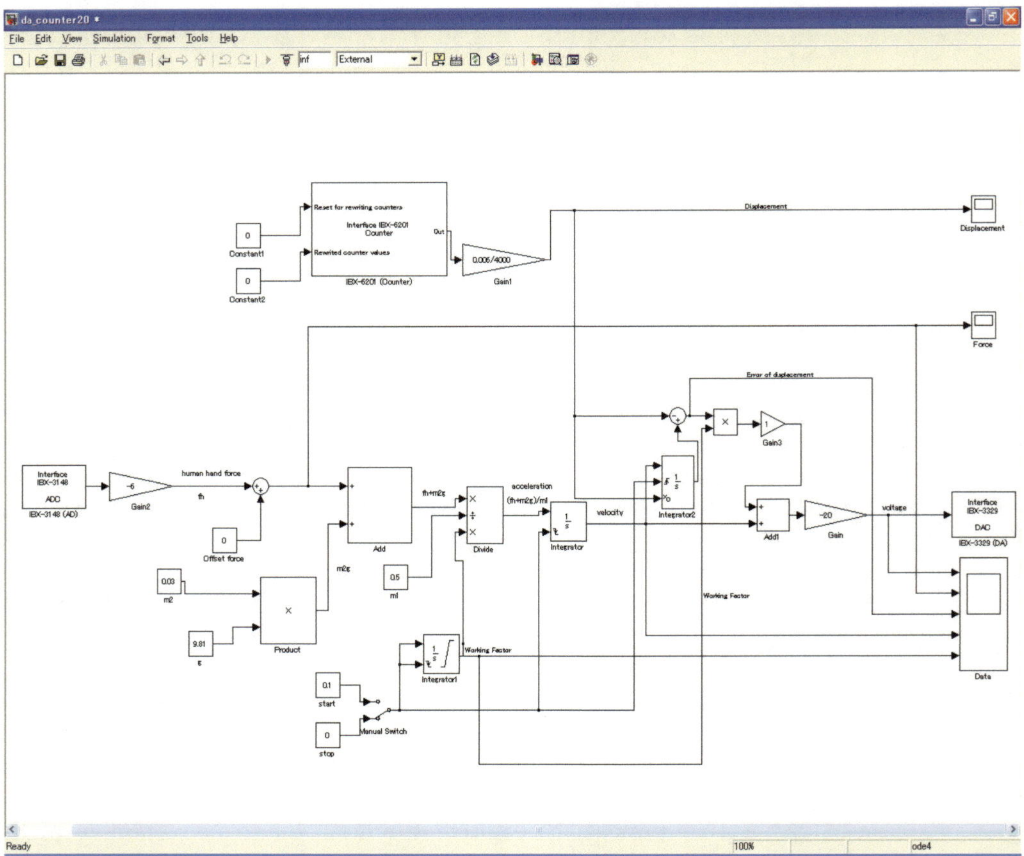

Fig. 6. The program for the simulation

The subject manipulated (from 'A' to 'B' as in Fig.4, distance between 'A' and 'B' was about 0.12 m) each size object with the robot system once for each m_1 and m_2 set separately. The task required the subject to manipulate the object approximately 0.1m, maintain the object for 1-2 seconds and then release the object. For each trial (for each m_1 and m_2 set for each size object), the subject subjectively evaluated the system for maneuverability as any one of the following alternatives:-

1. Very Easy & Comfortable (score: +2)
2. Easy & Comfortable (score: +1)
3. Borderline (score: 0)
4. Uneasy & Uncomfortable (score: -1)
5. Very Uneasy & Uncomfortable (score: -2)

All subjects evaluated the system for maneuverability as above for small, medium, large object independently for each m_1 and m_2 set. Load force and motions data were recorded separately for each trial.

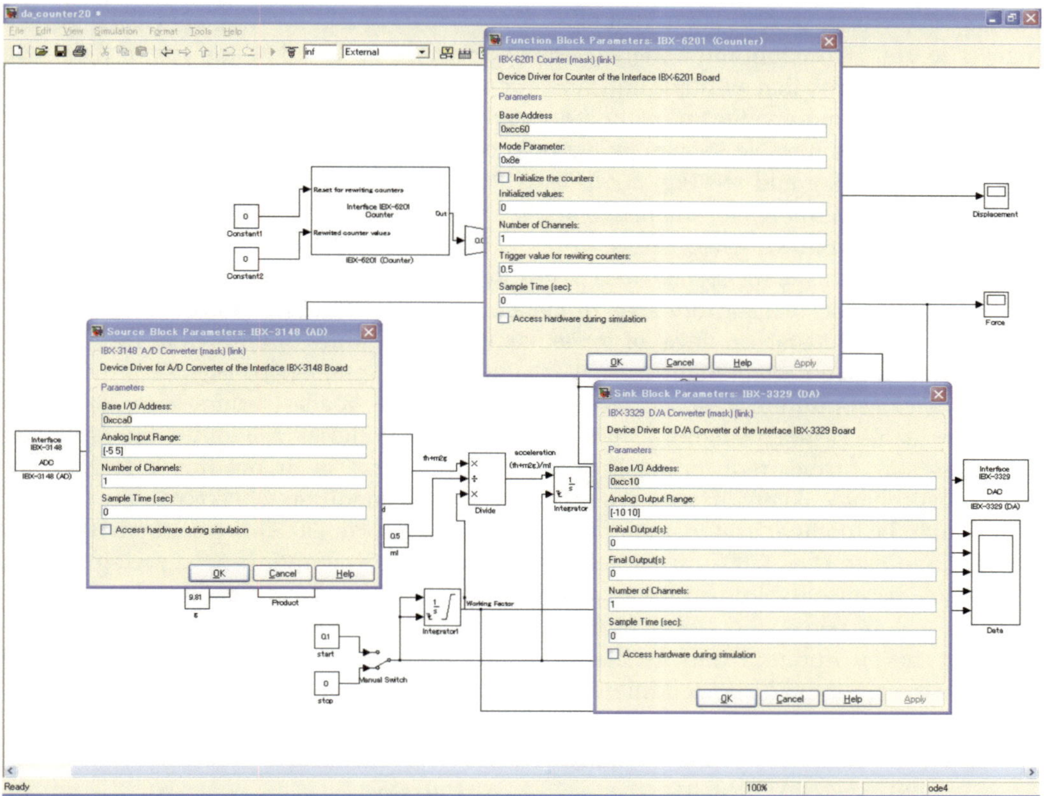

Fig. 7. Setting appropriate parameters for the custom-derived blocks.

Each subject after each trial also manually manipulated a reference-weight object horizontally on a table using right hand alone for reference weights. Weight of the reference-weight object was sequentially changed in a descending order starting from 0.1 kg and ending at 0.01 kg maintaining an equal difference of 0.01 kg i.e., 0.1, 0.09,…0.02, 0.01kg.The subject thus compared the perceived weight of the PAO to that of the reference-weight object and estimated the magnitude of the perceived weight following the psychophysical method 'constant stimuli'. Appearance of PAO and reference-weight object were the same.

m_1 (kg)	2.0	1.5	1.0	0.5
m_2 (kg)	0.09	0.06	0.03	

Table 1. Values of variables for the simulation

3.6 Experiment results

3.6.1 Optimum maneuverability

Mean evaluation scores of the system regarding its maneuverability for 12 m_1 and m_2 sets for each size object were determined separately. Table 2 shows the mean evaluation scores for the medium size object. Similar scores were also determined for large and small size objects. The results reveal that maneuverability is not affected by visual size of object. The reason may be that human evaluates maneuverability using haptic senses where visual size cue has no influence. However, haptic cues might influence the maneuverability.

The table shows that ten m_1 and m_2 sets got positive scores whereas the remaining two sets got negative scores. Results show that m_1=0.5kg, m_2=0.03kg and m_1=1kg, m_2=0.03kg got the highest scores. Hence, optimum maneuverability may be achieved at any one of these two conditions. We think that a unique and single condition for optimum maneuverability could be determined if more values of m_1 and m_2 were used for the simulation. The subjects felt very easy and comfortable to manipulate objects with the power assist system only when m_1=0.5kg, m_2=0.03kg and m_1=1kg, m_2=0.03kg. This is why these two sets were declared as the optimum conditions for maneuverability. Here, optimality was decided based on human's feelings following heuristics.

These findings indicate the significance of our hypothesis that we would not be able to sort out the positive sets (satisfactory level of maneuverability) of values of m_1 and m_2 from the negative sets (unsatisfactory level of maneuverability) of values of m_1 and m_2 for different sizes of objects unless we thought $m_1 \neq m_2 \neq m, m_1 \ll m, m_2 \ll m, m_1\ddot{x}_d \neq m_2 g$.

We see that the optimum/best sets are also the sets of the smallest values of m_1 and m_2 in this experiment. If much smaller values of m_1 and m_2 are chosen randomly, the perceived heaviness may further reduce, but it needs to clarify whether or not this is suitable for human psychology. Again, in zero-gravity or weightless condition when m_2=0, the object is supposed to be too light as it was studied by Marc and Martin (2002) in actual environment and by Dominjon *et al.* (2005) in virtual environment. It was found that the zero-gravity is not feasible because the human loses some haptic information at zero-gravity that hampers human's weight perception ability (Rahman *et al.*, 2009b).It is still not known whether the optimum sets are optimum only for the particular conditions of this experiment or they will persist as the optimum for all conditions in practical uses in industries.

m_1	m_2	Mean maneuverability score
1	0.06	+0.83(0.41)
2	0.06	+0.33(1.21)
0.5	0.03	+2.0 (0)
1	0.03	+2.0 (0)
1.5	0.03	+1.5 (0.55)
2	0.09	-0.17(0.98)
0.5	0.06	+1.0 (0)
1.5	0.09	-0.17(0.98)
0.5	0.09	+0.17(0.75)
1	0.09	+1.0 (0.63)
1.5	0.06	+0.67(0.52)
2	0.03	+1.17(0.41)

Table 2. Mean maneuverability scores with standard deviations (in parentheses) for the medium size object

3.6.2 Relationship between actual and perceived weight

We determined the mean perceived weight for each size object separately for m_1=0.5kg, m_2=0.03kg (condition 1) and m_1=1kg, m_2=0.03 kg (condition 2) as shown in Fig.8. We assumed m_2 as the actual weight of the power-assisted object. It means that the actual weight was 0.03kg or 0.2943 N for each size object for the two m_1 and m_2 sets. We compared the perceived weights of Fig.8 to the actual weight (0.2943 N) for each size object for m_1=0.5kg, m_2=0.03kg and m_1=1kg, m_2=0.03 kg. The figure shows and we also found in our previous research that m_1 does not affect weight perception, but m_2 does affect (Rahman et al., 2009a, 2011a). We also see that visual object sizes do not affect weight perception (Gordon *et al.*, 1991). Results for two-way (visual object size, subject) analyses of variances separately analyzed on perceived weights for the two m_1 and m_2 sets showed that variations due to object sizes were insignificant ($F_{2,\,18}<1$ for each m_1 and m_2 set).The reason may be that subjects estimated perceived weights using haptic cues where visual cues had no influences. Variations among subjects were also found statistically insignificant ($F_{9,18}<1$ for each m_1 and m_2 set).

The actual weight of the object was 0.2943 N, but the subjects felt about 0.052 N when the object was manipulated with the power assist robot system in horizontal direction. Hence, the results reveal that the perceived weight is about 18% of the actual weight if an object is manipulated horizontally with a power assist robot system. Its physical meaning is that the perceived weight of an object manipulated with power-assist in horizontal direction is 18% of the perceived weight of the same object manipulated in horizontal direction manually. This happens because the power assist robot system reduces the perceived weight through its assistance to the user. It is a well-known concept that a power assist robot system reduces the feeling of weight. However, it was not quantified. This research quantified the weight attenuation for horizontal manipulation of objects with the power assist robot system. As we found in our previous research, the perceived weight reduces to 40% and 20% of the actual weight if the object is vertically lifted (Rahman *et al.*, 2011a) or vertically lowered (Rahman *et al.*, 2011b) respectively. The weight perception is less for horizontal manipulation as the gravity force is compensated.

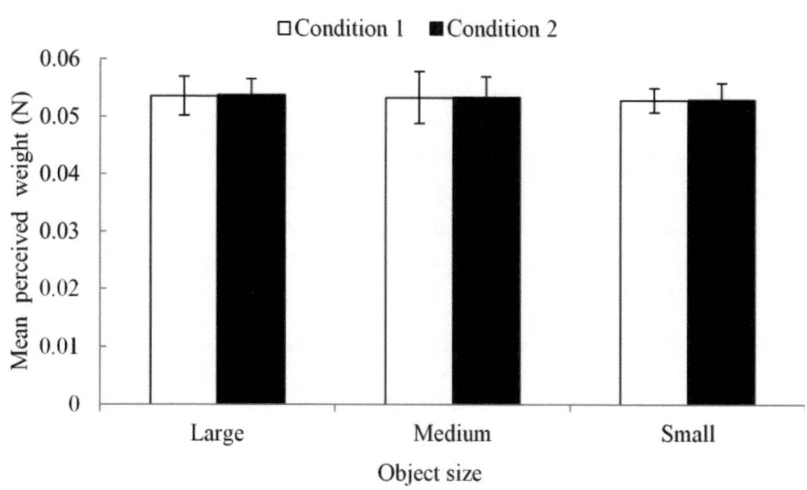

Fig. 8. Mean (n=10) perceived weights for different object sizes for condition 1 (m_1=0.5kg, m_2=0.03kg) and condition 2 (m_1=1kg, m_2=0.03 kg).

3.6.3 Force analysis

The time trajectory of load force for a typical trial is shown in Fig.9. We derived the magnitude of peak load force (PLF) for each object size for condition 1 (m_1=0.5kg, m_2=0.03kg) and condition 2 (m_1=1kg, m_2=0.03 kg) separately and determined the mean PLFs. The results are shown in Table 3. Results show that mean PLFs for condition 2 are slightly larger than that for condition 1. We found previously that both m_1 and m_2 are linearly proportional to peak load force. However, m_1 affects load force, but it does not affect weight perception. On the other hand, m_2 affects both load force and weight perception (Rahman *et al.*, 2011a). Here, we assume that larger m_1 in condition 2 has produced larger load force.

We have already found that subjects feel the best maneuverability at m_1=0.5kg, m_2=0.03kg and m_1=1kg, m_2=0.03 kg. On the other hand, actually required PLF to manipulate the power-assisted object should be slightly larger than the perceived weight (Gordon *et al.*, 1991), which is 0.052 N. We compared the perceived weights from Fig.8 to the PLFs (Table 3) for the large, medium and small objects and determined the excess in PLFs. The results show that subjects apply load forces that are extremely larger than the actually required load forces for condition 1 and 2. We also see that the magnitudes of PLFs are proportional to object sizes (Gordon *et al.*, 1991). We assume that the excessive load forces create problems in terms of maneuverability, safety, motions etc. that we discussed in the introduction.

3.6.4 Motion analysis

Fig.9 shows trajectories of displacement,velocity and acceleration for a typical trial. The figure shows that the time trajectories of load force and object's acceleration are synchronized i.e., when load force reaches the peak; acceleration also reaches the peak and so on. However, the trajectory of displacement is different from that of load force and acceleration i.e., the displacement is not entirely synchronized with load force and acceleration. Hence, we see that there is a time delay between PLF (peak acceleration as well) and peak displacement. Previously we assumed that the time delay is caused due to a delay in position sensing (Rahman et al., 2010b), but this research reveals that the time delay may be caused by the combined effects of the time constant of the position sensor and the delay in adjusting the situation and motions by the subject. We also assume that the time delay may cause the feeling of reduced heaviness of the object manipulated with the power assist robot system.

We derived peak velocity and peak acceleration for each trial and determined their means for each object size in each condition separately as shown in Table 4 and Table 5 respectively. The results show that the velocity and accelerations are large. We assume that the large peak load forces have resulted in large accelerations that are harmful to the system in terms of maneuverability, safety, motions etc.

m_1, m_2 sets	Mean PLFs (N) with standard deviations (in parentheses) for different object sizes		
	Large	Medium	Small
m_1=0.5kg, m_2=0.03kg	2.9131(0.1307)	2.6020(0.1151)	2.4113(0.1091)
m_1=1.0kg, m_2=0.03kg	2.9764(0.2009)	2.6554(0.1552)	2.4602(0.1367)

Table 3. Mean peak load forces for different conditions for different object sizes

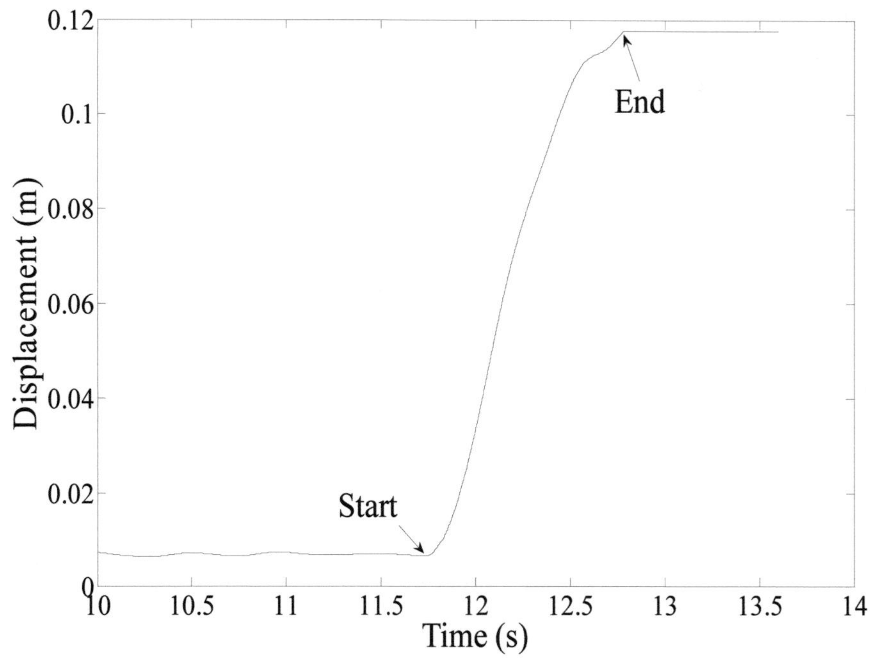
0.12
0.1
0.08
0.06
0.04
0.02
0
Displacement (m)
End
Start
10
10.5
11
11.5
12
12.5
13
13.5
14
Time (s)

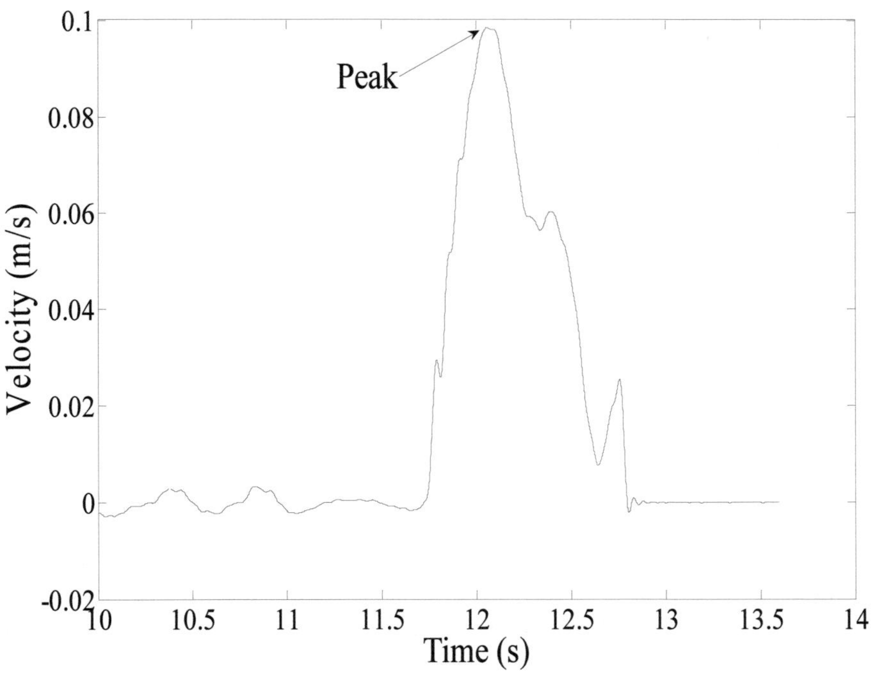
0.1
0.08
0.06
0.04
0.02
0
-0.02
Velocity (m/s)
Peak
10
10.5
11
11.5
12
12.5
13
13.5
14
Time (s)

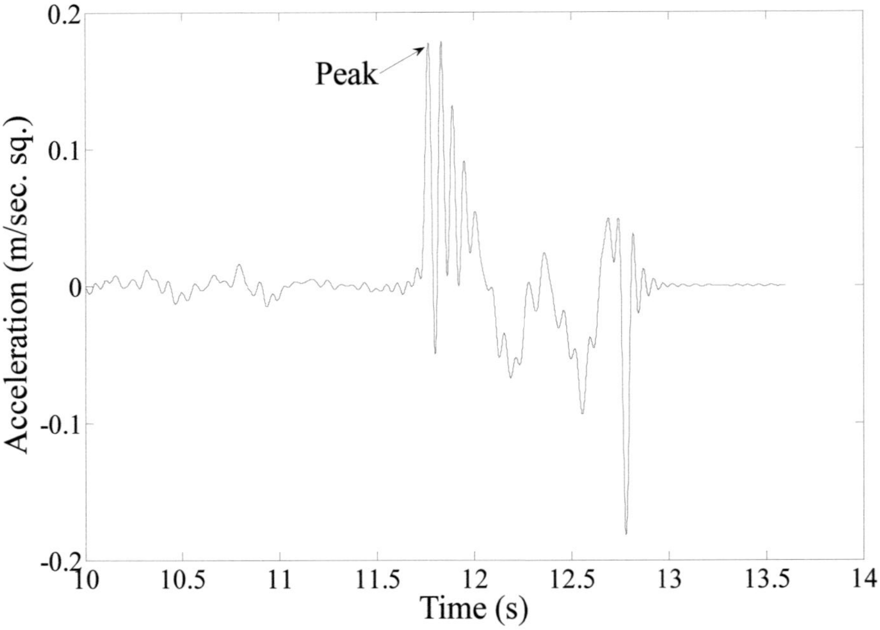

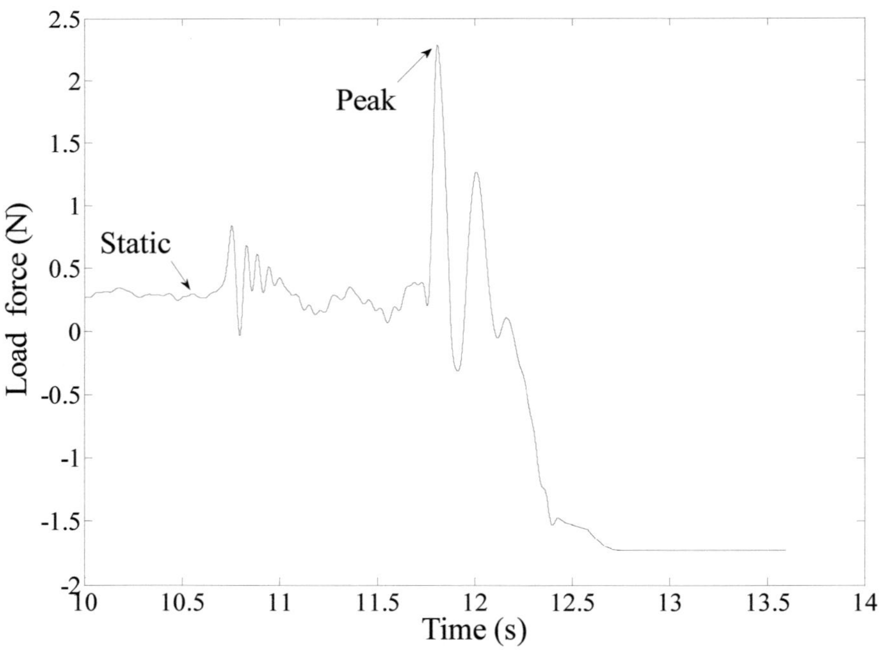

Fig. 9. Time trajectories of displacement , velocity , acceleration and load force for a trial when a subject manipulated the small size PAO with the system at condition 1 (m_1=0.5kg, m_2=0.03kg).

Object size	Mean peak velocity (m/s)	
	m_1=0.5kg, m_2=0.03kg	m_1=1.0kg, m_2=0.03kg
Large	0.1497(0.0149)	0.1557(0.0209)
Medium	0.1345(0.0157)	0.1399(0.0122)
Small	0.1098(0.0121)	0.1176(0.0119)

Table 4. Mean peak velocity with standard deviations (in parentheses) for different object sizes for different conditions

Object size	Mean peak acceleration (m/s²)	
	m_1=0.5kg, m_2=0.03kg	m_1=1.0kg, m_2=0.03kg
Large	0.2309 (0.0901)	0.2701 (0.0498)
Medium	0.2282 (0.0721)	0.2542(0.0153)
Small	0.1887(0.0298)	0.2134(0.0525)

Table 5. Mean peak accelerations with standard deviations (in parentheses) for different object sizes for different conditions.

4. Experiment 2: Improving system performances by a novel control

4.1 Experiment

Table 3 and Table 5 show that subjects apply too excessive load forces and accelerations that cause problems as we discussed in section 1. Experiment 2 attempted to reduce excessive load forces and accelerations by applying a novel control method.

The novel control was such that the value of m_1 exponentially declined from a large value to 0.5kg when the subject manipulated the PAO with the system and the command velocity of Eq.(6) exceeded a threshold. We found previously that load force is linearly proportional to m_1 and we also found that subjects do not feel the change of m_1 (Rahman et al., 2011a). Hence, reduction in m_1 would also reduce the load force proportionally. Reduction in load force would not adversely affect the relationships of Eq. (2) because the subjects would not feel the change of m_1. It means that Eq. (7) and Eq. (8) were used for m_1 and m_2 respectively to modify the control of Fig.5. The digit 6 in Eq. (7) was determined by trial and error. The novel control is illustrated in Fig.10 as a flowchart. The procedures for experiment 2 were the same as that for the experiment 1, but m_1 and m_2 were set as $m_1=6*e^{-6t} + 0.5$, m_2=0.03 (condition 1.a) and $m_1=6*e^{-6t} + 1.0$, m_2=0.03 (condition 2.a) for the simulation. Program for the simulation is shown in Fig.11. We here ignore presenting the simulation details for $m_1=6*e^{-6t} + 1.0$, m_2=0.03 because the concept and procedures for $m_1=6*e^{-6t} + 0.5$, m_2=0.03 and $m_1=6*e^{-6t} + 1.0$, m_2=0.03 are the same.

$$m_1=6 * e^{-6t} + 0.5 \tag{7}$$

$$m_2=0.03 \tag{8}$$

The system performances were broadly expressed through several criteria such as motion, object mobility, naturalness, stability, safety, ease of use etc., and in each trial in each scheme, the subjects subjectively evaluated (scored) the system using a 7-point bipolar and equal-interval scale as follows:

1. Best (score: +3)
2. Better (score: +2)

3. Good (score: +1)
4. Alike (score: 0)
5. Bad (score:-1)
6. Worse (score:-2)
7. Worst (score:-3)

4.2 Experiment results

4.2.1 Reduction in peak load forces and peak accelerations

We compared the mean PLFs of experiment 2 conducted at m_1=6 * e^{-6t} + 0.5, m_2=0.03 and m_1=6 * e^{-6t} + 1.0, m_2=0.03 to that of experiment 1 conducted at m_1=0.5, m_2=0.03 and m_1=1.0, m_2=0.03. The findings are shown in Table 6. Findings show that PLFs reduced significantly due to the control modification.

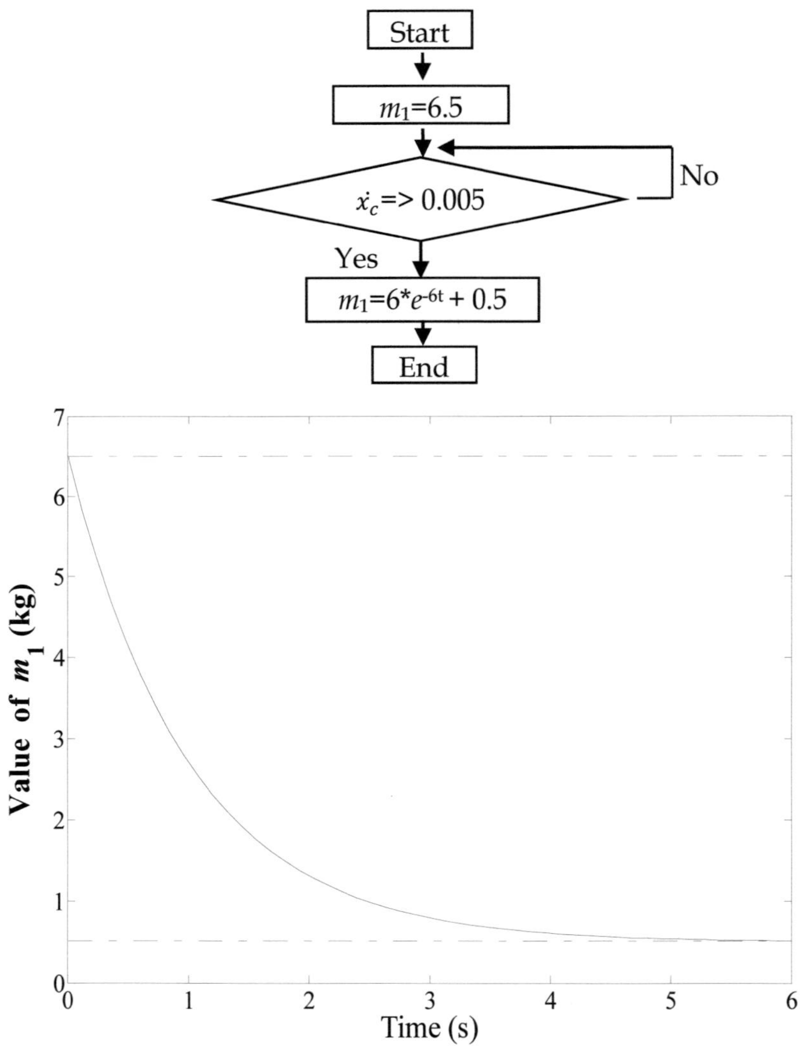

Fig. 10. Flowchart and hypothetical trajectory of inertial mass for the novel control technique.

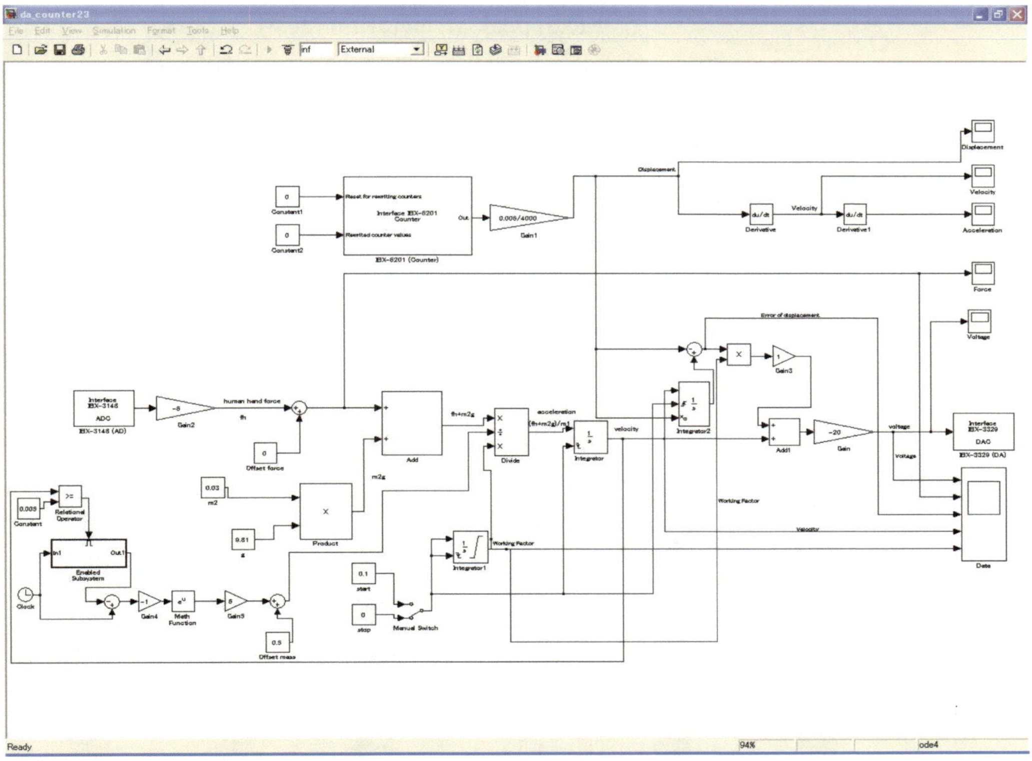

Fig. 11. The program for the simulation for the novel control method

Mean peak accelerations for different object sizes after the control modification are shown in Table 7. The results show, if we compare these to that of Table 5, that the peak accelerations reduced due to control modification. The reason may be that the reduced peak load forces after the control modification reduced the accelerations accordingly. The velocity did not change significantly due to the control modification.

4.2.2 Improvement in system performances

We determined the mean evaluation scores for the three objects separately. Fig.12 shows the mean scores for the small size object for both conditions. The scores for the large and medium size objects in each condition were almost the same as that shown in the figure. It means that the novel control was effective in improving the system performances.

m_1, m_2 sets	Mean PLFs (N) with standard deviations (in parentheses) for different object sizes		
	Large	Medium	Small
$m_1=6 * e^{-6t} + 0.5$, $m_2=0.03$	1.3569 (0.1154)	1.1123(0.0821)	0.9901(0.0910)
$m_1=6 * e^{-6t} + 1.0$, $m_2=0.03$	1.8646 (0.1707)	1.5761(0.1071)	1.0990 (0.0885)

Table 6. Mean peak load forces for different conditions for different object sizes after the control modification

Object size	Mean peak acceleration (m/s^2)	
	m_1=6 * e^{-6t} + 0.5, m_2=0.03	m_1=6 * e^{-6t} + 1.0, m_2=0.03
Large	0.1234 (0.0403)	0.1404 (0.0302)
Medium	0.1038 (0.0233)	0.1220 (0.0107)
Small	0.0884 (0.0311)	0.1008 (0.0164)

Table 7. Mean peak accelerations with standard deviations (in parentheses) for different object sizes for different conditions after the control modification

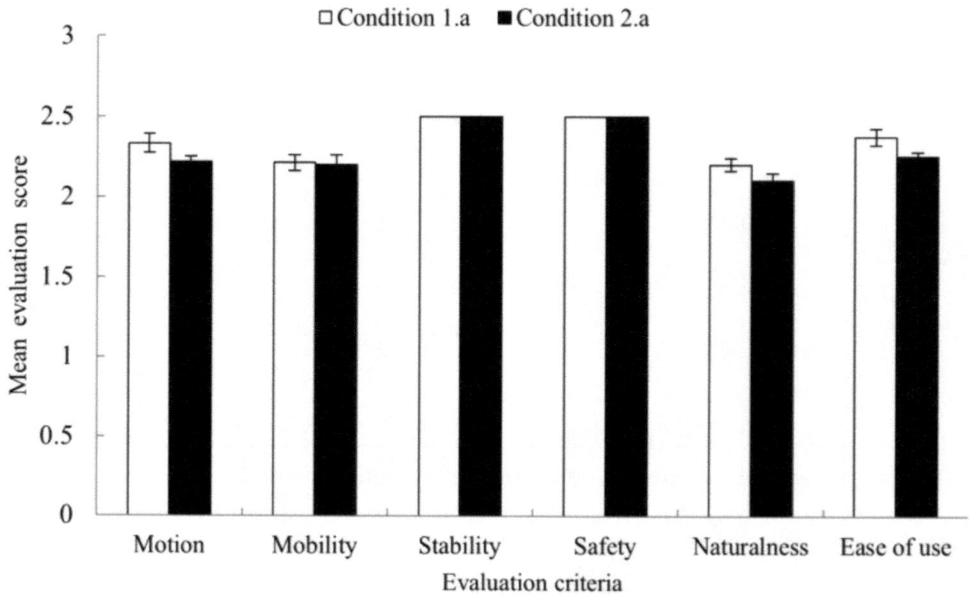

Fig. 12. Mean performance evaluation scores for small size object for condition 1.a (m_1=6 * e^{-6t} + 0.5, m_2=0.03) and condition 2.a (m_1=6 * e^{-6t} + 1.0, m_2=0.03) after the control modification.

5. Conclusions

In this chapter, we presented a 1-DOF power assist robot system for manipulating objects by human subjects in horizontal direction. We included human features in the robot dynamics and control. We determined optimum maneuverability conditions for manipulating objects with the robot system. We also determined psychophysical relationships between actual and perceived weights for manipulating objects with the robot system. We analyzed weight perception, load forces and motion characteristics. We implemented a novel control method based on weight perception, load forces and motion characteristics that improved the system performances through reducing the peak load forces and peak accelerations. The findings may help develop human-friendly power assist robot devices for manipulating heavy objects in industries such as manufacturing and assembly, mining, logistics and transport, construction etc. This chapter also provides a vivid example to the readers of how Matlab/Simulink is used to model and develop control system and interfaces between hardware and software for simulation and control of a robotic system. The findings of this chapter are novel and they enhance the state-of-the-art knowledge and applications of robotics, control system, simulation, Matlab/Simulink, psychology, human factors etc. We will verify the results using heavy objects and real robotic systems in near future. The system will be upgraded to multi-degree of freedom system. Distinctions in weight perception, load forces and motion characteristics between unimanual and bimanual manipulation of objects in horizontal direction will be investigated.

6. Acknowledgment

The authors are thankful to the Ministry of Education, Culture, Sports, Science and Technology of Japan for financial supports.

7. References

Bracewell, R.M., Wing, A.M., Scoper, H.M., Clark, K.G. (2003) 'Predictive and reactive co-ordination of grip and load forces in bimanual lifting in man', *European Journal of Neuroscience*, Vol.18, No.8, pp.2396-2402.

Ding, M., Ueda, J., Ogasawara, T. (2008) 'Pinpointed muscle force control using a power-assisting device: system configuration and experiment', *In Proc. of IEEE Int. Conf. on Biomedical Robotics and Biomechatronics*, pp.181 - 186.

Doi, T., Yamada, H., Ikemoto, T. and Naratani, H. (2007) 'Simulation of pneumatic hand crane type power assist system', *In Proc. of SICE Annual Conf.*, pp. 2321 - 2326.

Dominjon, L., Lécuyer, A., Burkhardt, J.M., Richard, P. and Richir, S. (2005) 'Influence of control/display ratio on the perception of mass of manipulated objects in virtual environments', *In Proc. of IEEE Virtual Reality*, pp.19-25.

Giachritsis, C. and Wing, A. (2008) 'Unimanual and bimanual weight discrimination in a desktop setup', M. Ferre (Ed.): *EuroHaptics 2008*, LNCS 5024, pp. 378–382.

Gordon, A.M., Forssberg, H., Johansson, R.S., Westling, G. (1991) 'Visual size cues in the programming of manipulative forces during precision grip', *Exp. Brain Research*, Vol. 83, No.3, pp. 477–482.

Hara, S. (2007) 'A smooth switching from power-assist control to automatic transfer control and its application to a transfer machine', *IEEE Trans. on Industrial Electronics*, Vol. 54, No. 1, pp.638-650.

Kawashima, T. (2009) 'Study on intelligent baby carriage with power assist system and comfortable basket', *J. of Mechanical Science and Technology*, Vol.23, pp.974-979.

Kazerooni, H. (1993) 'Extender: a case study for human-robot interaction via transfer of power and information signals', *In Proc. of IEEE Int. Workshop on Robot and Human Communication*, pp.10-20.

Kong, K., Moon, H., Hwang, B., Jeon, D., Tomizuka, M. (2009) 'Impedance compensation of SUBAR for back-drivable force-mode actuation', *IEEE Trans. on Robotics*, Vol. 25, Issue: 3, pp.512 - 521.

Kosuge,K., Yabushita, H., Hirata, Y. (2004) 'Load-free control of power-assisted cycle', *In Proc. of IEEE Technical Exhibition Based Conference on Robotics and Automation*, pp.111-112.

Lee, H., Takubo, T., Arai, H. and Tanie, K. (2000) 'Control of mobile manipulators for power assist systems', *Journal of Robotic Systems*, Vol.17, No.9, pp.469-477.

Lee, S., Hara, S., Yamada, Y. (2008) 'Safety-preservation oriented reaching monitoring for smooth control mode switching of skill-assist', *In Proc. of IEEE Int. Conf. on Systems, Man and Cybernetics*, pp.780–785.

Liu, G., Yan, Y., Chen, J., Na, T. (2009) 'Simulation and experimental validation study on the drive performance of a new hydraulic power assist system', *In Proc. of IEEE Intelligent Vehicles Symposium*, pp.966-970.

Lum, P.S., Reinkensmeyer, D.J., Lehman, S.L. (1993) 'Robotic assist devices for bimanual physical therapy: preliminary experiments', *IEEE Trans. on Rehabilitation Engineering,* Vol.1, No.3, pp.185-191.

Marc, O.E., and Martin, S.B. (2002) 'Humans integrate visual and haptic information in a statistically optimal fashion', *Nature,* Vol. 415, No.6870, pp.429-433.

Miyoshi, T. and Terashima, K. (2004) 'Development of vertical power-assisted crane system to reduce the operators' burden', *In Proc. of IEEE Int. Conference on Systems, Man and Cybernetics,* Vol.5, pp. 4420 - 4425.

Osamura, K., Kobayashi, S., Hirata, M., Okamoto, H. (2008) 'Power assist control for slide doors using an ideal door model', *In Proc. of IEEE Int. Symposium on Industrial Electronics,* pp. 1293 – 1299.

Rahman,S.M.M., Ikeura, R., Nobe, M., Sawai,H. (2009a) 'Design and control of a 1DOF power assist robot for lifting objects based on human operator's unimanual and bimanual weight discrimination', *In Proc. of IEEE Int. Conf. on Mechatronics and Automation,*pp.3637-3644.

Rahman, S.M.M., Ikeura, R., Nobe, M., Sawai, H. (2009b) 'A psychophysical model of the power assist system for lifting objects', *In Proc. of IEEE Int. Conf. on Systems, Man, and Cybernetics,* pp.4125-4130.

Rahman, S.M.M., Ikeura, R., Nobe, M., Sawai, H. (2010a) 'Study on optimum maneuverability in horizontal manipulation of objects with power-assist based on weight perception', *In Proc. of SPIE,* Vol. 7500, 75000P.

Rahman, S.M.M., Ikeura, R., Nobe, M., Sawai, H. (2010b) 'Displacement-load force-perceived weight relationships in lifting objects with power-assist', *In Proc. of SPIE,* Vol. 7500, 75000S.

Rahman, S.M.M., Ikeura, R., Nobe, M., Sawai, H. (2010c), 'Controlling a power assist robot for lifting objects considering human's unimanual, bimanual and cooperative weight perception', *In Proc. of IEEE Int. Conf. on Robotics and Automation,* pp.2356-2362.

Rahman, S.M.M., Ikeura, R., Hayakawa, S. and Sawai, H. (2011a) 'Design guidelines for power assist robots for lifting heavy objects considering weight perception, grasp differences and worst-cases', *Int. J. Mechatronics and Automation,* Vol. 1, No. 1, pp.46–59.

Rahman, S.M.M., Ikeura, R., Ishibashi, S., Hayakawa, S., Sawai, H., Yu, H. (2011b) 'Lowering objects manually and with power-assist: distinctions in perceived heaviness, load forces and object motions', *In Proc. of 4th IEEE International Conference on Human System Interactions, 19-21 May, 2011, Yokohama, Japan, pp.129-135.*

Seki,H.,Iso,M.,Hori,Y.(2002) 'How to design force sensorless power assist robot considering environmental characteristics-position control based or force control based-', *In Proc. of Annual Conf. of IEEE Industrial Electronics Society,*Vol.3,pp.2255-2260.

Seki,H.,Ishihara,K.,Tadakuma,S.(2009) 'Novel regenerative braking control of electric power-assisted wheelchair for safety downhill road driving', *IEEE Trans. on Industrial Electronics,* Vol. 56, No. 5, pp. 1393-1400.

Tanaka, T., Satoh, Y., Kaneko, S., Suzuki, Y., Sakamoto, N. and Seki, S. (2008) 'Smart suit: soft power suit with semi-active assist mechanism – prototype for supporting waist and knee joint', In Proc. of Int. Conf. on Control, Automation and Systems, pp. 2002-2005.